HEALTH PSYCHOLOGY

HEALTH PSYCHOLOGY

Theory, Research and Practice

DAVID F. MARKS
MICHAEL MURRAY
BRIAN EVANS
CARLA WILLIG

SAGE Publications
London • Thousand Oaks • New Delhi

© David F. Marks, Michael Murray, Brian Evans and Carla Willig 2000

First published 2000

 SAGE Publications Ltd
6 Bonhill Street
London EC2A 4PU

SAGE Publications Inc
2455 Teller Road
Thousand Oaks, California 91320

SAGE Publications India Pvt Ltd
32, M-Block Market
Greater Kailash – I
New Delhi 110 048

British Library Cataloguing in Publication data

A catalogue record for this book is available
from the British Library

ISBN 0 8039 7607 0
ISBN 0 8039 7608 9 (pbk)

Library of Congress catalog card number

Typeset by Mayhew Typesetting, Rhayader, Powys
Printed in Great Britain by The Cromwell Press Ltd,
Trowbridge, Wiltshire

CONTENTS

AUTHOR BIOGRAPHIES

DAVID F. MARKS is Head of the Health Research Centre and Professor of Psychology at Middlesex University, London, UK. Previously he has held positions at the University of Sheffield, UK, and the University of Otago, New Zealand. His previous books include *The Psychology of the Psychic* (1980, with R. Kammann), *Theories of Image Formation* (1986), *Imagery: Current Developments* (1990, with J.T.E. Richardson and P. Hampson), *The Quit For Life Programme: An Easier Way to Stop Smoking and Not Start Again* (1993), *Improving the Health of the Nation* (1996, with C. Francome), *Dealing With Dementia: Recent European Research* (2000, with C.M. Sykes) and *The Psychology of the Psychic* (Revised Edition) (2000). He was elected Chair of the Special Group in Health Psychology of the British Psychological Society and Convenor of the Task Force on Health Psychology of the European Federation of Professional Psychologists' Associations. He is Editor of the *Journal of Health Psychology*.

MICHAEL MURRAY is Professor of Social and Health Psychology in the Division of Community Health, Memorial University of Newfoundland, Canada. Previously he has held positions at St Thomas' Hospital Medical School, London, UK and at the University of Ulster, Ireland. His previous books include *Smoking Among Young Adults* (1988, with L. Jarrett, A.V. Swan and R. Rumen) and *Qualitative Health Psychology: Theories and Methods* (1999, with K. Chamberlain). He served as Chair of the Health Psychology Section of the Canadian Psychological Association and was founding editor of the *Canadian Health Psychologist*. He is an Associate Editor of the *Journal of Health Psychology*.

BRIAN EVANS teaches psychology at Middlesex University, London, UK where he is programme leader of the MSc degree in Psychology and Health. Previously he has held positions at the University of Sussex, UK, and at Concordia University, Montreal, Canada. He is interested in the analysis of psychological research and theory in its socio-political context and his previous publications include *IQ and Mental Testing: An Unnatural Science and Its Social History* (1981, with B. Waites).

CARLA WILLIG teaches psychology at City University, London, UK. Previously she has held positions at Plymouth and Middlesex Universities. Her research is primarily concerned with the relationship between discourse and practice, particularly in relation to risk taking. She has published journal articles and book chapters on the discursive construction of trust and sexual safety, and she has contributed to theoretical and epistemological debates concerning social constructionist psychology. She edited *Applied Discourse Analysis: Social and Psychological Interventions* (1999) and is a member of the Editorial Board of the *Journal of Health Psychology*.

COPYRIGHT ACKNOWLEDGEMENTS

The authors and publishers wish to thank the following for permission to use copyright material:

Figures 1.1 and 2.1: The World Bank; Oxford University Press.

Figure 1.2: Margaret Whitehead; The King's Fund.

Figure 1.3: John Spicer and Kerry Chamberlain; SAGE Publications Ltd.

Figure 2.6: Samuel Odom, C. A. Peck, H. Hanson, P. J. Beckman, A. P. Kaiser, J. Lieber, W. H. Brown, E. M. Horn, I. S. Schwartz/Indiana University.

Figure 2.7: Richard Wilkinson; *The British Medical Journal*.

Figure 3.1: Vivian Nutton; Cambridge University Press.

Figure 5.1: *Private Eye*, Pressdram Ltd.

Figure 5.2: Tom Cox; Macmillan Press Ltd.

Figure 6.1: The Department of Health.

Table 6.1: Gary Egger, G.Swinburn; *The British Medical Journal*.

Figure 6.2: Geoffrey Webb; Edward Arnold.

Figure 7.1: The British Museum.

Box 7.2: National Union of Students.

Figure 8.1: Karen Conrad, B. R. Floy, D. Hill; Taylor and Francis Group Ltd.

Table 8.1: Carlo DiClemente; University of Illinois at Urbana-Champaign.

Figures 9.1 and 9.2; Table 9.1: Anne Johnson; Blackwell Science Ltd.

Tables 9.2 and 9.3: Susan Miller Campbell, Letitia Anne Peplau, Sherrine Chapman DeBro; Cambridge University Press.

Table 10.3: Jay Coakley; Human Kinetics Publishers Inc.

Figure 11.1: Howard Leventhal.

Box 12.3: M. Stewart and D. Roter; SAGE Publications Inc.

Box 12.4: Mary Klein Buller and David B. Buller, *The Journal of Health and Social Behavior*.

Tables 13.1 and 13.2: Donald Meichenbaum and Dennis C. Turk; Plenum Publishing Corporation.

Table 14.3: James Maxwell Glover Wilson; The World Health Organization.

Table 14.5: Susan Michie and Theresa M. Marteau; The British Psychological Society.

Table 15.1: Jostein Rise; John Wiley & Sons Ltd.

Every effort has been made to trace all copyright holders, but if any have been overlooked, the publishers will be pleased to make the necessary amendments at the first opportunity.

PREFACE AND ACKNOWLEDGEMENTS

This book provides an account of health psychology as an applied field with special relevance to health promotion and disease prevention. It aims to dig below the surface to expose the underlying theoretical assumptions of the field and critically to analyse its methods, evidence and conclusions. The importance of psychological processes in the experience of health and illness is being increasingly recognized. Evidence for the role of behaviour and emotion in current trends of morbidity and mortality is accumulating; much research has also been conducted on the effects of stress and psychological dispositions on the onset, course and management of physical illness.

Health psychology is growing rapidly and health psychologists are in increasing demand in health care and medical settings. In the USA, the single largest area of placement of psychologists in recent years has been in medical centres. Psychologists have become vital members of multidisciplinary clinical and research teams in rehabilitation, cardiology, paediatrics, oncology, anaesthesiology, family practice, dentistry, and other medical fields. In Europe, health psychology is becoming recognized as a new health profession and theory and policy are being put into practice through improvements in training (Marks et al., 1998). In the first 20 years of its development the focus has been clinical in nature (Marks, 1996); in the next decades, however, more effort needs to be directed towards creating effective methods of disease prevention and health promotion, especially with reference to the behavioural risk factors of smoking, drug and alcohol use, diet, sedentary lifestyles, responses to stress and unsafe sexual behaviour.

Health psychology has a crucial role to play in helping the development and evaluation of health promotion interventions. Psychologists will be doing this in close collaboration with communities, other professionals, and policymakers. Changes in policy and practice are urgently needed to increase equity and enhance the well-being of the most vulnerable members of society. This book therefore adopts a preventive perspective with a focus on positive health enhancement.

Health psychology is a richly interdisciplinary field requiring an understanding of the cultural, socio-political and economic roots of behaviour and experience. The authors of this textbook use an interdisciplinary perspective to illustrate health psychology's relevance to a world in which social, economic and political changes have not kept pace with industrial, scientific and medical achievements. The gap between the 'haves' and the 'have-nots' widens, the population is ageing, and the impacts of learned helplessness, poverty and social isolation are increasingly salient features of society. In preparing to deal with these issues, all those concerned with health promotion and disease prevention will require more in-depth understanding not only of the complexities of human behaviour, but of the lived experience of health, illness and health care. By integrating both quantitative and qualitative approaches, this book is intended as a small step in that direction.

Key terms are identified by bold italics and defined in the Glossary at the end of the book. The authors collectively would like to thank and acknowledge the assistance of the following people and organizations: Elizabeth Durrant, Nick Heather, Catherine Marie Sykes, Lynne Segal, the Health Education Authority, and Alcohol Concern; MM gives special thanks to his wife Anne and two sons Matthew and Daniel for keeping him happy and healthy.

PART 1

HEALTH PSYCHOLOGY IN CONTEXT

This book provides an overview of the field of health psychology studied as a natural and human science. In Part 1 we are concerned with the economic, structural and cultural context of health and illness experience. Chapter 1 introduces and defines the concept of health and reviews the development of health psychology as a new field of inquiry. The value of an interdisciplinary approach is suggested and links with other disciplines and professions are described. The role of frameworks, theories and models is discussed. It is proposed that the psychology of health, illness and health care needs to be considered in economic, political, ecological, social and cultural context.

Chapter 2 discusses the contextual factors produced by the macro-social environment, the economic and societal factors which operate across and within societies and structure the health experience of populations, communities and individuals. The chapter examines the influence of economic, educational and health-care system variables on life expectancy. It proceeds by discussing socio-economic status (SES), gender, age, race, and ethnicity in the light of the body of evidence suggesting that *inequality* is a persistent characteristic of our health-care systems.

Chapter 3 examines the ways in which health and illness have been construed across time and place. Western biomedical procedures often tend to be viewed as 'scientific' and 'evidence based' while the medical systems of other cultures and 'complementary' therapies are seen as 'unscientific' or 'magical'. These assumptions need to be evaluated in the light of studies conducted with participants from different cultures and ethnic groups who make their own accounts of health and illness and act upon them in positive and functional ways. Anthropological and sociological studies of health and medicine have generated a range of theories and concepts which enhance the psychological study of health and illness.

1 HEALTH PSYCHOLOGY AS A NEW FIELD OF INQUIRY

The desire for the prolongation of life . . . we may take to be one of the most universal of all human motives. Kenneth Arrow (1963, p. 75)

OUTLINE

This chapter introduces health psychology as a new field of inquiry. Health psychology is considered a hybrid of natural and human science. The case is made for adopting an interdisciplinary approach. Necessary links with other disciplines and professions are described. We examine the nature of theories and models within health psychology and argue that health experience and behaviour need to be considered in their full economic, political, ecological, social and cultural context.

WHAT IS HEALTH?

The attainment and preservation of health reaches to the very core of human existence. In its broadest sense, *well-being* is an overarching concern for every human being, group and society. Health is described and explained in various discourses which are socially constructed. The concepts of 'health', 'mind' and 'body' vary across time and place, but for all cultures and cosmologies they play a fundamental role in the experience of being human.

The word 'health' is derived from Old High German and Anglo-Saxon words meaning 'whole', 'hale' and 'holy'. Historically and culturally there are strong associations with ideas of wholeness, holiness, cleanliness, sanitariness, sanity, goodness, saintliness and godliness. There are equally strong associations between the concepts of disease, disorder, disintegration, uncleanness, unsanitariness, insanity, badness, evil and the work of the devil. An emphasis on health as wholeness and naturalness was present in ancient China and classical Greece where health was seen as a state of 'harmony', 'balance' or 'equilibrium' with nature. These beliefs are found in many healing systems to the present day.

Galen (AD 130–199), the early Greek physician, followed the Hippocratic tradition in believing that *hygieia* (health) or *euexia* (soundness) occur when there is a balance between the hot, cold, dry and wet components of the body. The four bodily humours were believed to be blood, phlegm, yellow bile and black bile which were hot and wet, cold and wet, hot and dry, and cold and dry respectively. Diseases were thought to be caused by external 'pathogens' which disturbed the balance of the body's four elements: hot, cold, dry and wet. Galen believed that the body's 'constitution', 'tempera- ment' or 'state' could be put out of equilibrium by excessive heat, cold, dryness or wetness. Such imbalances might be caused by fatigue, insomnia, distress, anxiety, or by the residues of food resulting from the wrong quantity or quality. These accounts have similarities to some of today's cross-cultural images of health (Chapter 3) and also recent ideas about personality, illness and stress (Chapter 4) and the common belief that colds and coughs, which create an excess of phlegm, are caused by exposure to cold and wet conditions.

Concepts of health and illness are embodied in the everyday talk and thought of people with different languages, cultures and religious groups. For obvious reasons it is difficult, if not impossible, to establish any single universally acceptable account. The World Health Organization (WHO) published a definition of health in 1946 which it hoped would have fairly universal application. This now well-known definition states that health is: 'the state of complete physical, social and spiritual well-being, not simply the absence of illness'. Although it can be seen to be abstract and idealistic, the WHO definition is both positive and inspirational. It may never be possible to reach it, but it sets a target that is well worth striving for.

But even the WHO definition has some important elements missing. The physical, social and spiritual dimensions are all undeniably a necessary part of well-being. However, social factors are embedded within cultures and this should not be left purely as an implicit assumption. Economic forces also play a crucial role in determining the well-being of societies and individuals, as we shall see in the next chapter. There is also an important psychological aspect to well-being which cannot be neglected in a definition of health, especially in a book about health psychology. But psychological processes are more than discrete events occurring in an individual mind, they are embedded in a social world, a world of interaction with others. It is therefore customary in certain contexts to describe psychological processes as 'psychosocial' processes, highlighting the social embeddedness of all things psychological. This is especially the case in the context of health, illness and health care, where the key psychological processes are also intimately social in nature.

Therefore the WHO definition of health needs to be revised in the light of all of the above. We provide this new definition in Box 1.1.

BOX 1.1   DEFINITION OF HEALTH

Health is a state of being with physical, cultural, psychosocial, economic and spiritual attributes, not simply the absence of illness.

How we define health has implications for theory, practice, policy, and health promotion. The term 'health promotion' was first used in 1974 by the Canadian Minister of National Health and Welfare, Marc Lalonde (1974) who argued persuasively that health and illness are not dependent only on medical conditions but also on the environment and conditions of living. The World Health Organization (1986) defined health promotion as: 'the process of enabling people to increase control over, and to improve their health. To reach a state of complete physical, mental and social well-being an individual or group must be able to identify and to realise aspirations, to satisfy needs, to change or cope with the environment . . .' (p. i).

This health promotion approach provides a unifying concept for those who recognize the need to make changes in the ways and conditions of living in order to improve health. Health professionals are more than providers of services, they can be seen as agents of change, facilitating the empowerment of individuals and communities to increase their control over and to improve their health (Marks, 1999). The theories and research health psychology have as yet been only partially applied to the practice of health promotion (Bennett and Murphy, 1997). However, as we shall see, health psychology has much to offer to a multidisciplinary approach that considers both the environmental context and behaviour as key determinants of health.

EPISTEMOLOGIES FOR STUDYING EXPERIENCE AND BEHAVIOUR

Traditionally, there have been two primary theories of knowledge, or epistemologies, for studying and trying to understand human behaviour and experience. The first is the *natural science* approach that analyses behaviour and experience in a manner similar to the way in which physicists, chemists or biologists conduct investigations in the form of experiments to search for a single, 'true' account of reality. The second is the *human science* approach that explores behaviour and experience with the objective of discovering underlying meaning or understandings. The field of health psychology includes research from both traditions.

The two approaches have different objectives and are not necessarily mutually exclusive. The natural science approach aims to identify causal relationships between variables. It asks 'why does x happen?' and it attempts to generate accurate predictive models. By contrast, the human science approach aims to access meanings and the texture of human experience. It asks 'how does it feel to experience x?' and it produces detailed descriptions and sometimes also explanations of human action.

The first, natural science tradition is well represented by the ***medical model*** and its more recent offshoot, the ***biopsychosocial model*** for health research. In the medical model all health and illness phenomena are understood to be biochemical or physical in nature and the mind as activity of the nervous system. Engel's (1977) biopsychosocial model challenged the medical model with the proposal that health and illness are a consequence of physical, psychological and cultural variables. The three Ps of the biopsychosocial model – people, prevention, psychology – can be contrasted with the three Ds of the medical model – diagnosis, disease, drugs. However, both the medical and the biopsychosocial model share the assumptions of a single reality discoverable through the methods of natural science.

Critics have suggested that the biopsychosocial model remains essentially biomedical and that its theoretical basis has yet to be properly worked out (e.g. Armstrong, 1987; Ogden, 1997). However, while the precise causal pathways appear to be complicated and remain somewhat elusive, new psychological theories and approaches see non-physical events as having great significance in health, illness and health care. Whatever one's epistemological predilections, the study of health psychology is concerned with developing a better understanding of the psyche and the body and the relationships between the two.

The second epistemology in the human science tradition is represented by research concerning *discourse, narrative* and social representations. People's accounts of health and illness are an interesting and illuminating topic of study in their own right. Much of the research on health and illness narratives has been influenced by *social constructionism* (Stainton-Rogers, 1991). From this perspective, there is no single, fixed 'reality' but a multiplicity of descriptions or 'drafts' each with its own unique pattern of meanings. Mulkay (1991, pp. 27–8) suggests the existence of: 'many potential worlds of meaning that can be imaginatively entered and celebrated, in ways which are constantly changing to give richness and value to human experience'. One of the best known ways of studying these 'worlds of meaning' has been to analyse the social psychological functions of different accounts using a so-called discursive approach (Potter and Wetherell, 1987). This was influenced by Berger and Luckmann (1966) who argued that there is no single or true reality, but that reality is a social construction. Earlier intellectual forbears were Pascal, Marx and Nietzsche. All believed that conscious thinking is constructed within a particular socio-historical context.

However, social constructionists continue to engage in a lively debate regarding the extent to which social constructions are grounded in material reality (see Parker, 1998). Relativist social constructionists, inspired by Nietzsche, emphasize the flexibility of discourse and the sense in which language can be said to construct reality. Critical realist social constructionists, inspired by Marx, acknowledge that discourses construct different versions of reality but they argue that the material world cannot accommodate all constructions equally well (see also Nightingale and Cromby, 1999).

In addition to wide variations in health beliefs between cultures, there is significant within-culture diversity. Folk beliefs, knowledge and practices among individuals from different communities and social groups rub shoulders with each other and with the health-care professionals in a virtual Tower of Babel. These diverse beliefs meld with practices and lifestyles in accord with people's worldviews and values. Wide discrepancies frequently occur between patients' and the scientifically schooled knowledge and beliefs of the health-care professionals. Such differences probably underlie and directly contribute to the communication problems which are frequently evident between health-care professionals and patients (see Chapters 13 and 14).

THE NEED FOR A CROSS-CULTURAL PERSPECTIVE

Theories in health psychology provide accounts of how psychological processes affect individual health experience. In evaluating these theories it must be acknowledged that they are cultural products of the predominantly English-speaking world of the USA, Europe and British Commonwealth. More specifically, many of health psychology's theories are extensions and adaptations of US/European cognitive and social psychology from 1950 to 1990. During this time there was a resurgence of research in artificial, laboratory environments using structured psychometric instruments, questionnaires and performance tests designed to reveal the mechanisms underlying human behaviour. Although these methods were popular and influential, it has been argued that they often lacked 'ecological validity' (Neisser, 1976), or, in other words, that the findings could not be generalized to the world that lies outside the laboratory. Critics have suggested that the laboratory experiment and the questionnaire are subject to more bias than their proponents are willing to admit (Harré, 1979; Gergen, 1985; Potter and Wetherell, 1987; Radley, 1994; Stainton-Rogers, 1996).

North American/European psychological theory can be viewed as part and parcel of an *indigenous* psychology which may be inapplicable to cultures outside (Heelas and Lock, 1981). This view was supported by Lillard (1998) who catalogues evidence that 'European American' folk psychology shows major differences from the folk psychologies of other cultures. Folk psychology is a mixture of beliefs and values showing multiple cultural variations.

One prominent example of a non-universal cultural value which is deeply embedded in US/European societies is that of *individualism*. Individualism dictates that individuals are responsible for their own health (Brownell, 1991). Over-concern with personal responsibility for health can lead to victim blaming and an atmosphere in which 'we are worrying ourselves half to death' (L. Thomas, 1979, p. 38 cited by Brownell, 1991). Brownell warned that the 'tendency to overstate the impact of personal behaviour on health' could feed the victim-blaming ethos which is already strong in western societies (Brownell, 1991, p. 303).

Cross-cultural psychology emphasizes cultural diversity and casts a sceptical eye over the *ethnocentrism* of mainstream psychology. This approach considers national or large group samples as the unit of analysis rather than individuals. Research on cross-cultural studies of health has focused primarily on mental health (e.g. Dasen et al., 1988) and there has been relatively little attention paid to physical health. A truly cross-cultural approach to health psychology is at a relatively early stage of development. However, it is clear that there is a need for more understanding of cross-cultural differences in concepts of health and illness and in the methods used for preserving well-being and healing the sick.

WHAT IS HEALTH PSYCHOLOGY?

BOX 1.2   HEALTH PSYCHOLOGY: A DEFINITION

Health psychology is an interdisciplinary field concerned with the application of psychological knowledge and techniques to health, illness and health care.

Box 1.2 provides a working definition that is relatively easy to remember. In discussing this definition further, we can say that the primary objective of health psychology is to promote and maintain the well-being of individuals, communities and populations. The primary focus is normally *physical* rather than *mental* health although, like the two sides of a coin, these aspects are impossible to separate. At a theoretical level, health psychology is concerned with understanding the relationships between mind and body as these affect the overall state of an individual's well-being. At a practical level, it is concerned with intervening in the interface between the individual, the health-care system, and society.

A comprehensive but slightly more complicated definition was proposed by Joseph Matarazzo in 1982. This is presented in Box 1.3.

BOX 1.3   HEALTH PSYCHOLOGY: MATARAZZO'S (1982) DEFINITION

Health psychology is the aggregate of the specific educational, scientific, and professional contributions of the discipline of psychology to the promotion and maintenance of health, the prevention and treatment of illness, the identification of aetiologic and diagnostic correlates of health, illness, and related dysfunction and to the analysis and improvement of the health care system and health policy formation. (Matarazzo, 1982, p. 4)

This definition has been adopted by the American Psychological Association's (APA) Health Psychology Division, the British Psychological

Society's (BPS) Division of Health Psychology, and by other similar professional and scientific organizations. It serves as health psychology's 'official' definition and has become the 'gold standard' for defining the field.

In recent years, the social context of health issues is receiving more recognition and, consequently, health psychologists are increasingly working beyond the level of the individual, with families, workplaces, organizations, communities and populations. The field of health psychology is already very broad, but it is becoming even broader. Notice that Matarazzo's definition includes 'the analysis and improvement of the health care system and health policy formation'. In fact, health psychology is relevant to any activity, process or policy which has the potential to impact upon individual or community well-being in the broadest sense of the term.

Health psychology grew rapidly during the 1980s and 1990s. By the late 1990s, over 6,000 psychologists had become members of the APA's Health Psychology Division 38, having become one of the largest in the association. At the same time in the UK, the BPS Division of Health Psychology had nearly 1,000 members, and similar organizations are being established across the world.

Health psychology's rapid growth can be attributed to three factors. First, during the 1970s and 1980s there was increasing awareness of the vast amounts of illness and mortality which are determined by behaviour. Epidemiological research suggests that *all* of the leading causes of death in western societies are associated with *behaviour*. This means that many deaths are preventable if effective interventions can be found. Table 1.1 lists the major causes of death in England and Wales during 1997 together with the associated behaviours which are known to be risk factors for the diseases and events causing these deaths. It can be seen that the behaviours responsible for the majority of deaths are:

- smoking, both active and passive;
- poor diet;
- excessive alcohol consumption;
- lack of exercise;
- stress;
- driving carelessly or at speed

In addition to the above behavioural risk factors, a large number of deaths could be prevented with earlier detection or screening.

A second significant factor in the cultural evolution of health psychology has been a strengthening of the ideology in western societies that *individuals are responsible for their own health*. This ideology places the responsibility for good health onto the individual and behoves each individual person to become an expert on his or her own health and how this may be affected by the lifestyle he or she is leading. A number of lucrative industries have grown up which focus on the perceived needs of consumers who have been

TABLE 1.1 **Leading causes of mortality and associated behaviours, England and Wales, 1997 (Office for National Statistics, London, 1998)**

Cause	Number of deaths	Associated behaviours
Diseases of the circulatory system	229,585	• Smoking (active and passive) • Poor diet • Excessive alcohol consumption • Stress (?) • Lack of exercise • Lack of early detection • Poor adherence to treatment
Malignant neoplasms	135,771	• Smoking (active and passive) • Poor diet • Excessive alcohol consumption • Lack of early detection
Diseases of the respiratory system	93,435	• Smoking (active and passive) • Lack of early detection
Diseases of the digestive system	20,559	• Poor diet • Smoking (active and passive) • Stress (?)
External causes of injury and poisoning (including motor accidents)	16,615	• Driving at speed • Excessive alcohol consumption • Not wearing safety equipment
Diseases of the genitourinary system	6,776	• Unprotected sex • Lack of early detection
Other	55,311	• Many of the above
Total	558,052	

repeatedly exhorted to live a 'healthy lifestyle'. The fitness industry, diet industry, designer running shoes, low-fat yoghurts, light alcohol drinks, low tar and even non-combustible cigarettes are all testimony to the explosion of commercial interests catering for our every health wish and fear. The promotion of healthy behaviours by governmental organizations is therefore strongly linked to commercial exploitation of the so-called healthy lifestyle. At the same time, the perceived political correctness of health advocacy has led to a backlash in the form of accusations of 'health fascism' by commercial 'front' organizations appealing to ideas of human liberty and choice which suggest that adult consumers should be free to smoke, drink, and eat as much as they like if they choose to do so.

The ideology of personal responsibility for health is a core part of the cultural value of individualism which was already mentioned above. Individualism assumes that each individual person is a self-contained unit, requiring minimum levels of sharing, caring and interdependency. This value is particularly strong in those regions where health psychology has developed the fastest – the USA, northern Europe and Australia. This view suggests that there is really no such thing as 'society' or 'community', that people primarily should only look after themselves and their families.

A third trend promoting health psychology has been a disenchantment with biomedical health care. In spite of its very high costs (Figure 1.1),

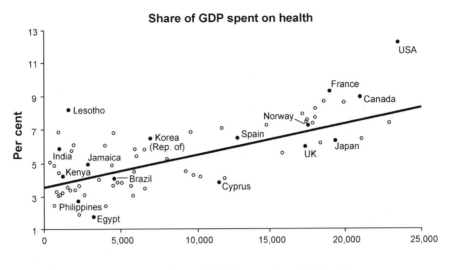

FIGURE 1.1   ***Income and health spending in 70 countries (World Bank, 1993, p. 110, Fig. 5.1; reproduced with permission)***

health-care systems are perceived by some to be inefficient, ineffective and producing low levels of satisfaction. The poor quality of communication experienced by patients with doctors and others in the health-care system has been a particularly strong focus of complaints and criticism. The dominance of the medical model has been heavily criticized since the 1970s (Illich, 1976a and b) and the decline of disease in the twentieth century, attributed by doctors to the efficacy of modern medicine, has been attributed by some to be due mainly to better hygiene and reduced poverty (McKeown, 1979).

Disenchantment with the medical model and a growing awareness of the importance of psychological and social influences on health and illness have led social scientists and others to propose new ways of conceptualizing health and illness. Psychosocial factors have been claimed to be as important or more important than the purely biological causes of well-being. This position led to the development of the biopsychosocial model (Engel, 1977). This new model has been a major influence in the evolution of health psychology as a new field of study.

For many reasons therefore, health psychology has become an exciting, dynamic and popular field. Many new books and journals have appeared and there is considerable attention from the media. Health promotion programmes are increasingly employing psychological knowledge and approaches in a variety of interventions. Primary health care physicians are employing more clinical, counselling and health psychology expertise, while surgeons, anaesthetists and many other clinicians are to an increasing extent applying health psychology research and practice in their clinical work.

A primary role of the health psychologist is to improve the psychosocial conditions for the promotion and maintenance of health. The study and enhancement of the psychosocial resources available to the individual person are a core focus of the field. However, the gap between theory and practice is larger than it should be and needs to be narrowed. As we shall see in Chapter 2, there are some fairly severe constraints on the ability of health workers positively to influence health because of the significant social and economic determinants which structure the health of individuals and communities. It is important to recognize these limits in designing and setting the objectives for interventions. In order to help make genuine improvements to the health-care system and health policy formation, psychologists need to be fully aware of the social and economic context in which they, the other professionals and communities live and work. This is why, in writing this book, the authors give high priority to the context of health psychology and to its interdisciplinary and inter-professional links.

Ethics

David Seedhouse (1998) stated: 'The health world is so conceptually disoriented it sometimes seems it may never achieve its moral potential. Mostly we bumble along – perpetually troubled by territorial squabbles and inadequate resources – blind to the intellectual challenge that must be met if health work is to become all it can be' (p. 23). While most people who work in health fields will recognize these problems, what is Seedhouse referring to when he speaks of 'moral potential'?

An important consideration in all health research and practice is ethics. These are principles whereby the practitioner and researcher think and act. According to Seedhouse (1998): 'Health work is moral work . . . Ethics is the key to health work's new era' (p. 34). Often health-care decisions are made with very little conscious thought about the rights and wrongs of doing things one way rather than another. However, there is a need to be aware of the ethical implications of even everyday decisions and choices which influence the information provided, intervention given and evaluation or follow-up made. The active participation of the person(s) on the 'receiving end' of interventions can only really be achieved when an ethical perspective is first applied to the situation and that such a perspective confirms the value of what is offered when all the costs and benefits have been openly considered.

Health psychologists work within the ethical codes of their national and regional professional boards and societies. Psychologists working in the USA are guided by the American Psychological Association's Ethical

Principles (APA, 1992). European psychologists are guided by the Meta-Code of Ethics produced by the European Federation of Professional Psychologists' Associations (EFPPA). This states: 'Psychologists . . . strive to help the public in developing informed judgements and choices regarding human behaviour, and to improve the condition of both the individual and society.' These four principles should operate in everyday working practice: (1) Respect for a person's right and dignity; (2) Competence; (3) Responsibility; (4) Integrity (EFPPA, 1997).

HEALTH PSYCHOLOGY AS AN INTERDISCIPLINARY FIELD

The study of health psychology is linked to branches of many health and social sciences including medical anthropology, medical sociology, medical ethics, social policy, health economics, epidemiology, medicine, surgery and dentistry. Health psychology overlaps extensively with two highly related fields: *behavioural health*, concerned with preventing illness and enhancing health, and *behavioural medicine*, concerned with integrating the behavioural and medical sciences. In some contexts, all three terms (health psychology, behavioural health and behavioural medicine) can be used interchangeably, especially when the focus is on health behaviour rather than people's experience of health more generally.

Matarazzo's definition of health psychology requires activity across a broad range of areas. In fact the field needs to be pegged out rather flexibly because of all the different contexts and settings where psychology could play a role, once they are investigated from a psychological perspective. There is always a new application around the corner waiting to be discovered and the most exciting research topics often lie between existing disciplines. There is enormous untapped potential waiting to be explored.

An increasingly important set of applications occur in the context of clinical work with patients. This is the field of *clinical health psychology*. This is a large and complex field in its own right.

Interdisciplinary approaches bring theory and knowledge from cognate disciplines into new, more powerful synthesis. Health is a multifaceted construct which lends itself to an interdisciplinary approach. Similarly, health care is a catch-all term applied to an infinitude of situations involving many different providers and users with a vast array of different needs. Without major contributions from other disciplines and fields it seems doubtful that health psychology can provide a meaningful account of the psychological aspects of health, illness and health care. A case can therefore be made for an *interdisciplinary* approach. As health psychology progresses we can see a process of bridge building which creates new points of contact with a broad spectrum of social, biological and health sciences. Through an evolutionary process, a new interdisciplinary field is being created between psychology and the many related fields.

THEORY IN HEALTH PSYCHOLOGY

Theory in health psychology consists of three broad types which vary according to their level of generality: there are *frameworks*, *theories* and *models*. Frameworks have some of the characteristics of paradigms as described by Kuhn (1970) as they refer to a complete system of thinking about a field of inquiry. However, unlike paradigms which include explicitly stated assumptions, laws and methods, frameworks are looser and less developed in nature, but are intended to be of general application.

Examples of frameworks in the fields of health and health care would be the so-called medical model and the more recent biopsychosocial model. However, these have been consistently referred to as *models* in the literature and, to avoid confusion, we will do the same here. It is necessary to consider theory building at its most general level and for this we reserve the term 'framework'.

An example of a *framework* for considering the general determinants of health is presented in Figure 1.2 (Dahlgren and Whitehead, 1991; Whitehead, 1995).

This framework has a multi-layered, onion-like structure which places the individual at the centre, endowed with fixed factors of age, sex and genetic factors, but firmly surrounded by four layers of influence consisting of individual lifestyle, social and community influences, living and working conditions and general socio-economic, cultural and environmental conditions. This framework has six characteristics:

1. It is concerned with all the determinants of health in general and not simply with the course of events during the treatment of illness.
2. It places the individual at the core but acknowledges the primary determining influence of society through the community, living and working conditions, and the surrounding socio-economic, cultural and environmental conditions.
3. It places each layer in the context of its neighbours reflecting structural constraints upon change.
4. It has a true interdisciplinary flavour and is not merely a medical or quasi-medical model of health.
5. It makes no imperialist claims for any one field over others.
6. It acknowledges the complex nature of health determinants.

Different theories and models are needed which vary in purpose and level of specificity for differing settings and contexts. However, there is a need for a general paradigm for understanding the health of the individual within which more specific theories and models can be nested. Such a paradigm should attempt to represent in an explicit, detailed and meaningful way the constraints upon and links between individual well-being, the surrounding community and the health-care system (Marks, 1996). As yet, no such general paradigm exists.

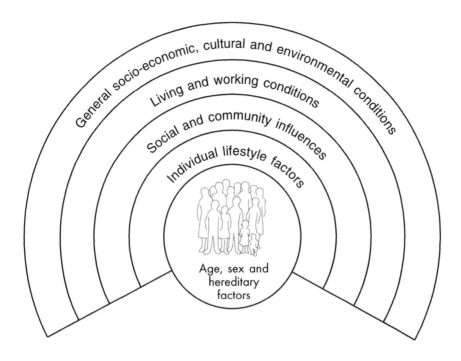

FIGURE 1.2   **A framework for the determinants of health (Dahlgren and Whitehead, 1991, p. 23; reproduced with permission)**

The next level of generality in theory building is the *theory*. The status of health psychology as a scientific endeavour rests upon its ability to provide explanatory accounts or theories of health experience and behaviour. Much current theory is intended to meet scientific criteria of accurate prediction and verifiability. Examples of theories in health psychology are those which are primarily concerned with the psychological resources needed to cope effectively with changing circumstances brought about by major life events including illness. Such resources may be classified into five main categories: economic, psychological, biological, social and spiritual. Processes which fall into these categories are: socio-economic status, resilience, immuno-competence, social support and beliefs respectively. Theories in each of these areas will be presented in this text.

Many theories in health psychology have consisted of *flowchart models*. Such models have focused upon informational processes in the heads of individuals as these influence, and are influenced by, social and physiological processes directly or indirectly related to health or illness. An example of a flowchart model is provided in Figure 1.3. This provides a hypothetical model of processes which are claimed to be related to hypertension (Spicer and Chamberlain, 1996).

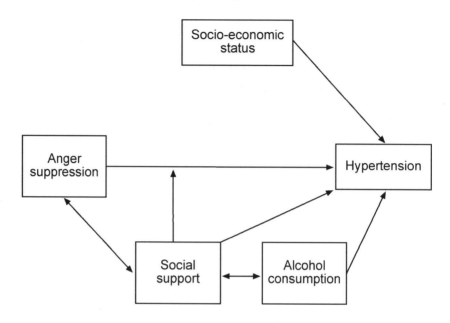

FIGURE 1.3 ***A flowchart representing a hypothetical model of hypertension (Spicer and Chamberlain, 1996, p. 163; reproduced with permission)***

The model proposes that hypertension is *influenced* by anger suppression, social support, alcohol consumption and socio-economic status. The level of influence may be either *causal*, at the strongest level of association, or *correlational*, at a weaker level of association. The model also suggests that social support is influenced by anger suppression and alcohol consumption and that social support moderates the relationship between anger suppression and hypertension.

Flowchart models can be analysed on three distinct levels: the theoretical level consisting of the constructs and causal relations; the measurement level containing the variables which map onto the constructs; and the statistical level which maps the statistical relationships between variables onto the theoretical relationships. The statistical analysis of flowcharts is becoming an ever more technical discipline in its own right and there are sophisticated computer programs designed especially for this purpose (Bentler, 1989; Byrne, 1994).

At the theoretical level, flowcharts often contain a mix of constructs from ontologically distinct domains which are nevertheless believed to be causally connected. Causal connectedness between these constructs is indicated by the lines and arrows which are drawn between boxes. These lines and arrows attempt to give a form of explanatory coherence and scientific meaning to the model. Thus, the flowchart model has a significance which appears to place it within a natural science epistemology of knowledge and understanding.

In fact, the hypertension model in Figure 1.3 is a complex of constructs selected from five domains or levels:

1   Hypertension is a *physiological* construct.
2   Anger suppression is a *psychological* construct.
3   Alcohol consumption is a *behavioural* construct.
4   Social support is a *social* construct.
5   Socio-economic status is a *sociological* construct.

This analysis suggests that there are, embedded in this flowchart, some deep, unanswered philosophical questions about the mechanisms for translating between the different levels of the system. For example, how does anger suppression (a psychological process) *cause* hypertension (a physiological process)? Normally, health psychologists do not attempt to answer (or even ask!) such questions at a philosophical level, but they remain significant questions nevertheless. The health psychologist attempts to collect as much empirical evidence as possible to confirm or disconfirm the anger suppression hypothesis by measuring hypertension directly and anger suppression via questionnaires, interviews or observation in the same group of participants. It is then possible to investigate statistically whether there is a link, causal or otherwise, between anger suppression and hypertension.

One alternative way of interpreting a flowchart is to see it as an essentially narrative device in the form of a diagram which can be given a particular scientific meaning. This kind of analysis is more in tune with the human science approach. Following extensive elaboration carried out by unpacking of the flowchart boxes and more detailed explication of how the contents of each box affects the others, a 'story' is being told by the model which can be allowed gradually to unfold.

To give the hypertension model a truly *causal* interpretation, the five constructs need to be connected and compatible so that the links become genuinely causal. One solution to the 'arrow problem' is to see that bio-psychosocial constructs can actually operate on multiple levels. One example of a multi-level construct is that of 'emotion'. Emotion is said to operate simultaneously on at least three different levels – sociological, psychological and physiological (Lazarus et al., 1980).

Thus, 'anger suppression' in the hypertension model operates on all three of these levels. However, it is at the physiological level that anger suppression can causally influence hypertension. A similar explanatory exercise needs to be performed with each of the eight interconnecting arrows in the model. This exercise may have a complexity that is belied by the bold simplicity of the arrows and the surface definition of the connected constructs. However, the flowchart model is an important conceptual device in the construction of scientific accounts of health and illness.

Health psychology draws much of its appeal from its claim that, by including the psychosocial, there is the possibility of providing a more meaningful, 'human' account of health, illness and health-care issues. New theories are created by employing psychological constructs to weave an account which provides fresh understanding. However, if a theory is to have any scientific value, its assumptions and contents have to be stated in a fully explicit and precise manner. The existence of unexplained assumptions has been a stumbling block for acceptance of the biopsychosocial model as an improvement upon the medical model.

Although the rhetoric of creating a challenge to the medical model attracted attention to the biopsychosocial model, this challenge in the name of psychology and the social sciences is not seen by everybody to be sufficiently radical or persuasive (e.g. Ogden, 1997). This means that a stronger case must be made on behalf of psychosocial models if the traditional medical model is to lose pole position in western thinking about health, illness and health care.

RESEARCH METHODS IN HEALTH PSYCHOLOGY

As a new field, health psychology has many different research questions and consequently requires many methods for potentially answering them. As the field develops, researchers are learning to ask better questions and are developing theories, models and methods which are appropriate to those questions. The role of theory has already been described above. Methodology is of equal importance in the testing of theories or models and in putting theory into practice. In applying health psychology to the real world of health care and promotion, it is necessary that practical applications are properly evidence based. Many of psychology's traditional methods are quantitative in nature, placing emphasis on the reliable measurement of variables in the context of controlled investigation including experimentation. Other qualititative methods are concerned with the exploration and analysis of health or illness experience. Qualitative approaches are gradually becoming more accepted (Murray and Chamberlain, 1998). However, the ongoing debate concerning the merits and demerits of these two broad approaches is likely to continue for some time into the future. In essence, these different methods complement each other and both have a positive role to play in painting a more complete picture of psychology and health.

It is inappropriate to suggest that any of the methods is 'better' than any of the others. There is no absolutely 'right' way of gathering information. Which method is to be recommended entirely depends upon the question being asked and the all-important context. There are therefore many different methods and research designs in health psychology. The list below includes (in alphabetical order) both methods of data collection and analysis.

action research: this type of research is concerned with the process of change and what else happens when change occurs. The investigator acts as a facilitator or resource who responds to the situation as it changes and helps the situation to develop in a desirable direction as perceived by the various parties concerned. Action research is particularly suited to consultancy work when an organization or system or method requires urgent improvement.

case studies: retrospective written reports on individual people, groups or systems.

cross-sectional studies: involve obtaining responses from a sample of respondents on one occasion only. With appropriate randomized sampling methods, the sample can be assumed to be a representative cross-section of the population(s) under study and it will be possible to make comparisons between sub-groups (e.g. males vs. females, older vs. younger people, etc.).

diary techniques: any data collection method in which the data are linked to the passage of time. They often involve self-report but they may also contain information about observations of others.

direct observation: directly observing behaviour in a relevant setting, for example, patients waiting for treatment in a doctor's surgery or clinic. The observation may be accompanied by recordings in written, oral, auditory or visual form. Several investigators may observe the same events and reliability checks conducted. Direct observation includes casual observation, formal observation and participant observation.

discourse analysis: a set of procedures for analysing language as used in speech or texts. It focuses on the language and how it is used to construct versions of 'social reality' and what is gained by constructing events using the particular terms being used. It has links with ethnomethodology, conversation analysis and the study of meaning (semiology).

ethnographic methods: seek to build a systematic understanding of a culture from the viewpoint of the insider. Ethnographic methods are multiple attempts to describe the shared beliefs, practices, artefacts, knowledge and behaviours of an intact cultural group. They attempt to represent the totality of a phenomenon in its complete context in its naturalistic setting.

focus groups: one or more group discussions in which participants focus collectively upon a topic or issue usually presented to them as a group of questions; although sometimes as a film, a collection of advertisements, cards to sort, a game to play, or a vignette to discuss. The distinctive feature of the focus group method is its generation of interactive data (Wilkinson, 1998).

historical analysis: the use of data produced from memory, historical sources, or artefacts.

interviews (structured or semi-structured): a structured interview schedule is a prepared, standard set of questions which are asked in person, or perhaps by telephone, of a person or group of persons concerning a particular research issue or question. A semi-structured interview is much more open ended and allows the interviewee scope to address the issues which he/she feels relevant to the topics being raised by the investigator.

longitudinal designs: involve measuring responses of a single sample on more than one occasion. These measurements may be *prospective* or *retrospective*, but prospective longitudinal designs allow greater control over the sample, the variables measured and the times when the measurements take place.

meta-analysis: a systematic and integrative statistical analysis of the results from a number of research studies which may be combined because they asked a similar research question. The analysis is often based on the calculation of the mean effect size in which each study is weighted according to the number of participants.

multivariate analyses: use information about more than one independent variable in a statistical analysis of data. Multivariate techniques include multiple regression and correlation, path analysis, factor analysis, multi-dimensional scaling, analyses of cross-classified data, logistic regression, multivariate analysis of variance, discriminant analysis, and meta-analysis. (For a useful summary of these techniques, see Grimm and Yarnold, 1995.)

narrative approaches: seek insight and meaning through the acquisition of data in the form of stories concerning personal experiences (Murray, 1997a). These approaches assume that human beings are natural storytellers and that the principle task of the psychologist is to explore the different stories being told.

questionnaires: many constructs in health psychology are measured using questionnaires consisting of a standard set of items with accompanying instructions. Ideally a questionnaire will have been demonstrated to be both a reliable and a valid measure of the construct(s) it purports to measure. A useful portfolio of such measures is available for researchers (Johnson et al., 1995). This portfolio contains a representative set of questionnaires in the following domains: pain and pain behaviours; stress, emotion and life events; coping; social support; health status and health-related quality of life; illness, symptoms, disability and recovery; expectations, experience and evaluations of health care; individual and demographic differences; causal and control beliefs; beliefs and knowledge about health and illness; health related behaviour.

randomized controlled trials (RCTs): these involve the systematic comparison of interventions using a fully controlled application of one or more interventions or 'treatments' with a random allocation of participants to the different treatment groups.

single case experimental designs: these are investigations of a series of experimental manipulations on a single research participant.

surveys: systematic methods for determining how a defined sample of participants respond to a set of standard questions attempting to assess their feelings, attitudes, beliefs or knowledge at one or more particular times.

The studies described in this textbook have used one or more of the above methods and designs. Progress in health psychology follows creative problem solving by many different individuals and groups using a multiplicity of skills and expertise of which the implementation of methodology is but one. Methods need to be appropriately matched to both theory and practice. For a useful source of information on research methods for health psychology, see Breakwell et al. (1995).

HEALTH PSYCHOLOGY IN SOCIAL CONTEXT

Health psychologists work in a variety of settings which include health promotion units, primary health care, general hospitals, companies and organizations, academic departments and research units. Some of the more traditional settings are clinical environments with medical agendas and practices. Although health psychologists frequently argue against the medical model and in favour of the biopsychosocial model (e.g. Broome and Llewellyn, 1995), it has to be acknowledged that the majority of practice still occurs in the context of clinical medicine.

The biopsychosocial model has been vigorously advocated by psychologists and others concerned with the health of the individual considered as a totality. However, as yet there has been no significant paradigm shift in clinical medicine and, although it has some vocal proponents, the biopsychosocial model has not replaced the medical model in hospitals and clinics. Health-care services, for the most part, remain dominated by medical rather than psychosocial concerns. Health-care services sometimes appear as if they are designed as much for the convenience of doctors and nursing staff as for the well-being of patients. In spite of attempts to improve older, ineffective systems of care, most health-care delivery remains heavily medicalized even when any evidence that it is effective remains absent.

The socio-political environment of many health-care systems has been described sociologically as a 'medical hegemony'. This refers to the power and leadership held by medical doctors over other staff groups working in the health-care system and, of course, the patients. The scale and scope of the work of paramedical staff and psychologists depends largely upon the decisions of health service managers and medical consultants. Clinical health psychology practice is therefore embedded in medical agendas with all the associated discourse, practices and technologies. The power imbalance between health-care professionals is replicated in their relationships with patients and it has been argued that this has profound implications for the delivery of care (Kreps, 1996a).

There has been little critical analysis of health psychology in its socio-political context. Equally there has been hardly any awareness or discussion of the implications of the individualistic nature of western culture, psychology and health-care systems for the current development of the field. Health psychology to the present day should perhaps be more aptly termed 'illness psychology' as its main focus is illness behaviour and illness management (Marks, 1996). There is a need for an explicitly social orientation such as the framework presented in Figure 1.2.

A fully social orientation considers health psychology within society as a whole. It includes the study of well-being from a multicultural perspective in its full social context. It studies health as well as illness, preventive care as well as cure, and considers the individual primarily as a social being and a creator of meanings. It considers the macro-social factors operating at global and societal levels in addition to the more microscopic processes occurring at the level of individual human beings. The political economy has a multitude of effects on well-being (Doyal, 1979; McKinlay, 1984) and health psychologists must give more attention to this. There is also a need for more studies of the cost-effectiveness of psychological interventions in comparision to pharmacological or other medical treatments so that the benefits can be weighed against the costs of these various treatment modalities.

From this perspective, health psychology is viewed as a strongly inter-disciplinary field having many links with other human sciences and also with the humanities and literature. In attempting to address issues shared with other disciplines, health psychology is inevitably a highly social and practical field of inquiry.

The future challenges and opportunities for the health psychology field are considerable. The Global Burden of Disease (GBD) study projected mortality and disability in the next 25 years (Murray and Lopez, 1997). The evidence from the GBD Study suggest that health trends will be determined mainly by the ageing of the world's population, the decline in mortality from communicable, maternal, perinatal and nutritional disorders, the spread of HIV, and the increase in tobacco-related mortality and disability (Murray and Lopez, 1997). Leading causes of disability are predicted to be:

- ischaemic heart disease;
- unipolar major depression;
- road traffic accidents;
- cerebrovascular disease;
- chronic obstructive pulmonary disease;
- lower respiratory infections;
- tuberculosis;

- war injuries;
- diarrhoeal diseases;
- HIV;
- dementia.

Many of the these causes of disability and mortality are psychologically or behaviourally mediated. In particular, tobacco, dietary fat, alcohol, driving and unprotected sex are highly significant risk factors. In the future, those with expertise in the understanding, prediction and control of behaviour will play a key role in the promotion of health, the modification of risk and the prevention of disability and mortality.

FUTURE RESEARCH

1 Critics have suggested that the biopsychosocial model remains essentially biomedical and that its theoretical basis has yet to be properly worked out. Research is needed at a basic conceptual and theoretical level to unravel the biopsychosocial model and to specify more clearly the differences between it and the medical model.
2 Transcultural studies of health, illness and health care are needed to facilitate communication and understanding of mechanisms and systems of healing among different cultural, ethnic and religious groups.
3 The benefits of applying psychological theories, methods and interventions need to be studied and communicated in a more convincing fashion to health-care purchasers and providers.
4 There is a need for more studies of the cost effectiveness of psychological interventions in comparision to pharmacological or other medical treatments so that the benefits can be weighed rationally against costs.
5 Action research is needed to learn how to implement changes in systems of care, putting theory and research into practice.

SUMMARY

1 Talk and thought about health varies considerably across time and place. There is no universally acceptable account of health and illness. Health is a positive state of being with physical, cultural, psychosocial, economic and spiritual attributes, not simply the absence of illness.
2 Health psychology is concerned with the application of psychological knowledge and techniques to health, illness and health care. Its primary objective is to understand and to help improve the well-being of individuals and communities. The primary focus is on physical rather than mental health, although these are not easily separable in practice.

3   There are three contrasting approaches to the understanding of health and health care. First, the medical model views all health and illness phenomena as purely biochemical or physical. Second, the biopsychosocial model, a development of the first approach, assumes that health and illness are determined by a combination of physical, psychological and cultural factors. Third, the human science approach which is more concerned with the quality of health and illness in everyday experience from an individual point of view.

4   Health psychology grew rapidly during the last quarter of the twentieth century. The field's growth can be attributed to three factors: (a) increasing evidence that much of the illness and mortality is caused by lifestyles and health-damaging behaviour; (b) a strengthening of the philosophy in industrialized countries that individuals are responsible for their own health; (c) increasing disenchantment with the medical model and its dominance of health care.

5   Health psychologists work according to an ethical code agreed by national and regional boards and societies. Four key principles of such codes are: (1) respect for a person's rights and dignity; (2) competence; (3) responsibility; (4) integrity. These principles apply equally to researchers, teachers/trainers and practitioners.

6   The biopsychosocial model has been put forward as a challenge to the medical model. It suggests that health is created by psychosocial as well as biological determinants. However, the model requires further work and radical revision may be necessary before the medical model can be finally replaced.

7   Theory building in health psychology occurs at three levels of generality: (a) the level of frameworks; (b) the level of theories; (c) the level of specific models.

8   Health psychology has a broad scope with many diverse, interesting and complex questions and consequently requires many methods for answering them. Both quantitative and qualitative methods are essential for a full understanding of the psychology of health experience and behaviour.

9   There is a need for more understanding of cultural differences in concepts of health and illness and in the methods used for preserving well-being and healing the sick. The cross-cultural approach to health psychology is at an early stage of development.

10 The implications of individualism for the nature of current theory and practice in health psychology need to be critically analysed.

11 A social orientation is necessary if we are to understand health behaviour and experience in the context of society and culture. Such an orientation includes the study of well-being from diverse interdisciplinary and cross-cultural perspectives. It focuses upon health as much as illness, preventive care as much as cure, and considers families, groups, and communities as much as individuals.

12 Health psychology has the potential to become a socially relevant, non-ethnocentric and immensely practical application of knowledge about the nature of being human.

KEY TERMS

behavioural health
behavioural medicine
biopsychosocial model
discourse
ethnocentrism
flowchart model
framework
health
health psychology
indigenous

individualism
inequality
interdisciplinary
medical model
model
narrative
social constructionism
theory
well-being

2 THE MACRO-SOCIAL ENVIRONMENT AND HEALTH

The health and survival of children depend on many factors: on the health of their fathers and mothers; on the survival skills of their families; on the relative peace or violence in their communities; on the economic and political status of their nations; on whether the wages that people earn or the land they till provide enough to eat; on the availability, quality and cost of education, health services, water, shelter and transportation; on the ability of people to organize and defend their rights; on local consumption of alcohol, tobacco and narcotics; on who has power over whom; on war . . . on military expenditures relative to public service expenditures; on international trade relations; on preservation or destruction of the environment; on how far a mother has to walk to get firewood or cow manure for cooking . . . on undermining of grassroots movements . . . on whether the banks will be permitted to continue protecting their billions by taking away food, health care and education from destitute children. (Werner, 1992, p. 10)

OUTLINE

This chapter describes the economic and societal context for the study of health psychology. Global trends and health variations between and within societies are discussed. The chapter then describes and discusses the relationship between health experience and social position as indicated by socio-economic status, gender, and ethnicity. The explanation of health variations creates an important challenge for health psychology.

GLOBAL HEALTH TRENDS

The health of human populations is shaped by historical, political and economic forces which are unpredictable and uncontrollable. Societies are dependent upon their economic power and shifts in the balance of power between themselves and others. The health of individuals is dependent upon the communities to which they belong and on the balance of economic power between the individual members. All are influenced by powerful economic forces which are impossible for anyone to control.

On a global scale, human well-being is determined by a host of factors, the most significant being droughts, famines, epidemics, wars and poverty.

In spite of all of these, life expectancy has increased almost everywhere and there has been a dramatic decrease in both infant and adult mortality. These improvements have resulted largely from a decline in the occurrence of fatal infectious diseases. However, there are still a large number of such deaths annually (16.4 million in 1993, one-third of all deaths) and the massive regional differences that existed in 1950 remain almost unchanged to the present day (Figure 2.1).

Of 5.6 billion people in the world population, 4.4 billion live in developing countries. The greatest influence on health at the global level is *poverty*. There are many different definitions of poverty but one defines it as 'a level of income below which people cannot afford a minimum, nutritionally adequate diet and essential non-food requirements' (UN Development Programme, 1995). Half of the world's population lacks regular access to treatment of common diseases and most essential drugs. In the mid-1990s there were approximately 15 million refugees and 15 million internally displaced persons.

In 1995 the World Health Organization (WHO) renewed its global strategy, Health for All. In launching this strategy, the WHO's then Director-General, Dr Hiroshi Nakajima (1995), suggested that a two-track society divided by poverty is a 'global time bomb'. Nakajima warned that if poverty alleviation policies fail, further improvements in global health would be impossible to achieve. The WHO (1995) report presented some striking statistics. In industrialized countries, two-thirds of all deaths occur after the age of 65 while, in developing countries, two-thirds of all deaths occur before the age of 65, and nearly one-third before the age of 5. In spite of the overall improvements in health, there are huge inequities which, if anything, are increasing.

The greatest cause of ill health and early mortality is poverty. The health effects of poverty are tangible in both industrialized and non-industrialized countries and the biological mechanisms are the same. The major impacts of poverty on health are caused by the absence of:

- safe water;
- environmental sanitation;
- adequate diet;
- secure housing;
- basic education;
- income generating opportunities;
- access to health care.

The most common health outcomes are infectious diseases, malnutrition and reproductive hazards (Anand and Chen, 1996).

In 1991, the number of people living in extreme poverty was estimated by Oxfam to be approximately 1.1 billion – one-fifth of the world's population. It was also estimated that the wealthiest fifth of the world's population controlled 85% of global *gross national product (GNP)* and 85% of

Life expectancy at birth (years)

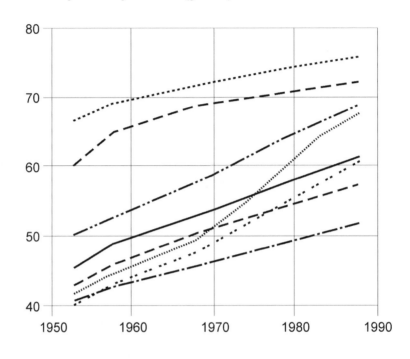

—·—·—·—   **Sub-Saharan Africa**

— — — — — ·   **India**

....   **China**

————————   **Other Asia and islands**

—··—··—··   **Latin America and the Caribbean**

·· ·· ·· ·· ·· ·   **Middle Eastern crescent**

— — — — — ·   **Former socialist economies of Europe**

·············   **Established market economies**

FIGURE 2.1 *Trends in life expectancy by demographic region, 1950–90 (World Bank, 1993, p. 23, Fig. 2.1; reproduced with permission)*

world trade, while the poorest fifth controlled only 1.4% of GNP and 0.9% of world trade (Oxfam, 1991). In the 1990s, the gap between the 'haves' and 'have-nots' continued to widen and it appears most unlikely that it will narrow within the next 50 to 100 years.

The WHO (1995) report stated that poverty causes 12 million deaths annually in children under the age of 5; one-quarter of these deaths arise from acute lower respiratory tract infections and one-quarter from diarrhoea and dysentery. The WHO estimated that malnutrition is an underlying cause in 30% of child deaths and produces growth retardation in 230 million children and severe wasting in another 50 million. Among adult deaths, poverty accounts annually for up to 2.7 million deaths from tuberculosis and 2 million from malaria. Maternal mortality, running at 500,000 deaths a year in 1995, is associated with high fertility and poor access to health services (Kevany, 1996).

INEQUALITIES BETWEEN COUNTRIES

Studies of life expectancy

Evidence from a wide variety of sources suggests that the average life expectancy is higher when income differences are relatively small and societies are more socially cohesive (Wilkinson, 1996). It has been suggested that the same basic principles determine the health of populations in both rich and poor countries (Rogers, 1992). However, recent analyses conducted by one of the authors suggest that the relationships between ecological variables and life expectancy is quite different for poor and rich nations (Marks, 1999).

Two important predictors of life expectancy are gross national product per capita (GNPpc) and *income distribution*. GNPpc is calculated using the World Bank Atlas method which measures the total domestic and foreign value added claimed by residents converted to US dollars. Income distribution is measured by examining the percentage share of income or consumption taken by the lowest and highest income groups in a society. For example, in one of the poorest countries, Tanzania, in 1991, the best off 20% of households controlled 62.7% of the country's income while the worst off 20% controlled only 2.4% of income. In one of the richest nations, the USA, in 1985, the best off 20% of households controlled 41.9% of the country's income while the worst off 20% controlled only 4.7% of income (World Bank, 1993). However, GNPpc and income inequality are independent predictors of life expectancy and of health.

Among rich countries, GNPpc and income inequality are the most significant predictors of longevity, GNPpc having a positive effect and income inequality a negative effect (Wennemo, 1993). However, Marks (1999) found that female secondary education participation rates are also positively associated with higher average longevity. More surprising was

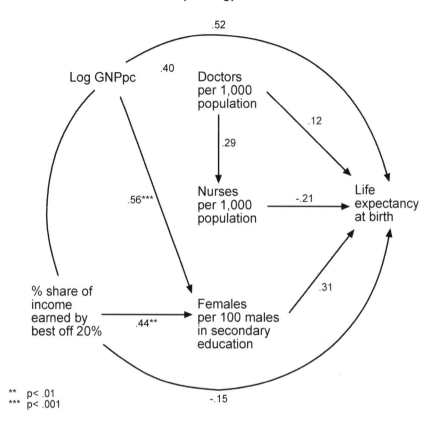

Note: The diagram here (and also the one in Figure 2.4) shows the results of a multivariate analysis called 'path analysis'. A multiple regression is performed with each variable on the left hand side of an arrow (an 'endogenous' variable) treated as independent variable and each variable on the right hand side of an arrow being treated as a dependent variable. For example, a multiple regression is performed in which 'life expectancy at birth' is a dependent variable while log GNPpc, % share of income earned by best-off 20%, females per 100 males in secondary education, doctors per 1,000 population, and nurses per 1,000 population are independent variables. The number printed beside each arrow is the path coefficient, a parameter that indicates the magnitude of the direct effect of one variable on another while controlling for the other variables (see Grimm and Yarnold, 1995).

FIGURE 2.2 *The statistical relationship between life expectancy and economic, educational and health service variables in 20 rich countries (Marks, 1999, p. 10)*

the finding that when GNPpc, income inequality and female secondary education participation rates are all controlled, the average life expectancy in a country is independent of expenditure on health services, and of the numbers of doctors and nurses (Figure 2.2).

These findings place into context the widely held assumption that if national health services are allocated more resources, they will necessarily reduce ill health and keep populations living longer. It has been

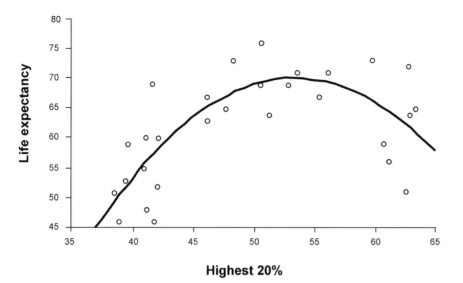

$$Y= -194.132 + 9.865 * X -.092 * X^2; R^2=.543$$

FIGURE 2.3 *The relationship between life expectancy and income distribution in poor countries (Marks, 1999, p. 12)*

acknowledged for some time that the health service has only a limited role to play in the production of a healthy population. There are limits to health care and when those limits are reached, further health gains appear to follow economic and social changes, not increased expenditure on biomedical health care.

Among poor countries, ecological influences show a more complex pattern. Although GNPpc and female secondary education participation rates both have large effects on life expectancy, *income distribution* shows a curvilinear relationship with life expectancy (Figure 2.3). The reason for this remains uncertain but it may be related to changes in the labour market when larger income differences between unemployed, employed workers, farmers and factory owners are created during the early stages of industrialization. Unlike rich countries, however, the more doctors and nurses there are, the higher the average life expectancy. So in these countries, the more medical care there is available, the longer the average life span. However, the total amount spent on health care per head of population is not significantly related to life expectancy (see Figure 2.4).

This analysis and others in the literature suggest that GNPpc and income inequality both have a large influence on the average life expectancy of a population. Also, when GNPpc and income inequality are controlled, female literacy is a significant predictor of life expectancy. In poor countries having a high level of female participation in secondary

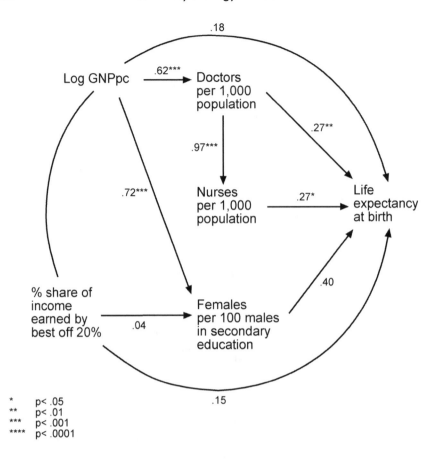

FIGURE 2.4 **The statistical relationship between life expectancy and economic, educational and health service variables in 20 poor countries (Marks, 1999, p. 12)**

education is as important as having large numbers of doctors and nurses while, in rich counties, variations in female secondary education have a larger influence on life expectancy than variations in the numbers of doctors and nurses. This study suggests that, over and above the resulting equalization of opportunities, educating girls has a highly beneficial effect on a society's health. This is a reflection of the fact that the higher the quality of a mother's education, the more effective she can be in promoting the health of her family.

In industrialized countries, future improvements in health can be expected if income growth is accompanied by a more equitable distribution of income. If a society has a highly uneven distribution of income and contains a high proportion of citizens living in poverty, then spending more on health care is unlikely to improve health. This is illustrated by the

USA which spends a higher proportion of its GNP on health care than any other country (14%) and yet ranks twelfth for average life expectancy.

Poverty is linked to debt

If poverty levels are to be significantly reduced it is necessary for wealthier countries to allocate more resources to the development of poorer countries, but not in the form of further loans. If the WHO's Health For All strategy is going to have any chance of success, health must be given a higher priority in global development policies. International debt has a major impact on poverty. In sub-Saharan Africa which contains 34 of the 41 most indebted countries, the proportion of people living in absolute poverty (on under one dollar per day) is growing. Human well-being in sub-Saharan African countries is among the worst in the world. Consider the following indicators:

- Two-thirds of Africans live in absolute poverty.
- More than half lack safe water.
- Seventy per cent are without proper sanitation.
- Forty million children are not in primary school.
- Infant mortality is 55% higher than in other low-income countries.
- Average life expectancy at 51 is 11 years less.
- The incidence of malaria and tuberculosis is increasing.

A large part of the cause of these problems is sub-Saharan Africa's international debt. It pays at least four times more on debt repayments than on health care for its citizens. The worst case is Mozambique which in 1998 owed nearly five times more than its annual national income. UNICEF estimates that 500,000 children die every week because of the debt crisis (Logie and Benatar, 1997). In 1995 the Jubilee 2000 campaign was started in the UK with the aim of getting the unpayable debt of 50 of the world's poorest nations written off by the end of the year 2000. This would cost no more than US$100 billion, about the same as the amount which in 1997 the International Monetary Fund (IMF) promised to loan one country, South Korea, because its economic collapse threatened the value of stocks on financial markets in New York, London and Tokyo.

The World Bank's (1993) *World Development Report 1993: Investing in Health* contains evidence that the post-1950 decline in mortality in developing countries can be attributed to policies which:

- make investments to reduce poverty;
- make health expenditure more cost effective;
- increase the effectiveness of public health measures;
- improve essential clinical services;
- improve schooling, particularly for girls;
- improve the rights and status of women.

The evidence suggests that, in addition to new biomedical discoveries and technologies, some dramatic economic changes are needed if we are to experience further health improvements during the twenty-first century. Among these changes, the cancellation of unpaid debts of the poorest countries and income redistribution within the richest countries have the potential to bring health improvements to match those of the last 50 years of the twentieth century. On the other hand, if current trends continue, the health of many national populations will actually worsen.

The nature of health-care systems

A society's system of health care is a salient manifestation of its desire to care for its most vulnerable members. A health-care system mirrors a country's political ideology. One informative illustration of this principle is the British National Health Service (NHS) founded in 1948. It will be helpful throughout this section to use the NHS as an example of more general principles. The NHS was based on a *welfare model* of health care following the principles of Fabian socialism. A welfare model aims to provide a free, comprehensive service regardless of age, socio-economic status, gender, sexual preference, race or religion. The NHS is the largest employer in Europe. The political climate of Margaret Thatcher's government of the late 1980s brought the 'NHS reforms' and created an internal market of purchasers and providers similar to that operating in the USA. These changes followed principles of 'value for money' and cost containment within a new internal *market model* of competing providers. Similar changes were made to the health-care system in New Zealand.

In the market model, purchasers or insurers pay for services and the provision of care depends upon contracts and the ability to pay. General practitioners (GPs) could become direct purchasers of care and become independent and competitive businesses while fulfilling clinical responsibilities to patients and trying to keep up with medical developments.

Another important aspect of a health service is the distribution and supply of drugs, technology and expertise controlled by a multinational medical-industrial complex of organizations. Whatever principles shape the organization at a structural level, huge numbers of personnel, products and equipment are necessary to operate the system requiring considerable amounts of expenditure. In spite of repeated attempts to increase efficiency, health-care costs continue to rise. The British NHS costs about 3% more each year to run and many commentators believe the service remains chronically underfunded. Policy analysts have suggested that efficiency gains have been accompanied by rising inequities in the quality and distribution of care.

In 1996 the WHO drew up a charter which held that the fundamental value underlying health-care reform is the improvement of people's health, *not* cost containment (Box 2.1).

> **BOX 2.1   WHO'S LJUBLJANA CHARTER: SUMMARY**
> **(RICHARDS, 1996)**
>
> European health care systems should be:
>
> Driven by values of human dignity, equity, solidarity and professional ethics
>
> Targeted on protecting and promoting health
>
> Centred on people, allowing citizens to influence health services and take responsibility for their own health
>
> Focused on quality, including cost effectiveness
>
> Based on sustainable finances, to allow universal coverage and equitable access
>
> Orientated towards primary care

The impact of health service reforms on health outcomes is difficult to evaluate. In the NHS, for example, one impediment to rational appraisal was the refusal of the health ministry to introduce changes in a pilot region to investigate benefits and any unexpected costs (e.g. administrative costs) before changing the system nationally. Those with an interest in showing positive results often choose a purely descriptive approach, measuring changes in performance or activity by demonstrating more admissions or shorter waiting times. However, the quality of patient *experience* is rarely systematically assessed by measuring patient satisfaction or health outcomes before and after a reform. The evaluation of health care is a multi-disciplinary exercise in which the health psychologist can work collaboratively with other professionals and make a significant contribution.

One way of evaluating health service changes is to survey health-care personnel regarding their perceptions of the changes in quality of care. This approach can be illustrated by a study which assessed the impact of the NHS reforms through random surveys of GPs, consultants, surgeons and public health physicians (Francome and Marks, 1996). The latter group is responsible for purchasing health care for their district populations. The study examined the implications of the contracting process of the internal market on the quality of patient care. The study confirmed the view of many commentators that the NHS changes led to an upsurgence of managerialism in which managers – the 'grey suits' – had taken over from the medical consultants – the 'white coats' – as the power brokers in hospitals. Following the changes, health care was perceived as having become increasingly determined by costs rather than clinical need. Many believed that a two-tier system had developed in which the patients of fund-holding GPs were able to obtain faster treatment than those of non-fundholders. As a result of the changes, one of the founding principles – equity – had been eroded and some patients lost trust in doctors (Francome and Marks, 1996).

Health-care systems are under constant review and subject to reform and change on a regular basis. Some commentators suggested that the British and other European health reforms failed to improve the health of communities when considered as a totality. Some have suggested that it is inappropriate to treat health care as a marketplace in which competition over quality and price is used to squeeze more health care from a dwindling supply of resources. Richards argued:

> There should be a return to the ideology of health as a public good where the rights of individuals are balanced more equitably with the health needs of the whole community. Control of spending on health care will not be achieved by minor adjustments to the mix of public and private sectors. A more radical approach is necessary, based on a much more critical look at current provision. (Richards, 1996, p. 1622)

Health-care policies and reforms are controversial with competing values and principles dividing the various protagonists into camps. Some improvements follow from audits of existing services to determine how much they contribute to health gain in relation to their costs. Improvements at a more structural level follow social and economic reforms which focus on poverty, deprivation and improved education.

As suggested above, there is little evidence that, in industrialized countries, allocating even more expenditure to health care is likely to make any further improvements to life expectancy. The *World Development Report* (1993) stated that between 1960 and 1980 worldwide the number of hospital beds rose from 5 million to almost 17 million, more than doubling per capita supply. Between 1955 and 1990, the number of physicians increased from 1.2 million to 6.2 million. However, the report concluded that cost-effective public health and clinical interventions are best delivered at district, community or household levels, not in expensive specialized hospitals where 30 to 80% of national expenditures on health services are allocated. This suggests that billions of dollars are being spent every year for relatively little added value in return.

In the industrialized world it has become fashionable for health services to be restructured in a search for greater efficiency and value for money. However, the evidence suggests that this is tinkering which has little if any positive impact on public health. Structural changes at societal level through policies which bring greater equity in income distribution and the reduction of poverty are necessary if we are to achieve health gains in the twenty-first century which are comparable to those of the twentieth century.

INEQUALITIES WITHIN COUNTRIES

In spite of the massive allocation of public resources to health care, *inequalities* are one of the most striking features of any health-care system.

Inequalities must be taken seriously because of their pervasiveness, magnitude and continuation into better off social groups (Carroll and Davey Smith, 1997). In reviewing health inequalities in 14 countries, Benzeval et al. (1995) concluded:

> People who live in disadvantaged circumstances have more illnesses, greater distress, more disability and shorter lives than those who are more affluent. Such injustice could be prevented, but this requires political will. . . . Health inequalities are endemic characteristics of all modern industrial societies, but the size of the differential varies between countries and over time, indicating that there is nothing fixed or inevitable about having such a health divide. (Benzeval et al., 1995, p. xvii)

This evidence demonstrates that premature mortality rates, illness and disability are higher among the more disadvantaged sections of each national population: Australia (National Health Strategy, 1992), Belgium (Lagasse et al., 1990), Finland (Valkonen, 1993), France (Desplanques, 1984), Germany (Helmert and Shea, 1994), Ireland (Nolan, 1990), Italy (Piperno and Di Orio, 1990), the Netherlands (Mackenbach, 1993), Norway (Dahl, 1993), Spain (Kunst and Mackenbach, 1994), Sweden (Vågerö and Lundberg, 1989), Switzerland (Lehmann et al., 1990), the UK (Fox and Benzeval, 1995) and the USA (Pappas et al., 1993). The evidence shows substantial indications that health variations reflect the social and economic circumstances of individuals.

Inequalities will only be reduced by adopting a thoroughly multi-layered approach. Whitehead (1995) identified four different levels for tackling health inequalities:

1   Strengthening individuals.
2   Strengthening communities.
3   Improving access to essential facilities and services.
4   Encouraging macro-economic and cultural change.

These four levels correspond to the four layers of influence in Whitehead's 'onion model' of the determinants of health outlined in Chapter 1 (see Figure 1.1). Some health psychologists would want to include an extra level between the individual and the community, for the household or family (Valach et al., 1996). Psychologists do not usually talk quite so simplistically about 'strengthening' individuals, but analyse the personal characteristics and skills associated with positive health (e.g. self-efficacy, hardiness, sense of coherence, social skills). In fact, as we shall see later, developing interventions aimed at individual health beliefs and behaviours are a core feature of psychological theory, research and practice.

However, interventions aimed at tackling inequalities at an individual level have shown mixed results. There are four possible reasons. First, people living and working in disadvantaged circumstances have fewer resources (time, space, money) with which to manage the process of change. Second, health-threatening behaviours such as smoking tend to increase in difficult or stressful circumstances as they provide a means of coping (Graham, 1993). Third, there may have been a lack of insensitivity to the difficult circumstances in which people work and live which constrain the competence to change. Fourth, there has been a tendency to blame the victim. For example, cancer sufferers may be blamed for the disease if they are smokers on the grounds that they are responsible for the habit which caused it.

Overall, efforts directed at the individual level have been inconclusive and small scale. Because many health determinants are beyond the control of the individual, psychological interventions aimed at individuals are likely to have limited impact on public health problems when considered on a wider scale. This suggests that there is a need for psychologists to work beyond the individual level, with families, communities, work sites and community groups.

Benzeval et al. (1995) suggested that efforts to tackle inequalities typically have two shortcomings: (1) Excessive attention is given to the health experiences of white males of working age as compared to women, older people and minority ethnic groups. More attention must be given to the health concerns of these under-served groups. (2) The policy areas dealt with in detail – housing, income maintenance, smoking and access to health care – are insufficiently comprehensive as an agenda for tackling inequalities. Tackling health inequalities at the level of services to individuals is insufficient. The correction of inequalities in health demands 'a wide-ranging and radical reshaping of economic and social policies' (Benzeval et al., 1995, p. 140). In other words, action in the form of policy change is required to bring about macro-economic and cultural change.

SOCIO-ECONOMIC STATUS (SES)

In the remainder of this chapter, we examine health variations and their potential causes and psychosocial mediators. One of the most significant is socio-economic status (SES). We describe the health gradient correlated with SES and outline different explanations for its existence. We also briefly outline and discuss the factors of relative deprivation, gender and ethnicity and explore the psychosocial implications of their association with variations in health.

Socio-economic status (SES) is an important factor in health, illness and health care. SES is usually defined in terms of occupation, education or income, but it is a complex and multi-dimensional construct which defies simple definition. The SES construct has traditionally been analysed from a sociological perspective and has been found to control large amounts of the variance in health outcomes (Adler et al., 1994; Carroll et al., 1996; Carroll and Davey Smith, 1997). The construct needs to be unpacked for its

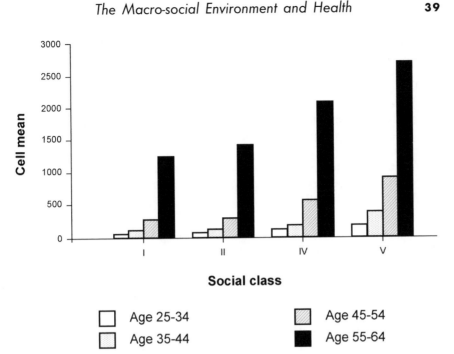

Note: Social class III has been omitted because its historical run was broken in 1961 when it was sub-divided.

FIGURE 2.5 ***Mean annual death rates (all causes) per 100,000 men by age and social class, 1991–93, for England and Wales (computed from Blane et al., 1997, Table 1)***

psychological content because the mediators of SES effects on health experience are likely, at least in part, to be behavioural and psychosocial.

Data from many hundreds of quantitative studies show that SES is strongly correlated with illness and mortality. The Black Report (1980/1988) provided the first major national review of the issue in the UK. The relationship between mortality and SES is known as a *health gradient* because plots of mortality rates against SES reveal a continuous gradient of increasingly poor health as SES changes from high to low. Figure 2.5 shows male all-cause mortality plotted against social class for England and Wales for 1991–93. Similar gradients exist in the USA (Adler et al., 1994) and throughout industrialized countries.

Complementing the quantitative data, qualitative data concerning people's experience of health and illness derived from discourse provides insights into the mediators of gradients. Chamberlain (1997) reviewed evidence from qualitative research concerning how people from upper and lower SES positions understand health and illness (e.g. Calnan and Williams, 1991a and b). These studies interviewed small groups of middle-class and working-class women and men classified on the basis of their occupations, producing a 'white-collar' and 'blue-collar' distinction. Several differences are evident between these two groups.

Blair (1993) analysed the language used by middle-class and working-class groups and concluded that working-class people tend to use more physicalistic terminology in their accounts of health and illness while middle-class people are more mentalistic and person centred. Contact and communication with professionals can be affected by their class relationship with patients so, not surprisingly, surgeons and doctors are often perceived as 'upper' class by working-class patients, while nurses are seen as more 'down to earth':

> You know how it is, those bloody doctors and their big words. That's enough to scare the shit out of anyone. I don't know what the hell they're talking about. I didn't have no bloody education like them. Why should I take the stuff they give me when I don't know what the hell they're talking about. (Jim, lower SES). (Chamberlain, 1997, p. 402)

Meanings of health show class-related differences. Working-class men and women see health in a more utilitarian way concerned with an absence of disease, being able to work and get through the day without feeling ill. Middle-class people see health as a value concerned with feeling good and having energy to indulge in leisure activities. Chamberlain (1997), however, suggests a more complex picture with four differing views of health. The *solitary* view, presented by lower SES participants, sees health as involving only physical components of energy, lack of symptoms and a good diet. The *dualistic* view, held only by lower and some higher SES people, sees health as having both physical and mental aspects, which act in parallel and independently of each other. The *complementary* view, presented mainly by upper SES people, sees physical and mental elements as integrated together in an alliance. The *multiple* view, held by higher SES people, sees multiple aspects to health – physical, mental, emotional, social, spiritual – as interdependent, interconnected, in balance in health and out of balance in illness. These comparative studies are few in number and have been conducted in only a few countries, primarily in New Zealand. Further studies are needed to explore the relationship between social positioning and health experience.

Explaining the health gradient

Looking at the overall picture, it may be concluded that SES produces a complicated mixture of impacts on the health of individuals. Wilkinson (1992) suggested that 'social consequences of people's differing circumstances in terms of stress, self-esteem, and social relations may now be one of the most important influences on health' (p. 168). Carroll et al. (1996)

suggest that the SES–health gradient is a consequence of class-related differences in social support and personal control. Both help to ameliorate stress and differ significantly in the predicted direction. An alternative formulation suggests that depression, hostility, stress and social ordering could be responsible for the SES–health gradients and that individual control over life circumstances might be a higher order variable (Adler et al., 1994). Both theories give a primary role to stress and personal control.

For a more complete account, it is necessary to consider the differing experiences and behaviours in the life cycle of individuals of differing SES. Important though feelings of personal control undoubtedly are, it is necessary to contextualize individual developmental history within family, social and ecological systems (see Box 2.2).

BOX 2.2 BEHAVIOURS AND EXPERIENCES ASSOCIATED WITH LOW SES

- low weight births
- family instability
- child abuse, poor diet/nutrition
- poor educational outcomes
- parental smoking
- parental drinking
- parental lack of exercise
- low household income
- poor housing
- overcrowding
- environmental pollution
- unemployment or unstable employment
- occupational hazards
- poorer access to health services
- heavier smoking
- heavier drinking
- lack of exercise
- lower personal control
- less social support

The risk-factors in Box 3.2 can be considered from an *ecological perspective* or *systems theory approach*. Bronfenbrenner's (1979) ecological approach conceptualized developmental influences in terms of four nested systems:

- *microsystems*: families, schools, neighbourhoods;
- *mesosystems*: peer groups;
- *exosystems*: parental support systems, parental workplaces;
- *macrosystems*: political philosophy, social policy.

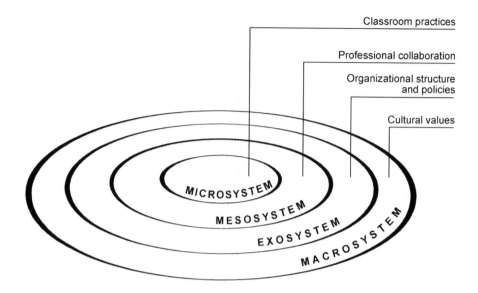

FIGURE 2.6 *Bronfenbrenner's ecological systems model (Odom et al., 1996, pp. 18–30; reproduced with permission)*

These systems form a nested set, like a set of Russian dolls, microsystems within mesosystems, mesosystems within exosystems and exosystems within macrosystems (Figure 2.6).

Ecological theory assumes that human development can only be understood in reference to the structural ecosystems. We have already suggested a general systems framework for understanding the determinants of health and illness in Chapter 1 (Figure 1.2). Of key importance is the principle that it is the *perceived environment* and not the so-called 'objective' environment which affects human behaviour and experience.

Any explanation of the SES–health gradient needs to consider psychosocial systems that structure inequalities across a broad range of life opportunities and outcomes, health, social and educational. As illustrated in Box 3.2, in comparison to someone at the high end of the SES scale, the profile of a low SES person is one of multiple disadvantage. The disadvantages of low SES accumulate across all four ecosystems: families, schools, neighbourhoods (microsystems); peer groups (mesosystems); parental support systems, parental workplaces (exosystems); and political philosophy and social policy (macrosystems).

Davey Smith et al. (1994) argue that it is the *accumulation* and *clustering* of adverse physical, material, social and psychological effects which explain the health gradient. While each factor alone can be expected to produce a relatively modest impact on mortality, the combination and interaction of many kinds of ecosystem disadvantage are likely to be sufficiently large to generate the observed gradient.

Four explanations of the gradient have been proposed: artefactual, social selection, behavioural, and materialist. The evidence suggests that the first two factors are incapable of accounting for the gradient. The second two factors appear to be more plausible, but unfortunately they are not easy to separate. This is because the social structure both distributes the exposure to environmental hazards and sets the conditions for the behaviours which damage or promote health (Davey Smith et al., 1994).

Materialist explanations propose that factors outside the individual's control expose some sections of the population to a hazard and not others, or differentially exposes the whole population (Blane et al., 1997). There are four major domains in which these variations occur. First, exposure to *air pollution* is likely to depend upon income. Where a person lives, for example, near main roads or industrial plants, is dependent upon income as is the quality of protection afforded by a vehicle a person owns to exhaust fumes. Second, the *diet* is implicated by epidemiological studies in 35% of all cancer deaths (Doll and Peto, 1981) and also in cardiovascular disease. Income determines the range of foods to which an individual has access and so it can perhaps be assumed that a significant proportion, perhaps one-half, of the dietary effect on total mortality could be caused by materialist factors, less than 15% of all deaths (Blane et al., 1997). Third, four major causes of mortality are associated with *occupational hazards*: cancer, cardiovascular disease, accidents and respiratory disorders. Blane et al. suggest that 10% of all deaths could be caused by occupational hazards. Fourth, the *quality of housing* is strongly related to both income and health. Although no precise figure can be attributed to the housing factor as an overall cause of mortality, there is a strong link between poor housing and bad health (SCOPH, 1994).

Blane et al. (1997) suggest that these four materialist causes of mortality combine and accumulate across the life span in the same individuals bringing about interactive and additive effects on increasing the risk of serious life-threatening conditions among those sectors of the population who are most exposed. These materialist factors are separate from the behavioural and psychosocial differences that also exist between people of differing SES.

Studies in many countries have shown that people with lower SES have a higher behavioural risk profile. Cavelaars et al. (1997) analysed the gradients in behavioural risk factors in 11 European countries using data from the Eurobarometer survey. This survey has been conducted twice each year since 1970 on people over 15 years of age in all countries of the EU. The Eurobarometer measures public attitudes towards the EU and its policies. Between 1987 and 1991 respondents were also asked about their consumption of cigarettes, alcohol and vegetables, and also about their weight and height from which a body mass index could be computed. Cavelaars et al. investigated inequities between high and low education groups in each country. Of particular interest was the observation of a north–south difference in behavioural risk inequalities for heavy smoking and infrequent vegetable consumption in men, with larger inequalities in northern European countries than in southern European countries. This pattern matches the gradients for ischaemic heart disease in men, which also show larger gradients in the north and smaller gradients in the south. The data of Cavelaars et al. suggest that the behavioural factors of smoking and diet contribute to the SES-related health gradient.

Taylor et al. (1997) describe the features of 'healthy' and 'unhealthy' environments:

> Across multiple environments, unhealthy environments are those that threaten safety, that undermine the creation of social ties, and that are conflictual, abusive or violent. A healthy environment, in contrast, provides safety, opportunities for social integration, and the ability to predict and/or control aspects of that environment. (Taylor et al., 1997, p. 411)

Unhealthy environments are associated with chronic stress and 'the lower one is on the SES continuum, the greater the amount of hassle and time needed to address basic tasks of living' (Taylor et al., 1997, p. 419).

As noted above, both behavioural and material circumstances vary with SES. It is impossible to decide with the presently available information how much each of these causes is contributing to the gradients in illnesses and deaths. Understanding the material and behavioural causes and the interactions between the two is a priority for further research.

RELATIVE DEPRIVATION

In addition to striking the health gradients discussed above, there is evidence that *relative deprivation* plays an independent role in mediating health experience. Much of the evidence for relative deprivation has been discussed by Richard G. Wilkinson in *Unhealthy Societies* (1996). Wilkinson (1992) found a correlation of 0.90 between life expectancy at birth and the proportion of income going to the least well-off 70% of the population (after controlling for GNP per head of population). Major structural shifts during the 1980s and 1990s made income distribution in many western countries less equitable. In the UK the percentage of households existing on below half the average income changed from 9% in 1979 to 24% in 1990–91 (Millar, 1993). In countries where the income gap widened, life expectancy increased less than in countries where the gap narrowed (Figure 2.7).

Kaplan et al. (1996) found a correlation of 0.62 ($p<.001$) between the percentage of household income received by the less well off 50% and all-cause mortality across the 50 states in the USA. Kaplan et al. (1996) also found that income inequality is associated with a wide range of social indicators including high rates of low birth weight, homicide, violent crime,

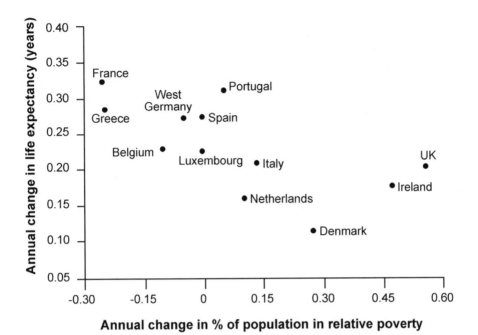

FIGURE 2.7 *Annual rate of change in life expectancy and in the proportion of the population in relative poverty in 12 European community countries, 1975–85. (Wilkinson, R.G., 1992, p. 304; reproduced with permission)*

work disability, smoking, sedentary activity, unemployment, imprisonment, recipients of income assistance and food stamps, and poor educational outcomes. A similar US study using different measures by Kennedy et al. (1996) obtained findings which were consistent with those of Kaplan et al. (1996). Lynch and Kaplan (1997) discuss the methodological and measurement problems associated with these researches and conclude that it is the 'appraisal of well-being that may provide a psychosocially mediated link between income inequality and health status . . . so that even those with good incomes might feel "relatively deprived" compared to the super rich' (p. 308).

Kennedy et al. (1998) investigated the influence of income distribution and socio-economic status on self-rated health status in a sample of over 200,000 US civilians who were non-institutionalized (that is, non-incarcerated and non-hospitalized) aged 18 years or older. Data were collected on income distribution in each of the 50 US states. The Gini coefficient was used to measure statewide inequalities in income. The objective of the study was to determine the effect of inequalities in income within a state on self-rated health status while controlling for individual characteristics such as socio-economic status. Random probability samples of individuals in each state were collected by the 1993 and 1994 behavioural risk factor surveillance system, a random digit telephone survey. The survey collected information on an individual's income, education, self-rated health and other health risk factors.

The results showed that when personal characteristics and household income were controlled for, individuals living in states with the greatest inequalities in income were 30% more likely to report their health as fair or poor than individuals living in states with the smallest inequalities in income. This study found that:

1 Inequality in the distribution of income is associated with an adverse impact on health independent of the effect of household income.
2 The effects of income distribution on self-rated health are not limited only to those in the lowest income groups; those in the middle income groups in states with the greatest inequalities in income rated themselves as having poorer health than those in middle income groups in states with the smallest inequalities.
3 The effects of income inequality on self-rated health are as strong as other individual risk factors.
4 Social and economic policies that affect income distribution may have important consequences for the health of the population.

We saw above that countries or states with a higher equality of income distribution have populations with relatively high life expectancy. It was suggested by Wilkinson (1996) that these socio-economic trends are created by the greater *social cohesion* and social support existing in more egalitarian societies. For people suffering the highest levels of distress and poverty, social integration and support can literally be life or death issues. Interpersonal processes within networks of relationships entail the giving, receiving and sharing of support of different kinds (informational, emotional and material).

Interpersonal processes are also engaged in evaluating and comparing one's own socio-economic position with others. The process of *social comparison*, and downwards comparison in particular, is included in judging self-worth, setting aims and ambitions and making changes to lifestyle and health behaviours. A negative downwards comparison is likely to be associated with only fair or poor self-ratings of well-being, which in turn are associated with higher rates of morbidity and mortality.

The consequences of social comparison need to be considered in socio-historical context. People of many backgrounds, nationalities and cultures now share similar aspirations. Once upon a time the 'American dream' gave North Americans the idea that they could drive Cadillacs, own houses with swimming pools, play the stock market and vacation in exotic places such as Hawaii or the Caribbean. Similar albeit lower key aspirations have been inculcated among Europeans. Yet, as the gap between the rich and the poor widens, the economic realities for many people are dramatically different and the widening wealth gap can only bring increased levels of hopelessness, frustration and failure. This reality–actuality gap is the 'feel-bad' factor of psychosocial alienation associated with the killer disorders of industrialized societies, cancer, cardiovascular disease, tobacco addiction, alcoholism and obesity. There are good reasons for expecting that the prevalence of alienation and stress will be higher in countries or states where the income distribution is most skewed. The impact of differences in socio-economic position on health are likely to be psychosocially mediated through a sense of worthlessness, low self-esteem, and hopelessness. Thus, economic inequality can be seen as a new pathogen in contemporary societies.

GENDER

Major differences occur across place and time in the health prospects of men and women. Recent research has focused on the political, psychosocial and economic implications of gender. According to a medical textbook from the 19th century: 'child-bearing is essentially necessary to the physical health and long life, the mental happiness, the development of the affections and whole character of women. Woman exists for the sake of the womb' (Holbrook, 1871, pp. 13–14; cited in Gallant et al., 1997). Attitudes have changed and, supported by policy and legislation, women's health is near the top of the health researcher's agenda. These changes have been supported in the USA by the foundation by the National Institutes of Health in 1990 of the Office of Research on Women's Health (ORWH) leading to a number of special research projects, reports and symposia across many health disciplines including psychology.

In industrialized societies today men die earlier than women but women have poorer health than men (Macintyre and Hunt, 1997). In 1996 in the UK boys had a life expectancy of 74.4 years compared with 79.7 years for girls. This excess mortality of 5.3 years in males in 1996 increased over the course of the twentieth century from only 3.9 years in 1900–1910. However, the evidence suggests that from the paleolithic period to the industrial revolution men lived longer than women, 40 years as compared to 35. Also, in less developed countries (e.g. India, Bangladesh, Nepal and Afghanistan) women still live longer than men (WHO, 1989). Thus, there are significant historical and cultural differences in gender-related health. To complicate the picture further, the SES–mortality gradient appears to be steeper for men than for women while illness rates, treatment rates, absenteeism and prescription drug use are generally higher for women (Macintyre and Hunt, 1997).

Women have higher morbidity rates but lower mortality rates. Women suffer more non-fatal chronic illnesses and more acute illnesses. They also make more visits to their family physicians and spend more time in hospital. Women suffer more from hypertension, kidney disease and auto-immune diseases such as rheumatoid arthritis and lupus (Litt, 1993). They also suffer twice the rate of depression. Men, on the other hand, have a shorter life expectancy, suffer more injuries, suicides, homicides and heart disease.

In addition to biological factors, the political and economic causes of gender-related health differences are complex and multi-faceted. These differences need to be considered in their full context, including policy issues, SES, psychosocial factors, lifestyle differences, life cycle changes and violence. Chronic conditions such as cancer, depression and anxiety also show gender-related differences which merit theoretical analysis.

Psychosocial and lifestyle differences are likely to play a major role in mediating gender-related health differences. In industrialized societies women suffer more from poverty, stress from relationships, childbirth, rape, domestic violence, sexual discrimination, lower status work, concern about weight and the strain of dividing attention between competing roles of parent and worker. Financial barriers may prevent women, more than men, from engaging in healthier lifestyles and desirable behaviour change (O'Leary and Helgeson, 1997).

Social support derived from friendships, intimate relationships and marriage, although significant, appears to be of less positive value to women than to men. Although physical and mental well-being generally benefit from social support, women often provide more emotional support to their families than they receive. Thus, the loss of a spouse has a longer and more devastating effect on the health of men than on that of women (Stroebe and Stroebe, 1983). The burden of caring for an elderly, infirm or dementing family member also tends to be greater for females in the family than for males, especially daughters (Grafstrom, 1994). Gallant et al. (1997) have made a useful review of the literature on the psychological, social and behavioural influences on health and health care in women. While the health of women is a focus for renewed efforts in health care, the health of men cannot be taken for granted. Men are more likely to suffer diseases of the cardiovascular system, more often suffer a violent death and die younger.

ETHNICITY

Empirical evidence suggests that the health of minority ethnic groups is generally poorer than that of the majority of the population. This pattern has been consistently observed in the USA between African-Americans (or blacks) and whites for at least 150 years (Krieger, 1987). There has been an increase in income inequality in the USA which has been associated with a levelling off or even a decline in the economic status of African-Americans. The gap in life expectancy between blacks and whites widened between 1980 and 1991 from 6.9 years to 8.3 years for males and from 5.6 years to 5.8 years for females (NCHS, 1994b). Under the age of 70, cardiovascular disease, cancer and problems resulting in infant mortality account for 50%

of the excess deaths for black males and 63% of the excess deaths for black females (Williams and Collins, 1995). Similar findings exist in other countries. Analyses of three censuses from 1971 to 1991 have shown that people born in South Asia are more likely to die from ischaemic heart disease than the majority of the UK population (Balarajan and Soni Raleigh, 1993).

There are many possible explanations for these persistent health differences between people of different races who live in the same country and are served by the same educational, social, welfare and health-care systems (Williams and Collins, 1995; Williams et al., 1997). First, the social practice of *racism* means that minority ethnic groups are the subject of discrimination at a number of different levels. Such discrimination could lead directly or indirectly to health problems additional to any effects related to SES, poverty, unemployment and education. Discrimination in the health-care system exacerbates the impacts of social discrimination through reduced access to the system and poorer levels of communication resulting from language differences.

Second, *ethnocentrism* in health services and health promotion favours the needs of majority over minority groups. The health needs of members of minority ethnic groups are less likely to be appropriately addressed in health promotion which in turn leads to lower adherence and response rates in comparison to the majority population. These problems are compounded by cultural, lifestyle and language differences. For example, if interpreters are unavailable, the treatment process is likely to be improperly understood or even impaired and patient anxiety levels will be raised. The lack of permanent addresses for minority ethnic group families created by their high mobility makes communication difficult so that screening invitations and appointment letters are unlikely to be received.

Third, health status differences related to race and *culture* are to a large extent mediated by differences in SES. Studies of race and health generally control for SES and race-related differences frequently disappear after adjustment for SES. Race is strongly correlated with SES and is even sometimes used as an indicator of SES (Williams and Collins, 1995; Modood et al., 1997).

Fourth, differences in health-protective behaviour may occur because of different cultural or social norms and expectations. Fifth, differences in readiness to recognize symptoms may occur also as a result of different cultural norms and expectations. Sixth, differences could occur in access to services. There is evidence that differential access to optimal treatment may cause poorer survival outcomes in African-Americans who have cancer in comparison to other ethnic groups (Meyerowitz et al., 1998). Seventh, members of minority ethnic groups are more likely to inhabit and work in unhealthy environments because of their lower SES. Eighth, there could be genetic differences between groups which lead to differing incidence of disease and some diseases are inherited. There are several well-recognized examples, including sickle cell disorder affecting people of African-Caribbean descent, thalassaemia, another blood disorder which affects people of the Mediterranean, Middle Eastern and Asian descent, and Tay-Sachs disease which affects Jewish people.

Other possible mechanisms underlying ethnicity differences in health are differences in personality, early life conditions, power and control, and stress (Williams and Collins, 1995; Taylor et al., 1997). Research is needed with large community samples so that the influence of the above variables and the possible interactions between them can be determined.

FUTURE RESEARCH

1   The SES variable needs to be unpacked in more detail if our understanding of the mechanisms of health and illness is to make genuine progress. More research is necessary to understand the effects of disadvantage – both absolute and relative – on individual and population health.

2   Further studies are needed to investigate the psychological and material mediators of health gradients.

3   Qualitative studies of the health experiences of people from different socio-economic backgrounds is of particular importance to our understanding of the psychological mechanisms underlying health variations. Further qualitative studies are needed to explore the relationship between social positioning and health experience.

4   Transnational research is needed to unravel the links between relative deprivation and health. What kinds of psychological and social processes are at stake here? Is lack of social cohesion the mediator of the relationship between health and relative deprivation as suggested by Wilkinson? Do social comparisons also play a role?

SUMMARY

1   The greatest influence on health is poverty. Of 5.6 billion people in the world population, 4.4 billion live in developing countries. Half of the world's population lacks regular access to treatment of common diseases and most essential drugs. Globally, the burden of death and disease is much heavier for the poor than for the wealthy.

2   Inequities are one of the most pervasive features of health-care systems. There is evidence that for both wealth and health, the gap between the 'haves' and the have-nots is becoming wider between and within populations.

3   Health in rich, industrialized countries can be expected to improve if income growth is accompanied by a more equitable income distribution. When a society contains a large proportion of citizens living in poverty and a highly uneven distribution of income, spending more money on doctors, nurses and health care appears to produce little health gain. Improving female literacy has more impact on overall life expectancy than increasing expenditure on health care.

4   Health in poor countries is related to GNPpc, income distribution, and female literacy. However, it is also correlated with the numbers of doctors and nurses.

5   It is necessary for wealthier countries to allocate more resources to development of poorer countries. If the WHO's Health For All strategy is going to have any chance of success, health must be given a higher priority in global development policies. The international debts of the poorest countries must be cancelled so that they can afford to spend more on health care and education.

6   Health-care systems undergo continuous change and reform. The aim of such changes is to increase efficiency and slow the steady escalation of costs. Health services provide a mixture of private insurance schemes, state funding, and voluntary provision. Critics have questioned the applicability of a market model to health care.

7   Socio-economic status (SES) is strongly related to health, illness and mortality. It has been suggested that health gradients are a consequence of class-related differences in social cohesion, stress and personal control.

8   Similar arguments can be applied to the influence of relative deprivation. Inequality in the distribution of income is associated with an adverse impact on health independent of the effect of household income. Data collected by Kennedy et al. (1998) suggest that the effects of income distribution on self-rated health are not limited only to those in the lowest income groups; those in the middle income groups in states with the greatest inequalities in income rated themselves as having poorer health than those in middle income groups in states with the smallest inequalities.

9   The effects of income inequality on self-rated health are as strong as other individual risk factors. Social and economic policies that affect income distribution may have important consequences for the health of the population.

10   Gender differences in health, illness and mortality are significant and show striking interactions with culture, history and SES.

11   The health of minority ethnic groups is generally poorer than that of the majority of the population. Possible explanations include racial discrimination, ethnocentrism, SES differences, behavioural and personality differences, cultural differences and other factors. Discrimination in the health-care system could exacerbate the impacts of social discrimination by virtue of reduced access to the system, poorer levels of communication and poorer compliance.

12   Ethnocentrism in health services and health promotion marginalizes minority groups leading to lower adherence and response rates in comparison to the majority population. Differences in culture, language, lifestyle, health-protective and health-seeking behaviours are likely to compound the problems of racism and ethnocentrism. Health status differences related to race and culture appear to be partly mediated by differences in SES.

KEY TERMS

culture	poverty
ecological approach	racism
ethnicity	relative deprivation
ethnocentrism	social cohesion
gross national product (GNP)	social comparison
health gradient	socio-economic status (SES)
income distribution	systems theory
inequalities	welfare model
market model	

3 CROSS-CULTURAL IMAGES OF HEALTH

There is no such thing as human nature independent of culture. (Clifford Geertz, 1973, p. 229)

OUTLINE

The way people react to illness is rooted in their broader health belief systems which in turn are culturally immersed. This chapter provides some examples from the work of medical historians and medical anthropologists who have investigated how health belief systems vary across time and society. It considers the different expert health belief systems which have historically existed in western society and contemporary popular belief systems. It also considers several non-western health belief systems.

CONTEXT

We are cultural beings and an understanding of health beliefs and practices requires an understanding of the cultural and indeed of the historical and social context within which we live. It is impossible to extract humans from the context which gives them meaning. Historians and anthropologists have conducted substantial research into the historical and cultural embeddedness of health beliefs. Early in this century, W.H. Rivers, the famous physician-anthropologist, promoted interest in the cultural relativity of health practices. He dismissed the idea that the health practices of people in the developing world were a mixture of disconnected and meaningless customs. Instead, he argued that they were 'inspired by definite ideas concerning the causation of disease' (Farmer and Good, 1991).

Culture is all around us and pervades our very being. Anthropologists have developed an inclusive definition of culture:

> Above all a system of meanings and symbols. This system shapes every area of life, defines a world view that gives meaning to personal and collective experience, and frames the way people locate themselves within the world, perceive the world, and believe in it. Every aspect of reality is seen as embedded within webs of meaning that define a certain world view and that cannot be studied or understood apart from this collective frame. (Corin, 1995, p. 273)

An understanding of people's reactions to illness requires an understanding of these culturally specific, indigenous health belief systems.

CAUSAL ONTOLOGIES AND MORAL DISCOURSE OF SUFFERING

Each society has developed its own understanding of health and illness. Shweder et al. (1997) have described seven general systems of understanding which they have termed ontologies of suffering. Each of these systems are locally developed ways of understanding illness and suffering which are in turn linked with ways of intervening to alleviate suffering. Table 3.1 summarizes these *causal ontologies*.

Murdock (1980) conducted a survey of the explanations of illness in 139 societies. He found that in sub-Saharan Africa there was a preference for explanations based upon moral transgressions. In East Asia, the preference was for interpersonal explanations and in the circum-Mediterranean region he found that witchcraft explanations for death and suffering were widespread.

Park (1992) conducted a further analysis of Murdock's data and argued that on a worldwide scale the 'big three' explanations were interpersonal, moral and biomedical. In their review of this evidence Shweder et al. (1997) claimed that the *moral discourse* was the pervasive underlying explanatory framework in many societies. In light of this they conducted detailed analysis of the moral discourse of the residents of the city of Bhubaneswar, Orissa in India. From this they identified three moral dimensions which are summarized in Table 3.2

In western societies the dominant moral discourse is that of autonomy which focuses on the rights of the individual. As Porter (1997) argued: 'the West has evolved a culture preoccupied with the self, with the individual and his or her identity, and this quest has come to be equated with (or reduced to) the individual body and the embodied personality, expressed through body language' (p. 7). In health care this leads to the rights of the individual patient having paramount importance. This discourse pervades much of contemporary medical ethics.

As discussed in Chapter 2, in western discourse the individualistic focus is promoted as natural, while alternative concerns are disparaged. The anthropologist Clifford Geertz (1973) describes the relative character of this focus as follows:

> The Western conception of the person as a bounded, unique, more or less integrated motivational and cognitive universe, a dynamic centre of awareness, emotion, judgement, and action organised into a distinctive whole and set contrastively both against other such whole and against a social and natural background is, however incorrigible it may seem to us, a rather peculiar idea within the context of the world's cultures. (Geertz, 1973, p. 229)

TABLE 3.1 *Causal ontologies of suffering (Shweder et al., 1997)*

Causal ontologies	Explanatory references	Therapy
Biomedical	Western: genetic defects, hormone imbalances, organ pathologies, physiological impairments	Direct or indirect ingestion of special substances, herbs and roots, vitamins, chemical compounds
	Non-western: humors, bodily fluids, juices	Direct or indirect mechanical repair (e.g. surgery, massage, emetics) of damaged fibres or organs
Interpersonal	Western: harassment, abuse, exploitation	Avoidance or repair of negative interpersonal relations
	Non-western: sorcery, evil eye, black magic	Talismans, magic
Sociopolitical	Oppression, political domination, adverse economic or family conditions	Social reform
Psychological	Unfulfilled desires and frustrated intentions, forms of fear	Intrapsychic and psychosocial interventions, e.g. meditation, therapy
Astrophysical	Arrangement of planets, moon or stars	Wait with optimism for change
Ecological	Stress, environmental risks	Reduction of stress and environmental hazards
Moral	Transgressions of obligation or duty, ethical failure	Unloading one's sins, confession, reparation

TABLE 3.2 *Moral discourses of suffering (Shweder et al., 1997)*

Discourse	Focus	Content
Autonomy	Individual	Harm, rights, justice
Community	Family and community	Duty, interdependence
Divinity	Divine design	Sacred and natural order

The pervasiveness of the individualistic ethos in Western society is also evident in a number of psychological studies which have attempted to characterize cultural variations in people's ways of thinking and acting. One frequently cited study is that by Hofstede (1980) who analysed national differences in responses to employee morale surveys conducted by a large American multinational corporation. Factor analysis of the responses identified four dimensions: power distance, uncertainty avoidance, masculinity/ femininity, and individualism/collectivism. Of these four, the most investigated dimension is individualism vs. collectivism.

Individualist cultures emphasize the separateness and uniqueness of its members whereas collectivist cultures emphasize group needs and inter-connectedness (Matsumoto et al., 1996). For example, in Hindu society the community and divinity discourses are more prominent. An understanding of these dimensions is important for understanding cultural variations in health belief systems.

HEALTH BELIEF SYSTEMS

As societies have evolved they have developed various *health belief systems*, knowledge of which is sometimes confined to those who undergo specialized training. This has given rise to the separation of what have become known as expert or technical beliefs systems as opposed to the traditional folk or indigenous systems. These systems are not discrete but interact and are in a process of constant evolution. Although the majority of people in any society organize their world through indigenous belief systems the character of these is connected in some form with the expert belief system.

Kleinman (1980) distinguished between three overlapping sectors of any health-care system: the professional, the folk and the popular. The popular sector is 'the lay, non-professional, non-specialist, popular culture arena in which illness is first defined and health care activities initiated' (p. 50). The professional sector comprises the organized healing professions – their representations and actions. The folk sector is the non-professional, non-bureaucratic, specialist sector which shades into the other two sectors. In view of the central role of health in our self-definition, these different health sectors both reflect and contribute to broader worldviews.

Although this threefold division is widely cited, other researchers (e.g. Blumhagen, 1980) have preferred a simpler twofold division into pro-fessional and popular realms. 'Systematicity, coherence and interdependence are aspects of the professional belief systems' (Blumhagen, 1980, p. 200). Conversely, the lay health belief system can appear disconnected. This broad classification avoids an accusation that certain specialized health belief systems are classified as folk when they have limited status in society although they may have an extensive codification of health complaints and treatments. These two broad belief systems interact such that the lay person can draw upon more specialized knowledge but also the specialist will make use of more popular knowledge. Further, both ways of thinking about health draw upon a more general worldview and are located within a particular local and political context. Blumhagen (1980) also argues that these two health belief systems should be con-sidered distinct from the individual belief system which the individual uses to understand their personal experience of illness. An understanding of popular health beliefs requires an understanding of the dominant expert health belief systems.

WESTERN HEALTH BELIEF SYSTEMS

Classical views of health

In the west the classical view of health and illness derived from the Graeco-Arabic medical system. *Galenic* medicine provided an expert system developed from the Greeks, in particular the work of Hippocrates and his colleagues. Their major contribution was in offering a naturalistic explanation of health and illness. A central concept in Galen's formulation was balance which was equated with health and imbalance which implied ill health (see also Chapter 1). Balance was conceived as a balance of bodily fluids or humours. They identified four main fluids: bile, phlegm, blood and black bile. These seemed to vary with the seasons such that an excess of phlegm was common in the winter leading to colds, while an excess of bile led to summer diarrhoea. Figure 3.1 shows a plan of the Hippocratic humoral system.

Not only could these four humours be linked to the four seasons, but they were also linked to the four primary conditions of hot, cold, wet and dry. Further, in Roman times they linked the four humours with the elements of air, fire, earth and water, with four types of fever, four periods of the day, four colours, four tastes. Medieval scholars added four temperaments, four Evangelists and four music tones (Nutton, 1995).

Besides a focus on understanding natural processes, the Galenic tradition also placed responsibility on individuals to look after themselves. Ill health was a consequence of natural processes, not a result of divine intervention. In many ways Galen's ideas not only prefigured but also continue to influence much of contemporary health beliefs.

Christian ideas

Galenic ideas dominated the expert system of medicine in Europe for almost two millenia. However, during the Middle Ages in Europe, Galen's work became confined more to the learned few and other ideas based upon religion became more commonplace. Illness was often seen as punishment for humankind's sinfulness. Herzlich and Pierret (1987) in their historical study of popular beliefs about health and illness note the interweaving of naturalistic and religious explanations:

> The disorders of the body . . . have their correspondence in the corruption of both the air and morals. This breakdown of order encompasses the phenomena of nature, those of the organism, and the conduct of human behaviour. But over all of this hovers the will of God. In the last analysis, it is he who sends illness to us. (Herzlich and Pierret, 1987, p. 103)

Indeed, this belief was written into the Book of Common Prayer: 'Whatsoever your sickness is, know you certainly, that it is God's visitation'

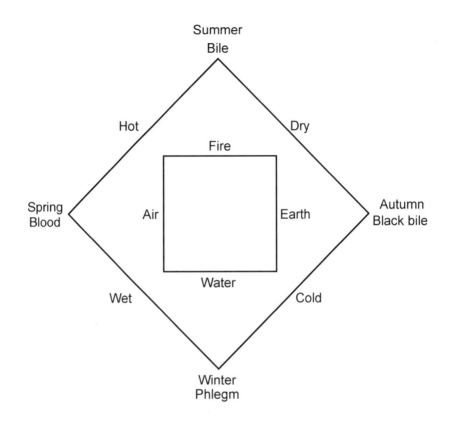

FIGURE 3.1 *Hippocratic humoral system (Nutton, 1995, p. 25; reproduced with permission)*

(Anselman, 1996, p. 229). The Church's seven deadly sins even came to be associated with pathological conditions of the body. For example, pride was symbolized by tumours and inflammations, while sloth led to dead flesh and palsy (Thomas, 1997).

Christianity drew upon different traditions. The ascetic tradition scorned concern for the body and instead promoted acts such as fasting and physical suffering, which supposedly led to spirituality. Indeed disease could be welcomed as an opportunity to purify the soul through suffering. With the Protestant Reformation this belief was replaced with the idea that the body had been given to humans by God. It was the individual's religious duty to look after and care for the body. Illness was seen as a sign of weakness and neglect. To honour God required living a healthy life and abstaining from excess, especially in terms of sex and diet.

Up until the Reformation, and later, the priest played an important role in healing. Wear (1985) noted that religious writers frequently made reference to the body. He remarked on the works of several seventeenth-century religious figures. For example, Robert Horne described the body as the 'Temple of God' which it was necessary to keep pure and clean. He quotes from the work of William Perkins (1612):

> Whereas our bodies are God's workmanship, we must glorify him in our bodies, and all the actions of body and soul, our eating and drinking, our living and dying, must be referred to his glory: yea we must not hurt or abuse our body, but present them as holy and living sacrifices unto God. (cited in Wear, 1985, p. 63)

These ideas were widely promulgated in the new Protestant reformation. The way to heaven was through attention to health behaviour; it was also linked to a social morality. The rich were wrong to indulge themselves while there was so much poverty and suffering.

Despite the authority of the Church, these religious interpretations began to decline with the growth of medical science. For example, Anselman (1996) in his analysis of the diaries of an eighteenth-century woman notes that 'her distinctive understanding of illness remains fundamentally physical rather than metaphysical' (p. 229). While in terms of the expert belief system there has been increasing acceptance of a naturalistic view of disease, the moral basis of health continues to underlie much of contemporary health belief. Indeed, Thomas (1997) argues that in the late twentieth century 'the association between health and "clean living" has been intensified' (p. 29).

Biomedicine

During the Enlightenment a new way of knowing the world attained dominance. Hepburn (1988) describes the Enlightenment as having two streams of thought. The first was the acceptance of the distinction between superstition and reason. The second was the emergence of positivism which emphasized that science based upon direct observation, measurement and experimentation gave direct access to the real world. This approach concentrated attention on material reality and a conception of the body as distinct from the mind. A central figure was Descartes (1596–1650) who conceived of the human being as composed of mind and body. The former was not open to scientific investigation whereas the latter could be conceived as a machine: 'I would consider myself primarily as having a face, hands, arms, and this entire machine composed of bones, and flesh, as it appears in a corpse, of which I designate through the name of body' (cited by Benoist and Cathebras, 1993, pp. 860–1).

The eighteenth century saw the rise of individualism in western society. In previous eras the group or collective organized ways of thinking and acting, which in turn was interconnected with the physical and spiritual world. Professional understanding of health and illness became more closely entwined with knowledge of the individual physical body. Foucault (1976) described how between the mid-eighteenth and mid-nineteenth centuries the 'medical gaze' came to focus on the interior of the human body. The symptoms of illness now became signs of underlying pathophysiology. Foucault noted that the change in perspective of the physician was illustrated in the change in the patient query from 'How do you feel?' to 'Where does it hurt?' For this new physician the stethoscope became the symbol of having insight into the bodily interior. Treatment centred on changing the character of this physiology either by medical or surgical means.

Foucault argued that this concern with the passive individual body reflected wider social changes. The view of the body as 'something docile, that could be surveilled, used, transformed and improved' was reflected not only in the growth of hospitals, but also prisons, asylums and schools. As Williams and Calnan (1996) noted: 'From this perspective, modern medicine is seen as part and parcel of a wider, more extensive, system of disciplinary techniques and technologies of power which are concerned with the moral regulation and 'normalization' of the population through the medical regimen' (p. 1610).

This approach to the study of health and illness has become known as *biomedicine*, cosmopolitan or allopathic medicine (Leslie, 1976). It came to dominance for several reasons including the fact that it was in accord with a broader view of humans, its alliance with physical science and the steady improvement in the health of the population which was attributed to medical intervention. Le Breton (1990) noted that the focus on the body is in accord with the western emphasis on the individual. 'One of the functions of the body becomes that of marking the frontiers of the individual' (see Benoist and Cathebras, 1993). Further, the separation of mind and body 'offers a subtle articulation of the person's alienation from the body in Western society, but this alienation is found, as well, in every sphere of economic and political life' (Benoist and Cathebras, 1993). Biomedicine separates the person from the body.

Friedson (1970) described how the coming to dominance of the biological approach was not without resistance. It required strong political action to organize the profession of medicine and to take legal action against other health practitioners. Throughout there was the dismissal of alternative perspectives and the assertion that biomedicine was the central force which had led to the substantial improvements in society's health. Biomedicine was based upon a positivist epistemology which supposedly gave it access to an outside reality. Only this approach was the true approach. All other approaches could be disparaged.

Biopsychosocial models of health

The dominance of this biomedical system has come in for substantial challenge both from the scientific establishment and the public. Initially, this was reflected in a call for more attention to the psychological and social aspects of health. This led to the development of the *biopsychosocial model* of health and illness (Engel, 1977). According to Engel (1980) the various aspects of health and illness can be organized in a hierarchy from the biosphere and society down through the individual's level of experience and behaviour to the cellular and subatomic level. All of these levels interact and need to be considered if we are to understand health and illness. With varying degrees of enthusiasm this model has in many respects replaced the basic biomedical model.

In addition, the increasing evidence of the link between social and behavioural factors and health has led to the promulgation of a health promotion ethic by the medical establishment with an emphasis on personal responsibility for health. Crawford (1980) argued that 'in an increasingly 'healthist' culture, healthy behaviour has become a moral duty and illness an individual moral failing'. Admittedly, the adoption of a more biopsychosocial approach to health care, especially by general practitioners, is sometimes met with hostility by patients who have accepted the basic biomedical model (Jaber et al., 1991). Steinert and Rosenberg (1987) suggest that this might explain why some people feel concerned that their physician is becoming too involved in their psychosocial problems.

Criticisms of the biomedical model also led the World Health Organization to propose an extensive definition of health as a state of complete physical, mental, and social well-being, not the mere absence of disease or infirmity. This definition widened the scope of health care to consider not only the well-being of the individual but also of the community. In Chapter 1 an even wider definition was offered, encompassing the economic, political and spiritual domains. Currently, much of health care in western society is attempting to shift from a concern with bodily processes to concern with the wider concept of quality of life (e.g. McGee and Jenkinson, 1997).

Alternative medicine

The late twentieth century has witnessed increasing criticism of medicine. Indeed it has been argued that a process of de-medicalization is taking place. In this period known as 'late modernity' there is widespread questioning of the scientific method (Williams and Calnan, 1996). This is reflected in medicine where there is evidence of increasing fracture between the high technology medicine on the one hand and the more psychosocial practice on the other (Armstrong, 1983).

The apparent failure of biomedicine to solve the big medical problems such as cancer and AIDS has led to an increased cynicism and a turn to alternative health systems. In the USA, Eisenberg et al. (1993) found that more visits are made to providers of unconventional therapy than to primary care physicians. Indeed, it was estimated that Americans spend as much on complementary medicine as on hospitalizations. In a series of studies, Furnham and his colleagues have investigated the reasons behind the growth of *alternative medicine*. Vincent and Furnham (1996) found in a survey of users of complementary medicine in Britain four main reasons for their usage:

1   The perceived ineffectiveness of orthodox medicine.
2   The belief that complementary medicine would be effective.
3   Valuing the perceived emphasis on treating the whole person.
4   A desire to take an active role in maintaining their health.

In another study of a sample of German adults, Furnham and Kirkcaldy (1996) found that those who used complementary practitioners had a more health-conscious lifestyle. Calnan and Williams's (1992) study of lay people in Britain found a considerable degree of ambivalence about the value of modern medicine, particularly high-tech medicine.

Popular views of health in the west

Evidence from a series of studies of popular beliefs about health and illness in western society illustrate the interaction of what can be described as the classic, the religious, the biomedical and the lifestyle approaches to health and illness. Probably the most influential study of western lay health beliefs was carried out by Herzlich (1973). She conducted interviews with a sample of French adults and concluded that health was conceived as an attribute of the individual – a state of harmony or balance. This had such components as physical well-being, plenty of physical resources, absence of fatigue, psychological well-being, evenness of temper, freedom of movement, effectiveness in action and good relations with other people. Illness was attributed to outside forces in our society or way of life.

This concern with balance could be said to reflect an older more traditional view of health and moves beyond the individual to relation-ships with the social and physical world. The laypeople also referred to illness in terms of both organic and psychosocial factors. On their own organic changes did not constitute illness. Rather, for the layperson 'physical facts, symptoms and dysfunctions have, of course, an existence of their own, but they only combine to form an illness in so far as they transform a patient's life'. The ability to participate in everyday life constitutes health, whereas inactivity is considered the true criterion of illness.

Herzlich's study was seminal because it provoked further research into popular health beliefs. However, symbolic culture does not exist inde-pendently from the physical and material circumstances of the community; rather they have a complex dialectical relationship. Thus, to understand somewhat more of Herzlich's findings requires recognition of her sample, which was largely French middle-class adults supplemented with some rural workers. These health beliefs were perhaps more typical of this group of people than groups from poorer social situations.

Other studies have explored how lay perceptions of health and illness are rooted in the social experience of people, in particular sub-cultures. D'Houtaud and Field (1984) conducted a large open-ended survey of over 4,000 French adults. Content analysis of their replies revealed 6,172 responses which were subsequently coded into 41 categories and then into 10 broader themes. There was a clear pattern in the preference for these themes across the social classes. The higher and middle-class adults preferred a definition of health in terms of a hedonistic use of life, in terms of their body and in terms of equilibrium and of vitality. Conversely, those from lower more manual social classes preferred a definition in terms of the value of health, psychological well-being, hygiene and absence of sickness.

In considering these variations, D'Houtaud and Field argue that 'it is not difficult to discern in such complementary representations of health the reflection of the corresponding roles of mastery on the one hand and of execution of social tasks on the other' (p. 48). The health beliefs are not things in themselves but are intimately related to the immediate social experience of the adults.

Blaxter (1990) analysed the definitions of health provided by over 9,000 British adults in the health and lifestyles survey. She classified the responses into nine categories (Table 3.3).

In analysing the responses across social classes, Blaxter (1990) noted considerable agreement in the emphasis on behavioural factors as a cause of illness. Indeed, she commented on the limited reference to structural or environmental factors, especially among those from working-class backgrounds. Despite this, other studies have found widespread scepticism about health promotion campaigns. Williams and Calnan (1996) suggest that the growth of the self-help consumer movement in health care is another symbol of popular opposition to the passive patient model of biomedicine. They noted that this opposition 'can be located within the broader socio-cultural and political framework of self-determination and a reclaiming of control over the body, self and wider environment' (p. 1617).

Blaxter (1990) also found evidence of gender differences. The women were more likely to define health in terms of personal relationships. In their study of working-class women's views of cancer, Murray and McMillan (1988) also found that the women made repeated reference to their families when describing the disease. For them, health and illness were not simply characteristics of their individual body but rather involved their relationships with others.

Chamberlain (1997) noted a series of social class differences in his review of several studies of laypeople's perceptions of health. In a series of studies he and his colleagues found that while people from both high and low SES groups perceived health as functional and important for everyday

TABLE 3.3 **Popular definitions of health (Blaxter, 1990)**

- Health as not-ill: the absence of physical symptoms.
- Health despite disease.
- Health as reserve: the presence of personal resources.
- Health as behaviour: the extent of healthy behaviour.
- Health as physical fitness.
- Health as vitality.
- Health as psycho-social well-being.
- Health as social relationships.
- Health as function.

purposes, there were certain differences in the locational justification for this. Whereas lower SES people emphasized the role of health in their ability to work, higher SES people referred more to their ability to participate in leisure activities. They distinguished between four different lay views of health:

1   A solitary view which emphasized physical aspects and was only reported by lower SES participants.
2   A dualistic view which combined both physical and mental aspects of health but in a non-integrated fashion. This was used by both lower and higher SES participants but especially by the former.
3   A complementary view of health which integrated both physical and mental dimensions and was used predominantly by higher SES participants.
4   A multiple view of health which included physical, mental, emotional, social and spiritual dimensions. This was only used by higher SES participants.

However, indigenous health beliefs go beyond descriptive dimensions to consider underlying etiology. Moscovici (1984), in his discussion of social representation theory, suggested that people rarely confine their definition of concepts to the descriptive level. Rather lay descriptions often include reference to explanations. This is apparent in a study of lay descriptions of health and illness by Stainton-Rogers (1991). Stainton-Rogers used Q-sort methodology to identify the concepts used by a sample of British adults to explain health. She identified eight different accounts of health and illness (Table 3.4)

It would seem that in western society there exists a range of competing accounts of health and illness. Although the biomedical explanation remains the dominant account, other explanations reach back to more traditional accounts. Thus the various ontologies of suffering described by Shweder et al. (1997) are present in the everyday accounts of laypeople in western society. They are not mutually exclusive but are adopted by people depending upon circumstances. These ontologies are also apparent in the indigenous health beliefs of other cultures.

TABLE 3.4 **Popular explanations of health (Stainton-Rogers, 1991, pp. 138–54)**

- The 'body as machine' account which considered illness as naturally occurring and 'real' with biomedicine considered the main form of treatment.
- The 'body under seige' account which considered illness as a result of external influences such as germs or stress.
- The 'inequality of access' account which emphasized the unequal access to modern medicine.
- The 'cultural critique' account which was based upon a sociological worldview of exploitation and oppression.
- The 'health promotion' account which recognized both individual and collective responsibility for ill health.
- The 'robust individualism' account which was concerned with every individual's right to a satisfying life.
- The 'willpower account' which defined health in terms of the individuals ability to exert control.

NON-WESTERN VIEWS OF HEALTH

The biomedical perspective has come to a position of dominance throughout the world, reflecting the imperialistic expansion of western society more generally. Alternative health-care systems have tended to be disparaged by biomedicine. Leslie and Young (1992) state that the 'derogation of Asian medical theories and epistemologies was not an isolated event. Rather, it was an expression of a more general cultural phenomenon' (p. 3). Being based upon a positivist perspective, the practitioners of biomedicine believed that they had access to a reality 'that exists prior to and independent of people's attempts to understand and control it' (p. 3). As such, alternative perspectives were seen as basically wrong.

However, alternative professional systems of health care continue to exist in large parts of the world, especially in Asia. Further, as migrants have moved to other countries they have taken their health beliefs with them. In the major western metropolitan centres there is now extensive availability of health-care systems other than biomedicine. This has led to a feedback into western ways of thinking about health and illness, especially among those who are disenchanted with biomedicine (Furnham and Forey, 1994).

Chinese views of health

The Chinese perspective views health as the result of a balance between and within the various systems both internal and external to the person. Disease is perceived as the consequence of disharmony or disequilibrium. This view of health and illness reflects a broader worldview which emphasizes interconnectedness and balance (Quah and Bishop, 1996).

Chinese medicine rests upon the religion and philosophy of Taoism. According to this view the universe is a vast and indivisible entity and each being has a definite function within it. Each being is linked in a chain in harmony. 'Violating this harmony is like hurling chaos, wars, and catastrophes on humankind – the end result of which is illness' (Spector, 1991, p. 243). The balance of the two basic powers of yin and yang governs the whole universe including human beings. Yin is considered to represent the male, positive energy which produces light and fullness. Conversely, yang is considered the female, negative force which leads to darkness and emptiness. A disharmony in yin and yang leads to illness. A variety of methods including acupuncture and the use of herbal medicines can be used to restore this harmony.

Within Chinese culture human suffering is traditionally explained as the result of destiny or ming. Cheng (1997) quotes the Confucian teacher Master Meng: 'A man worries about neither untimely death nor long life but cultivates his personal character and waits for its natural development; this is to stand in accord with Fate . . . All things are determined by Fate, and one should accept what is conferred' (p. 240). An important part of your destiny depends upon your horoscope or pa-tzu. During an individual's life, his or her pa-tzu is paired with the timing of nature. Over time these pairings change and create the individual's luck or yun.

Buddhist and Taoist beliefs are also reflected in Chinese medical belief systems; for example, good deeds and charitable donations are promoted. Heavenly retribution is expected for those who commit wrongs. This retribution may not be immediate but it will be inevitable. An important concept in this respect is pao which has two types – reciprocity and retribution (Cheng, 1997). In mutual relationships reciprocity or give and take is expected. When this does not occur some form of retribution will take place.

These views of health and illness are not only codified within Chinese medicine but influence everyday lay beliefs about health and illness both in China and in Chinese communities around the world. Several examples illustrate this. Cheng (1997) conducted interviews with a sample of Chinese workers in Hong Kong who had sustained hand injuries. He found that many of the workers, especially the older ones, explained their injuries in terms of fate or predestination. For example, one worker said: 'The injury was predestined. You were bound to be hurt no matter how careful you were. Something like a ghost blinded your eyes. No way for you to be careful! It couldn't be escaped in any way!'

Others referred to the role of retribution for some wrong which the individual may have committed in a previous life. One mentioned the role of his pa-tzu or horoscope. Admittedly, this did not mean he was condemned to misfortune. If he changed his life course then the pairing with his pa-tzu may become more harmonious. His belief in the role of fate enables the person to escape blame for the event but still maintain a belief that they have control over their lives. Cheng (1997) gives the example of a Mr Pang who says: 'Everything is predestined. Although my ming [fate] is not good, you know. I haven't looked down upon myself for the past years.'

Bishop and Teng (1992) investigated how Chinese Singaporean students describe illness. They found they used not only the dimensions of seriousness and contagiousness which were used by western students (see Chapter 11) but also a third dimension which was concerned with the extent to which the disease was perceived as related to behaviour or the Chinese concept of 'heatiness' ('hot' vs. 'cold'). In a similar study (Tan and Bishop, 1996), further evidence was found for this three-dimensional model although this time the third dimension was concerned with the degree to which a disease is perceived in terms of blocked 'qi' or energy. They reconcile these two findings by suggesting that blocked 'qi' and 'heatiness' both include the concept of internal imbalance or energy which is a central concern in Chinese medicine.

In a subsequent study it was found that the preference for Chinese illness concepts and for seeking help from practitioners of traditonal Chinese medicine (sinsehs) were related to the extent of Chinese culture orientation as measured by their agreement with a series of Chinese values (Quah and Bishop, 1996).

These lay belief systems remain strong within immigrant communities. For example, Frye (1991) interviewed a sample of Cambodian refugee women in California. She found that they explained health and illness within a traditional Buddhist worldview. Again, this approach emphasizes the central importance of balance and harmony within one's life. For these women a disturbance of this equilibrium resulted in a state of internal 'bad wind'. Using various wind releasing strategies such as 'coin rubbing', equilibrium could be restored. Equilibrium could be maintained by avoidance of competitive behaviour, respect for individuality, nurturance of the weak and peaceful co-existence with the natural world. Despite the availability of western medicine facilities, the women preferred to travel considerable distances to access a Cambodian physician.

This study also illustrates the importance of social balance or interconnectedness rather than individualism. Kleinman et al. (1995) examined the social course of epilepsy in interior China and the Chinese tradition of understanding suffering as a social experience. They quoted the parent of one patient with epilepsy:

> His disease brings our family so much trouble. The heaviest burden is in our hearts. I'm always crying about it. I have no money to give our son treatment. Wouldn't it be better for me to die? Others have sons in order to have blessings in their old age. But what do I have? I'll only reap hardships and worry as long as I live. There is no one in my family to look after him. (Kleinman et al., 1995, p. 1325)

Blackhall et al. (1995) also found evidence of this more collectivist approach to health among Korean and Mexican Americans. They surveyed a large sample of American seniors from four ethnic backgrounds: Korean, Mexican, African and European about their attitudes toward patient autonomy. They found that the Korean and Mexican Americans placed greater emphasis on family decision making. Illness was not simply a property of the individual but had implications for the whole family who should be consulted about treatment plans.

Ayurvedic medicine

The Ayurvedic system of medicine is based upon the Sanskrit words meaning knowledge (veda) needed for longevity (ayus). This system remains extremely extensive in India. It is estimated that 70% of the population of India and hundreds of millions of people throughout the world use ayurvedic medicine (Schober, 1997). According to this system which is based on Hindu philosophy both the cosmos and each human being consists of a female component, Prakfti, which forms the body, and a male component, Purusa, which forms the soul. While the Purusa is constant, the Prakfti is subject to change. The body is defined in terms of the flow of substances through channels. Each substance has its own channel. Sickness occurs when a channel is blocked and the flow is diverted into another channel. When all channels are blocked the flow of substances is not possible and death occurs. At this stage the soul is liberated from its bodily prison (Trawick, 1992).

The task of Ayurvedic medicine is to identify the blockages and to get the various essences moving again. The different forms of imbalance can be corrected through both preventive and therapeutic interventions based on diet, yoga, breathwork, bodywork, meditation and/or herbs (Schober, 1997).

As with the Chinese medical system, the Ayurvedic system pervades much of popular beliefs about health and illness thoughout the Indian sub-continent and among Indian communities in other parts of the world. However, Ayurvedic medicine has not gained the hegemony of western biomedicine, even within India. There is a variety of other competing health belief systems which has led to the development of a pluralistic health culture made up of several different systems. In an interview study of a community in Northern India, Morinis and Brilliant (1981) found evidence not only of Ayurvedic beliefs, but also 'unami' (another indigenous health system), allopathic, homeopathic, massage, herbalist, folk, astrologic and religious systems. They note that while these systems may formally seem to conflict, their study participants could draw on some or all of them to help explain different health problems.

Further, the strength of these beliefs is related to the immediate social situation and the roles and expectations of the community. For example, Winkvist and Akhtar (1997) conducted interviews with a sample of women from an urban slum and in a village near Lahore, Pakistan about their health beliefs. In that society, the major medical system is a mixture of biomedicine and 'unami' medicine which is a version of Galenic medicine. They found that the women's definitions of health reflected their social context:

For them, health did not constitute a separate, personal attribute that could be discussed as an end by itself. Rather, health was a reflection of the expected roles of these women as wives and daughters-in-law. Health meant physical strength for village women and women of lowest SES, and mental strength for city women and women of low SES. Women of medium SES were less involved with hard labor and household maintenance, and hence health was related to cultural qualities such as cleanliness and neatness. (Winkvist and Akhtar, 1997, p. 1489)

As with other societies, these women's popular health beliefs do not simply reflect the dominant expert health belief system but are adjusted to accommodate to changing social and material circumstances (see Chamberlain, 1997).

African medical systems

In Africa, a wide range of traditional medical systems continues to flourish. These include a mixture of herbal and physical remedies intertwined with various religious belief systems. As Porter (1997) notes, belief systems which attribute sickness to 'ill-will, to malevolent spirits, sorcery, witchcraft and diabolical or divine intervention . . . still pervade the tribal communities of Africa, the Amazon basin and the Pacific' (p. 9). In a more developed assessment Chalmers (1996) summarized the African view as reflecting 'a belief in an integrated, independent, totality of all things animate and inanimate, past and present' (p. 3). As with other traditional health systems a central concept is balance. 'Disturbances in the equilibrium, be they emotional, spiritual or interpersonal, may manifest in discordance at any level of functioning' (Chalmers, 1996, p. 3).

Two dimensions are paramount in understanding African health beliefs: spiritual influences and a communal orientation. It is common to attribute illness to the work of ancestors or to supernatural forces. Inadequate respect for ancestors can supposedly lead to illness. In addition, magical influences can be both negative and positive, contemporary and historical. Thus, illness can be attributed to the work of some malign living person. The role of the spiritual healer is to identify the source of the malign influence.

Rather than the individualistic orientation of western society, African culture has a communal orientation. Thus, the malign influence of certain supernatural forces can be felt not just by an individual but by other members of his or her family or community. 'The nuclear family, the extended family, the community, the living and the deceased as well as their ultimate relationship with God are intimately linked in the African view of health and illness' (Chalmers, 1996, p. 4). Thus intervention may be aimed not only at the sense of balance of the individual but also of the family and the community.

Mulatu (1995) investigated the illness causal beliefs of a large sample of Ethiopian adults. Factor analysis of their replies identified four causal dimensions: psychological stressors, supernatural retribution, biomedical defects, and social disadvantage. Psychological stressors and supernatural retribution were considered more important causes of psychological than of physical illnesses. He also found a relationship between these causal beliefs and treatment choices, attitude to patients and demographic characteristics. For example, belief in supernatural retribution was associated with use of religious prayer, holy water, consulting traditional healers and both traditional and modern medicine. Finally, there was also a relationship between education and causal beliefs such that the less educated placed more emphasis on supernatural causes. It was suggested that this reflects the extent of acculturation to the western biomedical model of illness.

As with other medical systems, immigrant communities have brought their health beliefs to their new countries of residence. Landrine (1997) criticized studies of North American health beliefs which have largely ignored the distinctive culture of black Americans. Semmes (1996) noted that African slaves maintained their pre-slavery health beliefs, practices and indigenous healers. When they gained emancipation black Americans found they were denied access to medical care. As a consequence they relied on their indigenous healers and over time developed a unique African-American folk medicine. He suggests that in contemporary North America many blacks are returning to this medical system as they feel rejected or excluded by what they perceive as the racism of white American health care.

CULTURE AND HEALTH BELIEFS

It is apparent that how people organize their beliefs about health is intertwined with their broader belief systems. Culture is not simply part of traditional communities but pervades all our lives. We are all cultural beings. The definition of health as a quality of the individual body is something peculiar to biomedicine. Other cultures both within and outside western society prefer a more social definition of health which emphasizes the relationship between the individual and the world. These alternative belief systems are not fixed and separate but are in a process of constant change.

FUTURE RESEARCH

1   Through access to historical documents, psychologists can assist in expanding our understanding of the evolution of contemporary health beliefs.
2   Understanding of popular health beliefs requires an understanding of their social and cultural context.
3   The increasing development of alternative health care in western society requires ongoing research.

4   In most large industrialized societies cultural minorities make use of a variety of competing health belief systems. There is a need for research to explore how these interact with the more dominant health belief systems.

SUMMARY

1   Human thought and practices are culturally immersed.
2   Different ways of explaining health and illness are apparent in different societies. These are known as causal ontologies.
3   The moral discourse of suffering is a particularly pervasive health discourse.
4   Systems of health can be considered as either expert or folk. These two systems are not separate but interactive.
5   The western view of health has moved through various stages from the classic to the religious and then the scientific.
6   The scientific view of health or biomedicine is the most dominant view in contemporary society but other health belief systems remain popular.
7   In contemporary society there is increasing interest in various alternative therapies.
8   Chinese medicine is an expert health belief system which remains popular in China and among Chinese migrants in other societies.
9   Ayurvedic medicine remains popular in other parts of Southern Asia.
10   In Africa there is a wide variety of other health belief systems which emphasize spiritual aspects and a communal orientation.

KEY TERMS

alternative medicine
biopsychosocial model
biomedicine
causal ontologies

Galenic medicine
moral discourses
systems of health

PART 2

HEALTH BEHAVIOUR AND EXPERIENCE

In Part 2 we review theory and research concerned with those health behaviours and experiences most relevant to the major causes of illness and death in industrialized societies. Part 2 begins with a review of the evidence for links between personality and health. This is followed by chapters on each of the major behavioural risk factors in contemporary living:

- stress;
- poor diet;
- excessive alcohol consumption;
- cigarette smoking;
- unprotected sexual exposure;
- lack of physical activity.

Each chapter offers practical recommendations concerning how the relevant theory and research can be applied to improve current systems of health care.

4 HEALTH AND THE INDIVIDUAL

Ills of the body may be cured by physical remedies or by the power of the spirit acting through the soul. Paracelsus (Hartman, 1973, p. 49)

OUTLINE

This chapter examines the influence of individual differences in personality and other psychological dispositions on illness. Beginning with the history of the distinction between physical and psychological disorders, it goes on to consider the Freudian analysis of hysteria and other psychosomatic disorders. This is followed by a brief account of the school of psychosomatic medicine and theories about the relationship between psychological dispositions and organic disorders. An analysis of the problems involved in investigating and explaining links between personality and physical illness is followed by an assessment of contemporary research with particular reference to coronary heart disease and cancer.

PSYCHOLOGICAL AND PHYSICAL DISORDERS

Let us begin by making a rough and ready distinction between psychological disorders, such as anxiety and depression, and physical disorders, such as infectious diseases and cancer. A straightforward and natural way of understanding their causation is to propose that psychological disorders are best explained by psychological causes, such as stress, traumatic experiences, childhood problems and the like, while physical disorders are attributable to physical causes, such as viruses, bacteria and carcinogenic agents. Following on from this it seems natural that psychological disorders should be treated by psychological means, such as psychotherapy and behaviour therapy, while physical disorders are best treated medically.

Nowadays everybody knows that this is an oversimplification. Psychological disorders ranging from serious mental illness to relatively mild cases of depression are commonly attributed to biochemical imbalances, often thought to be genetic. Some of these views are supported by DNA research and there is an increasing vogue for drug treatments in preference to psychotherapy. On the other hand, it also remains fashionable to believe that people with certain kinds of personality may be particularly susceptible to heart disease or cancer and that stress is a principal factor in the causation of much physical illness. Holistic treatments and complementary therapies for physical diseases frequently have a large psychological component including stress management programmes, relaxation, breathing exercises and meditation.

Historically the most influential doctrine has been the Hippocratic one which presupposes that there is a physical basis for all disorders, whether physical or psychological, and which dates back to the fifth century BC. As we saw in Chapters 1 and 3, according to Galen's theory, psychological and physical disorders are both attributable to an imbalance of the four bodily *humours*, blood, phlegm, black bile and yellow bile. Little scope was left for psychological causation and this theory only really lost its hold on western thinking in the 1850s. When Galen noted that *melancholy* women were more likely to get breast cancer than *sanguine* women he was not putting forward a psychological hypothesis. Although the psychological characteristics of melancholy correspond roughly to the modern concept of depression, Galen took the view that breast cancer and melancholy were jointly attributable to humoral imbalance, in this case to an excess of black bile (see Sontag, 1991, p. 54).

As an indication of the grip these ideas had on medical thinking in western Europe, the black bile theory of depression was still being articulated in 1836 by Johannes Freidreich, professor of psychiatry in Würzburg, together with the view that mania was caused by an excess of yellow bile, psychosis by an excess of blood, and dementia by an excess of phlegm (see Shorter, 1992, p. 15). One feature of the doctrine of the four humours which even today finds its echo in psychological theory is Galen's description of the four *classical temperaments* (see Box 4.1).

BOX 4.1   THE FOUR HUMOURS AND MODERN PERSONALITY THEORY

In the second century AD Galen described four temperaments which characterize individuals possessing an excess of each of the four humours. The *sanguine* has an excess of blood, the *choleric* of yellow bile, the *phlegmatic* of phlegm and the *melancholic* of black bile. As descriptions of personality types they were still in use during the second half of the twentieth century. In his influential theory of personality the late Hans Eysenck proposed two basic dimensions of personality, extravert-introvert and stable-unstable, and developed a personality test to measure them. Both dimensions were assumed to be measurable along a continuum with extreme examples towards either end and the average person in the middle. Although he considered the reduction of personality to four qualitatively different types to be an oversimplification, Eysenck (1965) pointed out that the classical temperaments do correspond quite closely with four extremes which can be identified using his personality test: the *stable extravert* (sanguine), *unstable extravert* (choleric), *stable introvert* (phlegmatic) and *unstable introvert* (melancholic).

The humoral theory was eventually abandoned following the founding of the modern science of cellular pathology by Rudolf Virchow in the 1850s. This was the key that opened the door to contemporary understanding of physical diseases. Since there were no obvious indications that cellular pathology could account for psychological disorders, the door was also open for the development of purely psychological explanations, notably by Sigmund Freud.

In recent years the wheel has come full circle. Advances in our understanding of neurotransmitters and the development of DNA research, together with criticism of the cost and efficacy of psychotherapy, has led to an increased enthusiasm for purely physical accounts of psychological disorders with the ancient imbalance theories based on the four humours replaced by theories which attribute these disorders to biochemical imbalances whose causes are genetic.

The historical dominance of the humoral theory and the modern ascendancy of organic medicine has not entirely inhibited speculation of the opposite kind, that psychological factors may play a part in causing physical diseases and influencing recovery. This is evident in the freedom with which modern medical practitioners and the general public deploy the concept of *stress related disease*. A good historical example is provided by Dogen (1200–1253), the founder of the Soto school of Japanese Buddhism. Admonishing his pupils not to regard illness as a hindrance to performing their spiritual practices, he remarked:

> I suspect that the occurrence of illness stems from the mind. If you lie to a hiccuping person and put him on the defensive, he gets so involved in explaining himself that his hiccups stop. Some years ago when I went to China, I suffered from diarrhoea while aboard ship. A violent storm arose, causing great confusion; before I knew it, my sickness was gone. This makes me think that if we concentrate on study and forget about other things, illness will not arise. (Dogen's *Shobogenzo Zuimonki* quoted in Masunaga, 1972, p. 91)

Sontag (1991, pp. 22–6, 53–6) provides many European and North American examples. In England in the late sixteenth and seventeenth centuries it was widely believed that the happy man would not get plague. In 1871 the physician who treated Alexander Dumas for cancer wrote that among the principal causes of cancer were 'deep and sedentary study and pursuits, and feverish and anxious agitation of public life, the cares of ambition, frequent paroxysms of rage, violent grief'. At about the same time in England, one doctor advised patients that they could avoid cancer by being careful to bear the ills of life with equanimity; above all things, not to 'give way' to any grief. At this time also TB was often thought to come from too much passion afflicting the reckless and sensual or else to be a disease brought on by unrequited love. In fact TB was often called consumption and hence the appearance in the English language of metaphors such as consuming passion.

The rapid march of organic medicine since the 1850s led to a declining enthusiasm for such explanations among medical practitioners. Having obtained a medical education which was second to none in the 1880s, Freud was always careful to avoid any temptation to propose psychological explanations for physical disorders. In recommending that psychoanalytic training should be restricted to those already qualified in medicine, he made a sharp distinction between *neuroses* and organic disorders. Only the medically trained psychoanalyst would have the skills necessary to decide whether a patient's symptoms needed to be investigated as indicating possible organic disorder or whether they should be treated as neurotic symptoms.

Freud's caution was understandable. His own theories originated from the study of cases of **hysteria**, patients who had symptoms which appeared to indicate serious neurological or other physical disorders, but for which there turned out to be no underlying physical cause (see Box 4.2). Hysteria was a major problem for the rapidly developing science of neurology towards the end of the nineteenth century. If a patient has lost the use of a limb, is unable to speak or feel any sensation in part of her body, and lacking the advantage of having a modern brain scanner, how do you tell whether you are dealing with a hysterical symptom or a brain tumour?

BOX 4.2 HYSTERIA: THE CASE OF ANNA O

Psychological theories of hysteria first came to prominence as a result of the collaboration between Sigmund Freud and the Viennese physiologist Josef Breuer. From 1880 to 1882 Breuer treated a patient who became known as 'Anna O' and who proved to be of great importance in the history of psychoanalysis. Anna suffered from a spectacular range of hysterical and other symptoms including paralysis and loss of sensation mainly on the right side of her body, disturbances of eye movements and vision, occasional deafness, multiple personality and loss of the ability to speak her native German. As a result of this last symptom, Breuer was obliged to talk to her in English over which she retained a perfect command. When she was asked to recall previous occurrences of each of her symptoms while under hypnosis Anna invariably arrived at previously forgotten memories of distressing incidents which had occurred while she had nursed her dying father. As a result of this the symptom temporarily disappeared. For example, the paralysis of Anna's right arm disappeared after she recalled having had the hallucination of a large black snake while sitting at her father's bedside. Anna O's true identity was much later revealed to be Bertha Pappenheim and she went on to become a well-known feminist who campaigned on problems of single mothers, children in orphanages, prostitution and the white slave trade. Just how successful was her treatment for hysteria is still a matter of controversy and she herself remained ambivalent about the value of psychoanalysis, once remarking that it depends very much on the ability of the psychoanalyst whether it is a good instrument or a double-edged sword. For further details, see Sulloway (1980).

Freud's research in this area led him to develop what is probably the most influential and controversial theory of the human mind ever proposed. Although he did not consider it appropriate to use it to explain susceptibility to organic disorders, some of his twentieth-century followers did take this step and introduced the *psychosomatic approach* to psychoanalysis. Some of the theoretical ideas of this psychosomatic tradition have been a major influence on the thinking of today's health psychologists, as will be shown later in this chapter. But first let us take a closer look at hysteria or *psychosomatic disorders*, since this subject is as controversial today as it was when Freud began his investigations.

HYSTERIA AND PSYCHOSOMATIC DISORDERS

The medical theorists of ancient Greece first used the word **hysteria** to refer to anomalous physical complaints which they believed occurred only in women. Favouring physical explanations, they regarded it as a gynæcological disorder caused by the womb moving away from its normal position. At the beginning of Freud's career it was still usually thought of as a feminine disorder and either explained on a physical basis in as fanciful way as the ancient Greeks, or else dismissed as malingering.

By the end of the nineteenth century, as a result of the pioneering work of Charcot, Breuer and Freud, it had become widely accepted that hysterical disorders are not restricted to women, that sufferers are not merely malingerers but are unaware of the causes of their condition, and that these causes are psychological rather than physiological (for detailed accounts of this early work on hysteria and subsequent developments in the twentieth century, see Sulloway, 1980; Shorter, 1992).

Although the pioneers brought to light cases of male hysteria it still appeared to be predominantly suffered by women, and this is still generally thought to be the case today. For most hysterical disorders, 80% to 90% of sufferers are women. The main exception is the case of *shell shock* or *battle neurosis* which was common among troops in World War I, but much less so in World War II, an interesting historical change to which we will return shortly.

By using the newly discovered techniques of hypnosis, the pioneers were able to show that hysteria may be caused psychologically, but outside the awareness of the sufferer. Hysterical symptoms could be induced in any hypnotisable person by the use of *post-hypnotic suggestion*, and the symptoms of hypnotisable patients could often be relieved, unfortunately only temporarily, in this way. While this does not actually rule out the possibility that there is an organic basis to hysteria, it certainly made it a lot easier for Freud to put forward his bold psychological hypotheses.

Freud and Breuer (1895) reported that, by using hypnosis and later the psychoanalytic technique of *free association*, they enabled their hysterical patients to recover traumatic memories which had previously been inaccessible and which appeared to have been the cause of their symptoms. These traumatic memories were frequently of sexual abuse, often occurring in childhood and involving a parent or close relative. Freud believed that the causes of hysterical symptoms were always sexual, whereas Breuer believed that any traumatic experience could cause them, a view which would subsequently receive support from the occurrence of shell shock.

Nowadays, the Freud–Breuer controversy seems of relatively minor significance in comparison with the controversy which has erupted as a result of Freud's subsequent theoretical shift from the sexual abuse theory of hysteria to his theory of infantile sexuality, and especially his claim that most of the repressed memories of sexual abuse which his patients recovered were not memories of real events at all, but of childhood fantasies. Traditionally regarded by psychoanalysts as a key discovery, this has been denounced by Masson (1992) and others as a cover-up of the reality of widespread sexual abuse of children. The controversy has been further fuelled by critics of Freud who believe that psychoanalytic techniques do not really lead to the spontaneous appearance in the mind of incidents of sexual abuse, whether real or imagined, but that psychoanalysts use elaborate interpretive devices to brainwash their patients into inventing false memories (Crews, 1997). A useful account of these confusing and increasingly acrimonious controversies is given by Segal (1996).

Whatever the truth is as to their causes, the fact remains that hysterical symptoms do produce a great deal of human misery. It also still seems reasonable to suppose that, in some way or other, unconscious psychological mechanisms are at work. The most useful recent contribution to the subject has been Edward Shorter's study of the history of psychosomatic illness in the modern era (Shorter, 1992). He analyses a well-known but little understood phenomenon, the large differences in the types of symptom which have been reported in different historical periods. The spectacular symptoms reported by Charcot and others in the late nineteenth century, symptoms of an apparently neurological condition, are nowadays encountered by neurologists only rarely in a working lifetime. While Charcot certainly exaggerated the dramatic character of the symptoms and encouraged his patients to do so, there is little doubt that they were common enough and that their virtual disappearance is a real change.

Shorter makes a similar case for the almost complete disappearance of shell shock between World War I and World War II. On the other hand, he argues that today's hysterics display symptoms which were relatively uncommon in the past, usually consisting of pain or fatigue. Common psychosomatic pains include persistent non-organic pain in the face and mouth, such as *burning-mouth syndrome*, headaches, apparent heart attack and chest pain, back pain, abdominal pain and pain in the limbs. This modern epidemic of pain symptoms has been matched by a similar epidemic of diffuse symptoms of fatigue, variously attracting the labels of *myalgic encephalomyelitis (ME)*, *fibrositis* and *chronic fatigue syndrome (CFS)* (see Box 4.3).

BOX 4.3   ME AND CHRONIC FATIGUE SYNDROME

In July 1955, 200 people were admitted to the Royal Free Hospital, London, with symptoms similar to those nowadays referred to either as 'myalgic encephalomyelitis' (ME) or 'chronic fatigue syndrome' (CFS). Subsequently 70 doctors and nurses at the hospital were also taken ill and the hospital had to close for two months. No cause was ever discovered and psychiatrists concluded that it was a case of mass hysteria. CFS first appeared in the USA in 1984 where 160 cases of a new mystery illness were diagnosed in Incline Village, a prosperous small town near Lake Tahoe, Nevada. The symptoms reported were quite diffuse but suggestive of a viral infection together with prolonged and debilitating fatigue. As in the case of the Royal Free syndrome, extensive laboratory tests failed to identify any pathological agent. Since then a huge number of further cases of ME or CFS have been reported, together with a failure to identify any organic cause, leading the majority of doctors and medical researchers to conclude that the condition is psychosomatic. Although the terms ME and CFS are modern ones, the actual symptoms are more or less identical to those referred to as neurasthenia in the period around the beginning of the twentieth century. This widespread phenomenon was also investigated by researchers who failed to find a viral cause. Freud was convinced that it was caused by excessive masturbation, an hypothesis which was disproved by the early pioneers of sex research who showed that there was no relationship between reported frequency of masturbation and symptoms of neurasthenia. Orthodox medical opinion eventually came round to the view that the cause was purely psychological and closely linked to depression. For further information on the history of neuresthenia, ME, CFS and related conditions see Shorter (1992), Sulloway (1980) and Showalter (1997). Showalter has put forward the controversial hypothesis that ME and CFS are part of a very large-scale contemporary hysterical epidemic which includes not only these syndromes but also phenomena such as Gulf War Sydrome, recovered memory of childhood sexual trauma, multiple personality syndrome, satanic ritual abuse and alien abduction.

The topic of hysteria seems destined always to provoke controversy. The reader who contemplates Shorter's list of modern psychosomatic complaints will appreciate that it is contentious. Debate about the organic reality of these conditions has been acrimonious, especially recently in the case of ME and CFS. Sufferers remain convinced of the physical reality of their condition. Media presentations have generally been sympathetic to this view and a minority of doctors also believe that an underlying organic basis may be present. In such circumstances, the prevailing medical view that the conditions are psychosomatic is easily cast as the villain of the piece. Yet there are good arguments in favour of the prevailing medical orthodoxy. No organic abnormalities have been discovered after extensive research and the social composition of sufferers has the typical character of earlier examples of hysteria, being very largely female, white and middle class.

The shifting character of psychosomatic symptoms and the intense controversies about their physical reality are elegantly and plausibly explained by Shorter. He regards psychosomatic illness as physical symptoms produced by the action of the unconscious mind and argues that an essential feature of the condition is a need to convince doctors of the reality of the patients' illness. Shorter states:

> One factor that conveys a history is the doctor's attitude. Patients want to please doctors, in the sense that they do not want the doctor to laugh at them and dismiss their plight as imaginary. Thus they strive to produce symptoms the doctor will recognise. As doctors' own ideas about what constitutes 'real' disease change from time to time due to theory and practice, the symptoms the patients present will change as well. These medical changes give the story of psychosomatic illness its dynamic: the medical 'shaping' of symptoms. (Shorter, 1992, p. 1)

In a medical environment in which brain scanners are readily available, hysterical patients are unlikely to convince neurologists that they are suffering from a brain tumour; but in a world in which new viruses continue to appear, sometimes not easy to isolate in the laboratory, then plausible symptoms of infectious disease are much more likely to be taken seriously.

If Shorter's analysis is correct, then three conclusions can be drawn. First, Freud and Breuer deserve great credit for emphasizing the reality of the suffering of the hysteric and her need to be taken seriously and given sympathetic medical attention. Second, if they were wrong in their various theories about the causes of hysterical symptoms, if neither traumatic memories nor infantile sexuality provide adequate explanations, then it is essential to discover what are the underlying psychological mechanisms. Third, careful attention needs to be given to the question: how does a doctor or therapist go about treating a patient or client whose symptoms are psychosomatic, but who is deeply committed to the belief that they are physical symptoms requiring medical treatment?

THE PSYCHOSOMATIC APPROACH IN PSYCHOANALYSIS

A useful survey of the psychosomatic tradition in psychoanalysis is given by Brown (1964). The first theorist to extend Freud's ideas on the unconscious mechanisms underlying hysterical and other neurotic disorders and to apply them to organic diseases was Georg Groddeck (1866–1934). In contrast to most psychoanalysts, his writing is refreshingly free from technical jargon. *The Book of the It* (Groddeck, 1979/1923) is an entertaining mixture of sense and nonsense, ranging from ingenious and plausible interpretations of everyday phenomena to some of the wildest and most extravagant speculation to be found anywhere in the psychoanalytic literature. Unfortunately for our present purposes, most of Groddeck's more plausible observations are concerned with general aspects of human sexuality, following along largely Freudian lines, whereas his wildest and most idiosyncratic views are those concerned with the causes of physical illness. He was deeply impressed by Freud's observations that hysterical symptoms were often meaningful to the sufferer, at least at an unconscious level, sometimes symbolically and sometimes quite directly expressing a wish. A simple example might be an hysterical pregnancy occurring in an infertile woman or one with no partner. In *The Unknown Self* Groddeck extended the idea that symptoms may be meaningful to all physical diseases and wrote: 'In other words, without Freud and psychoanalysis, we should not know what we do now, that every illness has a meaning to the sufferer, that it is intentional, consciously or unconsciously, and that it can be treated by discovering this intention, this meaning' (Groddeck quoted by Brown, 1964, p. 90). Brown outlines Groddeck's position as follows:

> Georg Groddeck . . . propounded a somewhat bizarre and largely intuitive theory based upon his experiences in analysing cases of heart disease, nephritis, cancer, and other serious organic illnesses. The individual according to this theory does not live his own life and has little to do with his fate. He is, in fact, lived by the 'It' which seems to be conceived as a compound of the Freudian 'Id' with the wisdom of the Jungian collective unconscious. It was the 'It' which decided when the individual would be born, and it also decides when he will die, whether or not he will succeed, and when and how he becomes ill. Every disease, from a wart to a cancer, is an expression of the omnipresent and omnipotent 'It'. For example, a woman with a small wart on the inner aspect of her thigh was told by Groddeck that she wished to become a man and had therefore produced (or, rather, her 'It' had produced) a miniature penis. A woman with a tumour of the uterus had obviously developed the tumour because, lacking a child, the 'It' had caused this deadly substitute 'child' to grow within her. A fracture case would be asked: 'Why did you break your arm?' and a case of laryngitis: 'Why did you wish to be unable to speak?' (Brown, 1964, pp. 89–90)

The evidence offered by Groddeck is purely anecdotal and most people would regard his views on the causes of physical illness as absurd, but is it necessarily ridiculous to propose that a real physical illness can sometimes come about as the result of an unconscious impulse? To take a fairly extreme example, if we accept that, in the case of an hysterical pregnancy, many of the physical symptoms of a real pregnancy can be brought about by an unconscious wish, is it not conceivable that, on some occasions, a real heart attack can occur in someone who has an unconscious wish to commit suicide?

The argument is perhaps more easily made in the case of accidents. Freud gave many examples of unconsciously motivated accidents, notably in 'The Psychopathology of Everyday Life' (1901). In one, a spurned lover, apparently by accident, stepped in front of a car when he happened to meet the woman in the street, and was killed before her eyes. The fact that some people tend to be *accident prone*, that is, to have far more than their fair share of accidents, has been extensively documented and much discussed by members of the psychoanalytic schools such as Karl Menninger and Theodor Reik.

Menninger (1938), following Freud, took the view that we sometimes have an unconscious wish to punish ourselves as a kind of penance for some wrongdoing or guilty thought, and that in some guilt laden individuals this can manifest itself quite frequently as accident proneness. The problem, as with most psychoanalytic explanations, is that it is extremely difficult to see how unconscious motivation can be convincingly demonstrated. While the existence of accident proneness is not doubted, it is not easy to find a satisfactory way to test the psychoanalytic explanation against the alternative and prosaic explanation that some people are just a lot more clumsy or inattentive than others.

Rather than propose that the symptoms of organic disease always have a symbolic meaning for the sufferer, an alternative and more influential approach from the psychosomatic schools has been based on the concept of unrelieved tension. When certain problematic emotions, such as anxiety, depression, aggression and sexual impulses, cannot be effectively discharged or rechannelled, they can have physiological consequences which predispose the individual to develop specific organic diseases. An extreme example is provided by Wilhelm Reich, whose capacity for extravagant speculation rivals that of Groddeck, but who is also partly responsible for present day speculation about the existence of a *cancer prone personality*. In his early work, *Character Analysis*, Reich (1949) examined body postures and put forward the hypothesis that, in certain individuals, characteristic emotional states can become frozen in their outward expression as fixed body postures that can have disease consequences. For example, a posture which causes constriction of the chest cavity could result in a shallow and unhealthy pattern of respiration, eventually leading to the development of respiratory disorders such as asthma.

In his later work Reich became increasingly preoccupied with his theory that the successful release of sexual energy during orgasm was the key to psychological well-being and that the damming up of this energy in neurotic individuals could lead to cancer. He attributed the cancer which killed Freud to sexual problems in his marriage. In *The Cancer Biopathy*, Reich (1948) developed these ideas with the pseudoscientific notion of *orgone energy*, a form of energy which he falsely believed to exist in the universe, detectable by measuring instruments, channelled in the nervous system and discharged in psychologically healthy individuals at the moment of orgasm. Reich had parted company with most of his fellow psychoanalysts by this time in his career and the wild science fiction quality of his writing is nowhere more evident than in the following passage, quoted by Susan Sontag: 'There is a deadly orgone energy. It is in the atmosphere. You can demonstrate it on devices such as the Geiger counter. It's a swampy quality . . . Stagnant, deadly water which doesn't flow, doesn't metabolize. Cancer, too, is due to the stagnation of the flow of the life energy of the organism' (Sontag, 1991, p. 68).

Sontag notes that: 'cancer is felt to be what he thought it was, a cosmic disease, the emblem of all the destructive, alien powers to which the organism is host'. Reich's cancer theories are clearly pseudoscientific and absurd, but his idea that cancer may be caused by some block in the individual's normal flow of emotional energy has proved influential. The belief that psychological factors play an important part in the initial causation and subsequent disease course of cancer was widely held by many psychosomatic thinkers. By the mid-1950s when their influence was at its height, Leshan and Worthington (1956), reviewing research in this area for the *British Journal of Medical Psychology*, drew the following conclusions:

> As one examines these papers, one is struck by the fact that there are consistent factors reported in studies which gathered material in different ways. There appear to be four separate threads which run through the literature. These are (1) the patient's loss of an important relationship prior to the development of the tumour; (2) the cancer patient's inability successfully to express hostile feelings and emotions; (3) the cancer patient's unresolved tension concerning a parental figure; (4) sexual disturbance. (Lesham and Worthington, 1956, p. 54)

Views such as these are still widely held, although seldom by cancer specialists. They are often used to justify complementary therapies which aim to teach sufferers how to beat cancer by the power of the mind. This is all very well if they work, if psychological dispositions really do play a significant part in the causation and development of cancer. If not, as Sontag and others have pointed out, the propagation of these beliefs may be profoundly undesirable:

> In Karl Menninger's more recent formulation: 'Illness is in part what the world has done to a victim, but in larger part it is what the victim has done with his world, and with himself . . .' Such preposterous and dangerous views manage to put the onus of the disease on the patient and not only weaken the patient's ability to understand the range of plausible medical treatment but also, implicitly, direct the patient away from such treatment. (Sontag, 1991, pp. 47–8)

Of all the theorists in the psychosomatic tradition, the one who has contributed most to modern health psychology is Franz Alexander, the

Chicago psychoanalyst, who in *Psychosomatic Medicine* (1950), combines psychoanalytic theory with hypotheses about physiological mechanisms, principally involving the *autonomic nervous system (ANS)*. He emphasizes the distinction between the *sympathetic* division of the ANS, which roughly speaking controls emotional arousal and fight-or-flight emergency reactions of the organism, and the *parasympathetic* division which, again roughly speaking, controls relaxation and the slowing down of functions activated by the sympathetic division.

According to Alexander, sustained activity in either branch of the ANS without the counterbalancing effect of the other can have disease consequences. Sympathetic overstimulation contributes to cardiovascular disease, diabetes and rheumatoid arthritis, while parasympathetic overstimulation contributes to gastrointestinal disorders including dyspepsia, ulcers and colitis. Sympathetic overstimulation may occur as a consequence of prolonged stress, a point to which we will return in the next chapter, but Alexander also thought that some personalities may be predisposed to the overstimulation of one of the two branches of the ANS at the expense of the other.

Alexander's theories led to the development in contemporary health psychology of the distinction between the *Type A* and *Type B personalities* and their differential susceptibility to cardiovascular disease, and to recent related work on hostility and cardiovascular disease. We will consider this work shortly but, before doing so, it is necessary to examine the logic underlying empirical research linking personality to physical disease and some of the pitfalls in its interpretation.

EXPLAINING LINKS BETWEEN PERSONALITY AND DISEASE

It is generally agreed today that the psychosomatic approach in psychoanalysis and the proponents of psychosomatic medicine failed to produce convincing evidence of links between psychological dispositions and illness or to demonstrate that their therapeutic interventions were effective (Walker and Shelton, 1985; Holroyd and Coyne, 1987). They were criticized for much the same reasons that psychoanalysis has been criticized more generally (Webster, 1995; Crews, 1997). Their theories were highly speculative and relied on elaborate interpretations of clinical data rather than controlled statistical studies. They also suffered from the defect of being retrospective, seeking to 'explain' patients' illnesses as 'caused' by psychological dispositions already known to the clinician, rather than prospective, making predictions about future illness on the basis of present psychological dispositions.

The period since the 1960s has seen the growth of a large empirical literature on the statistical relationship between personality, as assessed by a wide variety of standardized tests, and physical illness. These studies often derive their hypotheses from the earlier speculations of the psycho-somatic approach but seek to rectify its defects by carefully analysing statistical evidence. There is, however, one major defect which cannot be overcome because it is intrinsic to this type of research. The evidence is obtained from correlational investigations rather than true experiments and, as a consequence, findings are open to a wide range of interpretations. Obviously no investigator can assign personalities at random to experimental participants and then study their subsequent proneness to illness. All that the investigator can do is to administer personality tests to the participants and obtain measures of their illness status. Statisticians constantly remind us that it is not possible to infer causation from correlation and, in the case of personality–illness correlations, it is possible to illustrate this by considering a range of important problems of interpretation. These will now be considered.

Direction of causality

Psychological dispositions may be a cause of physical illness but they are also a consequence of it. This is a particular problem for cross-sectional studies which assess personality traits and illness status (present illness or illnesses experienced in the past) at the same time. For example, if patients with a history of coronary illness have higher scores on anxiety and depression than healthy controls, should we conclude that anxiety and depression are risk factors for coronary illness or that a history of coronary problems can cause people to become more anxious and depressed? Obviously the causal direction cannot be inferred from this type of study. The flaw may seem trivially obvious but it is surprising how many cross-sectional studies are to be found in the literature on personality–illness links.

The problem cannot always be resolved by conducting prospective studies to investigate the relationships between the current personalities of healthy volunteers and future illness. The reason for this is that many major illnesses take a long time to develop and it is frequently the case that patients have experienced unusual and disturbing symptoms for some time before a diagnosis is given. It is therefore possible that psychological dispositions which appear to be a cause of subsequent illness are in fact a consequence of symptoms of developing illness occurring prior to diagnosis. Prospective studies are clearly far superior to cross-sectional studies but they do not necessarily eliminate the problem of the direction of causality.

Background variables

A correlation may be found between two variables A and B when there is neither a direct effect of A on B, nor of B on A, but because a third *background variable* X has an effect on both. Galen's explanation for the association he believed to exist between melancholy and breast cancer is a good illustration. Here an excess of black bile is the background variable which he hypothesized to be a cause of both melancholy and breast cancer. As a further illustration, suppose that some people have a history of childhood illness which leaves them constitutionally weak and prone to further illness. Suppose also that this history of childhood illness has had a deleterious effect on their personality development, perhaps by limiting their opportunities for social development. The inclusion of a number of such individuals in a sample along with constitutionally stronger individuals who have had a healthy childhood could produce a non-causal correlation in the sample between adult personality and adult proneness to illness, because both are influenced by childhood illness. Further examples of background variables, notably genetic predispositions, are discussed by Holroyd and Coyne (1987) and Suls and Rittenhouse (1990).

Self-reported illness and the distress-prone personality

Stone and Costa (1990) and Cohen and Williamson (1991) point out that much health psychology research relies on self-reported illness rather than biologically verified disease status. This does not only apply to minor ailments such as colds and flu. The diagnosis of angina pectoris, for example, is frequently based on patients' reports of chest pain.

Stone and Costa argue that this reliance on self-reported illness is particularly unsatisfactory when considering research into links between personality and illness. They point out that there is extensive evidence that psychological distress is associated with somatic complaints but not with organic disease. Since many personality tests scores may be interpreted, at least to some extent, as measures of distress, it follows that correlations between test scores and self-reported illness may provide a false indication of a link between personality and disease when all that they really show is that neurotic individuals are the ones most likely to complain of being ill.

However, it should not be assumed that any discrepancy between self-reported illness and biologically verified illness is necessarily an indication of neuroticism. Adler and Matthews (1994) note that there is evidence that perceived health predicts mortality independently of biological risk factors leading them to conclude that self-reported health provides useful information over and above direct biological indications.

Dimensions of personality

Personality testing is not an exact science and there is little agreement as to what the basic dimensions of personality really are, or even whether the question is worth asking. Three influential theories have been those of Eysenck (1947), who argued initially that there were only two dimensions, extraversion and neuroticism (see Box 4.1), and subsequently added a third, psychoticism, Cattell (1950) who believed he had identified 16, and McCrae and Costa (1985) who settled for five. These so-called 'Big Five' personality traits consist of extraversion/introversion, agreeableness/ antagonism, conscientiousness, neuroticism/emotional stability, and openness to experience (McCrae and Costa, 1985). Jerram and Coleman (1999) assessed whether these 'Big Five' personality traits could be related to health behaviour in a sample of 50 British older people. Neuroticism was associated with a higher number of reported medical problems, negatively perceived health status and a higher frequency of visits to the doctor. Openness and agreeableness were associated with positive health perceptions. The authors conclude that since associations are evident for each of the personality traits, the 'Big Five' personality traits should be included in research on health behaviour.

A problem that arises in research using personality tests is that similar questions can often be found included in tests which are supposed to be measuring different traits so that, not surprisingly, scores for the same group of individuals given both tests may be highly intercorrelated. Just taking some of the measures which are frequently used in research into the links between personality and illness, the individual who scores high on anxiety is also likely to score high on depression, neuroticism and *pessimistic explanatory style*, and correspondingly low on self-esteem, *self-efficacy, hardiness*, internal *locus of control* and *sense of coherence*. The common element which may run through all of these measures is probably best labelled, following Stone and Costa as *distress proneness*. Further factors may also be common to some but not all of the tests. Given that the tests used vary from study to study as do the measures of physical illness, anyone seeking to understand the mechanisms by which personality may be linked to illness is confronted with major problems of interpretation.

Physiological mechanisms versus health behaviour

Psychological dispositions may be linked to illness either by virtue of physiological characteristics with which they are associated or more indirectly because of their relationship to health behaviour. The proponents of psychosomatic medicine, especially Franz Alexander, believed in the existence of physiological mechanisms linking personality to illness, usually involving differences in the functioning of the sympathetic and parasympathetic divisions of the autonomic nervous system.

Health psychologists who conduct research into the relationship between personality and illness are also primarily interested in physiological pathways. However, it is generally acknowledged that more prosaic explanations for correlations between personality and illness may be derived from the fact that personality differences are often associated with differences in health behaviour (Miller et al., 1996; Suls and Rittenhouse, 1990).

Characteristics such as anxiety, depression, neuroticism and hostility have been variously shown to be associated with levels of smoking and alcohol consumption, diet and exercise, sleep disturbance, likelihood of seeking medical advice in the early stages of a disease and the likelihood of adhering to recommendations subsequently. Any of these variables, or some combination of them, could be invoked to account for an empirical correlation between personality and illness.

Further problems arise if we consider the relationship between personality and *stress* and *social support*, two variables which have also been shown to be associated with physical illness. Stress and social support are normally thought of as environmental influences on the individual as distinct from personality which, as it were, comes from the inside. But the two types of variables cannot be so easily separated. The competitive individual is likely to seek out stressful situations while the anxious individual avoids them; the individual with high self-esteem may attract social contact while the depressive discourages it. Once again empirical correlations between psychological dispositions and physical illness may be found not because of the existence of direct underlying physiological mechanisms, but as an indirect consequence of associations between personality and other variables which influence physical health.

THE TYPE A/B PERSONALITY, HOSTILITY AND HEART DISEASE

The concept of the Type A personality was introduced by Friedman and Rosenman (1974) to describe psychological characteristics which they believed to be associated with proneness to coronary heart disease (CHD). The Type A personality is: highly competitive and achievement oriented, does not suffer fools gladly, always in a hurry and unable to bear delays and queues, hostile and aggressive, active and choleric, reads, eats and drives very fast, and is constantly thinking what to do next, even when supposedly listening to someone else. In contrast to this the Type B personality is relaxed, laid back, lethargic, even-tempered, amiable and philosophical about life, relatively slow in speech and action, and generally has enough time for everyone and everything. The Type A personality has much in common with Galen's choleric temperament, the Type B with the phlegmatic (see Box 4.1).

The classification of individuals as Type A or B has traditionally been made on the basis of a structured interview (Rosenman, 1978) in which people are not only asked questions about their Type A/B modes of behaviour but also provoked into directly manifesting such behaviour by being subjected to pauses and delays in the interview, deliberately interrupted and challenged about their answers to questions. Their responses to these provocations enable the interviewers to refine their ratings of Type A/B characteristics. The structured interview (SI) is generally considered to be the best method for assessing the Type A/B personality but many researchers have adopted the less time consuming approach of using standardized self-report questionnaires of which the *Jenkins Activity Survey (JAS)* has been most commonly used. This simply asks questions about Type A/B modes of behaviour.

In their discussions of links between personality and illness, health psychologists have always given pride of place to the research on the Type A personality and heart disease. The reason for this is that the first reports of well-designed, large-scale prospective studies based on initially healthy volunteers were very impressive. The key study was the Western Collaborative Group Study (WCGS) in which over 3,000 Californian men, aged from 39 to 59 at entry, were assessed as Type A or B using the SI and followed up initially over a period of eight and a half years, and later extending over 22 years. In an influential report on the results at the eight and a half year follow-up, Rosenman et al. (1975) found that Type As were twice as likely as Type Bs to suffer from subsequent CHD. Of the sample 7% developed some signs of CHD and two-thirds of these were Type As. This increased risk was apparent even when other risk factors assessed at entry, such as blood pressure and cigarette smoking, were statistically controlled for.

Similar results were subsequently published from another large-scale study conducted in Framingham, Massachusetts, this time with both men and women in the sample (Haynes et al., 1980). By the early 1980s, it was confidently asserted that Type A characteristics were as much a risk factor for heart disease as high blood pressure, high cholesterol levels and smoking.

Subsequent research has failed to support these early findings. When Ragland and Brand (1988) conducted a 22-year follow-up of the WCGS they painted a different picture. Early reports appeared to have exaggerated the significance of the Type A risk and three subsequent follow-ups yielded inconsistent findings. Using mortality as the crucially important measure, Ragland and Brand found:

> Type A/B behaviour was positively but not significantly associated with coronary heart disease in the first and third intervals, significantly negatively associated . . . in the second interval and not associated in the fourth interval. The results confirm the importance of the traditional coronary heart disease risk factors, and raise a substantial question about the importance of Type A/B behaviour as a risk factor for coronary heart disease mortality. (Ragland and Brand, 1988, p. 462)

This result and a number of other negative findings, as well as some positive ones, led to a re-evaluation of Type A/B research at the end of the 1980s when the burgeoning literature was extensively reviewed (Booth-Kewley and Friedman, 1987; Matthews, 1988; Evans, 1990). It became clear that the bulk of the positive findings came from cross-sectional studies rather than prospective studies. Positive prospective findings also tended to come from population studies of initially healthy volunteers, while studies of high risk individuals who already had symptoms of coronary disease either failed to show a relationship with the Type A/B personality or produced a reverse finding with Type As actually having better outcomes than Type Bs. Evans (1990) considers a number of statistical artefacts which may account for this as well as the engaging hypothesis that, while healthy Type As may be more at risk than Type Bs, following an initial diagnosis Type As are more likely than Type Bs to modify their risky health behaviours, thereby giving themselves a better long-term prognosis.

Reviewers also discovered that studies using the SI to assess personality were much more likely to produce positive results than those using questionnaires, especially the JAS. In seeking to explain this, it was noted that the SI assessments only correlated modestly with those based on the JAS. Further analysis of component scales which contributed to the SI assessments revealed that only one of these components, which mainly indicated hostility, was implicated in the relationship between Type A/B and CHD. Since the JAS does not include items assessing hostility, this also explains the generally negative findings from research using it to predict CHD.

This last finding led to a rapid decline in Type A/B research in the 1990s together with a new enthusiasm for research into the relationship between hostility measures and subsequent illness. Reviewing developments in health psychology for the *Annual Review of Psychology* in 1994, Adler and Matthews found that prospective studies in the period from 1989 to 1994 produced no evidence that the Type A personality is at greater risk for CHD than the Type B, while also noting and encouraging the emergence of research using measures of hostility instead.

As in the case of the Type A/B personality, research on hostility and health is divided between studies using SI methods to assess hostility and those using questionnaires, usually the *Cook-Medley Ho Scale* (for details of these and other assessment methods, see Smith, 1992). Corresponding to the findings of Type A/B research, research using the SI has produced more positive findings than research using self-report questionnaires. In a detailed review of the literature Miller et al. (1996) located eight studies using SI methods and combined the results to yield a small positive relationship between hostility and CHD. Research using the Ho scale has mostly failed to show a significant relationship with CHD although, curiously, it is rather more predictive of all-cause mortality, at roughly the same level as that between the SI and CHD. It should, however, be emphasized that the statistical relationship between measures of hostility and health is a weak one. Certainly hostility cannot be regarded as a substantial health risk of similar magnitude to that of cigarette smoking or high blood pressure, for instance.

There are many echoes of earlier discussions about Type A/B research to be found in those concerning hostility and health. In analysing possible explanations for the statistical relationship, both Smith (1992) and Miller et al. (1996) consider differences in physiological reactivity and the tendency of hostile people to indulge more in high risk health behaviours, to be subjected to higher levels of stress and to attract less social support than average. Again mirroring earlier discussions of the Type A/B personality dimension, they point out that hostility has many distinct subcomponents, including cynicism, mistrust, verbal and physical aggressiveness, overt and experienced aggressiveness. They propose that more attention should be given to subcomponents in order to discover which are most health hazardous. Recently, for example, cynicism has been identified as the possible culprit (Lepore, 1995). Given the generally weak statistical associations which have been found so far between hostility measures and health outcomes, it remains an open question whether researchers in this field are engaged on an exciting search for the truly toxic dimension of personality as far as CHD is concerned, a dimension with demonstrable physiological pathways to heart disease, or whether they are on a wild goose chase.

FURTHER STUDIES OF LINKS BETWEEN PERSONALITY AND ILLNESS

If we look beyond the Type A/B personality, hostility and heart disease, we find that much of the remaining research on links between personality and illness is concerned with what might be termed positive and negative prevailing moods or 'affectivity'. Researchers have sought to demonstrate that positive dispositions (e.g. optimism, high self-esteem) are associated with good health and negative dispositions (e.g. depression, pessimistic explanatory style) are associated with poor health. As we have already pointed out, these measures are all intercorrelated so that it is misleading to consider research under separate headings for distinct dimensions of personality. It amounts to much the same thing to show, for example, that persons scoring high on a test measuring depression have an increased risk of heart disease as it is to show that those scoring high on a test measuring optimism have a reduced risk. It is also important to bear in mind that persons with negative dispositions are more likely than those with positive dispositions to report illness when not actually ill and also to indulge in hazardous health behaviours, such as cigarette smoking and heavy drinking. With these cautions in mind we will now consider the research findings.

The widely held belief that depression is an important factor in the onset and subsequent development of cancer now appears to be without foundation. Adler and Matthews (1994) reviewed three recent large-scale prospective studies of the relationship between depression and both the incidence of and mortality from cancer. In these studies initially healthy samples of up to 9,000 were followed up over periods ranging from 10 to 20 years and no association was found between depression and either cancer onset or mortality.

Similar findings have been reported from follow-up studies of patients who have been treated for cancer. For example, Barraclough et al. (1992) followed up 204 patients who had received surgery for breast cancer over 42 months after surgery. They used a very detailed interview schedule, which included the assessment of prolonged major depression before surgery and during the follow-up period. They found no relationship at all between depression and relapse. Relapse was also unrelated to stressors, including bereavement, long-term social difficulties and lack of a confiding relationship.

A spectacular exception to the general run of negative findings on personality and cancer was the research of the late H.J. Eysenck, R. Grossarth-Maticek and their associates. Eysenck (1988) claimed that personality variables are much more strongly related to death from cancer than even cigarette smoking. In two subsequent papers the two researchers appeared to have identified personality types that increase the risk of cancer by about 120 times and heart disease by about 25 times (Grossarth-Maticek and Eysenck, 1991; Eysenck and Grossarth-Maticek, 1991). They also claimed to have tested a new method of psychological treatment which can reduce the death rate for disease prone personalities over the next 13 years from 80% to 32%.

These extraordinary claims were not received favourably by others working in this field. In a comprehensive and highly respected review of the field, Fox (1988) dismissed earlier reports by Eysenck and Grossarth-Maticek as 'simply unbelievable' and the 1991 papers, which were the first detailed accounts of their research, were subjected to devastating critiques by Pelosi and Appleby (1992, 1993) and by Amelang and Schmidt-Rathjens (1996). The 'cancer prone personality' was not clearly described and seems to have been an odd amalgam of emotional distance and excessive dependence. After pointing out a large number of errors, omissions, obscurities and implausible aspects of the data, in a manner reminiscent of Leon Kamin's now legendary analysis of Cyril Burt's twin data (Kamin, 1977), Pelosi and Appleby comment:

> It is unfortunate that Eysenck and Grossarth-Maticek omit the most basic information that might explain why their findings are so different from all the others in this field. The methods are either not given or are described so generally that they remain obscure on even the most important points; . . . Also essential details are missing from the results, and the analyses used are often inappropriate. (Pelosi and Appleby, 1992, p. 1297)

Turning to less contentious research, Adler and Matthews (1994) reviewed findings linking positive and negative dispositions to illness and they report a fairly perplexing set of contrasting findings. For example, Peterson et al. (1988), in a 35-year follow-up of 99 graduates of the Harvard University classes of 1942–44, found that pessimistic explanatory style, as assessed in tests taken by the participants while undergraduates, was predictive of poor physical health in later life assessed by physicians. Yet in stark contrast to this, Friedman et al. (1993) found that children who had been rated by their parents and teachers as having a good sense of humour and being optimistic and cheerful were more likely than other children to die early in adulthood.

Another somewhat counter-intuitive finding is that of Reed et al. (1994) who investigated the relationship between realistic acceptance and survival time of men suffering from AIDS. They found that those who were assessed as showing a realistic acceptance of their deteriorating condition and eventual death had a mean survival time which was nine months less than those who were assessed as being unduly optimistic. In an earlier review of research concerning mental health Taylor and Brown (1988) concluded that overly positive self-evaluations, exaggerated perceptions of control and mastery and unrealistic optimism, far from being associated with psychological difficulties, were actually associated with good mental health. Reed et al. appear to have shown that this surprising result extends even into the field of physical health.

Another personality variable which has been of interest to health psychologists over the last 20 years is the notion of locus of control. Originally formulated by Rotter (1954), this concept was applied to health beliefs by Wallston et al. (1978) who developed the *Multidimensional Health Locus of Control (MHLC) Scale*. This questionnaire has three subscales measuring the extent to which people attribute their state of health to their own behaviour (internal locus), and/or external factors including both powerful others, especially medical professionals, and chance or fate. The internal locus of control scale has much in common with the concept of self-efficacy (Bandura, 1977). In both cases the main focus of research interest has been not so much to investigate direct links with physical health but rather to show that they are predictive of the adoption of positive health behaviours and the avoidance of negative ones.

In a detailed review of research on the topic, Norman and Bennett (1996) found that the results were mixed and they concluded that the relationship between locus of control and health behaviour is a weak one, a conclusion which was recently confirmed by a large-scale study of a representative sample of 11,632 people who completed the MHLC in Wales (Norman et al., 1998). In this study, all three health locus of control dimensions were found to correlate significantly with a health behaviour index, with those engaging in more positive health behaviours scoring higher on the internal dimension ($r = 0.05$), lower on powerful others ($r = 0.09$) and lower on chance ($r = 0.16$). These are low correlations indicating a very weak predictive relationship and leaving more than 95% of the variance in health behaviour unaccounted for. Self-efficacy appears to be a rather better predictor of health behaviour and it has been argued that it is the best available predictor (Schwarzer, 1992).

In conclusion, the evidence for direct links between individual personality and biologically verified health status is very weak. Popular beliefs in these links, the confident assertions of theorists in the psychosomatic tradition and the convictions of practitioners of complementary therapies have to date received little support from well-designed empirical studies. The evidence for links between personality and health behaviour is rather better but still modest. The modern trend in health psychology to focus more directly on health behaviour, how it becomes established and what causes change, seems potentially a more productive approach. This in turn suggests that levels of analysis beyond that of the individual and towards populations and population groups may be the best way forward.

FUTURE RESEARCH

1   There is a need for clarification of the role of psychological factors in conditions such as chronic fatigue syndrome where there is controversy as to whether they have an organic basis. This could usefully be extended to conditions suspected of being psychosomatic in children, to determine whether child psychotherapists are correct in their view that children tend to *somatize* psychological distress. Research could also evaluate the effectiveness of psychotherapeutic interventions for these conditions.

2   There is also a need for clarification of the structure of personality with particular reference to health in order to reduce or eliminate the problem of overlapping measures.

3   Investigations to distinguish between personality variables which are associated with biologically verified illness as distinct from those which are associated with reported illness for which there appears to be no organic basis.

4   Studies to establish which dimensions of personality are directly associated with health relevant physiological variables and which are primarily associated with health behaviours.

5   Outcome studies to assess the effectiveness of interventions designed to modify psychological dispositions, such as hostility, which are suspected of being health hazardous. It would be particularly valuable to assess whether interventions can improve the prognosis for those already diagnosed as suffering from organic disease.

6   Where personality variables are linked primarily to health behaviours, it would be useful to establish whether interventions designed to modify health behaviour (e.g. smoking cessation programmes) could be more effective if they took account of personality assessments of participants.

SUMMARY

1   From the Ancient Greeks to modern times orthodox medical practitioners have usually believed that there is a physical basis to all illness, including psychological disorders. Traditional explanations based on the Hippocratic doctrine of the four humours have now been replaced by the *medical model*, a science of pathology and the belief that psychological disorders are caused by biochemical imbalances, often thought to be genetic.

2   The modern history of psychological explanations for physical symptoms begins with Freud's theories of hysteria, physical symptoms of illness for which no organic basis could be discovered.

3   Clinical cases of hysteria of the type studied by Freud are relatively rare nowadays, but it has been argued that the earlier symptoms have been replaced by new symptoms such as chronic fatigue syndrome.

4   The psychosomatic approach was developed by psychoanalysts who extended Freud's theories of hysteria to provide psychological explanations for the causation of real organic disorders such as heart disease and cancer.

5   Proponents of the psychosomatic approach generally failed to produce convincing evidence in support of their hypotheses. However, the theories of Franz Alexander on the physiological mechanisms which could underlie the relationship between the psychology of the individual and organic disease have led to modern conceptions of the Type A personality and stress as contributors to cardiovascular disease.

6   Health psychologists have found it very difficult to determine whether personality is associated with susceptibility to physical disease directly through physiological mechanisms, indirectly by way of health behaviour, or whether the data are best explained by statistical artefacts and flaws in the design of the studies from which they are obtained.

7   Earlier indications that the Type A personality is a risk factor for cardiovascular disease have not been confirmed by more recent studies. Attention has now shifted to hostility which does seem to be a risk factor, although much less so than traditional risk factors such as high blood pressure or cigarette smoking.

8   There is no clear-cut evidence that personality variables are associated with increased risk of cancer.

9   Studies investigating the long-term effects on health of optimism and pessimistic explanatory style have yielded conflicting findings.

10 Realistic acceptance has been found to be associated with decreased survival time of men suffering from AIDS.

11 Internal *locus of control* is only very weakly associated with positive health behaviours. *Self-efficacy* shows an overall stronger relationship, yet the level of prediction is still relatively modest. Overall, evidence for any substantial link between personality and health is lacking.

KEY TERMS

accident proneness

chronic fatigue syndrome (CFS)

hardiness

humours (doctrine of the four
    humours

hysteria (conversion hysteria)

locus of control

myalgic encephalomyelitis (ME)

pessimistic explanatory style

psychosomatic disorders

psychosomatic medicine

self-efficacy

sense of coherence

Type A/B personality

5 STRESS AND COPING

Though the faculties of the mind are improved by exercise, yet they must not be put to a stress beyond their strength. (John Locke, 1690)

OUTLINE

This chapter discusses theoretical models of stress and coping and research on stress as a cause of physical illness. It begins with a critical discussion of the stress concept and gives an account of stimulus, response and interactional models of stress and coping. Consideration is given to the effects of stress on the immune system and to the ways in which people react to traumatic stress. A discussion of the methodological problems involved in research on stress and illness is followed by an examination of the evidence linking stress to cardiovascular disease, cancer and infectious diseases.

WHAT IS STRESS?

It is frequently asserted that stress has become a major feature of modern living, caused particularly by changes in the type of work that we do, by the breakdown of traditional family structures, and by many features of the contemporary urban environment. Stress is thought to be a principal cause of psychological distress and physical illness and millions of working days every year are believed to be lost as a consequence of this. The ability to cope successfully with stress is frequently held to be the key to human happiness (Figure 5.1).

But what exactly do we mean by stress, and how convincing is the evidence in support of these popular beliefs? If you ask people what they mean by stress you will find that their answers fall into one of three categories, each of which finds its echo in the academic literature on theories of stress. The first type of answer is that stress is 'when you are under a lot of pressure', or 'when things are getting on top of you'. This is essentially the position taken up by theorists who put forward *stimulus models* of stress, theorists who have variously tried to catalogue and present a taxonomy of environmental stressors or to devise measures of the relative stressful impact of life events ranging in severity from bereavement, divorce and job loss to having one's car wheel clamped or paying a visit to the dentist. These life event measures have in turn been used to investigate the role of stress as a cause of physical illness.

"Keep blowing"

FIGURE 5.1   **Coping with a life event stressor (Private Eye, 4 October 1996, p. 22; reproduced with permission)**

The second type of answer concentrates on the physical and psychological feeling of 'being stressed' or 'completely stressed out' with symptoms such as headaches, poor concentration, insomnia, bodily tension and fatigue. This position is taken by theorists who develop *response models* of stress, theorists who concentrate on the physiology of stress and who investigate possible mechanisms linking stress to physical illnesses such as coronary disease and viral infections, by way of the cardiovascular and immune systems respectively. Response models have also provided the impetus for the introduction of stress management programmes which focus on controlling the physiology of stress using techniques such as relaxation and breathing exercises, yoga, meditation, aerobics and other forms of physical exercise.

The third type of answer is that stress is 'when you think you can't cope' or 'when you have too much strain put on you and you don't have the resources to deal with it'. This is the position developed in *interactional models* of stress by theorists who argue that stress occurs when there is an imbalance between the perceived demands placed on the individual and the ability to meet those demands, often described as *coping resources*. These models are attractive because they overcome a problem inherent in stimulus and response models, that individuals differ as to what events or demands they find stressful and in the way that they respond to these events and demands. They have led to the study of coping methods and to the development of techniques aimed at helping individuals to overcome stress by increasing the effectiveness of their coping methods. These are taught in *stress management workshops* and *stress innoculation training*.

It needs to be pointed out that not everyone agrees that the development of general theories of stress is a viable scientific objective. For example, while it seems worthwhile to study the effects respectively of bereavement, living in noisy environments and of poor role definition at the workplace, it is not necessarily the case that such studies would yield results which had enough points in common to be incorporated into a general theory of stress. Several critics have pointed out that stress is an umbrella term which has been applied to so many quite different phenomena as to become virtually meaningless from a scientific point of view (Averill, 1989; Brown, 1996). In an effort to encompass such diverse phenomena theories may have become so vague and ambiguous that they lack any practical value. But if the stress concept is such a nebulous one, why has it come to play such a significant role in popular discourse and media presentations? This question has been taken up by a number of authors who have analysed stress as a social construct (Young, 1980; Pollock, 1988; Averill, 1989; Radley, 1994; Brown, 1996). Consider now two illustrations of the way in which a social analysis can be useful.

First, stress is often used as a device for legitimating behaviour which might otherwise be seen as the result of anxiety, neurosis or personal inadequacy. For example, to phone up your workplace to say that you will not be coming in today, or to excuse yourself for not taking an exam on the grounds that you are too worried, not sleeping well, too tired, or simply feel inadequate would not be considered acceptable. To give as the reason that you are suffering from stress, preferably supported by a letter from a doctor or counsellor, could be considered perfectly reasonable. In spite of the differences between stimulus, response and interactional models of stress, what they all have in common is that they draw attention to current events in one's life or one's immediate environment as provoking a reaction, rather than focusing exclusively on the individual. But it may very well be that an inability to cope with the demands of everyday life may be more appropriately seen as indicative of a long-standing psychological problem such as anxiety or depression. To appreciate the power of words, consider the effect of replacing the statement that someone suffers from agoraphobia with the statement that they find public places highly stressful. The two statements may be equally true, even synonymous, yet the effect of using the two forms of language is likely to be quite different.

Second, stress often has the function of explaining the otherwise inexplicable, whether this be psychological or physical symptoms or actual illness. Suppose that someone has a consultation with the doctor after suffering a heart attack. The doctor is expected to provide an explanation as to why the heart attack occurred. Does the patient smoke, drink a lot of alcohol, eat too much especially fatty foods, have a history of high blood pressure, or avoid exercise? If the answer to all these questions is 'no', the next question is likely to be, 'have you been experiencing a lot of stress lately?'; a question to which most people are likely to reply 'yes', especially if they are urgently seeking an explanation for an otherwise inexplicable complaint. But is the explanation a valid one or merely a convenient pseudoexplanation? Clearly the role of stress in the aetiology of physical illness needs to be investigated just as carefully as any other proposed causal agent.

STRESS AS A STIMULUS

The impression given by the mass media is that stress research has advanced to the point when it should be technically possible to estimate the number of days by which one's life has been shortened as a result of individual stressors. Moving house, having one's car stolen and getting divorced each score a certain number of points and the grand total points score for any individual might then be used to calculate his or her life expectancy. This type of belief is a testament to the popularization of the stress concept in the mass media, but it does not have any basis in empirical research. It probably has its origins in misunderstandings of some pioneering research conducted by Holmes and Rahe (1967) into the types of life events which people rate as being most stressful. They began by choosing 43 probably stressful life events, and then asked 400 US adults to rate the relative amount of readjustment that they judged would be required by each of the 43 events. The 10 highest rated of these are listed in Box 5.1. Holmes and Rahe then used their results to construct a *social readjustment rating scale (SRRS)* that assigns points values to different stressors and which has subsequently been used in research on the relationship between stress and physical illness.

BOX 5.1   STRESSFUL LIFE EVENTS AND DAILY HASSLES SCALES

Listed below in order of severity are the 10 life events rated as highly stressful by a sample of the US adult population studied by Holmes and Rahe (1967), and the 10 daily hassles endorsed most frequently by a New Zealand student population studied by Chamberlain and Zika (1990) using a scale derived from Kanner et al. (1981).

	Life events		Daily hassles
1	Death of spouse	1	Not enough time
2	Divorce	2	Too many things to do
3	Marital separation	3	Troubling thoughts about future
4	Jail term	4	Too many interruptions
5	Death of close family member	5	Misplacing or losing things
6	Personal injury or illness	6	Health of a family member
7	Marriage	7	Social obligations
8	Fired at work	8	Concerns about standards
9	Marital reconciliation	9	Concerns about getting ahead
10	Retirement	10	Too many responsibilities

Some researchers felt dissatisfied with the SRRS because many of the events listed in it occur relatively rarely in anyone's life. There was a desire for a scale that reflected to a greater degree the day-to-day variation experienced by people in levels of the stress to which they are exposed. This led Kanner et al. (1981) to devise, using similar techniques to those of

Holmes and Rahe, two further scales, a *hassles scale* consisting of everyday events that cause annoyance or frustration, and an **uplifts scale** consisting of events that make them feel good. Of the two, the hassles scale has been the more widely used for research which parallels that using the SRRS. Box 5.1 lists as an example the findings of Chamberlain and Zika (1990), using an adaptation of the Kanner et al. scale, of the 10 most frequently endorsed hassles by a sample of 161 students in New Zealand.

The SRRS, the hassles scale and research using them have been the subject of extensive criticism since their original publication (Schroeder and Costa, 1984; Dohrenwend and Shrout, 1985; Harris and Brown, 1989). These criticisms focus on the choice of items for inclusion in the scale, items which often seem highly arbitrary, vague, ambiguous, insensitive to individual differences and sometimes likely to assess the individual's level of neuroticism rather than experienced life event stress.

The arbitrariness of items included in the scales is probably inevitable. It is trivially easy to think of stressful life events and hassles that have not found their way into the existing scales, but a complete listing of all such events would be endless. The vagueness and ambiguity of some items is a more serious problem. Items such as *change in recreation* or *change in responsibilities at work*, taken from the SRRS, and most items on the hassles scale can be criticized in this way. Items such as bereavement may also create problems because bereavement may have very different stressful impacts on different people as a function of length and quality of relationship, whether or not the death was unexpected, and so on.

Much of the research linking physical illness to stressful life events has consisted of retrospective studies in which participants are asked about life event stress occurring prior to the onset of physical illness. These studies have been criticized because, as we have already pointed out, people who have recently been ill may very well be predisposed to recollect and report recent stressful life events to a greater extent than control group individuals who have remained well. Any such tendency will obviously lead to an overestimation of the association between stress and illness. The inclusion of vague and ambiguous items in the scales is clearly likely to maximize the differential reporting of stressful life events.

The question as to whether the scales may be partially measuring neuroticism arises because they include a lot of items such as *too many things to do* or *troubling thoughts about the future* which could equally find a place in a scale designed to measure anxiety and depression. This leads to a problem in interpreting the results even of prospective studies which investigate the association between scores on life events and hassles scales and subsequently occurring physical illness over a period of time. In principle this can establish whether stress really does predict the development of illness. Most prospective studies have relied on self-reports of illness; but it is highly probable that neurotic individuals will not only give high scores on life events and hassles scales but also be more likely to interpret minor symptoms as indicative of physical illness than individuals low on neuroticism. Here an empirical association between stress and illness may occur as a result of a reporting bias rather than a genuine causal link. A better approach is to rely on biologically verified assessments of illness.

Recent researchers investigating stress–illness links have shown a trend away from the use of standardized checklists in favour of the structured interview techniques developed by Brown and Harris (1978, 1989). Their *life events and difficulties schedule (LEDS)* is used to assess, classify and rate the severity of stressors, making allowance for individual circumstances. Originally developed to study the social origins of depression in women, the LEDS has since been used to study links between life event stress and physical illness (Harris, 1997).

In addition to their use for developing measurement scales for research into the effects of stress, stimulus models of stress have also produced some useful theorizing about the nature of stressful stimuli. One approach has been to distinguish between qualitatively different types of stressor and a useful fourfold classification has been put forward by Elliot and Eisdorfer (1982):

1   *Acute, time-limited stressors*: examples could be being threatened in the street or taking the driving test.
2   *Stressor sequences*: examples could be selling one's house or losing one's job.
3   *Chronic, intermittent stressors*: examples could be deadlines for journalists or premenstrual tension.
4   *Chronic stressors*: examples could be medical emergencies for doctors or living in cramped and overcrowded conditions.

These distinctions are useful for anyone investigating responses to stress because both psychological and physiological effects of each type of stressor are likely to be quite different. A further distinction, introduced by Spielberger (1966, 1972), can be made between physical threats and ego threats, threats to the physical and phenomenological self respectively. Spielberger argues that everyone reacts in much the same way to physical threats, while only individuals high in trait anxiety experience large increases in anxiety in response to ego-threats. Each of these examples illustrates the need for stress researchers to move away from using stress as a single umbrella category and seeking uniform effects on all individuals, and to move towards a more fine-grained analysis which concentrates on specific types of stressor and takes note of individual differences.

STRESS AS A RESPONSE

Since any catalogue of potential stressors is endless and individuals differ greatly as to what they find stressful, an alternative is to seek to identify a characteristic stress response which occurs whatever the nature of the stressor. This could theoretically include physiological, psychological and behavioural consequences of stress, although in practice researchers have tended to concentrate on physiological effects, especially those which may be associated with the development of physical illness.

Research on the physiology of stress originated in the work of Walter Cannon in the first half of the twentieth century. Cannon's theories revolve around the concept of *homeostasis*, whereby the physiological mechanisms of the body are considered as feedback systems functioning as far as possible to maintain a steady state. Homeostatic balance is disrupted not only by basic bodily needs, as in the case of hunger and thirst, but by any environmental stimulus which disrupts the body's state of equilibrium (e.g. excessive heat or cold, bacterial and virus infections, emotion provoking stimuli), thereby causing a reaction which has the function of reestablishing the inner balance. Anything which disrupts equilibrium may be regarded as a stressor (Cannon, 1932).

Under Cannon's influence, Hans Selye began a programme of animal experimentation into the physiological effects of noxious stimuli and other environmental stressors from the early 1930s until shortly before his death in 1982 (Selye, 1956, 1976). He argued for the existence of a generalized response, known as the *general adaptation syndrome (GAS)*, which occurs whenever the body defends itself against noxious stimuli. The GAS occurs primarily in the pituitary-adrenocortical system and consists of three stages, an *alarm reaction* in which the body's defences are mobilized, a *resistance stage* in which the body adapts to the stressor, and an *exhaustion stage* in which the body's capacity to resist finally breaks down. The GAS may be likened to the process whereby an individual, confronted by sudden unexpected financial demands, takes out a bank loan (alarm reaction), and uses it to meet these demands (resistance stage) until further income is received and the loan repaid (recovery) or bankruptcy results (exhaustion stage). Selye particularly drew attention to the abnormal physiology of the animal during the resistance stage which, if protracted, could lead to what he called the *diseases of adaptation*. These include ulcers, cardiovascular disease and asthma.

Although Selye's views have been very influential in the history of stress research, they are no longer widely accepted following extensive criticism by Mason (1971, 1975). He argued that the body's reaction to different stressors is not uniform at all. Those common physiological reactions which Selye did find were caused by the emotional reaction of the animal to the stressor rather than to a direct physiological effect. In many studies of the effects of stress, laboratory animals have been exposed to some highly unpleasant conditions and it seems likely that researchers have been effectively studying the physiology of fear. It is not easy to find a justification for this type of animal experimentation and the results of such studies will not be considered any further.

The tradition of psychosomatic medicine, which was introduced in the last chapter, spans a similar historical period as the work of Cannon and

Selye but focuses much more on the human response to stress. Franz Alexander and his associates drew a distinction between the temporary and biologically adaptive changes in the physiology of the animal facing an emergency necessitating flight or fight and the protracted and maladaptive physiological changes taking place in the anxious or stressed human being. Of particular significance are the physiological changes which are activated by the sympathetic branch of the autonomic nervous system:

> Sympathetic stimulation is necessary when the individual is confronted by actual danger or the need for increased activity, but when he is angry or afraid about events of yesterday or the possible events of tomorrow what was intended as an emergency reaction becomes a prolonged and chronic one. For example, the useful temporarily raised blood-pressure of emergency may become the pathological and permanently raised blood-pressure of prolonged resentment and frustration. Another difference between animals and human beings is the capacity of the latter to see emergencies in situations where the danger is not to life and health but only to pride or self-respect. For instance, the student before an examination shows the rapid pulse, the pallor, and other changes which were biologically intended for life-or-death situations, and even more so the neurotic with for example claustrophobia becomes anxious and his sympathetic system is stimulated in a situation where there is no objective danger at all but only a symbolic one. (Brown, 1964, p. 94)

The proponents of psychosomatic medicine emphasized the effects of stress and anxiety on the cardiovascular, gastro-enteritic and respiratory systems. Some of their theories have an attractive plausibility, but their broad theoretical sweep and the range of physiological mechanisms proposed was never matched by an appropriate level of careful empirical research. Health psychologists have made some progress in investigating the relationship between stress and cardiovascular disease, but other areas considered by the schools of psychosomatic medicine remain, from a research point of view, largely virgin territory. At present the two most active areas of investigation into responses to stress are, first, the study of the effects of stress on the immune system, usually referred to as *psychoneuroimmunology (PNI)* and, second, the study of the long-term effects of extreme or traumatic stress, usually referred to as *post-traumatic stress disorder (PTSD)*. We will now consider these two areas of research.

Psychoneuroimmunology (PNI)

The AIDS epidemic was a major cause of recent interest in psychological influences on the immune system, but there are also other considerations. The immune system is implicated not only in the body's defences against all infectious diseases but also in cancer and in *autoimmune diseases* such as rheumatoid arthritis. If psychological factors can be shown to have a significant role as causes of *upregulation* and *downregulation* of the immune system, then it is possible that psychological interventions could play an important role in the treatment of a very wide range of diseases.

O'Leary (1990) provides a comprehensive analysis of research into stress, emotion and human immune function and further reviews are given by Herbert and Cohen (1993), Bachen et al. (1997) and Evans et al. (1997). Maier and Watkins (1998) attempt to synthesize current knowledge from an evolutionary perspective to account for psychological and behavioural effects of physical illness as well as the effects of stress on the immune system. These authors all emphasize that the immune system is a very complicated one involving a range of different types of cell with distinct functions. A brief synopsis of these is given in Box 5.2.

BOX 5.2   CELLS OF THE HUMAN IMMUNE SYSTEM (O'LEARY, 1990; BACHEN ET AL., 1997)

The main cells of the immune system are *leucocytes*, usually known as white blood cells. The three most important types of leucocytes are *granulocytic cells*, *monocytes/macrophages* and *lymphocytes*. These in turn divide into the following categories:

granulocytic leucocytes: the main types are *neutrophils* which are *phagocytes* (eating cells) that engulf and destroy bacteria, *eosinophils* which similarly engulf antigen-antibody complexes, and *basophils* which have effects which promote the migration of other immune cells to the region.

monocytes/macrophages: these cells have a number of functions including 'recognition' of certain carbohydrates on the surfaces of microorganisms.

lymphocytes: these cells usually have the function of attacking specific targets. They can be subdivided into *B cells*, *NK cells* and *T cells*. B cells produce antibodies which proliferate rapidly, thereby controlling infection. NK (natural killer) cells destroy virus infected and tumour cells. T cells further subdivide into *T helper cells*, which enhance immune responses by stimulating the replication of immune system cells and antibodies, *cytotoxic T cells*, which destroy virus, parasite and tumour infected cells, and *T suppressor cells*, which inhibit immune responses.

It can be seen that the human immune system is not simple. Much as one might like to do so, it is not possible to talk in a general sense of heightened or reduced immunity, because the immune system is volatile with changes constantly taking place in one or more of its parts, so that at any particular time one measure may indicate heightened immunity while another may indicate reduced immunity. Furthermore, the preponderance of different kinds of immune cells varies considerably among healthy individuals and in the same healthy individual from day to day, so that the demonstration of a statistically significant effect of a psychological variable does not necessarily entail that it has clinical significance as regards disease outcomes.

Research on stress and immunity can be broadly divided into studies of the short-term effects of *acute stressors* and of the longer term effects of *chronic stressors*. Acute stressors which have been studied include sleep deprivation, space flight, taking examinations, exposure to the objects of phobias such as snakes, violent exercise, loud noises, electric shocks and attempting to solve difficult or impossible problems. Chronic or long-term stressors which have been studied include bereavement, unemployment, marital conflict, separation and divorce, and caring for relatives suffering from Alzheimer's disease. No study has investigated the effects of any particular stressor on all aspects of immune function and it is therefore necessary to piece together findings from different studies in order to obtain a general picture.

It has been a fairly consistent finding that chronic stress is associated with some degree of downregulation of immune systems with changes noted particularly in the number of NK cells, the total number of T cells and the proportion of T helper cells to T suppressor cells. Findings for the effects of acute stressors have been more variable with some indications of upregulation, some of downregulation and some null findings. Studies which have used a variety of different measures of immune function have also produced contrasting findings for different aspects of the immune system. Evans et al. (1997) argue that, on balance, the results are consistent with the interpretation that the effects of stressors are to produce an initial upregulation followed by longer term downregulation, but they emphasize that more research is needed to provide definitive answers. O'Leary (1990) also reviews research on the effects of psychosocial interventions on immune function and concludes that there is some indication of immunological enhancement in participants who have been trained in relaxation techniques and who practice them regularly; the effects of other types of intervention have yet to be convincingly demonstrated.

There is general agreement that a number of methodological difficulties need to be overcome before we can safely conclude that stress has direct effects on the immune system with disease consequences. First, it is important to distinguish between direct effects of stress and other physiological pathways which may be activated by stressors such as sleep deprivation and space flight. Second, it is necessary to rule out indirect effects that may be obtained when stressors provoke health hazardous behaviours, such as smoking and alcohol consumption, which may in turn have effects on the immune system. Third, where significant effects of stress on immune function have been adequately demonstrated, it is also necessary to show that these effects have clinical significance as regards disease outcomes. We shall return to this last point later in this chapter when we examine research on the relationship between stress and biologically verified disease.

Post-traumatic stress disorder (PTSD)

Can a characteristic response to stress be found in individuals who have been subjected to extreme levels of stress, such as soldiers returning from battlefields, victims of rape and other violent crimes and survivors of disasters such as earthquakes, floods and nuclear accidents? The term PTSD was introduced by researchers studying psychological symptoms reported by soldiers returning to the USA from the Vietnam War and subsequently extended to studies of other exposures to traumatic stress. It was first accepted as a diagnostic label by the American Psychiatric Association in 1980. The symptoms which are most often used to characterize PTSD are insomnia, nightmares, flashbacks, problems of memory and concentration, acting or feeling as if the event is recurring and a greatly increased sensitivity to new stressful events (Brewin et al., 1996; Baum and Spencer, 1997). A variety of physiological changes have also been found in persons suffering from PTSD (Ver Ellen and van Kammen, 1990; Charney et al., 1993; Shalev and Rogel-Fuchs, 1993).

As in the other areas of enquiry which focus on reactions to stress, our understanding of PTSD is complicated by the existence of large individual differences. Not everyone exposed to traumatic stress develops the symptoms of PTSD. Prevalence rates among individuals exposed to extreme stressors vary widely according to the nature of the stressor, most commonly from 10% to 30% (Green, 1994). There are also large individual differences in the types of symptoms encountered and their severity. Neither is it clear whether reactions to different kinds of traumatic stressor are basically the same or whether they depend on the particular character of the stressor.

The physiological differences found between those who suffer from PTSD and those who do not are real enough, but it has not been established whether they have occurred as a result of traumatic stress, or whether they are pre-existing characteristics of the physiology of individuals who are predisposed to react to traumatic stress by developing the symptoms of PTSD. Such individuals may also suffer from pre-existing psychological problems, including substance abuse, lifetime major depression, panic attacks and other anxiety disorders (Keane and Wolfe, 1990; Baum and Spencer, 1997). This in turn raises the question, in any particular case, as to whether the traumatic stressor is the primary cause of subsequent psychological reactions or the straw that breaks the camel's back.

While there has been at least one recent attempt to develop a theoretical model of PTSD (Brewin et al., 1996), others question its usefulness as a clinical diagnosis (Robins, 1990). A trenchant critique is given by the Canadian anthropologist Allan Young (1995) who combines an historical analysis of the concept with an ethnographic study conducted in a psychiatric unit specializing in the treatment of PTSD. He argues that PTSD is not, as its proponents would have us believe, a psychiatric condition which has been vividly described throughout human history, but rather a cultural phenomenon of the modern era. He traces it to the work of Freud and others in the late nineteenth century, work which has contributed to the *medicalization* of certain types of human unhappiness. While not disputing the extent of the suffering which is caused by traumatic experiences, he does challenge the usefulness of the diagnosis of PTSD as a step towards helping people to deal with them.

Whatever the merits of Young's analysis, it must be admitted that therapeutic interventions for PTSD have not so far been very successful. Shalev et al. (1996) reviewed the results of studies using many alternative forms of treatment, including pharmacological, behavioural, cognitive, psychodynamic, group and family therapies, hypnosis, inpatient treatment and rehabilitation. They concluded that the effects are rarely better than a modest reduction in the severity of symptoms and suggest that, for patients suffering from chronic PTSD, the treatment aim should probably be rehabilitation rather than cure.

INTERACTIONAL MODELS OF STRESS

A number of theorists have sought to overcome the problems of stimulus and response models by conceptualizing stress as a relationship between the individual and the environment and developing interactional models. The most influential of these was first put forward by Lazarus (1966) and developed by Lazarus and Folkman (1984). In this model psychological stress is defined as 'a particular relationship between the person and the environment that is appraised by the person as taxing or exceeding his or her resources and endangering his or her well-being'. A distinction is made between *primary appraisal* whereby an event may be perceived as benign and non-threatening, potentially harmful, threatening to one's self-esteem, or challenging, and *secondary appraisal* in which an assessment is made of one's ability to cope with the threat or challenge. Stress occurs whenever there is a mismatch between perceived threat and perceived ability to cope.

These ideas have been developed at considerable length in a number of books and articles, but they do raise the question as to whether they amount to much more than just another way of saying that stress is when you think you cannot cope. Although this may seem a modest enough assertion, it can in fact be criticized for its implication that stress results only from a purely subjective mismatch between demands and coping resources. One can ask, what about the person who thinks that they can cope when objectively the demands of the situation exceed the person's actual ability to cope? Are such optimists not stressed?

This problem is partially solved by Trumbull and Appley (1986) who extended the model of Lazarus and Folkman by proposing that stress can occur whenever either the real or the perceived demands exceed either the real or the perceived capacity to cope. This is all very well as far as it goes, but it might be felt that Trumbull and Appley's definition is so broad and all-encompassing that it amounts to no more than a statement of the obvious. A critical question might be, what is the relative importance of mismatches between real demands and coping resources and those between perceived demands and coping resources in determining whether an individual suffers the effects of stress?

Using the terminology introduced in Chapter 1, it is probably better to think of interactional models of stress as *frameworks* for thinking about the subject rather than specific theories or models. Another way of representing an interactional framework is the flowchart model of Cox (1978) shown in Figure 5.2. One of the useful features of this flowchart is that it incorporates feedback between responses, demands and appraisal. For example, behavioural responses, depending on whether they are appropriate or inappropriate, may result in a reduction or an increase in actual demand; psychological defence mechanisms may become activated leading to changes in the cognitive appraisal of mismatches between perceived demand and perceived capability, and so on.

Hobfoll (1989) criticizes interactional models of stress for failing to generate scientifically testable hypotheses. Both he and Schönpflug (Schönpflug, 1986; Schönpflug and Battmann, 1988) put forward new and substantially similar interactional models of stress and coping which, they argue, can lead to testable hypotheses and can best be described as *economic models*. In these models human behaviour is seen as functioning primarily to gain *resources* and to avoid the depletion of resources. Hobfoll defines stress as a reaction to the environment in which there is: (a) the threat of a net loss of resources; (b) the net loss of resources; (c) a lack of resource gain following the investment of resources. He defines resources as those objects, personal characteristics, conditions, or energies that are valued by the individual or that serve as a means for attainment of these objects, personal characteristics, conditions or energies and cites as examples mastery, self-esteem, learned resourcefulness, socioeconomic status and employment.

Sociologists might find much of interest in the emergence of such triumphantly capitalist models of human psychology at the present time. As for testable predictions, the most clear cut one is that a net gain in resources can never be a source of stress. This contrasts with some older theories which have regarded all change as potentially stressful. To Hobfoll and Schönpflug, winning a large sum of money, gaining promotion and an increased salary at work, or moving to a new and more desirable neighbourhood would not normally be a source of stress. This certainly presents an interesting challenge to the ingenuity of researchers. Deriving other testable predictions is more difficult, mainly because it is not easy to see how resources such as mastery, self-esteem and learned resourcefulness can be measured in a sufficiently uniform manner to be fed into a model in order to derive predictions.

One consequence of the emergence of interactional models of stress has been the development of checklists designed to assess the individual's predominant coping strategies. An example is the *COPE* questionnaire

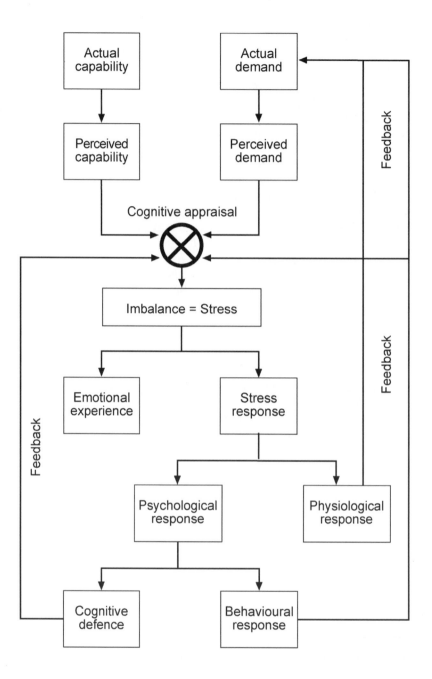

FIGURE 5.2 *Flowchart for an interactional model of stress (Cox, 1978, p. 19; reproduced with permission)*

devised by Carver et al. (1989) which consists of 14 subscales each consisting of a number of items for which the individual tested indicates agreement or disagreement on a four-point scale. The 14 subscales with an example of a checklist statement from each are shown in Box 5.3.

BOX 5.3   ASSESSING COPING STRATEGIES: THE COPE SCALE (CARVER ET AL., 1989)

In the COPE scale, you are asked how you respond when confronting difficult or stressful events in your life. To each item you use the following rating system:

1 I usually don't do this at all.
2 I usually do this a little bit.
3 I usually do this a medium amount.
4 I usually do this a lot.

The 14 COPE subscales with an example of a checklist item from each (the complete version contained four items per subscale) are:

1 **Active coping**: I take additional action to get rid of the problem.
2 **Planning**: I try to come up with a strategy about what to do.
3 **Suppression of competing activities**: I put aside other activities in order to concentrate on this.
4 **Restraint coping**: I force myself to wait until the right time to do something.
5 **Seeking social support for instrumental reasons**: I ask people who have had similar experiences what they did.
6 **Seeking social support for emotional reasons**: I talk to someone about how I feel.
7 **Positive reinterpretation and growth**: I look for something good in what is happening.
8 **Acceptance**: I learn to live with it.
9 **Turning to religion**: I seek God's help.
10 **Focus on and venting of emotions**: I get upset and let my emotions out.
11 **Denial**: I refuse to believe that it has happened.
12 **Behavioural disengagement**: I give up the attempt to get what I want.
13 **Mental disengagement**: I turn to work or other substitute activities to take my mind off things.
14 **Alcohol-drug disengagement**: I drink alcohol, or take drugs, in order to think about it less.

Coping scales have been criticized for adopting a 'blunderbuss' approach to the complex mechanisms involved in coping with different types of stressor, and failing to take account of the fact that individuals may vary greatly in the types of coping they adopt in different stressful situations (Somerfield, 1997). They may also be criticized for relying too much on introspective judgements unsupported by other types of evidence. If it is a feature of the psychology of stress that people tend to behave irrationally when exposed to high levels of stress, then the reports of individuals about their personal ways of coping may be particularly inaccurate. The psychoanalytic theory of anxiety and the defence mechanisms, which has been lucidly described by Brenner (1955, Chapters 3–5) is a fertile source of ideas about coping methods; but it rests on the assumption that our most consistently used defence mechanisms are largely unconscious. For example, *denial*, the refusal to acknowledge the existence of a real danger, may be observed when an individual ignores or denies the significance of symptoms of life-threatening disease, but it is unlikely to be a fully conscious process. How is such an individual likely to respond to the denial items on the COPE questionnaire when asked, for example, how often when confronted with stressful life events, he or she 'refuses to believe that it has happened'?

DOES STRESS MAKE US MORE SUSCEPTIBLE TO PHYSICAL ILLNESS?

This question has generated more research than any other topic in health psychology and it is easy to see why. If stress can be shown to be an important factor influencing susceptibility to disease, then the possibility exists that interventions designed to reduce stress levels, or to help individuals to cope better with unavoidable stress, may reduce the incidence of disease and assist the recovery of those who are already ill. Looked at in this way, stress management might one day make a contribution to the prevention and cure of disease to match that already made by vaccination and antibiotics.

The popular belief that stress is a major cause of physical illness is not convincingly supported by existing research findings, but neither is the opposite belief that stress plays only an insignificant role. The problem is that it is extremely difficult to carry out good research in this area and most of what has been done is open to a range of possible interpretations. We have already noted two shortcomings which apply to the majority of studies. Retrospective studies may have a substantial response bias because people are more likely to recall experiencing stress in periods preceding illness than at other times. All studies which rely on self-reports of illness may have a response bias because people who consider themselves to be suffering from stress are more likely than non-stressed individuals to interpret minor ailments as symptoms of illness.

The better designed studies which investigate the association between exposure to stress and subsequent and biologically verified illness may still present problems of interpretation. It has been shown that people who are experiencing stress are more likely than others to indulge in health hazardous behaviour such as heavy smoking and drinking, drug taking, poor diet, inadequate sleep and lack of exercise (Schachter et al., 1977; Cohen and Williamson, 1988). Thus it could be that stress acts only indirectly as a cause of illness insofar as it influences health behaviour.

Some might argue that if stress causes people to indulge in hazardous health behaviour and if this in turn results in physical illness, then it makes perfectly good sense to conclude that stress causes illness. But this may not be sound reasoning. For example, suppose that it is shown that, for a random sample of the population, periods of stress are associated with an increased likelihood of developing chest infections. This result is then shown to be entirely attributable to the fact that stressed smokers greatly increase the amount they smoke, thereby making themselves more vulnerable to chest infections. Non-smokers do not develop chest infections when stressed and non-stressed heavy smokers are just as prone to chest infections as stressed heavy smokers. Under these circumstances it would not make sense to say that stress causes chest infections, only that smoking does. For this reason, it seems sensible for stress–illness research to concentrate on links where there may be direct physiological pathways, by way of the cardiovascular or immune systems, rather than indirect ones which occur as a consequence of changes in health behaviour.

The methodological problems which we have discussed so far are all likely to lead to inflated estimates of the strength of the association between stress and illness. Further issues have been raised which point in the opposite direction, to the possibility that current research may produce underestimates. These issues derive partly from work on the relationship between personality and illness which was considered in Chapter 4. One argument is that some individuals possess personal characteristics which make them immune to the effects of stress. Among the personal characteristics which have been suggested as having this function are the sense of having control over one's successes and failures, or internal *locus of control* (Suls and Mullen, 1981); a sense of *self-efficacy* (Bandura, 1977); a *hardy personality* (Kobasa, 1979); and an ability to perceive one's world as meaningful and manageable, or *sense of coherence* (Antonovsky, 1987). If stress only causes illness in people with vulnerable personalities, then it may be misleading to calculate the size of the effect of stress on illness by using general population samples which include many who are relatively immune to these effects.

A further issue is the potential mediating effect of *social support* on the relationship between stress and illness. There is extensive evidence that people with strong networks of social support live longer and enjoy better health than relatively isolated individuals (House et al., 1988; Uchino et al., 1996). The relationship appears to be a causal one and not simply a consequence of unhealthy individuals attracting less support, or of people with socially unattractive personalities (e.g. hostility) also being prone to illness. Uchino et al. note that high quality social support appears to have beneficial effects on aspects of the cardiovascular, endocrine and immune systems. In seeking to explain this relationship one influential hypothesis is that social support has a *buffering effect* against the effects of stress, so that stress is only likely to cause illness among individuals with relatively low levels of support (Cohen and Wills, 1985). Uchino et al. argue that evidence from a number of studies demonstrates the existence of such stress-buffering effects.

If the above considerations are valid, then stress is only likely to have a strong effect on susceptibility to illness among individuals who score low on internal locus of control, self-efficacy, hardiness and sense of coherence, and who have a low level of perceived social support. Therefore, studies of stress–illness links which are based on representative population samples may greatly underestimate the potential effects of stress because they include many individuals for whom the effect is likely to be small. Would-be researchers who consider these issues alongside our previous observations on factors which may lead to overestimates of the effect of stress on illness might be excused if they were to throw up their hands in despair. As a research topic it is not an easy one and certainly no study published to date has succeeded in overcoming all or even most of the potential problems. Nevertheless recent and relatively well-designed studies have thrown up a number of interesting findings, particularly in the areas of coronary heart disease, cancer and infectious diseases, and to these we now turn.

Coronary heart disease (CHD)

Most of the research on the association between psychological characteristics and CHD has been concerned with the Type A personality (see Chapter 4). Reviewing the literature in 1988, Krantz and Raisen were unable to find any convincing evidence that stress could be regarded as a proven coronary risk factor. In 1994, Adler and Matthews were able to locate a number of relevant findings, some positive, some negative. In a 12-year follow-up study of 2,000 healthy men, Rosengren et al. (1991) found that those who had initially reported substantial stress were more likely to experience coronary artery disease subsequently, even after controlling for the effects of smoking, alcohol abuse and lack of physical exercise. In contrast, in a six-year follow-up of 12,000 men who were at high risk, Hollis et al. (1990) found no relationship between stress and subsequent mortality. Similarly Levav et al. (1988) found no increased mortality over 10 years for Israeli parents who had lost a son, and Avis et al. (1991) found no increased mortality over five years for US women whose partners had died.

Studies of workers in Germany, Finland and Sweden, with follow-up periods ranging from six to 10 years, all found an association between assessments of job strain and subsequent risk of CHD, including mortality (Haan, 1988; Siegrist et al., 1990; Falk et al., 1992), but Reed et al. (1989) found no such relationship in an 18-year follow-up of 4,000 Hawaiian men of Japanese ancestry. Adler and Matthews (1994) concluded that there is a need for further research covering a wider range of national and ethnic groups and with more female samples.

Cancer

Chen et al. (1995) found evidence of a substantial association between life event stress and breast cancer. They gave the Brown and Harris Life Events and Difficulties Schedule (LEDS) to 119 women who were referred for biopsy of a suspicious breast lesion. They found that those who had experienced severe stress in the previous five years were more than three times more likely to be diagnosed as having breast cancer than those who had not. This is an impressive finding but it needs to be treated with caution since other researchers have failed to find evidence of an association. In a detailed review of 29 published studies from 1966 to 1997 Petticrew et al. (1999) concluded that the evidence did not support the hypothesis of a causal relationship between stressful life events and onset of breast cancer.

Since breast cancer may take five years to develop to the point where it is clinically detectable, it is also arguable whether stress is a causal factor in initial onset or subsequent development of the condition. Although an earlier retrospective study by Ramirez et al. (1990) had indicated that stress is a major predictor of relapse in those who have already been treated for breast cancer, an elegant prospective study by Barraclough et al. (1992) produced a negative result. They carried out a 42-month follow-up study of 204 patients who had received surgery for breast cancer and found no relationship between LEDS assessed life event stress and subsequent relapse.

In view of the very conflicting character of these findings, no firm conclusions can at present be drawn about the relationship between stress and breast cancer. Studies which have considered the subsequent occurrence of all forms of cancer following periods of stress have generally failed to find evidence of an association. There is, for example, no indication of a higher cancer rate among the bereaved (Fox, 1988), and Keene (1980) found no increased rate of cancer among former prisoners of war. Further discussion of cancer occurs in Chapter 8.

Infectious diseases

If stress causes changes in the immune system then this could obviously lead to altered susceptibility to infectious disease. We have already seen that there is extensive evidence that stress does have statistically significant effects on a variety of measures of immune functioning, but that these effects are generally well within the range of normal variation for healthy people. This leaves the question open as to whether they are sufficiently large to lead to altered susceptibility to disease. The only way to find out is to examine the evidence for a direct relationship between stress and the incidence of infectious disease. Over the last 10 years Sheldon Cohen and his associates have been conducting a thorough and detailed analysis of this issue.

Cohen and Williamson (1991) dismissed evidence drawn from retrospective studies and all studies which rely on self-reported illness for reasons which we have already explained. Much of the research in this area is concerned with minor viral infections, such as the common cold, and these are likely to be particularly susceptible to reporting bias. For example, a mild sore throat and headache may be self-diagnosed as a viral infection by the more hypochondriacal individual while others will attribute the same symptoms to staying up too late at a party in a smoky atmosphere. It is easy to see how correlations may occur between such self-reported illness and perceived levels of stress, even if there is no true causal relationship between stress and susceptibility to viral infections.

A further problem pointed out by Cohen and Williamson is that stress may be associated with greater exposure to viruses, perhaps because stressed individuals seek the company of others to a greater extent than non-stressed individuals. An illustration of this methodological problem is given in Box 5.4. An ingenious way of avoiding the difficulty comes from *viral challenge studies* in which volunteers are deliberately exposed to viruses, usually cold viruses, and then followed up to determine whether those reporting high levels of stress prior to exposure are more likely than others to catch the virus, biologically verified by the researchers.

Reviewing viral challenge studies up to 1990, Cohen and Williamson found that the results were inconclusive with some evidence of an effect of stress on susceptibility to the common cold but contrasting evidence that stress is unrelated to susceptibility to influenza. Reviewing subsequent research, Cohen and Herbert (1996) describe three further viral challenge studies all confirming that stressful life events are predictive of increased susceptibility. In one study of 394 volunteers, Cohen et al. (1991, 1993) found that stress levels predicted increased likelihood of catching five different cold viruses and that the higher the level of reported stress, the greater the susceptibility. These results were replicated in a study by Stone et al. (1992) and, in a third study, Cohen et al. (1995) found that negative affect just prior to viral exposure was associated with more severe colds. In contrast to an earlier study the effect was also found for influenza.

BOX 5.4   STRESS AND EXPOSURE TO VIRAL INFECTIONS:
A RESEARCH PROBLEM

A popular source of volunteers for health psychologists studying stress and illness has been medical students taking examinations. However, as a method for studying the effect of stress on susceptibility to viral infections, the method is deeply flawed. Can you see why?

While it is true that taking examinations is very stressful for medical students, it is also the case that sitting in an examination hall with a large number of other students for several hours is likely to provide a high level of exposure to whatever minor viruses happen to be around at the time. Note also that, prior to taking examinations, for several days or more, students are likely to spend a lot of time alone in their own rooms preparing for the examinations, and relatively little time socializing with other students. They are unlikely to be exposed to viruses. After the examinations the reverse is the case. Students spend very little time on their own and a great deal of time socializing, once again at the mercy of whatever viruses are around. Researchers are likely to find that these students develop the symptoms of viral infections consistent with exposure at or shortly after the high stress period of taking examinations but only rarely consistent with exposure in the period prior to the examinations. They might draw the unwarranted conclusion that students have a heightened level of immunity in the stressful period prior to the examinations and a much reduced level afterwards.

On a cautionary note, Cohen and Herbert point out that none of the studies previous to 1996 obtained biological data to indicate whether increased susceptibility was caused by immunosuppression. It is possible that differential susceptibility may be linked to other differences in health behaviour between the stressed and non-stressed participants. Although there were controls for levels of smoking and alcohol consumption, it is possible that differences existed in other relevant factors such as sleep disturbance and diet.

The one other extensively researched infection is herpes, both oral (cold sores) and genital. These are latent viruses which continue to reside in the host after the initial infection has cleared up but which reappear from time to time. Sufferers have long suspected that recurrence is associated with periods of stress and a number of studies have been undertaken to see whether this is true. The evidence to date is rather inconsistent both for oral and genital herpes. One well-designed study found that there is an association between stress and herpes recurrence but that this is an indirect consequence of the association between stress and susceptibility to colds and influenza (Hoon et al., 1991). Catching a cold or influenza can trigger the recurrence of herpes.

A question discussed frequently in recent years is whether stress is a factor in the onset or development of HIV/AIDS. Not everyone exposed to the HIV virus becomes infected and the rate at which the disease progresses varies enormously. Since much of this variability is currently unexplained it is not surprising that there has been considerable interest in the possibility that stress is a factor. Unfortunately the topic is an extremely difficult one to investigate. It is rarely possible to know when an individual was initially exposed to the HIV virus with any degree of precision and subsequent diagnosis and disease progression is associated with much stress, lifestyle changes and the occurrence of other infections, so that it is practically impossible to disentangle the variables. Although stress cannot be ruled out as a factor, Cohen and Herbert were unable to find any convincing evidence that it is. They pointed to a need for long-term follow-up studies with large samples to find out whether psychological interventions such as stress management programmes have any value in reducing the rate of progression of the disease.

FUTURE RESEARCH

1 Analysis of *stress discourses* among and between people and health professionals to establish more clearly the ways in which the concept of stress functions in society.
2 Studies focusing on the psychological and physiological effects of different types of stressor (e.g. bereavement, excessive work load, physical assault). Such research need not proceed on the assumption that very general psychophysiological models of stress are being tested.
3 Research into the effects of stress on the gastro-enteritic and respiratory systems in addition to its effects on the cardiovascular and immune systems.
4 Assessment of the effectiveness of therapeutic interventions including especially those designed to alleviate the psychological effects of traumatic stress and the physiological effects of stress for those already suffering from or at risk for *stress related diseases*.
5 Prospective stress–disease studies which combine measures of a wide variety of physiological characteristics (e.g. of the immune system) with biologically verified assessments of disease status.
6 Clarification of the relationship between stress, physiological reactions, health behaviours, social support and *stress immunizing* personality characteristics using large-scale population based studies.

SUMMARY

1 Stress is sometimes conceptualized as environmental stimuli or life events which impinge on the individual, sometimes as a particular type of response or reaction to stressful events, and sometimes as a mismatch between demands placed on the individual and the perceived ability to cope with these demands.
2 Various methods have been proposed for assessing life events stress. The main problem is that individuals differ greatly as to what they find stressful. For this reason structured interviews are to be preferred to standardized questionnaires.
3 Investigations into physiological reactions to stress have identified many different types of reaction. Physiological reactions vary considerably from individual to individual and according to the nature of the stressor.
4 Significant effects of stress on the immune system have been demonstrated although it is not yet clear whether these effects are large enough to alter susceptibility to disease.

5   A variety of physiological and psychological effects associated with exposure to traumatic stress have been shown to exist, although it is arguable whether they can be used to establish *post-traumatic stress disorder* as a psychiatric condition.

6   Interactional models of stress are intrinsically attractive because they take account of individual differences in reactions to stress and methods of coping. They have the disadvantage that they depend very much on the reliability of subjective assessments and, for this reason, may not be scientifically testable.

7   Empirical studies of the relationship between stress and disease have frequently been unsatisfactory because they are *retrospective* and rely on self-reported stress and illness. They also frequently fail to distinguish between physiological effects of stress and influences on health behaviour.

8   Theoretical models of the relationship between stress and disease are difficult to test because they involve complex interactions between stress, social support and personality variables.

9   There is no convincing evidence for a significant role of stress in the aetiology and prognosis for cardiovascular disease and cancer.

10 *Viral challenge studies* have established that stress does increase susceptibility to some infectious diseases, especially colds and flu. It has not yet been established whether this association is the direct result of effects on the immune system or indirectly caused by changes in health behaviour.

KEY TERMS

COPE
general adaptation syndrome
   (GAS)
hardiness
hassles scale
homeostasis
locus of control
post-traumatic stress disorder
   (PTSD)

psychoneuroimmunology (PNI)
self-efficacy
sense of coherence
social readjustment rating scale
   (SRRS)
stress inoculation training
stress management workshops
uplifts scale
viral challenge studies

6   FOOD AND EATING

You are what you eat.

OUTLINE

This chapter focuses on the part played by food and eating in the changing patterns of illnesses and deaths in affluent societies. Our interest as health professionals and researchers is motivated by the possibility that improvements in food habits can be expected to reduce the prevalence of cancers, cardiovascular diseases, obesity, diabetes, osteoporosis and dental disease. The chapter explores the impact of changes in lifestyle during human evolutionary history, examines the ecology of eating in affluent societies and reviews the epidemiological evidence on the influence of diet on health. The chapter then considers the role played by conditioning, culture and cuisine. Finally, we suggest guidelines for dietary health communication, education and promotion in communities and populations.

EATING, DRINKING AND OBESITY

From the cradle to the grave, many of the most significant, social and pleasurable activities in human experience are centred on eating and drinking. Eating and drinking are much more than simply ways of satisfying hunger and thirst, they are also social activities that are rich in symbolic, moral and cultural meanings. Changes in diet, lifestyle and social organization during our evolutionary history have produced a mixture of beneficial and deleterious effects on health. Eating the 'right' balance of foods and setting the 'right' balance between energy input from eating and drinking and energy expenditure through activity and exercise are of critical importance. Eating preferences and habits are influenced by a complex interaction of processes that include conditioning, customs and culture.

The increasing prevalence of obesity is a primary focus for concern. Like other 'diseases of affluence', *obesity* has multiple causes that include genetic predisposition, culture, family eating patterns, lack of positive role models, individual food choices and lifestyle, in particular lack of physical activity. Traditionally, attitudes to obesity have reflected moral positions concerning gluttony and sloth. In the late 1990s as many as one in five adolescents in the USA were classified as being 'overweight', this pre-valence having doubled during the last 30 years of the twentieth century (Boyle and Morris, 1999). Similar trends are evident across the entire industrialized world. A pan-EU survey on consumer attitudes to physical activity, body weight and health carried out in 1997 found that 11% of the EU population were underweight, 48% normal weight, 31% overweight, and 10% obese (European Commission, 1999). The *Allied Dunbar National Fitness Survey* (1992) showed that in 1990 48% of men and 40% of women in England were overweight. These percentages had increased from 39% and 32% respectively in only 10 years. In 1991 in another national survey, approximately 15% of the English population were found to be obese, with a **body mass index (BMI)** of at least 30 (White et al., 1993). The same survey suggested that prevalence of obesity is 50% higher in men and 100% higher in women in social classes IV and V than in those in classes II and I. What is happening to bring about these changes?

One explanation is that people are becoming significantly less active than was previously the case. National surveys suggest that average activity and fitness levels have been declining since 1950. In the Allied Dunbar survey seven out of 10 men and eight out of 10 women were found to be taking insufficient exercise to achieve any health benefit, although 80% of the population believed themselves to be fit. However, one-third of men and two-thirds of women were unable to continue walking at a moderately brisk pace (3 mph) up a slight gradient (1 in 20) without becoming breathless, finding it very demanding and having to slow down or stop (see Chapter 10). The pan-European survey found that obese people in the EU are more likely to be physically inactive for longer hours in their leisure time and more likely not to participate in any physical activity (European Commission, 1999).

Another factor is income. Income is strongly associated with dietary quality (Low Income Project Team, 1996). This is because in low-income households the food budget often acts as a reserve when demands for other items including alcohol, tobacco or bills must be met. Figure 6.1 presents a framework for the determinants of food and nutritional security (Williams and Dowler, 1994).

Effective methods of health promotion and behaviour change are needed at a population level. Such initiatives need to be created using building blocks from psychology, nutrition and epidemiology. However, it is necessary to build on a solid foundation of evolution, history and culture. Attempts to provide explanatory accounts of eating and diet purely in terms of individual behaviour cannot be expected to succeed. Evolution, history and culture are significant contextual determinants of why we eat what we eat and when and how we eat it. As Rozin (1984) reminds us, 'people eat food, not nutrients' (p. 603).

In the first part of this chapter we discuss food and eating from the perspectives of evolution, ecology and epidemiology. This discussion informs the second part that focuses on conditioning, culture and cuisine.

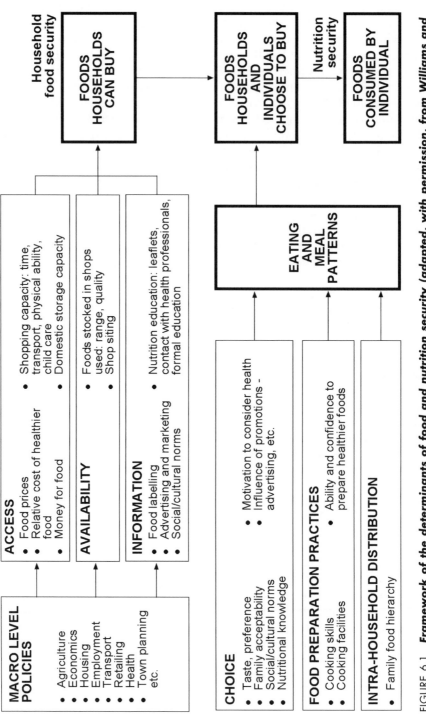

FIGURE 6.1 **Framework of the determinants of food and nutrition security (adapted, with permission, from Williams and Dowler, 1994, p. 4)**

AN EVOLUTIONARY PERSPECTIVE

The study of human evolution and pre-history provides a useful perspective on contemporary ways of life, especially aspects related to food, eating and energy. Early humans can be traced to sites in Africa dating approximately 2.5 million years BP (before the present) when the tool-making *Homo habilis* (or 'handy man') lived in the Olduvai Gorge in Tanzania. The Olduvai hominids were hunter-gatherers, killing and processing their food with weapons and tools fashioned from pieces of volcanic obsidian (Lamb and Sington, 1998). They may have communicated using an early form of speech. Early hominids evolved at a time when the temperature of the earth was cooling and the northern hemisphere was becoming increasingly glaciated. In fact, the ice sheets have advanced and retracted several times during the last million years when the earth's surface temperature has shifted dramatically by up to an average of 10°C every few thousand years (Lamb and Sington, 1998).

Allowing 25 years for each generation, it can readily be calculated that 100,000 generations of humans separate contemporary *Homo sapiens* from our early hominid ancestors *Homo habilis*. In evolutionary terms this is not very many generations for changes to occur. Another species of hominids, *Homo erectus*, is dated from about 1.8 million years BP and contemporary *Homo sapiens* from about 130–100,000 years BP. The survival of the genus *Homo* over the last 2.5 million years can be attributed to a very high adaptability to geological and climatic variations. An efficient body temperature control system enabled body temperatures to remain at equilibrium. The ability to discover, hunt, fish, gather and process foods throughout the entire range of terrain and circumstances on earth, and having a communication system and social organization to support the nomadic way of life, must have aided human survival.

For 99.5% of evolutionary history, members of genus *Homo* lived as nomadic 'hunter-gatherers'. Then, at the start of the Holocene 10,000 years ago, following the last major retreat of polar ice which had reached Britain 18,000 years ago (Lamb and Sington, 1998), a significant change occurred. At the beginning of this period of climatic stability, groups of humans began permanent settlements as agricultural communities and the 'agricultural revolution' had begun.

Because phylogenetic evolution is quite slow, it can be reasonably assumed that the genetic make-up of contemporary humans remains adapted to a nomadic existence of gathering and hunting (Powles, 1992). Contemporary humans are not fitted to the forms of social organization that exist today in post-agricultural, post-industrial societies. The ecological niches to which genus *Homo* became adapted over 2.4 million years are found today in only a few inaccessible places where wheat fields, supermarkets and televisions are nowhere to be seen. The evidence suggests that contemporary *Homo sapiens* remains phylogenetically adapted to a hunter-gatherer lifestyle in ways that are compromised by agriculture, urbanization and advanced technology.

The vast majority of human populations live in cities, towns and villages. However, contemporary urban lifestyles, the associated social structures and surrounding ecology appear to be sub-optimum as far as our health is concerned. This idea has implications for the understanding of food and eating, and for health psychology more generally. The 'hunter-gatherer hypothesis' receives general support from a variety of observations.

The era of the hunter-gatherer

The evidence for and against the hunter-gatherer hypothesis can be evaluated in the light of studies of contemporary groups of hunter-gatherers. Four groups have been studied: Australian aboriginals; the San (or 'Bushmen') of the Kalahari Desert, especially of the !Kung language group; pygmies in the Congo Basin; and the Hadza of East Africa (Powles, 1992). There have also been studies of nomadic peoples in Siberia, Lapland and Greenland.

Hunter-gatherers typically lived in bands of 10 to 50 persons with an average band size of perhaps 25. Band composition was fluid. Temporary shelters were built near water and, when food and water supplies were abundant, a band would remain in settlement for several months. A number of bands or 'tribes' of perhaps 500 to 5,000 individuals would speak a common language. Population density was below one person per square kilometre. Property was a burden as it had to be carried manually and so, except for a few essential clothes, utensils and weapons, hunter-gatherers would have had hardly any permanent personal possessions. Concepts of ownership, scarcity and territory, and the associated psycho-social issues, were irrelevant to hunter-gatherers. Animals such as horses, camels or reindeer were used for transportation and for their milk, meat and skins. The time at which fire was discovered, enabling heating and cooking of raw foods, remains uncertain.

It is believed that early hunter-gatherers spent less time working, building shelter and obtaining food than most humans did following the agricultural revolution. The !Kung San typically spend 2.0 hours per day and the Arnhem Land Aborigines 4.5 hours per day collecting food. It appears likely that about 75% of food energy would have been gathered from vegetable sources by women and the remaining 25% from hunting of animals mainly by men. Powles (1992) estimated the average daily *energy expenditure* for four different historical periods. These estimates suggest that the average daily energy expenditure for a 65 kg male in post-industrial society is 3.5 megajoules (MJ) compared to 4.4 MJ among hunter-gatherers, a difference of more than 25%. In comparison to the 9.3 MJ expended by a labourer in industrial society, however, the difference is much larger at 62%. Yet, the evidence suggests that nomadic, or even early post-industrial, levels of obesity were nothing like those of today.

Even larger differences in energy expenditure may have existed for women – traditionally the principal food gatherers, water collectors, cooks, cleaners, child rearers and child carriers. In most societies nearly all aspects of food getting show differential gender involvement with women being responsible for the majority of food-related activities (Fieldhouse, 1996). In pre-literate societies, three-quarters of over 200 food-related situations were the exclusive province of women. Hunting and fishing tended to be done by males while grinding grain and fetching water were done predominantly by women (Murdock, 1937). In contemporary Africa, women are responsible for 75% of agricultural production, 30% of the ploughing, 50% of planting, 50% of livestock care, 60% of harvesting, 70% of weeding, 85% of food processing, and 95% of domestic work (Fieldhouse, 1996).

A study reviewed by Powles among !Kung Bushmen observed that a child is carried by the mother for a distance of 2,400 km each year in the first two years of life, 1,800 km in year three, and 1,200 km in year four, giving a total of 7,800 km (4,900 miles) over four years. These exceed average activity levels among contemporary adult western women by a wide margin. Reductions in energy expenditure in women may have exceeded that of men; this is consistent with the observation that obesity is generally more common in women than in men (Webb, 1995).

In addition to possible differences in energy expenditure there are differences in diet. Natural ecosystems provide a diet of wild foods that is both varied and plentiful. For example, North American Indians used hundreds of plants in their diets including stinging nettle, common purslane, milkweed, clover, pond-lily, dandelions and fiddleheads (Fieldhouse, 1996). Over 13,000 insects have been classified as edible. In 1950, the Groote Eylandt Aborigines ate 19 large land animals, 76 birds, 97 fish, 39 crustaceans and 82 plants. This diet is adequate both in quality of nutrients and quantity of energy supplied. The evidence suggests that protein, mineral and vitamin intake among hunter-gatherers would have been generally above 'recommended levels'.

For hundreds of thousands of years of human evolution, the capacity to store fat easily was advantageous for survival. Ice Age hunter-gatherers needed to store fat to survive the winters and long journeys in search of food. When the ice retracted and temperatures increased, foods became more accessible and activity levels declined. Thus a metabolic feature promoting survival became a risk factor for diseases that previously had rarely existed.

The agricultural revolution

The agricultural revolution is dated at about 10,000 years BP when humans in the Middle East began settlements in fertile valleys and river deltas. This development meant that humans lived for the first time in densely

populated villages and towns. Wheat, barley and other cereals were culti-
vated and sheep and goats were kept in captivity and slaughtered to
provide a ready supply of meat. For the first time people acquired
and retained ownership of property and land. The revolution spread
through Europe, reaching Britain about 5,000 years ago. Population density
increased dramatically from less than four persons per square kilometre to
100 or more persons per square kilometre. In fertile river valleys, densities
would have increased several hundredfold. Settlement made it easier for
individuals to survive protracted or severe bouts of illness or disability.
New forms of social organizations could be established to promote health
and provide aid to the sick. However, with the stabilizing influence of
settlement and civilization came a number of adverse consequences (see
Box 6.1).

**BOX 6.1   HYPOTHESIZED ADVERSE CONSEQUENCES OF
AGRICULTURAL SETTLEMENT (MARKS, 2000)**

- Food supplies became more dependent on local weather conditions and
  hazards, e.g. floods, droughts, earthquakes and volcanoes.
- The diet became less varied and balanced.
- Malnutrition, anaemia and osteoporosis became more prevalent.
- Average levels of activity and energy expenditure decreased.
- The prevalence of bowel and respiratory infections increased.
- New pathogens and epidemics were possible.
- The birth rate increased.
- Warring over territory became more likely.
- Social problems related to population density and ownership became
  more prevalent.
- Psychosocial and socio-economic stresses related to population density,
  property, status and self-esteem became more significant.

The industrial revolution and beyond

About 200 years or eight generations ago the next stepping stone in human
social evolution was laid – the industrial revolution: the steam engine
and, later, the internal combustion engine, the electric motor, light bulb
and telephone. These new systems of transportation and communication
had radical effects on lifestyles. In spite of huge technological progress,
however, large amounts of hard work, often in adverse conditions, were
necessary for the working population. Subsequently many other new technologies, notably the jet engine, nuclear energy and the digital computer
enabled further changes in lifestyle.

The contemporary era of television, computers, satellites, mobile phones
and the Internet is bringing many benefits to working efficiency and
communication. Labour-saving products in the form of washing machines,

dryers, microwave ovens and dishwashers have brought further reductions in energy expenditure in tasks of daily living. The availability in every supermarket of 'instant' or ready-to-eat dinners, desserts and snacks for consumption during a busy schedule of sedentary work and television viewing means that food preparation and cooking is increasingly being moved from the kitchen to the food-processing industry. Food production is undergoing continuous change and consumer interest is growing in the safety of genetically modified foods that have entered the food chain. The contribution of the food industry to the quality of food and eating in the population is becoming ever more crucial (International Life Sciences Institute, 1998). In general the industry will be unlikely to make improvements purely on a voluntary basis. Health only becomes a higher priority than profit when there is a heavy consumer demand backed by policy and legislation.

Summary

Contemporary lifestyles are very different to those of the hunter-gatherer, who enjoyed a diverse and plentiful diet consisting of meat, vegetables, fruit, berries, nuts, minerals and vitamins, complemented by supplies of uninfected water. The diet contained moderate amounts of salt, no refined sugar and little or no alcohol or tobacco. High levels of energy expenditure occurred during seasonal journeys alternating with sedentary periods when activity was at moderate levels. The agricultural and industrial revolutions brought increased risk of infectious diseases, 'diseases of affluence', technological change and an ever more sedentary lifestyle.

AN ECOLOGICAL MODEL

In this section we consider the implications of the hunter-gatherer hypothesis for the contemporary ecology of food and eating. A primary focus for this discussion will be *fat*, in people who are perceived – or perceive themselves – to be fat, in foods, and the relationship between the two. A concern with fatness and thinness has dominated the discourses of diet and dieting during the past few decades. Ogden (1992) suggested that the widespread concern with dieting among western women has become the modern-day equivalent of Chinese foot binding, corsets and breast binding. These were all ways of controlling, managing or 'mastering' the female body. Ogden (1992) stated: 'The majority of dieters have a problem with feeling fat, not with being fat, but the dieting industry does not distinguish between the two' (p. 16).

A pan-European survey asked a sample of 15,239 people representative of the population to indicate which of nine figures best described their current and ideal body image. An underweight body image was chosen by 55% as their ideal, in comparison to only 37% who felt that their body image was in the underweight category. The disparity between ideal and current body image was generally greater for females than males. Of the population 1% was found to be underweight and yet trying to lose weight. Ninety per cent were females, predominantly in the 15–24 age group (53%) and 25–34 age group (24%) with secondary (53%) or tertiary (40%) level education (European Commission, 1999). The high value placed on thinness in affluent societies today is not evident in other cultures, for example, in Africa or the Pacific Basin, nor was it seen as especially desirable in previous eras when a fulsome figure was perceived as attractive or a symbol of power and status.

The obesity debate has focused on two main subjects: fatty foods and fat people. First, considering the issue of fatty foods, in most western countries the proportion of food energy derived from fat is close to 40% as compared to a recommended level of 30–35%. *Triglyceride* is the main component of dietary fats and oils and the principle form in which fat is stored in the body. Triglyceride is composed of three fatty acids attached to a glycerol molecule. These acids are saturated (S), monounsaturated (M) and polyunsaturated (P). The proportions of these three acids varies across different fats and oils, butter having 64%, 33% and 3%, olive oil having 15%, 73% and 13%, and rape seed oil (canola) having 7%, 60% and 33% respectively. The P:S ratio is therefore approximately 0.05 for butter and almost 5.00 for canola.

Keys et al. (1959) measured total serum *cholesterol* levels in two groups of men who were given diets that varied in the degree of saturation of fat but matched for total fat content. Diet A that had a P:S ratio of 0.16 produced a much higher serum cholesterol level than diet B with a P:S ratio of 2.79. Cholesterol has been implicated as a causal factor in *coronary heart disease* (Brown and Goldstein, 1984). The findings of Keys et al. led many to conclude that fats and oils with a low P:S ratio like butter or coconut oil were high risk food items while olive oil and rape seed oil were lower risk. This analysis led to a negative health image for food items containing high amounts of saturated fat (Webb, 1995) triggering health promotion campaigns with the aim of reducing saturated fat in western diets. However, it is important to distinguish between two different fractions of cholesterol that are low-density lipoprotein (LDP) and high-density lipoprotein (HDP). High levels of LDP are positively associated with cardiovascular disease while high levels of HDP are negatively associated with cardiovascular disease. The different types of fatty acids have a complex set of effects on raising or lowering LDP and HDP. This complicates the issue and presents a considerable challenge to nutritional health promotion.

A second focus in the obesity debate has been the investigation of the characteristics of people who are classified overweight or obese. The excess weight gain of obese individuals is due mainly to the increase in *adipose tissue* mass that is 85% fat. Traditional models of obesity have placed the cause at one of two levels: (i) individual overweight and obese people have been blamed for their 'sloth' and 'gluttony'; (ii) overweight and obese people are assumed to have a genetic predisposition to lowered metabolic rate (Webb, 1995).

The first of these causes is seen as potentially controllable, but only in those people who possess 'strong will power' or high 'self-efficacy' (Bandura, 1977). In attributing the responsibility for obesity to the individual, it is necessary to take into account the particular context consisting among other things of biological, social, ecological and psychological barriers to change (Chapters 9 and 10). Working with obese people at an individual level is the primary activity of organizations such as Weight Watchers and has been an active area of research and practice in clinical psychology.

The idea that there is a genetic cause or predisposition to the development of obesity is the second major theory. This theory provides little hope to those affected as obesity is seen as irreversible within present technology. Biological influences on body fat levels include age, sex, hormonal factors and genetics. In spite of the discovery of the so-called 'ob' gene and its product leptin in mice (Zhang et al., 1994), the development of treatments for human obesity is a remote possibility because the genetic influences on obesity are known to be polygenic. On present evidence, biological influences on fatness appear to be unalterable and are likely to remain so in the foreseeable future.

The ecological approach to obesity is an alternative view to traditional approaches based on individual behaviour or biology. The ecological approach sees obesity in the context of the individual's relationship to the surrounding environment. Egger and Swinburn (1997) proposed three main influences on equilibrium levels of body fat, biological, behavioural, and environmental. Obesity is not a pathological disorder of individuals requiring treatment but a normal end result of living in an environment that produces obesity. Contemporary post-agricultural, post-industrial society is said to be *obesogenic* because it generates too high an equilibrium level of fatness across the whole population relative to average activity levels. In order to solve the obesity problem it is necessary to understand, measure and alter the characteristics of the environment, not attempt to address the problem at the level of the individual.

This ecological theory is based on the *fat balance equation* which states:

> Rate of change of fat stores in the body = rate of fat intake − rate of fat oxidation. (Swinburn and Ravussin, 1993)

Total energy is the mediator of weight gain that, under contemporary conditions, is interchangeable with fat energy. The intake of fat is a significant component of total energy intake while total energy expenditure is the main determinant of fat oxidation. A reduction of dietary fat within an otherwise varied diet leads to weight loss. However, weight loss tends to be associated with rebound weight gain due to physiological defences against weight loss. In an environment that promotes obesity, there is also a high equilibrium point of fat stores.

To calculate the macronutrient intake in the diet as a percentage of total energy, the following energy equivalents are used:

1 g fat yields 9 kcal
1 g protein 4 kcal
1 g carbohydrate 3.75 kcal
1 g alcohol 7 kcal

These figures mean that a person who consumes 100 g of fat in a 2,200 kcal diet is obtaining:

$100 \times 9 \times 100/2{,}700 = 90{,}000/2{,}700 = 33.3\%$ of energy as fat (Webb, 1995).

Although the proportion of energy from fats and oils has decreased in western countries since the 1960s, this reduction is attributed mainly to reductions in food *energy intake* rather than a shift to a lower fat diet (Webb, 1995). However, what seems to be clearly established is the fact that the average level of energy intake is falling more slowly than the average level of energy output. This energy imbalance has created the conditions for increases in average weight levels and prevalence of obesity.

If we are to see reductions in the prevalence of obesity, the average energy expenditure of the population needs to be significantly increased while the average energy intake across the population further reduced. Yet over the last few decades population average energy expenditure has been decreasing as a consequence of labour-saving technology. Without intervention at a policy level, a new culture of enhanced physical activity for the entire population seems a long way off. This means that the currently high prevalence of obese and overweight people is likely to remain evident for some considerable time.

Environmental influences on food intake and physical activity can be divided into those concerned with the wider environment and those having a close proximity to the individual 'distal' and 'proximal' influences respectively. There is a vast range of environmental influences that affect what and how much is eaten, by whom, and under which circumstances. As Egger and Swinburn (1997) point out, these influences are frequently underrated. Examples of these influences are shown in Table 6.1.

Summary

While environmental influences remain uncontrolled, obesity rates will not fall. Policy changes and regulation of the food industry are necessary to improve the quality of food products. New policies aimed at raising activity levels are necessary. Interventions targeted at dietary change can also be expected to have positive effects. But what kind of changes in diet

TABLE 6.1 **Environmental influences on food intake and physical activity (Egger and Swinburn, 1997, p. 478; reproduced with permission)**

Type of environment	Physical environment		Economic environment		Sociocultural environment	
	Food	**Activity**	**Food**	**Activity**	**Food**	**Activity**
Macro	Food laws and regulation	Labour saving devices	Food taxes and subsidies	Cost of labour versus automation	Traditional cuisine	Attitudes to recreation
	Food technology	Cycleways and walkways	Cost of food technology	Investment in parks and recreational facilities	Migrant cuisines	National sports
	Low fat foods	Fitness industry policies	Marketing costs	Costs of petrol and cars	Consumer demand	Participating versus watching culture
	Food industry policies	Transport system	Food prices	Costs of cycleways	Food status	Gadget status
Micro	Food in house	Local recreation facilities	Family income	Gym or club fees	Family eating patterns	Peers' activities
	Choices at school or work cafeterias	Second cars	Other household expenses	Owning equipment	Peer attitudes	Family recreation
	Food in local shops	Safe streets	Subsidized canteens	Subsidized local events	Pressure from food advertising	School attitude to sports
	Proximity of fast food outlets	Household rules for watching TV and video	Home grown foods	Costs of school sport	Festivities	Safety fears

and food production should health promotion and psychology policy be aiming for? To answer this question, it is necessary to review recent findings from the field of *epidemiology*.

EPIDEMIOLOGICAL STUDIES OF DIET AND HEALTH

Fat and fibre

Epidemiology has contributed a large number of studies on the influence of diet on illness and mortality. From their review of the cancer field, Doll and Peto (1981) concluded that approximately 35% of all cancer deaths can be attributed to diet as compared to the 30% that are attributable to tobacco. Earlier ecological studies correlated national mortality rates with average animal fat intakes and found that average animal fat intake in grams per day was strongly associated with age adjusted death rates. However, ecological studies are confounded by numerous variables that have no theoretical relationship to mortality (e.g. GNP) and yet have as strong a correlation as average daily fat intake. Recently there have been controlled prospective studies, systematic reviews and *meta-analyses* to draw upon.

A major focus for epidemiological research has been dietary fat and fibre in the form of meat, cereals, fruit and vegetables. Animal-derived foods are high in fat but contain almost no fibre. Fruit and vegetables contain high amounts of fibre but no fat. One approach to study the impact of contrasting amounts of fat and fibre in the diet is by comparing the mortality and illness rates of meat eaters and non-meat eaters. Although meat consumption increases the risk of cancers of the colorectum, breast and prostate, until recently the evidence of reduced illness and mortality among vegetarians has not been conclusive.

Key et al. (1998) compared the mortality rates of vegetarians and non-vegetarians among 76,000 men and women who had participated in five prospective studies. This meta-analysis analysed the entire body of evidence collected in prospective studies in western countries in the period 1960 to 1981. The original studies were conducted in California (2), Britain (2) and Germany (1) and provided data concerning 16- to 89-year-old participants for whom diet and smoking status information was available. The results were adjusted for age, sex and smoking. Vegetarians were defined as those who did not eat any meat or fish (n = 27,808). Participants were followed for an average of 10.6 years when 8,330 deaths occurred. The results showed that vegetarians as a group contained a lower proportion of smokers and current alcohol drinkers, a higher proportion of high exercisers and had a consistently lower body mass index.

The death rate ratio for ischaemic heart disease for vegetarians versus non-vegetarians across the five studies was 0.76 (95% CI 0.62–0.94). The all cause mortality ratio was 0.95 (95% CI 0.82–1.11). The reduction in mortality among vegetarians varied significantly with age at death, younger ages at death being associated with much lower rate ratios: 0.55 for deaths under 65; 0.69 for deaths between 65 and 79; 0.92 for deaths between 80 and 89. When the group of non-vegetarians was subdivided into regular meat eaters and semi-vegetarians who ate fish only or ate meat less than once a week, there was evidence of a significant dose-response effect. The ischaemic heart disease death rate ratios compared to regular meat eaters were 0.78 in semi-vegetarians and 0.66 in vegetarians. These data suggest that vegetarians have a lower risk of dying from ischaemic heart disease than non-vegetarians. However, none of the data for other causes of death were statistically significant. This could be attributed to the numbers of deaths from these other causes being smaller, lowering statistical power. Like any epidemiological study, this study could not control for all relevant factors and could be subject to confounding. For example, vegetarians may differ from carnivores in many ways that could not be controlled for (e.g. in exercise levels, use of drugs, religious beliefs and health values).

Other studies have found an association between diet and cancer. Block et al. (1992) reviewed the role of fruit and vegetables in cancer prevention and concluded that 132 of 170 studies indicated a significant protective effect for cancers at all sites including prostate.

Ness and Powles (1997) reviewed ecological, *case-control*, cohort studies and unconfounded trials in humans concerning fruit, vegetables and cardiovascular disease conducted during the period 1966 to 1995. All studies in the review reported on fresh fruit and vegetables or a nutrient that could serve as a proxy. Many of the studies found a significant protective association for coronary heart disease and stroke with consumption of fruit and vegetables or surrogate nutrients. The protective effect appeared to be stronger on stroke than on coronary heart disease.

Willett et al. (1993) conducted the Nurses Health Study in the USA using a prospective longitudinal design with 121,700 nurses whose diet and cancer incidence were studied in 1980, 1984, 1986 and 1988. Willett found no evidence of a positive association between fat intake and the incidence of breast cancer. However, alcohol consumption and weight gain were found to be significant risk factors for breast cancer.

A review by Cummings and Bingham (1998) stated: 'What is remarkable about the diet-cancer story is the consistency with which certain foods emerge as important in reducing risk across the range of cancers.' They concluded: vegetables and fruit are protective for almost all of the major cancers. Consumption of meat, especially red meat and processed meat, is linked with bowel, breast, prostate and pancreatic cancer. Alcohol is a significant risk factor for upper gastrointestinal cancer, liver cancer and breast cancer.

Salt

Salt (sodium chloride) has long been associated with essential hypertension. Ecological studies suggest that populations with low salt intake such as the Kalahari Bushmen have low incidence of hypertension in comparison to societies such as the UK and USA where salt intake and hypertension incidence are both high (Webb, 1995). However, there are many confounding variables in these ecological studies which could explain this link: high physical activity, low levels of obesity, low alcohol and tobacco use and high potassium intake in those groups with low salt diets.

In a controlled study, Law et al. (1991) correlated blood pressure and salt intake from 24 populations and concluded that there was a highly significant relationship for both developed and undeveloped societies that increased with age and baseline levels. The findings of many studies suggest that populations with lower mean salt intake have a lower blood pressure and a less steep rise of blood pressure with age. Much of the salt in western diets, perhaps 80%, comes from processed food. There is a need to restrict the salt content of processed foods requiring regulation of the food industry.

Sugar

Sugar or sucrose appeared in the west in the eighth century (Mintz, 1997). Sugar is a disaccharide composed of one unit of glucose and one of fructose, which is found in fruits and vegetables, particularly sugar beet and sugar cane, from which it is extracted and purified to make white sugar, brown sugar, treacle or syrup. It is used as a sweetener and preservative by food processors. It has been strongly linked with the development of obesity, maturity onset diabetes and the rotting of teeth (dental caries). However, the increasing obesity rates can be attributed in part to the prominence in our diet of the 'empty' calories of sugar which carry no nutritious value.

Caffeine

Caffeine is the most popular drug on earth with more than 80% of the world's population consuming it daily (James, 1997). It is consumed mainly in coffee, tea, drinking chocolate, cocoa and cola drinks and provides slight psychoactive effects on arousal and mood. In the form of coffee, it has achieved symbolic status as a recreational, exotic and even erotic beverage. Consumption varies across countries with four of the highest consumers being the UK, Sweden, Canada and the USA with average daily levels of 444, 425, 238 and 211 mg (Gilbert, 1984).

Because of its widespread usage even small increases in relative risk for heart disease or cancers could have large absolute effects. James (1997) reviews evidence from hundreds of studies concerning caffeine's psycho-pharmacological and epidemiological effects. James suggests that caffeine use *could* account for 9–14% of cases of coronary heart disease, 17–24% of stroke cases and could contribute to adverse reproductive outcomes when used in pregnancy. However, these estimates require further research.

Summary

The diet for cancer prevention is high in fruit, vegetables and cereals and low in meat and fat. This diet will also help prevent other chronic diseases including coronary heart disease, hypertension and obesity. There would be health benefits if people also consumed less sugar, salt and caffeine and ate more fruit, vegetables and cereals, and consumed low amounts of alcohol. The International Life Sciences Institute (1998) has suggested that these principles are not new since they correspond to the lifestyle of most people at the beginning of the twentieth century: 'In the hundred years since then, humans have not been able to adapt their behaviours and lifestyles to rapid environmental change' (p. 11).

PSYCHOLOGICAL, SOCIAL AND CULTURAL ASPECTS OF FOOD AND EATING

Conditioning and early experience

Following Pavlov's (1927) studies of conditioned reflexes, learning and conditioning became the main focus of research on food preferences and aversions. Although experience generally determines food choices, sweet tastes and possibly fatty tastes are innately attractive while bitter tastes are innately avoided. Capaldi (1996) suggests that preferences for foods are modifiable in four ways:

1 Mere exposure.
2 Flavour-flavour learning: flavours that are repeatedly associated with an already preferred flavour such as saccharin will themselves become preferred. A sweetener produces liking in almost any other food with which it is mixed.
3 Flavour-nutrient learning: flavours that are repeatedly associated with a nutrient such as a protein become preferred.
4 Taste aversion learning: this occurs when a novel taste solution (the conditioned stimulus or CS) is followed by an unpleasant stimulus (the unconditioned stimulus or UCS) that produces transient gastro-intestinal illness or vomiting (the unconditioned response or UR) (Garcia et al., 1966). The learning of taste aversion follows the principles of generalization, extinction and latent inhibition (Schafe and Bernstein, 1996). However, it differs from Pavlovian conditioning in having a rapid acquisition, tolerance of long delays between the CS and US, and selective associability in which particular CS–US pairs produce aversion and not others. This type of learning is adaptive in animals that need to sample foods and learn rapidly to differentiate between positive and toxic foods. However, taste and food aversions are also quite common in humans, for example, specific types of alcohol (gin or whisky) as a result of nausea caused by over-imbibing on the first occasion of use.

The overall flavour of food is conveyed by the senses of taste, smell and chemical irritation. The foetus receives its first nutrients in the amniotic fluid that is a potential carrier of flavour and odour (Mennella and Beauchamp, 1996). By term the human foetus has swallowed quite large amounts of amniotic fluid (200–760 ml daily) and has been exposed to glucose, fructose, lactic acid, pyruvic acid, citric acid, fatty acids, phospholipids, creatinine, urea, uric acid, amino acids, proteins and salts (Mennella and Beauchamp, 1996). The amniotic fluid and mother's milk are both primed by a maternal diet that is unique and so may have similar aromatic profiles providing a 'thread of chemical continuity between the pre- and postnatal niches' (Schaal and Orgeur, 1992). Studies of foetal swallowing and of preterm infant sucking even suggest that a preference for sweet flavours is evident before birth (Tatzer et al., 1985). This evidence suggests that preferences for flavour and smell are influenced very early in life. In fact the earliest and most emotional life events revolve around eating and drinking and, as Rozin states, the taking and giving of food are, from the very first, 'exquisitely social' (Rozin, 1996, p. 235).

Culture and cuisine

Culturally shared eating habits provide a sense of belonging; they are an affirmation of cultural and social identity, are kept with pride and not readily altered. Food preferences and eating habits are acquired in the context of family power dynamics, moral values, culture and cuisine. Culture is the major determinant of what and when we eat and, to a lesser degree, how much we eat. Food habits and preferences are among the last characteristics of a culture to be lost during immigration into a new culture. Rozin suggests that sociocultural factors are so important in determining food choices that if you can ask only one question, the question should be: 'What is your culture or ethnic group?' (Rozin, 1996, p. 235). A second useful question would be: 'What is your religion?'

Culture is the sum total of a group's learned behaviour and preserves traditions, especially those concerned with eating habits: 'Culture is learned. Food habits are acquired early in life and once established are likely to be long-lasting and resistant to change. Hence the importance of developing sound nutritional practices in childhood as a basis for life-long healthy eating' (Fieldhouse, 1996, p. 3). Moral influences concerned with power and control are also key features of family eating practices. Mintz (1997), for example, states:

> In any society, the act of eating can be encumbered with moral overtones – as can the act of not eating when others eat. Such acts take on their power as means of scoring moral points in contrast to their opposite: either of eating some things and not others; or of eating or not eating at all . . . to redefine ingestion as an arena for the acting out of moral principles is a distinctively human achievement. (Mintz, 1997, p. 173)

Eating and drinking habits are central to socialization that occurs during infancy in the family and influenced principally by mothers, usually the main getter and preparer of food for the family. The immediate family is the dominant influence on the child, establishing cultural and culinary practices and preferences and the rules by which different foods may be eaten in particular combinations or meals.

Recent studies have explored the role of family dynamics and parental influences on the food choices of adolescents. Rozin (1996) points to what he calls the 'family paradox', the lower than expected correlations between parents' and childrens' food preferences. However, the evidence suggests that food preferences established by mid-adolescence appear to continue well into adult life (Kelder et al., 1994). Of particular interest is the establishment of preferences for snacks, sweet foods, fruit and vegetables. Boureaudhuij (1997) investigated the establishment of family food rules in infancy and its impact on food choices and consumption in adolescence. Adolescents and young adults aged 12 to 22 who reported more permissiveness in their family at age 10 were found to be eating more fat and sweet foods and more snacks. They reported more unhealthy food choices in their families. Hill et al. (1998) conducted interviews with a teenager and principal food shopper/meal preparer in each of 20 Pakeha (European) families in Auckland, New Zealand. The study observed that although teenagers generally believed that fruit and vegetables were 'good for you', their consumption was influenced by their independence from parental control in different eating situations, their perceptions of the desirability of different foods and their participation in sports. The investigators concluded that there is a need to market fruit and vegetables as attractive and nutritious in competition with the snack foods that are heavily promoted on television and which generally contain high amounts of sugar, salt or fat.

In industrialized societies, variations in traditional family structures have occurred as a result of social changes and new working patterns. These changes have brought more variation to traditional patterns of eating communal family meals. However, meal structures are adhered to rather inflexibly and the scope for innovations may be more limited than nutritional health education desire (Douglas and Nicod, 1974).

A significant role within these rather stable cultural and family influences is played by cuisine, a style of cooking with particular ingredients, flavours and modes of preparation and rules about orders and combinations (Rozin, 1982). These culinary principles tend to be culture specific to some extent. Cuisine is nationally or regionally based and so we speak of French, Italian, Indian, Japanese and Chinese cuisine, although these broad categories need to be subdivided into more specific culinary groups, e.g. Cantonese, Szechwan, etc. The type of cuisine defines written or oral rules concerning how food sources are gathered or killed, prepared and combined into meals. Fieldhouse (1996) reviews this topic in some detail and concludes: 'Our unwillingness to accept just anything as food betrays the notion that food is consumed for nourishment of the body alone. Food also nourishes the heart, mind and soul' (p. 76).

Dietary health information, communication and promotion

As we have seen, the 'western diet' is associated with cardiovascular diseases, cancer, diabetes, osteoporosis and dental disease. Among the six leading causes of death in western societies (e.g. see Table 1.1) at least four are associated with nutritional factors or excessive alcohol consumption. In this light, many international and national expert committees have recommended dietary standards and there have been many health promotion campaigns. Public debates about food and eating have been fuelled by scientific findings that have not always been easy to interpret, leading to food scares, distrust of authorities and other negative reactions. Webb (1995) provides an excellent discussion of these and other issues from a nutrition and health promotion perspective. Before developing interventions and policy based on epidemiological studies, however, the psychological, social and cultural aspects of these epidemiological imperatives need to be considered. They may create greater obstacles and opportunities for improving the diet than is generally acknowledged.

A popular theme for health education campaigns in the latter part of the twentieth century has been the 'diet–heart hypothesis'. This is based on the evidence that coronary heart disease is associated with raised cholesterol levels (see Figure 6.2). Health education publications in the 1980s and 1990s dedicated considerable space to the desirability of a diet that is low in fat and cholesterol. However, the issue of serum cholesterol reduction is complicated by the existence of different fractions of cholesterol, as previously mentioned (see p. 130). High levels of LDP are positively associated with cardiovascular disease while high levels of HDP are negatively associated with cardiovascular disease. If this information is not handled well, there is the potential to create confusing and inconsistent health messages.

To effect behaviour change, health promotion messages must be *simple*, *clear* and *consistent*. Unfortunately, dietary health communications have sometimes been the opposite, creating much confusion. One example is the controversy over cholesterol, butter and margarine. For many years it was believed that butter was bad for health because of its high content of saturated fats causing high levels of serum cholesterol. Health-conscious consumers switched to margarine. Subsequently it was claimed that margarine could be equally unhealthy and many consumers switched back to butter. These responses were associated with confusion and distrust of health messages in the dietary field.

The confusion created by dietary health communication is a source of comment in the mass media. For example, 'A Food Lover's Guide to Fat' (Shapiro, 1994) in *Newsweek* posed questions and answers in the following way:

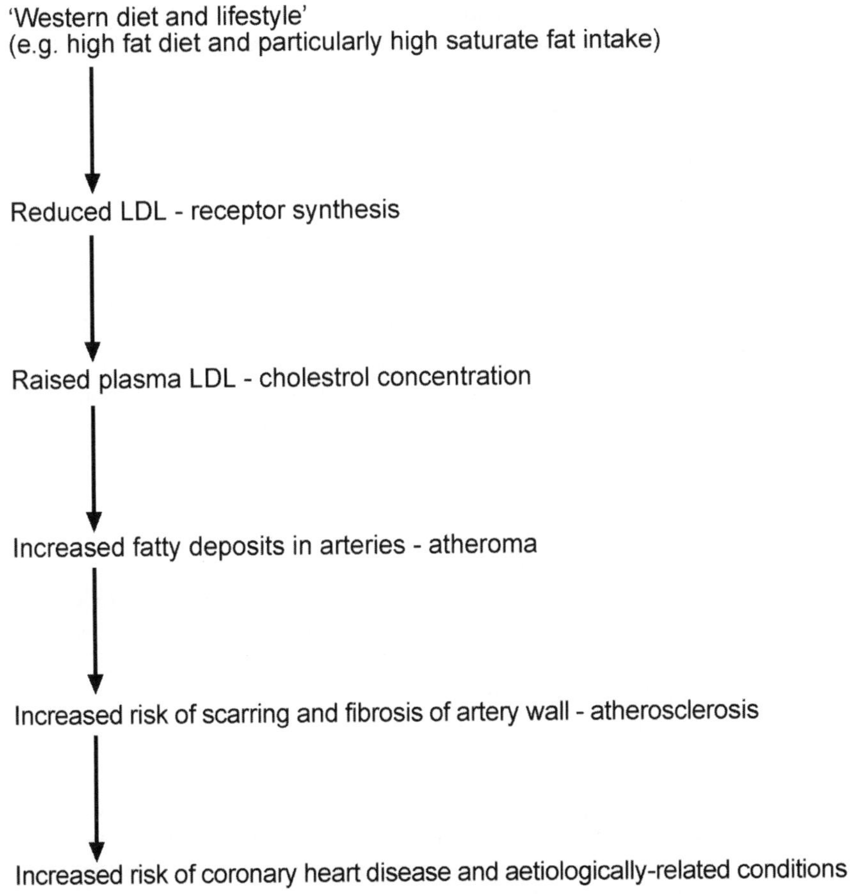

'Western diet and lifestyle'
(e.g. high fat diet and particularly high saturate fat intake)

↓

Reduced LDL - receptor synthesis

↓

Raised plasma LDL - cholestrol concentration

↓

Increased fatty deposits in arteries - atheroma

↓

Increased risk of scarring and fibrosis of artery wall - atherosclerosis

↓

Increased risk of coronary heart disease and aetiologically-related conditions

FIGURE 6.2 ***The diet–heart hypothesis (Webb, 1995, p. 195; reproduced
with permission)***

Q: How much fat should I eat?
A: Good question. Unfortunately, there's no single good answer . . .

Q: Is cutting fat the best way to lose weight?
A: 'The percentage of fat you eat doesn't seem to make much difference'
(Walter Willett). 'Obesity is caused by too many calories. Fat's a good place
to begin'(Marion Nestle). 'There's a lot of controversy in this area' (John
Potter).'

This article parodies the situation and leaves the reader wondering what to
do. At the same time that all this attention was being focused on dietary
fat, relatively little attention was being paid to the issues of dietary sugar,
salt and caffeine. Campaigns have also ignored the possibility that a

pressure to change diet can bring about deleterious physical and psychological effects including depression and even suicide if certain nutrients become deficient in particularly vulnerable people (Hartley, 1998).

Individuals acquire their knowledge about health through schooling, the media, medical practitioners, community nurses, information from industry, product labels, public health campaigns and other sources (International Life Sciences Institute, 1998). It is essential that communication provides correct information in a form that is understood by the target audience. Dietary guidelines are usually formulated in terms of *nutrients*. Consumers buy and eat *foods* and so they need to be able to translate recommendations about nutrients into how best to purchase foods. Effective nutritional health promotion involves interaction and collaboration of nutritionists, epidemiologists, psychologists, educators, professional communicators, journalists, medical doctors, industrialists and legislators. For each target population group, it is necessary that common efforts be directed to:

- Agreeing a set of dietary guidelines based upon **systematic reviews**.
- Designing simple, clear and consistent health communications.
- Implementing programmes which target relevant health professionals.
- Then, supported by the relevant health professionals, targeting the relevant community groups.
- Evaluation of process and outcome.

For many reasons, a population or community level approach to disease prevention and health promotion is more effective than individual approaches. Community approaches have a higher impact, provide a more efficient use of funds and are more cost effective (Tolley, 1985). For example, a small reduction in dietary fat made by a large proportion of the population is expected to lead to greater improvements in population health than large changes made by a relatively few people (Rose, 1992).

Fieldhouse (1996) proposed five characteristics of dietary innovations:

1   The perceived advantage of change; the higher this is the more rapid the rate of adoption.
2   Compatibility with existing values and needs (i.e. the culture).
3   Simple to understand and use.
4   'Trialability': the degree to which an innovation may be experimented with on a limited basis.
5   Observability: the degree to which the outcomes are visible to others.

Boyle and Morris (1999) review community nutrition programmes in the USA. Winett et al. (1989) and Bennett and Murphy (1997) discuss community health promotion from a psychological perspective.

FUTURE RESEARCH

1   The hunter-gatherer hypothesis could be tested by investigating the health of groups and communities who belong to similar cultures but differ with respect to hunter-gatherer characteristics, e.g. agriculturalists vs. pastoralists. If the influences of diet, smoking, alcohol consumption and accidents can be controlled, it should be possible (at least in principle) to determine whether pastoralists have higher levels of well-being, lower rates of chronic illness and live longer than agriculturists, as predicted by the hypothesis. One supportive study in Burkina Faso found that the agriculturalist Mossi people were more stressed and marginalized than the pastoralist Fulani people (Van Haaften and Van de Vijver, 1996). Further studies should be conducted with actual hunter-gatherers and matched sedentary control groups to determine how such differences translate into illness and mortality rates.

2   The quest for thinness on well-being and body weight requires further study, particularly in girls and women. Role models in the fashion and entertainment industries are almost always 'Twiggy' thin, often in anorexic proportions. The relationship between contemporary ideal images of thinness and the increasing prevalence of obesity warrants further study.

3   Much of the discussion of risk factors for coronary heart disease focuses on dietary fat, LDL and HDL cholesterol. However, many other dietary factors including fibre, several minerals and vitamins and non-nutrient substances also influence the development of this disease, as well as many non-dietary factors such as smoking and exercise. Rather than focusing on cholesterol alone, studies are needed to explore how disease prevention can best be applied with vulnerable population groups concerning all known risk factors.

4   The fast food industry has become a major provider of food and drink. The implications of fast food for future nutrition and cultural food values deserve further study.

5   More study is needed at a policy level to explore the best ways of working with the food industry, both manufacturing and retail, to improve the quality of food at affordable prices.

SUMMARY

1   Many of the most important activities in human existence centre on eating and drinking. More than simply satisfying the biological drives of hunger and thirst, eating and drinking are symbolic, moral and culturally embedded activities.

2   Eating a balanced diet and setting an optimum balance between energy input and energy expenditure are important aspects of health.

3   Among the six leading causes of death in affluent societies, at least four are associated with nutritional factors or excessive alcohol consumption. Cancer, coronary heart disease, stroke, obesity and other 'diseases of affluence' are all associated with the western lifestyle, especially diet.

4   Obesity has multiple causes that include genetic predisposition, culture, family eating patterns, lack of positive role models, individual food choices and lifestyle, in particular lack of physical activity.

5   Anthropological evidence suggests that human beings spent 95.5% of our evolutionary history living as hunter-gatherers. The evidence suggests that the genetic make-up of contemporary humans remains adapted to a nomadic existence of hunting and gathering. The hunter-gatherer hypothesis suggests that contemporary humans are not yet optimally fitted to the psychosocial conditions of post-agricultural, post-industrial societies.

6   The agricultural revolution brought many changes to health, diet and lifestyles. Food supplies became more dependent on local weather conditions and hazards; the diet became less varied and balanced; fat consumption increased; average levels of activity and energy expenditure decreased; the prevalence of bowel and respiratory infections increased; new pathogens and epidemics were possible; the birth rate increased; warring over territory became more likely; social problems related to population density and ownership became more prevalent; psychosocial and socio-economic stresses related to population density, property, status and self-esteem became more significant.

7   Changes in industrialized societies over the last 200 years have produced a mixture of beneficial and deleterious effects on human health. One of the most significant during the twentieth century was a significant reduction in energy expenditure as a consequence of labour saving devices and new forms of transportation.

8   The ecological approach to obesity analyses eating in the context of the surrounding environment. In this approach obesity is not seen as a pathological disorder of individuals requiring treatment but a normal end result of living in an obesogenic environment, one that is designed in such a way that obesity in a high proportion of the population is an inevitable outcome.

9   Epidemiological evidence suggests that a diet that is high in fruit, vegetables and cereals and low in meat and fat is protective against cancer. This diet will help prevent other chronic diseases, including coronary heart disease, hypertension and obesity. There are further health benefits if people consumed less sugar, salt and caffeine.

10 Food preferences are influenced very early in life. The earliest and most emotional life events revolve around eating and drinking. The basic mechanisms for establishing these preferences are learning and conditioning in the context of family power dynamics, moral values, culture and cuisine. Culturally shared eating habits provide a sense of belonging, affirm cultural and social identity and are not readily altered.

11 A community approach to disease prevention and health promotion has many advantages compared to individual approaches. Population approaches have a higher impact, are more efficient and cost effective.

12   Interventions at a population level require an agreed set of dietary guidelines following systematic reviews, simple, clear and consistent health communications, targeting firstly the relevant health professionals, then the relevant population groups and communities.

KEY TERMS

adipose tissue
body mass index (BMI)
case-control study
cholesterol
coronary heart disease (CHD)
energy expenditure
energy intake
epidemiology

fat
fat balance equation
meta-analysis
obesity
obesogenic
systematic reviews
triglyceride

7 ALCOHOL AND DRINKING

Dionysus discovered and bestowed on men the service of drink, the juice that streams from the wine-clusters; men have but to take their fill of wine, and the sufferings of an unhappy race are banished, each day's troubles are forgotten in sleep – indeed this is our only cure for the weariness of life. (Euripides, The Bacchae, trans. P. Vellacott, 1954)

OUTLINE

This chapter discusses theories and research on the psychology of drinking and the causes, treatment and prevention of alcohol problems. It begins with a brief history of attitudes to alcohol and the emergence of the theory that alcoholism is a disease which can only be cured by lifelong abstinence. An analysis of the physical and psychological dangers of heavy drinking is followed by an examination of contrasting theories about its causes. The chapter concludes with a discussion of the relative merits of different approaches to the treatment and prevention of alcohol problems.

THE BLESSING AND CURSE OF ALCOHOL: HISTORICAL BACKGROUND

The fermentation process which produces alcohol from yeast, fruit and grain is a very simple one, often occurring naturally, and methods for producing alcoholic beverages seem to have been invented and widely used in most ancient civilizations. They were certainly familiar to the Babylonians, Egyptians and Greeks and to the Chinese who also invented distillation for the production of strong liquor. Unlike the production of wine and beer, the distillation of liquor is complicated; although known about, its use has been rare in many cultures.

Distilled spirits did not become generally available in England until the eighteenth century when, because of their relative cheapness, they were popular with the working class. This was the subject of deep social concern, at least among the educated middle classes. William Hogarth's prints, *Beer Street* and *Gin Lane* (Figure 7.1), illustrate the prevailing view by contrasting the pleasant and supposedly harmless effects of drinking beer with the dire consequences of drinking spirits. Notice the general sense of industriousness and well-being in Beer Street; many people are working and the only shop that is boarded up is the pawnbrokers. In Gin

FIGURE 7.1 Hogarth's Beer Street and Gin Lane (© The British Museum; reproduced with permission)

Lane nobody is working except the busy pawnbroker and there is a grim depiction of emaciation, death and the neglect of children. The frequently stated belief of the time that 'Drink is the curse of the working classes' was later turned into sharp social criticism when Oscar Wilde observed that 'Work is the curse of the drinking classes'.

An ambivalent attitude towards alcohol is characteristic of many earlier cultures and is nowhere better expressed than in Euripides' tragedy, *The Bacchae*, written about 414 BC. We have already quoted above the words which Euripides puts into the mouth of the seer Teiresias on the benign effects of alcohol as a cure for the weariness of life. This is in stark contrast to the views of the protagonist Pentheus, which parallel those of the modern prohibitionist. Enraged at having been taken prisoner by Pentheus, Dionysus, the God of wine, abandonment and revelry exacts a cruel revenge. The Bacchae, women of Thebes who include Pentheus's mother, take to the woods under the influence of Dionysus to perform their secret rites, believed by Pentheus to involve much drinking of wine, dancing naked, sexual abandon and extreme savagery.

Pentheus intends to put a stop to this but his motives are not pure. He has a prurient interest in spying on the activities of the Bacchae and Dionysus takes advantage of this to trick them into killing him. The tragedy reaches its culmination when Pentheus's mother, not realizing that it is her own son and in a frenzied state, carries his head on a pole into Thebes. The play has much contemporary relevance as a meditation on the consequences of the hedonistic pursuit of ecstasy; equally it comments on the dangers of trying to suppress it and on the dubious motives of the stern moralists and killjoys who wish to do so.

Modern attitudes to alcohol as a social problem are illustrated by the history of the **temperance societies** initially in the USA and spreading to many other countries over the last 150 years (Critchlow, 1986; Levine, 1978, 1980; Heather and Robertson, 1997). Alcohol has commonly been perceived as the principal cause of violence, crime, sexual immorality, poverty through loss of employment, broken homes and child neglect. Temperance societies, a misnomer since they promote abstinence and prohibition rather than moderation, began with the Washingtonian movement of the 1840s and continue to the present day as Alcoholics Anonymous, which has branches in almost every North American town of any size and in many other countries. These societies have typically been organized by reformed alcoholics with the mission to help others to become abstinent. Their influence has been enormous not only in bringing about the era of prohibition from 1920 to 1934 but also in establishing as received medical opinion the debatable hypothesis that alcoholics can never return to moderate drinking but can only be cured by remaining abstinent for the rest of their lives.

Heather and Robertson (1997) point out that several distinct views about alcohol have either co-existed or been confused by the temperance societies. Historically, it is useful to distinguish four viewpoints: the *moral position* that heavy drinking is a sin for which the individual must take full responsibility; the *addiction model* that alcohol is a highly addictive substance to which any regular user can become enslaved; the *disease model* that certain at-risk individuals are bound to become alcoholics if they drink at all, while others can get away with it; and the *learning model* that heavy drinking is basically just a habit that can in principle be corrected to any required degree. Clearly, these views can be overlapping. Temperance societies usually adopt a strong element of the moral position, requiring participants to make public admissions of guilt and repentance, while at the same time adopting elements of the disease model in viewing the alcoholic as a victim and the addiction model in viewing alcohol as the villain of the piece.

The influence of the temperance societies on William James, the father of North American psychology, can be seen in the following extract from the famous section on habit in his *Principles of Psychology*:

> Every smallest stroke of virtue or of vice leaves its never so little scar. The drunken Rip Van Winkle, in Jefferson's play, excuses himself for every fresh dereliction by saying, 'I won't count this time!' Well! he may not count it, and a kind Heaven may not count it; but it is being counted none the less. Down among his nerve-cells and fibres the molecules are counting it, registering and storing it up to be used against him when the next temptation comes. (James, 1950/1890, p. 127)

THE DANGERS OF DRINKING

No one who has ever got drunk and suffered a subsequent hangover, or even simply seen other people in this state, would doubt that regular heavy drinking is likely to result in ill health, cause accidents and play havoc with the lives of the drinkers and their families. There is plenty of evidence to support this and none to contradict it. The problem arises when we consider the effects of light to moderate drinking. On the face of it, it would seem implausible that anything which has such deleterious effects in large quantities could actually have beneficial effects in smaller quantities. Yet much publicity has been given to evidence suggesting that light drinking may protect the individual against heart disease and many drinkers will attest to its beneficial effects in promoting relaxation and a sense of well-being, counteracting the effects of stress, reducing social inhibitions and, in the words of Euripides' Teiresias, acting as a 'cure for the weariness of life'. In short, is it true that alcohol is good in moderation, bad in excess? To throw light on this question we will consider separately the evidence linking drinking to physical ill health, accidents and psychosocial problems. A brief summary of the risk factors which we identify is given in Box 7.1.

BOX 7.1   RISKS INCURRED BY THE CONSUMPTION OF ALCOHOL

Risks which can be incurred on any single occasion of heavy drinking

- Driving, industrial and household accidents; falls, fires, drowning.
- Domestic and other forms of violence as perpetrator.
- Domestic and other forms of violence as victim.
- Unwanted pregnancies following unprotected sexual exposure.
- HIV or other sexually transmitted diseases following unprotected sexual exposure.

Risks incurred by regular heavy drinking

- Death from liver cirrhosis.
- Irreversible neurological damage.
- Possible increased risk of cardiovascular disease and certain cancers.
- Problems caused by alcohol dependence.
- Exacerbation of pre-existing difficulties such as depression and family problems.
- Loss of employment, reduced career prospects.

Risks incurred by women who drink during pregnancy

- Fetal alcohol syndrome.
- Spontaneous abortion.
- Low birth weight babies.

Physical health

Prolonged heavy drinking has been shown to be a cause of *liver cirrhosis*, a serious condition which frequently results in death. Schmidt (1977) analysed data from 20 countries and found that there was a close relationship between per capita alcohol consumption and deaths from cirrhosis, the correlation between the two variables being 0.94. Similarly, changes in levels of alcohol consumption within countries are closely tracked by changes in cirrhosis rates. As an example, Saunders (1985) considers Finland where alcohol was banned from 1919 to 1932, subject to tight controls until around 1960 and increasingly liberalized until 1975, since when increasing restrictions have again been introduced. The large changes in levels of alcohol consumption over time were found to be associated with similar large changes in deaths from cirrhosis.

Surveying mortality statistics for England and Wales, the Office of Population Censuses and Surveys (1994) found that there were 3,056 deaths (1,753 men and 1,303 women) from cirrhosis in 1992, of which 967 (56%) of the cases in men and 540 (41%) in women were alcohol related.

These deaths occurred mainly among long-term heavy drinkers. Sherlock (1995) estimates that 20 units of alcohol daily for 5 years is the minimum associated with cirrhosis. In contrast to the heavy drinker, the moderate drinker is taking a relatively small risk of sustaining serious liver damage.

The Royal Colleges of Physicians (1991) reported that heavy drinking is associated with a substantial increased risk of strokes in men, although there is no clear evidence of a similar increase in risk for women. In a 21-year follow-up study of 5,766 Scottish men, Hart et al. (1999) found that those drinking 35 units or more a week were at twice the risk of death from stroke than light or moderate drinkers. Another form of brain damage known to be caused by drinking is **Wernicke-Korsakoff syndrome**, a condition characterized by severe impairment of short-term memory, confusion and visual disorders. Fortunately, it is rare and mainly confined to those who have drunk heavily over a long period of time.

The evidence linking alcohol to cancer is sometimes unclear because heavy drinkers are usually also cigarette smokers, to such an extent that it has often proved difficult to separate out statistically the effects of alcohol over and above the known carcinogenic effects of cigarette smoking (Popham et al., 1984). One form of cancer which has been clearly shown to be associated with heavy drinking is liver cancer, but this normally occurs in individuals who already have cirrhosis. Drinking has also been shown to be associated with cancers of the mouth and throat. One extensive review conducted by two leading epidemiologists, concluded that the 3% of all cancers may be attributable to alcohol (Doll and Peto, 1981). Reviewing evidence on the association between drinking and breast cancer, the Royal Colleges of Physicians (1991) considered that the evidence is inconsistent with some studies finding an increased risk even at quite low levels of consumption while others have found no evidence of an association. They concluded: 'Any elevation of risk with alcohol is likely to be modest (25–50%) but would be important since cancer of the breast is the commonest cancer in women.'

Drinking during pregnancy has been shown to be associated with a significant risk of damage to the unborn child. Heavy drinking is the main cause of **fetal alcohol syndrome** in which the child suffers from a particular type of facial abnormality as well as mental impairment and stunted growth (Pratt, 1982). Relatively low levels of drinking have also been linked to below average birth weight and an increased risk of spontaneous abortion. It is still unclear what, if anything, constitutes a safe level of drinking during pregnancy, or whether the risks are mainly restricted to certain periods of fetal development (Forrest et al., 1991). Current medical opinion is that the pregnant woman is best advised not to drink at all throughout her pregnancy.

Before turning to the question of the possible health benefits of light to moderate drinking, it is necessary to be a little more precise about what is meant by 'light', 'moderate' and 'heavy' drinking. The units used to indicate levels of safe drinking in an easily accessible form vary from country to country. We will adopt the British system in which one unit equals one glass of wine of average strength (11% to 12% alcohol), half a pint of normal strength beer or lager, or a single measure (1/6 gill) of spirits (whisky, gin, vodka). It is important to bear in mind that strong wines and beers may contain up to twice this amount of alcohol.

Since 1986, British medical authorities have recommended that the limit of safe drinking is 21 units a week for men and 14 for women, and this was reaffirmed more recently after a full review of the evidence (Royal Colleges of Physicians, 1995). Using these figures as a guideline, we will consider moderate drinking to be at or slightly below the level of 21/14 units a week for men/women; less than half of that level will be regarded as light drinking and anything over 42/28 units will be regarded as heavy drinking.

Room and Day (1974) put forward the hypothesis that light to moderate drinkers may enjoy better health than both teetotallers and heavy drinkers. Since then a large number of studies have been conducted, many of which appear superficially at least to support this hypothesis. Klatsky et al. (1981) studied the relationship between drinking habits and mortality rates of more than 2,000 people over a 10-year period and found that those who took up to 14 units a week had lower mortality rates than non-drinkers; the non-drinkers had about the same mortality rates as those who took from 21 to 35 units a week.

The benefits, if they are genuine, of light to moderate drinking seem to be mainly associated with a reduced risk of death from heart disease. In a large New Zealand study Jackson et al. (1991) found that taking up to 42 units a week was associated with a reduced prevalence of heart disease in comparison with non-drinkers and heavier drinkers. Doll et al. (1994) analysed data for 12,321 male British doctors born between 1900 and 1930 who have been investigated from 1978 to date and found that regular drinkers had lower rates of heart disease than non-drinkers. They also examined all cause mortality and concluded that this increased progressively with amount drunk above 21 units a week.

The results of these and other studies are not entirely consistent with each other, especially for the purpose of establishing upper limits for safe drinking, but they are at least consistent with the statement that men and women who drink up to 21 and 14 units a week respectively are not taking any significant risk with their physical health. The additional claim that light to moderate drinking is actually beneficial to health is more open to doubt. Although non-drinkers do have higher mortality rates than drinkers, this may be only because the category of non-drinkers includes a substantial number of individuals who have given up drinking because of poor health. This is a useful illustration of the statistician's dictum that *correlation does not entail causation*. It could be that not drinking causes poor health but, equally well, it could be that poor health causes not drinking. Most people, if asked to bet which of the two propositions is true, would probably choose the latter. It is also supported by the analysis by Shaper et al. (1988) of data from 7,000 middle-aged men, which confirmed that those who suffered from health problems cut down or abstained from drinking.

Some studies have attempted to overcome the problem by distinguishing between ex-drinkers and non-drinkers and still claim beneficial effects for light drinking, but it is not clear that they have succeeded in overcoming the methodological problems inherent in collecting questionnaire data on this issue. Shaper (1995) and Marks (1995) criticize the methodology of the Doll et al. (1994) study and argue that the data are consistent with the interpretation that alcohol has no health beneficial effects, but only injurious effects which increase in a dose-dependent way as a function of amount consumed.

Following an extensive analysis of data from 10 North American studies, Fillmore and her colleagues (Fillmore et al., 1998a, 1998b; Leino et al., 1998) conclude that, when appropriate statistical controls are made for confounding effects, there is no evidence that abstinence is associated with a greater mortality risk than light drinking. This has been confirmed in a Scottish study by Hart et al. (1999). Furthermore, the Royal Colleges of Physicians (1995) point out that any beneficial effects which might exist are counterbalanced by the fact that alcohol certainly contributes to hypertension (high blood pressure) and conclude that 'the evidence does not justify any suggestion that abstainers would benefit their health if they started to consume alcohol.'

Accidents

The reader of the last section might reasonably draw the conclusion that, for the light to moderate drinker, the dangers of drinking are not very great. Why then did McGinnis and Foege (1993) claim that alcohol is one of the three leading contributors to preventable death in the USA and Stinson et al. (1993) claim that, after AIDS, it is the leading contributor to death among young people? The reason is that alcohol is a factor in a substantial proportion of accidental deaths.

In Britain the Department of Transport (1996) carried out an analysis of data on road traffic accidents in which one or more of the drivers involved either failed or refused a breath or blood test. In 1996 there were 10,850 drink-drive accidents including 540 deaths. Pedestrians who are killed in road accidents are also likely to have been drinking. In an earlier report (Department of Transport, 1992), it was estimated that about half of pedestrians aged between 16 and 60 killed in road accidents had more alcohol in their bloodstream than the legal drink-drive limit. This fact is certainly supported in any driver's experience of travelling through urban areas after pub closing time at night.

Studies conducted in a number of countries indicate that alcohol is implicated in many attendances at hospital accident and emergency departments (Cherpitel, 1993; Waller et al., 1998). Williams et al. (1994) reported that 50% of adults admitted to a hospital surgery unit with a head injury were obviously drunk. Alcohol has been shown to play a significant role in deaths from falls, fires, industrial accidents and deaths from drowning (Eckhardt et al., 1981; Plueckhan, 1982; Tether and Harrison, 1986).

Psychosocial problems

The regular use of alcohol often gives rise to the problem of alcohol dependence. There has been some debate about the usefulness of the concept of alcohol dependence as a clinical category, an issue which will be discussed in the next section. However, for present purposes, we will follow Edwards (1986) and consider it to have some or all of the following characteristics:

- Drinking assuming priority over all other activities.
- Increased tolerance leading to heavier drinking to achieve the same effect.
- Withdrawal symptoms when unable to drink the usual amount.
- Awareness of a need to control drinking combined with an inability to do so.

Morgenstern et al. (1997) have shown that alcoholism is often found among people with a range of personality disorders. Similarly, Miller and Brown (1997) point out that drinking problems are common among those being treated for other mental health problems, making it more difficult to provide effective therapy. Alcohol is also frequently implicated in suicide, homicide and other violent crime, both as perpetrator and as victim. The British Medical Association (1989) estimated that alcohol is associated with 60–70% of homicides (one-third of victims being intoxicated at time of death), 75% of stabbings, 70% of beatings and 50% of fights or domestic assaults.

To what extent is alcohol to blame? This raises all of the usual chicken-and-egg problems of interpreting statistical correlations. For example, does drinking incite people to commit crimes or do criminals drink to reduce their fear before carrying out the crimes which they have already decided to commit? Do people take to drink in an effort to ameliorate their psychological problems, or are these problems caused by heavy drinking? Probably the most sensible response which can be made to this latter question at the present time is to reiterate the well-known health education slogan: 'If you drink because you have a problem, then you will end up with two problems.'

THEORIES OF DRINKING AND ALCOHOL DEPENDENCE

To understand the motivation for drinking and problems of dependence it is best to begin by considering the psychological effects of alcohol. Alcohol is popularly associated with beliefs about the loosening of inhibitions and the suppression of unpleasant emotions, especially anxiety. This explains why it is consumed in social gatherings such as parties and weddings, when people are expected to interact in a much more relaxed and informal way than they would otherwise, and also why heavy drinking is common among people with psychological problems.

The belief that social drinking is harmless and solitary drinking dangerous arises because the periodic loosening of social inhibitions is seen as a healthy activity whereas drinking to ameliorate the effects of psychological problems seems unhealthy. Drinking does not deal with the cause of the problem and is likely to create dependence. This distinction between social and solitary drinking is a useful one although it is also an oversimplification. Social drinkers who always drink heavily in social gatherings may run a high risk of developing dependence, while people who usually have a couple of drinks on their own to 'switch off' after a period of very demanding work may only be taking a small risk.

The view that the major motive for drinking is to reduce anxiety is often referred to as the ***tension reduction hypothesis*** (Blane and Leonard, 1987; Sayette, 1993; Sayette and Hufford, 1997). Some versions of this hypothesis have focused primarily on the direct effect of alcohol on the nervous system, but in recent years there has been a shift of opinion towards models that account for the anxiety reducing effects as indirect consequences of the effect of alcohol on information processing. Hull (1981) proposed that alcohol makes cognitive processes more shallow and reduces awareness of information which could lead to a negative self-evaluation. Others have proposed that it works by altering responses to stress (Levenson et al., 1980; Sayette, 1993). A detailed analysis of the relationship between alcohol and emotional arousal is given by Stritzke et al. (1996).

Let us now turn from the general theoretical question of why people drink to the question as to why some people develop drinking problems. Here a number of contrasting theoretical perspectives need to be considered. They are not mutually exclusive in the sense that this can sometimes be said of theories in the natural sciences. The discerning reader will notice various ways in which elements of each can be consistent with elements of the others. They are best thought of as reference points which are useful aids to thinking about the issues.

Genetic theories

Genetic theories propose that some people have an inherited predisposition to develop drinking problems. However, even if it is true, this should not be taken as implying that it is inevitable that they will do so. To take an analogy, some people may have an inherited proneness to develop heart disease, but whether or not they will do so still depends on whether they smoke, eat fatty foods and so on. The risks are greater for some people than for others. Similarly, there could be many environmental reasons why drinking problems develop in those who have an inherited predisposition and also in those who do not.

Much depends on the relative potency of hereditary and environmental factors. At one extreme it is sometimes suggested that certain people are 'born alcoholics', destined to succumb to alcoholism as soon as they take their first drink. Organizations such as Alcoholics Anonymous see their mission as rescuing such unfortunate people by showing them how to achieve total abstinence and maintain it against all temptation. Perhaps surprisingly, this *biological determinist* view is also attractive to manufacturers of alcoholic drinks. They can argue that the born alcoholic is bound to have a drink and become alcoholic sooner or later, however much the availability of drink is restricted. The rest of us can drink as much as we want without running the risk of becoming alcoholic. As Rose et al. (1984) point out, using many different examples, biological determinism is always attractive to those who wish to evade responsibility for creating or failing to solve social problems.

At the opposite end of the spectrum to the biological determinist view is the *environmentalist* view that, in the same circumstances, everyone is equally likely to develop a drinking problem. This view is implicitly held by those who adopt the addiction model and place all the blame for drinking problems on alcohol, which they consider to be a highly addictive substance. The third view, the middle way as it were, is that outlined in the first paragraph of this section: both heredity and environment play a part in determining whether people develop drinking problems. It is this view which receives most support from the research evidence.

It has been clearly established that alcohol problems tend to run in families. The children of heavy drinkers are more likely to become heavy drinkers themselves than children whose parents do not drink heavily (Sher, 1991). However, this cannot be taken as evidence of an inherited predisposition as it could equally well be that patterns of drinking are learned, especially as a result of identification with the same sex parent.

One way of assessing hereditary effects is to compare the concordance rates for drinking in *monozygotic* (MZ, identical) and *dizygotic* (DZ, fraternal) *twins*. The theory behind this is that both types of twin grow up in the same family environment so that a greater concordance for the 100% genetically similar MZ twins than for the 50% similar DZ twins is evidence of genetic effects. The data turns out to be suggestive rather than conclusive. Heather and Robertson (1997) reviewed a number of studies, most but not all of which found higher concordance for MZ twins. Assessment of the potency of heredity is not possible from these studies because the crucially important size of the difference between MZ and DZ concordance rates varies greatly from study to study. It also varies according to what patterns of drinking are assessed. One study found the greatest hereditary effect for chronic alcoholism, in comparison with moderate to heavy drinking, while another found the greatest effect for teetotalism in comparison with all other patterns of drinking. The shortcomings of MZ/DZ comparisons for assessing heredity have been analysed by Rose et al. (1984). For example, MZ twins spend much more time in each other's company than DZ twins and thus may be more likely to acquire the same patterns of drinking for non-hereditary reasons.

The other main way of assessing hereditary effects is to examine whether adopted children grow up to acquire similar drinking habits to their biological parents, or whether they are more influenced by their adopting parents. As with MZ/DZ comparisons, the evidence tends to confirm the existence of hereditary effects, but assessing the relative potency of heredity and environment proves to be impossible, partly because of unexplained variation in the results obtained from different studies and partly because of inherent methodological weaknesses in adoption studies. Goodwin and his colleagues (Goodwin, 1976) found that male adoptees who had an alcoholic biological parent were four times more likely than controls to become alcoholic. However, when they looked at the category of *problem drinker* as distinct from alcoholic, no evidence of hereditary effects was found. They also found no evidence of hereditary effects when they considered alcoholism in female adoptees.

In contrast to the Goodwin studies, which were conducted in Denmark, a Swedish study (Bohman et al., 1981; Cloninger et al., 1981) found that female adoptees whose biological mothers were alcoholic were three times more likely than controls to become alcoholics themselves. They analysed data for both male and female adoptees and attempted to assess environmental effects through the adoptive home as well as genetic effects (drinking habits of biological parents). They concluded that genetic and environmental effects were both equally strong for males whereas genetic effects were stronger for females. However, their results were not entirely clear cut as they varied considerably for different categories of problem drinking. Cloninger (1987) attempted to resolve the problem by proposing the existence of two different types of alcoholism, one of which is inherited exclusively down the male line, the other equally for both sexes. Alternative typologies have also been proposed (Babor et al., 1992) but the evidence on which they are based is methodologically flawed and inconsistent (Heather and Robertson, 1997).

There are many methodological problems in evaluating adoption studies (see Rose et al., 1984), not least because people who release children for adoption and people who adopt are very atypical samples of the general population and because characteristics of the biological parents are often taken into account by adoption agencies in choosing a suitable adoptive home. These problems, together with the variation between the findings of superficially similar studies, lead to the conclusion that, although there is enough evidence to show that there is some degree of genetic predisposition towards different patterns of drinking, it is not possible to assess how important they are in comparison with environmental effects.

It should be noted that the genetic pathways which predispose people towards particular patterns of drinking are unlikely to be straightforward as in the case of eye colour or blood groups. There has been one recent attempt to demonstrate a specific genetic locus for alcoholism (Blum et al., 1990), but it has received only modest support from subsequent research (Heather and Robertson, 1997). As with other forms of human behaviour, there are likely to be a multitude of complex genetic routes which may make some individuals more likely than others to become problem drinkers. For example, there may be inheritable differences in the way that alcohol is metabolized, so that some people find its effects pleasant, others unpleasant, some find it takes more alcohol, others less, to achieve the same effect. There may be differences in genetic predisposition to experience anxiety, so that some are predisposed to drink more than others on discovering that it temporarily suppresses anxiety. One could discuss, in the same way, a genetic predisposition to take valium or prozac, or indeed to eat high fat foods such as hamburgers, as discussed in Chapter 6. There may also be inherited differences in personality characteristics, such as extraversion, which in turn influence the likelihood of becoming a regular social drinker.

Finally, it is worth asking what would be the advantage of having a better assessment of hereditary influences on alcohol consumption? The obvious answer is that it could prove valuable for preventative purposes. Anyone with a heavy drinking parent could be advised to examine carefully the characteristics of their parent's drinking and their own in order to take measures to avoid falling into the same trap. But now consider what would follow if environmental influences predominate. Since we know that alcohol abuse tends to run in families, an important environmental influence would be from parent to child. People with heavy drinking parents should still be advised to examine the drinking habits of their parents and themselves to avoid making the same mistakes. Thus it appears that there is little to be gained for practical purposes by carrying out studies designed to provide better estimates of the relative importance of hereditary and environmental influences on alcohol consumption and dependence.

Addiction, disease and dependency theories

The fascinating history of these interrelated theories has been surveyed by Heather and Robertson (1997) and McMurran (1994). It appears that they all have their origins in the activities of the temperance societies and other evangelical anti-drink campaigners rather than being the natural outcome of dispassionately conducted medical and psychological research. Yet evangelical campaigners have succeeded in influencing medical opinion to the point that disease and dependency theories have become medical orthodoxy despite a lack of adequate evidence to support them.

The earliest clear statements of addiction theories can be traced back to the classic works of Benjamin Rush of Philadelphia and Thomas Trotter of Edinburgh, published respectively in 1785 and 1804. These men replaced the view of habitual drunkards as moral degenerates by one in which they are victims of a disease of addiction. Once the disease is established, the victims lose all voluntary control over their drinking. They have become incapable of resisting their craving for the 'demon drink'. Rush and Trotter succeeded in popularizing their belief that alcohol is a highly addictive substance 70 years before this was done for opium.

Later disease theories focused increasingly on the at-risk individual who has a predisposition to become alcoholic once he or she starts drinking. Although a predisposition to become alcoholic does not have to be hereditary (we have already mentioned that it may be the result of upbringing), nevertheless the concept of the born alcoholic proved attractive to disease theorists. In common with earlier addiction theories, these theories emphasized craving and loss of control. The difference was that, for the new disease theorists, alcohol is only highly addictive for a small number of people. The rest of us can drink with impunity. This change of emphasis proved attractive, especially to a North American society which had abandoned prohibition, embraced personal liberty and responsibility and has a powerful drinks industry.

During the 1950s the disease theory gained a tremendous impetus through the work of E.M. Jellinek at the Yale Centre for Alcohol Studies. He was also closely associated with Alcoholics Anonymous and the World Health Organization (Jellinek, 1960). He insisted that a sharp distinction could be drawn between heavy drinkers, who might be causing physical damage to themselves but were not physically dependent on alcohol, and alcoholics, in whom metabolic changes have resulted in physical dependence. A curious feature of Jellinek's theory is his distinction between *gamma alcoholics*, who typically lose control and cannot stop after the first drink, and *delta alcoholics*, who drink steadily and maintain control of the amount drunk, but find it impossible to abstain for even quite short periods of time. This distinction appears to have occurred to Jellinek as a result of observing differences between the patterns of out-of-control excessive drinking typically found, for example, in Anglo-Saxon countries and the continuous but controlled heavy drinking typically found in the Mediterranean wine-growing countries. It is strange that an observation which might have led to an interesting study of drinking as a cultural phenomenon should have led instead to a nosology of alcoholic diseases.

From the mid-1970s and again in conjunction with the World Health Organization, the disease theory was being revised and extended, notably by Gross and Edwards, to become the *alcohol dependence syndrome* (Edwards and Gross, 1976; Edwards, 1986). In this new conceptualization Jellinek's sharp distinction between physical addiction and psychological dependence was abolished and the syndrome was viewed instead as a psycho-physiological disorder. The descriptions given by Edwards and

Gross are not always very clear and tend to change from one publication to another. Sayette and Hufford (1997) summarize Edwards's more recent accounts as including some or all of the following symptoms:

- Tolerance: a diminished effect of alcohol, usually accompanied by increased consumption.
- Withdrawal symptoms following reduced consumption.
- Consumption of larger amounts or for a longer time period than was intended.
- Persistent desire or unsuccessful efforts to cut down or control drinking.
- Excessive time spent obtaining, consuming or recovering from the effects of alcohol.
- Reduction of important activities due to drinking.
- Continued drinking despite knowing that it is causing or exacerbating a physical or psychological problem.

The concept of the alcohol dependence syndrome has been sharply criticized by Shaw (1979, 1985) who points out that much woolly thinking lies behind it. Most people, on reading the above list of symptoms, would conclude that anyone who drinks regularly would exhibit one or more of them to some degree. As a list, it seems consistent with the idea that, rather than being a disease, alcohol dependence is an arbitrary point which can be chosen on a continuum from the light social drinker to the street dwelling 'wino'. Yet proponents of the syndrome insist that it is a clinical entity, admittedly with somewhat varying symptomatology, which only applies to a relatively small number of people who suffer from it.

One should not, of course, 'throw out the baby with the bath water'. No theory of alcohol use can afford to neglect the phenomena of physical dependence associated with prolonged heavy drinking and most clearly manifested in the spectacular withdrawal symptoms which can occur. These include the most unpleasant to be found among all drugs and involve tremors ('the shakes'), sweating, nausea, vomiting, hallucinations ('pink elephants') and convulsions. Indeed, Lerner and Fallon (1985) note that in a significant number of cases sudden withdrawal can actually prove fatal. The phenomena of psychological dependence also need to be addressed by any theory of alcohol use. While alcohol dependence syndrome may be poorly defined as a clinical entity, the psychological problems which are often associated with heavy drinking certainly need to be explained.

Psychoanalytic theories

Freud did not devote very much time to the question of the causes of alcohol problems but, as with so many topics to which he turned his attention, his speculations are interesting albeit difficult to test empirically.

He put forward two main suggestions. The first, outlined in his classic 1917 paper, 'Mourning and Melancholia', is that the alcoholic is fixated at the oral stage of psychosexual development, the breast feeding stage. Freud distinguished between the early oral dependent stage, where gratification is primarily obtained from the taking in of milk, and the oral sadistic stage, associated with the appearance of teeth, biting and consequent weaning. The oral dependent personality is supposed to be basically very passive, excessively focused on the mouth as a means of obtaining gratification, and seeking to regress to an infantile state in which there is no clear differentiation between fantasy and reality.

The concept of oral dependent fixation can be used to account for alcoholism, eating disorders, smoking, thumb sucking and oral sex. Some degree of oral fixation is assumed to be present in everyone, but especially in the alcoholic who drinks in order to regress to the world in which fantasy and reality are one and the same. The oral character of drinking, together with the anxiety reducing and sleep inducing properties of alcohol, make it an ideal activity for the oral dependent personality. Whatever the merits of Freud's hypothesis, it is certainly amusing to contrast the machismo image of drinking among young men with one in which people who drink themselves into a stupor recreate the world of the baby who sucks contentedly at the breast and then nods off to sleep.

In 1930, in another classic paper, 'Three Contributions to the Theory of Sex', Freud outlined a second proposal on the causation of alcoholism, in this case derived from his theories about paranoia and homosexuality. He thought that the phenomenon of men drinking together in exclusively male groups is an expression of latent homosexual wishes. A failure to achieve satisfactory sexual relationships with women, itself a consequence of the latent homosexuality, would 'drive men to drink' in the company of other men. But when the repressed homosexual wishes threatened to become conscious, the drinker would rush back to his female partner and then become suspicious to a paranoid extent that she was having sex with other men, the very men he unconsciously wished to have sex with himself.

The self-destructive character of prolonged heavy drinking was analysed by Karl Menninger (1938), the Freudian disciple whose ideas about accident proneness were briefly touched upon in Chapter 4. He argued that unconscious self-destructive impulses, which can manifest themselves in alcoholism, suicide and accident proneness, have their origins in rage initially directed at the child's parents and later repressed because they cause guilt. Self-destructive behaviour can be seen as serving two extremely aberrant purposes, simultaneously redirecting the repressed rage at the self and, by inflicting punishment, atoning for the original guilt-inducing wish. The long, slow suicide which often seems to be the essential feature of the career of the alcoholic is thus explained.

Freud's concept of *secondary gain* can also be usefully applied to alcohol problems. Just as hypochondriacs are often seen to be using their condition to avoid work and to get people at their beck and call, so can it be seen that sufferers from many kinds of neurosis often exploit their condition in order to gain attention, avoid things that they do not wish to do and generally manipulate people around them. It is easy to see how patterns of drinking can function in this way and not only in the regular heavy drinker: 'It's your fault for getting me drunk' or 'I only did it because I was drunk' can provide a convenient way of evading responsibility for the person who commits a sexual indiscretion or beats their partner. Here alcohol has the double function of releasing the inhibitions which might otherwise prevent the impulse from being acted on, while simultaneously being held to blame as if it were the drink that performed the action rather than the drinker. In the case of the alcoholic, it is possible to see here some dangers in adopting the medical or disease model. If alcoholics think of themselves as victims of a disease over which they have no control, not only will they avoid taking responsibility for actions carried out while under the influence of drink, but they will also avoid taking responsibility for drinking, which may make it difficult or impossible to help them.

Learning theory and the controlled drinking controversy

Learning theorists consider drinking problems to develop as a result of the same learning mechanisms that are at work in establishing patterns of 'normal drinking'. They argue that the reasons why some people become problem drinkers and others do not lie in their particular personal histories of learning to drink, their present social environment insofar as it provides opportunities and encouragement to drink and in physiological variables that may make the effects of alcohol more pleasurable or positively reinforcing for some people than others.

Operant conditioning is a term used originally by B.F. Skinner (1938) to denote the type of learning which occurs when animals are trained to respond in a particular way to a stimulus by providing rewards after they make the appropriate response. In the classic experiment, hungry rats were confined in small boxes and trained to press a bar in order to obtain food pellets. This phenomenon, which was of course well known to animal trainers, pet owners and the parents of small children long before it was 'discovered' by psychologists, has some applicability to the understanding of problem drinking. Of particular importance is the _gradient of reinforcement_, the fact that reinforcement which occurs rapidly after the response is much more effective in producing learning than delayed reinforcement. In the case of drinking alcohol, a small amount of positive reinforcement, such as reduced anxiety, that occurs fairly soon after drinking, may cause a strong habit to develop in spite of the counterbalancing effect of a large amount of negative reinforcement (hangover, divorce, loss of employment) which occurs much later.

Drinking, eating, smoking, drug and sexual addictions all have the 'irrational' characteristic that the total amount of pleasure gained from the addiction seems much less than the suffering caused by it. According to learning theorists, the reason for this lies in the nature of the gradient of reinforcement. Addictive behaviours are typically those in which pleasurable effects occur rapidly after the addictive behaviour while unpleasant consequences occur after a delay. The simple mechanism of operant conditioning and the gradient of reinforcement is able, as it were, to overpower the mind's capacity for rational calculation.

Classical conditioning refers to the process, first investigated about 100 years ago by the Russian physiologist Ivan Pavlov, whereby a response which occurs as a natural reflex to a particular stimulus can be conditioned to occur to a new stimulus. In Pavlov's early experiments a bell was rung shortly before food was placed in a dog's mouth, thereby eliciting salivation as a physiological reflex. After a number of pairings of bell and food Pavlov found that the dog salivated when the bell was rung unaccompanied by food.

An interesting application of conditioning theory to the explanation of drug dependence, tolerance and withdrawal is the *compensatory conditioned response model* (Siegel, 1975). Initially, when a drug is taken a physiological *homeostatic* mechanism comes into operation to counteract its effects. In the case of alcohol, which has a depressing effect, the homeostatic mechanism activates the nervous system in order to maintain balance. In the regular drinker this gradually produces tolerance so that increasingly large quantities of alcohol are required to produce the same effect. Furthermore, the homeostatic response of nervous activation may become conditioned to stimuli normally associated with drinking, such as situations where drinking has frequently taken place in the past. If conditioned drinkers are in such situations but do not drink, the conditioned response of nervous activation will not be balanced by the effects of alcohol and the resultant unpleasant state of excessive activation is what is known as a withdrawal state. In this way classical conditioning can account for the close connection to be observed between the phenomena of tolerance and withdrawal.

The compensatory conditioned response model has had considerable influence on addiction studies, but has been challenged by a number of alternative models that use conditioning theory to account for the phenomena of addiction. Three models that have received particular attention are those of Wikler (1980), Stewart et al. (1984) and Robinson and Berridge (1993). Drummond et al. (1995) provide a useful survey of this now highly technical subject.

Social learning theorists argue that classical and operant conditioning provide incomplete explanations of human learning, which also frequently depends on observation and imitation. Bandura (1977) has been particularly influential in emphasizing the importance of learning by imitation and linking it to his concept of *self-efficacy*, a personality trait consisting of having confidence in one's ability to carry out one's plans successfully. People with low self-efficacy are much more likely to imitate undesirable behaviours than those with high self-efficacy. Heather and Robertson (1997) give a useful discussion of the application of these principles to drinking. Patterns of drinking by parents are observed by children who may then imitate them in later life, especially the behaviour of the same sex parent. In adolescence, the drinking behaviour of respected older peers may also be imitated, and subsequently that of higher status colleagues at work, a phenomenon which may explain the prevalence of heavy drinking in certain professions such as medicine and journalism.

Can individuals with drinking problems ever resume moderate levels of drinking, or is total abstinence their only realistic goal? Because they regard heavy drinking as essentially a habit rather than a disease, learning theorists have taken the view that a return to moderate drinking can, at least in some cases, be a viable objective. Although not necessarily the preferred objective, moderation is a viable objective nevertheless. This apparently modest and cautious view has provoked an extraordinary amount of criticism, especially in the USA where a belief that lifelong abstinence is the only cure is deeply entrenched, often taking on the character of a moral crusade. The evidence which has accumulated over the last 40 years points clearly in favour of the learning theorists.

In an early study, Davies (1962) investigated the subsequent drinking history of 93 patients who had been diagnosed as *alcohol addicts* and treated at the Maudsley Hospital, London, with a programme aimed at abstinence. He found that seven of them had resumed moderate drinking and had maintained this over at least five years. This finding was confirmed in a number of further studies including the large scale Rand study (Armor et al., 1976) in which 589 male alcoholics, who had been treated at abstinence orientated treatment centres throughout the USA, were followed up 18 months after treatment: 12% were found to be drinking moderately. In a subsequent four-year follow-up of 922 male alcoholics who had attended the same treatment centres, Polich et al. (1980) found that 18% had resumed normal drinking. Nordström and Berglund (1987) followed up 70 alcoholic men who appeared to be well adjusted an average of 21 years after treatment and found that 21 were social drinkers while 11 were abstainers.

Similar results were found in a number of studies into spontaneous changes in people's drinking habits. Clark and Cahalan (1976) interviewed 615 men in San Francisco on two occasions about four years apart and found considerable fluctuation between moderate drinking, light drinking and abstinence. Further studies revealed spontaneous remission rates from problem drinking varying from 4% to 42% (Imber et al., 1976; Smart, 1976).

The relative merits of treatment programmes which aim for a return to moderate drinking and those which aim for abstinence have been discussed in several helpful reviews (Miller and Hester, 1986; Rosenberg, 1993; Heather and Robertson, 1997). A return to controlled drinking seems to be a viable objective for people with less severe forms of dependence provided that they are well motivated. For those with severe dependence, abstinence is to be preferred as the objective, although much again depends on level of motivation. As we shall see in Chapter 8, similar arguments apply to the control of smoking.

In the case of elderly, homeless 'winos' with a long history of severe dependence, a reduction in daily intake is probably the only realistic goal of an intervention. A recent development in Britain has been the establishment of *wet houses* which provide accommodation and activities designed to reduce the amount of drinking which takes place, while, in contrast to traditional establishments, not actually prohibiting consumption on the premises. This form of intervention combines practical help to those who most need it together with sensible expectations of those with a severe drinking dependency.

PREVENTION AND TREATMENT OF ALCOHOL PROBLEMS

Prevention

Bruun et al. (1975) reviewed the evidence concerning public policy and the prevention of alcohol problems in a book which rapidly established itself as the key treatment of the topic. Its findings have since been extended and brought up to date by Griffith Edwards and his colleagues in association with the World Health Organization (Edwards et al., 1994; Holder and Edwards, 1995). Central to both the earlier and the more recent works are their arguments in favour of the *population based approach*, which incorporates the principle that the most effective policies for reducing alcohol problems are those which reduce average levels of consumption in the population. These policies include high levels of taxation for alcoholic drinks and restrictions on access, such as limiting opening hours for bars and imposing tight controls on which shops can sell alcohol and the hours during which they can do so.

These views are opposed by the drinks industry because reduced per capita consumption means smaller profits. Neither are they popular with governments who fear that restrictions on availability and high taxation would be unpopular with the electorate and with the drinks industry, which is a powerful pressure group. For example, Heather and Robertson (1997) pointed out that in 1979 the newly elected Conservative government took the unusual step of suppressing a government policy review document initiated by the previous Labour government on alcohol policy. The document was subsequently leaked to Bruun and was in line with his own recommendations regarding a population based approach. A survey conducted shortly afterwards showed that 74 (i.e. more than one in ten) members of parliament including government ministers had a financial interest in the drinks industry.

Heather and Robertson (1997) describe recent attempts by the British drinks industry to influence academic debate. For example, shortly before the publication of the Edwards report in 1994, the Portman Group, a 'front' organization for the British drinks industry, sent prepublication copies which they had been able to obtain to leading academics with a substantial financial offer if they would anonymously contribute to a critical response. Following adverse publicity the project was eventually dropped. Edwards (1998) argues that academics should not accept funding from drinks industry front organizations such as the Portman Group, which seek to promote alcohol consumption in highly unethical ways. He suggests that the drinks industry would have a 'pariah' status unless it changes its ways: 'The drinks conglomerates are very clearly targeting young people, as witnessed by their woeful behaviour over "alcopops". They are trying to target the developing world in a way highly reminiscent of the tobacco manufacturers.' (For further discussion of the links between policy, industrial pressure groups and unhealthy behaviours at the individual level, see Chapters 6 and 8.)

In opposition to the population based approach, the argument favoured by the pro-alcohol lobby can be called 'why spoil everybody's fun?' This argument is expanded as follows. Alcoholics are a small minority who will probably continue to drink heavily however highly it is taxed and however much access is restricted. Their condition is probably inherited and unlikely to be changed by any measures short of total prohibition. For the vast majority of the population, alcohol problems can best be prevented by educational initiatives on sensible approaches to drinking. Why then, hit the pockets of the normally drinking majority, and restrict their opportunities to enjoy drinking, in a probably unsound strategy to protect a small minority?

These views may sound reasonable but they are not supported by scientific evidence. In examining the dangers to physical health of heavy drinking, we have already referred to the close relationship between per capita alcohol consumption and deaths from liver cirrhosis, the latter a clear indicator of prolonged heavy drinking. One example was the analysis by Saunders (1985) of the very large changes in average levels of consumption in Finland this century as a result of periods of restrictive legislation followed by periods of liberalization. These changes were associated not only with corresponding changes in rates of liver cirrhosis, but also in hospital admissions for alcoholism, arrests for drunkenness, road traffic accidents, where the driver had been drinking and arrests for driving while under the influence of alcohol. Kendell et al. (1983a, 1983b) conducted a similar analysis of the effects in Scotland of a large increase in tax on alcohol. They found an 18% fall in consumption, equally for light drinkers and heavy drinkers, and a corresponding reduction in alcohol-related fights and road traffic accidents.

One area of legislation to control the dangers of alcohol use, which more and more countries are adopting, is strictly enforced drink-driving laws with severe penalties for offenders. It is now almost universally agreed that this has played an important role in reducing traffic fatalities. It even commands the support of the drinks industry which, in view of the high level of public support for the laws, would be foolish to oppose it. The other main preventative measures that have been much analysed are health education programmes, such as leaflets and booklets which explain the dangers of excessive drinking and provide guidelines for 'sensible drinking'. Unfortunately, the evidence here indicates that they are ineffective. Health education generally appears to improve knowledge about the effects of alcohol and attitudes to it but has no effect on the amounts actually consumed (Ashley and Rankin, 1988), which perhaps explains why it is another approach that the drinks industry is happy to support.

Although this may seem an unnecessarily cynical view, there are some reasons for taking it seriously. Heather and Robertson (1997) point out that the drinks industry derives a good part of its profits from very heavy drinkers. In a survey of Scottish drinking habits, Dight (1978) estimated that 3% of the population were responsible for 30% of total alcohol consumption. The loss of this source of profits would be crippling to the drinks industry. Hence the continued profitablity of the industry requires the existence of a substantial percentage of very heavy drinkers. This provides another salient example of a conflict of interest between good public health and profits in industry.

Given that at present governments of alcohol-consuming countries are unlikely to make major changes to the taxation and availability of alcohol, the failure of existing health education programmes to curb excessive drinking is worrying. The obvious answer is to find ways to improve these programmes. We have already noted that advice to cut down from general practitioners can be effective and this is clearly one minimal form of intervention which could be implemented further, as in the case of cigarette smoking. Other front line professionals who could also provide controlled drinking advice include social workers, probation officers and community nurses.

Important features of any health message are who it comes from and to whom it is directed. For example, drinking among young people is frequently associated with independence from authority and a loosening of social and sexual inhibitions. In these circumstances, drinking advice from traditional authority figures may be counterproductive. Peer group propaganda may be much more effective as in the case of the 1998 campaign of the British National Union of Students, an example of which is discussed in Box 7.2.

BOX 7.2   DRUNK BLOKES ARE EASY TO GET INTO BED

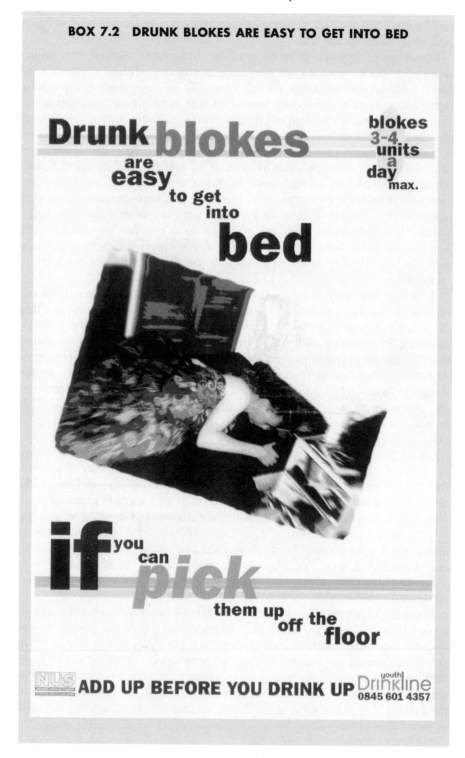

This advertisement, distributed to British universities and colleges in 1998 by the National Union of Students, is designed to correct the misapprehension, fostered by drinks industry advertising, that getting drunk enhances sexual pleasure. It also ingeniously reverses the traditional male view, and the subject of mothers' warnings to daughters since time immemorial, that women can be easily seduced if plied with drink. As for the human male, in the words of the porter in Macbeth, 'it provokes the desire, but it takes away the performance; therefore much drink may be said to be an equivocator with lechery'. Perhaps more could be made of this fact in the health promotion literature. It is certainly not lost on the drinks industry who recently advertised a very low alcohol Australian lager (Swan Light) with the slogan, 'Don't turn your didgeridoo into a didgeridon't!'

Figure reproduced with kind permission of the National Union of Students.

TREATMENT

One of the most striking aspects of the treatment of alcohol problems is the contrasting approaches taken in different countries. In the USA and Canada treatment programmes are almost always aimed at total abstinence, while in Britain a return to moderate drinking has increasingly become the treatment goal (Rosenberg, 1993). North American programmes are usually based on specialist treatment centres which have a strong medical orientation, dominated by psychiatrists who subscribe to a disease model of alcoholism. In Finland, on the other hand, alcohol problems are regarded as essentially social problems and dealt with primarily by social workers (Heather and Robertson, 1997). These differences have been shaped by social forces and, until recently, have rarely involved any serious critical analysis of the evidence for the efficacy of the programmes. For example, Miller and Brown (1997) note that the specialist US treatment programmes for alcohol and drug problems are among those least supported by scientific evidence. The same can be said for the other main American option, Alcoholics Anonymous, which is usually unwilling to expose itself to controlled trials to test for efficacy (Heather and Robertson, 1997).

Where the comparative efficacy of different treatment programmes has been evaluated, the predominant finding has been that *cognitive-behavioural* programmes are the most cost effective and also likely to produce better results than other types of treatment, including counselling and psychotherapy (Miller et al., 1995; Finney and Monahan, 1996; Miller and Brown, 1997). Recent evidence suggests that a particularly effective technique is *motivation enhancement therapy* which has been analysed in some detail by Miller (1996). This approach is in direct contrast to the confrontational tactics traditionally adopted by therapists treating addictions, in which every effort is made to overcome the client's supposed resistance to acknowledging that she has a problem, aggressively to challenge any dishonesty and to break down her defences. Instead the motivation enhancing therapist tries to create a warm empathic relationship with the client and uses a gentle and indirect approach in order to boost her self-esteem and encourage her to become aware of the gulf that exists between the negative characteristics of her current drinking habits and positive feelings about herself as a person. Further effective therapeutic techniques include social skills training, not least those needed to abstain or drink moderately in situations where others are drinking heavily, and training in psychological strategies designed to prevent a full-blown relapse from occurring after a single occasion of relapse (Marlatt and Gordon, 1985).

One finding which has been confirmed by a number of investigators is that *brief interventions* can be as effective as more extensive ones. In a very large five-year study known as Project MATCH, 1,726 people with drinking problems were divided into three groups receiving respectively: (a) a programme which aimed to encourage attendance at Alcoholics Anonymous; (b) coping skills therapy; (c) motivation enhancement therapy. Motivation enhancement therapy proved just as effective as the other two, although it consisted of only four as against 12 sessions over a 12-week period (Project MATCH Research Group, 1997).

Studies conducted in Sweden and Britain have both demonstrated the effectiveness of simple interventions in which heavy drinkers make periodic visits to general practitioners, who advise them on cutting down drinking (Kristensson et al., 1983; Wallace et al., 1988; Richmond and Anderson, 1994). In a World Health Organization study of very brief interventions (Babor and Grant, 1992), 1,655 heavy drinkers in 10 countries were given one of: (a) a 20-minute assessment only (control group); (b) assessment plus five minutes interview with a health worker who advised them to cut down; (c) assessment, advice and 15 minutes counselling on a habit breaking plan; (d) assessment, advice and extended counselling consisting of at least three further sessions. Men in all three intervention groups performed equally well, cutting down 25% more than the control group. In the case of women all four groups showed equally reduced consumption so that, for them, the mere fact of having been assessed was sufficient to motivate them to cut down.

These findings could have considerable significance for public policy. The cost effectiveness of brief interventions appears to be relatively high and they offer health-care systems excellent value for money. However, Heather (1995) sounds a cautionary note. He points out that the evidence for the effectiveness of these interventions comes from *opportunistic interventions* rather than those aimed at individuals who specifically seek help for alcohol problems. In the latter case the evidence for the effectiveness of such interventions is lacking. Here it is important to make a distinction between brief interventions, such as motivation enhancement therapy, that are effective for people who request help but which still require a substantial amount of the therapist's time distributed over a number of sessions, and minimal opportunistic interventions, such as when someone is advised to cut down by a doctor.

FUTURE RESEARCH

1 Clarification of the health risks and possible benefits of light to moderate drinking, including heart disease, various cancers and risks to the unborn child.
2 Epidemiological studies to determine the causal role of alcohol in psychosocial problem areas including different types of crime, marital and family problems, suicide and psychological disorders.
3 Studies to assess the relative merits of abstinence versus controlled drinking as an objective for people with drinking problems. What types of client are best advised to aim respectively for abstinence and for moderation?
4 Investigations to establish what are the physiological and psychological characteristics of dependence, tolerance and withdrawal. Comparative testing of alternative conditioning models.
5 Evaluation of the effectiveness and cost effectiveness of interventions using long-term follow-ups and appropriate controls. Currently the most promising appear to be brief opportunistic interventions by medical practitioners and, for those actively seeking help, motivation enhancement therapy and cognitive-behavioural therapy by health psychologists.
6 Research into the cost effectiveness of alternative approaches to the prevention of alcohol problems, including taxation, restrictions on availability, educational and other health promotion initiatives.

SUMMARY

1 Most cultures have had an ambivalent view of the use of alcohol, its benefits and undesirable effects.
2 There is a sharp conflict between the medical or disease model of alcoholism, particularly prevalent in North America, where lifelong abstinence is considered to be the only cure for the alcoholic, and psychological models based on learning theory, more common in Europe, where drinking in moderation is considered a viable objective, at least for some types of heavy drinker.
3 Drinking has been shown to cause liver cirrhosis, strokes, various cancers and, in the case of drinking during pregnancy, damage to the unborn child. Most of these risks are confined to the heavy drinker. However, in the case of drinking during pregnancy there is evidence that risk may begin at quite low levels of consumption.
4 The greatest physical risk taken by the moderate drinker and the occasional binge drinker is the risk of accidental injury or death, especially, but not exclusively, traffic accidents.
5 It is not clear to what extent problem drinking causes psychological disorders or is a consequence of pre-existing disorders. However, whichever is the case, drinking has the effect of exacerbating these disorders and making them more difficult to treat.

6   Alcohol has been shown to be associated with a large proportion of homicides and assaults, both as perpetrator and as victim.

7   It has proved difficult to assess the relative contribution of hereditary and environmental factors to the development of different patterns of drinking; on balance, the evidence suggests that both factors make a substantial contribution.

8   The nature of physical and psychological dependence on alcohol is not well understood; at present, conditioning/learning models represent the most promising approach.

9   For heavy drinkers who have not actively sought treatment for their problems, advice to cut down or stop drinking given by doctors is the most effective known intervention.

10   For those who seek help, motivation enhancement therapy is at least as effective as the combative, confrontational approach usually associated with the disease model of alcoholism.

11   The most effective methods for preventing alcohol problems are measures which have the effect of reducing overall levels of consumption, including high taxation and restricted availability. However, in most countries in the west the drinks industry acts as a powerful lobby against these measures and few politicians would risk unpopularity by introducing them.

KEY TERMS

alcohol dependence syndrome
classical conditioning
cognitive-behavioural therapy
compensatory conditioned
    response model
delta alcoholic
fetal alcohol syndrome
gamma alcoholic
gradient of reinforcement
homeostasis

liver cirrhosis
motivation enhancement
    therapy
operant conditioning
opportunistic intervention
self-efficacy
temperance societies
tension reduction hypothesis
Wernicke-Korsakoff syndrome

8 TOBACCO AND SMOKING

This vice brings in one hundred million francs in taxes every year. I will certainly forbid it at once – as soon as you can name a virtue that brings in as much revenue.
(Napoleon III, 1808–73)

OUTLINE

It is 50 years since research confirmed the connection between smoking and ill health. This discovery was followed by a series of reports by medical societies and government departments advising people not to smoke. With the accumulation of evidence on the negative aspects of smoking, most western governments promoted various measures to reduce the **prevalence** of smoking. These measures met with substantial success such that the prevalence of smoking has fallen steadily in most industrialized societies. Recent studies have confirmed the ill effects of passive smoking of environmental tobacco smoke. However, a large number of people continue to smoke. Indeed, the evidence suggests that the overall prevalence of smoking in young people in the USA and Britain started to increase again in the mid-1990s. The aim of this chapter is to document the extent of smoking and factors which help explain its continued popularity and to discuss why people take up smoking and what steps can be taken to reduce the prevalence.

PREVALENCE AND DISTRIBUTION OF SMOKING

Although tobacco was popular during the nineteenth century, it was largely smoked using pipes and confined to men. The development of cigarettes towards the end of the nineteenth century was followed by a rapid increase in tobacco consumption. In the first half of the twentieth century, cigarette smoking became an immensely popular activity, especially among men in the western world. In the USA cigarette consumption doubled in the 1920s and again in the 1930s (Breslow, 1996) and peaked at about 67% in the 1940s and 1950s (Giovino et al., 1994). In Britain it was estimated that the prevalence among men reached almost 80% during the same period (Wald et al., 1988). However, following the accumulation of evidence on the health hazards of smoking the prevalence has declined overall, although sex, social class, regional and other differences have developed.

The classic study by Doll and Hill (1952) linking smoking with cancer was followed by reports by the Royal College of Physicians in Britain (1962) and the Surgeon General in the United States (US Department of

Health, Education and Welfare, 1964) demonstrating the harmful effects of smoking. Studies conducted in the 1990s confirmed the ill effects of the passive smoking of environmental tobacco smoke (Environmental Protection Agency, 1992; Department of Health, 1998). By 1994 the prevalence of smoking had dropped to about 25% to 30% in both the USA and Britain. This decline was most pronounced among white, middle-class men. In Britain, only 16% of professional men and women smoked compared with 48% of men and 36% of women from unskilled manual occupations (Smyth and Browne, 1992).

Graham (1996) considered the sex differences in the prevalence of smoking across Europe between 1950 and 1990. During this period there was a consistent decline in the prevalence of smoking among men from about 70–90% to about 30–50%. However, among women the same period saw a rise in the prevalence of smoking followed by a slow decline reaching 20–40% in 1990. The initial rise in prevalence was led by women from professional backgrounds, but they have also led the decline such that today smoking is more common among women from poorer backgrounds. In less developed and developing countries there is substantial evidence that the prevalence of smoking continues at a high rate and is actually increasing (e.g. Peto et al., 1992). These increasing prevalence rates are caused by the extensive promotion of tobacco by the industry.

'The European Health and Behaviour Survey' (Steptoe and Wardle, 1996) found national variations in smoking behaviour across that continent. More than 40% of men in Austria, Greece, Norway and Portugal smoked, while less than 25% smoked in Belgium, Finland, Hungary and Sweden. In general the prevalence of smoking was lower among women and lowest (10%) in Finland.

There is also evidence of ethnic differences in smoking rates although these often intertwined with *socio-economic status* (SES) differences. Winkleby et al. (1995) found that although there was little difference between college educated whites and hispanics in smoking prevalence; among those with limited education the smoking prevalence among whites was twice that among hispanics.

National surveys have also clearly established a growing link between smoking and various indicators of social deprivation. In Britain a national survey of health and lifestyles (Cox et al., 1987) found that smoking was linked with such indicators as a history of mental illness and use of tranquillizers. Smoking is more prevalent among people on low incomes, the unemployed and those who are divorced or separated. Finally, smoking is linked with alcohol consumption, caffeine intake and other drug use.

ADVERTISING AND THE SOCIAL CONTEXT OF SMOKING

Tobacco advertising appears to play a significant role in creating an accepting social context for tobacco and smoking. Almost everybody, smoker and non-smoker alike, must be aware of the ads and their accompanying health warnings through their continued presence on billboards, on racing cars and in magazines seems an affrontery to common-sense notions of health promotion. Yet, given the huge numbers of people who die from smoking related diseases, it seems illogical that tobacco companies are allowed legally to advertise their harmful products. However, many issues are interwined and the abolition of tobacco advertising is not as simple and straightforward as it might first appear.

First, there is the argument that there is a lack of evidence to suggest that tobacco advertising significantly influences smoking behaviour. Schudson (1993) questioned the 'magical potency' of tobacco advertising by pointing out that most advertisements are directed to target audiences who already use a product. The industry claims that advertisements simply try to interest the customer in switching brands of a product they already use. A large number of econometric studies have found either no overall relationship between advertising and sales or a small, statistically significant positive relationship. However, the results of such studies are equivocal as much depends on who supplies data for the studies: the tobacco industry or the public health authorities (Schudson, 1993). Schudson (1993) supported his view that advertising has limited impact on encouraging tobacco consumption by highlighting the fact that health messages in the mass media have not been very effective in discouraging smoking. However, the impacts of tobacco advertising and health messages in the media are hardly comparable given the different budgets which are at least ten to one in favour of the industry.

The issue of banning tobacco advertising is further tangled when politics are included. The epitome of this can be seen within the European Union (EU) which, on the one hand, supports and finances the tobacco industry through the Common Agricultural Policy, and on the other, recognizes the health effects of tobacco in funding its 'Europe Against Cancer' campaign. However, in financial terms, the former greatly exceeds the latter.

Tobacco growers are part of a strong agriculture lobby and assisted by a hugely powerful cigarette manufacturing lobby. Some member states have a vested interest in providing financial assistance to tobacco growers. They want to maintain the economic well-being of the tobacco producing areas and they are unwilling to risk losing the votes of the smokers in their electorates. Despite this, attempts have been made to persuade tobacco growers to change their crops. Yet the fact remains that in 1994 the EU provided ECU 1,165 million in tobacco subsidies and a mere ECU 15 million to the 'Europe Against Cancer' campaign (Ludvigsen and Roberts, 1996).

The EU's conflict of interest is made all the stronger by the consideration that, by killing off smokers, the tobacco industry is actually helping the economy. Europe is facing a demographic change in which the birth rate is decreasing and life expectancy is increasing (Eurostat, 1992). Therefore smokers who die before the average life expectancy are helping to reduce expenditure on an already expensive elderly population. Between 4% and 5% of the UK government's revenue comes from tobacco sales tax.

In July 1997 the British New Labour government launched an 'Anti-Smoking Summit' with high profile speakers including government ministers, policymakers and entrepreneur Richard Branson. A wide range of interests was represented from the media, business, the arts and sport to the medical professions and health charities. A full range of issues was considered such as the scope of the advertising ban, consumer protection issues, prices, tax and fiscal measures, public education, smoking in public places and helping people stop smoking. Tessa Jowell claimed, 'This initiative is at the heart of our public health policy, it has strong public support, and is my personal number one priority.' A letter circulated by Prime Minister Tony Blair refers to the need for intersectoral action: 'Action is needed not just from Government, but all sectors of society . . . The medical profession, business, the media, sporting bodies, local communities, indeed all those who set standards and influence opinions in society, have an important role to play'.

This summit sent a wave of optimism among those concerned with tobacco control. However, allegations of political 'sleaze' soon came to the fore and optimism turned to despair. It was revealed that the government wanted to argue that Formula One motor racing should be exempted from an EU draft directive on banning tobacco advertising. It was suggested that the main reason for this U-turn was the government's acceptance of a £1 million donation from Formula One chief, Bernie Ecclestone. Other suggestions got caught up in the scandal, including the Prime Minister's personal enthusiasm for Formula One and pressure from Germany's Chancellor Kohl as part of a trade-off for allowing Britain to take part in a committee running the new EU central bank. Tobacco taxes are a major source of revenue and the German government opposes the EU-wide ban on tobacco advertising.

Pressure from the European Commission brought a compromise in which the UK government accepted a draft directive that would give Formula One exemption from the tobacco advertising ban for a fixed period. Finally, in December 1997 a tobacco advertising ban directive was passed by the EU Health Council. Britain backed the agreement which was secured by 62 votes – the minimum number needed. Germany and Austria opposed the agreement and Denmark along with Spain, which had previously supported the ban, abstained. Spain admitted it had changed its mind 'for political reasons' as a favour to Germany (Bates, 1997).

The directive was finally voted through in May 1998. The ban outlaws tobacco advertising and sponsorship and is to be fully in force in 2006. Individual governments will have the power to implement the ban in a shorter time frame if they wish. Under the directive, print media will have to stop carrying cigarette advertisements within four years and sponsorship of sporting events not organized at a world level will be illegal after five years, while sponsorship of events organized at a world level will have to end by October 2006 at the very latest.

The tobacco and publishing industries were quick with their accusation that the directive would disrupt the harmony of the single market. Yet, before the directive was passed two EU committees had challenged it on the grounds that it breached the principle of the single market. However, the EU parliament's legal service pointed out that the directive was legally sound as they had a duty to ensure a high level of human health protection (ASH Burning News, 1998).

The EU has come close to clearing some of the complexities of banning tobacco advertising. This is an important beginning. The laws will now have to go through a process of implementation in each member state, thus giving the tobacco industry time to devise cunning alternative ways to lure people to smoke. With committment and a freeing from political rhetoric, member states are a powerful force against the tobacco industry. Time will show just how much these developments in banning tobacco advertising have been due to real committment or more political rhetoric to further knot the whole issue.

THEORIES OF SMOKING

The resistance shown by smokers to large-scale campaigns to discourage the practice has prompted a massive amount of research to help to explain the continuing popularity of smoking. It is agreed that smoking is an extremely complex practice involving a mixture of biological, psychological and social processes.

Biological theories of smoking

Nicotine, the main active ingredient in tobacco smoke, is a substance which if taken in large quantities can be toxic. However, delivered in small amounts via cigarette smoke it has a range of psychophysiological effects including tranquillization, weight loss, decreased irritability, increased alertness and improved cognitive functioning (Rose, 1996). The apparent conflict between the stimulant physiological effect of nicotine and reports of relaxation has been called the 'nicotine paradox' (Nesbitt, 1973). One explanation for this paradox is that smoking appears relaxing because the smokers are often in a state of mild nicotine withdrawal which is relieved by the cigarette which returns the nicotine level in the body to 'normal' (Hughes, 1991; Foulds and Ghodse, 1995).

Over time the smoker seems to develop a *physical dependence* on nicotine. In the USA several tobacco companies have publicly admitted that smoking is addictive. In 1997 the smallest of the big five US tobacco companies (the Liggett Group) admitted that it had raised the nicotine content in cigarettes to increase their addictiveness (Porter, 1997). Documents of several large US tobacco companies during the period 1962 to 1984 were obtained by Slade et al. (1995). These revealed that the companies considered nicotine to be the active pharmacological substance in tobacco smoke and in the early years explicitly referred to *addiction*. The debate about the addictive qualities of nicotine continues (see Stolerman and Jarvis, 1995). Evidence for this is available from both epidemiological and experimental studies.

In terms of consumption patterns, in the early 1990s male smokers were averaging 17 cigarettes per day while female smokers were averaging 14. Very few smokers were less than daily smokers indicating the ongoing need to smoke. Further, within five minutes of waking approximately 14% of smokers reported having a cigarette and over 50% within 30 minutes (NOP, 1992). Even after the occurrence of a serious smoking induced disease, many smokers return to smoking. For example, Davison and Duffy (1982) found that 50% of smokers who had undergone surgery for lung cancer resumed smoking.

According to survey evidence most adult smokers (83%) claim they wish they had never started and almost one-third report that they had given up smoking for at least a day in the past year (Gallup and Newport, 1990). Even for those who manage to quit, the long-term success is poor. Hatziandreu et al. (1990) found that 93% of those smokers who try to give up resumed regular smoking within one year. This figure is supported by a large number of randomized controlled trials which find that only 5–6% of smokers trying to stop without treatment can remain abstinent for one year (Law and Tang, 1995).

The experimental work of Schachter and his colleagues (e.g. Schachter et al., 1984) developed the nicotine regulation model of smoking. According to this model there is a physiological regulatory mechanism which monitors the level of nicotine in the brain. When this falls below a certain level the individual feels the need for another cigarette. Admittedly, this model is not so straightforward since smokers will smoke nicotine-free cigarettes when there are no others available and will go for lengthy periods without a cigarette, e.g. on an airline flight. Further, the role of nicotine is variable. Hajek et al. (1995) drew attention to the 10–18% of smokers who have been classified as light smokers. These smokers smoke five or less cigarettes a day which would not be sufficient to maintain a high level of nicotine. Further, these light smokers are not distributed randomly in the population but are more common among those from higher levels of education (Hajek et al., 1995) and among blacks (Kabat et al., 1991).

Admittedly, not all people smoke or exhibit a desire to smoke. This raises the suggestion that perhaps there is a *genetic* component. A number of twin studies from different continents have produced evidence of strong genetic link in the risk of smoking. Heath and Madden (1995) reviewed the evidence from national twin studies in Scandinavia and Australia. In their predictive model genetic factors increased both the likelihood of becoming a regular smoker ('initiation') and of these smokers becoming long-term smokers ('persistence'). In a large follow-up survey of the smoking practices of male twin pairs from the US Vietnam Era Twin Registry, True et al. (1997) found that genetic factors accounted for 50% of the risk of smoking and environmental factors accounted for a further 30%. In addition, genetic factors accounted for 70% of the risk variance of becoming a regular smoker whereas environmental factors were not important. Carmelli et al. (1992) found that the evidence for a genetic component was stronger among light smokers.

According to evolutionary psychologists, the persistence of behaviour patterns such as smoking must reflect some evolutionary value. With the decline in the overall prevalence of smoking there has emerged what Pomerlau (1979) has described as a group of 'refractory' smokers who are more likely to have a variety of other problematic patterns of behaviour and cognition such as depression, anxiety and bulimia/binging. In ancient times these patterns may have been biologically adaptive or neutral. However, in contemporary society, a more active fight or flight response is inappropriate. Smoking would be valuable to this population because it can produce small but reliable adjustments to levels of arousal. While smoking may be hazardous to health, Pomerleau suggests that the introduction of other forms of nicotine administration raises new questions. In countries where the prevalence of smoking is still high, the smoking population presumably includes many less dependent smokers. These less dependent smokers would have less physiological need for smoking. Evolutionary approaches to addictions tend to ignore the psychological and social influences that create the conditions for tobacco use (Marks, 1998). It is to these influences that we now turn.

Psychological theories of smoking

Probably the most frequently used model of smoking is that based on learning theory. Basically, it argues that people become smokers because of the positive reinforcement they obtain. The mechanisms are similar to those described in Chapter 7 in reference to alcohol and drinking. Initially, smoking is physically unpleasant (to a greater extent than is the case for alcohol) but this is overruled because of the social reinforcement from peers. The pleasant associations of smoking then generalize to a range of other settings. In addition, the smoker learns to discriminate between those situations in which smoking is rewarded and those in which it is punished. He or she also develops responses to a number of *conditioned stimuli* (both internal and external) which elicit smoking. Smoking can be conceptualized as an escape/avoidance response to certain aversive states (Pomerlau, 1979). The smoker will light up a cigarette to escape or avoid an uncomfortable situation.

In 1966 Tomkins proposed his affect management model of smoking which was subsequently revised and extended by Ikard et al. (1969) who conducted a survey of a national (US) probability sample. In a factor analysis of the responses they identified six smoking motivation factors: reduction of negative affect, habit, addiction, pleasure, stimulation and sensorimotor manipulation. Subsequent surveys by Coan (1973) and Costa et al. (1980) produced similar factors. Livison and Leino (1988) found that women more than men reported that they smoked for reduction of negative affect and pleasure.

In their study of smoking among young adults, Murray et al. (1988) added two additional reasons: boredom and nothing to do. In a survey they asked young adults to indicate which of these factors were important reasons for smoking in different situations. In all situations relaxation and control of negative affect were considered the most important reasons. At home boredom was also considered important, perhaps reflecting these young people's frustration with family life. At work addiction was considered important, perhaps reflecting the extent to which it disrupted their work routine, while socially habit was rated important.

According to Zuckerman (1979) individuals engage in *sensation seeking* so as to maintain a certain level of physiological arousal. More specifically, Zuckerman (1984) emphasized that sensation seeking was designed to maintain an optimal level of catecholaminergic activity. Carton et al. (1994) found in a French sample that smokers scored higher on a measure of sensation seeking, in particular on disinhibition, experience seeking and boredom susceptibility subscales. They suggest that from a physiological perspective these sensation seekers have a low level of tonic arousal and seek exciting, novel or intense stimulation to raise the level of cortical arousal. This argument is very similar to that of Eysenck et al. (1960) who found that smokers scored higher on measures of *extraversion*. This personality dimension is also supposed to reflect a lower level of cortical arousal which could be raised by engaging in risky activities such as smoking.

Besides sensation seeking and extraversion, a variety of personality characteristics have been found to be associated with smoking. In a sample of Scottish adults, Whiteman (1997) found that smoking was associated with hostility. However, they accept that 'presence of an association does not help in determining if the relationship is causal'. Indeed, they hypothesize that deprivation of smoking which was required for the study may have increased hostility.

A variety of different types of studies have found that stress is associated with smoking. Schachter et al. (1984) found that among smokers, consumption was higher in experimental stressful laboratory situations. Lindenthal et al. (1972) found in a survey that people with higher self-reports of stress were more likely to be heavy smokers. In a study of nurses' smoking practices, Murray et al. (1983) found that those who reported the most stress were more likely to smoke. This relationship remained after controlling for the effect of family and friends' smoking practices. Finally, in a macro-social study, Colby et al. (1994) found that those US states which had the highest levels of stress as measured by a range of social indicators also had the highest levels of smoking and of smoking related diseases.

Social theories of smoking

Smoking is a social activity. Even when the smoker smokes alone he or she still smokes in a society where cigarettes are widely available and promoted. A number of qualitative studies have considered the social meaning of smoking. Murray et al. (1988) conducted detailed interviews with a sample of young adults from the English Midlands. These suggested that smoking had different meanings in different settings. For example, at work going for a cigarette provided an opportunity to escape from the everyday routine. As one young factory worker said:

> We would say we were going to the toilet and have a quick cigarette . . . As long as they [management] didn't catch you. If they caught you, well, you'd be in trouble, sort of thing. But it was alright. We used to go in about every hour, something like that. (Murray et al., p. 49)

For these workers, to have a cigarette meant to have a break and conversely not to have a cigarette meant not to have a break. The cigarette was a marker, a means to regulating their work routine.

Outside work, smoking was perceived as a means of reaffirming social relationships. For those young people who went to the pub, the sharing of cigarettes was a means of initiating, maintaining and strengthening social bonds. Those who did not share cigarettes were frowned upon. One young man explained when he smoked:

> Only, basically, when somebody else has one. Say we're all out in a group, say, and we're all crashing [sharing] the fags [cigarettes] and that. Say it's somebody else's turn, I'd wait for them to get one out. I wouldn't light one of my own. I'd wait for him to get his out and if it's my turn, I'd just wait about ten minutes and get mine out . . . I can't handle that, people who just smoke on their own. It doesn't seem right. (Murray et al., 1988, p. 65)

Graham's (1976, 1987) series of qualitative studies has provided a detailed understanding of the meaning of smoking to working-class women. In one of her studies (Graham, 1987) she asked a group of low-income mothers to complete a 24-hour diary detailing their everyday activities. Like the young workers in the study by Murray et al. (1988), smoking was used as a means of organizing these women's daily routine. For example, one woman said:

> I smoke when I'm sitting down, having a cup of coffee. It's part and parcel of resting. Definitely, because it doesn't bother me if I haven't got a cigarette when I'm working. If I'm busy, it doesn't bother me, but it's nice to sit down afterwards and have a cigarette. (Graham, 1987, p. 52)

Further, for these women smoking was not just a means of resting after completing certain household tasks but also a means of coping when there was a sort of breakdown in normal household routines. This was especially apparent when the demands of childcare became excessive. Graham describes smoking as 'not simply a way of structuring caring: it is also part of the way smokers re-impose structure when it breaks down' (p. 54). She gives the example of one woman who said:

> If it's nice, I send them [children] out or ask them to play in the bedroom but normally I will sit in the kitchen and have a cup of coffee and a cigarette . . . The cup of coffee calms me best, then a cigarette and then it's just being on my own for a few minutes to sort of count to ten and start again. (Graham, 1987, p. 54)

Graham (1987) argues that for these women smoking is an essential means of coping with everyday difficulties. It is also a link to an adult consumer society. Through smoking the women were reaffirming their adult identity.

Smoking is not only embedded in the immediate material circumstances in which the smoker lives, but also in the wider social and cultural context within which smoking is widely promoted. Admittedly, in most western societies there are considerable restrictions on the sale and promotion of cigarettes. Despite these, tobacco manufacturers continue to find ways to promote their products, e.g. through the sponsorship of sporting and cultural activities. In the USA it is estimated that the tobacco companies spend approximately $6 billion per annum on advertising and promotion (Emmons et al., 1997). As illustrated above, the tobacco industry is a powerful lobby group having considerable influence on government and policymaking.

ACQUISITION OF SMOKING

Natural history of smoking

Numerous *cross-sectional* and *longitudinal surveys* have confirmed that adolescence is the key period for the development of smoking. In childhood, smoking is rare but on entry to adolescence experimentation with cigarettes becomes more commonplace. Early to mid-adolescence is the period when there is the most rapid increase in the incidence of smoking.

A longitudinal study by Chassin et al. (1996) which followed a cohort of adolescents through until their late twenties confirmed the importance of adolescence in the establishment of smoking. They found that 59.3% of those who were adolescent smokers smoked in adulthood compared with only 9.6% of adolescent non-smokers. The majority of adult smokers began smoking in early adolescence. However, there was also evidence of an increase between adolescence and early adulthood suggesting a subgroup of late-onset smokers who begin smoking after leaving high school. There was also evidence of instability in smoking habits during adulthood which was due to individuals quitting smoking but then starting again. In addition, those smokers who got married and became employed were more likely to succeed in quitting. Chassin et al. suggest that this indicates what they describe as the importance of social role influences on smoking.

Stages of smoking acquisition

In the process of becoming a smoker the individual can be viewed as progressing through several stages. Leventhal and Cleary (1980) proposed the stages of preparation, initiation, becoming, maintenance and cessation. The first three stages are often collectively termed *acquisition* which refers to the period in early adolescence when experimentation with cigarettes increases rapidly. During mid-adolescence a sub-group of the majority who experiment with cigarettes gradually begins to use them on a more regular basis.

The *transtheoretical model* (Prochaska and DiClemente, 1983) provides more detailed understanding of the processes involved in both the acquisition and *cessation* of smoking among adolescents. In a survey of tenth and eleventh grade students, Pallonen et al. (1998) were able to classify them into an expanded nine stages of change continuum, three of which were considered acquisition stages (*Precontemplation, contemplation* and *preparation*). The non-smokers, especially those in the precontemplation stage reported the least exposure to smoking in their social environment. The largest difference between the three acquisition stages was in terms of friends' smoking behaviour which was much higher in the preparation stage.

In terms of the perceived pros and cons of smoking there was a steady increase in the perceived coping pros of smoking across the three acquisition stages, but little change in the perceived social pros and the perceived cons. This led Pallonen et al. (1998) to conclude that 'nonsmokers' positive expectations of smoking as a helpful coping mechanism advance the cigarette smoking acquisition process' (p. 319). Admittedly, this is for a sample of 16–17 year olds. Among a younger sample the social pros may be more important. Four temptations to try smoking were rated by the students. At the beginning of the acquisition process socializing and plain curiosity were the most important temptations, but regulation of negative and positive affective states became more important in the later stages.

DETERMINANTS OF SMOKING

Conrad et al. (1992) conducted a review of the findings of 27 longitudinal studies of the onset of smoking which were conducted between 1980 and 1990. They organized several hundred predictors of smoking identified under six domains into a hypothetical model which is illustrated in Figure

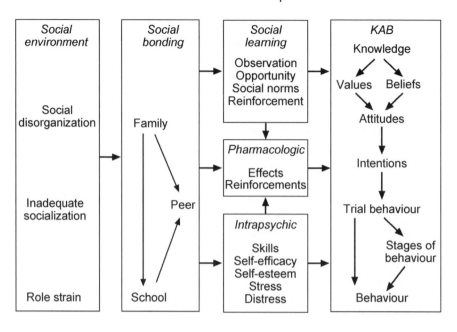

FIGURE 8.1 ***Six domains of the determinants of tobacco use (Conrad et al., 1992, p. 1714; reproduced with permission)***

8.1. This provides some indication of the many factors involved in the recruitment of teenagers to smoking. The model attempts to integrate the large amount of information.

This model is derived from large-scale survey data. Despite proposing links between domains within this hypothetical model, Conrad et al. concluded: 'Few researchers have tested competing theoretical models . . . Most studies have been based on different, unstated, or atheoretical orientations, so it is difficult to see a consistent pattern across studies.' Other researchers (e.g. Bauman, 1992; Jarvis, 1994) have also been critical of the inadequacy of much survey-based research. A major problem with the urge to find a predictor is that the endpoint is not fixed.

As Murray et al. (1988) stated earlier: 'While epidemiological surveys have provided a wealth of detail about the characteristics of young smokers and about the situations in which they smoke their methodology has tended to reify smoking. Smoking has been considered a fixed individual characteristic rather than an ongoing social and psychological process.' Thus, to understand the acquisition of smoking requires a more fine-grained analysis. However, attention to these 'determinants' or predictors of smoking during adolescence can inform us as to the character of those who adopt smoking during this period. The content of these domains has been further developed by Flay et al. (1992) who note that they fall broadly into the threefold division of social, psychological and biological.

Biological factors in recruitment to smoking

Pre-adolescence is the period of preparation. During this period children become increasingly aware of the character of cigarettes and why people smoke. Eiser et al. (1986) conducted interviews with a small sample of 7- to 8- and 10- to 11-year-olds. They found that both groups of children were aware to some extent not only of the health hazards of smoking but also of the social reasons for smoking. Further, more of the older children spoke of the supposed psychological relief provided by smoking.

Although the initial reaction to tobacco smoke is usually negative teenagers rapidly develop a taste for it. There is also evidence that from an early stage pharmacologic factors begin to play a role in the establishment of regular smoking. Young smokers report that smoking has a calming effect and that they crave cigarettes if they cannot smoke (McNeill, 1991). Admittedly, while this self-report of craving may be an exaggeration there is supportive evidence in that reports of craving are strongly associated with nicotine intake as measured by saliva analysis (Goddard, 1990). Further, within two or three years of smoking onset teenagers report difficulties in stopping (McNeill, 1991). Indeed, there is evidence that the tobacco industry collected data showing that signs of dependence are apparent among teenagers and they find it difficult to quit (Henningfield et al., 1998). In a recent study of high school students, Daughton et al. (1997) found that 52% of those who smoked felt that they were 'hooked' on cigarettes or that they would become addicted to them. Indeed, six out of ten of these young smokers felt that even giving up for three days would be difficult. However, the fact that biology is not the only explanation for difficulty quitting is illustrated in the comment by one young smoker in the study by Murray (1983): 'I have tried to stop but my friends keep smoking and offer me one I can't refuse. I do not come out at weekends because of them offering them to me.'

Psychological factors in recruitment to smoking

This domain includes a range of more psychological, interpersonal and behavioural factors. Although Conrad et al. (1992) identify an association between these factors and smoking among adolescents, other reviewers suggest caution. For example, Jarvis et al. (1990) argue that despite the large number of studies on the role of attitudes the evidence remains insufficient. Stacy et al. (1994) found that while attitudes were associated with smoking they did not predict smoking as measured 12 months later. They concluded that 'it is possible that attitude toward health behavior is useful empirically, theoretically, and practically only in the context of a more general theory' (p. 82).

The *theory of reasoned action* (TRA, Ajzen, 1985) and *theory of planned behaviour* (TPB, Ajzen, 1991) argue that smoking behaviour is predicted by behavioural intention which in turn is predicted by attitudes, social norms and perceived self-efficacy. Several studies have considered the value of all or parts of this model for predicting the uptake of smoking. In a longitudinal study of teenage smoking behaviour Flay et al. (1994) tested a version of the theory. They found that smoking initiation was predicted by intentions which were in turn predicted by negative outcomes expectation regarding smoking and ill health (a measure of attitudes), parents and friends social behaviour (an indirect measure of social norm) and refusal self-efficacy.

Several studies have found that perceptions of smoking norm predicted smoking. For example, Chassin et al. (1984) found that those teenagers who had an overestimate of the prevalence of smoking were more likely to adopt smoking. A related factor is the availability of cigarettes. Robinson and Klesges (1997) found that teenagers who had ready access to cigarettes were at greater risk of becoming smokers. Pierce et al. (1996) examined in some detail the role which perceived susceptibility plays in the transition from pre-experimentation to actual experimentation. They argued that adolescents who adopt smoking would be 'cognitively predisposed to smoking' (p. 358). By this they meant that they would both intend to and expect to adopt smoking. They found that those adolescents who were classified as susceptible (answered yes to at least one of the following: Do you think you will try a cigarette soon?; If one of your best friends were to offer you a cigarette, would you smoke it?; Do you think you will be smoking cigarettes one year from now?) were more likely to be smoking four years later.

A number of studies have asked children and teenagers why they smoke. Zoller and Maymon (1983) found that curiosity was the most common reason. Levitt (1971) found that pleasure, improvement in emotion and habit were common reasons. This seems to confuse initiation and maintenance motives. In a large survey of tenth grade students Sarason et al. (1992) found that curiosity, social norms and social pressure were most frequently given for initiation while pleasure and addiction were mentioned by current smokers. More girls than boys mentioned social norms and pressure to adopt smoking.

A variety of other intrapsychic variables have been found to predict smoking onset. In particular, indicators of rebelliousness and risk taking have frequently been found to predict smoking. Pederson et al. (1997) found that grade six students (11–12 year olds) who had tried smoking scored higher on depression, rebelliousness and social conformity. Admittedly, most of the studies have been cross-sectional in design. A study by Lipkus et al. (1994) considered to what extent personality measured on entry to university predicted smoking status 20 years later. They found that people who subsequently began smoking scored higher on measures of rebelliousness, impulsivity, sensation seeking and hostility. A related factor is pubertal timing. Tschann et al. (1994) found early maturers and those adolescents who reported emotional distress were more likely to be smokers.

Since adolescence has frequently been characterized as a period of stress it is not surprising that several researchers have considered the role of smoking as a means of coping with stress during adolescence. Wills and Shiffman (1985) suggest that people low in personal resources such as self-esteem, feelings of mastery and social support turn to smoking or other substance use because it is the only available means of coping with stress.

Social factors in recruitment to smoking

These factors are relevant to the *social learning, social bonding* and *social environment* domains. Having parents, siblings and peers who smoke strongly increases the risk of smoking among adolescents. There is a certain difference between studies in the reported relative effect of family members versus peers but all agree on the overall effect. It has been suggested that parents are more important at the preparation stage while peers become more important as the adolescents begin to experiment with cigarettes. Murray et al. (1985) found some evidence of sex linking in this relationship, indicating that an important process of adopting smoking was modelling the behaviour of the same sex parent. Further, this and other studies (e.g. Glendinning et al., 1997) have found a relationship between smoking and family structure with children from single parent families being more at risk. Conrad et al. also suggest that there may be a secular effect with parents having a lesser influence today than they did in previous years. These associations between adolescent smoking and smoking by their parents and peers has been explained as due to such processes as model-ling, accessibility, peer pressure and perceived social norm.

Various indicators of poor social attachment with parents have been found to be associated with increased risk of smoking. Strong attachment with parents is associated with a better sense of well-being and a greater capacity to handle stressful events (Greenberg et al., 1983). It has been suggested that teenagers with poor social attachment have a weaker self-image and a greater need to portray themselves to their peers as 'tough' or 'cool' through, for example, smoking (Leventhal and Cleary, 1980). In a longitudinal study of Scottish adolescents Glendinning et al. (1997) found that perceptions of family support were inversely related to smoking. This effect was raised when there was evidence of fewer parental controls. These effects were found to be independent of family socio-economic status (SES).

The social environment includes a group of distal variables described as social disorganization and role strain which are more common in families from low SES. Admittedly, the evidence with respect to this domain is inconsistent in view of the lower rate of smoking among black teenagers who tend to come from poorer family backgrounds (Flay et al., 1992).

This broad social category is sometimes expanded to include the public marketing of cigarettes. There is evidence linking adolescence cigarette consumption to advertising of particular brands. For example, a study of cigarette brand preferences among teenagers in the USA in the period 1989–93 found that the most significant change was an increase in the proportion of youth purchasing the three most heavily advertised brands. Several other historical analyses (e.g. Pierce et al., 1996; Pierce and Gilpin, 1995) have identified a clear association between increases in adolescent smoking and cigarette advertising campaigns. In a three-year follow-up study (Pierce et al., 1998) it was found that those who were aware of cigarette advertisements at baseline were more likely to experiment with cigarettes in the follow-up period. A regression analysis which controlled for family and peer smoking practices estimated that 34.3% of smoking among adolescents was attributable to tobacco advertising and promotional activities. In a content analysis of US magazines, King et al. (1998) found that those brands which became more popular among young people tended to be advertised in magazines with high youth readership.

SOCIAL MEANING OF SMOKING TO ADOLESCENTS

The majority of acquisition studies have been survey based. This reduces the opportunity to explore the perceived *meaning* of smoking to the young people. To understand these meanings requires more qualitative and ethnographic work to explore how young people perceive smoking within the context of their lives. An early attempt to understand smoking within the context of adolescents' lives was the study of English teenagers conducted by Murray and colleagues (Murray, 1983). He noted that adolescence is the period when young people begin to define and assert their identity among their peers. The character of this process reflects their immediate social context. In the case of working-class boys their social environment often offers little excitement and they hang about the streets waiting for something to happen. It is in this context that smoking acquires an important meaning. Not only is it a symbol of adult identity but the sharing of cigarettes also becomes a means of strengthening solidarity with peers and disrupting the boredom of street life. Further, for these young people restrictions on smoking can be perceived as yet another example of oppressive authority which should be resisted (cf. Brehm and Brehm, 1981). As one young working class girl said: 'So what if people do smoke? There's hardly anything you can do about it! I want to start smoking in the future and I wouldn't thank you for interfering or getting smoking banned.'

In a detailed qualitative and sociometric study of friendship patterns of a sample of Scottish schoolchildren, Michell and Amos (1997) found evidence that gender differences in the meaning of smoking and how it was intertwined with issues of style and social identity. Girls identified at the top of the pecking order and who projected an image of high self-esteem were more likely to smoke. These girls were more often described as 'good-looking' and being attractive to boys. They often hung out in the park after school rather than participating in organized activities. These girls did not feel under pressure to smoke. Rather they adopted smoking as part of the image of being cool, rebellious and sophisticated. It was seen as part of the 'top' girl package. One 11-year-old girl said: 'You don't want to be seen as a wee sad people.' To avoid this image she would wear her short skirt, jewellery and makeup and would smoke.

Admittedly in this study there was a small minority of girls who were low in the pecking order and who smoked. These girls did admit that they had felt bullied or coerced into smoking or that they smoked in order to be like the 'top' girls. These girls had poor social skills and low self-esteem. They felt they were not responsible for smoking themselves. For 'top' boys the desire to smoke was less clear cut. Michell and Amos (1997) suggested that they occupied an ambivalent position since smoking conflicted with their desire to be fit. Smoking was less important because they had other means, especially sports, of claiming a top position.

An important although neglected aspect of this study is the broader socio-cultural context within which the young people lived. The two schools investigated in this study had a varied catchment area which included private and public housing. However, the fact that 50% of the students were receiving free school meals, the Glasgow average, would suggest that a large proportion came from lower SES backgrounds. It is not simply that all 'top' girls smoked but rather those within a particular subculture did.

Wearing et al. (1994) in their review have drawn attention to the importance of the socio-cultural context. They refer to an American study by Lesko (1988) which identified two subcultures in a school she studied. There were the 'rich and popular' girls who were fashionably and expensively dressed and fitted with the classic 'good girl' image. Conversely, there were the 'burn outs' who challenged school discipline and enjoyed 'hanging out'. This latter group of girls smoked. In commenting on this study Wearing et al. (1994) note: 'Smoking . . . for the "burn outs" is a leisure activity which symbolizes resistance to the passive, sweet tempered, modest, restrained, domestic identity associated with traditional female identity and which for the "rich and popular" girls is being constructed in adolescence through school and leisure' (p. 632).

SES AND ETHNIC DIFFERENCES IN ADOLESCENT SMOKING

There is increasing evidence from large surveys in North America in the 1990s that the prevalence of smoking was higher among students from low SES backgrounds and among white students when compared to black and hispanic students (Kann et al., 1993). This led to a series of survey studies investigating SES and ethnic differences in the psychosocial factors associated with smoking.

Wills et al. (1995) found that in families with low levels of parental education there were also lower levels of parental support, lower self-esteem, less perceived control, more frequently reported life events and lower levels of academic and behavioural competence. Statistical modelling of the results found no direct effect of parental education on cigarette and substance use among teenagers, but rather the effect of low parental education was mediated through lower levels of parental support and academic competence, which in turn were related to less behavioural competence and higher levels of negative life events and affiliation with substance using peers. This would suggest that lack of parental support in these households make these young people more susceptible to smoking.

Robinson and Klesges (1997) found that African-American children reported stronger social support and feelings of success than European American children. Rebellious, risk-taking behaviour was less common among African-American children. Conversely, European American children reported more friends who smoked, perceived the prevalence of smoking to be higher, rated cigarettes more positively and viewed cigarettes as more accessible. However, there is a need for more detailed research on ethnic differences in the social meaning of smoking.

GENDER DIFFERENCES IN ADOLESCENT SMOKING

A series of reports in the 1990s indicated that in many western societies more girls than boys were adopting cigarette smoking (e.g. Gliksman et al., 1989; Miller and Plant, 1996). Much of the research which has focused on this issue has concentrated on investigating the gender differences in the perceived value of smoking as a means of controlling weight. Adolescence is the period when girls become particularly aware of society's emphasis on body size. Teenage girls are particularly concerned about being overweight. Smoking would seem to be one strategy used to control weight gain.

Charlton (1984) in a large survey of British teenagers found that girls were much more likely to agree that smoking controlled weight. In a survey of a large sample of US students in seven to ten grades (11–15 years old), French et al. (1994) found a strong association between various measures of dieting and smoking among girls but not among boys. Girls who reported symptoms of eating disorder, had tried to lose weight, feared weight gain or reported a strong desire to remain thin were more likely to report smoking. In the USA there is evidence that this belief is particularly pronounced among white girls. Heckler (1985) found that obesity is more acceptable in black culture and Camp et al. (1993) found in a survey of teenagers that white girls more frequently agreed that smoking helps control body weight.

The character of social activities enjoyed by teenage boys and girls needs also to be considered. While boys often remain involved in sport and other organized activities, girls become more involved in less organized activities. In a survey of English teenagers (Murray et al., 1983; Swan et al., 1990) it was found that smoking was more common among girls who got involved in such activities. Smoking for these girls had a variety of positive social meanings including affirming social bonds with their peers, asserting their adult status and regulating time.

SMOKING CESSATION

It was estimated that the proportion of ever-smokers who quit smoking increased from 30% in 1965 to 45% in 1987 (US Public Health Service, 1990). However, the speed of the decline seemed to have slowed in the 1990s, leading Pomerleau (1997) to suggest that smoking rates will finally asymptote at about 15–20%. The evidence from both clinical (e.g. Hjalmarson et al., 1994) and community (e.g. COMMIT, 1995) smoking cessation programmes have been disappointing. This has led to attempts to develop a more sophisticated understanding of the process of giving up smoking.

Biological aspects of cessation

It is well established that cessation of smoking by regular smokers leads to a variety of symptoms such as irritability, difficulty concentrating, anxiety, restlessness, increased hunger, depressed mood and a craving for tobacco (Stolerman and Jarvis, 1995). Important evidence that these withdrawal symptoms are due to the loss of nicotine is the finding that it is relieved by administration of nicotine but not of a placebo (Jarvis et al., 1982).

This evidence has led to the development of a variety of pharmacologic products aimed at aiding smoking cessation. These are designed to deliver nicotine directly rather than through cigarette smoke. The techniques developed include nicotine chewing gum, nicotine transdermal patch and a nasal spray or inhaler. Evidence from clinical trials has demonstrated that these techniques are effective (Stolerman and Jarvis, 1995). However, the individual smoker must still have the psychological motivation to use them.

Psychological aspects of cessation

Possibly the most influential psychological model which has been used in the design of health behaviour change programmes over the past decade has been the transtheoretical model of change (TTM). Historically, this model evolved from a review of over 300 theories of psychotherapy which led to the identification of 10 distinct 'processes of change' underlying these theories. In a subsequent empirical study with a sample of smokers the participants reported that they used different change processes at different times. From this work DiClemente and Prochaska (1982) developed a series of *stages of change*. Subsequent research has provided more detail on the character of the different stages and the processes which connect them. The following are the most important components of the model:

1 *Processes of change*: the character of the ten change processes and possible intervention strategies derived from them are summarized in Table 8.1. These processes have been grouped into two broad blocks: experiential (consciousness raising, self-re-evaluation, emotional arousal, environmental re-evaluation and social liberation); behavioural (counter-conditioning, stimulus control, reinforcement management, self-liberation and helping relationships).

2 *Stages of change*: the TTM argues that change proceeds through six stages which are summarized in Table 8.2. DiClemente and Velicer (1997a) note that initially they viewed *relapse* as a separate stage but now they accept that relapse is a process of reversal which can occur between any two stages. The experiential processes are more active in the early stages and the behavioural processes in the later stages. Of particular importance to interventions is the recruitment of smokers who are at the *action stage* and the ability to support recent ex-smokers during the *maintenance stage*.

3 *Decisional balance*: this reflects the relative weighting of the pros and cons of changing the behaviour. As the individual moves from the precontemplation stage to the preparation stage the pros of smoking decrease and the cons of smoking increase.

4 *Self-efficacy*: this concept, derived from Bandura (1977), is the situation-specific confidence which individuals have that they can maintain behaviour change. Individuals at the preparation stage have a higher sense of situational self-efficacy than those at the precontemplation stage.

5 *Temptation*: this is a measure of the intensity of urges in a particular situation to engage in a particular behaviour. The most common types of tempting situations are negative affect, positive social situations and craving. It is posited that situational temptation to smoke is higher among those at the precontemplation stage compared with those at the preparation stage.

Admittedly, much of the research in the development of this model was based on restricted samples. More recent research has considered its relevance to larger samples of smoking and found support. Fava et al. (1995) found general support for the stages and processes of change in a large sample of smokers. Further, they found using the three measures of

TABLE 8.1 **Processes of change: definitions and representative interventions identified in the transtheoretical model (DiClemente, 1993, p. 102; reproduced with permission)**

Process	Definition	Interventions
Consciousness raising	Increasing information about self and the problem	Observations, confrontations, interpretations, bibliography
Self-re-evaluation	Assessing how one feels and thinks about oneself with respect to the problem behaviours	Value clarification, imagery, corrective emotional experience, challenging beliefs
Self-liberation	Choosing and committing to act or believing in ability to change	Decision-making therapy, New Year's resolutions, logotherapy techniques, commitment enhancement techniques
Counter-conditioning	Substituting alternatives for anxiety related to addictive behaviours	Relaxation, desensitization, assertion, positive self-statements
Stimulus control	Avoiding or counter stimuli that elicit problem behaviours	Restructuring one's environment (e.g. removing alcohol or fattening foods), avoiding high-risk cues, fading techniques
Reinforcement management	Rewarding oneself or being rewarded by others for making changes	Contingency contracts, overt and covert reinforcement, self-reward
Helping relationships	Being open and trusting about problems with people who care	Therapeutic alliance, social support, self-help groups
Emotional arousal	Experiencing and expressing feelings about one's problems and solutions	Psychodrama, grieving losses, role playing
Environmental re-evaluation	Assessing how one's problems affect the personal and physical environment	Empathy training, documentaries
Social liberation	Increasing alternatives for non-problem behaviours available in society	Advocating for rights of the repressed, empowering, policy interventions

temptation suggested by Velicer et al. (1990) that those in the preparation stage were least tempted in positive/social and habit/addictive situations, but were more tempted in negative/affective situations.

Recently, the transtheoretical model has been extended by Dijkstra et al. (1997) who argued that smokers could be classified into four stages: immotives, precontemplators, contemplators and preparers. As their name

TABLE 8.2 **Stages of behaviour change (DiClemente and Velicer, 1997a, p. 39)**

Stage	Definition
Precontemplation	Not intending to take action in the foreseeable future
Contemplation	Intending to change
Preparation	Intending to take action in the immediate future and have developed a plan of action
Action	Have made specific overt modifications
Maintenance	Working to prevent relapse but do not apply change processes as frequently as in the Action stage
Termination	Behaviour change successful and individuals have zero temptation and 100% self-efficacy

implies, immotives are stuck in the sense that they are planning never to quit, at least in the short term. They also differed from precontemplators in the sense that they anticipated fewer long-term health consequences of smoking and had lower levels of self-evaluation. Precomtemplators do have some desire to quit but not within the next six months.

In a large follow-up study of a large sample of smokers Dijkstra et al. (1998) found further evidence of these four stages. In a factor analysis they identified four pros of quitting: long-term health consequences; short-term health consequences; social consequences; self-evaluative consequences. They identified one con of quitting factor which emphasized various perceived negative consequences; and two quitting self-efficacy factors – one with regard to social situations and one regarding emotional situations. The precontemplators scored higher on all the pros of smoking and on the measures of self-efficacy. When these smokers were followed up three and 14 months later their initial stage of readiness was found to predict their subsequent smoking behaviour.

This model has attracted considerable debate. For example, Bandura (1997) argued that the stages are artificial and do not reflect the constant process of change. Prochaska and Velicer (1997b) replied that the stages are not a substitute for processes but rather an attempt to specify when and where such processes operate. Farkas et al. (1996) found in a prospective study that a measure of addiction was a better predictor of subsequent smoking status than the initial stage of change. Prochaska and Velicer (1997a) argue that they were not comparing like with like and that 'the stage effect has been replicated in over 60 a priori predictions and has failed in about six conditions'. Most researchers (e.g. Stockwell, 1996) feel that despite various criticisms the model is still a useful and robust approach to understanding smoking cessation. There have been various attempts to deepen the theoretical base of the model. For example, Sutton (1996) argued that intention to quit is the central construct in the model and that in previous work (e.g. Sutton, 1989) it had been found that intention coupled with motivation (based upon the theory of reasoned action) predicted smoking cessation.

However, there still remains the concern that this model does not sufficiently consider the social aspects and meaning of smoking.

SOCIAL ASPECTS OF CESSATION

Smoking activities are deeply embedded in everyday social activities and
a society where cigarettes are widely promoted. Cessation attempts must
take these aspects into consideration. Hughes (1996) in his review of
trends in smoking cessation programmes refers to the increasing social
gradient in smoking prevalence. Smoking is becoming confined to people
who live in poor circumstances. As Graham (1987) has demonstrated, for
many of these people smoking serves an immediate positive social
function such that attempts to discourage smoking among them will be
resisted.

Stewart et al. (1996) conducted a qualitative study of the role of smoking
in the lives of such women and their perception of smoking cessation
efforts. In reading the interviews with these women Stewart et al. felt that
'due to the pressing nature of the participants' life circumstances, many
were caught in a daily struggle for survival. Consequently, the long-term
benefits of quitting had little relevance for them'. Smoking was a means of
coping with the 'stress, chaos and crises in their lives'. In addition, the
women felt that they did not have the self-esteem and confidence to quit
smoking. For example, one woman said:

> Probably the one thing that would help me [quit] would be to get my self-esteem
> back up . . . because it is not good any more like it used to be like. Like I diet so
> many times in my life and that doesn't help, and everything else. Like I feel bad
> about myself. There are a lot of different situations in my life, and maybe if I
> could better myself in certain ways . . . if I could get a job. (Stewart et al., 1996,
> p. 48)

As regards attempts to quit, the women mentioned lack of social support
from their partners, immediate family and friends. They felt that if there
were peer support groups it would be easier to quit. In concluding, Stewart
et al. emphasized the disempowering character of the immediate social
circumstances of these women's lives. Smoking cessation efforts need to
provide not only social support but attempt to enhance the women's sense
of control and mastery through changing their social conditions.

Finally, social attempts at smoking cessation need also to address the
widespread promotion and availability of cigarettes. Reviews of the impact
of national bans on cigarette advertising in countries like Norway and
Finland found they were followed by a decline in tobacco consumption
(Laugesen, 1992). As regards availability, Townsend et al. (1994) has shown
a clear association between the price of cigarettes and consumption. Further,
it was smokers from lower incomes who were most affected by increase in

the price of cigarettes. They suggest that social policy should take into consideration the effect on their living conditions of increased price.

PSYCHOLOGICAL THERAPY FOR SMOKERS

Smoking places a massive burden on physical and social well-being, industrial productivity and the health-care systems. Mortality shows a dose–response relationship to consumption so that stopping smoking before middle age produces almost the same life chances as never smoking at all (Doll et al., 1994). Quitting smoking or, if that is impossible, reducing cigarette consumption, add years to the lives of young or middle-aged smokers. There are also substantial social and socio-economic benefits when measured across the entire population. Thus, quitting smoking or, if that fails, reducing smoking, are both viable targets for a smoking cessa-tion programme. In order to achieve these aims, it is necessary for an intervention to help smokers to control both their physical and *psycho-logical dependency* on smoking.

There has been increasing interest in the development of *cognitive-behavioural therapy (CBT)* for the control and change of smoking and other health-related behaviours. These therapies can be delivered as a brief intervention of one or more sessions to groups of smokers who feel moti-vated to stop. An example of a brief intervention using CBT is the *QUIT FOR LIFE (QFL) Programme* developed by one of the authors (Marks, 1993). This encourages a steady reduction of cigarette consumption over seven to 10 days followed by complete abstinence. The QFL programme is delivered in several alternative ways: as a group therapy of 10 sessions, as a self-help programme following a single, one-hour group therapy session, or on the internet.

The programme uses a spectrum of 30 cessation methods in a self-help package consisting of a handbook, a cassette tape by the BBC's Nick Ross, reduction cards, a progress chart and other necessary materials. QFL is an adaption of a system originally called the 'Isis Programme' in New Zealand where it has been running almost continuously since 1979 (Sulzberger et al., 1979). The Isis Programme integrated new and existing methods which, from a reading of the scientific and self-help literature, looked particularly promising. A preliminary observational study suggested that the therapy could be particularly effective when delivered to groups of self-referring smokers (Marks, 1992).

A list of the methods used in the self-help version of QFL is presented in Table 8.3.

Unlike many other behavioural methods, QFL requires a *gradual reduction* of cigarette consumption over a period of seven to 10 days. A set of targets is used directed towards a 50% reduction each day (see Figure 8.2). Of particular importance is the objective of increasing the smoker's confidence or *self-efficacy* that he/she will be able successfully to make

TABLE 8.3 **Methods used in the Quit for Life programme (Marks, 1993, p. 18)**

Method
1   Rubber Band around Pack
2   Record all Smoking on Card
3   Program 1 (NURD)
4   Enter Daily Total on Chart
5   Program 2 (WE STD)
6   Keep a List of Triggers
7   Program 3 (EASY)
8   Meditation
9   Imagery Rehearsal
10 Program 4 (NOGO)
11 The Eight Steps and Sensitization
12 Music Therapy (Side 2, Cassette)
13 Win the Argument Game
14 List Personal Benefits of Quitting
15 Plan Your D-Day
16 Try Different Ways of Relaxing
17 Rehearse Positive Programs
18 Increase Activity
19 Distraction
20 Buddy System
21 Willpower
22 Learn Fail-Safe Procedure
23 Develop Eating Control Programme
24 Rules for Snacking
25 Develop Exercise Programme
26 Relapse Prevention
27 Assert Non-Smokers' Rights
28 Deconstruct Tobacco Advertising
29 Develop Time Management Skills
30 Prevent Stress and Strain

the change from smoker to non-smoker. The attempt to increase self-efficacy is a persistent and unflagging component of the therapy. It is essential that the therapist is constantly vigilant concerning the smokers' ever more creative rationalizations as they proceed towards their 'D-Day', the first 24-hour period when they are not expected to smoke at all.

One of QFL's techniques, Program 1, is illustrated in Figure 8.3. This is based on a *computer metaphor* employed to explain what happens when a person becomes a smoker, maintains the habit for a period of time and then decides to quit smoking. Smokers are invited to imagine that the brain is a sophisticated biological computer, or 'biocomputer', consisting of the central nervous system (or hardware) and learned 'programs' (or software) which enable the nervous system to process information. In order to quit smoking, it is suggested that the smoker must alter the software or 'programming' which currently dictates that the smoking must occur in a fixed and uncontrollable way. Following the computer metaphor, it is necessary

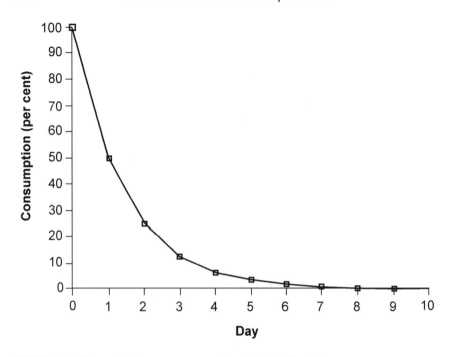

FIGURE 8.2 ***The reduction targets set by the Quit for Life programme***
(Marks, 1993, p. x)

for the smoker to eliminate his/her pro-smoking software and to restore
non-smoking software. This requires a period of systematic *re-program-*
ming, achieved by systematic repetition during the act of smoking when
pro-smoking 'programs' are replaced by new, anti-smoking 'programs'.

The smoker repeats a four-line 'program', coded by the mnemonic NURD,
while actively smoking a cigarette. As the 'program' is repeated over and
over while engaged in smoking activity, the pleasure of smoking and desire
to smoke are expected to diminish. This technique is one of 30 methods
available within QFL and is not expected to be sufficient on its own.

The QFL Programme is divided into two stages, reduction and relapse
prevention. It is further subdivided into 10 sections spaced across a period
of three months. The reduction stage begins on a Tuesday and finishes on
the following Monday, Tuesday, Wednesday or Thursday with D-Day.
Relapse prevention begins immediately after D-Day and continues formally for 12 weeks. This stage incorporates an element of nicotine replacement therapy (NRT) during a period of 10–30 days immediately following
D-Day when smokers may use a low dosage level gum or patch.

The self-help version of QFL was evaluated in a randomized controlled
trial (Marks and Sykes, 1999). For this evaluation, the control treatment
consisted of a self-help booklet constructed by health promotion specialists,
typical of the treatment provided by health promotion clinics: *Stopping*

Program 1

As I smoke I realise that:

this cigarette is giving me no satisfaction	N
this is an unpleasant experience	U
this cigarette its making me feel rotten	R
I am losing the desire to smoke	D

The following condensed version may help you to memorize Program 1:

NO SATISFACTION	N
UNPLEASANT	U
ROTTEN	R
DESIRE	D

From now on, you should smoke every cigarette deliberately and with concentration

FIGURE 8.3 **A diagram illustrating the use of one of Quit for Life's techniques, program I (Marks, 1993, p. 22)**

Smoking Made Easier (SSME, Health Education Authority, 1992). SSME recommends a staged approach: preparing to stop; stopping; staying stopped. The preparation stage consists of clarifying reasons for stopping, becoming ready to stop and making an action plan. Smokers are recommended to stop suddenly, using their will power, rather than gradually to reduce their consumption. Smokers are advised to choose a day, get support from family and friends, review the action plan the day before, plan a suitably healthy reward for the end of the first day, and another for the end of the first week and the first month. They should plan ahead and telephone the national Quitline, GP or health centre for further help. Once smokers have stopped they are exhorted to think positively, take care, not play games, keep busy, avoid alcohol, refuse or break up cigarettes offered by friends, learn to relax and to ring the national Quitline for advice and support.

In this trial, 260 participants were recruited from the North London population and randomly allocated to one of the two treatment conditions (Marks and Sykes, 1999). Outcome measures consisted of point abstinence rates and reduction scores at three, six and 12 months. The abstinence and reduction data were validated using breath carbon monoxide readings. The 12-month follow-up revealed that 23 of 116 (19.8%) QFL participants were abstinent, compared to six of the 104 (5.8%) contactable control participants. Ten (8.6%) of the QFL group but none of the control group reported a reduced consumption. Approximately one in four (33/116 or 28.4%) of participants were abstinent or had a significantly lower cigarette consumption 12 months after the treatment compared to one in 17 (6/104 or 5.8%) of the controls. These changes in tobacco consumption were validated by breath carbon monoxide readings.

Cost effectiveness is the cost of delivering each treatment to a sufficient number of self-referred smokers to produce one quitter/reducer. CBT may be delivered in a most cost-effective way to groups of smokers in one or more therapy sessions. The evidence suggested that QFL is at least three times more cost effective than the control treatment. In 1998 in the UK, nicotine replacement therapy (NRT) costs approximately £180 per smoker to deliver a 10% chance of abstinence at one year post-treatment. In this case, CBT would be 26 times more cost effective than NRT. CBT is more efficacious and cost effective than other treatments by quite a large margin. Brief psychological therapies have the potential to make a significant impact on the prevalence of smoking if the means can be found for disseminating therapies in an efficient and cost-effective manner.

FUTURE RESEARCH

1   There is still limited understanding of the social basis of cigarette smoking among young people. In particular, there is a need for increased understanding of the social, ethnic and gender variations in the dynamics of smoking among young people.

2 Although there have been a plethora of prevention programmes there is still a need for greater understanding of the variations in their effectiveness.
3 More research on the influence of tobacco advertising on the uptake of smoking in young people is necessary in those countries where advertising is still permitted. The evidence is likely to be significant in eventually gaining a worldwide advertising ban.
4 Randomized controlled trials of psychological therapy in comparison to nicotine replacement therapy are necessary to determine their relative efficacy and cost effectiveness.

SUMMARY

1 About 25% of adults in most western societies smoke, while prevalence rates in the developing world are higher than this and are increasing.
2 The prevalence of smoking varies according to sex, social class and ethnicity.
3 Biological, psychological and social factors contribute to the continued popularity of smoking.
4 The uptake of smoking occurs largely in adolescence and appears to be associated with parental and peer smoking.
5 Various social and psychological factors are of prime importance in understanding the recruitment of teenagers to smoking.
6 Most smokers report difficulty in quitting the habit.
7 The transtheoretical model describes the process of quitting as progressing through several stages.
8 Social, biological and psychological factors are involved in the process of smoking cessation.
9 Brief psychological therapies for smoking cessation based on cognitive-behavioural therapy are showing considerable promise, with high efficacy and cost effectiveness. Health-care systems need to build their capacity and infrastructure to increase public access to psychological therapies.
10 The final solution to tobacco control will require a multi-level approach consisting of economic, political, social and psychological interventions.

KEY TERMS

acquisition
action stage
addiction
cessation
cognitive-behavioural therapy (CBT)
conditioned stimuli
contemplation stage

cost effectiveness
cross-sectional studies
longitudinal designs
maintenance stage
physical dependence
precontemplation stage
preparation stage
prevalence

psychological dependency
QUIT FOR LIFE (QFL)
   Programme
relapse
relapse prevention
self-efficacy
sensation seeking

socio-economic status (SES)
stages of change
theory of planned behaviour
   (TPB)
theory of reasoned action
   (TRA)
transtheoretical model

9 SEXUAL BEHAVIOUR AND EXPERIENCE

Discourses of sexuality . . . are often inadequate, contradictory and fragmented, leading to unexpected and often undesirable (and undesired) material outcomes whether they meet in Parliament, the classroom, the parking lot or in bed. (Ingham and Kirkland, 1997, p. 173)

OUTLINE

This chapter provides a brief overview of the study of sexual behaviour in its historical context. This is followed by a discussion of five contemporary approaches to the study of sexual behaviour. These revolve around a behavioural, physiological, cognitive, relationship and meaning-centred focus. These approaches are illustrated and critically evaluated.

SEXUALITY AND HEALTH

Sexual behaviour is of relevance to health psychologists for a number of reasons. First, sexual behaviour constitutes an excellent example of the mind–body interdependence which interests health psychologists. Second, sexual behaviour can have very serious physical and emotional consequences such as pregnancy or sexually transmitted disease. These consequences have major implications for the individual's psychological well-being. Third, sex is very much a social activity during which two (or more) individuals' minds and bodies meet. Since much of health psychology's theorizing is derived from social psychology, health psychologists can be expected to have something to say about sexual interaction. However, the study of sexual behaviour (or *sexology*) has historically been a truly interdisciplinary field in which epidemiologists, medics, sociologists, psychologists and other social scientists work together.

SEXOLOGY IN HISTORICAL CONTEXT

Preceding the nineteenth century a purely moral approach to sex prevailed. A fundamental divide between reproductive and non-reproductive sexuality meant that reproduction was the only moral justification for sexual indulgence. Any non-reproductive sexual act was referred to and condemned as 'sodomy'. (The meaning of this term has changed since then and it is now taken to refer to anal sex.) However, it was acknowledged that sodomy could potentially be practised by anyone. Thus, it was perceived as a temporary aberration rather than a stable preference or even identity.

A more medico-scientific approach to sex emerged in the nineteenth century. This involved classification of sexual practices into 'normal/ healthy' and 'abnormal/unhealthy'. It also meant that sexual practices were seen as an expression of an inherent trait rather than as aberrant behaviours. As a result, sexual types were constructed: the 'homosexual', the 'sadist', the 'masochist', the 'transvestite', and so forth. Krafft-Ebbing's *Psychopathia Sexualis* (1887) presents an inclusive catalogue of sexual perversions.

Weeks (1985) shows how the emergence of sexology in the nineteenth century served to replace religious authority (and its concern with morality) with scientific authority (and its concern with disorder and abnormality). However, the new focus upon sexual pathology and perversion was based upon widespread assumptions of what constituted 'normal sexuality'. Sexologists studied those individuals who did not conform to sexual norms and expectations. They did not explore what 'ordinary people' actually did sexually, that is, to what extent norms and expectations actually reflected the lived reality of people's sexual lives.

It was only in the middle of the twentieth century that researchers began to describe, rather than judge or pathologize, human sexual behaviour. Scientists became aware that there was a profound lack of knowledge about normal *sexuality*. On the basis of their literature review preceding their large-scale survey of Americans' sexual behaviours, Kinsey and his colleagues noted that 'the scientific understanding of human sexual behaviour was more poorly established than the understanding of almost any other function of the human body' (Kinsey et al., 1953, p. 5). Even today, the study of sexual behaviour remains one of the most underdeveloped fields in the human sciences (Johnson and Wellings, 1994).

Researchers have used a range of different methods in order to find out about people's sexual experience. The following five approaches have informed contemporary psychosexual research:

1   Sex surveys.
2   Laboratory studies of sexual activity.
3   Study of social cognitions about sex.
4   Study of sexual experience within close relationships.
5   Study of sexual meanings.

SEX SURVEYS

Sex surveys adopt a behavioural focus. They employ large-scale survey methods in order to provide descriptive data about a population's sexual habits. Sex surveys usually involve the collaboration of researchers from a variety of disciplines, including epidemiologists, sociologists and psychologists. Sex surveys are designed to obtain descriptive information about a particular population's sexual behaviour patterns. Such surveys typically include questions about age at first sexual intercourse, frequency of intercourse, sexual orientation, use of contraception and number of sexual partners. Many surveys also include questions about sexual knowledge (e.g. about reproductive processes and sexually transmitted diseases) and attitudes (e.g. towards pre-marital sex, homosexuality and monogamy).

Sex surveys tend to be carried out in response to particular social and/or medical concerns of the day such as teenage pregnancies in the 1970s or the spread of the human immunodeficiency virus (HIV) in the 1980s. The choice of questions included in any one survey tends to reflect such concerns. For example, earlier studies (e.g. Kinsey et al., 1948) are characterized by a focus upon the experience of orgasm, whereas later studies (e.g. Johnson et al., 1994) are more interested in the use of sexual risk reduction strategies (i.e. contraception and *safer sex practices*).

Sex surveys are a relatively recent development. Before 1950 few attempts had been made to chart sexual practices in a representative sample of the general population. In the nineteenth and early twentieth century, the study of sexuality was largely confined to what was defined as deviant sexuality. The short history of sex surveys is characterized by two attributes. First, researchers have encountered strong resistance from powerful individuals and institutions who argued that sexual surveys were socially and/or morally inappropriate. For example, Kinsey et al. (1948, 1953) encountered public and official opposition to their study of sexual behaviour of American males and females, including the threat of lawsuits by a medical association. Forty years later, in Britain, Johnson et al. (1994) were refused government funding of a large-scale study into sexual attitudes and lifestyles on the grounds that it was intrusive and unacceptable to the British people. Similarly, in the USA, funding for a national survey of sexual behaviour was withdrawn in response to government opposition to the nature of the survey (Aldhous, 1992).

The second characteristic of sex surveys is that they tend to reveal much greater diversity of sexual practices than is publicly acknowledged within the culture. It appears that human sexual behaviour is extremely flexible and that people have a wide range of sexual preferences, both with regard to the types of activities as well as the frequencies with which these are engaged in.

The Kinsey reports (Kinsey et al., 1948, 1953)

Alfred Kinsey, an American biologist, instigated the first mass sex survey. He and his colleagues analysed data obtained from interviews with 5,300 males and 5,940 females. These interviews covered between 300 and 500 questions about a wide range of aspects of sexual experience, lasting an average of two hours each. The interview agenda covered social and economic data, marital histories, sex education, physiological data, masturbation, nocturnal dreams, heterosexual and homosexual histories, as well as animal contacts. The researchers also examined materials such as sexual diaries, calendars, personal correspondence, scrapbooks and photographic collections, paintings and drawings as well as toilet wall inscriptions and graffiti.

Kinsey and his colleagues were keenly aware of the lack of scientific studies of human sexuality. The reason for this absence was, they felt, the 'almost universal acceptance, even among scientists, of certain aspects of [sexual] behaviour as normal, and of other aspects of that behaviour as abnormal' (1948, p. 7). By contrast, Kinsey et al. set out to chart sexual practices without preconceptions as to what was rare or common, normal or abnormal, or socially or morally desirable or significant.

The findings vindicated their non-judgemental approach. They found high incidences and considerable frequencies of sexual behaviours which had been publicly regarded as both rare and abnormal. For example, they found that more than a quarter of teenage males had experienced homosexual activity to the point of orgasm. Of male teenagers and men in their early twenties 10% had had extramarital homosexual contacts. By the age of 45, 37% of men and 13% of women had experienced homosexual activities to orgasm. Again, challenging socio-moral assumptions, Kinsey et al. found that by the age of 40, 50% of males and 26% of females had experienced extramarital coitus.

Overall, the authors stressed the similarity of the sexual response in men and women, particularly with regard to the physiological nature of orgasm. The major difference between males and females was that women's sexual activities were more discontinuous, that is they were found to occur more sporadically. In addition, there was more variability of sexual behaviour within the female sample, that is women were found to differ more among themselves than did men.

Evaluation of the Kinsey survey

REPRESENTATIVENESS
Even though the Kinsey sample included a wide range of participants varying in age, education levels, religious affiliation, occupation and geographical location, there was a bias towards better educated, professional, urban Protestants living in the northeastern quarter of the USA. In addition, the authors excluded data obtained from black respondents on the grounds that this sample (n = 934) was too small to allow for comparative analysis of sub-groups within the sample, as well as from white women who had served prison sentences (n = 915) on the grounds that this sample's responses were so different from the rest that its inclusion would have distorted the data.

Participants were selected on the basis of their membership of social groups such as religious, community, professional or trade union groups or educational or penal institutions. Although this method of sampling avoided problems associated with the low response rates in probability sampling as well as self-selection biases associated with recruiting volunteers, it excluded individuals who were not members of social groups. This is a major problem in a sex survey since social group membership may well be a relevant variable in the determination of sexual practices. In addition, many respondents came from single-sex institutions such as colleges, prisons and the armed forces which may have inflated the reporting of homosexual encounters (Tatchell, 1996).

RELIABILITY AND VALIDITY

Reliability and validity checks were carried out on the data by way of internal consistency assessments and re-takes of histories (reliability), as well as comparisons of spouses' and male–female data (validity). Both reliability and validity were found to be good, with the exception of a large discrepancy found between males' and females' reportings of pre-marital coitus.

The interviews were conducted by the four researchers themselves. Kinsey alone carried out 57.6% of the interviews, taking 7,036 sexual histories. This ensured that interviewers were well trained as well as experienced. However, the four researchers were all male which almost certainly influenced the responses obtained from the female respondents. Recent researchers noted that both male and female respondents prefer to be interviewed about sexual matters by a female interviewer (e.g. Johnson et al., 1994).

Gender-specific issues such as women's fear of rape were handled in a way which feminist critics would soon come to see as grossly inadequate. However, later sex surveys by feminists such as *The Hite Report* (Hite, 1976) had their own specific problems with sampling and interpretation (see Segal, 1994).

National survey of sexual attitudes and lifestyles (Johnson et al., 1994)

The emergence of the sexually acquired infection with the human immunodeficiency virus (HIV) and its continuing spread throughout the 1980s and 1990s highlighted the importance of scientific studies of sexual lifestyles and attitudes. Johnson et al. (1994) carried out the largest representative sample survey of sexual lifestyles ever undertaken in the British population. A total of 18,876 women and men aged between 16 and 59 took part in the survey. Its objectives were twofold:

- to provide data which would increase understanding of transmission patterns of HIV and other sexually transmitted diseases (epidemiological focus);

- to obtain information which would be helpful in designing effective HIV/AIDS education interventions (psychosocial focus).

In order to obtain relevant data, a team of trained interviewers administered the questionnaire within the context of a personal interview. Core questions about sexual lifestyle covered age at first intercourse, numbers of heterosexual and homosexual partners, frequency of sex, experience of different practices and so on. Attitudinal questions, administered to a subsection of the sample (n = 5,000), assessed attitudes towards premarital, extramarital as well as homosexual sex. Particularly sensitive questions were administered by way of self-completion booklets.

FINDINGS

Premarital sex was found to be near universal. Median age of first intercourse decreased from 21 for the oldest female cohort to 17 for the youngest. The ages were 20 and 17 for male cohorts respectively. Non-use of contraception at first intercourse has declined steadily over recent decades, and was reported by fewer than a quarter of women and a third of men aged 16 to 24. However, when intercourse occurs before age 16, contraception is much less likely to be used.

Condoms are the most popular form of contraceptive at first intercourse. There was marked variability between individuals in the number of sexual partners they reported. Over the last five years, 65.2% of men and 76.5% of women reported no or only one sexual partner, whereas 1% of men reported more than 22 partners and 1% women more than 8. The range of the number of sexual partners over a lifetime was zero to over 4,500 for men and zero to 1,000 for women. Men and women in the 16 to 24 age group reported the greatest number of sexual partners, with 11.2% of men and 2.5% of women of this age group reporting over 10 partners in the last five years. The authors argue that the large difference between numbers of heterosexual partners reported by males and females suggests that there must be some overreporting by men and/or underreporting by women.

Extramarital sex: 4.5% of married men and 1.9% of married women reported more than one sexual partner in the last year. Among single people the figures were 28.1% of men and 17.5% of women. Among cohabiting couples, 15.3% of men and 8.2% of women reported more than one sexual partner in the last year. Among separated, widowed or divorced respondents aged 25 to 44, the figures were 40% of men and 16% of women.

When taking into account the last five years, multiple partnerships were reported by 68% of men and 50% of women in the sexually active 16 to 24 age group. Monogamy was prevalent in the 45 to 59 age group (90% of men; 95% of women). For the entire sample, 15.1% of men and 7.6% of women reported concurrent relationships over the past five years.

Married people are far more likely to be monogamous. Cohabiting individuals' behavioural patterns are more similar to those who are single. Only 43.1% of cohabiting men and 59.9% of cohabiting women reported monogamy over the past five years, with 24.3% of men and 12.7% of women reporting concurrent relationships.

Frequency of sexual activity: the median frequency reported by women aged 20 to 24 was five times in the last four weeks and for women aged 50 to 54 it was once in the last four weeks. Men aged 25 to 29 reported having sex five times in the last four weeks, whereas for 50- to 59-year-old men it was twice. The highest median frequency of any age group was five times in the last four weeks.

Homosexual behaviour: 92.3% of men and 95.1% of women reported exclusively heterosexual experiences. Some kind of homosexual experience was reported by 6.1% of men and 3.4% of women, with 3.6% of men and 1.7% of women reporting genital contact. Within the last two years 1.4% of men and 0.6% of women had had a same-sex partner. Men aged 35 to 44 were most likely to have had homosexual experience at some time in their lives (over 7%). Exclusively homosexual behaviour appears to be rare. Over 90% of both men and women who reported same-sex partners also had experience of heterosexual sex.

Contraception (see Figures 9.1 and 9.2): 17.6% of sexually active men and 21.1% of sexually active women reported no use of contraception in the past year. Contraceptive use decreases with age. The three contraceptive methods most commonly relied on are the pill (28.8% of women and 30.4% of men); the condom (25.9% of women and 36.9% of men); and male or female sterilization (23.3% of women and 21.4% of men). Even though contraceptive use increases with numbers of partners, a substantial minority of those with five or more partners in the past year do not report condom use (39.6% of women and 28.4% of men). This gives cause for concern within the context of HIV transmission.

Sexual attitudes (see Table 9.1): pre-marital sex is fully accepted by three-quarters of respondents, whereas extramarital sex was considered to be always or mostly wrong by nearly 80% of the sample. Monogamy was seen to be the appropriate form of sexual expression within a regular relationship for all age groups. The views of men and women were most divided on the question of casual sex: 35.8% of men regarded one-night stands as always wrong, whereas 62.45% of women were of this view.

Views on homosexuality were the most polarized within the sample: 70.2% of men and 57% of women regarded sex between two men to be always or mostly wrong (64.5% and 58.8% for sex between two women). One in five respondents believed homosexual sex to be not wrong at all. Abortion is seen as always or mostly wrong by 37.7% of women and 33.1% of men.

Overall, those without experience of a particular behaviour are more likely to perceive it as being wrong.

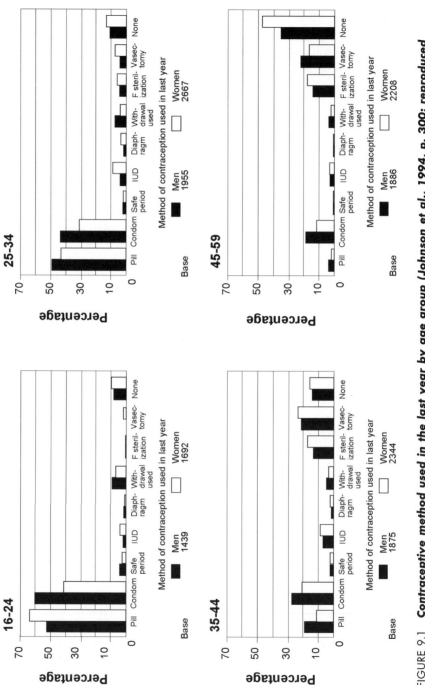

FIGURE 9.1 **Contraceptive method used in the last year by age group (Johnson et al., 1994, p. 300; reproduced with permission)**

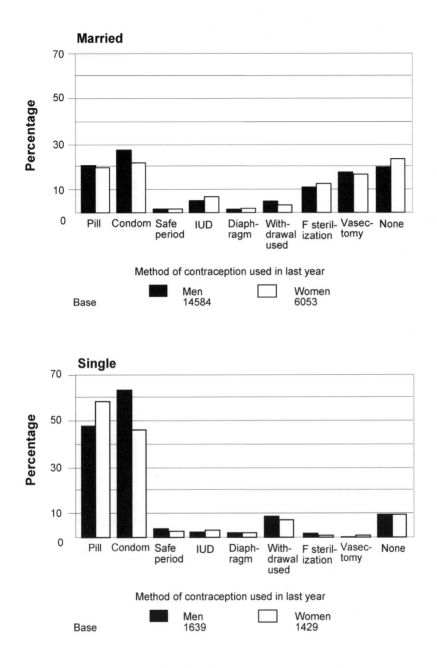

FIGURE 9.2 **Contraceptive method used in the last year by marital status (Johnson et al., 1994, p. 301; reproduced with permission)**

TABLE 9.1 **Views on selected sexual relationships and encounters (Johnson et al., 1994, p. 237; reproduced with permission)**

	Always wrong (%)	Mostly wrong (%)	Sometimes wrong (%)	Rarely wrong (%)	Not wrong at all (%)	Base
Sex before marriage						
Men	4.7	3.5	10.7	7.6	73.5	8,242
Women	5.8	5.0	15.0	8.1	66.1	10,191
Sex outside marriage						
Men	47.0	31.8	17.4	1.1	2.7	8,155
Women	55.6	28.6	13.7	0.9	1.2	10,258
Sex outside live-in relationship						
Men	35.8	32.7	19.6	2.9	9.0	8,083
Women	46.9	32.7	14.3	1.6	4.5	10,210
Sex outside regular relationship						
Men	28.9	30.6	22.5	5.5	12.6	8,082
Women	37.6	32.4	18.2	3.9	8.1	10,178
One-night stand						
Men	35.8	21.7	17.8	6.5	18.2	8,067
Women	62.4	20.3	10.6	2.3	4.4	10,251
Sex between two men						
Men	60.8	9.4	6.4	3.9	19.6	8,022
Women	46.2	11.7	10.7	6.1	25.3	9,629
Sex between two women						
Men	51.2	13.3	9.2	4.7	21.7	7,951
Women	46.6	12.2	10.2	5.9	25.0	9,667
Abortion						
Men	16.8	16.3	41.2	8.0	17.7	7,642
Women	17.7	19.9	42.1	7.5	12.8	9,458

Evaluation of the survey

REPRESENTATIVENESS

The survey obtained a systematic probability sample of around 20,000 people using the postcode address file as the sampling frame, with an acceptance rate of 71.5% (among households where an eligible respondent could be identified and interviewed). The postcode address file is the file of current postal addresses kept by the Royal Mail and is likely to have generated a reasonable level of representativeness of the general population. However, this method of sampling excludes the homeless and its use of self-completion booklets required literacy among participants (Stanley, 1995).

VALIDITY AND RELIABILITY

Administration of the survey was preceded by a two-year development period during which qualitative work, piloting as well as a feasibility study were carried out. This ensured that terminology, question formulation and ordering, accuracy of memory and willingness to disclose intimate information using different formats (e.g. face to face, self-completion booklet, showcards) had been thoroughly explored before the questionnaire was designed. However, the choice of formal as opposed to vernacular terms to refer to sexual organs and practices, together with precise, technical definitions, though preferred by both interviwers and respondents, may have inhibited (some) respondents in their talk. The use of formal terminology tends to locate the interview within a clinical context, with its connotations of health and illness. This may have led respondents to simplify and homogenize their answers.

In addition, some of the questions included in the survey need to be placed within their social and legal contexts. For example, anal intercourse is illegal in England and Wales which almost certainly affected respondents' willingness to report it. Similarly, the widespread condemnation of homosexual sex identified by the survey highlights the hostile social environment within which reporting of such activities is still taking place. This may have resulted in underreporting of experiences of same-sex contacts.

General problems with sex surveys

There are a number of methodological problems shared by all sex surveys. First, people who agree to answer questions about their sexual habits, whether verbally or in writing, may well differ systematically from those who refuse. As a result, sex surveys do not access the full range of sexual information potentially available and are therefore limited in their representativeness.

Second, strong sociocultural norms and expectations with regard to sexuality may lead respondents to misrepresent their sexual habits and experiences. It has been suggested that women downplay the nature and extent of their sexual activities, whereas men exaggerate theirs (e.g. Kinsey et al., 1948, 1953; Johnson et al., 1994).

Third, the identity of the interviewer may influence the validity of the responses obtained. For example, Davis (1992) suggests that around one-third of gay men would not disclose their sexual identity within the context of a large-scale sex survey. Thus, social desirability biases may limit the validity of a sex survey's findings.

Fourth, another concern with validity arises from the formulation of the questions included in a sex survey. There appears to be a great deal of ambiguity surrounding sexual terminology. For example, Hunt and Davis (1991) found that the term 'sexual partner' was interpreted in many different ways by their gay male respondents, ranging from describing someone with whom genital contact had occurred (48.2%) through someone orgasm had been experienced with (25.9%), to someone with whom a bed has been shared, naked (22.3%). Furthermore, the range of response options including presuppositions implied by question formulations (e.g. 'Have you ever' as opposed to 'When did you last') can restrict information obtained.

Fifth, the choice of sexual vocabulary, such as vernacular or medical, provides a discursive context within which sex is considered. Such a context may facilitate the revelation or withholding of particular types of information. Kinsey et al. (1953) drew attention to the ways in which terminology can shape responses obtained: 'Syphilis may be rare . . . although bad blood may be more common . . . The existence of prostitutes in the community may be denied, although it may be common knowledge that there are some females and males who are hustling' (pp. 61–2).

Finally, it is important to remember that sex surveys can only provide information about that which they have been designed to measure. As a result, those sexual practices and experiences which the researchers were not aware of at the design stage of the survey cannot emerge through the survey. Thus, sex surveys using forced choice or multiple choice questions preclude the identification of the unexpected. Such procedures therefore provide, at best, an incomplete account of the sexual experiences of the population. In addition, because the extent of biasing is unknown, the statistical reliability of the findings remains uncertain.

LABORATORY STUDIES OF SEXUAL ACTIVITY

These studies adopt a physiological focus. They aim to obtain accurate descriptions of the physiological processes which accompany human sexual activity. Laboratory studies of the *human sexual response* constitute a later development in the scientific study of human sexuality. Such studies involve observation and physiological measurement of the body's response to sexual stimulation. This requires the presence of researchers and/or measurement instruments during human sexual activity. Levels of arousal and other physiological changes can be measured by attaching electrodes to relevant body parts as well as insertions of micro-cameras into the body.

One major problem with laboratory studies of this type is the inevitability of obtaining biased (i.e. non-random) samples of participants through self-selection: the willingness to be observed during masturbation or intercourse is unlikely to be randomly distributed across the population.

Study of the human sexual response (Masters and Johnson, 1966)

The best-known laboratory study of the human sexual response is Masters and Johnson's (1966) pioneering work. They set out to answer two general questions:

- What happens to the human male and female as they respond to effective sexual stimulation?
- Why do men and women behave as they do when responding to effective sexual stimulation? (Masters and Johnson, 1966, p. 10).

The authors recruited 382 women and 312 men, most of whom were between 21 and 40 years of age, to take part in their study. Over a period of 11 years, they observed more than 10,000 sexual response cycles in the context of various forms of masturbation and heterosexual penetrative intercourse. A major focus of the study was orgasmic expression in women.

FINDINGS

Masters and Johnson identified the sexual response cycle, a sequence of stages of sexual arousal taking the individual from initial excitement to a plateau phase, on to orgasm and finally into a resolution phase. Male and female sexual response cycles were found to follow the same pattern. Masters and Johnson provide detailed descriptions of physiological changes in various organs which take place during the sexual response cycle. They observe that the human physiological reaction to elevated levels of sexual tension is not confined to the primary or secondary organs of reproduction. Rather, there is evidence of sexual arousal throughout the entire body. This takes the form of widespread vasocongestion as well as myotonia (muscle tension). For both women and men, physiologically more intense orgasms were obtained through masturbation. For women, orgasms were also more frequently and more consistently produced through self-manipulation.

Evaluation of the study

The major shortcoming of the study revolves around the selection of participants. Masters and Johnson's sample was drawn from the academic community associated with a large university hospital complex in the USA. In addition, a precondition for participation in the study was 'facility of sexual responsiveness' and 'essential normalcy of the reproductive viscera' (ibid., p. 12). This meant that those people who did not experience what the researchers' defined as 'normal' or 'healthy' sexual responses were not included in the study. Furthermore, participants had to have a 'positive history of masturbatory and coital orgasmic experience' (ibid., p. 311). In this way, the researchers prejudged the very categories they set out to investigate.

Masters and Johnson's research questions refer to responses to 'effective' sexual stimulation. Tiefer (1995), in a thorough deconstruction of Masters and Johnson's sexual response cycle, draws attention to the inherent circularity of the research questions: 'effective' sexual stimulation is defined as that which induces the complete sexual response cycle. As a result, the researchers' finding that the cycle is a universal human phenomenon follows almost by definition. It appears that rather than researching what actually happens to a wide range of men and women during sex, Masters and Johnson demonstrated what could be achieved by a selected group of enthusiastic volunteers who fulfilled a set of predetermined criteria. Thus,

Masters and Johnsons's sexual response cycle constituted a physiological potential rather than a universal reality.

However, it is important to remember that an awareness of a human potential, of what it is possible to do or experience, can motivate people to bring about a desired change in their performance and/or competency. Masters and Johnson did not claim that their sample was representative of the general population or that most people did experience the complete sexual response cycle regularly. Rather, they saw their research as a way of providing information which could help individuals to learn how they could gain access to sexually satisfying experiences (see also Masters and Johnson, 1966). However, what they described was restricted to two particular kinds of sexual activity – penetrative heterosexual intercourse and masturbation.

General problems with laboratory studies

Laboratory studies of sexual activity lack *ecological validity*. This is to say, the social and physical environment within which sexual activity takes place in these studies is so far removed from its real-life context that their findings must be treated with caution. In addition, individuals who agree to take part in such studies are unlikely to be representative of the general population. They are likely to be more confident about their sexual performance and more liberal in their sexual attitudes than those who do not take part.

On a more conceptual level, it has been argued that laboratory studies of sexual behaviour contribute to the *medicalization* of sexuality (e.g. Tiefer, 1995). Here, sex is perceived as a simple and universal *biological* function which all humans are expected to perform in the same way. If they do not, treatment is required in order to re-establish what is considered to be the natural sexual response. As a result, those whose sexual experiences do not match the 'healthy human sexual response' identified in the laboratory are diagnosed as suffering from sexual dysfunction. This can undermine people's acceptance and enjoyment of alternative forms of sexual pleasure such as those which do not involve penile penetration. Ironically, just as homosexuality was removed from the Diagnostic and Statistical Manual for the categorization of mental illness in the early 1970s, sexual dysfunctions have been defined as psychiatric disorders by the American Psychiatric Association.

STUDY OF SOCIAL COGNITIONS ABOUT SEX

These studies use questionnaires in order to measure beliefs, attitudes and perceptions held by individuals. They are theoretically informed and aim to predict sexual behaviour, or at least behavioural intentions.

Psychological studies of sexual behaviour are often informed by theories and methods associated with the social cognition framework (see Chapters 10 and 11). Such studies seek to obtain information about individuals' cognitions concerning sex and to explore the relationship between these cognitions. For example, researchers may investigate the extent to which a person's attitudes towards particular sexual practices allows us to predict their intention to engage in these practices. Cognitive studies of sexual behaviour frequently set out to test existing models of health behaviour within the context of sexual health. They are usually motivated by the desire to understand why people take sexual risks, such as unprotected sexual intercourse and how such risk taking may be reduced. In recent years, numerous studies of young people's knowledge and attitudes regarding HIV/AIDS and safer sex practices have been published. One study of this type is described in Chapter 11 (Rise, 1992).

Researchers using social cognition models within the context of sexual risk taking argue that people's sexual behaviour is mediated by attitudes rather than knowledge. This is said to explain why widespread awareness of the mechanisms for sexual transmission of HIV has not led to a correspondingly widespread change in sexual practices. A number of social cognition models have been used to study contraceptive use and/or safer sex practices. The health belief model, protection motivation theory and the theory of reasoned action/planned behaviour have all informed studies of sexual risk taking (e.g. Van der Velde and Van der Pligt, 1991; Terry et al., 1993; Abraham and Sheeran, 1994).

It appears that the theory of reasoned action is better suited to account for sexual choices than the health belief model or protection motivation theory because social norms and interpersonal considerations play an important role in sexual behaviour (e.g. Rise, 1992; Sheeran and Abraham, 1995). Also, it has been found that more positive attitudes towards condoms are associated with greater past and/or intended future use of condoms (e.g. Catania et al., 1989; Pleck et al., 1990).

Example of a study of social cognitions about sex: attitudes and experiences of heterosexual college students

Campbell et al. (1992) investigated the relationship between attitudes towards condom use and actual condom usage. Participants were 393 unmarried, heterosexual American undergraduate students, aged 18 to 24. A 20-item measure of condom attitudes assessed beliefs about condoms in four domains: comfort and convenience, protective effectiveness, interpersonal aspects and sexual sensation (see Table 9.2 for all items). There was also a single item measure of general attitudes towards condoms ('How positive or negative are your personal feelings about you/your partner using a condom?'). Students with sexual experience (66%) were also asked whether they had ever used condoms and whether they had

TABLE 9.2 ***The condom attitudes items (Campbell et al., 1992, p. 278;***
reproduced with permission)

Comfort and convenience
 1   Condoms are easy to obtain.
 2   Condoms are expensive. (R)
 3   An advantage of condoms is that you don't need a prescription from a physician.
 4   It would be embarrassing to be seen buying condoms in a store. (R)
 5   Modern condoms are reasonably comfortable for the man to wear.
 6   Condoms are messy and awkward to dispose of. (R)
 7   Condoms are convenient and easy to carry.
 8   Condoms are difficult for a man to wear. (R)

Efficacy
 9   The use of a condom is an effective method of birth control.
10   Condoms are not effective because they often break easily. (R)
11   The use of a condom is a good way to prevent getting sexually transmitted diseases.
12   Condoms do not offer reliable protection. (R)

Interpersonal
13   Discussing the use of a condom with a partner can improve communication.
14   The use of a condom might be embarrassing to me or to my partner. (R)
15   The peace of mind gained from using a condom can improve a sexual relationship.
16   Interrupting lovemaking to use a condom spoils the mood. (R)

Sexual sensation
17   A problem with condoms is that they reduce sexual stimulation. (R)
18   The use of a condom can actually enhance sexual pleasure for both myself and my
     partner.
19   Sex doesn't feel as natural with a condom. (R)
20   The thinking ahead that is needed when using a condom adds excitement to lovemaking.

Scores for items followed by (R) were reversed before computing means, so that higher scores
indicate more positive attitudes. Each item was rated on a 5-point scale from 1 (strongly
disagree) to 5 (strongly agree). Items were presented in a random order without headings.

used condoms the last time they had sex. Intention to use condoms in the
future was measured by asking the subjects to assess the likelihood of
them using condoms with a hypothetical new sexual partner.

The results showed that women had more positive attitudes towards
condoms. Men were concerned about the effects of condoms on sexual
sensation. Women worried more about getting a sexually transmitted
disease from a new partner. For women, past condom use was best predicted by positive general attitudes towards condoms as well as less
negative attitudes towards the effects of condom use on sexual sensation.
For men, feeling positive about the interpersonal aspects of condom use as
well as having positive general attitudes towards condoms were significant predictors of past condom use. For both women and men, intended
condom use in the future was best predicted by positive general attitudes
towards condoms and positive views about the interpersonal aspects of
condom use. In addition, those students who had had fewer sexual
partners were more likely to say that they would use a condom in the
future. For women only, increased worry about contracting a sexually

TABLE 9.3   **Regression analyses predicting expected use of a condom with a new partner (Campbell et al., 1992, p. 284)**

Predictor	Women			Men		
	Standard coefficient	SE	t	Standard coefficient	SE	t
Single-item condom attitude rating	.15	.03	4.82***	.27	.04	6.22***
Comfort and convenience	.06	.11	0.52	.12	.11	1.05
Efficacy	.09	.07	1.31	.06	.10	0.64
Interpersonal	.21	.08	2.82**	.35	.10	3.66***
Sexual sensation	.10	.05	1.88	-.02	.08	-0.28
Worry about disease	.24	.04	5.74***	.03	.05	0.62
Number of sexual partners	-.13	.03	-4.19***	-.11	.04	-2.77**
	$R^2 = .53$			$R^2 = .50$		
	$F = 19.05***$			$F = 17.23***$		

* $p < .05$. ** $p < .01$. *** $p < .001$.

transmitted disease (STD) also predicted intention to use condoms in the future (see Table 9.3).

This study suggests that there are gender differences regarding attitudes towards condoms as well as condom usage. Women and men worry about different aspects of condom use and have different reasons for using (or not using) condoms in the past. However, intended condom use was associated with similar considerations for both men and women.

General problems with the cognitive approach

There are several problems with the cognitive approach. Studies measuring social cognitions about sexual practices rely upon questionnaires which presuppose that cognitions are stable entities residing in people's heads. They do not allow for *contextual variables* which may influence social cognitions. For example, an individual's attitude towards condom use may well depend upon the sexual partner with whom they anticipate having sexual contact. It may depend upon the time, place, relationship and physiological state (e.g. intoxication) within which sex takes place. As a result, the attempt to predict actual behaviour from decontextualized attitude measures is unlikely to succeed. In addition, it can be argued that sexual intercourse, which is a joint activity, is less likely to be shaped by individual cognitions than solitary health behaviours such as flossing or exercising. The variance in sexual behaviour controlled by social cognition variables is generally modest (around 20% or less) (e.g. Abraham et al., 1992; Campbell et al., 1992).

Another problem with the cognitive approach is its reliance upon self-reports for past sexual behaviour. As discussed within the context of sex surveys, there are limitations to the accuracy with which individuals report their own sexual practices. Most social cognition studies measure behavioural intentions rather than actual behaviour. This may generate higher correlations between attitude and behavioural measures. However, the relationship between intentions and behaviours is by no means a direct one. More research needs to explore the ways in which intentions are/are not translated into behaviours.

Finally, the vast majority of social cognition studies of sexual behaviour has focused upon young heterosexual people and gay men, who are perceived to be most vulnerable to HIV infection. However, Johnson et al. (1994) found that people who are divorced, widowed or separated report higher rates of risky sexual practices than those who are single. Also, most heterosexual women in the USA suffering from STD infections have become infected by a partner with whom they have had a long-term involvement (Reiss, 1991). Thus, there is a need for studies of older and/or cohabiting/married heterosexuals' sexual decision-making.

STUDY OF SEXUAL EXPERIENCE WITHIN CLOSE RELATIONSHIPS

Studies of this type use questionnaires, interviews, diaries and observation in order to investigate sexual experience and behaviour in close relationships. They explore how a sexual relationship begins, how partners come to have sex for the first time and how sexual partners communicate about sex. They also assess frequency of sex and sexual satisfaction within different types of relationship. Finally, a relationship focus allows researchers to examine the role played by sexuality within a close relationship and its part in relationship processes such as conflicts or break-ups.

Sexual satisfaction within a particular relationship has been the focus of many studies. For example, Kurdek (1991b) found no significant differences between sexual satisfaction among gay, lesbian, heterosexual unmarried and heterosexual married couples. Greeley (1991) observed that sexual satisfaction was higher for younger respondents. However, earlier studies suggested reverse trends, with married adults enjoying sex more in middle age than in the earlier years of their marriage (e.g. Brown and Auerback, 1981), and lesbians being more satisfied with the sex in their relationships than heterosexual women (e.g. Coleman et al., 1983). Frequency of sex within a relationship has consistently been found to be associated with sexual satisfaction (e.g. Blumstein and Schwartz, 1983; Greeley, 1991).

It is important to bear in mind that such associations do not imply a causal relationship between the two variables. For example, it is possible that both frequency of sex and sexual satisfaction are not directly causally related, and that another third variable (such as overall relationship satisfaction or conflict) gives rise to both. There appears to be a positive association between sexual satisfaction and relationship satisfaction (Sprecher and McKinney, 1993). Greeley (1991) suggests that sexual satisfaction is a contributing factor to marital happiness. This claim is compatible with the finding that sexual problems play an important role in relationship break-ups for both heterosexual and homosexual couples (e.g. Cleek and Pearson, 1985; Kurdek, 1991a). However, it is possible that post break-up studies artificially increase sexual explanations of the break-up. This could occur either because people remember deteriorating sexual relations most vividly and therefore identify them as the cause of the break-up, or because references to sexual problems are a socially acceptable way of accounting for relationship break-ups.

General problems with the study of sexual relationships

Studies of sexual behaviour with a relationship focus have generated a wide range of findings which can help to answer questions about sex in close relationships. However, there are a number of conceptual and methodological problems with such studies. First, key variables used in such studies are based upon rather narrow definitions at best, and remain unspecified at worst. For example, 'satisfaction' is a key concept investigated by numerous studies. It is either left undefined and assessed with a single question, such as 'How much sexual satisfaction do you get out of your sexual relationship?' (e.g. Greeley, 1991), or it is measured with multi-item scales which assess different dimensions of sexual satisfaction, such as levels of fun, closeness, excitement or enjoyment experienced (e.g. Hudson et al., 1981; Pinney et al., 1987). In both cases, participants respond on Likert-type scales (e.g. from 1 'very much' to 5 'not at all').

The problem with both types of measures is that they do not allow researchers to find out what 'sexual satisfaction' may mean to respondents, and how these meanings may vary between groups and across contexts. For example, it may be that women and men differ in their definitions of 'satisfaction' or even in the extent to which they perceive sexual satisfaction to be important. For some people, satisfaction may be synonymous with having experienced an orgasm, whereas for others it may signify feeling happy and relaxed, or it may simply mean that they do not experience any sexual dysfunctions. Furthermore, questionnaire items tend to ask very general and abstract questions, divorced from particular contexts. This obscures the fact that people's sexual relations take place within specific settings and that these may give rise to varied sexual experiences which cannot be evaluated globally. For example, the item 'Sex is fun for my partner and me' (from Hudson et al., 1981) does not allow a respondent to report great sex on Sunday mornings and lousy sex on weekday nights. Quantitative averaging of such varied experiences does not capture the diverse range of experience of an individual's sex life.

Sprecher and McKinney (1993) note a number of further shortcomings with this research method. They draw attention to the fact that the widely used questionnaire based self-report measures are vulnerable to self-report bias (under and overreporting) as well as memory problems. Much of what participants report may be reconstructions of events based on culturally available sexual scripts rather than accurate reports of what actually occurred. Another problem concerns generalizability. Much of the research has been conducted with predominantly white, middle-class, heterosexual volunteers, often college students. Findings cannot, therefore, be generalized to other sociocultural groups.

STUDY OF SEXUAL MEANINGS

Since the mid-1980s, studies of sexual behaviour have emerged which focus upon *sexual meanings*. This approach is informed by a social constructionist perspective. Here, the objective is to understand what people do by reference to the *meanings which they attribute to their actions*. Thus, a focus upon sexual meanings moves beyond attempts to describe sexual habits or to identify and measure relevant cognitions about sex. Instead, these studies aim to understand how people 'make sense' of their sexual experience and how people's lay theories about sex inform their sexual practices.

For example, Plummer (1996) argues that people's sexual experiences are organized by culturally available 'sexual stories'. These change throughout history and thus allow different sexual meanings to be constructed at different times. Sexual stories provide interpretive frames which make particular sexual identities available. For example, the identity of the gay man/lesbian woman becomes available in the 'coming out' story. Social constructionist studies of sexuality do not aim to reveal the truth about people's sexual lives; rather, they explore how people construct or make a particular sense of their sexual lives. In order to do this, researchers examine transcripts of semi-structured interviews, letters, diaries and/or naturally occurring conversations about sex.

The continuing spread of AIDS has prompted social constructionist researchers to use these methods in order to find out why even those people who know the facts about the transmission of HIV are still reluctant to adopt safer sex practices. For example, Holland et al. (1991) found that young heterosexual women's conceptualization of sex in terms of love and romance informed their choice of sexual practices, namely penetrative sex without condoms. The authors suggest that condoms carry symbolic meanings which undermine their use in heterosexual love relationships.

Similarly, Ingham et al. (1992) observed that a social construction of sex as something mystical and uncontrollable allows people to justify and accept unsafe sexual behaviour as 'natural'. Safer sex practices are not easily compatible with the notion of 'passion' which involves the loss of control and rationality. From within this discourse, a sexual encounter which requires planning and negotiation is perceived as premeditated and therefore not consistent with love and passion (Willig, 1994). Discursive constructions of sexual activity, safer sex and contraception position those who use such constructions in particular ways, and these positionings have implications for sexual practice (Willig, 1998). For example, Harden and Willig (1998) found that young people's discursive construction of contraceptive methods was gendered which meant that they were reluctant to use the male pill or the female condom.

The social constructionist approach is *anti-essentialist* because it conceives of human sexuality as a set of potentialities which may or may not be realized within differing social, cultural and historical contexts. In this sense, sex is not 'a natural act' (see Tiefer, 1995), but rather a social practice.

Example of a study of sexual meanings: constructions of condom use and their implications for sexual practice

Willig (1995) investigated the question: How is 'condom use' discursively constructed by heterosexual adults, and how do such constructions position speakers? The participants were 14 heterosexual British adults aged 22 to 56. Semi-structured interviews included questions about the nature of HIV disease, its social and political implications, as well as the participants' personal feelings about HIV and AIDS. Interview transcripts were analysed using Parker's (1992) version of the discourse analytic method. This facilitated a systematic exploration of the ways in which the discursive object, in this case 'condom use', was constructed in the texts.

The results showed that participants framed their accounts of condom use almost exclusively within a marital discourse. This discourse constructs marriage and its equivalent, the 'long-term relationship', as a condition incompatible with condom use. Participants' assumptions regarding the nature of such relationships – as safe by definition and based upon trust – together with their awareness that relationships can 'go wrong', positioned them in such a way that they felt unable to request safer sex from their partners. In order to communicate to their partner that they could be trusted not to engage in extramarital sex, respondents took the risk of unprotected sex with their partner.

It was concluded that 'condom use' was constructed as incompatible with the 'long-term relationship'. The practice of unprotected sex fulfils a communicative function which is perceived to be instrumental to the maintenance of long-term sexual relationships.

General problems with the study of sexual meanings

Studies of sexual meanings tend to be based on small samples. Semi-structured interviewing is a very time-consuming method of data collection. Transcription of one hour's worth of interviewing takes approximately 10 hours. As a result, it is hard to tell how widespread discursive constructions identified in any one study might be within a particular population. Small-scale qualitative studies of this kind can only demonstrate the availability and contextualized deployment of particular discursive formations. Ideally, studies of sexual meanings ought to be conducted in clusters, whereby constructions identified in one study are then traced in further studies with different respondents, in different contexts. For example, marital discourse described by Willig (1995) may or may not be available to gay men and lesbians. It may or may not be deployed in naturally occurring conversations. However, most studies of sexual meanings remain isolated and consequently fail to integrate findings from diverse research projects.

At a more theoretical level, it has been argued that social constructionist approaches to the study of sexuality fail to address questions about bodily and psychic processes and their role in the constitution of sexual desire (e.g. Segal, 1994). By exclusively focusing on discourse and representation, the body is reduced to a blank slate inscribed with meanings.

FUTURE RESEARCH

1   It has been pointed out (e.g. Giddens, 1992) that social scientific research, as it reaches the public domain, establishes a new context within which social behaviour takes place. This is to say, social research feeds back into and so changes that which it studies. For example, survey information about sexual habits can change social and moral norms in society. Johnson et al. (1994) note that the Kinsey reports sold 200,000 copies in the first two months after publication and that their exposure of sexual diversity in the USA had major implications for sexual ethics. Thus, the study of sexual behaviour ought to include studies which reflexively explore the ways in which the dissemination of research findings are taken up and assimilated into their surrounding culture.

2   Segal (1994) draws attention to sexology's failure to theorize desire. She argues that a pervasive biological reductionism has informed studies of sexual behaviour which have consequently sought to measure orgasms and sexual satisfaction, thus reducing the sexual encounter to 'joint masturbatory homework' (ibid., p. 113). Little research has attempted to find out what attracts us sexually to particular others, how sex acts are experienced subjectively, what constitutes sexual pleasure, the role of fantasy in desire, what 'sexual passion' means and how it comes about. More work is needed which addresses these questions.

3   Tiefer (1995) expresses her concern about the colonization of sex research by a discourse of health and illness. She shows how the location of sexuality within the conceptual model of health and the health industry constitutes a particular choice. This, she argues, results in the construction of sexual activity as a fundamentally biophysical phenomenon which is studied by those who are trained medically rather than

those who know about culture and learning. Tiefer suggests that this serves to individualize sexual problems, such as impotence, by locating their cause within the sufferer's body, rather than to explore their social causes. Further work is needed which attempts to link individual sexual experiences to wider social discourses about sex and sexuality.

SUMMARY

1 In the nineteenth century a medico-scientific approach to sexuality emerged in the industrialized world. This approach involved the classification of sexual behaviours as either 'healthy' or 'unhealthy' and the construction of sexual types. Research was generally prescriptive and much of sexology pathologized those whose sexual preferences deviated from social norms.

2 Contemporary psychosexual research focuses on the behavioural, physiological, cognitive, relationship and meaning centred dimensions of human sexual experience. Research methods include large-scale surveys, laboratory experiments, questionnaire studies and interviews.

3 Sex surveys adopt a behavioural focus. They employ large-scale survey methods in order to provide descriptive data about a population's sexual habits. They reveal much greater diversity of sexual practices than is publicly acknowledged within the culture.

4 Methodological problems with sex surveys include limited representativeness of samples, strong effects of desirability bias and demand characteristics, ambiguity surrounding sexual terminology and the limitations of closed question formats.

5 Laboratory studies of sexual activity adopt a physiological focus. They aim to obtain accurate descriptions of the physiological processes which characterize human sexual activity. Laboratory studies allow researchers to identify and map human potential rather than to describe habitual behaviours.

6 Laboratory studies of sexual behaviour have limitations. They lack ecological validity. Participants are unlikely to be representative of the general population. In addition, laboratory studies tend to reduce human sexual experience to its purely biological function.

7 Cognitive studies of sexual behaviour are concerned with people's beliefs about and attitudes towards sexual matters. They tend to utilize social cognition models in order to study the relationship between cognitions about sex and sexual behaviour.

8 Social cognitions control only around 20% of the variance in sexual behaviour. Cognitive studies are limited because they do not consider the role of contextual variables, the importance of negotiation with a sexual partner and the mechanisms by which behavioural intentions are translated into actual behaviour.

9 Some studies of sexual experience have a relationship focus. They explore the role of sex in close relationships. Sexual satisfaction within close relationships has been the object of many studies. There appears to be a positive association between sexual satisfaction and relationship satisfaction.

10 Methodological problems with relationship focused studies include narrow definitions of key variables, self-report bias, reliance on participants' memories of events and limited generalizability due to restrictive sampling.

11 Recent studies of sexual experience have focused on the sexual meanings people attribute to their actions. Diverse and changing sexual 'stories' and 'discourses' have been identified and their implications for sexual practice have been explored.

12 Studies of sexual meanings can be criticized for their limited generalizability due to small sample sizes and their heavy dependence upon context. In addition, their exclusive focus on discourse and representation ignores the materiality of the human body and its role in sexual experience.

KEY TERMS

anti-essentialist view of human sexuality

biological reductionism

ecological validity

human sexual response cycle

medicalization

safer sex practices

sex survey

sexology

sexual meanings

sexuality

10 EXERCISE AND ACTIVITY

By equating certain types of behaviour with virtue and others with vice, the secular moralists . . . threaten to undermine the critical task of educating the public in general . . . to the very real dangers lurking behind everyday behavioural choices.
(Howard M. Leichter, 1997, pp. 360–1)

OUTLINE

Recent years have seen an increased interest in, and promotion of, exercise and physical activity. This chapter reviews the background to this 'exercise movement' and summarizes the evidence linking exercise with health. It considers the wide variations in participation in exercise and the social and psychological factors associated with these variations. It then considers the varying meanings of exercise within different social contexts and strategies which have been used to promote greater participation.

PHYSICAL ACTIVITY AND HEALTH

The enthusiasm for physical activity as a means of promoting health has waxed and waned over the centuries (MacAuley, 1994). In ancient China exercise was encouraged as a means of improving health. Similarly, in ancient Greece gymnastic activity was considered a means of treating disease. However, others urged caution about exaggerating the benefits of physical activity. For example, the famous physician Galen (c. 200–129 BC) who had so much influence on western medicine, cautioned against excessive involvement in athletics:

> While athletes are exercising their profession, their body remains in a dangerous condition, but when they give up their profession they fall into a condition more powerless still; as a fact, some die shortly afterward; others live for a little time, but do not arrive at old age . . . Athletes live a life quite contrary to the precepts of hygiene, and I regard their mode of living as a regime far more favourable to illness than to health.

The advent of scientific medicine in the last century provided an opportunity to clarify the value of sustained exercise on health. For example, John Morgan (1873) studied the longevity of oarsmen who participated in the Oxford and Cambridge boat race. He found that their life expectancy was 2.2 years longer than that predicted from contemporary life tables, thus disputing popular wisdom of those days. Since then there have been sustained attempts to identify the relative contribution of physical exercise on physical and mental health.

Physical health

The past ten years has seen a steady accumulation of evidence confirming the benefits of exercise in terms of physical health. Initially, this evidence was correlational but now there is experimental evidence. A meta-analysis of the contribution of physical activity to the prevention of coronary heart disease concluded that physically inactive individuals are twice as likely to develop coronary heart disease (CHD) as are people who engage in regular physical exercise (Berlin and Colditz, 1990).

In 1991 the American Centers for Disease Control and Prevention and the American College of Sports Medicine convened a panel of experts to review the evidence. In their report (Pate et al., 1995) they concluded that 'cross-sectional epidemiologic studies and controlled, experimental investigations have demonstrated that physically active adults, as con-trasted with their sedentary counterparts, tend to develop and maintain higher levels of physical fitness' (p. 403). They added that research demonstrated a clear link between physical fitness and reduced risk for several chronic diseases. In view of this evidence, they recommended that 'every US adult should (daily) accumulate 30 minutes or more of moderate-intensity physical activity that can be accumulated in relatively short bursts' (p. 404).

This recommendation emphasized that it was not necessary to engage in prolonged vigorous exercise. Rather 'gardening, housework, raking leaves, and playing actively with children can also contribute to the 30-minute-per-day total if performed at an intensity corresponding to brisk walking. Those who perform lower-intensity activities should do them more often, for longer periods, or both'. These recommendations emphasized the importance of what could be described as everyday physical activity which was within the grasp of most people rather than the more intense vigorous activity often rejected by lay people.

A more recent report provided further evidence of the beneficial effects of regular moderate physical activity. In 1996 the US National Institute of Health convened a consensus conference to review the evidence. The subsequent report (NIH Consensus Development Panel, 1996) concluded that 'accumulating scientific evidence indicates that physical inactivity is a major risk factor for CVD'. They recommended similar guidelines as the previous report and affirmed that 'intermittent or shorter bursts of activity (at least 10 minutes), including occupational, non-occupational, or tasks of daily living, also have similar cardiovascular and health benefits if per-formed at a level of moderate intensity (such as brisk walking, cycling, swimming, home repair, and yard-work) with an accumulated duration of at least 30 minutes per day' (p. 23). Further, they suggested that the low

TABLE 10.1 *Physical activity and mental health: biological mechanisms (based on Plante and Rodin, 1990)*

- Increases in body temperature due to exercise result in short-term tranquillizing effects.
- Regular exercise facilitates stress adaptation because the increase in adrenal activity increases streroid reserves which can then be available to counter stress.
- Reduction in resting muscle activity potential after exercises helps release tension.
- Exercise enhances neurotransmission of noradrenaline (norepinephrine), serotonin and dopamine leading to improved mood.
- Exercise leads to the release of endogenous morphine-like chemicals synthesized in the pituitary gland leading to enhanced feelings of well-being.

rate of participation in regular physical activity may be due to the misperception that vigorous continuous activity was necessary to reap the health benefits. They caution that risk of injury increases with increased intensity and frequency of activity.

The recommendation that moderate exercise provides a protective effect continues to be debated. For example, Winnett (1996) argues that intensity of exercise, not frequency or duration, is the critical variable associated with fitness, strength and health outcomes.

Mental health

As with physical health the past decade has seen a series of reports of experimental studies confirming the beneficial effects of exercise on mental health. Glenister (1996) reviewed eleven randomized controlled trials (RCTs) which produced evidence for a positive effect of exercise on patients suffering from depression.

Plante and Rodin (1990) reviewed the impact of physical activity on the psychological health and well-being of non-clinical populations. They concluded that exercise improves mood and well-being and reduces anxiety, depression and stress. They also reported positive effects on self-concept, self-esteem and self-assurance. They suggested five biological mechanisms underlying the connection between physical activity and mental health which are detailed in Table 10.1.

However, it is not simply biological processes but also psychological processes which explain the connection between exercise and mental health. Plante and Rodin (1990) suggest eight psychological processes that may be involved in explaining the improvement in mood following exercise (Table 10.2).

Although, most contemporary evidence confirms the beneficial psychological effects of even limited physical exercise (Gauvin and Spence, 1996), there is still contrary evidence from laboratory research. For example, in a carefully designed study Gauvin et al. (1997) found no mood-enhancing effects of an acute exercise programme administered to a sample of physical inactive participants. They argued that much of the previous research was conducted using volunteers whereas their study focused on a sedentary

TABLE 10.2 *Physical activity and mental health: psychological processes (based on Plante and Rodin, 1990)*

- Improved physical fitness provides people with a sense of mastery, control, and self-sufficiency.
- Exercise is a form of meditation that triggers an altered and more relaxed state of consciousness.
- Exercise is a form of biofeedback that teaches exercisers to regulate their own autonomic arousal.
- Exercise provides distraction, diversion, or time out from unpleasant cognitions, emotions, and behaviour.
- Since exercise results in the physical symptoms associated with anxiety and stress (e.g. sweating, hyperventilation, fatigue) without the subjective experience of emotional distress, repeated pairing of the symptoms in the absence of associated distress results in improved psychological functioning.
- Social reinforcement among exercisers may lead to improved psychological states.
- Exercise may act as a buffer, resulting in decreased strain caused by stressful life events.
- Exercise competes with negative affects, such as anxiety and depression, in the somatic and cognitive systems.

population. They concluded that future research should consider the effect of exercise on different populations.

PARTICIPATION IN PHYSICAL ACTIVITY

Modern lifestyle

We discussed in Chapter 6 the evidence that human beings traditionally required considerable energy expenditure for survival. In ancient times the hunter-gatherer needed to expend substantial energy on a regular basis so as to ensure access to food and shelter (Park, 1988). This need to expend substantial energy remained well into this century and continues in much of the developing world. However, the rapid increase in technology in industrialized societies over the past generation has led to a much more sedentary lifestyle. This decline in physical activity is a consequence of the reduced need for energy expenditure in all spheres of human life, including work, transportation and home maintenance. Technological developments in entertainment have reduced the role of physical activity in leisure time (King, 1994). In describing the implications of this change in lifestyle Blair et al. (1992) remarked that 'humans evolved to be active animals and may not be able to adapt well to the modern sedentary lifestyle'.

The steady accumulation of evidence linking physical activity with improved health status has been followed by a 'fitness boom' in the 1970s and 1980s (King, 1994). Superficially, it would seem that involvement in physical activity and exercise has increased substantially in popularity. For example, in the 1980s, approximately $8 billion was spent by Americans annually on sportswear, $1 billion on exercise equipment, $1 billion on athletic footwear and $50 million on books about exercise and diet (Legwold, 1995). However, results of large national surveys indicate that most adults in industrialized societies still prefer a sedentary lifestyle although with substantial regional variations.

In the USA the National Health Interview Survey estimated that only 14% of American adults engage in vigorous physical activity 3 or more times a week, a further 24% engage in moderate physical activity 5 or more times per week and 24% engaged in no physical activity (National Center for Health Statistics, 1994b). The Behavioral Risk Factor Surveillance System (USCDCP, 1993) estimated that 58% of American adults are sedentary (i.e. engage in no or irregular leisure-time activity). The Canadian Health Promotion survey (1990) also found a limited involvement of adults in leisure-time physical activity (LTPA). They classified just under half of Canadian adults (48%) as high LTPA (at least 15 minutes vigorous exercise at least three times per week).

In Britain, according to the *Allied Dunbar National Fitness Survey* (1992) only 20% of women and 30% of men are taking sufficient physical exercise to benefit their health. Booth et al. (1993) found in a survey of over 4,000 Australian adults that 22% were physically inactive, 40% exercised occasionally and only 38% exercised regularly and planned to continue. Admittedly an indication of the popular belief in the benefits of exercise was apparent in the finding that about half of those who did not exercise regularly were thinking about doing some. Scandinavian countries would seem to have a more active lifestyle. In Finland, Helakorpi et al. (1994) found that only 60% of males and 61% of females reported engaging in vigorous physical exercise at least twice a week. This had increased steadily from 43% of males and 40% of females in 1978.

Variation in participation

Most studies confirm that there are substantial age and sex variations in participation in physical activity. For example, the British General House-hold Survey (OPCS, 1985) found that there was a steady decrease in par-ticipation in outdoor activities from 55% and 36% among 16- to 19-year-old males and females to 17% and 6% of 70+ year olds. During adolescence there is a steady decline in participation in physical activity. North American surveys have estimated that while 70% of 12 year olds report participation in vigorous physical activities, this declines to 42% of men and 30% of women by 21 years (NIH Consensus Development Panel, 1996).

Participation in physical exercise is also linked to socio-economic and education background. The proportion of adults in the US National Health Interview Survey (National Center for Health Statistics, 1994b) reporting a sedentary lifestyle was 32% among lower-income people compared to 24% in the general population. In the Australian survey (Booth et al., 1993) 42% of those with tertiary education participated in regular exercise compared to 33% of those with sub-secondary education. In the British Whitehall study it was found that while only 5% of men in the highest grade did not participate in moderate or vigorous exercise, 31% of those in the lowest grade did not (Marmot and Davey Smith, 1997).

There is also evidence of significant ethnic variations although these are often confounded by socio-economic and educational variations. In the USA several studies have found that black women are less active than white women (Folsom et al., 1991). The Behavioral Risk Factor Surveillance System (USCDCP, 1993) found that in general ethnic minorities were less involved in physical activities. Among women a sedentary lifestyle was reported by 68% of African Americans compared to 56% of non-Hispanic whites. A similar pattern was apparent among men.

EXERCISE AMONG CHILDREN

There are substantial variations in the extent of participation of children in physical activity. Sex, socio-economic and ethnic variations are apparent from an early age. Simons-Morton et al. (1997) conducted a large survey of over 2,400 third grade (8- to 9-year-old) children in four US states. They found that not only did boys participate significantly more in moderate to vigorous physical activity but they also participated more in sedentary activities. Specifically, boys spent more time than girls watching television and playing video games. The ethnic differences in physical activity were not significant after controlling for other demographic variables. However, there were differences between states with California students reporting most moderate to vigorous physical activity and Louisiana students reporting the least.

Gottlieb and Chen (1985) considered the character of physical activity among a sample of 2,695 seventh and eight grade students (12–14 year olds) in Texas. They found that the female students were more likely than the males to participate in running, swimming, dancing, skipping, tennis, roller skating and volleyball. These activities were largely classified by sporting experts as individual, non-competitive and potentially aerobic activities. The male students preferred team, competitive, non-aerobic activities. Gottlieb and Chen concluded that this evidence of sex typing in sporting activities reflected 'the importance of socialization within the family unit and later through the peer group for gender differences'. They also found evidence of ethnic differences. After controlling for father's occupation, Anglos were more likely to engage in individual, non-competitive, aerobic type activities (bicycling, swimming, tennis, frisbies, roller skating and golf). Blacks favoured competitive team sports such as basketball and also dancing, while Mexican-Americans preferred baseball. Gottlieb and Chen suggest that this reflects the varying ethnic-related opportunities for success in sporting activities in the USA and the availability of role models.

Hasbrook (1986) found that gender differences in sporting participation interacted with socio-economic status. Among girls, those from poorer social backgrounds were less likely to participate in physical activity whereas among boys there was no relationship with social position. Oygard and Anderssen (1998) also found that teenage girls with higher levels of education were more physically active whereas again among boys there was less evidence of a relationship with level of education.

Predictors of children's participation

Initial attempts to explain children's participation in sporting activities focused on parental modelling. Moore et al. (1991) found that more active parents are more likely to have more active preschool children. Simons-Morton et al. (1997) found that a generalized measure of support for physical activity from parents, teachers and peers predicted extent of physical activity among the children. Thus, as with other behaviour patterns, children's activity levels are modelled on those of their parents and they are encouraged by their parents to behave in a similar manner.

In an attempt to distinguish between parental influence and children's attributes Stucky-Ropp and DiLorenzo (1993) conducted a study in a mid-western American town which involved structured interviews with over 200 10- to 12-year-old children and their mothers. Statistical analysis of their findings showed that the children's reported enjoyment of physical activity was the most salient *predictor* of exercise behaviour. In addition, the mothers' perceptions of barriers to exercise (e.g. lack of time) and mothers' reports of family support were important. There were also some sex differences. Boys' activity was also predicted by their perception of modelling and support of exercise behaviour by family and friends, whereas girls' activity was more predicted by presence of exercise-related equipment at home and parental modelling. These results confirm the central role of family environment in establishing an interest in physical activity among children.

As children move into adolescence it would be expected that the influence of parents would decline. Reynolds et al. (1990) explored this issue with longitudinal data on 743 14- to 16-year-old students from the control condition of the Stanford Adolescent Heart Health Program. They collected baseline data on these teenagers and then followed them up four and 16 months later. At four months the best predictor of physical activity for both males and females was baseline activity. For boys, self-efficacy (confidence that they could exercise despite obstacles) was a non-significant predictor but not social influence which included the activity levels of family and friends. This would suggest the development of a more independent lifestyle. For girls social influence was important as was perceived stress and intention. At 16 months baseline activity remained important for boys but not self-efficacy, perhaps another indicator of their changing lifestyle and the conflicting influences. For girls, self-efficacy was important.

Social meaning of sport for young people

Much psychological research into the development of physical activity has adopted a deterministic model such that it is assumed that participation is 'caused' by a combination of social and psychological variables. This approach ignores the active role of the young person in deciding whether or not to become involved and the social context within which physical activity occurs. A limited number of studies have adopted this more social perspective.

Kunesh et al. (1992) conducted a detailed investigation of the school play activities of a sample of 11- to 12-year-old girls in central USA. In interviews the girls reported that they found physically active games at home and at school enjoyable. However, in the school playground the girls preferred to stand in a group and talk while the boys participated in various games. When the girls did participate in games they were often criticized by the boys for their supposed inferior skill performance. To avoid this negative treatment the girls excluded themselves. The girls reported that when playing at school they felt nervous and embarrassed. These findings would suggest that while at an early age boys and girls both enjoy physical activities by the time they reach puberty the girls feel that they are being excluded.

As they enter adolescence the gender difference in participation in physical activities becomes more pronounced. From a series of interviews with young people from southeast London, Coakley and White (1992) identified five factors which help explain young people's decisions about participation in sporting activities (Table 10.3).

This study emphasized that perceived identity was a central concern in the extent and character of sports preferred. Young people actively sought out or rejected involvement in certain physical activities dependent upon a variety of factors including previous experiences and ongoing changing circumstances. As Coakley and White (1992) state: 'young people become involved in sport through a series of shifting, back-and-forth decisions made within the structural, ideological, and cultural context of their social worlds' (p. 21). Further:

> Young people do not get socialized into sport in the sense that they simply internalize or respond to external influences; nor do young people get socialized out of sport in the sense that they drop out in response to external influences. Instead, sport participation (and nonparticipation) is the result of decisions negotiated within the context of a young person's social environment and mediated by the young person's view of self and personal goals. Neither participation nor nonparticipation is a 'once and for all time' phenomenon explainable in terms of a quantitative, cause-effect methodological approach. (Coakley and White, 1992, p. 34)

TABLE 10.3 **Young people's decisions about sport participation (based on Coakley and White, 1992)**

1 *Consideration of the future, especially the transition to adulthood:* certain sports are accepted and others rejected depending upon their perceived adultness. Teenagers reject those games which they perceive as childish. Young women in particular become less involved in sporting activities which they perceive as having little connection with the female role.

2 *Desire to display and extend personal competence and autonomy:* young people become involved in sporting activities to the extent to which it extends their feeling of competence and autonomy. Again, there are gender differences with the young women being less likely to define themselves as sportspersons even if they are actively involved in physical activities. For them, sports is often perceived as a more masculine activity.

3 *Constraints related to money, parents and opposite-sex friends:* access to material resources is an important factor in explaining whether young people participate in certain sporting activities.
   In addition, the young women emphasize the importance of parents who seem to adopt a much more controlling influence on their general social lives. Further, the extent of participation in sporting activities is affected by whether or not the young women have a boyfriend. It is often the boyfriend who initiates leisure activity and restricts or encourages participation in sporting activities. Indeed, the young women seem to give their own interests a low priority in order to maintain their relationships with their boyfriends.

4 *Support and encouragement from parents, relatives, and/or peers:* young people report that they are often actively encouraged by family or friends to participate in certain physical activities. The young women in particular note the importance of having a friend to accompany them to sporting activities.

5 *Past experiences in school sports and physical education:* many young people report certain negative school experiences which colour their attitudes to physical activities. In particular, young women comment on how school physical education was associated with feelings of discomfort and embarrassment. Young men seem to have more pleasant memories of school sport.

PARTICIPATION OF ADULTS IN PHYSICAL ACTIVITY

An increasing amount of psychological research is being aimed at explaining the variations in the extent of participation in physical activity among adults. Most of this research has focused on identifying the social and psychological predictors of exercise or sports behaviour (e.g. King et al., 1992; Sallis et al., 1992a; Hawkes and Holm, 1993; Dzewaltowski, 1994). Frequently, these studies have used various social cognition models of health behaviour. The most popular have been the Health Belief Model and the theories of reasoned action and planned behaviour. Recently, there has been a rapid increase in the number of reports using the transtheoretical model of change.

Health belief model

The *Health Belief Model (HBM)* was originally developed by Rosenstock (1966). According to the model (Figure 10.1), a person's readiness to take a health action is determined by four main factors:

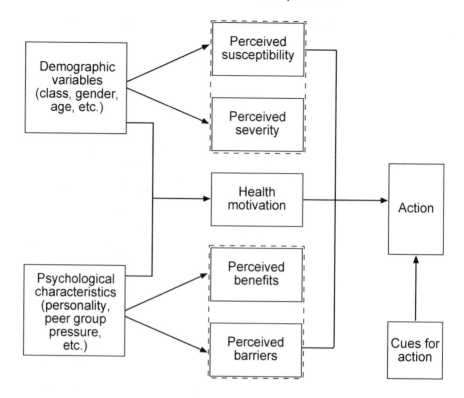

FIGURE 10.1 ***The Health Belief Model***

- the perceived susceptibility of the disease;
- the perceived severity or seriousness of the disease;
- the perceived benefits of the health action;
- the perceived barriers to performing the action.

In addition, Becker and Mainman (1975) included general health motivation as a fifth factor. More recent revisions of the theory (Becker and Rosenstock, 1984) have also included three further factors in the HBM. These supplementary factors are demographic variables, psychosocial variables and structural variables, in particular knowledge of the disease and contact with the disease. More recently 'cues to action' has been added as an additional explanatory variable (Figure 10.1) This proliferation of variables led Oliver and Berger (1979) to describe the HBM as 'more a collection of variables than a formal theory or model' (p. 113).

Several studies have used all or, more usually, portions of the HBM to explain participation in physical activity. In particular, researchers have considered to what extent perceived benefits of and barriers to physical activity explain participation. Dishman (1986) classified the main perceived barriers into four categories: effort, time, health limitations and obstacles. However, it is possible that these barriers are more justifications for lack of participation rather than explanations of it. Further, Sallis et al. (1992b) found that when these benefits of and barriers to exercise were considered along with a host of other predictive factors they did not emerge as important.

The Canadian Health Promotion Survey found that two-thirds of Canadians believed that exercise would benefit their health (Canada Fitness Survey, 1984). Further, it was apparent that those who reported increasing their exercise level did so mainly because of their increased knowledge of the risks of remaining sedentary. The Canada Fitness Survey found that the most frequently cited barriers for lack of participation in exercise were lack of time, injury, illness, poor weather and inconvenience. Lee (1993) suggested that the identification of these external barriers may act as a means of avoiding personal responsibility for lack of exercise.

Theories of reasoned action and planned behaviour

The *theory of reasoned action (TRA)* was developed by Ajzen and Fishbein (1980). This model proposes that exercise behaviour is predicted by intention to engage in such behaviour which in turn is predicted by the individual's attitude towards exercise and the perceived social norm. The attitudinal component is in turn a function of the perceived consequences of participating and a personal evaluation of those consequences. Further, the perceived norm is a function of the perceived expectations to participate and the motivation to comply with those expectations. Godin (1994) conducted a review of studies adopting the TRA and concluded:

> It has proven to be very helpful in understanding the decision-making process underlying exercise behavior . . . approximately 30% of the variance in intention to exercise seems to be explained by the attitudinal component. The normative component is less consistently associated with intention to exercise and does not appear to be a stable variable for the interpretation of exercise behavior. (Godin, 1994, p. 1392)

The *theory of planned behavior (TPB)* developed by Ajzen (1985) introduced perceived behavioural control into the basic model and suggested that, besides the attitudinal and social norm components, whether someone intended to behave in a certain way depended upon the extent to which they believed they had control over a particular behaviour (Figure 10.2). This concept was derived from Bandura's (1977) concept of self-efficacy. Godin (1994) found that the introduction of the behavioural control variable in studies of exercise participation increased the proportion of the variance explained.

Godin and his co-workers (Collete et al., 1994) also applied an extended version of this model to explain the intention of a sample of adults to take up a physical exercise. In a survey of over 350 Canadian adults they found

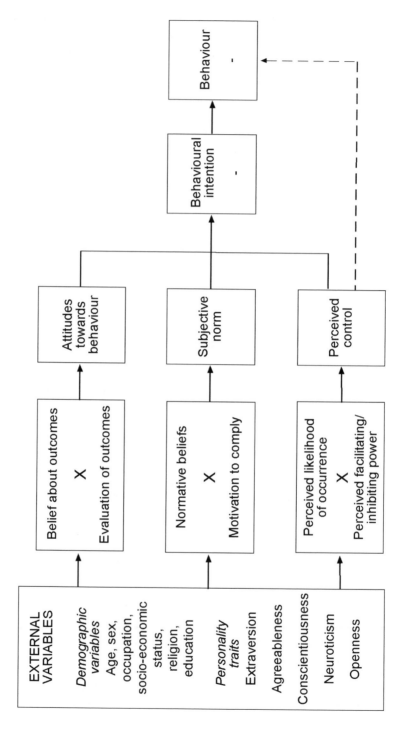

FIGURE 10.2 **The theory of planned behaviour**

that the four best predictors of intent to participate were current physical activity, age, attitude toward exercise and personal normative belief. With regard to the attitude, the high intenders were more likely to consider exercise enjoyable, interesting, exciting, pleasant, good and useful. Colette et al. (1994) suggested that the significance of personal normative belief reflects the individuals' belief that they are the ones who decide whether or not to take action. Unlike other studies self-efficacy did not predict intention to participate.

Hawkes and Holm (1993) combined elements of the HBM with the TRA and with Cox's (1982) theory of client health behaviour (TCHB) to examine gender differences in exercise determinants. They found that for both men and women the most important statistical predictors were social influences and health self-determinism. The social influence concept was derived from the TRA while health self-determinism was a measure of intrinsic health motivation derived from the TCHB. However, the various model variables still only explained a small proportion of the variance in long-term physical activity participation, suggesting that other factors are important.

Self-efficacy

Bandura's (1986) social learning theory has been used extensively to explain participation in physical activity. In particular, Bandura's argument that perceived *self-efficacy* is the common cognitive mechanism that mediates behavioural responses has been applied. Bandura argued that whether a person persists in a particular behaviour in different circumstances depends upon his/her perception of individual mastery over the behaviour. Bandura suggested that this sense of self-efficacy develops through personal experiences of success, but also from verbal support from others and the perceived level of physiological arousal. Several researchers have found that perceived self-efficacy does indeed predict participation in physical activity (e.g. Broman, 1995). However, since involvement in the behaviour can enhance feelings of self-efficacy, Sallis et al. (1989) questioned the value of this variable as a predictor in cross-sectional studies.

Transtheoretical model (TTM)

The *transtheoretical model* was originally developed by Prochaska and DiClemente (1983) to explain why anti-smoking messages were more successful for some people than for others. According to the TTM, people adopting a new behaviour move through a series of stages of change within which they utilize different processes to support the changes. These stages are described in Chapter 8. Movement across the stages is dependent on decisional balance and perceived self-efficacy. Decisional balance is a cognitive assessment of the relative merits of the pros and cons of the exercise behaviour while self-efficacy is the belief in one's ability to perform the exercise.

Marcus and her colleagues (Marcus and Simkin, 1994) have used this theoretical framework to describe the extent of participation in physical activity and have linked it with other *social cognition* models. Marcus et al. (1992a) found that those who were regularly participating in physical activity (action or maintenance stages) scored higher on a measure of self-efficacy. They concluded that this suggests that those who are at the early stages (precontemplation and contemplation) have little confidence in their ability to exercise.

In a large survey of Australian adults, Booth et al. (1993) classified people into the various stages of change in terms of their readiness to participate in exercise. They found that while there was little gender difference those in the lower stages of change categories tended to have a lower level of education. This accords with previous work on social variations in exercise.

What's wrong with social cognition models of exercise?

Social cognition models (SCMs), such as those described above, have focused on identifying the determinants of physical activity. Stainton-Rogers (1991) provided a coherent critique of these models describing them as portraying 'thinking as a passive, mindless activity rather than an active striving after meaning, and portray people as thinking-machines rather than as aware and insightful, open to being beguiled by convincing tales and rhetoric, and inventive story-tellers' (p. 55).

More than this they locate the thinking in the head of the individual rather than as something which unfolds in interaction with others leading to an individualistic focus in health promotion (Becker, 1992). A social interactionist views the individual as part of a group and of a society. His or her behaviour, thoughts and beliefs can be considered as unfolding in interaction with the groups and society as a means of adapting to changing circumstances. Their decision to become involved in physical activity is the result of an ongoing engagement with their immediate social world. Further criticisms of SCMs can be found in Chapter 15.

Social context of exercise

There have been attempts to develop a more social interactionist understanding of physical activity. These argue that the extent to which people engage in physical activity is related to the character of their everyday social experience. Calnan and Williams (1991a and b) conducted detailed interviews with a sample of middle-aged men and women from the southeast of England. The participants were from different social backgrounds. They found clear social class differences in perceptions of exercise. Those from working-class backgrounds perceived exercise in relation to everyday tasks, activities and duties at home and at work. They adopted a functional definition of health and fitness. For them their ability to 'exercise' their everyday tasks both confirmed and reaffirmed their health. For example, one farm-worker said: 'I get enough exercise when I am working on the farm shovelling corn all day, you get enough exercise. In the garden out there, I take the dog for a walk, yet I get enough exercise' (p. 518). They tended to be satisfied with their physical health which they could enhance during their everyday activities.

Middle-class people tended to perceive exercise as not being part of their everyday activities. They preferred to define it with reference to recreational or leisure activities which they sometimes felt they could not engage in because of lack of time. Fitness for these individuals was defined in terms of athleticism not in ability to perform everyday tasks. This group also made more reference to the health-promoting effects of exercise in terms of 'well-being' and relief from routine daily obligations. In discussing these class differences in perceptions of exercise Calnan and Williams (1991a and b) referred to the work of Bourdieu (1984) who suggested that whereas working-class people express an instrumental relation to their bodily practices, middle-class people engage in health practices which are 'entirely opposed to (such) total, practically oriented movements' (p. 214).

In a similar type of study, Mullen (1992) explored the meaning of health behaviour such as exercise within the context of work. He interviewed a sample of Scottish men from different social backgrounds. It is apparent that the men from working-class backgrounds spoke of work as exercise and as often being good for their health. For example, one man said: 'Ah think working has a good effect, hard work; it hasn't done me any harm. Ah think if you do anythin' that keeps you fit you know . . . you're usin' your muscles all the time you know an' ye get up the next day fresh an' ye enjoy yer, ye look forward to a holiday then right enough' (p. 77).

Mullen (1992) does not specifically explore social class differences although he does note that sedentary (more middle-class) occupations were described in terms of lack of exercise, e.g. 'desk bound' or 'spending a lot of time in the car'. Thus, as reported by Calnan and Williams (1991a and b), exercise was defined by these people as an activity outside work.

In a large-scale survey of young people's physical activity in Norway, Oygard and Anderssen (1998) also considered the importance of the meaning of exercise and the physical body. In discussing the relationship between social class and exercise they also refer to the work of Bourdieu (1984) who suggested that this relationship derives from social class differences in attitude toward the body. In our society the legitimized body emphasizes both inner and outer characteristics. While the former is concerned with the healthy body, the latter refers to the fit and slim body. The middle and upper classes are more able to produce this legitimized body since it requires investment in time and money. Working-class people with less time free from necessity have a more instrumental view of their body and view concern with exercise and fitness as pretentious. Conversely, middle-class people with more leisure time and resources to expend promote a cult of health and a concern with physical appearance.

Murray and Jarrett (1985) examined gender differences in perceptions of health and health maintenance. They conducted detailed interviews with a sample of young people and found that young men were more likely to define health in terms of fitness and health maintenance in terms of physical activity which improved their ability to perform. Young women preferred diet and weight control which improved their physical image. Other studies (e.g. Hayes and Ross, 1987) have found that concern for bodily appearance is the most important reason for physical activity among females. However, this concern with bodily image is closely linked with social position.

In their survey Oygard and Anderssen found that level of education was positively associated with extent of participation in physical activity among females but not among males. In reviewing this finding, they refer to the suggestion that concern with the body is more common among those belonging to the cultural elite who are more anxious about their appearance and their 'body for others' (Bourdieu, 1984, p. 213). Oygard and Anderssen concluded: 'For females in higher social positions, it may be of importance to show others who they are by developing healthy and "delicate" bodies, i.e. they are more concerned with the inner and outer body than females in lower social positions' (1998, p. 65). However, they also added more prosaically that the lesser involvement of less educated females may be due to them having limited access to leisure facilities. They found little relationship between education and physical activity among males and suggest that this may reflect the greater promotion of male sporting activities and the greater integration of physical activity into male culture.

CULTURAL CONTEXT

It is important to note that physical activities are conducted within a wider social and cultural context which promotes different ideals. For example, participation in sport is particularly promoted in North American society. There the muscular physique is presented as the ideal male form. Luschen et al. (1996) note that the emergence of those body-building exercises which are aimed at building muscular strength and fitness 'reflects a bodily culture that is in line with American values of masculine prowess' (p. 201). They add that 'activities like American football, weightlifting, and boxing set a premium on brute physical force and place much less emphasis on endurance and relaxation' (p. 202). Ability to attain this physical shape is promised to those who participate in various fitness gyms. However, access to these somewhat elite facilities is generally restricted to those with money, although there has been a move in some countries to make exercise the subject of a GP's prescription, for example, in the UK. In addition, aggressive sporting activities are also promoted among the middle class as a training ground for developing an aggressive business attitude, not to mention the making of useful social contacts.

A related issue is the role of religion. Certain forms of Christianity have traditionally held a negative view of excessive concern about the body (see Chapter 3). It has been suggested that this is a reason for the poorer performance of Catholic societies in sporting events (Curtis and White, 1992). Conversely, in more Protestant or secular societies concern with body shape and performance is promoted. Indeed, Turner (1984) argues that contemporary concern for the body could be described as the new Protestant ethic:

> The new ethic of managerial athleticism is thus the contemporary version of the Protestant ethic, but, fanned by the winds of consumerism, this ethic has become widespread throughout the class system as a lifestyle to be emulated. The com-modified body has become the focus of a keep-fit industry, backed up by fibre diets, leisure centres, slimming manuals and outdoor sports. (Turner, 1984, p. 112)

An understanding of the variations in the extent of participation in physical activities requires attention not only to the various psychological processes but also to the sociocultural context within which they have meaning and which promote or discourage involvement in such pursuits.

PROMOTING PHYSICAL ACTIVITY

With the increase in evidence demonstrating the physical and mental benefits of physical activity and exercise, governments and health auth-orities have become keen to promote greater participation. Unfortunately, the evidence suggests that many of these campaigns have not been very successful. Large scale-media campaigns have not proven very effective in increasing participation (Marcus and Simkin, 1994). This has led to the development of more focused interventions aimed either at the whole community or particular groups within the community.

Population based strategies

A series of recent interventions which have attempted to increase partici-pation in communities have been based upon various psychological models, especially the transtheoretical model. Marcus et al. (1992b) designed an exercise intervention for volunteers recruited from a community. The character of the intervention was matched to the initial stage of change of the volunteers. On follow-up there was evidence of a significant increase in involvement in exercise commensurate with the initial stage. Admittedly, this study was not a controlled trial (Marcus et al., 1996). In a subsequent randomized controlled trial, however, Marcus et al. (1994b) found further supportive evidence. At three months follow-up the subjects in the stage-matched group showed stage progression (i.e. greater interest or involvement in exercise) while those in the standard group showed stage stability or regression.

In a review of randomized controlled trials of physical activity promotion in general populations Hillsdon et al. (1995) found evidence for the effectiveness of various intervention strategies. Those trials which were most effective had the following common features:

- home-based programmes;
- unsupervised, informal exercise;
- frequent professional contact;
- walking as the promoted exercise;
- moderate intensity exercise.

They noted that the character of the interaction between the professional and client may be more important than the actual behavioural technique (cf. Najavits and Weiss, 1994).

Interventions aimed at high-risk groups

An alternative to the large-scale interventions aimed at the general population are those which focus on high-risk groups. There is increasing interest in the value of exercise for elderly people or those who suffer from particular health problems. The initial interventions were often opportunistic but more recent attempts have been carefully designed to identify the characteristics of effective programmes.

Several psychological characteristics have been found to be associated with involvement of particular groups of patients in exercise programmes. Dishman and Gettman (1980) found that self-motivation was associated with participation. Wilhelmsen et al. (1975) found that social support increased involvement. Other studies which have investigated the role of health beliefs and attitudes have found inconsistent results. For example, Morgan et al. (1984) found little difference between exercise adopters and non-adopters in their responses to questions from the Health Belief Model (HBM).

Mirotznik et al. (1995) conducted a retrospective study to assess the value of the Health Belief Model for explaining participation in a coronary heart disease exercise programme. They found that while general health motivation and perceived severity of CHD positively predicted attendance, the perceived benefits of exercise did not.

Clarke and Eves (1997) found partial support for the value of the transtheoretical model to explain the willingness of a sample of sedentary adults to participate in an exercise programme prescribed by their family doctor. They classified the participants into the precontemplation, contemplation and preparation stages reflecting the fact that at this stage they had not begun the programme. The cons of participation in the exercise programme

TABLE 10.4 ***Behavioural strategies to improve adherence to exercise programmes (based on Robinson and Rogers, 1994)***

- *Stimulus control*: providing cues which remind people of the programme.
- *Consequent control*: providing rewards and punishments for participation.
- *Cognitive behaviour modification*: increasing people's belief that they have control over the design and conduct of the programme.
- *Behavioural treatment packages*: combining behavioural and cognitive strategies.

decreased across the stages as predicted although there was little change in the pros. The barriers to participation identified were lack of support, lack of facilities, dislike of exercise and lack of time. The importance of dislike of exercise declined across the stages while the importance of lack of facilities increased. The finding that lack of time was used as frequently by those in the precontemplation as those in the preparation stage was interpreted as evidence that it is more a justification for lack of participation rather than a convincing reason.

ADHERENCE TO EXERCISE PROGRAMMES

A common problem with exercise programmes is that while many people sign up for such programmes it has been estimated that 50% or more drop out after a short period of participation (Dishman, 1986). Robinson and Rogers (1994) identified four behavioural stategies associated with increased adherence which are summarized in Table 10.4.

However, Robinson and Rogers concluded that this is a very schematic outline and there is a need for further research into the dynamic nature of the exercise behaviour change process.

Further, these stategies are largely focused at the individual. They ignore the social context and the social meaning of exercise and physical activity. Social approaches attempt to widen the traditional individual change approach to include: 'changes in social networks and structures, organizational norms, regulatory policies, and the physical environment as a means of enhancing long-term maintenance of the target behavior' (King, 1994, p. 1406).

FUTURE RESEARCH

1 Despite the evidence linking exercise with various indicators of health there is still a need to explore the specific impact of exercise interventions on different populations.
2 There is evidence of a changing involvement of children and youth in physical activity. Research could consider the character of these changes.

3   Physical activity has different meanings for different sub-groups of population. Research is needed to develop our understanding of these different meanings.
4   Programmes to promote greater participation in physical exercise are often based upon limited understanding of the different meanings of exercise. Participatory action research offers an opportunity to increase our understanding of different groups perceptions of physical activity programmes.
5   Involvement in sporting and physical activity is closely linked to people's social and economic circumstances and the socio-cultural context. There is scope for further research on the social embeddedness of exercise.

SUMMARY

1   Interest in exercise has waxed and waned over the years. The past generation has witnessed increasing interest in the health benefits of exercise.
2   Results of several comprehensive surveys indicate that moderate degrees of physical activity have both physical and psychological benefits.
3   There is some evidence to suggest that excessive exercise can have negative health effects.
4   A large proportion of the populations of western societies are sedentary.
5   The degree of participation declines during adolescence, especially among girls.
6   In adulthood, participation is lesser among females, those from poorer social positions and those from ethnic minorities.
7   Various psychological factors have been found to be associated with partici- pation in both childhood and adulthood.
8   The meaning of exercise is linked to the varying social contexts.
9   Exercise participation programmes can be either population based or aimed at high risk groups. The main problem with both forms of programme is adherence which is generally low.

KEY TERMS

Health Belief Model (HBM)   theory of planned behaviour (TPB)
predictors   theory of reasoned action (TRA)
self-efficacy   transtheoretical model of change
social cognition   (TTM)

PART 3

HEALTH PROMOTION AND DISEASE PREVENTION

Part 3 is concerned with some of the major processes in health promotion and disease prevention. We review in turn psychological theory and research on:

- beliefs and explanations;
- communication: messages and meanings;
- compliance and empowerment;
- immunization and screening;
- health promotion.

We give some emphasis to the theoretical and methodological issues of work in this field which falls squarely within the interface between research and practice. Whenever possible we indicate the practical implications of research for the improvement of health-care delivery.

11

BELIEFS AND EXPLANATIONS

The description of health beliefs obtained from accounts shows that these do not constitute a logically tight system, but often operate in an apparently inconsistent fashion. (Alan Radley, 1994, p. 60)

OUTLINE

The traditional biomedical approach to illness defines it in terms of physical symptoms and underlying physical pathology. Health is defined as the absence of such symptoms and pathology. However, as historians of medicine have emphasized, this is not the only approach although in our society the discourse of medicine about illness is so loud that it tends to 'drone out all the others' (Herzlich and Pierret, 1987, p. xi). Psychologists have used a variety of theoretical perspectives to investigate popular beliefs about illness. This chapter summarizes some of this research. In particular, it contrasts the research which has used a cognitive perspective with that which has used a discursive, narrative or social representation perspective.

COGNITIVE APPROACHES

Illness perceptions

The most developed cognitive model of illness was initially proposed by Howard Leventhal and his colleagues (Leventhal et al., 1989). This was derived from the Leventhal group's initial work on the impact of fear communication. They found that, irrespective of the level of fear, the message was effective if it produced a plan of action. This led them to infer that the key factor was the way the threat was represented or understood. They developed a *dual processing model* to accommodate the representation of fear and of the threat (Figure 11.1), an influential model that has undergone some elaboration by Leventhal (1999).

This model led the Leventhal group to explore more fully how lay people represented specific threats such as illness. They conducted open-ended interviews with a sample of patients suffering from various diseases. From this information they proposed a self-regulation model of illness which suggested that lay people's thoughts on illness can be organized along four dimensions. Lau and Hartman (1983) suggested that since these dimensions were derived from a sample of patients with an acute, time-limited illness

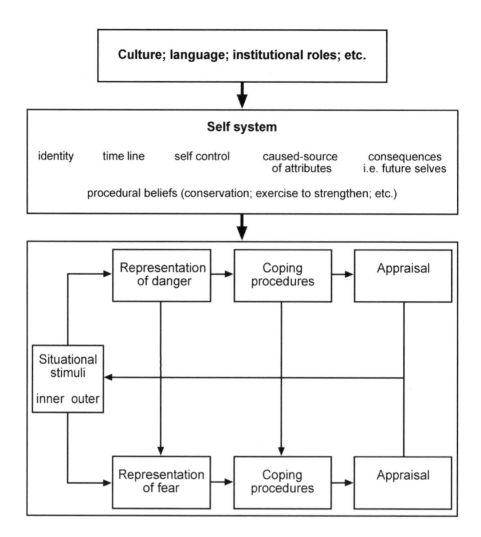

FIGURE 11.1 *A self-regulating model for coping with illness (Leventhal, 1999)*

TABLE 11.1 *Dimensions of illness perceptions (Leventhal et al., 1980; Lau and Hartman, 1983)*

- *Identity*: the signs, symptoms and the illness label.
- *Consequence*: the perceived physical, social and economic consequences of the disease, and the felt emotional consequences.
- *Causes*: the perceived causes of the disease.
- *Time line*: the perceived time frame for the development and duration of the illness threat.
- *Cure*: the extent to which the illness is responsive to medical treatment.

experience it was necessary to introduce a fifth dimension to cover those illnesses which were resistant to treatment (Table 11.1).

Schober and Lacroix (1991) used evidence from seventeenth- and eighteenth century writings to suggest that the cognitive structure of illness representation was 'invariant in time' (p. 18). Admittedly, the content of the dimensions would be different and reflect contemporary medical wisdom.

There have been various attempts to develop a measure of these different illness dimensions. Turk et al. (1986) developed a 38-item Implicit Models of Illness Questionnaire (IMIQ) which was designed to operationalize the five lay illness dimensions. They also added items to measure perceived personal responsibility and disruptiveness. The scale was administered to a sample of diabetic educators, diabetic patients and college students. Factor analysis of their scores revealed four slightly different dimensions:

1 *Seriousness*: which included items concerned with the seriousness of the disease.
2 *Personal responsibility*: the extent to which the person is perceived as responsible for the onset and/or resolution of the disease.
3 *Controllability*: the extent to which the disease is perceived as controllable by the individual or outside forces.
4 *Changeability*: the extent to which the disease changes over time.

Turk et al. (1986) suggested that these four dimensions more accurately reflect the subjective personal experience of the disease as opposed to the more objective description provided in Leventhal's model. However, there have been mixed results by other researchers in attempts to measure these various dimensions.

Schiaffino and Cea (1995) applied the IMIQ to a larger sample of people with different diseases. A factor analysis of their scores identified four factors:

1 *Curability*: this was a combination of Leventhal's cause, cure and time-line dimensions.
2 *Personal responsibility*: this includes causes, consequences and identity components which have a common characteristic referring to the extent to which the person is perceived as responsible for the disease.
3 *Symptom variability*: this was somewhat similar to the original time-line dimension and to Turk et al.'s control and changeable factors.
4 *Serious consequences*.

Schiaffino and Cea concluded that the search for a universal description of underlying dimensions is perhaps misguided since the dimensions may vary over illnesses.

Weinman et al. (1996) developed another questionnaire to measure the original five dimensions. They subsequently used this measure in a longitudinal study to investigate the relationship between illness representations and work behaviour after myocardial infarction (Petrie et al., 1996).

They found several interesting relationships. Subsequent attendance at a rehabilitation course was significantly predicted by a stronger belief during admission that the illness could be cured. Return to work was predicted by perception that the illness would last a short time and have less serious consequences. In conclusion, they noted that these popular illness beliefs 'seem to be largely formed by information before becoming ill [and] are quite consistent over time'. Weinman and Petrie (1997) suggested that the study of illness perceptions, or more specifically the cognitive representations of illness, can be used as a new framework for understanding how people react to illness.

One common feature in these models of lay illness cognitions is a basic time perspective. Attention to this perspective provides a means of integrating the different dimensions into three broad categories:

1   Looking back at the possible causes of the disease.
2   Looking at the present character of the disease in terms of its label, symptoms and severity.
3   Looking forward to the time-line and consequences of the disease.

This framework allows us to consider much of the research on illness cognitions.

Causes of disease

According to the basic tenets of attribution theory people attempt to provide a causal explanation for events in their world particularly if those events are unexpected and have personal relevance (Heider, 1958). Thus it is not surprising that people will generally seek a causal explanation for an illness, particularly one which is serious.

Taylor et al. (1984) interviewed a sample of women who had been treated for breast cancer. They found that 95% of the women had a causal explanation for their cancer. These causes were classified as stress (41%), specific carcinogen (32%), heredity (26%), diet (17%), blow to breast (10%) and other (28%). They also asked the women who or what they considered responsible for the disease and found that 41% of the women blamed themselves, 10% blamed another person, 28% blamed the environment and 49% blamed chance. The patients were also asked whether they felt any control over their cancer and they found 56% felt they had some control.

Weiner et al. (1972) suggested that we can classify attributional dimensions along three dimensions:

1   *Locus*: the extent to which the cause is localized inside or outside the person.
2   *Controllability*: the extent to which the person has control over the cause.
3   *Stability*: the extent to which the cause is stable or changeable.

Various researchers have used these dimensions to explore illness cognitions with greater or lesser success.

Swartzman and Lees (1996) considered the character of the causal explanations of various physical symptoms. Initial classification of the suggested causes revealed fourteen categories. A revised version of these was then rated by another sample of students. Multi-dimensional scaling analysis of the scores suggested three dimensions which they labelled: non-physical–physical; stable–unstable; and controllable–uncontrollable. The latter two labels are comparable to two of the original attributional dimensions. However, the physical–non-physical dimension has not been previously identified. Physical causes included 'physical activity' and 'physical constitution' while non-physical causes included personality, mood and stress.

Murray and McMillan (1993a) asked a sample of over 700 adults to rate the relative importance of 24 potential causes of cancer. Factor analysis of their ratings revealed five factors which were labelled:

- Stress (which contained items referring to stress, worry, loneliness, unemployment).
- Environment (including such items as air pollution, work conditions, asbestos, nuclear radiation, a knock or hurt, X-rays and promiscuity).
- Health-related (such factors as childbirth, antibiotics, breast-feeding, virus or infection).
- Behaviour (fatty foods, smoking, drinking).

Heredity and chance did not load heavily on any of these factors. Although some of these factors could be redefined along the classic attributional dimensions, others (e.g. health-related) were more specific and would suggest that people combine general and specific casual explanations.

Causal attributions are not things in themselves but are the basis of plans for action. How the person explains an event partly determines how that person subsequently copes with that situation. Affleck et al. (1987) interviewed a sample of men who had been hospitalized for a heart attack. The most common causes for the heart attack were stress and personal behaviour. They found that attributing the cause to stress (external, uncontrollable) was predictive of greater morbidity over the following eight years. According to Turnquist et al. (1988) being able to identify a potential cause of an illness, irrespective of the character of that cause, is an important predictor of subsequent adjustment.

Immediate characteristics of the disease

An important feature of medical investigation of disease is the drawing together of symptoms which occur together and the identification of symptom clusters. There is evidence to suggest that the layperson follows a similar strategy.

Bishop and his colleagues suggested that lay people bring meaning to physical symptoms by relating them to disease prototypes. Bishop and Converse (1988) found that laypeople were able to provide a disease label for sets of physical symptoms and vice versa. During socialization we learn which symptoms are associated together such that when we are giving minimum symptomatic details of a particular illness, we can confidently predict other symptoms.

Bishop (1987) identified certain dimensions which lay people use to organize physical symptoms. Using multi-dimensional scaling he identified four dimensions which he termed contagiousness, location in body, psychological cause, and degree of activity disruption. He subsequently refined these to two basic dimensions: seriousness and contagiousness (Bishop, 1991a). He suggested that lay people use these two basic dimensions to organize their impressions of different symptoms associated with various diseases.

Consequences of disease

Diseases can be short term or long term, acute or chronic, responsive to treatment or not. All of these features can be considered as consequences of disease or illness. What are the implications of the illness for the person? In their model Leventhal et al. considered not only the physical consequences but also the psychological and social. Weinman and Petrie (1997) found that the illness dimension which best predicted return to work among a sample of patients with heart attack was the perceived consequences of the illness. Moss-Morris et al. (1996) found a similar finding with patients suffering from chronic fatigue syndrome.

One consequence which is partly ignored is the character of the treatment. For many lay people the treatment is the illness and vice versa. Murray and McMillan (1988) asked lay people to define cancer. They found that one of the most important definitions was the character of the treatment for cancer.

Illness cognitions among children

The cognitive perspective has been used by several researchers to explore the development of illness concepts among children. Bibace and Walsh (1980) interviewed children of different ages about their concepts of illness. They then coded the children's replies into Piaget's (1930) stages of cognitive development. Children between the ages of 2 and 6 years provided more pre-logical explanations. At this age the most common explanation for illness was contagion. People became ill because they were close to certain contagious objects or persons. Between 7 and 10 years children offer more concrete-logical explanations. At this age the children explain illness in terms of internalization and contamination. The person is required to come into physical contact with the source of the illness and possibly to ingest it. Finally, 11-year-olds' explanations were more formal-logical. The children offer a more physiological explanation referring to internal physiological processes. Kister and Patterson (1980) also referred to Piagetian concepts and suggested that young children explain illness in terms of 'immanent justice' – a form of punishment for a transgression.

Several commentators (e.g. Burbach and Peterson, 1986) have questioned the methodological adequacy of these and comparable studies. Siegal et al. (1990) found that young children were reluctant to use contagion to explain toothache but correctly used it to explain getting a cold. They suggested that in previous work 'rather than lacking knowledge of the causes of illness, [the children] may simply have misunderstood the procedural requirements of the interview. They also found no evidence that illness is described in terms of immanent justice. They suggested that in previous research the children may have attempted to comply with the suggestion of an adult interviewer that adults may be so powerful that children who are naughty will be inevitably punished' (p. 160).

Bird and Podmore (1990) argued that the apparent age differences in children's illness beliefs are more a function of access to knowledge than to cognitive development. In their study they interviewed children about health and illness and found that their replies were not detailed enough to allow reliable coding into Piagetian stage categories. They found little support for the claim that younger children prefer external contamination and that older children are more aware of internal processes. Older children were found to mention a broader range of knowledge sources such as parents, television and school.

Another problem with much of the research on children's illness beliefs is that it has been conducted largely on healthy children (Eiser, 1985). It would not seem unreasonable to expect that sick children would have different illness beliefs. Eiser et al. (1984) compared children with diabetes with a matched group of healthy children. They found the children did not differ much in their knowledge of the causes of various illness other than diabetes. However, healthy children were more likely to define health as 'not being ill' or 'body working properly'.

Collecting information about illness cognitions

One problem with the social cognitive approach to the study of illness beliefs is that it tends to ignore the context within which the beliefs are expressed. Abraham and Hampson (1996) argue that culture-bound, self-presentational processes influence the character of the replies which people give in such studies. However, they suggest that it is possible to take account of these processes.

An example of a study which attempted to control for this self-presentation effect is that by Landrine and Klonoff (1994). They suggested that studies of causal explanations of illness often neglect supernatural causes because people feel embarrassed to admit belief in such causes.

They asked a sample of American college students to generate causes of illness and found supernatural causes were freely mentioned by only 4.7% of the sample whereas 66.4% of the sample rated such causes as important when they were provided.

This study suggests that illness beliefs are not located in the heads of the individuals but that rather they are joint creations which partly reflect the character of the relationship between the individual and the interviewer. This criticism has led to the development of other approaches.

SOCIAL APPROACHES

Illness discourse

A major problem with cognitive approaches to the study of illness perceptions is that it presents them as static and asocial phenomena which exist within the minds of the individual, i.e. it abstracts the perceptions out of the meaning making context within which they must be generated. An alternative perspective which attempts to present a more dynamic and social approach is that offered by various discursive psychologists. Their focus is on the character of the *discourse* and the context within which it occurs rather than on the structure of the inferred beliefs. They deliberately consider the immediate and broader social context within which beliefs are articulated. For them the communicative nature of language is the focus of attention rather than inferred underlying beliefs (Potter and Wetherell, 1987).

Middleton (1996) used this approach to explore talk in a parent group for children with chronic renal failure. He argued that this talk is more than 'a display of inner workings of minds' but is 'part of the process of making [their] health care experiences socially intelligible' (p. 244). Rather than breaking the talk down into elemental beliefs, he attempted to understand it as part of the process of making sense of illness within a social context. Middleton suggests that an important component of such talk is that it contains many contradictory elements and expressions of uncertainty. These elements are not deficiencies but rather are seen as being 'used to establish common understandings concerning what it is to care for chronically ill children' (p. 257). Further, the talk is more than self-presentation which can be ironed out by careful assessment but rather part of the broader collective process of meaning making.

Similarly, Blaxter (1993), in her study of working-class women in Scotland, noted that in their talk about illness with the researcher the women were simultaneously developing an understanding: 'alternatives are tried out, rejected, associated with each other, traced from one period of life to another'. Examples are given of different cases and the different factors that might apply are reasoned out (p. 133). It is not as if there are simple cognitive representations which can be extracted from the minds of the women but rather they develop their understanding of health and illness in interaction – testing out ideas with their interlocutor.

In an earlier study, Cornwell (1984) illustrated the importance of the immediate context in soliciting accounts of health and illness. She investigated the health beliefs and practices of working-class people resident in the East End of London. She noted that the character of their replies changed as she got to know the research participants. This led her to distinguish between private and public accounts. The public accounts are the more socially acceptable versions which would often make reference to biomedical terms which is the acceptable scientific language of our society. The private accounts referred more to personal experience or the experience of friends and family which often contradicted that of the medical establishment.

Cornwell (1984) stressed that intrinsic to the traditional research interview is a *power imbalance* which is more pronounced when the interviewee is from a working-class background. In this situation the middle-class interviewer is inviting a certain account which emphasizes the more publicly acceptable beliefs.

Farr (1978) made a similar point in his critique of the work of Herzlich (1973) who argued that her interviews with laypeople would suggest that they tend to perceive the individual as the source of health and society or way of life as the source of illness. However, Farr (1978) indicated that such an explanation would be predicted on the basis of **attribution bias** (Ross, 1977) which suggests that the layperson has a tendency to attribute the cause of good events (e.g. health) to self and bad events (e.g. illness) to external factors. This tendency would be especially pronounced in an interview setting such that Herzlich's findings are at least partly reflective of the context within which the information was collected.

Radley and Billig (1996) have provided a detailed commentary on the discursive context within which health beliefs are generated. They suggest that private and public accounts interpenetrate. Although storytelling may be a means of revealing private beliefs it can also be used to substantiate or to subvert public beliefs. Healthy and sick people approach the issue from different perspectives: 'the healthy have much to say about their illness experience, while the sick are often at pains to show their "normality"' (p. 225). Since the interviewer is usually a healthy person, the sick person feels strongly 'the need to *legitimate* [their] position'. This emphasizes that the 'accounts are situated in a rhetorical context of potential justification and criticism' (p. 226). Although this commentary was aimed at qualitative interview research, a similar comment can be made about quantitative questionnaire studies of health and illness beliefs.

Balshem (1991) also commented on the role of the interviewer in collecting accounts of cancer. In her study of working-class women she found that the accounts differed depending upon the context within which they were obtained. In general, however, she argued that the working-class women in her study argued against the dominant medical discourse which explained cancer in terms of personal behaviour. Indeed, some of the women preferred to adopt these behaviours as a means of rebellion against authority.

Overall, these discursive approaches argue that illness discourse is an active and social creation which reflects the attempts of the person or persons to make sense of a problematic situation. Thus, the character of the discourse is variable and needs to be considered with reference to the immediate and broader social context within which it is generated.

Illness narratives

Recently, there has been a growth of interest in the stories which people tell about illness experiences. Narrative psychologists (Sarbin, 1986) argue that *narrative* construction is an intrinsic part of making sense of the world. The process of creating a narrative enables the person to give meaning to a crisis. Before the narrative there is merely a disjointed sequence of events. In creating the narrative the person selects some pieces of information and ignores others and pieces a story together. Admittedly this process is not conducted in isolation but as part of a wider process of social engagement. As such, many narrative psychologists would locate their work within the broader framework of discursive psychology (Murray, 1997a).

According to narrative psychology people generate stories about illness experiences (Murray, 1997a). The construction of these narrative accounts enables the person to grasp its meaning and to begin to exert some control over it. The character of these stories varies depending upon a variety of factors such as previous experience and public repertoires (Murray, 1997b). Some stories may offer the prospect of advancement, while others offer decline. Several psychotherapists (e.g. Neimeyer, 1995) have suggested that the aim of therapy is to assist the client in developing a new more personally enhancing story.

Murray (1997b) analysed the written accounts of a sample of women who had breast cancer. He found that the accounts were organized into a similar storyline with a beginning, a middle and an end. The beginning was the period before cancer which was often characterized as a time of innocence. The middle of the story was the diagnosis and the subsequent medical treatment. The end was the period of reassessment of identity and reintegration into society. In closing their story the women frequently emphasized the positive features of having cancer – it had given them an opportunity to reassess their lives. It was also apparent that the women were aware of the therapeutic benefits in telling their stories. They explicitly referred to this process of sense making. Through the process of *emplotment* (Ricoeur, 1981) the women were able to take control over a crisis event and transform it into a life-enhancing moment.

The literary critic Anatole Broyard (1992) provided an account of his experience of cancer from which he subsequently died. In his account he explicitly draws attention to this process of emplotment:

My initial experience of illness was a series of disconnected shocks, and my first instinct was to try to bring it under control by turning it into a narrative. Always in emergencies we invent narratives. We describe what is happening, as if to confine the catastrophe. When people heard that I was ill, they inundated me with stories of their own illnesses, as well as the cases of friends. Storytelling seems to be a natural reaction to illness. People bleed stories, and I'm a blood bank of them. (Broyard, 1992, pp. 19–20)

Robinson (1990) invited people with multiple sclerosis (MS) to write about their illness. They provided a range of stories which varied substantially. It was possible to identify a pattern in them similar to that suggested by Gergen and Gergen (1986). The majority of the narratives could be classified as 'progressive' in that the patients described their disease as providing an opportunity for personal advancement. Others were classified as 'stable' and a minority as 'regressive'.

This preference for a progressive narrative reflects both social and personal processes. In western society the dominant health narrative is that not only can illness be positive but that the person can exert control over their illness (see Saillant, 1990). Adopting a progressive narrative allows the patient to transcend the physical infirmity of MS. DelVecchio et al. (1994) in their study of patients with epilepsy also suggest that in organizing their narrative accounts the patients can 'negotiate right action in the face of uncertainty' (p. 838).

Frank (1993) suggested that the central point in any crisis narrative is an epiphany when the actor begins to reassess their position in the world. This can occur at any time during the course of an illness but subsequently the sick person sees the illness in a new light. It is at this stage that the illness story turns from a regressive narrative into a progressive narrative. Admittedly not all sick persons encounter such an epiphanous moment. As Frank (1993) stated: 'Insofar as changing your life is an historically defined project, so the general possibility of epiphanies is also socially constructed. To experience an epiphany requires a cultural milieu in which such experiences are at least possibilities, if not routine expectations' (p. 42).

The temporal character of the illness narrative does not have to be coterminous with the physical character of the illness. For example, Robinson (1990) noted that for some people, the diagnosis of illness meant the end of their lives – their life narrative ended, there was no prospect of progression. As he points out for some people 'a personal story may be ended before a life has physically finished'. For these people the suffering and dislocation of illness provides no prospect of renewal.

Hyden (1997) proposed three types of illness narrative. The first type, illness as narrative, is the process whereby illness is expressed and articulated through narrative. The second type, narrative about illness, is the way physicians and others organize their knowledge about illness. The third type is narrative as illness. This is the process by which a narrative or an insufficient narrative generates an illness. It is this third type which has led to the suggestion that therapy can be construed as narrative reconstruction – the development of a more healthy story.

An important aspect of the illness narrative is that it integrates and situates much of the information which is considered in a rather isolated and fragmented manner by the cognitive psychologists. Blaxter (1993) makes a similar point in her description of lay people's descriptions of illness: 'a . . . notable feature of the accounts was the strain to connect, to present a health history as a chain of cause and effect, with each new problem arising from previous ones' (p. 137). Further, Baumeister and Newman (1994) note that one of the defining characteristics of narratives is that they can accommodate inconsistencies. Similarly, Blaxter (1993) notes that the lay people in her study 'were perfectly capable of holding in equilibrium ideas which might seem opposed: the ultimate cause, in the story of the deprived past, of their current ill-health, but at the same time their own responsibility for "who they were"; the inevitability of ill-health, given their biographies, but at the same time guilt if they were forced to "give in" to illness' (p. 141).

A further feature of narratives is that they serve to orient the individual towards the illness and the social world. Maines (1993) described that narratives can be considered as conveying an argument. As with the discursive psychologists, narrative psychologists emphasize the importance of the social context within which the story is being told (Murray, 1997b). The ill person can tell a different story to the doctor, to her peers and to the researcher – it depends on what message she is trying to convey.

Finally, narratives can move from the level of the personal to that of the societal or political and vice versa. Farmer (1994) noted how stories are involved in the creation of *social representations*. Specifically, he noted in his study of social representations of AIDS in Haiti that as specific stories began to circulate about cases of people with AIDS, social representations about the disease developed. Further, Plummer (1996) noted how public stories about illness which are circulated through the media impinge on the individual who in turn interprets and experiences illness through them. Murray (1996) has also commented on the public circulation of written autobiographies as contributing to a shared illness narrative. The readers of these autobiographies learn a language for describing their illness.

Social representations of health and illness

Illness beliefs do not simply exist within the heads of individuals but emerge and change in everyday social interaction. To understand their nature requires an understanding of these broader societal belief systems. Several studies have used social representation theory to explore popular beliefs about health and illness. The most influential has been the classic study by Claudine Herzlich (1973). From her interviews with a sample of French adults Herzlich concluded that a central concept in the popular definitions of health and illness is activity. For most lay people to be active means to be healthy while to be inactive means to be ill. Herzlich distinguished between three lay reactions to illness:

1   *Illness as destructive*: the experience of those actively involved in society.
2   *Illness as liberator*: the experience of those with excessive social obligations.
3   *Illness as an occupation*: the experience of those who accept illness and feel they must contribute to its alleviation.

People are aware of these different reactions and not only adopt one or another of these strategies depending upon time and circumstance, but also characterize other individuals as belonging to a particular category.

An important characteristic of social representations is that they are not passive characteristics but part of the dialectic process of engagement between the individual and the social world. Moscovici (1984) refers to two particular processes, **anchoring** and **objectification**, which organize social representations. The first is the process whereby unfamiliar concepts are given meaning by connecting them with more familiar concepts, whereas the second is the process whereby a more abstract concept acquires meaning through association with more everyday phenomena. Several researchers have used these concepts to explore popular views of particular illnesses.

Joffe (1996) conducted detailed interviews about AIDS with a sample of young adults from London and from South Africa. She also conducted a content analysis of media campaigns. She notes that historically mass incurable illnesses have been anchored to the 'other'. In the case of AIDS this process is shown in the anchoring of that disease in the supposed aberrant behaviour of others. This process serves a protective function by distancing the person from the risk of contracting the disease. However, a certain amount of 'leakage' has occurred as it became apparent that AIDS could be spread via the blood supply and among heterosexuals. The process of objectification transforms an abstract concept into an image. Joffe (1996) noted that the media images of tombstones and coffins concretized the fear associated with AIDS.

Joffe (1996) argues that the potential for modifying social representations of disease is limited since they serve the function of preserving the status quo in a culture. They not only make the social world remain familiar and manageable but also maintain the dominance of certain ideas. Admittedly, certain organized groups within society can subvert these dominant ideas. Markova and Wilkie (1987) have shown how the gay movement in Britain contributed to a reassessment of the dominant image of AIDS as belonging to a supposedly deviant minority group which in terms of religious beliefs were themselves to blame for contracting the disease. Instead, it was recharacterized as a disease which could affect heterosexual as well as gay individuals.

INTEGRATION

One way of integrating these different approaches to the study of illness beliefs is by considering the levels of psychological analysis proposed by Doise (1986). Doise suggested that a reason for the confusion between different social psychologists was that they operated at different levels of analysis. He suggested that we should distinguish between research which was conducted at the *intrapsychic* level of analysis from that which is conducted at the *interpersonal*, *group* and *societal* levels.

Murray (1993) considered the value of these different levels for organizing research on representations of illness. At the intrapsychic level are the cognitive illness beliefs and to a lesser extent the narrative accounts. At the interpersonal and positional levels are the discursive and narrative accounts while at the societal level are the social representations.

Until now health psychology has tended to focus on describing the cognitive representations and to ignore the social and cultural context within which health and illness beliefs are generated. It has also assumed that these beliefs are emitted by the individual rather than being a social and active process by which the person attempts to make sense of the world of illness within a particular social context. Attention to the other levels of analysis enables consideration of these contextual factors. The consideration of health psychology in its full context of society and culture requires integration of the cognitive and social perspectives.

FUTURE RESEARCH

1   Illness beliefs evolve over time and place. There is a need for a greater understanding of the evolution of health beliefs.
2   Illness beliefs are not fixed but constantly changing. Health psychologists need to be involved in mapping these changes within specific sub-cultures.
3   Theoretically, health psychologists need to explore the conceptual connections between illness and health discourse.
4   The interconnctedness of illness discourse and bodily processes is still poorly understood. There is a need for a concerted programme of theoretical work in this area.

SUMMARY

1   Psychologists have used a variety of theoretical perspectives to investigate popular beliefs about illness. Two major approaches have been a cognitive perspective which analyses the way individuals think about health and illness as processes and a social perspective which includes discursive, narrative and social representation approaches.

2   Cognitive approaches have consisted of asking patients to rate aspects of illness experience along scales and then to factor analyse the scale ratings to develop illness dimensions such as 'identity', 'causes', 'time line', 'consequences' and 'cure'.

3   One common feature of models of lay illness cognitions is a basic time perspective in three broad categories:
  (a) looking back at the possible causes of the disease;
  (b) looking at the present character of the disease in terms of its label, symptoms and severity;
  (c) looking forward to the time line and consequences of the disease.

4   The power of the cognitive approach is that causal attributions can be assumed to be the basis of plans for action. How the person explains an event partly determines how that person subsequently copes with that situation. This has many implications for the communication and delivery of health care.

5   However, the evidence suggests that illness beliefs may not be located in the heads of individuals as stable, fixed entities, but rather that they are joint creations partly reflecting the character of the relationship between the individual and the interviewer. Not surprisingly, different samples and methods have yielded different illness dimensions and it seems unlikely that these dimensions are fixed or stable over time and place. It is also evident that health and illness beliefs may often be logically inconsistent.

6   Because the cognitive approach to the study of illness beliefs has tended to ignore the social and cultural context within which the beliefs are expressed, other approaches for the description and analysis of health beliefs have been developed.

7   An alternative perspective attempts to present a more dynamic and social approach to representations of illness and health. Three ways of looking at health beliefs from a more social perspective are to examine discourse, narrative and social representations.

8   Discourse analysis attempts to provide an alternative perspective which focuses on the character of the discourse and the context within which it occurs rather than on the structure of inferred beliefs. Discourse theorists consider the immediate and broader social context within which beliefs are articulated. For them the communicative nature of language is the focus of attention rather than inferred underlying beliefs.

9   The narrative approach analyses stories about illness experiences. The construction of narrative accounts enables the person to grasp its meaning and to begin to exert some control over it. The character of these stories varies depending upon a variety of factors such as previous experience and public repertoires. Some stories may offer the prospect of advancement, while others offer decline.

10 Social representation theory provides another way of exploring popular beliefs about health and illness. Illness beliefs do not simply exist within the heads of individuals but emerge and change in everyday social interaction. To understand their nature requires an understanding of these broader societal belief systems.

11   The consideration of health psychology in the full context of society and culture requires integration of the cognitive and social perspectives concerning how health and illness are represented by individuals.

KEY TERMS

anchoring

attributions

attribution bias

discourse

illness perceptions

(to) legitimate

narrative

objectification

power imbalance

social representations

12

COMMUNICATION:
MESSAGES AND MEANINGS

Words and language are not wrappings in which things are packed for the commerce of those who write and speak. It is in words and language that things first come into being and are. (Steiner, 1978, p. 41)

OUTLINE

This chapter focuses on interpersonal health communication. Three approaches to the study of doctor–patient communication are described: the 'deviant patient' perspective; the 'authoritarian doctor' perspective; and the 'interactive dyad' perspective. Three widely used research tools are examined, illustrated and critically evaluated: interaction analysis systems, questionnaires and qualitative textual analysis. Six recent trends in the study of interpersonal health communication are introduced. They are concerned with gender differences, 'compliance', the impact of computers, culture, the role of communication in coping with illness and counselling.

HEALTH COMMUNICATION

Health communication is communication in any form which contributes to the promotion of health. Thus, health promotion is the objective, whereas health communication is the means through which this objective is to be achieved. Not all measures which aim to promote health depend upon communication (e.g. fencing around dangerous sites; fitting cars with seatbelts). However, health psychologists' involvement with health promotion has been primarily concerned with communication. Thus, from a health psychology point of view, health promotion and **health communication** cover very similar, if not the same, ground. This is reflected in the editor's introduction to the *Journal of Health Communication* (Ratzan, 1996): 'Health communication is concerned with the use of ethical, persuasive means to craft and deliver campaigns and implement strategies that promote good health and prevent disease' (p. v).

Thus, the study of health communication is relevant to public health promotion efforts such as media campaigns as well as to the health promotion activities of health-care professionals including doctors. Public health communication has already been discussed in Chapter 11; this chapter focuses upon interpersonal health communication. The bulk of the literature in this field is concerned with doctor–patient communication within the surgery setting. However, it is necessary to bear in mind that health promotion activities are carried out in some form by all health-care professionals (HCPs) and HCP–patient communication is a key issue for health psychologists. This chapter critically reviews the major theories and research methods, and introduces recent trends and future directions.

DOCTOR–PATIENT COMMUNICATION

Why is it important?

Communication is an essential, and sometimes the only, route to information about the patient's physical and/or mental state. Early identification of symptoms and thus diagnosis and treatment are made possible through the patient's verbal descriptions of the discomfort they experience. In turn, the doctor, nurse or counsellor provides the patient with crucial information about necessary adjustments in lifestyle as well as treatment directives. All of these can be lifesaving. Also, it has been suggested that effective communication can have a therapeutic effect in itself (e.g. Radley, 1994). Although the major focus has been on verbal communication, non-verbal communication can also be important in interpersonal settings.

Limitations of doctor–patient communication

Despite its importance in the healing process, doctor–patient communication is not always effective. According to Ley (1982) communication is the least satisfactory aspect of the doctor–patient encounter: about one-third of patients in the UK say they are dissatisfied. Furthermore, patients' understanding and memory of what they have been told by the doctor is limited. In addition, and possibly as a consequence, one-third to one-half of outpatients do not comply with doctors' advice (Office of Inspector General, 1990, Chapter 14). Finally, a substantial proportion of patients' problems remain undisclosed and undetected (Maguire, 1984). In spite of a huge amount of research published in journals which are highly accessible to health-care professionals, the proportion of dissatisfied patients remained surprisingly, and disappointingly, constant over 25 years (Ong et al., 1995).

Improvements in the quality of doctor–patient communication could generate significant benefits for both patients and service providers. These include greater *patient satisfaction* with health-care services, increased patient adherence to treatment regimens, decreases in anxiety and distress on the part of patients as well as improved health promotion. In addition, improved disease prevention, quicker recovery from surgery as well as shorter lengths of stay in hospital would benefit the tax payer (Ley, 1988; Kaplan et al., 1989).

APPROACHES TO THE STUDY OF DOCTOR–PATIENT COMMUNICATION

The 'deviant patient' perspective

Early studies focused on patient characteristics in their attempt to account for failures in doctor–patient communication. For example, Balint's (1964) psychoanalytic approach assumed that in their presentations to the doctor, patients were routinely masking the 'real' problem and that it was the doctor's task to uncover it. Another popular early research question was 'what is it about the patient that makes him/her a defaulter?' (See Box 12.1.)

BOX 12.1 APPROACHES TO THE STUDY OF DOCTOR–PATIENT COMMUNICATION

Perspective	Methods
'Deviant patient'	Questionnaires Interaction analysis systems
'Authoritarian doctor'	Interaction analysis systems Questionnaires
'Interactive dyad'	Conversation analysis Discourse analysis

However, the search for patient characteristics responsible for non-adherence to treatment regimens met with little success. Instead, it was found that there was a link between patient satisfaction and *compliance* (e.g. Ley, 1982): satisfied patients were more likely to co-operate with their doctor's advice. This, together with wider social developments of the late 1960s which challenged traditional concepts of 'authority', led to a shift of focus onto the role of the doctor.

The 'authoritarian doctor' perspective

In this approach researchers looked at the ways in which doctors use their authority in order to control the doctor–patient interaction. Much emphasis was placed upon the inbuilt asymmetry in the doctor–patient interaction. In a classic study, Byrne and Long (1976) identified different doctors' styles of communicating with patients. They analysed audio-taped interactions from 71 GPs and approximately 2,500 patients and identified four diagnostic styles and seven prescriptive styles used by the doctors. These styles constitute a continuum from 'patient-centred' to 'doctor-centred' styles. A *patient-centred style* makes use of the patient's knowledge and experience through techniques such as silence, listening and reflection, whereas a *doctor-centred style* makes use of the doctor's knowledge and skill, for example, through asking questions. Byrne and Long observed that doctors adopted a habitual style which they tended to use with most patients. Some doctors were more controlling than others.

The major criticism of doctors' traditional communication style was that it was characterized by working to rigid agendas, little listening to patients' accounts and little open discussion of treatment options. A more patient-centred approach was called for. It was suggested that patient-centred styles increase patient adherence as well as satisfaction (e.g. Stewart, 1984). One corollary of this approach was the attempt to provide medical students with effective training in doctor–patient communication (e.g. Maguire, 1984; Maguire et al., 1989).

However, success has been limited. Recent studies have also not found as strong and positive a relationship between patient-centredness and satisfaction (Winefield et al., 1996). Kreps (1996a) advocated a consumer orientation to health care and health promotion in order to address the imbalance of power between providers and consumers. Until this power imbalance is corrected, training in communication skills is unlikely to succeed (Meeuwesen et al., 1991).

The 'interactive dyad' perspective

In the 1990s the focus on doctor–patient communication shifted again. Researchers began looking at the *communicative event* to which both doctor and patient contribute. Thus, both doctor and patient are seen to be shaping the conversation as they make use of culturally available discursive resources. Both doctor and patient use language in order to achieve interpersonal objectives, such as disclaiming or attributing responsibility for the patient's ill health or projecting a 'brave face' to avoid categorization as a hypochondriac. The 1990s ended with the assertion that 'doctor (or nurse) knows best' should have no place in modern health care (Coulter, 1999).

A focus on the communicative event as a joint achievement can shed light on the reasons for communication failure. For example, serious mis-understandings can arise when the doctor takes at face value patient statements which are in fact designed to communicate relational or self-presentational meanings, such as responding 'Fine, thank you' when being asked 'How are you?' (e.g. Coupland et al., 1994).

The importance of non-verbal communication in the form of eye contact, facial expression, gestures and other forms of communication has also been highlighted (Bensing, 1991). A focus on the communicative event, as opposed to the individual characteristics of doctors and/or patients, also allows the role of culture specificity in doctor–patient interactions to be explored.

METHODS USED TO STUDY DOCTOR–PATIENT COMMUNICATION

Three methods for the study of doctor–patient communication can be identified: interaction analysis systems; questionnaire studies; qualitative textual analysis.

Interaction analysis systems

Researchers in the field have used a range of methods to explore doctor–patient communication. The most widely used research tool to date is the *interaction analysis system (IAS)*. This is an observation instrument which allows the researcher to identify, categorize and quantify features of the doctor–patient encounter. A large number of different interaction analysis systems have been developed. The most commonly used IASs include those devised by Bales (1950) and Roter (1977) (see Box 12.2). Here, audio- or video-recorded doctor–patient interactions are analysed by categorizing each statement into one of a large number of mutually exclusive and exhaustive content categories. For example, a doctor's statement could be classified as 'information giving', 'information seeking' or 'social conversation'. A related analytic approach is Stiles' Verbal Exchange Structure (e.g. Stiles et al., 1982; Stiles, 1996) which identifies sets of speech act categories that tend to occur together and which are designed to achieve certain objectives within an encounter.

BOX 12.2 INTERACTION ANALYSIS SYSTEMS (STEWART, 1984, p. 169)

This is an adapation of the system developed by Bales (1950). Interactions are broken into segments and each segment is coded by judges using the following categories:

1 *Shows solidarity, raises other's status, gives help, reward*
   Includes: greeting, expressions of thanks, invitations, friendly comments which 'breaks the ice', expressions of sympathy ('I can see how you feel'), giving approval or encouragement, giving support and reassurance, acting in a conciliatory fashion.
2 *Shows tension release, jokes, laughs, shows satisfaction*
   Includes: cheerfulness, enjoyment, euphoria, joking, laughing.
3 *Agrees, shows, passive acceptance, understands*
   Includes: respectful conformation, concurrence, endorsement ('exactly'), a sign interest ('Yes, M-hmmmm'), consent to a request, giving approval.
4 *Gives suggestions, direction, implying autonomy for other*
   Includes: proposing a solution, demonstrating how situation is to be defined, direct attempts to counsel, control exercised so that the consent of the other is recognized.
5 *Gives opinion, evaluation, analysis, expresses feeling, wish*
   Includes: introspection, musing, expression of hopes, wants, guiding principles ('I want to get it right this time'), evaluation of an action ('I must have been nervous to behave that way'), making an inference about a situation ('It seems to me that he is angry all the time').

6 *Gives orientation, information, repeats, clarifies, confirms*
   Includes: explaining, summarizing, reporting, giving past history of symptoms or problems in a comparatively neutral emotional tone, rephrasing, stating a fact.

7 *Asks for orientation, information, repetition, confirmation*
   Includes: expression of lack of knowledge, direct questions.

8 *Asks for opinion, evaluation, analysis, expression of feeling*
   Includes: open-ended non-directive leads, questions seeking an interpretation, expressions of an inability to make satisfactory inferences (here the request may be implicit and lack anxiety more typical of Category 11).

9 *Asks for suggestion, direction, possible ways of action*
   Includes: requests for proposed solutions, requests for crystallization of a concrete plan (the appeal must have the undertone of shared responsibility rather than dependence which would be more typical of Category 11).

10 *Disagrees, shows passive rejection, formality, withholds resources*
    Includes: behaviour which is over-cool, unappreciative, dubious, critical, disbelief, behaviour which evades, disregards (the rejection is of the idea rather than the person otherwise it would be scored in Category 12).

11 *Shows tension, anxiety, asks for help*
    Includes: expressions of impatience, strain, misgivings, stammering, panic, self-consciousness, nervous laughter, an admission of an ignorance, remorse, an apology, expressions of self-criticism, expressions of frustration, asking for aid, appealing to the other's good nature, requests for help by currying favour, acting martyred, self-pitying; showing a need to be supported and given affection.

12 *Shows antagonism, deflates other's status, defends or asserts self*
    Includes: attempts to control in which freedom of choice is non-existent, commands, expression of non-compliance, unwillingness, stubbornness, nagging, interruptions, warding off interruptions, belittling, maligning; expressions of moral indignation, being 'on one's guard', showing off, boasting, showing rage or belligerence perhaps by cursing.

In a meta-analysis of IAS studies of doctor–patient communication Roter (1989) identified six broad communication variables addressed in the studies. These include information giving, information seeking, social conversation, positive talk, negative talk and partnership building (see Box 12.3). Roter also notes that IASs were predominantly used to study the doctors', rather than the patients', *communication styles*. Thus, IAS research is most closely associated with the 'authoritarian doctor' perspective.

BOX 12.3 THE MOST WIDELY ASSESSED COMMUNICATION VARIABLES (ROTER, 1989, p. 186; REPRODUCED WITH PERMISSION)

Information giving	Gives information, opinion, suggestion, instruction, counsels or persuades, tries to motivate patient, give directions,

	instructs or teaches, % communication which is teaching, % communication which is educational, verbal explanation, gives information and orientation, problem related expressions, explains, discusses problem resolution, descriptive communication, edification, disclosure, advertisement, answers patient questions, volunteers explanation, volunteers information, gives medical information, discloses, gives information on or discusses: patient condition, nature of illness, cause, symptoms, diagnosis, current health treatment, drugs, non-medical treatment, medical treatment, self-care, prevention, prognosis, seriousness of condition, physical activity, diet, health promotion, lifestyle, mentions exam findings, discusses physical exam.
Information seeking	Asks questions, asks for information, asks for instructions, takes medical history, asks about compliance (open and closed questions), non-directive history taking, % of communication which is questions, time devoted to history taking.
Social conversation	Greetings, shows courtesy, introduces self, non-medical statements, personal remarks, social remarks, casual conversation, discusses social/family matters.
Positive talk	Agrees/shows understanding, shows approval, laughs, uses humour, tension release, shows solidarity, gives reassurance, offers support, encourages, shows empathy, calms patient, shows simple attention, % communication with positive affective content, socio-emotional cluster (personal remarks, laughs, agrees, approves), doctor–patient friendly rapport.
Negative talk	Disagrees/criticizes, confronts, shows antagonism or hostility, shows tension, negative affect, tension build up, anxiety/nervousness, speech errors, negative errors, negative interaction, bored.
Partnership building	Asks for patient's opinion, understanding, suggestions, questions, ideas, makes interpretation, reflects patients' statements, facilitates patient response.

EXAMPLE OF A STUDY USING AN IAS: STREET (1991)

The objective of this study was to explain systematic differences in information giving by doctors. It has been found that patients who are upper middle class, more seriously ill, more educated and middle aged receive more information from their doctors (e.g. Pendleton and Bochner, 1980;

Waitzkin, 1985). In order to identify possible causes of these differences, Street (1991) measured the following variables:

1   Patients' communicative style (e.g. question asking, affective expressiveness and opinion giving).
2   Patient characteristics (e.g. education, age, sex, anxiety).
3   Physicians' 'partnership-building' utterances (i.e. utterances which solicit/invite patients' questions, concerns and opinions).

Video recordings of doctor–patient interactions at a family practice clinic at a teaching hospital in the USA were transcribed. The following five verbal behaviours were coded:

1   Physicians' information giving.
2   Physicians' partnership building.
3   Patients' opinion giving.
4   Patients' affective expressions.
5   Patients' question asking.

Patients were found to ask few questions (only 4.1% of all patient utterances) and to offer few opinions (6.4%). Physicians rarely solicited the patients' concerns, opinions and questions (only 2.3% of all physician utterances were partnership building). The most powerful predictor of doctors' information giving was patients' question asking. Also, anxious patients received significantly more information from their doctors than did less worried patients. There was also a tendency for younger and more educated patients to receive more diagnostic information.

Thus, this study's findings suggest that differences in physicians' information giving are partially mediated by differences in patients' communicative style (i.e. via question asking). However, it would be wrong to conclude that patients' communicative style is the 'cause of' physician information giving, since patients' question asking is largely a response to physicians' partnership-building utterances.

Even though IAS studies are able to identify and quantify relevant communication variables in doctor–patient interactions, there are a number of shortcomings associated with this approach. First, it does not allow us to analyse sequencing in conversation. IASs can only tell us what types of utterances were made, by whom and how often. It does not allow us to explore who initiates particular turns and with what consequences. Second, it relies upon a literal reading of statements. As a result, rhetorical strategies such as irony or sarcasm and their communicative functions cannot be identified and analysed. These concerns have been taken up by more recent methods of analysis, such as conversation analysis or discourse analysis, to be discussed later in this chapter.

Questionnaire studies

A number of questionnaires have been developed (e.g. Norton, 1978) to measure patients' perceptions of doctors' communication style. Such questionnaires tend to be administered after a clinic visit, and they therefore rely upon the patient's memory of the actual interaction. Questionnaire items include statements about the manner in which the doctor interacted with the patient (e.g. 'The doctor deliberately reacts in such a way that I know s/he is listening') which the patient is asked to rate on a Likert-type scale (see Box 12. 4). Questionnaires are also used to measure patient satisfaction. A combination of questionnaires can be used in order to investigate the relationship between doctor's communication style and patient satisfaction (e.g. Buller and Butler, 1987). Questionnaires are predominantly used to study the doctors' rather than the patients' communication styles. Thus, questionnaire research tends to come from within the 'authoritarian doctor' perspective.

BOX 12.4   EXAMPLES FROM NORTON'S (1978) COMMUNICATION STYLES MEASURE (BULLER AND BULLER, 1987, p. 380)

Scale item

Affiliativeness
Very encouraging
Verbally acknowledges other's contributions
Very relaxed
Doctor's eyes reflect exactly what he/she is feeling
Extremely open
Open and honest
Usually leaves an impression
Leaves me with an impression I usually remember
The way doctor says something really leaves an impression on me
Leaves a definite impression
Very empathetic
Extremely attentive
Listens very carefully
Deliberately reacts in such a way that I know he/she is listening

Dominance/activity
Tends to come on strong
Dominates conversations
Verbally exaggerates to emphasize a point
Dramatizes a lot
Very argumentative
Constantly gestures when communicating

EXAMPLE OF A QUESTIONNAIRE STUDY (MAKOUL ET AL., 1995)

As part of a wider study of communication and decision making about prescription medication, Makoul et al. (1995) used questionnaires in order to study discrepancies between perceived and actual communication. They video-recorded 903 consultations involving 39 GPs and their patients in Oxford, UK. After the consultation, patients were asked to complete a questionnaire which included a section about their perceptions of communication during the consultation. Doctors' questionnaires included questions about their patients' characteristics as well as their own communication styles. Analysis of the video-recordings involved the use of checklists which allowed the researchers to record mention of a particular topic (e.g. risk, benefit of medication) as well as who initiated discussion of the topic.

The results showed that physicians most frequently mentioned the product name (in 78.2% of consultations) and instructions for use of the medication (86.7%), whereas patients remained extremely passive. There was little discussion of issues such as side effects or the patient's opinion about the medication. For example, physicians initiated discussion about the patient's ability to follow the treatment plan in only 4.8% of the consultations. However, analysis of the questionnaires revealed that both doctors and patients overestimated the extent to which these issues had been discussed during the consultation. The authors concluded that the observed pattern of communication about prescription medication does not contribute to the development of patients' decision-making competencies. In addition, they point out that the observed discrepancies between interactants' perceptions and actual communication cast doubt on communication studies which use self-report methods alone.

Questionnaire-based studies of doctor–patient communication rely upon participants' memories of their perceptions of the interaction. This introduces two sources of bias. First, memory may be faulty. Second, participants' perceptions at the time of the interaction may have been distorted. In addition, the use of closed, multiple-choice items does not allow participants to generate their own criteria for evaluating doctor–patient communication. This is to say, questionnaires may be of limited validity for individuals or groups of participants. Finally, patients may be reluctant to be critical of their doctors.

Qualitative textual analysis

Researchers have also employed qualitative methods of text analysis such as discourse or conversation analysis. These methods require accurate and detailed transcription of recordings of doctor–patient interactions. Interview transcripts are then subjected to fine-grained linguistic analysis. The aim is to identify the procedures which speakers use in order to manage their discursive objectives (e.g. changing topics, disclaiming responsibility, delivering advice, etc.). This involves paying close attention to turn taking and transitions from one topic to another. In addition, a transcript is read as a whole, with a focus upon the indexicality of language, rather than as a collection of independent statements. Researchers are thus able to explore the ways in which meaning is constructed and negotiated by participants and trace the consequences of such constructions in the text. This approach is informed by the 'interactive dyad perspective'.

EXAMPLE OF A DISCOURSE ANALYTIC STUDY (COUPLAND ET AL., 1994)
Coupland et al. were interested in the relationship between medical and socio-relational dimensions of doctor–patient talk. In particular, they wanted to know how the opening phases of consultations between doctors and elderly patients are achieved and how participants enter a medical frame of talk. An analysis of 85 audio-taped consultations at a geriatric outpatients clinic in the UK was carried out for this purpose. It was found that, typically, consultations were initiated by some form of socio-relational talk, however brief. Consultation openings tended to take the following form:

- Summons/approach (e.g. 'Come in.').
- Greetings (e.g. 'Hello there.').
- Dispositional talk (e.g. 'Do sit down. Won't keep you a minute.').
- Familiarity sequence (e.g. 'I think I saw you two weeks ago, didn't I, Mrs Smith?').
- Holding sequence (e.g. 'Let's have a look at your notes.').
- How-are-you type exchange (e.g. 'How are you feeling?').

In the vast majority of cases, all of the above were initiated by the doctor. Other exchanges, such as apologies (e.g. 'Sorry I'm late'), compliments (e.g. 'You look very smart today') or environmental talk (e.g. 'It's hot, isn't it?') can be inserted into the typical consultation opening sequence by either doctor or patient. The doctor's 'How-are-you?' (HAY?) commonly occurs after a holding sequence and constitutes the transition from preliminary talk to the medical frame. However, Coupland et al. identified a number of alternative formulations of the HAY? as well as different patient inter-pretations of the HAY? For example, a 'How are you today?' can elicit a socio-relational 'I'm fine, thanks' instead of the intended account of the patient's current medical complaint.

In general, Coupland et al. found that patients and sometimes also doctors did not immediately and categorically orient to the medical agenda. They conclude that patients as well as doctors played significant parts in negotiating how and when they should move into medically framed talk. This, they argue, is vital within the context of geriatric care since many of the consequences of illness for elderly patients are experienced socially (e.g. reduced mobility or reduced independence).

Qualitative textual analysis is extremely time consuming. Detailed transcription, including pauses, interruptions and repetitions as they take place in naturally occurring conversations, takes up to 10 hours per one-hour recording. Line-by-line linguistic analysis of discourse requires careful reading and re-reading of the text. Researchers tend to analyse small numbers of transcripts in great detail. As a result, it is impossible to ascertain how common the discursive strategies and practices identified by any one study might be in a particular population. In other words, qualitative textual analysis does not allow us to generalize.

Another criticism of this method is that it conceives of the doctor–patient interaction as an entirely localized event. This fails to take into account power relations which pre-exist the doctor–patient encounter. That is to say, what is said by patient and doctor is not simply a product of their interaction but it reflects their respective roles and status within society. We need to look beyond the text in order to identify such factors.

Triangulation: combining methods of analysis

Even though the three methodological approaches to the study of doctor–patient communication have been discussed separately, there is no reason to believe that they are mutually exclusive alternatives. To the contrary, it could be argued that the best studies of communication would have to use a combination of methods in order to provide a comprehensive account of conversational dynamics and their outcomes. For example, the discovery by Makoul et al. (1995) that both patients and doctors overestimated the extent to which certain topics had been discussed during the consultation was only possible on the basis of a combination of questionnaire data and transcripts of the actual consultation. Triangulation of methods of data collection and analysis allows the researcher to obtain more than one perspective on the same phenomenon. Questionnaires reflect participants' perceptions of the interaction. IASs provide quantitative information about prominent features of the interaction. Textual analyses trace the discursive constructions and negotiations of meanings which constitute the interaction. As a result, triangulation can shed light on the limitations of any one method. For example, Makoul et al. (1995) were able to conclude that self-report methods alone are unlikely to provide accurate information about the communicative contents of a consultation.

Example of a study using a combination of quantitative and qualitative methods (O'Brien and Petrie, 1996)

O'Brien and Petrie (1996) examined the nature of patient participation in the medical consultation and its effect on patient understanding, recall and satisfaction. The authors used both quantitative and qualitative methods in order to obtain information about frequencies of types of patient participation (quantitative) as well as about the content of patient participation (qualitative). The consultations of 99 patients with joint pain from two hospitals in New Zealand were audiotaped and transcribed. The transcripts were coded using the Verbal Response Mode (VRM) coding system (Stiles et al., 1979) in order to determine the frequency and type of patient participation in each section of the medical interview. Patients' ability to remember and understand information presented during the consultation as well as patient satisfaction with the consultation were assessed immediately after the consultation via two verbally administered questionnaires. Transcripts from patients with the highest (n = 10) and the lowest (n = 10) scores on participation were selected for a qualitative analysis of the content of their consultations.

The quantitative analysis of consultation transcripts revealed that the majority of patient utterances in the history-taking section of the consultation provided information (i.e. edification and disclosure). The doctors' contribution to this part of the consultation consisted largely of questions and reflection. During the examination section, patients continued to offer information while doctors began to move from questions to edification, disclosure and interpretation. Patients asked more questions in the conclusion section than in any other part of the consultation. However, the overall number of questions asked by patients was small (13 on average per consultation). The conclusion section contained most of the doctors' information provision utterances (edification). On the basis of VRM coding, a patient participation score was obtained for each patient.

Analysis of the questionnaires revealed that patients best recalled medication name, other treatment instructions (such as X-rays and blood tests) and diagnosis, while instructions for taking medication, information about the diagnosis and the purpose of the prescribed medication were less well remembered. Understanding of medical information was also limited. There was no relationship between patient participation and recall and understanding. However, there was a significant negative correlation between patient participation in the history section of the consultation and satisfaction with treatment.

Qualitative analysis of interview transcripts suggested that patient participation was not necessarily constructive. Patients with high levels of participation tended to report symptoms in a random, unfocused manner and expressed anger and frustration. These consultations were also characterized by tensions and misunderstandings between doctor and patient, low levels of patient satisfaction and low levels of recall scores. By contrast, patients with the lowest participation levels showed very little emotion, complained little and confined their comments and questions to the specific symptoms which brought them to the clinic. In this way, the qualitative analysis was able to shed light on the negative relationship between high patient participation and satisfaction with treatment. High levels of participation often reflected an individual in distress, who was suffering from several health problems and who reported a history of unsatisfactory medical care. The authors suggest that there may be an optimal level of patient participation required for a constructive medical interview. They conclude by discussing possible ways in which constructive patient participation may be facilitated.

The use of triangulation constitutes a methodological challenge for most researchers. Such an approach requires considerable research skills in more than one research method. This is particularly important where researchers combine qualitative and quantitative methods. One of the risks associated with such triangulation is that researchers use a methodological approach with which they are not familiar and of which they have limited experience. As a result, a study using a combination of methods can be 'lopsided' in the sense that only one part of the study carries any scientific weight. For example, O'Brien and Petrie's (1996) qualitative analysis of consultation transcripts is not based upon any of the recognized forms of qualitative textual analysis. The authors do not provide any information about the way in which the texts were analysed or even which approach to the analysis of conversations had been adopted. As a result, their qualitative findings are difficult to evaluate.

GENERAL CRITICISMS OF WORK IN DOCTOR–PATIENT INTERACTION

A number of general criticisms can be made of the dominant trends in doctor–patient communication research to date. First, much of the research has attempted to identify general laws or categories that are applicable to doctor–patient interactions in general. However, Silverman (1987) points out that this may be an inappropriate goal given that a wide range of factors influence the nature of the interaction between doctors and patients. The patient's illness 'career' (i.e. early or late stage), the severity of the illness, the social status of the condition (i.e. Is it stigmatized? Does it attract research funds?), the technologies involved in treatment, the complexity of medical issues involved, as well as the location of the interaction (e.g. GP's surgery, hospital ward, specialist clinic) all shape the communicative event. As a result, it may be necessary to develop different theories and recommendations for these different types of doctor–patient interactions. Furthermore, diverse patient groups are likely to have diverse communication needs (e.g. children, the elderly, people with AIDS) which again need to be recognized.

BOX 12.5   GENERAL CRITICISMS OF WORK IN DOCTOR–PATIENT COMMUNICATION

Criticism: the search for universal laws and general categories.
Recommendation: include consideration of diverse patient communication needs.

Criticism: the focus upon general practice settings.
Recommendation: include other relevant health service settings.

Criticism: limited outcome measures.
Recommendation: include further measures of health status and quality of life.

For example, Silverman (1987) found that some parents of child patients actually want and expect the doctor to control the interaction and to make diagnostic and prescriptive decisions for them, in order to relieve them of the responsibility for their child's health. By contrast, people with AIDS constitute an extremely well-informed patient group whose knowledge about their condition often surpasses that of their doctors. Clearly, these two categories of clients require different communication styles from their doctors.

Second, the vast majority of research in the field takes place in the GPs' surgery. Other relevant settings such as hospital wards or family planning clinics are left relatively unexplored and so are patient interactions with other health professionals such as nurses, health visitors, midwives, dentists, receptionists and hospital doctors. There is no reason to believe that we are justified in extrapolating from findings from GPs' surgeries to other medical settings.

Third, researchers have tended to use patient satisfaction, adherence, as well as recall and understanding of information as *outcome measures* in order to assess the effectiveness of doctor–patient communication. However, it could be argued that a more relevant outcome measure would be actual health status as well as quality of life of the patient in the long term (Ong et al., 1995). These have been used least in empirical studies of doctor–patient communication to date.

RECENT TRENDS

Gender differences in physicians' communication styles

A number of studies have identified gender differences in doctors' communication styles (e.g. West, 1990; Meeuwesen et al., 1991). Female doctors are generally found to adopt more patient-centred communication styles whereas their male colleagues tend to be more directive and controlling. For example, West (1990) video-taped and transcribed 21 physician–patient encounters. She found gender differences in the ways in which physicians formulated directives. Male doctors typically used 'aggravated directives' such as imperatives (e.g. 'Take one of each four times a day'), need statements (e.g. 'I think you need to try and get out'), want statements (e.g. 'I want you to go ahead and get that light salt'), quasi-question directives (e.g.

'Why don't you jump up on the table?'), permission provisions (e.g.'You can start on the three months supply'), and directives by example (e.g. 'I would take one of those four times a day'). Aggravated directives demand action rather than answers in return and they imply an asymmetrical alignment between the parties in talk. By contrast, female doctors typically issued their directives in mitigated form, thus minimizing distinctions between themselves and their patients.

Mitigated directives include proposals for joint action (e.g. 'Maybe what we ought to do is stay with it'), singular suggestions (e.g. 'Maybe you can stay away from the desserts') and permission directives (e.g. 'Let me just say one thing'). Rates of compliance with doctors' instructions at the time of the consultation (e.g. to undress or lie down) varied with the form of directive used. Aggravated directives were less likely to elicit a compliant response. Female physicians' overall compliance rate was 67%, while male physicians achieved patient co-operation in only 50% of cases.

These findings resonate with the general literature of gender differences in communication (e.g. Tannen, 1991; Paludi, 1992) and suggest that gender-specific socialization carries over into the professional conduct of doctors. As mentioned above, patients' communication needs depend upon the nature of their illness and treatment requirements. Future research requires exploration of the relationship between physician's gender and communication style and patient communication needs.

Reconceptualization of 'compliance'

Patient compliance with medical instructions has been a major focus of research in doctor–patient communication. Compliance, defined as 'the extent to which the patient's behaviour . . . coincides with medical or health advice' (Haynes, 1979a), is generally seen to be one of the key objectives of doctor–patient communication. Compliance has been measured and its determinants have been explored by numerous researchers over the past 30 years or so. Recently, researchers have begun to question traditional conceptualizations of compliance. For example, Trostle (1988) argues that compliance research has defined patient behaviour in terms of professional expectations alone, thus reflecting (and reinforcing) the growing monopoly of the medical profession over the past century. Compliance research, according to Trostle, is ideological in that 'the very notion of compliance requires a dependent layperson and a dominant professional' (p. 1301). As a result, it fails to understand the complexity and legitimacy of patient behaviours which differ from clinical prescriptions.

In a study of 54 rheumatology patients Donovan and Blake (1992) found that non-compliance was largely the result of reasoned decision making. Qualitative analysis of semi-structured interviews with patients and audio-taped consultations with rheumatologists revealed that patients experimented with drug dosages and timing in order to manage side effects and effectiveness of drugs. Patients made decisions about compliance based on information gleaned from sources other than the rheumatologist, including their GPs, the media as well as family and friends. The authors propose that researchers and practitioners ought to be concerned with the provision of information which would allow patients to make informed decisions, rather than with compliance per se. Recent work has explored strategies for effectively communicating information about prescription drugs (Hammond, 1995). More detailed discussion of compliance and empowerment follows in Chapter 13.

The impact of computers on communication

In recent years the use of computers during the consultation process has become increasingly widespread. Many surgeries are now equipped with interactive computer systems which allow the doctor or nurse to update patient records, obtain patient histories as well as print out prescriptions in the presence of the patient. The impact of the presence of computers on communication in the medical context has only just begun to be explored.

Early studies (e.g. Brownbridge et al., 1988; Greatbatch et al., 1995) suggest that the use of the computer does indeed change the nature of the interaction. Through prompts and fixed sequencing of questions, the computer directs the flow of the interview. As a result, interviews can be longer and more detailed, but do not allow for 'small talk' which may reveal psychosocial concerns on the part of the patient. For example, Greatbatch et al. (1995) video-recorded consultations with general practitioners at an inner city practice before (n = 100) and after (n = 150) the introduction of a computer system. They found that the use of the computer was more prominent during the consultations than the prescription pad and pen had been. The presence of the computer led doctors to delay their responses to patients' utterances until after keystroke sequences had been completed. They confined their visual attention to the computer screen and restricted their contributions, particularly sociorelational ones such as expressions of sympathy and surprise and non-verbal ones such as laughter. Patients attempted to synchronize their conduct with the visible (changes on the screen) and audible (warning bleeps) manifestations of the workings of the computer system. Doctors' increasing familiarity with the system did not lead to changes in these practices. The authors conclude that use of the computer system adversely affected doctors' communication with their patients. Future research needs to assess the impact of computers on patient satisfaction as well as other outcome measures.

The role of culture in doctor–patient communication

Cultural differences play a role in how patients perceive and evaluate their doctors' conduct. For example, physicians' touch can lower patient satisfaction (e.g. Larsen and Smith, 1981) or it can be read as evidence of good care (e.g. Scarpaci, 1988). Similarly, telling the truth about a cancer diagnosis can be acceptable and expected in one culture, but perceived as cruel and unnecessary in another (Holland et al., 1987). The issue of organ donation is much more sensitive in some cultures than others and therefore requires special communication skills on the part of ICU doctors and nurses.

Randhawa (1995) discusses social and cultural factors which may be responsible for the shortfall of organ donors from within UK communities. Cultural concerns about cadaveric transplants (CAD) include violation of the sanctity of the deceased, the desire to be buried or cremated whole and/or religious convictions. Concerns about living related donor transplant (LRD) tend to be more social than cultural and revolve around family pressures and personal conflicts. Randhawa (1995) argues that health professionals need to be made aware of social and cultural factors which may deter potential donors. He calls for an assessment of existing hospital strategies towards organ procurement and their application in a multicultural society.

There is a need for further research into the ways in which culture mediates doctor–patient communication and its outcomes for patients. This is particularly important within the context of a multicultural society in which doctor–patient dyads do not necessarily share the same cultural background (see also Chapter 3).

The role of communication in coping with illness

Recently, health psychologists have begun to explore the ways in which communication mediates the illness experience itself. For example, the Relational Model of Health Communication Competence (Kreps, 1988) proposes that physiological and psychological health outcomes are influenced by health-care participants' level of communication competence. Competence is characterized by provider and consumer skills, such as empathic listening, verbal and non-verbal sensitivity, encoding and decoding skills and interaction management. Query and Kreps (1996) examined the relationship between lay caregivers' communication competence and their health outcomes within the context of Alzheimer's disease. Health outcome measures included social support and cognitive depression. Ninety care givers for patients with Alzheimer's disease completed three questionnaires measuring social support, communication competence and depression. Relationships between communication competence and social support (both extent of network and satisfaction) as well as competence and depression were non-significant. However, a linear combination of social support satisfaction and number of social supports significantly discriminated between caregivers high in communication competence and those low in competence. Thus, the results provide partial support for the Relational Model of Health Communication Competence.

Frey et al. (1996) discussed the ways in which communication practices within a residential facility for people with AIDS help residents cope with the loss of fellow residents. The use of particular discursive constructions (e.g. 'the military myth', 'the journey myth') as well as collective and private bereavement rituals, allow residents to manage the tensions of living and dying with AIDS. The authors argued that such communication practices can help residents avoid further depression of their immune system and cope better with their illness. More research into the effects of communication practices upon quality of life as well as physical health outcomes is needed.

Counselling within a medical context

The development of increasingly sophisticated diagnostic tests and screening procedures has highlighted the need for informed consent and patient choice. Genetic screening and the HIV antibody test, for example, provide the healthy individual with information which has major implications for their future health status. It may also require them to make significant lifestyle changes. The identification of an 'at risk status', therefore, has psychological consequences which need to be considered when testing is carried out. Pre-test counselling provides an opportunity for patients to consider advantages and disadvantages of testing and to make an informed decision about whether or not to do it. Post-test counselling helps the individual to make sense of the test result and to discuss ways in which they may cope with its implications.

It has been suggested that pre- and post-test counselling has reduced psychiatric morbidity in those who undergo the HIV antibody test (e.g. Chesney, 1993), although research in this area has yielded inconsistent results (Beardsell and Coyle, 1996). Silverman and his colleagues (e.g. Silverman et al., 1992a; Silverman et al., 1992b; Silverman, 1997) have conducted extensive research into the ways in which HIV counselling is managed in the UK. Using conversation analytic methods, they have identified two widely used communication formats: the interview format and the information delivery format. The former is based on a question and answer sequence, whereas in the latter the counsellor delivers information and the client offers response tokens such as 'yes' or 'mmm'. Silverman argues that both formats are functional in that they are designed to manage interactional and practical constraints. For example, the information delivery format allows the counsellor to address delicate issues within a tight time limit (10–15 minutes) by using indirect (e.g. 'when someone tests positive') and generalized (e.g. 'everyone needs to be really careful') formulations. By contrast, the interview format which allows for an exploration of the client's perspective is used in longer counselling sessions (40–45 minutes).

Michie et al. (1996b) analysed 131 routine consultations conducted in a genetics centre in the UK in order to find out what constitutes effective genetic counselling. Their study was designed to examine the extent to which genetic counselling influences outcomes. The authors used self-report questionnaires in order to measure inputs (e.g. the nature of the genetic problem, patient expectations and directiveness of the counsellor's consultation style) and outcomes (e.g. patient anxiety and patient satisfaction). The process of the consultation was examined on the basis of transcripts of audiotapes of the consultation. It was found that what both patient and counsellor bring to the consultation influences patient satisfaction and mood after the consultation. No causal association between what happens during the consultation and patient outcome was identified. However, the authors caution against the conclusion that genetic counselling is ineffectual and unnecessary by drawing attention to the possibility that responsive counsellors may be modifying their consultation style according to their perception of patient needs and expectations. As a result, associations between process and outcome variables would be masked.

Future research needs to include a comparison of matched recipients and non-recipients of genetic counselling. As new forms of screening and treatment emerge, health psychologists need to study the ways in which communication is used in their management. This is particularly important when screening practices and policies are still new and undeveloped and potentially open to psychological input.

FUTURE RESEARCH

1   Future research in doctor–patient communication must explore the communication needs of different patient groups, as well as the relationship between physician characteristics (e.g. gender, communication style, culture) and patient needs.
2   More attention needs to be paid to medical settings other than the doctor's office.
3   The relationship between doctor–patient communication and patient health status/quality of life also requires further work. In order to understand why patients do not follow physicians' advice, the notion of 'compliance' needs to be further unpacked.
4   Qualitative work can shed light on patients' reasons for not adhering to medical regimens.
5   The emergence of new technologies constitutes a challenge to health psychologists. Studies need to be designed and carried out in response to new developments in information technology, screening methods and treatment in order to trace their psychological implications.
6   The study of communication within a medical context has great potential for informing and improving communication practice. It is crucial that researchers spell out their findings implications for medical practice in a way which is accessible to practitioners.

SUMMARY

1   Communication is an essential and sometimes the only route to information about a patient's physical and/or mental state. However, communication is the least satisfactory aspect of the doctor–patient encounter and many studies have found that its effectiveness is limited.

2   There are three major approaches to the study of doctor–patient communication: (i) the 'deviant patient'; (ii) the 'authoritarian doctor'; (iii) the 'interactive dyad'. Questionnaires, interaction analysis systems and qualitative textual analysis are methods with which to study doctor–patient communication.

3   The interaction analysis system (IAS) is the most widely used research tool in doctor–patient communication to date. It is an observation instrument which allows the researcher to identify, categorize and quantify features of the doctor–patient encounter. Such features include 'information giving', 'information seeking' and 'social conversation'.

4   Both doctors' and patients' communicative styles, demographic as well as personal characteristics, can influence the nature and quality of the communicative event. For example, patients' question asking, anxiety state and educational background are associated with physicians' information giving (Street, 1991).

5   Typically, patients ask few questions and rarely offer their opinions during consultations with the doctor. Doctors do little to solicit patients' questions, concerns and opinions. In Byrne and Long's terms, doctor–patient communication remains doctor-centred.

6   Qualitative approaches to doctor–patient communication recognize that both doctor and patient shape the communicative event. Qualitative textual analysis aims to identify the discursive strategies that speakers use in order to manage their discursive objectives and to explore the ways in which meaning is constructed and negotiated by participants.

7   Studies have identified gender differences in doctors' communication styles. Female doctors adopt more patient-centred styles whereas their male colleagues tend to be more directive and controlling. These findings are in line with the general literature on gender differences in communication.

8   In recent years the use of computers during the consultation has become increasingly widespread. Studies suggest that the use of the computer changes the nature of the doctor–patient interaction. Computer-aided interviews tend to be longer and more detailed, but they reduce opportunities for sociorelational talk.

9   Health psychologists have begun to explore the ways in which communication mediates the illness experience. It has been suggested that physiological and psychological health outcomes can be influenced by health-care participants' communicative style, skills and practices.

10 Future research in doctor–patient communication should focus on the communication needs of different patient groups, the role of the setting in which communication takes place, the relationship between communication and health status and the implications of new technologies for doctor–patient communication.

KEY TERMS

communicative event

communication styles

compliance (also known as
  'adherence')

doctor-centred communication
  style

health communication

interaction analysis system (IAS)

outcome measures

patient satisfaction

patient-centred communication
  style

13

COMPLIANCE AND
EMPOWERMENT

Non-compliance is an unavoidable by-product of collisions between the clinical world and other competing worlds of work, play, friendship, and family life. (Trostle, 1988, p. 1305)

OUTLINE

Compliance is a term used to describe the extent to which patients comply with recommended treatment regimens. It is one of the most widely researched forms of health-related behaviour. Literally, thousands of articles have been published on the topic. There has been much debate about the assumptions underlying the term **compliance**. It has been suggested that it implies an excessively authoritarian stance on the part of the physician or other health professional which does not reflect recent changes within health-care systems. Alternative terms which reflect the current 'consumerist' approach to health care include 'adherence', 'co-operation', and 'collaboration'. This chapter summarizes some of the literature on why people do not follow medical recommendations and considers an alternative, patient-centred formulation of health care which focuses on the concept of **empowerment**.

CHARACTER OF COMPLIANCE

Forms of compliance and non-compliance

Compliance in health care takes two main forms: behavioural and medical. The former is concerned with health behaviours such as quitting smoking and the adoption of exercise which are considered in more detail in other chapters. Medical compliance can take a variety of forms and include those which are concerned specifically with medication including: having prescriptions filled, taking the correct dosage, taking the medicine at the correct times, remembering to take one or more doses and stopping the medication on time (Whitney et al., 1993). There are other forms of medical non-compliance including failure to keep appointments and insistence on discharge against medical advice (Meichenbaum and Turk, 1987).

Extent of compliance

The extent of compliance varies across the different forms of recommended behaviours. In general, most people do not comply with specific medical or health-care directives – at least not fully. While non-compliance would seem to be the norm, the extent of this non-compliance varies. Dunbar and Stunkard (1979) estimated that 20–80% of patients make medication errors and 25–60% stop taking their medication early. Haynes (1979b) estimated that non-compliance with drug treatment ranged from 42–62% and for appointment keeping it was about 50%. The US Chamber of Commerce (Whitney et al., 1993) estimated that over half of the 1.8 billion prescriptions written each year are taken incorrectly by patients. As a rough measure of compliance, Fiedler (1982) estimated that about a third of patients always comply, a third never comply and a third sometimes comply. While patients may comply with one treatment regimen they may not with another. For example, Orme and Binik (1989) considered compliance to different regimens among a sample of patients with diabetes. They found limited consistency across the different regimen demands.

Measurement of compliance

One reason for the wide variation in reports of compliance is the lack of agreement as regards measurement. Wright (1993) described three methods which are designed to increase accuracy of reports:

1   *Listening to patients*: unfortunately the evidence suggests that patients tend to over-report the extent to which they comply. For example, in one study of pediatric antibiotic usage (Gordis et al., 1969), 83% of parents claimed their children were taking the medication, yet 92% of the children's urine samples showed no sign of the drug (see comments on interviews by Radley and Billig, 1996).
2   *Counting tablets*: this technique is also subject to bias since all the patient may do is to take the pills out of the bottle and not consume them. For example, a study of patients with peptic ulcers found a disparity between compliance based on pill counts and that based on blood bromide levels (Roth et al., 1970).
3   *Assessing drug metabolite markers*: although these techniques can be accurate they are difficult to use over a lengthy period outside the hospital setting.

A major problem with these measurement strategies is the search for consistency. However, as discussed later, the sick person's behaviour is highly variable.

Consequences of non-compliance

In health terms it would seem that non-compliance has an overall negative impact on the health of society. Smith (1985) estimated that 23% of nursing home admissions in the USA were the result of non-compliance, while McKenney and Harrison (1976) estimated that 10% of hospital admissions were due to it. Gryfe and Gryfe (1984) estimated that among the elderly non-compliance contributed to as many as 15% of hospitalizations.

Certain forms of non-compliance are potentially more dangerous than others. Drash (1987) suggested that non-compliance with medication was the main reason for diabetic ketacidosis among children. Further, Smith (1985) estimated that every year in the USA several thousand hospital-izations for cardiovascular disease and over 100,000 deaths were at least partially due to non-compliance with the prescribed treatment.

One common health problem which apparently has a high rate of non-compliance is asthma. Despite the large number of drug education pro-grammes the proportion of people with asthma who do not comply with the recommended treatment remains high (Bender et al., 1997). In the USA it has been estimated that the direct and indirect costs of asthma in 1990 were over $6 billion (Weiss et al., 1992). Bender et al. (1997) suggest that a large proportion of this cost could be eliminated if compliance with medication was improved.

In assessing the benefits of compliance the positive effects need to be weighed against the potential negative effects. The term iatrogenesis was developed by Ivan Illich (1976a) to describe health problems which are caused by medicine. The estimates of the proportion of people admitted to hospital due to adverse drug reactions range from 6% to 22% (Nelson and Talbert, 1996). While a proportion of these may be due to non-compliance, others can be attributed to actually complying with the recommended drug therapy.

FACTORS ASSOCIATED WITH NON-COMPLIANCE

The large number of studies of medical compliance have frequently been criticized for their methodological limitations and conceptual weakness. For example, in their review of over 500 investigations, Sackett and Snow (1979) identified only 40 studies which satisfied a range of criteria they considered should be met. However, many reviews (e.g. DiMatteo and DiNicola, 1982; Meichenbaum and Turk, 1987) have identified a range of social and psychological factors which are frequently associated with non-compliance.

Patient characteristics

In terms of the broad social profile there has been some success in identifying the characteristics of the non-compliant patient. In general, the less social support and the more socially isolated the patients are, the less compliant they are. For example, in a study of treatment compliance in

TABLE 13.1 **Patient characteristics associated with compliance**
(Meichenbaum and Turk, 1987, p. 43; reproduced with permission)

Social characteristics	Personal characteristics	Health beliefs
Characteristics of individual's social situation	Demographics	Inappropriate or conflicting health beliefs
Lack of social supports	Sensory disabilities	Competing socio-cultural and ethnic folk concepts of disease and treatment
Family instability or disharmony	Type and severity of psychiatric disorder	
Parent's expectations and attitudes toward treatment	Forgetfulness	Implicit model of illness
Residential instability	Lack of understanding	
Environment that supports non-adherent behaviour		
Competing or conflicting demands		
Lack of resources		

an outpatient clinic for people with tuberculosis, it was found that homelessness was the only factor which predicted non-completion of therapy (Brainard et al., 1997). Further, individuals who came from unstable families were also found to be less compliant with medical treatment (Bender et al., 1997). In a study of compliance among diabetes patients Gray-Sevilla et al. (1995) found that adherence to medication was associated with higher levels of social support.

There has been much effort to identify the so-called 'non-compliant' personality. However, like much personality research in general (Mischel, 1968; see also Chapter 4), this has met with limited success. In reviewing the evidence, Hulka (1979) found no consistent relationship between age, sex, marital status, education, number of people in the household, social class and compliance. Admittedly, this is not to deny that specific groups of patients may be resistant to accepting certain types of treatment. For example, certain cognitive deficits or emotional upsets may reduce compliance. There is also evidence that people with a range of psychological problems are less likely to comply (e.g. Christiannse et al., 1989). Table 13.1 summarizes some of the patient characteristics associated with compliance.

Not surprisingly evidence suggests that the more the prescribed medication accords with the patients' belief systems, the more likely they are to comply with the treatment. Literally dozens of studies have confirmed the association between patients' health beliefs and compliance. In an attempt to bring some order to this plethora of research, some investigators have turned to the popular social cognitive models. Probably the most frequently used such model has been the **Health Belief Model**. Indeed, it was originally formulated to explain compliance with medical recommendations (Becker and Mainman, 1975). It argues that the extent to which a person complies depends upon perceived disease severity, susceptibility to

the disease, benefits of the treatment recommended and barriers to following the treatment (see also Chapters 10 and 15).

Varying degrees of support have been found for this model. For example,
Masek (1982) found that the more the patients perceive their condition to be
serious, the more likely they will be to comply with the recommended
treatment. However, Glasgow et al. (1997) found that perceived seriousness
of diabetes was not predictive of compliance. In a study of drug therapy
defaulting, Fincham and Wertheimer (1985) found that belief in the benefits
of medical care and low barriers to care predicted high compliance.
Glasgow et al. (1997) found that the perceived effectiveness of the treatment
was a better predictor of compliance in diabetes than the perceived barriers.

Social learning theory has also been used with varying degrees of success
to explain non-compliance. For example, Tillotson and Smith (1996) found
that although internal locus of control predicted compliance to a weight-
control programme for patients with diabetes, its importance was small and
depended on the degree of social support. In a study of patients with
rheumatoid arthritis Beck et al. (1988) found that patients' predictions
concerning their compliance (self-efficacy expectations) with treatment
predicted actual compliance.

These social cognitive models of compliance describe the beliefs which
are associated with or predict compliance. These models can be criticized
on both empirical and theoretical grounds. On empirical grounds the major
problem is that beliefs have not been found consistently to predict
compliance behaviour (DiMatteo and DiNicola, 1982). Theoretically, the
major problem is that these models reify the phenomenon. As such it
characterizes the behaviour as fixed and abstracted from the changing
social relations and the broader social context within which compliance
occurs. Treatment is not usually a one-off event but extends over a period of
time. In the case of chronic illness this period can be a lifetime. To understand compliance fully therefore requires an understanding of the social
context and how the patient integrates the treatment into his/her everyday
life.

Disease characteristics

Certain disease characteristics have been found to be associated with
compliance. Perhaps the most frequently mentioned disease characteristics
are the severity of the disease and visibility of the symptoms. The relationship with disease severity would appear not to be linear. A number of
studies have found that patients with asymptomatic chronic diseases
frequently do not comply with treatment (e.g. Miller, 1997). When the
symptoms are obvious and unwanted, the person is more likely to comply
with treatment which offers a promise of removing them. However, when
the prognosis is poor there is evidence that the rate of compliance is
reduced. For example, Dolgin et al. (1986) found compliance lower in those
cancer patients whose survival prospects were poor.

TABLE 13.2 **Treatment factors associated with non-compliance (Meichenbaum and Turk, 1987, p. 43; reproduced with permission)**

Preparation for treatment	Immediate character of treatment	Administration of treatment	Consequences of treatment
Characteristics of treatment setting	Characteristics of treatment recommendations	Inadequate supervision by professionals	Medication side effects
Long waiting time	Complexity of treatment regimen	Absence of continuity of care	Social side effects
Long time elapsed between referral and appointment	Duration of treatment regimen	Failure of parents to supervise drug administration	
Timing of referral	Degree of behavioural change		
Absence of individual appointment times	Inconvenience		
	Expense		
Lack of cohesiveness of treatment delivery systems	Characteristics of medicine		
	Inadequate labels		
Inconvenience associated with operation of clinics	Awkward container design		
Poor reputation of treatment facility			

Treatment factors

There are a large number of treatment factors associated with compliance. These are summarized in Table 13.2 under four broad temporal headings. Before the patient is actually prescribed a treatment, s/he has to obtain an appointment with the physician. The character of this process prepares or sets the scene for the physician's recommendations. Lengthy or inconvenient waiting times can lead to considerable frustration and an unwillingness to comply.

The more complicated the treatment prescribed, the less likely the patient is to comply fully. Admittedly, there have been attempts to simplify treatment regimens by providing patients with detailed information. However, the evidence suggests that compliance is still poor. One reason is information overload (Meichenbaum and Turk, 1987). In an attempt to cope with a very complicated treatment regimen the patient simply gets confused or ignores much of the information. Although physicians may explain the treatment, patients frequently do not understand or forget the instructions provided. Ley (1979) found that patients forget at least one-third of the information given by their physician. A variety of factors influences understanding. Basically, the more extensive and complex the instructions given, the less likely the patient is to recall it subsequently.

Svarstad (1976) found that when questioned shortly after a medical consultation over half the patients studied did not correctly report what their physician asked them to do.

There have been considerable attempts to improve knowledge by providing patients with written instructions. Studies have consistently found that instructions are frequently written at a level beyond that of the majority of recipients. For example, of 170 leaflets reviewed by Ley (1982) and Ley and Morris (1985), only 15% could be understood by 75% or more of the population. This led Ley and Florio (1996) to suggest the use of readability formulas in the development of written health information material. However, despite this endeavour to increase patients' understanding of treatment, there is limited evidence relating increased knowledge with compliance (Meichenbaum and Turk, 1987b).

Besides complexity, an important treatment characteristic is the actual length of the treatment regimen. Hulka et al. (1976) found that compliance declined with increased number of medications or doses. Sackett and Snow (1979) found that compliance with therapy declined with length of recommended treatment. They estimated that compliance with long-term therapy declined to approximately 50%, irrespective of illness or setting. Masur (1981) suggests that it is not the length of treatment which is the reason for this decline in compliance but rather the absence of symptoms. Long-term therapy is often recommended for chronic medical conditions which have few symptoms or for which there is no definite improvement in symptoms as a result of medication. In these cases the patient has no feedback on the benefits of medication. This lack of feedback undermines any motivation to comply with the medication. Leventhal (1986) found that when patients with hypertension were able to identify symptoms of their disease which were controlled by medication they were more likely to comply with it.

The actual character of the treatment is also important. For example, in the case of asthma it is the case that some people do not like taking inhaled medication while others do not follow the correct inhalation procedure, thus reducing overall compliance (McFadden, 1995). Understanding how the patient feels about a particular procedure or treatment is a necessary step in improving compliance.

It would perhaps be expected that those drugs with few *physical side effects* would be associated with higher compliance. It would seem that the social side-effects, in terms of stigma, are just as important (see section on empowerment). A related factor is the extent to which the treatment disrupts the patient's everyday life. There is a growing literature on intrusiveness suggesting that a major reason illness leads to impaired quality of life is that it intrudes into various domains of life. For example, Devins et al. (1996) argue that the physical disruption due to illness prevents a person participating fully in everyday life and accessing various pleasures and enjoyments. In the same way, certain forms of treatment can disrupt everyday life. As a means of reducing this disruption the person would reduce compliance with the treatment. Hunt et al. (1989) found that patients adjust their medication so as to balance control of symptoms with disruption of their lifestyle. Rundell and Weiss (1998), in comparing different side effects of treatment, found that constipation was associated with greater compliance than facial blotches, fatigue and sexual dysfunction. They concluded that when the side effects can be easily managed, compliance is higher.

Interpersonal factors

The character of the physician–patient relationship is at the centre of research into compliance. Although the role of physician's age in medical consultation would seem to be equivocal (Cockburn et al., 1987), it is well established that there are gender differences in both the quantity and quality of medical consultations. Female physicians spend more time with patients. In addition, they are also more attentive to patient needs, especially psychosocial needs (Maheux et al., 1990).

Much of the research on medical compliance has focused on the character of physician–patient communication. Physician styles in physician–patient communication have been classified as either 'patient centred' or 'authoritarian' (see Chapter 12). The *patient-centred* or affiliative style is designed to promote a positive relationship and includes behaviours such as interest, friendliness and empathy. The *authoritarian* or control-oriented style is designed to maintain the physician's control in the interaction. Not surprisingly, patients prefer those physicians who adopt the more affiliative style (Buller and Buller, 1987). Various related styles of physician interaction have been associated with compliance. DiNicola and DiMatteo (1982) suggested that patients are more compliant if their physician is warm, caring, friendly and interested. In behavioural terms the physician keeps good eye contact, smiles a lot and leans in towards the patient – all behaviours which are interpreted as demonstrating interest and consideration. Hall et al. (1988) found in their meta-analysis of 41 studies that patient satisfaction was associated with perceived interpersonal competence, social conversation and better communication as well as more information and technical competence.

Several studies have found an association between physician job satisfaction and aspects of compliance. McGlynn (1988) found that patients were more satisfied with those physicians who had high job satisfaction. DiMatteo et al. (1993) found that physician job satisfaction successfully predicted patient compliance two years later. Interestingly, compliance was also higher among those physicians with busier practices. It was suggested that this may reflect physician popularity. A related factor is the physician's sense of security. Since many conditions are resistant to standard medical interventions many physicians can experience a sense of inadequacy (Garrity, 1981). This, in turn, could lead to reduced job satisfaction and more conflict with patients. Indeed, when general practitioners receive complaints from their patients, they initially feel out of control, and may experience feelings of shock, panic, and indignation (Jain and Ogden, 1999).

Physicians and patients have a different view of health and illness. For example, St. Clair et al. (1996) compared the definitions of health provided by a sample of family physicians and those provided by a sample of patients with asthma. Whereas the former defined health in terms of absence of disease, the latter referred to 'being able', 'taking action' and 'physical well-being'. The more understanding the physician of the patient's belief system, the more compliant the patient is. For example, Ruiz and Ruiz (1983) found that Hispanic patients tend to comply more when their physician is more understanding of their cultural norms and practices.

An important although less explored factor is the physician's view of the patient. This overlaps with the physician's understanding of the patient's health beliefs and suggests that when the physician has a positive view of the patient then s/he will adopt a much more affiliative style of communication. This helps to explain the well-established social class effect that upper and middle-class patients receive more information and attention from physicians. For example, Taira et al. (1997) conducted a large survey of state employees in Massachusetts. According to the responses physicians were more likely to discuss healthy lifestyle issues such as diet and exercise with high income patients but they discussed smoking more with low income patients. Physicians frequently report more frustration with and less interest in lower and working-class patients (Hall et al., 1988).

Social and organizational setting

The medical consultation takes place in a social setting. Meichenbaum and Turk (1987) identified 10 setting characteristics potentially associated with non-compliance. Compliance is greater when the referral to a specialist is seen as part of the assessment rather than as a last resort, when care involves follow-up and is personalized, when appointments are individualized and waiting times are reduced, when treatment is available on site, when treatment is carefully supervised through home visits, special nursing care, etc., when there are good links between inpatient and outpatient services and when staff have a very positive attitude toward the treatment. In particular with long-term therapy, there is evidence that regular follow-up by the physician increases compliance (Bond and Monson, 1984).

It is not just the immediate medical context but the local social context, in terms of family and friends, which is important. If family members remind and assist the patient concerning their medication it would only be expected that the patient will be more compliant. Indeed, it has been suggested that the patient's partner's views of the medication prescribed is the most important factor in explaining compliance. Doherty et al. (1983) found that male patients whose wives strongly supported the treatment were more compliant. This concern with social context requires consideration of the broader socio-political context which conditions the character of health care and of compliance.

ALTERNATIVES TO COMPLIANCE

While the extensive literature on non-compliance has provided some insight into the character of the phenomenon, it has not contributed to its reduction. Indeed, Earker et al. (1984) have described it as the largest problem facing health care today. One of the main reasons for this lack of progress is that the majority of compliance research has been based upon a static model of the phenomenon which ignores the broader social context of health care and the dynamic nature of health and illness behaviour. An alternative more social and psychological approach requires an understanding of the role of medicine in our society and of the actual lived experience of illness and of managing illness.

The role of medicine

In western society medicine has been based upon power and authority. Since it is founded on the assumption that it has the monopoly on truth, it follows that patient non-compliance is a result of ignorance and/or deviance. Thus it is not surprising that Trostle (1998) describes the literature on compliance as 'a literature about power and control' (p. 1299). He argues that the increasing research interest in medical compliance is a reflection of 'a concern for market control combined with a concern for therapeutic power' (p. 1301). However, this very concern with maintaining power may carry with it an equal and opposite reaction evidenced by a reluctance of patients to comply.

According to reactance theory (Brehm, 1966), individuals believe they have the right to control their own behaviour. When this right is threatened they react and attempt to regain control over that behaviour and to prevent the loss of other freedoms. Basically, people do not like being pushed around and will attempt to subvert attempts to do so. In a revision of the original theory, Brehm and Brehm (1981) defined the concept of freedom as equivalent to that of control. People like to feel in control of their lives. Any attempt to reduce the sense of control over specific areas of our lives is a threat to the sense of freedom and is generally resisted.

The theory of psychological reactance has been used as an explanatory framework for non-compliance by Fogarty (1997). He argues that the more extensive and complex the treatment prescribed, the greater the threat to perceived freedom. Admittedly, this threat would be accepted if there was an indication that it was worthwhile. However, the very complexity of some regimens may sensitize the patient to additional threats to their freedom such that patients may become resistant to additional demands.

Non-compliance can thus be interpreted as a means of resisting medical dominance.

Frankenberg (1988) aptly described medicine as having a 'waiting culture'. The patient is expected to wait patiently in the waiting room. The more important the physician, the longer the waiting period. Frankenberg argues that 'being made to wait and not knowing what is to happen and when, is not an incidental of the cultural performance of sickness in biomedicine-dominated healing, it is central to the conversion of the suffering to the patient' (p. 137). It is a means of reducing the autonomy of the sick person and increasing the control of the physician. While some people may be happy to accept this situation, others may react with anger and frustration. But in the end, all patients must be patient.

Admittedly, not all patients are critical of the traditional authoritarian stance of the physician or feel the need to resist or not comply. Some people are more accepting of authority than others. In the late twentieth century, however, there was considerable public opposition to the idea of the all-powerful doctor and there were vocal demands for greater control over health care. Despite this apparent change in public attitudes, several researchers found that many people were still reluctant to adopt a more resisting, consumerist attitude. Haug and Lavin (1983) found that while younger and more educated patients were more consumerist in their attitude regarding their role in the doctor–patient encounter older patients were more accepting and accommodating.

Lupton (1997) investigated the impact of the supposed cultural shift on the attitudes of patients in Australia. She argued that contemporary popular advice is that the patient should adopt an active consumerist attitude to health care. Thus the patient is conceived as a rational autonomous being who can carefully weigh up the value of different services. The alternative, more traditional perspective is that of the unquestioning patient who passively complies with medical advice.

In her interviews with a sample of patients, Lupton found a more mixed picture. Many of the patients, especially the older ones, still preferred the passive patient role. Admittedly, they accepted that the traditional authoritarian image of the doctor had been challenged over the past generation as a result of publicity about medical negligence and sexual harassment. This resulted in a certain ambivalence about the doctor and a tension between adopting the consumerist or passive patient role. Thus while some patients would demand a more active role in their treatment and would be frustrated if they were denied it, many patients still preferred to adopt the traditional passive patient role.

As could be expected, the more consumerist stance of certain patients is not always welcomed by many physicians. Although several studies have shown that patients generally express a desire for information about their condition, many physicians are reluctant to disclose much information. In his study, West (1984) found that physicians often ignored patients' requests for information. Indeed it was found that patients' requests for more information were often met by challenges to their intelligence. Taylor (1979) suggested that so-called 'bad' patients – those who display anger and rebelliousness in hospital settings – may be reacting to the removal of freedoms and to restrictions on access to information. Conversely, the so-called 'good' patients – those who are more passive – may be too anxious to play a more active role in their encounters with medical staff.

Trostle (1998) suggested that 'the last decade's preoccupation with compliance is a consequence of the declining authority of the [medical] profession' (p. 1303). In traditional non-western societies the physician maintains the dominant role and the patient is more inclined to adopt a compliant stance. For example, Matsumoto et al. (1995) found that first generation Japanese-Americans were much more likely to report a willingness to comply than their second-generation peers. Conversely, in western society the demand for greater control over one's life conflicts with the traditional passive role and leads to greater resistance to medical advice.

Another feature of medical dominance is the power of the physician to define what is sickness. It is often assumed that the doctor typically makes the correct diagnosis and prescribes appropriate treatment. This is the ideal medical model. Thus non-compliance is the patient's fault. However, the evidence suggests that there are many sources of error on the part of the physician. For example, patients frequently attend with a variety of psychosocial problems, but these are often ignored by the physician. Bertakis et al. (1991) estimated that as many as 85% of patients who come to see their family doctor have some degree of psychological distress. As Mishler (1984) emphasized, scientific medical discourse does not contain language to handle these issues so the physician prefers to focus concern on biomedical matters which may be of limited concern to the patient. An example of the 'misdiagnosis' by physicians of women's health problems is provided in the study by Borges and Waitzkin (1995). They analysed a sample of doctor–patient interactions and found that typically the physician ignored contextual issues within which the women's health problems were located.

In a large study conducted over 11 sites in the USA, Bertakis et al. (1991) content analysed 550 physician–patient interviews. The interviews were tape recorded and patients completed a post-visit questionnaire. They found that physician questions about biomedical topics were negatively related to patient satisfaction while physician questions about psychosocial topics were positively associated with patient satisfaction. In addition, those patients whose physician dominated the interview reported less satisfaction. Bertakis et al. concluded that 'patients are most satisfied by interviews that encourage them to talk about psychosocial issues in an atmosphere that is characterized by the absence of physician domination'.

However, Waitzkin (1989) argues that the exclusion of discussion of the social context of health complaints is a 'fundamental feature of medical language . . . a basic part of what medicine is in our society' (p. 232). Not only does medical language ignore these social issues but medical treatment does not address these social issues. He suggests a redirection for medicine: 'by suggesting collective action as a meaningful option, medical professionals might begin to overcome the impact that its exclusion exerts'. To do this it needs to recognize the 'limits of medicine's role and the importance of building links to other forms of praxis that seek to change the social context of medical encounters' (p. 237).

Overall, there is much evidence to suggest that non-compliance is an implicit structural component of the contemporary medical-dominated health care system. To reduce non-compliance thus requires a reassessment of this system. It also needs an understanding of what it means to the patient to be ill.

LIVED EXPERIENCE OF CHRONIC ILLNESS

The extent to which people, especially those with chronic illness, comply with recommended treatment is enmeshed in their experience of living with illness. Compliance is not a fixed event but a changing process. A series of qualitative studies of illness have identified a number of processes which help us to understand the extent to which people accept the prescribed treatment regimens. Three of these processes are considered here.

Self-regulation

Individuals with chronic illness actively monitor and adjust their medication on an ongoing basis. It is not that they are recklessly ignoring professional advice but rather they are carefully regulating it according to a variety of factors. This is illustrated in the study conducted by Conrad (1985). Over a three-year period he conducted interviews with 80 individuals who had epilepsy about their life experiences with the disease. He noted that the individuals developed a personal 'medication practice' which best fitted with their self-image and their lifestyle. The patients realized the benefits of medication for seizure control and frequently stated that the medication helped them be more 'normal'. However, simultaneously the medication was seen as a daily reminder that they had epilepsy. They felt that reducing the medication was evidence that they were 'getting better'. Side effects were a frequently given justification for not complying with the recommended treatment. However, although side effects were mentioned they rarely referred to bodily side effects. Rather, they referred to social side effects. If the people with epilepsy felt that the medication was impairing their ability to handle routine social activities, they modified the medication to reduce this impact.

TABLE 13.3 **Reasons for self-regulation of medication (Conrad, 1985, pp. 34–5)**

- *Testing*: the way patients test the impact of varying dosages.
- *Controlling dependence*: the way patients assert to themselves and others that they are not dependent on the prescribed medication.
- *Destigmatization*: an attempt to reject the illness label and to be 'normal'.
- *Practical practice*: the way patients modified their dosage so as to reduce the risk of seizures, e.g. increasing the dosage in high stress situations.

Table 13.3 summarizes four reasons that Conrad suggested underlie individuals' preference to self-regulate the treatment rather than comply fully with the recommended regimen. These illustrate how non-compliance is a rational process whereby the individual carefully adjusts the medication to maximize its impact.

People carefully monitor the impact of prescribed medication and adjust the dosage accordingly. They do not simply follow the standardized instructions provided by the physician but rather adjust them to suit their own personal needs. This is illustrated in a study by Hunter et al. (1997) who looked at middle-aged women's usage of hormone replacement therapy (HRT). They interviewed 45 women and identified three broad themes within which the women talked about HRT:

1   *Hot flushes and night sweats*: the women would not take the medication when there were no symptoms, e.g. one woman said: 'I have no extraordinary symptoms, therefore I have no need of HRT' (p. 1544).
2   *Doctors' opinions and behaviour*: the women listened carefully to their doctor's advice and decided whether or not to take HRT, e.g. one woman said: 'I came to the doctor and had a discussion. I felt that I weighed up the advantages and disadvantages' (p. 1544).
3   *Taking hormones or medication for a 'natural' process*: the women were reluctant to take medication for something which they felt was natural. They sometimes referred to a similar concern with taking the contraceptive pill, e.g. 'I might consider it if I was suffering from symptoms which I felt I could not put up with. I'm a bit wary. I never really wanted to go on the pill because I'm always a bit wary of interfering with nature' (p. 1545).

This study illustrates that the patient's attitude to the recommended treatment is interwoven with their attitude to the illness and their attitude to their physician.

Fear of medication

From the physician's perspective, non-compliance can seem a foolhardy process. However, to the layperson non-compliance can be perceived as a means of reducing a variety of fears. This is illustrated in the findings of a study conducted by Donovan and Blake (1992). They investigated the extent to which a sample of people with various forms of arthritis complied with the recommended treatment. The study involved interviews and observations of 44 patients over a period of several years. They found that about half the patients did not follow the prescribed treatment. Detailed questioning of these patients revealed that they were carefully considering the implications of this non-compliance. It was not just a matter of obeying instructions or not – they were experimenting with dosages and timing. They were reluctant to follow the prescribed treatment for these reasons:

- fear of side-effects;
- fear of dependency;
- fear of reduced effectiveness;
- did not fit with lifestyle;
- drugs as a sign of weakness;
- drugs do not fit with health beliefs.

Similarly, Britten (1994) in her study of lay people's perceptions of medicines found that many people have a range of fears and anxieties about medication. This was especially the case among those people who reported that they often did not comply with prescribed medication. In her discussion, Britten comments on the physicians' urge to prescribe and suggests they should consider other options than medication.

Identity control

Medication compliance is also tied to the extent to which the patient accepts that s/he has an illness and wishes to control it. This is illustrated in the study by Adams et al. (1997). They conducted detailed interviews with a sample of asthma sufferers registered with a general practice in South Wales. Analysis of these interviews revealed that the extent to which the individuals complied with the recommended treatment (daily use of a curative and a prophylactic inhaler) was intimately bound up with how they defined themselves and their attitude to the illness. Three groups of patients, each with a particular pattern of medication, were identified:

1   *Deniers/distancers*: these were the individuals who argued that despite the medical diagnosis they did not have asthma but rather just 'bad chests'. They would fall into Goffman's (1963) 'discreditable' category and took steps to ensure that others were not aware of their diagnosis. They generally had a negative view of people with asthma (e.g. 'weakling' or 'wimp') and wished to avoid such a label. Although they took reliever medication when necessary, they were reluctant to take

prophylactic medication regularly. While the former helped their 'bad chest', the latter was a symbol that they were 'asthmatic'.

2   *Accepters*: these individuals reluctantly accepted that they had asthma. They also held a variety of negative associations of people with asthma. They emphasized that they were not stereotypical asthmatic people but rather more like certain individuals who were able to achieve despite having asthma, e.g. certain athletes. They defined asthma as a 'condition' which needed to be controlled. As such they not only took the reliever medication but also the prophylactic medication. However, these individuals emphasized that although they took their medication regularly they were not dependent on their doctor. Rather, they were proud that they controlled their asthma themselves, using the drugs, with limited contact with their physician. As one individual said: 'I don't need the doctor as long as the medication is working. I'd let him know if there was a problem. I just get repeat prescriptions' (p. 197).

3   *Pragmatists*: these individuals did not fall neatly into the previous two categories although they were closer to the accepters. All of them accepted that they had asthma but their notions of asthma and medication usage were somewhat idiosyncratic. Unlike the secrecy of the deniers and the public stance of the accepters this group adopted a more pragmatic attitude and practiced what Adams et al. described as a strategic policy of disclosure. This was related to their self-medication practices to which they adopted a pragmatic stance, e.g. 'I wouldn't take the inhaler in front of management.'

These studies illustrate that the extent of compliance with the recommended treatment is intertwined not only with the character of the disease but also with the patient's self-definition. Compliance or non-compliance is not only a means of managing symptoms but also of managing self-identity.

EMPOWERING PATIENTS

Implicit within this alternative approach to compliance is the concept of *empowerment* which is concerned with attempts to increase patient autonomy and control. Rather than attempting to control the patient which is implicit within models of compliance, empowerment attempts to increase patient autonomy. This approach is derived from the work of community educators and psychologists and defined as the process whereby 'people gain mastery over their lives' (Rappoport, 1987). Instead of imposing the views of the expert health professional, empowerment seeks to enhance the patients' self-understanding and the potential of self-care (Feste and Anderson, 1995).

The focus of this approach is the enhancement of the strengths and potential of the patient. Through dialogue the health professional seeks to understand the needs of the patient. Skelton (1997) suggests that the aim of patient education within this model is to 'blur' the boundaries between professional-as-teacher and patient-as-learner. Instead of the professional's health knowledge being considered paramount, the patient's lay health beliefs and knowledge is considered of equal or greater value. A central component of this understanding is the opportunity for patients to tell their stories. In describing this process Hunter (1991) notes that 'medicine has the power not only to rewrite the patient's story of illness but also to replot its course' (p. 139). Dependent upon the story that is handed back the patient will assess its relevance to their lives. As Hunter (1991) continues: 'if the two are widely disparate and the physician fails to recognize the distance between them, the interaction founders. The medicine will go untaken, the consultation unsought, the prescription unfilled' (p. 142).

Patient empowerment can aim to involve the patient more in health care through attention to patient needs or it can increase the patients' awareness of the broader social and political factors which adversely affect their health status. Admittedly, as Lupton (1997) found, not all patients wish to be actively involved in their personal health care or in taking broader collective action. It is for this reason that Skelton (1997) suggest a more localized approach which aims at the transformation of the power dynamic within the physician–patient dyad. Admittedly, the question remains regarding the extent to which this is possible when medicine maintains its powerful position in society.

FUTURE RESEARCH

1   New medical procedures and drugs are constantly being developed. While these can be efficacious in the controlled clinical trial setting, there is an ongoing need to assess the problems involved in their adoption in the community.
2   Different health problems require different forms of treatment. Research needs to consider the appropriateness of different interventions.
3   Similarly, not everyone will accept certain procedures. Further research is needed to explore the meaning of different treatments to different populations.
4   As attitudes to health care change, research needs to address the changing needs of different client groups and how these can best be addressed.
5   Finally, research needs to address how best to involve people more directly in all aspects of their health care.

SUMMARY

1   Compliance refers to the extent to which the patient follows the prescribed treatment regimen.
2   A wide range of social and psychological factors have been found to be associated with non-compliance. These factors are associated with the characteristics of the patients, the disorders they have, the treatments they are given, the relationships they have with their physicians and organizational factors.
3   Social characteristics associated with non-compliance include: characteristics of individual's social situation; lack of social supports; family instability or disharmony; parent's expectations and attitudes toward treatment; residential instability; an environment that supports non-adherent behaviour; competing or conflicting demands; lack of resources.
4   Personal characteristics associated with non-compliance include: demographics; sensory disabilities; type and severity of psychiatric disorder; forgetfulness; lack of understanding.
5   Health beliefs associated with non-compliance include: inappropriate or conflicting health beliefs; competing socio-cultural and ethnic folk concepts of disease and treatment; an implicit model of illness.
6   For summaries of the other data concerning the characteristics of compliant and non-compliant situations, see Tables 13.2 to 13.5.
7   An alternative approach is to consider the impact on patient behaviour of the socio-political role of the physician and the meaning of the health problem and of the prescribed medication for the patient.
8   Patient empowerment aims to involve patients in health care through listening to their needs not as recipients but as active partners in the process of health care. This requires an awareness of the broader social and political factors which adversely affect the health status of individual people and their communities.

KEY TERMS

authoritarian   Health Belief Model
compliance   patient-centred
empowerment   physical side effects

14 IMMUNIZATION AND SCREENING

An ounce of prevention is worth a pound of cure. (Anon)

OUTLINE

This chapter considers two main forms of disease prevention available within health care systems: ***immunization*** and **screening**. Although immunization for infectious childhood diseases is generally high in most industrialized countries, there is considerable variation over time and place. The various social and psychological factors which have been found to be associated with its uptake are reviewed. Most industrialized countries have introduced screening programmes for breast and cervical cancer yet many women are reluctant to participate. This chapter considers women's perceptions of these different programmes. Finally, recent genetic advances have held out the prospect of genetic screening programmes. Ethical and psychological factors associated with these programmes are reviewed.

IMMUNIZATION

Immunization is the procedure whereby those individuals who are most susceptible to contracting certain communicable diseases are administered a vaccine. This procedure is aimed at both immediate protection of individuals and also immunity across the whole community where the uptake rate is high. Over the years various vaccines have been developed for specific diseases. The characteristics of the ideal vaccine are summarized in Table 14.1.

Immunization has been described as one of the most successful examples of the primary prevention of disease (Woolf, 1996). Infectious diseases which were once the major causes of death and disability in both the industrialized and the developing world have now largely been eradicated. Vaccination programmes have led to the elimination of smallpox on a global scale and the near eradication of several other diseases, e.g. poliomyelitis. These vaccination programmes are generally targeted at specific subgroups of the population such as children, travellers and seniors. The most extensive programmes have been targeted at children.

TABLE 14.1 ***Characteristics of an ideal vaccine (Canadian Immunization Guide, 1989)***

- Confer long-lasting, preferably lifelong, protection against the disease.
- Inexpensive enough for large-scale use.
- Stable enough to remain potent during shipping and storage.
- No adverse effects on the recipient.

Although immunization has led to the decline of a range of life-threatening diseases it can also lead to a number of adverse reactions in a small number of individuals. Public health authorities have argued that in societal terms this risk is minimal when contrasted to the overall benefit to society (Hinman and Koplan, 1984). Despite the apparent success of mass immunization programmes there is evidence that a large proportion of at-risk individuals in western societies are not immunized against certain diseases.

Uptake of immunization among children

Studies in several western countries have found that immunization uptake among children is not universal. It has been argued that a major reason for the epidemics of measles in the late 1980s and early 1990s was the presence of large pools of susceptible children due to non-immunization (Schlenker et al., 1992). The incidence of whooping cough reported in the USA in 1993 was the highest since 1976 and twice that of 1992. Although vaccine safety has been vigorously promoted several widely reported cases of vaccine induced illness have been followed by a decline in immunization uptake.

A nine-city study conducted in 1991 in the USA found that only 10–38% of two-year-old children were fully immunized (US Center for Disease Control and Prevention, 1992). A subsequent report found a much higher rate of 67% among two-year-olds (US Center for Disease Control and Prevention, 1994). In the UK the uptake of pertussis vaccine fell from a high of 81% to a low of 32% in 1978 after concern about vaccine safety was widely reported in the mass media. The uptake of pertussis vaccine in the UK still lags behind that of many developing countries.

Not only have immunization programmes failed to achieve 100% uptake, but uptake has been found to be related to the social position of the child's family. The evidence suggests that there are lower rates of immunization among children from low income families (Marks et al., 1979). A study of the uptake of measles, mumps and rubella vaccine in 10 health districts in north London found that the rate ranged from 69% in one inner city district to 91% in one suburban or rural district where social conditions would be expected to be better (Li and Taylor, 1993). It was suggested that the low rate of uptake in the deprived inner city area may be due to the higher mobility of families living there leading to difficulties for the health authorities in tracing them and in arranging appointments. This study also found that immunization was lower in larger and one-parent families which are further indicators of social position.

New and Senior (1991) conducted detailed interviews with over 250 mothers from North West England. They found that mothers with lower educational qualifications, mothers living alone, mothers with large families and having a sick child were the best predictors of non-immunization. A study in the north of England (Reading et al., 1994) found that even after the establishment of an immunization programme, the relationship between immunization uptake and social deprivation remained. In this study the immunization of four birth cohorts between 1981 and 1990 was examined. Although there was an overall increase in uptake, the rates remained lowest in the children from the most deprived areas.

Immunization programmes and the role of health professionals

In order to maximize the uptake of immunization programmes, it is important that the service is not only accessible but that it is promoted by various health professionals. However, there is evidence to suggest that many health professionals are hesitant about promoting participation. In particular, there is evidence that family doctors have played a role in spreading the fear about vaccines. Indeed, a report in Britain (Peckham et al., 1989) concluded that the main obstacle to parents having their child immunized was misconceptions concerning contraindications by the family doctor. New and Senior (1991) in their interview study of mothers in North West England found that 53 out of 71 mothers who had not had their children fully immunized claimed that either their child was contra-indicated to pertussis vaccine or their doctor had advised them against it. Further, many of the mothers said they had received conflicting advice from different health professionals which led to confusion and loss of confidence in such advice. Indeed, some mothers said it was the actual attempt by the health professionals to convince them of the minimal risk which deterred them. As one mother said: 'Until they find a safe vaccine, one in 300,000 is still too large; I wouldn't play Russian roulette with my child.'

In addition to the family doctor, ancillary health staff can contribute to parents' anxiety about immunization. For example, Reddy (1989) conducted a survey of parents in a town in South East England. He found that a frequent reason given for non-vaccination was that their child was ill at the appointed time. However, Reddy found that when he telephoned the parents most of those children who were supposedly ill only had a minor cold. When questioned the parents said they were concerned about the dangers of vaccinating a sick child and that this concern had been shared by the health centre receptionist leading the parent to defer the appointment.

A study of parents in Utah (Lewis et al., 1988) found similar concerns. The most common reason given for non-immunization was that the child was ill at the time they were to be vaccinated. The authors noted that it is unlikely that these children were seriously ill but 'it is possible that, because of adverse media, parental worries, and concern about possible litigation, physicians and public health officials have been affected and failed to emphasize the importance of a young child receiving the complete immunization series and of not unnecessarily delaying immunization' (p. 286).

Parental reasons for non-immunization of children

Several studies have identified a variety of reasons expressed by parents for not having their children immunized. These have been summarized by Meszaros et al. (1996) under five categories (Table 14.2).

In their study, Meszaros et al. (1996) attempted to assess the relative importance of each of these explanations in a questionnaire survey of readers of *Mothering*, a popular magazine read by mothers in the USA. They found that the most important predictors of parents having their child immunized were the perceived dangers of the vaccine, doubts about medical claims that vaccines are effective, omission bias, belief that physicians overestimate the dangerousness of the disease, perceived ability to protect their child and perceived assessment of the likelihood of their child contracting the disease.

This fear of the adverse effect of immunization may be exaggerated in certain communities. In a study in England (Loewenthal and Bradley, 1996) it was found that the uptake of childhood immunization was particularly low among orthodox Jews. It was suggested by mothers interviewed that the main reason for their low uptake was their fear of a negative reaction, logistical difficulties and unsympathetic treatment by health staff. According to the health professionals, the mothers' fears were exaggerated because they lived in a close-knit community which perpetuated tales of bad reactions.

Besides these factors, an additional factor is the perceived relative risk. In a qualitative investigation of the views of a sample of inner-city parents in Baltimore, Keane et al. (1993) found that although some parents accepted that they or their children might be vulnerable to infectious diseases, other threats such as drugs, street violence and 'the wrong crowd' were considered more severe. Further, vaccines were viewed as only partly successful. The continued occurrence of chickenpox was frequently cited as evidence of vaccine failure.

A frequent explanation given by mothers in several studies is the natural/unnatural distinction. New and Senior (1991) found that whereas vaccination was perceived by some mothers as unnatural, by implication whooping cough was natural and therefore acceptable. Admittedly, some other women had weighed up the benefits and risks of immunization and

TABLE 14.2 **Parental reasons for non-immunization**
(Meszaros et al., 1996, p. 698)

- *Risk/benefit ratio*: perception that the risks of contracting the disease outweigh the benefits of being immunized.
- *Individual risk*: belief that the societal statistics which public health planners use do not apply to their child. Further, the parents believe that they can protect the child from exposure.
- *Ambiguity aversion*: aversity to options with ambiguous outcomes such that parents will prefer a straightforward Yes/No assessment of the likelihood of their child contracting a disease. When there is disagreement about potential risk they will err on the side of caution. Further, some parents may already be sceptical of medical information.
- *Omission bias*: preference for acts of omission over acts of commission.
- *'Free riding'*: assumption that since most of their children's peers have been vaccinated they are protected.

decided in favour of immunization. It would be expected that these were the women who were more accepting of the medical viewpoint, with all its doubts and confusions.

This natural/unnatural distinction was also alluded to in a large German study by (Weitkunat et al., 1998). They found that the most significant predictors of measles immunization were parental natural health orientation, advice of paediatrician, birth order position, dangerousness of measles, marital status, reliability of vaccination and smoking. They suggested that natural health orientation and advice of paediatricans may be interactive since individuals with a natural health orientation may select like-minded physicians. In a more detailed analysis of what they described as the subjective relevance of measles they found that those who assessed the likelihood of contracting measles as high and the latency as low were more likely to have their children immunized.

Parental concern about the possible risks of vaccination is also expressed in homeopathic beliefs. In a survey of parents of children in South West England (Simpson et al., 1995) it was found that the commonest reasons given for non-immunization of their children were homeopathy and religious beliefs. With regard to homeopathy, one parent said:

I believe that the body's defences are best strengthened by optimum nutrition and good hygiene and by allowing the body to experience normal illnesses without suppression during the normal course of events. To enhance this process I consult our family homeopath for acute and chronic assistance as necessary. I am actually thoroughly opposed to current practices in vaccination programmes; the onslaught of several vaccinations at once on a tiny body for the sake of convenience and getting them done, I find very disturbing. I am sure high prices are paid for this in terms of autoimmune diseases and weakened immune systems. (Simpson et al., 1995, p. 227)

Taken together these findings would suggest that while parents may be hesitant about having their child immunized because of their anxiety

TABLE 14.3 ***Prerequisites of screening (Wilson and Junger, 1968, p. 26j; reproduced with permission)***

- Condition sought should be an important health problem.
- Accepted treatment for patients with the disease.
- Facilities for treatment and diagnosis should be available.
- Recognizable latent or early symptomatic stage.
- Suitable test or examination.
- Test should be acceptable to the population.
- Natural history of the condition should be adequately understood.
- Agreed policy on whom to treat as patient.
- Cost should be economically balanced in relation to possible expenditure on medical care as a whole.
- Case finding should be a continuing process and not a once-and-for-all project.

about the potential risk, this image is compounded by media speculation and by the advice they receive from health professionals.

SCREENING

One of the main forms of secondary prevention is the early detection of disease through screening. This is the procedure whereby those sections of the population who are most at risk of developing a particular disease are examined to see whether they have any early indications of that disease. The rationale behind this strategy is that the earlier the disease is identified and treated, the less likely it is to develop into its full-blown form. Within public health circles there has been sustained debate as regards the value of this strategy.

Wilson and Jungner (1968) identified ten prerequisites for a successful screening programme (Table 14.3).

In western countries there have been several attempts to introduce mass screening for a limited number of conditions which satisfy all or most of these criteria. However, despite the supposed benefits of these programmes there has been a variety of problems in their implementation. It was generally assumed by their proponents that the major problem would be the introduction of the programmes. However, the problem has centred on the reluctance of at least a proportion of the targeted population to make use of these programmes and the unexpected negative side effects of participation.

Screening for breast and cervical cancer

Over the past decade there has been a concerted effort in most industrialized societies to introduce screening programmes for breast cancer. The reason for this is that it seemed to satisfy most of the criteria for screening previously outlined. It is currently the most prevalent or the second most prevalent form of female cancer in western society. In the

USA it is estimated that approximately 184,000 women are diagnosed with breast cancer each year and about 44,000 die from the disease (Parker et al., 1996). The American Cancer Society estimates that the lifetime risk of breast cancer for women is now one in eight (ACS, 1992). Not only is it widely prevalent, but its incidence is increasing by 1% to 2% per annum. The reason for this is unclear.

Partly in response to the epidemiological and medical evidence about the widespread prevalence of the disease and the association between stage of identification and success of treatment, there has been a demand not only from health authorities but also from women's organizations for the introduction of breast cancer screening programmes. Initially, the method favoured was breast self-examination, but due to queries about the accuracy of this procedure the favoured method is now mammography coupled with clinical breast examination by a health professional (Leitch, 1995). In most countries mammography programmes have been targeted at all women aged 50 to 69 years, although some countries will also attempt to cover younger and older women. The reason for the focus on the limited age band is because epidemiological evidence suggests it is the most cost effective in terms of case finding although there continues to be debate about the most appropriate age range (Fletcher, 1997)

Despite the widespread support for breast cancer screening and the estimates that it can lead to a reduction of up to 40% in mortality from that disease (Fletcher et al., 1993), a few critics have raised some cautions. For example, Skrabanek (1985) questioned the sensitivity and specificity of mammography and also queried the claimed value of early intervention. In reviewing the British data, Watmough et al. (1997) found that the introduction of breast cancer screening programmes has led to greater detection but not to a reduced mortality rate. A large Canadian study found contradictory results for women aged under 50 years leading Millar (1993) to call for caution. However, the majority view is that breast cancer screening is effective although it should continue to be monitored (Warren, 1988).

Cervical cancer is a much less prevalent condition. It is the eighth most prevalent form of cancer among women but the most common in women under 35 years of age. In the UK the disease accounts for about 1,850 deaths per annum while in the USA the figures are about 4,500 deaths per annum. The cause of the disease remains unknown although it is thought that a viral infection spread by sexual intercourse may be an important factor.

There is evidence that the precancerous stage of the disease can be detected at an early stage using a simple cervical smear test (pap test). Most western countries have introduced campaigns to encourage women to attend for regular smear tests, usually at least once every three to five years. Although cervical screening has been widely promoted there is also debate about its value. Raffle (1997) in a review of British figures indicated that the decline in deaths from cervical cancer preceded the establishment of screening programmes. McCormick (1989) argued that the overall costs to the nation in terms of expenditure and to the woman in terms of psychological distress outweighed the benefits in terms of increased life expectancy. There is obviously a need for continued surveillance.

Who participates in cancer screening programmes?

Evidence from several countries suggests that a large proportion of women do not avail of breast cancer screening programmes. Generally, screening rates are higher in Europe than in the USA (Vernon et al., 1990) The National Health Interview Study which is conducted regularly in the USA found that the rate of recent mammography among women aged 50 years and over was only 44% in 1992 although 70% of those aged 40 years and over reported ever having had a mammogram (US Center for Disease Control and Prevention, 1995). The 1994 National Population Health Survey found that 39% of women aged at least 35 years of age in Canada had never had a mammogram and 15% of those aged over 18 years had never had a pap test. For both tests, participation was lower for those with less education and lower income levels (Snider et al., 1996).

Admittedly with the introduction of mammography screening programmes in various countries over the past decade the proportion of women participating in such programmes has increased. The Mammography Attitudes and Usage Study (MAUS) found that the proportion of American women who reported ever having a mammogram increased from 64% in 1990 to 74% in 1992 (Horton et al., 1992). The US Center for Disease Control and Prevention (1995) reported an even bigger increase from 38% in 1987 to 68% in 1992. De Grasse et al. (1996) found that the proportion of women reporting being screened in Ottawa-Carleton, Canada increased from 60% to 83% between 1991 and 1994.

The pap test has been around for a longer period and its uptake is generally higher. In the USA the proportion of women having had a pap test was reported at 90% in 1992, although only 67% had been tested recently (US Center for Disease Control and Prevention, 1995). However, the extent to which women have the opportunity of having a pap test varies substantially. For example, Rang and Tod (1988) reported a study in which 810 women aged 35–59 years resident in London were invited to attend for a smear test. Only 25% responded, 30% of the invitations were returned as unknown and the remainder did not reply. A survey of community health councils in Britain found that the take-up rate to invitations for smears varied from 16% to 75% across health districts (Association of Community Health Councils, 1989).

Several studies have shown that use of cancer screening programmes is lower among women from low socio-economic status (SES) backgrounds (e.g. Horton et al., 1992; Bostick et al., 1994; Potvin et al., 1995; Frazier et al., 1996) and, to a lesser extent, among those from ethnic minorities. Admittedly, some studies have found less evidence of this trend. The US

Center for Disease Control and Prevention (1995) found few ethnic differences. It found that between 1987 and 1992 there had been substantial increases in uptake of mammography among black and hispanic women such that now they differ little from white women (see also Frazier et al., 1996).

Health service organization for cancer screening

Several studies have found that the most important factor in explaining variation in participation is the extent to which the woman's doctor recommends participation (National Cancer Institute, 1990). Further, Lurie et al. (1993) found that women are more likely to undergo screening with pap smears or mammograms if they see female rather than male physicians. There is evidence to suggest that physicians are often reluctant to advise mammography for a variety of reasons including scepticism about its effectiveness in general or for certain groups of women and fear of the effect of radiation. Smith and Herbert (1993) found that family physicians did not recommend mammography because they did not think the patients would participate, because the test was not available, because they were concerned about the radiation risk and because of the cost. Physicians are especially less likely to refer older women for screening (Costanza, 1992). Further, Frazier et al. (1996) found that black women were more likely to report that their physician had not recommended participation.

A further reason for the hesitancy among some physicians in the USA as to recommending screening is fear of litigation. It has been suggested that in the USA many physicians may be reluctant to talk about screening with their patients because of the public controversy about screening guidelines (Leitch, 1995). This could lead to anxiety among some physicians, bearing in mind that delayed diagnosis of breast cancer is one of the most common causes of malpractice complaint. In the USA women who have developed cervical or uterine cancer after smear tests have won legal cases because of inappropriate treatment. In commenting on these cases Austin and McLendon (1997) state that 'this trend is having a chilling effect on those professionals in the field of cytotechnology and cytopathology and potentially threatens the availability of this procedure for many of our patients' (p. 754).

More countries and regions are now establishing dedicated cancer screening programmes with postal invitations to women to attend on a regular basis. Despite these moves a proportion of women are still reluctant to participate in these programmes. Similarly, some women do not participate even when they are personally encouraged to attend by their physician (May et al., 1999). Sharp et al. (1996) found that a personal invitation by a woman's family doctor was as effective as a home visit from a nurse conveying the same message. However, despite the best intentions of family doctors many women fail to receive such personal invites because of inaccurate registers (McEwan et al., 1989). It has also been found that when those women who have not been screened for cervical cancer are sent an invitation from their family doctor most do not respond (Buehler and Parsons, 1997). This would suggest that other factors are important.

Health beliefs and cancer screening

This reluctance of many women to participate in screening programmes has contributed to a large number of studies which have investigated what women think about these services. Many studies of health beliefs have been based upon various social cognition models of health behaviour especially the *Health Belief Model (HBM)* and the *Theory of Reasoned Action* (TRA). These models argue that it is possible to identify a certain typical belief pattern which will predict use of health services such as screening. Although the models have not been statistically predictive, examination of individual components gives some insight into the reluctance of many women to participate in screening programmes.

In the case of breast cancer screening, the most frequently cited predictors are perceived susceptibility and perceived barriers. A meta-analysis of a large number of US studies (McCaul et al., 1996b) found a strong relationship between family history (actual risk) and *mammography* utilization but also a moderate relationship between perceived vulnerability (perceived risk) and use of mammography. In a UK study, Sutton et al. (1994) also found a relationship between perceived risk and attendance. Stein et al. (1992) found that perceived susceptibility to breast cancer was the best predictor of future intention to participate in mammography. However, they add that 'it is questionable . . . whether heightened feelings of susceptibility alone will sufficiently motivate women to obtain mammograms in the absence of a physician's recommendation' (p. 458).

Various barriers to attendance for mammography, both physical and psychological, have been reported. Rimer et al. (1989) found in their survey of women in the USA that those who did not attend for mammography had a stronger belief that screening was not necessary in the absence of symptoms, a preference not to think about it and a worry about the effect of radiation. Murray and McMillan (1993a) found that perceived barriers were the most important predictor of attendance for a smear test. The barriers they considered included dislike of the health service, fear of the examination, and fear of the result. McCaul et al. (1996b) found that women who worry about breast cancer are more likely to engage in various self-protective actions such as breast self-examination and attendance for mammography. Sutton et al. (1994) found a non-linear relationship with the highest attendance among women who were 'a bit worried', while those at the two extremes of worry were less likely to attend. They concluded that health promotion campaigns must balance advice to women on perceived risk with the negative impact of excessive worry. Other barriers reported include belief that a mammogram is appropriate only when there are symptoms, concern about radiation exposure, cost and access-related factors (Slenker and Grant, 1989).

With respect to benefits, several studies have indicated that the most frequently given reason for non-participation in cancer screening is that the women do not feel it necessary – they were healthy so they did not feel it was necessary to use it. It was thought that it was only necessary to have mammograms when one was sick (see Vernon et al., 1990). Mah and Bryant (1992) in their survey of rural women in Alberta found that the two most frequently given reasons for non-utilization of mammography was that the women had not been encouraged to do so by a doctor (37%) and that they felt they were healthy and did not need to use it (36%). Potvin et al. (1995) found that perceiving one's health as good was inversely associated with recent mammography. Harlan et al. (1991) found that the most frequently given reason for not having a cervical smear was not believing it necessary.

Although the HBM has been widely used in studies designed to predict attendance for breast cancer screening the results have not always been consistent. Bernstein Hyman et al. (1994) found that women who never scheduled a mammogram were more likely to perceive both fewer benefits of and barriers to mammography. They did not find any relationship between perceived susceptibility and mammography usage. They suggested that possibly other variables such as knowledge was a more important overriding factor. Many women are either unaware of the availability of the services or do not understand the character of the investigation. For example, Gregory and McKie (1991) found that many women did not understand that the early stages of *cervical carcinoma* are not accompanied by any symptoms. Similarly, Harlan et al. (1991) found that the main reason for non-participation in cervical screening was that women did not think it necessary because they did not have any symptoms. Rimer (1990) argues that since mammography occurs when there are no symptoms of breast cancer it takes 'almost an act of faith' to participate.

The *theory of reasoned action (TRA)* has met with some success in predicting cancer screening behaviour. In a large survey of women in Seattle, Montano and Taplin (1991) found that attitude and subjective norm both predicted participation in mammography as did affect which was a measure of the emotions associated with having a mammogram. They also found that facilitating conditions (a measure of logistics which is somewhat similar to the barriers factor in the HBM) and habit (a measure of previous use of mammography) also independently predicted usage.

Several researchers have used the *transtheoretical model of change (TTM)* (Prochaska and DiClemente, 1983) to explore the extent of participation in screening programmes. Rakowski et al. (1992) found that women who were classified as precontemplators (i.e. those who never had a mammogram and did not plan to have one) scored higher on a measure of negative beliefs including the beliefs that mammograms lead to unnecessary surgery and that they are only advisable if you have some breast symptoms. Skinner et al. (1997) found that action/maintainers were less likely to agree with the various psychological and physical barriers to screening.

There is a tendency in these health belief studies to adopt a *deficit model* to explain non-participation in screening. The women who do not use the service tend to be characterized as lacking in knowledge and concern about their health. This is especially the case when there are attempts to explain the lower utilization by women from low SES and from ethnic minorities. An alternative perspective is to view this non-attendance as a form of resistance to what is perceived as an unnecessary interference in their lives or even of something which could increase the likelihood of cancer (see Chapter 13). Several studies have explored this alternative perspective.

Meaning of cancer and cancer screening

Despite the advances in the treatment of cancer, or indeed partly due to the character of these advances, cancer remains the most feared disease in western society. Murray and McMillan (1993b) conducted a survey of a random sample of adults resident in Northern Ireland. They found that cancer was the most feared disease especially among women. The reason for this fear was because cancer was perceived as incurable and as leading to a painful death. Slenker and Spreitzer (1988) conducted a survey of a random sample of adults in Ohio. They found that not only was cancer the most feared disease but approximately half the respondents felt there was little you could do about the disease.

Several qualitative studies have explored women's fear of cancer and their reluctance to use the various screening services. Blaxter (1983) conducted interviews with women from Glasgow about their views on health and illness. She found that the women were reluctant to talk about cancer. Blaxter suggested that this lack of reference to cancer was a coping strategy used by the women to protect themselves from cancer: 'to talk about it was to invoke it, to speak briefly or in a lowered voice was to leave it sleeping'. Participation in screening would threaten this form of psychological defence.

Murray and McMillan (1988) conducted interviews with a sample of working-class women from Northern Ireland. Again they found evidence of a fear of cancer and a reluctance to interfere. One woman explained why she had not had a smear test taken:

> I think you have the fear, you see, of it. But they say they can get it in time . . . but sure how do they know they've got it in time. They don't know until they start opening you up and if they open you up, it would spread. So I would say, leave well enough alone. (Murray and McMillan, 1988, p. 42)

A similar finding was reported by Gregg and Curry (1994). They conducted detailed interviews with a sample of African-American low income women on their beliefs about cancer. Not surprisingly, they had a very negative image of the disease. They not only believed that cancer was deadly but they felt that if the cancer could be detected by mammography then it was already beyond cure. An example of this attitude is the case of the 62-year-old woman who had received a negative result from her pap test. Her reaction was a refusal to obtain a follow-up test:

> My last pap didn't come back good and they want me to go over to Grady, but I didn't go because I'm afraid they're going to tell me that I've got cancer. I've just had so much experience with cancer, and I know that if they operate on me its going to get worse. So I'm just going to prolong it as much as I can . . . We all go to die anyway . . . Its too late now. (Gregg and Curry, 1994, p. 524)

Balshem (1991) linked these negative beliefs about cancer with the life experiences of the women. She conducted an ethnographic study of a working-class community in Philadelphia which seemed very resistant to a health promotion campaign aimed at encouraging healthier lifestyles including attendance for breast cancer screening. When she interviewed these women, Balshem found that the health promotion message was counter to their experience. They believed that fate determined who got cancer and who survived. To look for cancer was to tempt fate; it was 'looking for trouble'. To quote Balshem: 'Challenging fate is a risky business. Cancer inspires not challenge but taboo.' Thus the women preferred not to think about cancer.

Other qualitative work would suggest that some women would prefer to conduct self-examination rather than attend a medical centre for investigation. For example, Tessaro et al. (1994) interviewed a sample of older African-American women and found that they did not think it necessary to use the health service since after self-examination they had found no lumps. Other women felt that they accepted lumps and bumps as part of life and were more concerned about other people's health rather than their own. One woman had this to say:

> I think the black woman don't realize herself she has a tendency to leave herself alone and worry about other people. So she doesn't have a chance to examine her body and see what is really wrong with it because she is so used to bumps and knocks and hurts until she ignores it. (Tessaro et al., 1994, p. 291)

Another important issue to consider is the sexual connotations of both breast and cervical cancer. Breasts are at the centre of a woman's sexual identity. Women fear breast cancer partly because of the threat to this identity (Murray and McMillan, 1988). Also, the evidence that a sexually transmitted virus may contribute to cervical cancer has been widely discussed. This has contributed to some women's reluctance to have a smear test. McKie (1993, 1995) considered the views of a sample of English working-class women. She found that in the minds of some of the women the test was associated with sexual promiscuity, a label which they did not want to have. By avoiding the test they sought to avoid the label.

Experience of cancer screening

Most of the research on cancer screening has concentrated on describing those factors associated with initial attendance. However, according to current guidelines women are expected to attend not once but on a regular basis. Few studies have examined this process of reattendance although the evidence does suggest that rate of attendance for follow-up is lower than for initial examination (Sutton et al., 1994; Tessaro et al., 1994; Otten et al., 1996). One important factor in reattendance is the woman's reaction to the initial test. Evidence suggests that this is not always positive.

Women will often find mammography screening painful. Keefe et al. (1994) reviewed several studies on the experience of pain during mammography and found that the percentage of women reporting pain varied widely across studies with a range of 1–62%. Admittedly, four of the eight studies reviewed by Keefe et al. (1994) found that at least one-third of the women reported some degree of pain during mammography. Lightfoot et al. (1994) reported that 40% out of a sample of 315 women undergoing screening mammography agreed that it hurt. Admittedly, it would seem that many will accept the pain and discomfort since it is short term and has long-term benefits. However, some are less accepting and indeed feel that the pain may actually increase their risk of cancer. For example, one woman commented in Eardley and Elkind's (1990) study: 'The straight answer is – if I don't have cancer now, I'll have it after this [the pressure of the machine].' Such a viewpoint may act as a disincentive for repeat mammography.

There is also evidence that cervical screening can be uncomfortable for some women. Schwartz et al. (1989) found in her survey of women in the East End of London that 54% rated having a smear test as painful or uncomfortable and 46% found it embarrassing. Again, such experiences would not be expected to encourage reattendance. In an interview study of women in New Zealand, it was found that smear tests were often described as unpleasant. Many of the women made reference to physical discomfort, humiliation and powerlessness (Wellington Women's Health Research Caucus, 1987).

Psychological consequences of cancer screening

In the initial haste to establish screening programmes, the psychological costs in terms of increased anxiety were overlooked. Recently, with the

publication of a series of more critical reports there has begun a reassessment. Wardle and Pope (1992) in reviewing the research organized it into
five groups:

1   *Impact of screening publicity*: although Skrabanek (1985) warned of the
    creation of a cancerphobia in society as a result of publicity campaigns
    for screening, the evidence for this is limited. Admittedly, several
    studies (e.g. Maclean et al., 1984; Eardley and Elkind, 1990) have found
    that women were alarmed when they received an invitation to attend.
    However, bearing in mind the evidence by McCaul et al. (1996b), it
    would seem that a certain rise in anxiety increases participation. Gram
    and Slenker (1992) found a lower level of anxiety about breast cancer
    among those who did not attend a mammography screening pro-
    gramme in Norway. However, as Sutton et al. (1995) suggest, excessive
    anxiety may act as a disincentive.
2   *Psychological costs of participation*: participation in screening pro-
    grammes is not always positive (Eardley and Elkind, 1990). The
    psychological effects may be disguised because of a selection effect
    such that the more anxious women avoid screening. Bowling (1990)
    has suggested that the middle-class women who tend to attend are
    more comfortable with the whole medical/scientific approach,
    whereas women from other social groups and cultures may be much
    more uncomfortable.
3   *Psychological costs of diagnosis of cancer*: not surprisingly the evidence
    suggests that a diagnosis of cancer is met by alarm and despair.
    Allebeck et al. (1989) found an increased rate of suicide among women
    positively screened in Scandinavia. Also of concern is the finding from
    the Swedish study that the increased rate of cardiovascular mortality
    following cancer screening offset the cancer mortality reduction
    (Anderson et al., 1988)
4   *Psychological response to diagnosis of abnormality*: although the screening
    test does not definitively identify cancer, evidence would suggest that
    any indication of abnormality is usually interpreted by the woman as
    such. Smith at al (1991) found that 95% of women who were told by
    mail that they had to return for further tests reported that they were
    upset or anxious. Until the possibility of cancer is ruled out these
    women will experience distress similar to being diagnosed with
    cancer. Indeed Lerman et al. (1991) found that this distress often
    continued after cancer had been ruled out. The extensive nature of this
    distress led Schmidt (1990) to conclude that the life years of mood
    impairment outweighed the benefits of cancer screening in terms of
    additional life years.
5   *Psychological costs of false positive diagnosis*: a large proportion of women
    with an initial positive diagnosis from the mammogram will later be
    declared negative on further examination. These are known as *false
    positive* cases. Not surprisingly, women will be extremely alarmed at

being informed that there may be something wrong. In a three-month follow-up of women who participated in mammography, Lerman et al. (1991) found that 47% of those who had suspicious readings reported that they had substantial anxiety about the procedure. This anxiety can last for a considerable period. In Norway, Gram et al. (1990) found that 29% of women with a false positive diagnosis reported anxiety about breast cancer compared to 13% of those with negative results.

The false positive result is followed by further anxiety provoking investigation which will include clinical examination and possibly surgery. In a 10-year follow-up, Elmore et al. (1998) found that one-third of the women who obtained some positive results were required to undergo additional investigations, including *biopsies*, even though it turned out that they did not have breast cancer.

Several studies have suggested that this anxiety remains even after the women have been cleared. Lerman and Rimer (1993) found that distress and anxiety continued after further examination had excluded cancer. Admittedly, not all women continue to experience anxiety. Although most cancer agencies will attempt to reduce anxiety by speeding up the process between evidence of a positive finding on the mammogram and subsequent surgical clearance, this is not always possible. An analysis of the tests conducted on a sample of women eventually declared false positive in Sweden found that they sometimes took up to two years (Lidbrin et al., 1996).

GENETIC SCREENING

The recent rapid advances in genetic research now hold out the prospect of genetic screening for different diseases. This can take various forms (see Lerman, 1997). *Carrier* testing investigates people who are likely to be carriers of the genes for such diseases as *cystic fibrosis* or *Tay-Sachs disease*. This form of testing is usually conducted in the context of reproductive decision making. Presymptomatic testing allows the identification of a disease before the symptoms actually develop. This form of testing is used to determine the person's risk of developing such late-onset diseases as Huntington's disease. Susceptibility testing is designed to test for a person's susceptibility to develop a disease, although whether or not that disease develops depends upon a variety of environmental and nutritional factors partly outside the person's control.

Although the general principles underlying genetic screening are similar to those of other forms of screening there are certain unique features. Lerman (1997) described several distinguishing features that need to be taken into consideration when investigating the psychological aspects (Table 14.4). These factors need to be accounted for in exploring the development of these services.

TABLE 14.4 *Features of genetic screening (Lerman, 1997, p. 4)*

- *Type of information*: genetic information is probabilistic and uncertain. In some cases you can say with certainty that a person will develop a disease but when is less clear (e.g. Huntington's disease). In other cases it is unclear whether the person will develop the disease at all (e.g. cancer).
- *Medical value*: control over disease onset is limited for certain diseases (e.g. cancer) and nonexistent for others (e.g. Huntington's disease).
- *Timescale*: the timescale is variable in that the results of genetic testing concern events which may occur far in the future.
- *Impact of results*: the results not only affect the individual but the family since genetic susceptibility is transmitted within families.

Psychological consequences of genetic screening

Unlike cancer screening, genetic testing is often initiated by individuals when they suspect that because of family history they may be carriers. Thus they would be expected to be in a heightened state of anxiety. Several studies have found a reduction in such anxiety following testing (Wiggins et al., 1992; Tibben et al., 1994). However, in some cases there was evidence of subsequent psychological distress. Lawson et al. (1996) found that of 95 individuals receiving the results of a test for Huntington's disease, two made plans for suicide and seven had clinical depression. Interestingly, there was no difference between those tested positive and those tested negative. Tibben et al. (1993) found that carriers tended to minimize the impact of the test results on their futures.

There is evidence that the positive effect of screening is only short term. At six-month follow-up Tibben et al. (1993) found that one-quarter of the carriers exhibited signs of psychopathology. They continued to follow the group for three years (Tibben et al., 1997) and found that for the first six months there was a rise in avoidant thoughts and a decrease in intrusive feelings. This was followed by a reversal of this pattern. It was suggested that this was evidence of a coping strategy whereby the carriers 'dose themselves' with tolerable levels of intrusive thoughts as they begin to process and accept the test results.

It was interesting to note the negative impact on some non-carriers (Huggins et al., 1992). This may partly be a reflection of survivor's guilt but also because the sympathy and support they had previously experienced was withdrawn when they were cleared.

Genetic screening can also have a dramatic impact on the family of the carrier. Hans and Koeppen (1989) found that partners often reacted with disbelief and denial. However, this turned to resentment and hostility as they became aware of the threat of transmission to their children. The partners can play an important role in helping the carrier cope with the diagnosis (Tibben et al., 1993).

The evidence of psychological impact of genetic screening has been followed by calls for greater provision of psychological support services

TABLE 14.5 **Possible advantages and disadvantages of childhood genetic testing (adapted from Michie and Marteau, 1996, p. 9)**

	Advantages	Disadvantages
Those with a faulty gene	Time to adjust and avoid emotional problems. Enables parents to help child prepare. Enables child and parents to prepare practically for the future. Allows child to take informed choices. Avoids problem of 'family secrets'. Child doesn't miss opportunity for testing. Relieves child's anxiety about future. Relieves parental anxiety.	Child's self-esteem and long-term adjustment may be impaired. Family's perception and treatment of child may be adversely affected. May lead to discrimination from others. May adversely affect marriage opportunities. May not have wanted to be tested if asked when older. May generate unwarranted anxiety before possible early signs.
Those without a faulty gene	Emotional relief. Able to plan life. Avoids adverse effects of later disclosure. Avoids pre-selection of the 'sick' individual inheriting the gene. Relieves anxiety about possible early signs.	Rejection by family for being unaffected. False reassurance about health status.

(Marteau, 1989, 1990). It is suggested that such services be made available both prior to testing such that the testees are fully aware of the issues and also afterwards so that they and their families can begin to come to terms with the findings (Boreani and Gangeri, 1996).

This is then followed by further anxiety provoking investigation which will include clinical examination and possibly surgery. Predictive genetic testing can be applied to children. This has a variety of implications which have yet to be researched. Michie and Marteau (1996) summarized the possible advantages and disadvantages (Table 14.5).

Some ethical issues

The prospect of widespread genetic screening has provoked sustained debate about the ethical issues. Harper (1992) voiced concern that the needs of individuals and families are being made subservient to broader eugenic goals. Stone and Stewart (1996) have claimed that the voice of the public is rarely heard in this debate. They argue that the advocates of genetic screening often falsely claim that their programmes are based on the public's right to know. Yet there is little evidence that the public wants to know. Stone and Stewart also raised a variety of other questions about genetic screening such as the ability of lay people to interpret genetic information, the competence of health personnel in explaining aspects of genetic screening and the use made of genetic information. Future programme development needs to consider these and other ethical issues.

In a review of the social impact and ethical implications of genetic testing, Davison et al. (1994) identified three areas of popular perception which have implications for predictive testing for Huntington's disease:

1   Both positive and negative results can lead to personal and family anguish. While the former is expected there is also evidence that those who are cleared suffer from survivor guilt and a feeling they do not belong to their family.
2   Some families who inherit the gene have developed ways of deciding who in the family will be sufferers. This lay procedure is undermined by medical investigation.
3   Knowing about possible futures may decrease the quality of a person's life. They note that this finding 'is not easily accommodated within the essentially rationalist or utilitarian philosophy underlying the idea of screening' (p. 354).

One particular aspect of remaining ignorant is that it allows the maintenance of hope. Many lay people are happy to tolerate uncertainty because of the hope that they will survive.

The premise of much genetic testing is that people understand the basic principles of inheritance. However, there is evidence that this is not always the case. In a qualitative interview study of members of families at risk of familial adenomatous polyposis (FAP), which geneticists consider almost 100% genetic, Michie et al. (1996) found that many referred to what they considered to be the vital role of the environment. Many of the family members also minimized the threat posed by the disease. While advising these people that they are at risk may be formally correct, it has immense implications for the future quality of their lives.

CONCLUSIONS ABOUT DISEASE PREVENTION

The development of immunization and screening programmes designed to prevent the onset of specific diseases offers tremendous promise for improving the health of society. However, in their design specific attention must be given to the human side of these interventions. Eardley et al. (1985) concluded their review of the reluctance of women to participate in cervical screening with the comment: 'When a programme of screening fails to take account of women's needs, expects women to take the initiative in making an appointment, and is organized in a way to suit the convenience of the provider rather than the user, then it is less likely that women will make use of the service.' Such comments are largely supported by the research evidence on the difficulties of implementing disease prevention services.

FUTURE RESEARCH

1   There are secular trends in immunization rates which are connected to media reports of adverse effects. There is a need further to understand how lay people interpret these reports.
2   Participation in cancer screening is related to age, social and ethnic factors. While there has been much quantitative research, there is a need for more qualitative research into the meaning of cancer and cancer screening within certain subgroups.
3   Genetic research premises a host of social, psychological and ethical issues. There is a need for an expanded programme of research to investigate both professional and public perceptions of genetic screening and the impact on different populations.

SUMMARY

1   Participation in immunization programmes is related to the social character of children's families.
2   The health professional plays a central role in deciding whether parents have their children immunized.
3   Parents have a range of fears and anxieties about immunization.
4   Many countries have implemented screening programmes for breast and cervical cancer.
5   Besides organizational details, the health professional, especially the family doctor, is central to explaining participation in these programmes.
6   Women have a variety of beliefs and fears about these programmes.
7   The so-called genetic revolution has many implications for screening.
8   Both the general public and people who are at risk of certain diseases have a variety of concerns about genetic screening.

KEY TERMS

deficit model
false positive
Health Belief Model (HBM)
immunization
mammography

screening
Theory of reasoned action (TRA)
Transtheoretical model of
    change (TTM)

15 HEALTH PROMOTION

It is now quite obvious that for many people their network of friends, neighbours, church relationships, and so on, provide not only support, but genuine niches and opportunities for personal development. (Julian Rappaport, 1981, p. 19)

OUTLINE

This chapter focuses upon the psychological dimensions of health promotion. Three major health promotion approaches are described: the behaviour change approach, the self-empowerment approach and the collective action approach. Health promotion interventions informed by each approach are described and critically evaluated. Two critiques of the western contemporary 'ideology of health promotion' are presented.

WHAT IS HEALTH PROMOTION?

Health promotion is any event, process or activity which facilitates the protection or improvement of the health status of individuals, groups, communities or populations. Its objective is to prolong life and to improve quality of life, that is to prevent or reduce the effects of impaired physical and/or mental health on those individuals who are directly (e.g. patients) or indirectly (e.g. carers) affected. Health promotion includes both *environmental* and *behavioural interventions*.

Environmental interventions target the built environment (e.g. fencing around dangerous sites) and involve legislation to safeguard the natural environment (e.g. maximum water pollution targets) as well as the production of goods (e.g. the ban on certain beef products). These measures are not usually influenced by those who are affected by them, although this can happen through collective action such as campaigns, boycotts or even elections. They do not necessarily require co-operation from those who benefit from them, and they do not typically involve communication with those targeted by them. This is to say, the effectiveness of environmental measures does not depend upon people's awareness of their existence.

'Ecopsychologists' and non-governmental organizations like Greenpeace are concerned with the development of sustainable environments which protect life and well-being. Researchers in psychophysics also have a contribution to make to this type of health promotion. For example, research into what types of sound are the most effective in attracting attention is a crucial part of the design of any auditory alarm system. A related topic is protection against hazards both natural and manmade and the communication of risk (Handmer and Penning-Rowsell, 1990). The United Nations designated the 1990s as the Decade for Natural Disaster Reduction and many governments, commercial and voluntary organizations and individuals are becoming increasingly concerned about risks and their management.

Behavioural *interventions* are primarily concerned with the consequences of individuals' actions. In recent years, this type of health promotion has focused upon the concept of *empowerment*. Empowerment is the process by which people increase their control over their physical, social and internal environments. Behavioural interventions include raising awareness and knowledge about health hazards, teaching technical (e.g. how to floss one's teeth; how to use a condom) and social skills (e.g. how to say no to drugs; how to negotiate condom use), as well as cognitive-behavioural techniques (e.g. how to practise progressive muscle relaxation; how to re-focus one's thoughts). All of these measures require the active co-operation of those who benefit from them and the use of persuasive and effective communication. The involvement of health psychologists is substantial. It includes social skills training, preventive health behaviour counselling, cognitive-behaviour therapy, education and advertising. This chapter focuses on behavioural interventions.

It is possible to identify three approaches which can inform health promotion interventions (Box 15.1).

BOX 15.1   THREE APPROACHES TO HEALTH PROMOTION

Behaviour change approach

Objective: to bring about changes in individual behaviour through changes in individuals' cognitions.
Process: provision of information about health risks and hazards.
Aim: to increase individuals' knowledge about the causes of health and illness.
Assumption: humans are rational decision-makers whose cognitions inform their actions.

Self-empowerment approach

Objective: to empower individuals to make healthy choices.
Process: participatory learning techniques.
Aim: to increase control over one's physical, social and internal environments.
Assumption: power is a universal resource which can be mobilized by every individual.

Collective action approach

Objective: to improve health by addressing socio-economic and environmental causes of ill health.
Process: individuals organize and act collectively in order to change their physical and social environments.
Aim: to modify social, economic and physical structures which generate ill health.
Assumption: communities of individuals share interests which allows them to act collectively.

These three approaches pursue different goals, utilize different means to achieve their goals and propose different criteria for their evaluation. However, they all aim to promote good health and to prevent or reduce the effects of ill health (French and Adams, 1986). These three approaches are considered in turn.

BEHAVIOUR CHANGE APPROACH

The goal of this approach is to bring about changes in individual behaviour through changes in the individual's cognitions. The approach is based upon the assumption that humans are rational decision-makers and therefore relies heavily upon the provision of information about risks and health hazards through the mass media as well as leaflets and posters. Information is presented as factual and attributed to an expert source. Here, health promotion is really synonymous with *health education* which aims to increase individuals' knowledge about the causes of health and illness. This approach is also known as 'information-giving model' (Aggleton, 1989).

As we saw in Chapter 10, psychologists have been developing theories about the relationship between knowledge, attitudes and behaviour for some time, known as *social cognition models (SCMs)*. These have been applied to a wide range of preventive health behaviours such as vaccination uptake, breast self-examination and contraceptive use. SCMs aim to predict the performance of behaviours and, by implication, to provide guidance as to how to facilitate their uptake by manipulating relevant variables (such as beliefs, attitudes and perceptions). It is suggested that there is a close relationship between people's beliefs, attitudes and intentions to act in particular ways. Consequently, by bringing about changes in beliefs it is hoped to bring about changes in behaviour.

For example, consider how the issue of smoking is dealt with by the Health Belief Model (HBM; Becker, 1974). Smokers deciding whether or not to give up smoking would be expected to consider:

- how susceptible they are to lung cancer and other smoking-related conditions;
- how serious these conditions are;
- the extent and value of the benefits of giving up smoking;
- the potential negative consequences of giving up smoking.

In addition, the HBM acknowledges the role of cues to action, internal (e.g. a symptom such as a smoker's cough) and external (e.g. information, advice or meeting someone with lung cancer), as well as health motivation, i.e. the importance of health to the individual.

The HBM has been applied to a wide range of health behaviours including the uptake of flu vaccinations, breast self-examination, anti-hypertensive regimens, mothers' adherence to regimens for their children and risk factor behaviours (e.g. seatbelt use, attendance at health check-ups, diets, etc.). Overall, the HBM is marginally successful in predicting health behaviours (see Janz and Becker, 1984; Harrison et al., 1992; Sheeran and Abraham, 1995). Each key variable of the HBM tends to be significantly correlated with the behaviour under study (e.g. Janz and Becker, 1984). This suggests that the variables identified by the HBM are relevant ingredients and contribute to the process which generates health behaviour. However, the variables of the HBM only *control* a relatively small amount of the *variance* in individuals' health behaviour (around 10% when combined). In other words, our ability to accurately predict health behaviour on the basis of the HBM is severely limited.

The theory of reasoned action (TRA; Fishbein and Ajzen, 1975) and its revised version, the theory of planned behaviour (TPB; Ajzen, 1985) propose that behaviour is informed by attitudes towards the behaviour as well as subjective norms about the behaviour, that is what significant others think one should do. These variables (and in the case of the TPB an additional variable: perceived control over the behaviour) combine to generate an intention to behave in a particular way, which is then used to predict actual behaviour. Attitudes and subjective norms are based upon beliefs held by the individual. So, for example, a woman's belief that birth control pills are a potential health risk and her belief that her friends and relatives would not approve of her taking such a risk are thought to generate a negative attitude towards taking birth control pills, as well as social pressure not to take them; thus giving rise to the intention to refrain from the use of birth control pills and, hopefully, to consider other forms of contraception.

The TRA and TPB have been used to predict numerous health behaviours, including smoking, alcohol consumption, contraceptive use/safer sex, health screening attendance, exercise, food choice and breast/testicle self-examination (see Sheppard et al., 1988; Ajzen, 1991; Conner and Sparks, 1995). Overall, the evidence suggests that TRA and TPB do contribute to our understanding of the antecedents of health relevant behaviours. Across studies TRA variables control between 43% and 46% of the variance and TPB variables control 50% of the variance in intentions to behave (Conner and Sparks, 1995).

However, it is important to bear in mind that the TRA and TPB do not actually predict behaviour but only the intention to behave. Thus, TRA and TPB variables control up to 50% of the variance in people's expressed intentions to behave. Unfortunately, correlations between intention to behave and actual behaviour are not perfect. They tend to range between 0.45 (Randall and Wolff, 1994, cited in Conner and Sparks, 1995) and 0.62 (van der Putte, 1993, cited in Conner and Norman, 1995), thus controlling only 20 to 38% of the variance. This means that TRA and TPB variables control only 10–20% of the variance in actual behaviour, leaving 80–90% of the variance uncontrolled.

A study using the TRA (Rise, 1992)

Rise (1992) used the TRA as a theoretical framework in order to study 'condom behaviour' defined as 'a decision based upon consideration of the expected consequences of using or not using condoms' (p. 185). A postal questionnaire about condom use was completed by 1,172 Norwegian adolescents aged 17 to 19 years and all non-virgins. The following variables were measured:

1   The intention to use condoms at the next intercourse (behavioural intention).
2   Beliefs about condom use, e.g. 'condoms protect me against sexually transmitted diseases' (behavioural beliefs).
3   Evaluation of behavioural beliefs and outcomes, e.g. 'How much do you fear STD?' (values).
4   Significant others' evaluation of the respondent's condom use (normative beliefs).
5   Importance of significant others' evaluation (motivation to comply).
6   Previous/habitual condom use (prior behaviour).

Items (2) and (3) together provided a measure of attitudes towards condom use; (4) and (5) combined assessed subjective norms. With the exception of prior behaviour, all variables were from the TRA.

Rise (1992) observed that *past behaviour* was by far the strongest predictor of intention to use condoms at the next intercourse. Next came subjective norm followed by attitude. All relationships were statistically significant (see Table 15.1). Behavioural beliefs related to pleasure and sensation (e.g. 'Condom use reduces my physical pleasure') discriminated best between intenders and non-intenders whereas traditional risk appraisal beliefs (e.g. 'Condom use protects me against STD') did not discriminate. Among normative beliefs, sexual partners' expectations had the best discriminatory power.

TABLE 15.1 *Correlations among attitudes towards condom use, subjective norms, prior behaviour and intention to use condoms at next intercourse (Rise, 1992, p. 190; reproduced with permission)*

	Attitudes	**Subjective norms**	**Prior behaviour**
Subjective norms	0.23	–	–
Prior behaviour	0.31	0.51	–
Intention	0.29	0.55	0.75

Rise's study confirmed the importance of subjective norms as well as attitudes in intention formation. However, the best predictor of intention to use condoms, prior behaviour, is not included in the TRA. The inclusion of this variable may increase the theory's predictive power. The finding that only some behavioural beliefs discriminate between intenders and non-intenders suggests that 'behavioural beliefs' should not remain a homogeneous category within the TRA framework. For example, it may be necessary to differentiate between beliefs about long-term and short-term outcomes of a *preventive health behaviour*. In this way, the importance of immediate pleasure and sensation as opposed to long-term consequences such as pregnancy or sexually transmitted diseases (STD) could be taken into account. However, the findings of this study relate to the particular context of sexual behaviour and may not be applicable to other health-relevant behaviours.

There are a growing number of social cognition models being used to predict health-relevant behaviours (Conner and Norman, 1995). In recent years, researchers have attempted to develop a more dynamic under-standing of health behaviour. For example, Weinstein (1988) proposes that individuals move through qualitatively different stages which characterize the precaution adoption process. Different variables become instrumental at different stages. Schwarzer's (1999) Health Action Process Approach also takes a more dynamic and process-oriented approach to health behaviour. However, despite the increasing range and complexity of social cognition models, it is possible to identify a number of shared charac-teristics on which to base a critique of the genre (Box 15.2).

BOX 15.2 CRITICISMS OF SCMS

1 SCMs are only concerned with cognitively mediated behaviours.
2 SCMs do not take into account the direct effect of impulse and/or emotion.
3 SCMs assume that the same variables inform different health behaviours.
4 SCMs assume that the same variables are relevant for diverse groups of people.
5 SCMs focus exclusively upon mental representations of the social world and do not take into account the direct effects of material, physical and social factors.
6 SCMs do not address the issue of joint decision making.

First, all SCMs conceptualize the individual as a rational decision-maker. Variables of relevance in SCMs are cognitions such as beliefs, attitudes and perceptions. This means that SCMs are only concerned with conscious, cognitively mediated health behaviours (e.g. the decision to buy a smoke alarm). However, it has been pointed out that many *health habits* occur routinely (Bennett et al., 1995) (e.g. brushing one's teeth in the morning) and do not involve conscious decision making.

Furthermore, SCMs do not take into account the role of impulse and/or emotion. Even where models do include the variable 'volitional control' (e.g. TPB, Ajzen, 1985), it is conceptualized as a conscious belief (in one's own efficacy) which the individual includes in his/her rational appraisal. However, situational pressure such as physical and emotional 'urges' as well as power relations can have a strong and direct influence on health-relevant behaviours such as contraceptive use and safer sex practices (e.g. Ingham et al., 1991).

Another assumption of SCMs is that a predictive model can be designed which is applicable to a wide range of health behaviours. In other words, it is assumed that the same variables (e.g. attitudes and subjective norm) inform different behaviours (e.g. attendance at dental check-ups as well as condom use). However, the predictive power of any one SCM varies depending on its context of application. There is rarely full confirmation for the Health Belief Model in the literature; rather, different variables appear to be important for different health behaviours.

Similarly, SCMs assume that the same variables are relevant to diverse groups of people. However, there is evidence to the contrary from studies which have identified different psychological antecedents of HIV-preventive behaviour for men and women, people of different ages, as well as people with different amounts of sexual experience (Abraham and Sheeran, 1994).

Another problem is that SCMs focus exclusively upon mental representations of the social world and their effects upon behaviour. They do not take into account the direct effects of material, physical and social factors. Thus, something like lack of access to health resources (e.g. healthy food, condoms, the local gym) can only feature as lack of volitional control (i.e. the belief that 'I cannot put the health behaviour into practice'), thus maintaining a focus upon the individual as opposed to his/her social and material location. As we have seen in Chapters 1 and 2, material, physical and social factors can place severe constraints on the individual's ability to act upon information. For this reason, health promotion programmes may instil a greater sense of frustration, hopelessness and lack of control, possibly even causing *decrements* in well-being.

Finally, decisions about health-relevant behaviours are conceptualized in SCMs as individual decisions. Yet many health behaviours arise out of an interaction between two or more people (e.g. condom use, smoking cessation, changes in diet), suggesting that the individual level of analysis is too narrow a focus for a theory of behaviour change.

Implications for health promotion practise

Even though social cognition models are concerned with behaviour change, there is little explicit discussion of exactly how their insights could inform the design of health promotion interventions (for exceptions, see: Tones, 1987; Abraham and Sheeran, 1994; Conner et al., 1994). This may be due to the assumption that once we have accurately and reliably identified the cognitive precursors of health-relevant behaviours, they will be amenable to easy manipulation. Alternatively, a reluctance to formulate concrete recommendations for practice may be a reflection of the pervasive and unfortunate divide that exists between academics and practitioners.

Whatever the reason, the preoccupation of SCM researchers with the prediction of behavioural intentions on the basis of social cognitions has prevented them from addressing the crucial question of how social cognitions are formed and how they can be changed. In other words, even if we could predict someone's behaviour on the basis of knowing their relevant beliefs, attitudes and/or perceptions, this would not tell us anything about if and how these could be modified.

One result of this reluctance to shift the focus from content (of beliefs or perceptions) to process (of belief formation or change) is that it creates the impression that the provision of relevant information is sufficient to induce changes in social cognitions. For example, accurate information about the spread and method of transmission of a disease, as well as the nature of its symptoms, could have a direct effect upon perceived susceptibility and severity, as defined by the HBM. Similarly, information about other people's opinions of those who do or do not engage in particular health-relevant behaviours could be expected to directly inform subjective norms, as conceptualized by the TRA. Even perceived behavioural control could be manipulated through the provision of information about the extent to which other people similar to oneself have succeeded in taking up a particular preventive health behaviour.

Thus, even though SCM theorists stress that information about a disease does not by itself generate behaviour change and that changes in attitudes and beliefs are required (e.g. Tones, 1987; Ross and Rosser, 1989), they are actually talking about a particular kind of information, namely biomedical, rather than information as such. In fact, it is suggested that other types of information are instrumental in bringing about changes in belief structure and consequently attitudes. For example, Tones (1987) suggests that 'teaching young people about the effects of various substances on the body might convince them of the damage which might be done' (p. 315); Abraham and Sheeran (1994) draw attention to the positive effects of 'providing heterosexual couples with instructions for condom use which included suggestions on how to eroticize them' (p. 176). Thus, it can be argued that SCMs share both the aim (i.e. to bring about individual behaviour change), and method (i.e. provision of information) of the behaviour change paradigm.

However, some SCM theorists who explored different methods of modifying social cognitions (e.g. Abraham and Sheeran, 1994) and their ideas will be discussed in the next section.

Critique of the behaviour change approach

The behaviour change approach attracts a number of criticisms (see Box 15.3). First, it is unable to target the major causes of ill health. Individual behaviour change, even when successfully implemented, cannot address socio-economic factors such as poverty, unemployment or environmental pollution. Its objective is change within the individual rather than change in the individual's environment. Second, the choice of what type of preventive behaviours to adopt lies with the 'experts' whose task it is to communicate this information to the public. As a result, recommendations and advice provided 'from above' can easily be seen to be incompatible with community norms, values and practices. In addition, receiving health advice in a top-down fashion can be a disempowering experience (Homans and Aggleton, 1988). Third, there is no direct link between knowledge, attitudes and behaviour. The behaviour change paradigm does not address the many variables other than cognitions about disease which inform human actions. Fourth, in its application the behaviour change paradigm tends to assume homogeneity among the receivers of its health messages. However, information is not received or processed uniformly by those to whom it is directed: mood, motivation, past experience, interest, perceived relevance, lay beliefs, group membership and many other factors mediate the way in which a message is 'heard' and interpreted.

BOX 15.3 CRITICISMS OF THE THREE APPROACHES TO HEALTH PROMOTION

Criticisms of the behaviour change approach
- is unable to target the major socio-economic causes of ill health;
- operates 'top-down';
- assumes that there is a direct link between knowledge, attitudes and behaviour;
- assumes homogeneity among the receivers of health promotion messages.

Criticisms of the self-empowerment approach
- it is assumed that rational choices are healthy choices;
- strong reliance upon simulation;
- inadequate concept of power.

Problems associated with the collective action approach
- vulnerable to lack of funding and to official oppositions;
- danger of creeping professionalization;
- problematic concept of 'community'.

In the light of these issues it is perhaps not surprising that the behaviour change approach has generally yielded relatively small effects on actual health behaviour when implemented in real-world interventions.

SELF-EMPOWERMENT APPROACH

The goal of this approach to health promotion is to empower individual people to make healthy choices. Self-empowerment can be defined as the process by which groups and individuals increase their control over their physical, social and internal environments (see Box 15.4 for examples of self-empowerment techniques). In order to facilitate self-empowerment, participatory learning techniques allow people to examine their own values and beliefs and explore the extent to which factors such as past socialization as well as social location affect the choices they make (Homans and Aggleton, 1988). Group work, problem-solving techniques, client-centred counselling, assertiveness training and social skills training as well as educational drama are forms of participatory learning. The self-empowerment paradigm, with its emphasis upon self-awareness and skills, resonates with what Stroebe and Stroebe (1995) refer to as the 'therapy model' of health promotion which deploys a wide range of psychological techniques such as cognitive restructuring, skill training and self-conditioning in order to help individuals act upon their intentions to adopt health behaviours.

Examples of therapeautic approaches using the techniques cognitive-behavioural therapy and motivation enhancement are described in Chapters 6, 7 and 8. However, the self-empowerment approach relies upon the individual person's inherent capacity to act rationally more than the therapy model does.

BOX 15.4   SELF-EMPOWERMENT TECHNIQUES

- Participatory learning
- Group work
- Problem solving
- Client-centred counselling
- Assertiveness training
- Social skills training
- Educational drama

Empowerment is the principle value of community psychology (Rappaport, 1987) with which the work described in this chapter has much in common. Empowerment has been described by Rappaport in the following terms:

> By empowerment I mean that our aim should be to enhance the possibilities for people to control their own lives. If this is our aim then we will necessarily

find ourselves questioning both our public policy and our role relationship to dependent people . . . Empowerment implies that many competences are already present or at least possible, given niches and opportunities. Prevention implies experts fixing the independent variables to make the dependent variables come out right. Empowerment implies that what you see as poor functioning is a result of social structure and lack of resources which make it impossible for the existing competencies to operate. It implies that in those cases where competencies need to be learned, they are best learned in a context of living life rather than in artificial programs where everyone including the person learning, knows that it is really the expert in charge. (Rappaport, 1981, pp. 12–13)

Self-empowerment is particularly popular within health education for young people. For example, peer pressure has been identified as a powerful obstacle to the adoption of healthy practices by young people. Here, self-empowerment techniques encourage young people to make independent decisions by developing their psychological resources to resist peer pressure, the so-called 'say no' technique. This has been attempted through assertiveness training, social skills training, inoculation to persuasive appeals and life skills training, with limited success (Hopkins, 1994, p. 335).

A range of HIV-preventive interventions for young people are informed by a self-empowerment rationale (Abraham and Sheeran, 1994). These include rehearsal of communication and interaction sequences which might be involved in condom purchase or sexual negotiation, questioning and challenging sexual scripts which do not allow space for negotiation of contraceptive use, peer education programmes, as well as group-based cognitive-behavioural programmes aiming to identify and then modify personal obstacles to HIV prevention. All of these involve reflexive self-appraisal as well as the acquisition of new skills. Abraham and Sheeran (1994) argue that such empowerment-based interventions can be effective in increasing perceived *self-efficacy* which has been shown to be a powerful predictor of intention formation and behaviour (e.g. Bandura, 1992). Thus, Abraham and Sheeran (1994) move beyond the more simplistic behaviour change/information giving approach, to manipulate SCM variables through empowerment techniques. Indeed, these authors also acknowledge the importance of power relations and cultural resources which require change at a community level.

An example of an empowerment-based intervention (Lugo, 1996)

The Resource Sisters/Compañeras Program was an empowerment education project for pregnant women in Orange County, Florida (Lugo, 1996). The programme focused on areas which had high rates of low birth weight babies, infant mortality, substance-exposed newborns and poverty. It was implemented in an inner city area, a rural section of the county and a quasi-suburban area. The programme was designed (a) to employ and

enhance the natural skills of women from the community (peer counsellors) to assist other women and foster collective problem solving; (b)
provide outreach and case management through home visits; (c) to
develop ongoing peer support groups.

Local women were recruited and trained to become peer educators. The
intensive three-week group training covered empowerment, resources,
needs assessment, case management, women's issues, problem posing,
prenatal health, labour and delivery and group facilitation. Trained peer
counsellors visited women in their homes who had been identified as high
risk (medically, demographically and/or psychosocially) by the state
screening programme. These visits provided an opportunity for individual
needs assessment and case management, as well as to encourage the
women to attend support group meetings. These meetings took place in
clients' neighbourhoods and their purpose was to be a forum where women
could define their own health issues.

The evaluation showed that around 20% of women who had been con-
tacted came to at least one support group meeting. Participation was
greatest in the rural community and was lowest among white women. Over
40% of women who had come to one group meeting returned several times.
Thus, obtaining a high level of initial participation seemed to be a challenge.

Issues raised and discussed by the women in the groups commonly
included personal violence, stress, relationships, parenting, physiological
and emotional changes during pregnancy and concerns with basic survival
(food, housing, etc.). The groups were a forum for discussion of individual
choices, decision making and self-care, as well as collective problem
solving. The groups developed social cohesion which was demonstrated
by contact among participants outside the group meetings. Peer counsellors reported an increased sense of empowerment and options since
working with the programme. However, after the first year of the programme there were no significant differences between clients' and non-
clients' low birth weight rates. Thus, the programme had not contributed
to improved pregnancy outcomes.

Lugo (1996) draws attention to the fact that the programme was exter-
nally imposed, as an alternative model for providing state-mandated case
management for at-risk pregnant women. This raises the question of
whether empowerment can occur within the context of a programme and a
circumscribed source of funding whose major purpose is individual
medical case management. Lugo (1996) proposes that the best promise for
success lies in efforts that hold empowerment and community development as core functions.

Implications for health promotion practise

The self-empowerment approach assumes that healthy choices are facilitated by increased personal control. Self-empowerment interventions aim
to provide a space in which individuals are able to understand themselves

as subjects of their own lives. Such interventions confront the challenge of enabling those who feel, and arguably also are, the most powerless in society to take control of their health. Self-empowerment also involves critical appraisal of the social and cultural factors which shape participants' health behaviours. As a result, participants may have to confront the reality of their social and economic powerlessness. This may be difficult to address within a personal empowerment group setting. Finally, self-empowerment workers need to negotiate the tensions between their roles as 'educator' and 'facilitator'. They need to be aware that the support they give may disempower clients.

Critique of the self-empowerment approach

There are a number of criticisms that can be made of the self-empowerment approach (see Box 15.3). First, there is an assumption that rational choices are healthy choices. However, there is evidence that people may engage in unhealthy or risky behaviours for perfectly rational reasons: e.g. mothers who refuse infant immunization because they consider it to be too risky or alternatively ineffectual (New and Senior, 1991); or some gay men who practise unprotected sex in order to maximize pleasure (Davies and Project Sigma, 1992). Second, self-empowerment techniques rely upon simulation: skills are practised in safe environments and artificial settings such as assertiveness training groups. It is assumed that skills acquired in this way can be transferred to real-life situations. However, it could be argued that powerful influences such as the fear of losing face, social reputations or loyalties which characterize real-life social situations are likely to interfere with such transference of skills. Third, the paradigm does not have an adequate concept of power (Homans and Aggleton, 1988). It is assumed that power is a potential resource which resides within the individual and can be mobilized through empowerment techniques. However, systematic inequalities with regard to access to material, social and psychological resources in society mean that people are not equal in their ability to put healthy choices into practice. In other words, the self-empowerment paradigm maintains a focus upon the individual as the locus of change and is therefore unable to address structural inequalities of power in society.

COLLECTIVE ACTION APPROACH

The aim of collective action is to improve health by addressing socio-economic and environmental causes of ill health within the community. Thus, this approach recognizes the close relationship between individual health and its social and material contexts, which consequently become the target for change. Individuals act collectively in order to change their environment rather than themselves. Therefore, the collective action approach constitutes the interface between the environmental and the behavioural approaches to health promotion in that it is concerned with the ways in which collectivities can actively intervene to change their physical and social environment.

It could be argued that self-empowerment is part of a social action process which culminates in the ability to take collective action. Therefore, a separation of the self-empowerment and collective action approaches may seem somewhat artificial. However, self-empowerment interventions typically limit themselves to the development of interpersonal skills in narrow settings and are therefore unlikely to constitute more than simply a first stage in a community empowerment process. Furthermore, self-empowerment can be a consequence rather than a precondition of collective action.

We can give three examples of collective health promotion. First, the WHO's **Healthy Cities Project** attempts to combine a community focus with an acknowledgement of the need to challenge pervasive inequalities in society. Set up in the mid-1980s, the Healthy Cities Project has involved over 400 communities to date. Its aim is to promote health in the urban context by identifying and counteracting aspects of urban life which impair health. Consistent with a collective action model of health promotion, this requires the active involvement of local communities, representatives of whom meet on a regular basis for a period of one year in order to identify health objectives and targets for change. This is followed by a two-year period of implementation and evaluation.

For example, in one German city, the community group identified weight as a health problem in the community and decided to approach butchers in the city with the request to develop a new low-fat sausage (Conner, 1994). In addition, the Healthy Cities Project aims to develop new ideas in public health. For example, research into the impact of poor housing on health (Hunt, 1993) found that levels of mould in the air had a direct and independent effect upon the health of children living in the dwellings. This study's findings were used to campaign for changes in housing conditions.

A second example is described by Raeburn and Rootman (1998) as 'People-Centred Health Promotion' (PCHP). They use the mnemonic PEOPLE to define their approach (Box 15.5).

BOX 15.5   THE ELEMENTS OF PEOPLE-CENTRED HEALTH PROMOTION (RAEBURN AND ROOTMAN, 1998)

- People-centredness
- Empowerment
- Organizational and community development
- Participation
- Life quality
- Evaluation

PCHP starts with people's everyday experience considered in a collective or community. The members of any community know best what their needs are and the role of the professional is seen as that of a *facilitator*. As described above, empowerment refers to people taking more control, building up 'strength', 'capacity' or 'resources' as a person, group or community. The concept of *personal control* refers to self-efficacy, sense of coherence, competence, effectiveness, and coping (discussed in more detail in Chapters 4 and 5). **Strength building** is concerned with the enhancement of skills, knowledge and competence, increasing assets and resources (Rappaport, 1987). PCHP considers people rather than individuals, i.e. 'people in their collectivity, rather than as isolated persons' (Raeburn and Rootman, 1998, p. 26). The PCPH approach advocates organization development, a change process or progression of changes as an organization is transformed to deal more effectively with the needs of the community.

According to Raeburn and Rootman (1998), the process of *community development* contains seven steps:

1 Participatory formulation of a philosophy of action and overall objectives.
2 Participatory planning of action through community needs assessment.
3 Consensual setting of time-limited goals.
4 Consensually agreed resource plans.
5 Allocation of tasks and actions to as many participants as possible.
6 Regular review of all major project goals and processes in a public forum.
7 Periodic assessment of outcomes.

Raeburn and Rootman (1998) describe several interesting case studies of health promotion projects involving empowerment and community development using the PCHP approach. These include the Superhealth Lifestyle Programmes, low cost community approaches to weight control, healthy eating and stress management.

A third example of community based approaches to health promotion is the concept of the *healthy living centre*. In the UK the government has allocated £300 million from the National Lottery 'New Opportunities Fund' to the development of healthy living centres over the period 1999–2003. This new initiative will lead to several hundred community projects focusing on the health of the most vulnerable 20% of the UK population. A healthy living centre provides health promotion of the kind that a community says it wants, not of the kind the government or health authorities believe that it needs.

Collective action as community empowerment

Outreach health education with intravenous drug using communities at risk of HIV infection provides a good example of the collective action approach (Rhodes and Hartnoll, 1991; Rhodes, 1994). Community *outreach* strategies aim to achieve subcultural change among target constituencies. Outreach involves the use of key members of the target community as indigenous workers who communicate a series of complementary risk reduction messages to other members of the community. In addition, such strategies can be incorporated within existing self-help initiatives which aim to achieve wider social and political change.

For example, the Junkiebonden, a federation of Dutch self-help groups, aims to initiate community change through campaigning for the modification of local and national drug policy. The Junkiebonden was involved in the setting up of the first syringe exchange in the Netherlands in 1984. Since then, it has distributed education and prevention materials to drug users and sex workers through outreach techniques. The Junkiebonden was set up from within the drug-using community and is run predominantly by current drug users. This was a grass-roots initiative which did not require external facilitation.

Evaluation of the needle exchange programme in Amsterdam has been positive. Since the establishment of the needle exchange network, the number of injectors has remained constant whilst the number of people joining treatment schemes has increased. The rate of HIV infections decreased. However, as Rhodes and Hartnoll (1991) point out, national and regional legislation and policing policies play a key role in the effectiveness of outreach work. Evidence from evaluations of needle exchange programmes in the USA and UK is less encouraging (e.g. Stimson et al., 1991).

Implications for health promotion practise

The aim of community outreach and development is to make contact with 'hard-to-reach' members of the population and involve them as fully active participants in health promotion actions. Those who are easily located by the outreach workers are less likely to be in need of their services (the *inverse care law*). Making contact repeatedly with members of a large, transient population such as homeless young people in large cities constitutes a major challenge to outreach workers. Also, it is important to distinguish between individual outreach, which aims to facilitate individual behaviour change through the provision of information and personal development, and community outreach, which aims to change community norms and behaviours. The former is associated with the self-empowerment approach.

Community development, with its emphasis upon collective ownership and control over health choices and health status, is much more likely to come into conflict with statutory health promotion agencies. This is particularly the case when marginalized communities such as drug users make choices which more dominant communities consider a threat to public health.

Community health promotion strategies may not be successful in all types of community. For example, drug users networks are primarily sustained because of functional needs such as dealing and scoring (Rhodes, 1994) rather than for political or social reasons. They do not share ritual celebrations of social identity as does the gay community in both the UK and USA. This, together with the absence of infrastructures for action, makes it more difficult to mobilize outreach strategies within such communities.

Critique of the collective action approach

It is clear that the collective action approach is deeply political. It involves the collective organization of those who are traditionally excluded from decision-making processes and a direct and active challenge to power relations associated with health and illness. As a result, health promotion initiatives using this approach have the potential to come into conflict with those whose interests lie with the status quo such as industry, employers, government departments and local councils which aim to make financial savings. Consequently, community action as a form of health promotion is vulnerable to lack of public funding and official opposition. In addition, there is a danger of creeping professionalization (Homans and Aggleton, 1988) whereby those involved in the initiative become removed from the grass-roots concerns of those they set out to represent. Finally, the notion of community, upon which the collective action paradigm depends, is itself problematic. For example, people who live in the same geographical space (or those who share a sexual preference, language, ethnic background, age group or social class) do not constitute homogeneous groups. The concept of community obscures the diversity of lifestyles which exists within such groups, and can therefore fail to address the diverse needs of people within a community. Furthermore, self-appointed community representatives can emerge who claim to speak for all members of the community but in reality represent the dominant group (see Box 15.3 for a summary).

Homans and Aggleton (1988) recognize the limitations which often prevent community initiatives from actually achieving social change, most crucially lack of resources, and propose an additional model (the socially transformatory model) which aims to bring about far-reaching change throughout society.

IS HEALTH PROMOTION EFFECTIVE?

Having considered the theoretical bases and given examples of different approaches to health promotion, it is time to address the question of *evaluation*. Evaluation of the effectiveness of health promotion initiatives is an extremely difficult undertaking. First of all, we need to differentiate between *outcome evaluation*, i.e. an assessment of changes brought about by the intervention, and *process evaluation*, i.e. an understanding of how and why the intervention worked. In addition, outcome evaluation can focus on a range of different criteria, such as behavioural (e.g. how many people have stopped smoking) or cognitive (e.g. the extent to which people's knowledge about the health risks of smoking has increased) or health status (mental or physical). Furthermore, there may be unintended consequences of an intervention, such as increases in anxiety which may be generated by provision of information about particular risks.

French and Adams (1986) specified evaluation criteria which are appropriate for different types of health promotion interventions. For example, a mass media campaign based on the principles of the behaviour change model would be best evaluated by measuring changes in compliance, morbidity and mortality rates, as well as knowledge increases, attitude and behaviour change, whereas self-empowerment would be assessed through self-reports of changes in self-esteem, lifeskills and independent decision making. However, it is important to bear in mind that a health promotion evaluation should only assess the extent to which a campaign has achieved its objectives and that these can be limited. For example, a campaign whose purpose it is to warn people about potential risks should not be evaluated by measuring behaviour change. In other words, campaign objectives and evaluation criteria need to be carefully matched.

In recent years, increasing emphasis has been placed upon evaluation and the need for evidence-based health promotion. Within a climate of financial pressures and budget cuts, public service expenditure needs to be cost effective. Governments and funding bodies are more likely to invest in health promotion projects which can been shown to work. In addition, there are ethical reasons for systematic evaluations: ineffective or counter-productive interventions should not be repeated, while effective interventions should be made available as widely as possible.

Hernes (1998) suggests that health care in general, including new technologies and remedies, suffers from similar limitations. The emerging evidence-based health-care movement promises to rectify this situation. However, it is important to remember that there are different types of evidence and that the evaluation design needs to be appropriate to the type of the intervention. Øvretveit (1998) points out that 'we are in danger of replacing indifference about effectiveness with a dogmatic and narrow view of "evidence"' (p. 1). Øvretveit (1998) adopts a pluralistic and practical approach to evaluation by providing an overview of the range of approaches and methods which can be used to evaluate health-care interventions.

THE 'IDEOLOGY OF HEALTH PROMOTION'

Health promotion is concerned with strategies for promoting health. It is assumed that (a) good health is a universally shared objective; (b) there is agreement on what being healthy means; (c) there is a scientific consensus about which behaviours facilitate good health. From this perspective, the real (and only) challenge for health experts and educators is to find effective ways of helping people to maximize their health.

However, there have been criticisms of this contemporary 'ideology of health promotion'. Evans (1988) was concerned that such an ideology can begin to drive health promotion interventions which instead ought to be informed by scientific evidence (both biomedical and psychosocial). Evans drew attention to programmes directed at lifestyle changes which are not unequivocally justified by biomedical research evidence, such as the recommendation to reduce cholesterol levels in the blood to prevent heart disease. Evans worried that 'by increasingly promoting presumably nonrisky behaviours, we may be contributing to a type of mass hypochondriasis resulting in an increasingly diminished freedom in human lifestyle and quality of life' (p. 207). This, he suggested, can result in an unhealthy obsession with exercise, an inability to enjoy a meal, as well as a reduction in spontaneity of lifestyle.

Lupton (1995) developed a critique of the *discourse of risk* prevalent in contemporary health promotion. She proposed that 'risk, in contemporary societies, has come to replace the old-fashioned (and in modern secular societies now largely discredited) notion of sin' (p. 89). This is achieved through the practice of health risk appraisals and screening programmes. Lupton likens these practices to religious confessions where sins are confessed, judgement is passed and penance is expected. Lupton points out that risk discourse attributes ill health to personal characteristics such as lack of will power, laziness or moral weakness. In this way those 'at risk' become 'risk takers' who are responsible for their own ill health as well as its effects upon others and society as a whole.

Lupton argues that risk discourse can have detrimental consequences for those positioned within it: being labelled at risk can become a self-fulfilling prophecy since people may feel reluctant to seek medical advice for fear of being reprimanded. Also, it can give rise to fatalism, as well as anxiety, uncertainty and fear, as, for example, for women 'at risk' of breast cancer who can experience their 'at risk' status as a half-way house between health and illness (Gifford, 1986, cited in Lupton, 1995).

The 'ideology of health promotion' has not gone unchallenged, however. Recent publications have explored the function and position of contemporary health promotion in an attempt to formulate alternatives to individualistic risk-based approaches (e.g. De La Cancela et al., 1998; MacDonald, 1998).

FUTURE RESEARCH

1   More studies which carry out systematic evaluations of health promotion interventions are needed. In order to be of use in informing the design of future interventions, such studies should specify whether they evaluate process or outcome or both. In addition, researchers

must ensure that intervention objectives and evaluation criteria are carefully matched and that unintended effects of the intervention are detected. This can be done through the use of qualitative research methods such as semi-structured interviewing of participants or participant observation.

2   There is a role for psychological studies of the processes involved in community action. Health psychologists need to shift their focus from the individual towards group processes in order to make full use of the collective action paradigm. For example, studies could aim to identify which factors motivate individuals to act collectively in responding to an environmental health hazard. Good settings for group health promotion projects are the family (Valach et al., 1996) or the household (Vinck et al., 1997).

3   SCM researchers are concerned with the prediction of behaviour on the basis of social cognitions. However, there is little research into how exactly health-relevant social cognitions may be successfully changed. Abraham and Sheeran (1994) proposed that self-empowerment techniques can be used in order to modify social cognitions. This hypothesis merits further investigation. Pre- and post-intervention measurement of relevant variables would allow us to identify the effects of self-empowerment techniques on participants' cognitions.

4   SCMs and the behaviour change approach do not address variables other than social cognitions which may have a direct effect upon health-relevant behaviours. In recent years, health psychologists have begun to draw on insights from social constructionism in order to explore the meanings and significations associated with health-relevant practices. For example, Gillies and Willig (1997) found that women smokers' framed their accounts of cigarette smoking within a discourse of addiction. This discourse constructs cigarette smoking as the consequence of physiological and psychological dependency. It positions the smoker as a victim of her addiction and can therefore have a disempowering effect. The ways in which symbolic meanings and significations associated with health-relevant practices limit and/or facilitate people's adoption of these practices require further investigation. This approach is particularly useful in exploring people's reluctance to adopt preventive health practices which they know to be beneficial. Recent social constructionist work has explored the implications of discourse analytic research for applied psychology including health promotion (Yardley, 1997; Willig, 1999).

SUMMARY

1   Behavioural health promotion interventions require the active co-operation of those who benefit from them and the use of persuasive and effective communication. Behavioural interventions include information provision and the teaching of behavioural, social and cognitive skills.

2   Three major approaches to health promotion are the behaviour change approach, the self-empowerment approach and the collective action approach. Each pursues different goals, utilizes different means to achieve its goals and proposes different criteria for intervention evaluation.

3   The behaviour change approach aims to bring about changes in individual behaviour through changes in the individual's cognitions. Social cognition models are utilized in order to make the link between knowledge, attitudes and behaviour. However, attempts by SCMs to predict behaviour on the basis of cognitions has led to disappointing results.

4   Criticisms of the behaviour change approach include its inability to target socio-economic causes of ill health, its top-down approach to education, its exclusive focus upon cognitions, its assumption of homogeneity among receivers of health messages and its individualism.

5   The self-empowerment approach aims to empower people to make healthy choices. Participatory learning techniques such as group work, client-centred counselling, social skills training and educational drama are used in order to increase participants' control over their physical, social and internal environments.

6   Criticisms of the self-empowerment approach include its assumption that rational choices are healthy choices, its reliance upon simulation in safe environments, its inadequate conceptualization of power and its consequent focus upon the individual as the target for change.

7   The collective action approach recognizes the close relationship between individual health and socio-economic factors. It aims to remove the socio-economic and environmental causes of ill health through the collective organization of members of the community. Self-help groups, outreach health education and the WHO Healthy Cities Project are examples of the collective action approach.

8   Health promotion interventions which use the collective action approach can encounter a number of difficulties. They can come into conflict with powerful bodies and they are vulnerable to lack of public funding and official opposition. Other problems include creeping professionalization and difficulties associated with defining and identifying communities.

9   The 'ideology of health promotion' can threaten the scientific basis of health promotion interventions. It can give rise to an unhealthy social obsession with exercise and diet and lead to the blaming of the victims of ill health.

10 Future research needs to include systematic evaluations of health promotion interventions, psychological studies of the processes involved in community action, as well as studies of the meanings and significations associated with health-relevant practices.

KEY TERMS

controlled variance (control/
   variance)
discourse of risk
empowerment
evaluation
health education
health habits
health promotion

Healthy Cities Project
intervention
inverse care law
outreach programme
preventive health behaviours
self-efficacy
social cognition models
   (SCMs)

GLOSSARY

Accident proneness: the alleged tendency of some individuals to have accidents more frequently than would be predicted by chance. First noted early in the twentieth century by the German psychologist Marbe, and analysed by proponents of *psychosomatic medicine* as caused by an unconscious wish to punish oneself.

Acquisition: the process of learning a response or taking up a specific behaviour through association or conditioning.

Action research: a type of research concerned with the process of change and what else happens when change occurs. The investigator acts as a facilitator or resource who responds to the situation as it changes and helps it to develop in a desirable direction as perceived by the various parties concerned. Action research is particularly suited to consultancy work when an organization or system or method requires urgent improvement.

Action stage: one of the stages proposed by the *transtheoretical model of change* in which a person takes specific actions with the aim of changing unwanted behaviour, bringing positive benefits to well-being.

Addiction: a term used to describe a person's physical and psychological dependency on an activity, drink or drug, seemingly beyond conscious control. Addiction is said to occur when there is: a strong desire to engage in the particular behaviour (especially when the opportunity to engage in such behaviour is not available); an impaired capacity to control the behaviour; discomfort and/or distress when the behaviour is prevented or ceased; persistence of the behaviour despite clear evidence that it is leading to problems (Gossop, 1989, pp. 1–2).

Adipose tissue: tissue in the body in which fat is stored as an energy reserve and which in excess leads to obesity.

Alcohol dependence syndrome: a psychophysiological disorder characterized by increased tolerance, withdrawal symptoms following reduced consumption, a persistent desire, or unsuccessful efforts to reduce or control drinking.

Alternative (or complementary) medicine: forms of health care which are not controlled by professional medicine and are based on non-orthodox systems of healing.

Anchoring: the process whereby unfamiliar concepts are given meaning by connecting them with more familiar concepts.

Anti-essentialist view of human sexuality: the view of human sexuality as a set of potentialities which may or may not be realized within differing social, cultural and historical contexts.

Attribution bias: the tendency to attribute positive things to oneself and negative things to others.

Attribution theory: theory of lay causal explanations of events and behaviours.

Attributions: perceived or reported causes of actions, feelings or events.

Authoritarian: a personality type or leadership style favouring obedience rather than freedom of expression.

Behavioural health: an interdisciplinary field dedicated to promoting the role of individual responsibility in the application of behavioural and biomedical knowledge and techniques to the maintenance of health and the prevention of illness (Matarazzo, 1980, p. 813).

Behavioural medicine: an interdisciplinary field concerned with the development and integration of behavioural and medical science knowledge and techniques relevant to health and illness and their application to prevention, diagnosis, treatment and rehabilitation (Schwartz and Weiss, 1978).

Biological reductionism: the assumption that all human experience can be directly traced to and explained with reference to its biological basis.

Biomedicine: a health system which identifies the cause of agreed diseases and symptoms as lying in certain physiological processes.

Biopsychosocial model: the view that health and illness are produced by a combination of physical, psychological and cultural factors (Engel, 1977).

Body mass index (BMI): the body weight in kilograms divided by the square of the height in metres; has a normal range of 20 to 25.

Case studies: retrospective written reports on individuals, groups or systems.

Case-control study: an epidemiological study in which exposure of patients to factors that may cause their disease (cases) is compared to the exposure to the same factors of participants who do not have the disease (controls).

Causal ontologies of suffering: causal frameworks for explaining illness and suffering.

Cessation: the process of stopping (ceasing) a specific behaviour, habit or activity; one possible outcome of the *action stage* in the *transtheoretical model of change*.

Cholesterol: a lipid produced in the body from acetyl-CoA and present in the diet.

Chronic fatigue syndrome (CFS): a syndrome identified in Nevada, USA, in 1984 and sometimes nicknamed 'yuppy flu', it is characterized by severe fatigue and other symptoms suggesting a viral infection and persisting over long periods of time. There is much current controversy as to whether it is a *psychosomatic disorder* or caused by an as-yet-unidentified virus. CFS is thought to be identical to *myalgic encephalomyelitis* (ME)

Classical conditioning: a learning process whereby a previously neutral stimulus (*conditioned stimulus, CS*) comes to evoke a certain response (unconditioned response, UCR) as a result of repeated previous pairings with a stimulus (*unconditioned stimulus, UCS*) which naturally evokes the response.

Cognitive-behavioural therapy (CBT): modification of thoughts, images, feelings and behaviour using the principles of *classical* and *operant conditioning* combined with cognitive techniques concerned with the control of mental states.

Cohort study: an epidemiological study that measures exposures to factors that may influence health in a group of people (cohort) and relates these factors to subsequent disease experience (in the follow-up).

Communication styles: different approaches to verbal interaction which are characterized by particular linguistic and rhetorical techniques and strategies such as listening or question asking.

Communicative event: a joint achievement which is the product of participants' strategic deployment of culturally available discursive resources.

Compensatory conditioned response model: influential model put forward by Siegel (1975) to account for the phenomena of addiction, such as tolerance, dependence and withdrawal, using the principles of *classical conditioning*.

Compliance: the extent to which a person's behaviour changes as a direct consequence of specific social influence: e.g. a measure of the extent to which patients (or doctors) follow a prescribed treatment plan; also known as 'adherence'.

Conditioned stimuli (CS): a stimulus that, because of pairing with another stimulus (*unconditioned stimulus, UCS*) which naturally evokes a reflex response, is eventually able to evoke that response (see *classical conditioning*). The acquisition is believed to occur when there is a positive contingency between two events such that event A is more likely in the presence of event B than in the absence of B.

Contemplation stage: the stage of intending to change at some, as yet unspecified time in the future; one of the stages of the *transtheoretical model of change*.

Controlled variance: the proportion of variance in a *dependent variable* which is statistically related to (or 'explained by') changes in one or more *independent variables* specified by a theory or model.

COPE: questionnaire devised by Carver et al. (1989) to assess the individual's predominant coping strategies in response to stress (see Box 5.3).

Coronary heart disease (CHD): restriction of the blood flow to the coronary arteries often evidenced by chest pains (angina) and which may result in a heart attack.

Cost effectiveness: method of economic analysis which takes account of both the effectiveness and the cost of an intervention. It requires the calculation of the cost of delivering an intervention to bring about a desired change in a threshold number (e.g. 1,000) of people, or alternatively the number of people likely to change their behaviour for a fixed cost (e.g. £10 million), as the direct consequence of the intervention, e.g. a health promotion campaign.

Cross-sectional studies: involve obtaining responses from a sample of respondents on one occasion only. With appropriate randomized sampling methods, the sample can be assumed to be a representative cross-section of the population(s) under study and it will be possible to make comparisons between different sub-groups, e.g. males vs. females, older vs. younger, etc.

Culture: 'a system of meanings and symbols. This system shapes every area of life, defines a world view that gives meaning to personal and collective experience, and frames the way people locate themselves within the world, perceive the world, and believe in it. Every aspect of reality is seen as embedded within webs of meaning that define a certain world view and that cannot be studied or understood apart from this collective frame' (Corin, 1995, p. 273).

Deficit model: an explanation used by health-care professionals to account for low compliance, e.g. women who do not use a screening service may be characterized as lacking in knowledge and concern about their health.

Delta alcoholic: an alcoholic who allegedly drinks steadily and maintains control of amount drunk, but is unable to abstain even for short periods of time.

Dependent variable: a variable which changes value as an effect of varying one or more *independent variables*; an *outcome* variable.

Diary techniques: any data collection method in which the data are linked to the passage of time. They often involve self-report but may also contain information about observations of others.

Direct observation: directly observing behaviour in a relevant setting, e.g. patients waiting for treatment in a doctor's surgery or clinic. The observation may be accompanied by recordings in written, oral, auditory or visual form. Several investigators may observe the same events and reliability checks may be conducted. Direct observation includes casual observation, formal observation and participant observation.

Discourse: talk or text embedded in social interaction presenting an account of the constitution of subjects and objects; an opinion or position concerning a particular subject.

Discourse analysis: a set of procedures for analysing language as used in speech or texts. It focuses on the language being used and how it is applied to construct versions of 'social reality' and what is gained by constructing events employing the particular terms chosen. It has links with ethnomethodology, conversation analysis and the study of meaning (semiology).

Discourse of risk: ways of talking and practices that attribute ill health to personal characteristics and construct an 'at-risk' status as a state in between health and illness.

Doctor-centred communication style: a communication style which primarily makes use of the doctor's expertise by keeping control of the interview agenda.

Ecological approach: a model or theory about health and behaviour that emphasizes environmental influences.

Ecological validity: the extent to which the environment within which behaviour or experience is studied captures the relevant features of the real-world environment.

Empowerment: any process by which people, groups or communities can exercise increased control or sense of control over aspects of their everyday lives, including their physical and social environments.

Energy expenditure: use by the body of chemical energy from food and drink or body stores during the processes of metabolism that is dissipated as heat, including heat generated by muscular activity; the day's total energy expenditure is measured in calories of heat lost.

Energy intake: the chemical energy in food and drink that can be metabolized to produce energy in the body; the day's total energy intake is measured in calories supplied by all food and drink consumed.

Epidemiology: the study of associations between patterns of disease in populations and environmental, lifestyle and genetic factors.

Ethnicity: pertaining to ethnic group or race.

Ethnocentrism: a bias in perception, thinking or principles stemming from membership of a particular ethnic or cultural group.

Ethnographic methods: seek to build a systematic understanding of a culture from the viewpoint of the insider. Ethnographic methods are multiple attempts to describe the shared beliefs, practices, artefacts, knowledge and behaviours of an intact cultural group. They attempt to represent the totality of a phenomenon in its complete context and naturalistic setting.

Evaluation: the assessment of the efficacy or effectiveness of an intervention, project or programme in terms of processes and/or outcomes.

False positive: an incorrect positive identification in a screening examination or test.

Fat: *triglycerides* that are either solid (e.g. butter, lard) or liquid (e.g. vegetable or fish oil) at room temperature.

Fat balance equation: states that the rate of change of fat stores equals the rate of fat intake minus the rate of fat oxidation.

Fetal alcohol syndrome: abnormality found in children whose mothers drink heavily during pregnancy, characterized by facial abnormalities, mental impairment and stunted growth.

Flowchart model: a diagrammatic representation of the relationships between processes and/or variables which are believed to be related to each other.

Focus groups: one or more group discussions in which participants focus collectively upon a topic or issue usually presented to them as a group of questions (or other stimuli) leading to the generation of interactive data.

Framework: a general representation for conceptualizing a research field or question.

Galenic medicine: health system derived from Greek and Arabic health beliefs.

Gamma alcoholic: an alcoholic who typically loses control and cannot stop after the first drink, although capable of abstaining totally for extended periods of time.

General adaptation syndrome (GAS): influential three-stage model of the physiological response to stress put forward by Hans Selye but no longer thought to be valid.

Gradient of reinforcement: principle applied mainly to *operant conditioning* whereby the acquisition of a learned response occurs more quickly, the more rapidly reward follows the occurrence of the response.

Gross National Product (GNP): the total output of a country's goods and services valued at market prices. The values for different countries can be compared by dividing by the size of the population (GNPpc).

Hardiness: personality trait first proposed by Kobasa and consisting of a high level of commitment, sense of control and willingness to confront challenges. Hardiness may protect the individual against the effects of stress.

Hassles scale: life events stress scale designed by Kanner and associates and focusing on everyday events that cause annoyance or frustration. See also *uplifts scale, social readjustment rating scale (SRRS)* and Box 5.1.

Health: a positive state of being which has physical, cultural, psychosocial, economic and spiritual dimensions, not simply the absence of illness.

Health Belief Model (HBM): psychological model which posits that health behaviour is a function of a combination of factors including the perceived benefits of and barriers to treatment and the perceived susceptibility to and seriousness of the health problem.

Health communication: the field of study concerned with the ways in which communication can contribute to the promotion of health.

Health education: the process by which individuals' knowledge about the causes of health and illness is increased.

Health gradient: the relationship between *socio-economic status (SES)* and mortality or morbidity that normally shows a monotonic increase as SES changes from low to high.

Health habits: routine behaviours acquired by learning or conditioning that protect health or put health at risk.

Health promotion: any event, process or activity which facilitates the protection or improvement of the health of individuals, groups, communities or populations.

Health psychology: an interdisciplinary field concerned with the application of psychological knowledge and methods to health, illness and health care.

Healthy Cities Project: a World Health Organization (WHO) intervention that aims to promote health in the urban context by identifying and counteracting aspects of urban life which impair health. The project seeks to enhance the physical, social and environmental well-being of the people who live and work in the participating cities.

Historical analysis: the use of data produced from memory, historical sources or artefacts.

Homeostasis: concept introduced by Cannon whereby the physiological mechanisms of the body are considered as feedback systems functioning as far as possible to maintain a steady state. Anything that disrupts the body's equilibrium may be regarded as a stressor, a conceptualization which was developed by Selye (see *general adaptation syndrome*).

Human sexual response cycle: a sequence of stages of sexual arousal taking the individual from initial excitement to a plateau phase, through orgasm, to resolution of sexual tension.

Humours (doctrine of the four humours): dating back to the physicians of ancient Greece, the belief that the body is essentially composed of four constituents or humours, blood, phlegm, black and yellow bile, and that diseases and psychological characteristics are attributable to an excess or shortage of one or more of the four.

Hysteria (conversion hysteria): physical symptoms which appear to indicate organic disease but where there is no clinical evidence of disease. Believed by some practitioners to be psychologically caused although this is normally denied vehemently by sufferers.

Identity control: term used to describe the process by which a person deliberately attempts to control the image they present to others.

Ideology of health promotion: the assumptions that good health is a universally shared objective and that there is scientific consensus about which behaviours facilitate good health.

Illness perceptions: beliefs about illness.

Immunization: medical procedure designed to protect susceptible individuals from communicable diseases by the administration of a vaccine. This procedure is aimed at both immediate protection of individuals and also immunity across the whole community where the uptake rate is high.

Incidence: the number of new cases of a disease occurring within a specific time period, e.g. one year.

Income distribution: the distribution of income across the population. It can be measured in terms of the percentage share of national income earned by the best off or worst off proportions of the population; e.g. in the USA in 1991 the highest 20% of the population received 41.9% of the total national income while the worst off 20% received 4.7%.

Independent variable: a variable which when manipulated is believed to effect or cause a change in a *dependent variable*; a *predictor* variable.

Indigenous: belonging to a particular culture, race, or tribal group.

Individualism: a cultural value that enshrines the personal control and responsibility of the individual.

Inequality: a difference in life opportunities that is correlated with social position or status, ethnicity, gender, age or any other way of grouping people.

Interaction analysis system: an observation instrument which identifies, categorizes and quantifies features of the doctor–patient encounter.

Interdisciplinary: a term used to refer to areas of study that cross the boundaries of established academic disciplines.

Intervention: the intentional and systematic manipulation of variables with the aim of improving health outcomes.

Interviews (structured or semi-structured): a structured interview schedule is a prepared standard set of questions which are asked in person, or perhaps by telephone, of a person or group of persons concerning a particular research issue or question. A semi-structured interview is much more open ended and allows the interviewee scope to address the issues which he/she feels to be relevant to the topics being raised by the investigator.

Inverse care law: the observation that the highest access to care is available to those who need it least (e.g. the more educated, articulate, affluent members of society) while the lowest access to care is available to those who need it most.

(To) legitimate: to justify one's position in the face of stigma, illness or invalidity.

Lived experience: a description of the phenomenology of a particular experience.

Liver cirrhosis: frequently fatal form of liver damage usually found among long-term heavy drinkers. Initially fat accumulates on the liver, enlarging it; this restricts blood flow, causing damage to cells, and scar tissue develops, preventing the liver from functioning normally.

Locus of control: personality traits first proposed by social psychologists and then adapted by health psychologists to distinguish between those who attribute their state of health to themselves, powerful others or chance.

Longitudinal designs: involve measuring responses of a single sample on more than one occasion. These measurements may be prospective or retrospective, but prospective longitudinal designs allow greater control over the sample, the variables measured and the times when the measurements take place.

Maintenance: the continued practice of or adherence to a specific health promoting behaviour, e.g. abstinence from smoking; one of the stages in the *transtheoretical model of change*.

Mammography: a method for imaging breast tissue of women using radiography.

Market model: a health-care system in which purchasers and providers make contracts concerning health services in terms of throughput, quality and price.

Medical model: a way of thinking about health and illness that assumes all health and illness phenomena are physiological in nature. According to this model, health, illness and treatments have a purely biological or biochemical basis.

Medicalization: the process by which experiences and practices which do not match those defined as 'natural' and 'healthy' are pathologized and treated as dysfunctional.

Meta-analysis: a quantitative literature review that combines the evidence from relevant previous studies, taking account of criteria for quality, allowing high statistical power.

Model: an abstract represention of relationships between processes believed to influence each other.

Moral discourses of suffering: language derived from moral principles used to describe and explain health and illness.

Motivation enhancement therapy: brief intervention developed by W.R. Miller for the treatment of alcohol and drug problems, that aims to boost the clients' self-esteem and motivation to change, in contrast to traditional, more confrontational approaches.

Multiple regression: a statistical technique based on correlations between variables enabling predictions to be made about dependent variables using a combination of two or more independent variables.

Multivariate analyses: use information about more than one independent variable in a statistical analysis of data. Multivariate techniques include multiple regression and correlation, path analysis, factor analysis, multidimensional scaling, analyses of cross-classified data, logistic regression, multivariate analysis of variance, discriminant analysis, and meta-analysis. For a useful summary of these techniques, see Grimm and Yarnold (1995).

Myalgic encephalomyelitis (ME): syndrome first observed in an epidemic at the Royal Free Hospital, London, in 1955, now usually thought to be identical to *chronic fatigue syndrome* and controversial for the same reasons.

Narrative: structured discourse which connects agents and events over time in the form of a story.

Narrative approaches: seek insight and meaning through the acquisition of data in the form of stories concerning personal experiences (Murray, 1997a). These approaches assume that human beings are natural storytellers and that the principle task of the psychologist is to explore the different stories being told.

Natural history: a description of the pattern of development of a disease, condition or specific behaviour.

Obesity: an excessive accumulation of body fat, usually defined as a body mass index (BMI) greater than 30.

Obesogenic: referring to an environment that exposes the population to a large number of foods and drinks that have a high percentage of fats.

Objectification: the process whereby a more abstract concept acquires meaning through association with everyday phenomena. The process transforms an abstract concept into a concrete image.

Operant conditioning: a learning process whereby a normally voluntary form of behaviour comes to occur with increasing frequency in a particular situation, or in the presence of a particular stimulus, as a result of previously and repeatedly having been rewarded in similar circumstances.

Opportunistic intervention: an attempt to modify health hazardous behaviour, such as smoking or heavy drinking, by a health professional, frequently a doctor, who has been consulted for other reasons.

Outcome: the result or effect of an intervention, e.g. the extent to which a particular doctor–patient communication has been effective.

Outreach programme: an intervention which aims to achieve subcultural change among hard-to-reach target constituencies in order to improve health outcomes.

Patient-centred communication style: a doctor's communication style which mobilizes the patient's knowledge and experience through techniques such as silence, listening and reflection.

Patient satisfaction: a measure of the extent to which patients' expectations of what a medical encounter ought to provide have been met (as judged by the patients).

Pessimistic explanatory style: tendency of some individuals to blame themselves for everything that goes wrong in their lives, believed to be associated with poor physical health.

Physical dependency: evidenced when a person experiences unpleasant physical symptoms when he/she stops using or reduces consumption of a drug, tobacco or alcohol.

Physical side effects: unwanted physiological effects that accompany medication.

Post-traumatic stress disorder (PTSD): long-term psychological and physiological effects of exposure to traumatic stress, including insomnia, nightmares, flashbacks, problems of memory and concentration, acting or feeling as if the event is recurring and a greatly increased sensitivity to new stressful events.

Poverty: the level of income below which people cannot afford a minimum, nutritionally adequate diet and essential non-food requirements.

Power imbalance: an unequal relationship between people that in certain contexts may result in distorted or unjust outcomes.

Precontemplation stage: the stage of knowing that a habit or behaviour is hazardous but without any intention to change it in the foreseeable future; one of the stages in the *transtheoretical model of change.*

Predictors: the independent variables in a statistical analysis (e.g. regression) that are expected to show significant relationships with the dependent variable(s).

Preparation stage: intending to take action in the immediate future, having developed a specific plan of action; one of the stages in the *transtheoretical model of change.*

Prevalence: the number of people with a disease or behaviour as a proportion of the population or sub-population at any point in time.

Preventive health behaviours: behaviours people choose to engage in with the aim of protecting and/or improving their health status.

Psychological dependency: a state associated with repeated activity or consumption of a drug or drink which leads to negative affect following reduced consumption or abstinence and a persistent desire or unsuccessful efforts to cut down or control the activity.

Psychoneuroimmunology (PNI): the study of the effects of psychological variables and especially stress on the immune system.

Psychosomatic disorders: physical ailments believed to be psychologically caused including *hysteria* and some conditions which have organic features such as ulcers and asthma.

Psychosomatic medicine: a precursor of modern health psychology which flourished from the 1930s to the 1950s, its proponents including Alexander and Dunbar believed that psychoanalytic theories about unconscious conflicts could be extended to explain susceptibility to various organic diseases.

Questionnaires: many constructs in health psychology are measured using questionnaires consisting of a standard set of items with accompanying instructions. Ideally a questionnaire will have been demonstrated to be both a reliable and valid measure of the construct(s) it purports to measure. A useful portfolio of such measures is available for researchers (Johnson et al., 1995).

QUIT FOR LIFE (QFL) Programme: a psychological therapy based on cognitive behavioural principles intended to help smokers quit smoking (Marks, 1993).

Racism: discrimination on the basis of race or skin colour.

Randomized controlled trials (RCTs): these involve the systematic comparison of interventions employing a fully controlled application of one or more interventions or 'treatments' using a random allocation of participants to the different treatment groups.

Relapse: going back to consumption of tobacco, alcohol or a drug after a period of voluntary abstinence.

Relapse prevention: strategies and procedures for reducing the likelihood of *relapse*.

Relative deprivation: the perception of being worse or better off than others.

Safer sex practices: those sexual practices that do not involve the exchange of bodily fluids which may contain the human immunodeficiency virus. Such bodily fluids are blood, semen and vaginal fluids.

Screening: procedure for the identification of the presence of certain diseases, conditions or behaviours in a community. Those sections of the population who are most at risk of developing a particular disease are examined to see whether they have any early indications. The rationale behind this strategy is that the earlier the disease is identified and treated, the less likely it is to develop into a fatal condition.

Self-efficacy: belief that one will be able to carry out one's plans successfully; a term proposed by Bandura (1977) and thought to be associated with positive health behaviours.

Self-regulation: process by which individuals monitor and adjust their medication on an ongoing basis.

Sensation seeking: a personality trait or type that is characterized by a strong desire for new sensations.

Sense of coherence: a personality trait originally proposed by Antonovsky to characterize people who see their world as essentially meaningful and manageable; associated with coping with stress.

Sex survey: a large-scale, questionnaire-based instrument which aims to provide quantifiable, descriptive data about a population's sexual habits.

Sexology: the scientific study of human sexual behaviour.

Sexual meanings: the significance which is attributed to sexual practices as a result of the application of sociohistorically and culturally variable and changing interpretive frames.

Sexuality: those aspects of human experience which are influenced by and/or expressive of sexual desire and/or practice.

Single case experimental designs: investigations of a series of experimental manipulations on a single research participant.

Social cognition: a cognitive model of social knowledge.

Social cognition models (SCMs): theories about the relationship between social cognitions, such as beliefs and attitudes, and behaviour, which aim accurately to predict behaviour or behavioural intentions.

Social cohesion: a measure of the degree to which members of a society, community or group support each other towards a common end for the good of all.

Social comparison: a process in which members of a society, community or group compare their own status or position with that of others.

Social constructionism: (1) the philosophical belief that there is no single, fixed 'reality' but a multiplicity of descriptions, each with its own unique pattern of meanings; (2) 'many potential worlds of meaning that can be imaginatively entered and celebrated, in ways which are constantly changing to give richness and value to human experience' (Mulkay, 1991, pp. 27–8).

Social readjustment rating scale (SRRS): measurement scale for life events stress developed by Holmes and Rahe and widely used in research on life events stress and illness. See also *hassles scale, uplifts scale* and Box 5.1.

Social representations: system of ideas, values and practices specific to a particular community which enables individuals to orient themselves in the world and communicate with each other.

Socio-economic status (SES): position or class based on occupation, education, or income.

Stages of change: the stages of precontemplation, contemplation, preparation, action, maintenance, and termination in the *transtheoretical model of change*.

Stress inoculation training: a self-instructional *cognitive-behavioural* method for stress management developed by Meichenbaum (1985), in which positive and useful responses to possible stressors are rehearsed.

Stress management workshops: training programmes in stress management usually delivered to groups, frequently lasting for a whole day or a weekend, and focusing on changing the way in which participants appraise situations as stressful and cope with stressful events.

Surveys: systematic methods for determining how a defined sample of participants respond to a set of standard questions attempting to assess their feelings, attitudes, beliefs or knowledge at one or more particular times.

Systematic reviews: reviews of the empirical literature concerning the efficacy or effectiveness of an intervention that consider all of the relevant studies taking account of quality criteria.

Systems theory: a theory concerned with structures, processes or relationships within communities, groups or families.

Temperance societies: originating in the USA in the nineteenth century, these societies, of which Alcoholics Anonymous is nowadays the best-known example, are dedicated to counteracting the harmful effects of drinking. Although the word temperance suggests drinking in moderation, temperance societies usually advocate teetotalism.

Tension reduction hypothesis: the hypothesis that people enjoy alcohol primarily because it reduces tension (anxiety, stress), rather than as a drug which directly produces positive moods.

Theory: a general account of relationships between processes believed to influence, cause changes in, or control a phenomenon.

Theory of planned behaviour (TPB): theoretical model which argues that behavioural intention is controlled by attitudes, subjective norms and perceived control.

Theory of reasoned action (TRA): theoretical model which argues that behavioural intention is controlled by attitudes and subjective norms.

Transtheoretical model of change: a model of behaviour change developed by DiClementi, Prochaska and others which attempts to identify universal processes or stages of change specified as *precontemplation, contemplation, preparation, action, maintenance* and termination.

Triglyceride: the main component of dietary fats and oils and the principle form in which fat is stored in the body; composed of three fatty acids attached to a glycerol molecule which are saturated, monounsaturated and polyunsaturated.

Type A/B personality: the Type A personality, in contrast to the Type B personality, is characterized by intense achievement motivation, time urgency and hostility and was until recently thought to be at much increased risk for heart disease.

Unconditioned stimulus (UCS): stimulus that evokes a response or reflex without training, e.g. a loud sound will naturally evoke a startle response.

Uplifts scale: life events scale designed by Kanner and associates (1981) to assess desirable events in contrast to their *hassles scale*.

Viral challenge studies: method of studying the relationship between stress and susceptibility to infectious disease in which volunteers are deliberately exposed to minor viruses, usually colds or flu, in order to determine whether those who have experienced higher levels of stress prior to exposure are more likely to contract the infection.

Welfare model: a welfare model aims to provide comprehensive health care to all members of a population regardless of age, socio-economic status, gender, sexual preference, race or religion.

Well-being: the state of 'wellness'; the general state of health of an individual.

Wernicke–Korsakoff syndrome: a form of irreversible brain damage sometimes found among long-term heavy drinkers, its symptoms include extremely impaired short-term memory, confusion and visual disorders.

BIBLIOGRAPHY

Abraham, C. and Hampson, S.E. (1996) 'A social cognition approach to health psychology: philosophical and methodological issues', *Psychology and Health, 11*: 223–42.

Abraham, C. and Sheeran, P. (1994) 'Modelling and modifying young hetero-sexuals' HIV-preventive behaviour: a review of theories, findings and educational implications', *Patient Education and Counseling, 23*: 173–86.

Abraham, C., Sheeran, P., Spears, R. and Abrams, D. (1992) 'Health beliefs and promotion of HIV-preventive intentions among teenagers: a Scottish perspective', *Health Psychology, 11*: 363–70.

Adams, S., Pill, R. and Jones, A. (1997) 'Medication, chronic illness and identity: the perspective of people with asthma', *Social Science and Medicine, 45*: 189–201.

Adler, N.E. and Matthews K.A. (1994) 'Health psychology: why do some people get sick and some stay well', *Annual Review of Psychology, 45*: 229–59.

Adler, N.E., Boyce, T., Chesney, M.A., Cohen, S., Folkman, S., Kahn, R.L. and Syme, S.L. (1994) 'Socioeconomic status and health', *American Psychologist, 49*: 15–24.

Affleck, C., Tenner, H., Croog, S. and Levine, S. (1987) 'Causal attribution, perceived benefits, and morbidity after a heart attack: an 8–year study', *Journal of Consulting and Clinical Psychology, 55*: 29–35.

Aggleton, P. (1989) 'Evaluating health education about AIDS', in P. Aggleton, G. Hart and P. Davies (eds), *AIDS. Social Representations. Social Practices.* London: Falmer Press. pp. 220–36.

Aggleton, P., Davies, P. and G. Hart (1994) *AIDS. Foundations For The Future.* London: Taylor & Francis.

Ajzen, I. (1985) 'From intention to actions: a theory of planned behavior', in J. Kuhl and J Beckmann (eds), *Action-control: From Cognition to Behavior.* Heidelberg: Spring. pp. 11–39.

Ajzen, I. (1991) 'The theory of planned behavior', *Organizational Behavior and Human Decision Processes, 50*: 179–211.

Ajzen, I. and Fishbein, M. (1980) *Understanding Attitudes and Predicting Social Behavior.* Englewood Cliffs, NJ: Prentice-Hall.

Aldhous, P. (1992) 'French venture where US fear to tread', *Science, 257*: 25.

Alexander, F. (1950) *Psychosomatic Medicine.* New York: Norton.

Allebeck, P., Bolund, C. and Ringback, E. (1989) 'Increased suicide rate in cancer patients: a cohort study based on the Swedish cancer Environment Register', *Journal of Clinical Epidemiology, 42*: 611–16.

Allied Dunbar, Health Education Authority, Sports Council (1992) *Allied Dunbar National Fitness Survey.* London: HEA and Sports Council.

Amelang, M. and Schmidt-Rathjens, C. (1996) 'Personality, cancer and coronary heart disease: further evidence on a controversial issue', *British Journal of Health Psychology, 1*: 191–205.

American Cancer Society (1992) *Cancer Facts and Figures – 1992.* Atlanta: ACS.

American Psychological Association (1992) 'Ethical principles of psychologists and code of conduct', *American Psychologist,* 47: 1597–1611.

Anand, S. and Chen, L. (1996) *Health Implications of Economic Policies.* New York: United Nations Development Programme (Discussion paper series).

Anderson, I., Aspegren, K., Janzon, K. et al. (1988) 'Mammographic screening and mortality from breast cancer: the Malmo mammographic screening trial', *British Medical Journal,* 297: 943–8.

Anselman, R.A. (1996) '"The want of health": an early eighteenth century self-portrait of sickness', *Literature and Medicine,* 15: 225–43.

Antonovsky, A. (1979) *Health, Stress, and Coping.* San Francisco: Jossey-Bass.

Antonovsky, A. (1987) *Unravelling the Mystery of Health: How People Manage Stress and Stay Well.* San Francisco: Jossey-Bass.

Armor, D.J., Polich, J.M. and Stambul, H.B. (1976) *Alcoholism and Treatment.* Santa Monica, CA: Rand.

Armstrong, D. (1983) *The Political Anatomy of the Body.* Cambridge: Cambridge University Press.

Armstrong, D. (1987) 'Theoretical tensions in biopsychosocial medicine', *Social Science and Medicine,* 25: 1213–18.

Arrow, K. (1963) *Social Choice and Individual Values,* 2nd edn. New York: Wiley.

ASH Burning News (1998) Emails 17/4/98 and 14/5/98.

Ashley, M.J. and Rankin, J.G. (1988) 'A public health approach to the prevention of alcohol related problems', *Annual Review of Public Health,* 9: 233–71.

Association of Community Health Councils (1989) *Cervical Cytology Screening: Getting it Right.* London: ACHC.

Austin, R.M. and McLendon, W.W. (1997) 'The Papanicolaou smear: medicine's most successful cancer screening procedure is threatened', *Journal of the American Medical Association,* 277: 754–5.

Averill, J.R. (1989) 'Stress as fact and artifact: an enquiry into the social origins and functions of some stress reactions', in C.D. Spielberger, I.G. Sarason and J. Strelay (eds), *Stress and Anxiety: Volume 12.* New York: Hemisphere. pp. 126–48.

Avis, N.E., Brambilla, J., Vass, K. and McKinlay, J.B. (1991) 'The effect of widowhood on health: a prospective analysis from the Massachusetts Women's Health Study', *Social Science and Medicine,* 33: 1063–2070.

Babor, T.F. and Grant, M. (eds) (1992) *Project on Identification and Management of Alcohol Related Problems. Report on Phase II: A Randomised Clinical Trial of Brief Interventions in Primary Health Care.* Geneva: World Health Organization.

Babor, T.F., Hoffman, M., DelBoca, F.K. et al. (1992) 'Types of alcoholics. I. Evidence for an empirically derived typology based on indicators of vulnerability and severity', *Archives of General Psychiatry,* 49: 599–608.

Bachen, E., Cohen, S. and Marsland, A.L. (1997) 'Psychoimmunology', in A. Baum, S. Newman, J. Weinman, R. West and C. McManus (eds), *Cambridge Handbook of Psychology, Health and Medicine.* Cambridge: Cambridge University Press. pp. 35–9.

Balarajan, R. and Soni Raleigh, V. (1993) *Ethnicity and Health. A Guide for the NHS.* London: Department of Health.

Bales, R.F. (1950) *Interaction Process Analysis: A Method for the Study of Small Groups.* Cambridge, MA: Addison-Wesley.

Balint, M. (1964) *The Doctor, his Patient and the Illness.* New York: International Universities Press.

Balshem, M. (1991) 'Cancer, control, and causality: talking about cancer in a working class community', *American Ethnologist, 18*: 152–71.

Bandura A. (1977) 'Self-efficacy: toward a unifying theory of behavior change', *Psychological Review, 84*: 191–215.

Bandura, A. (1986) *Social Foundations of Thought and Action: A Social Cognitive Theory.* Englewood Cliffs, NJ: Prentice-Hall.

Bandura, A. (1992) 'Exercise of personal agency through the self-efficacy mechanism', in R. Schwarzer (ed.), *Self-efficacy: Thought Control of Action.* Washington: Hemisphere. pp. 3–38.

Bandura, A. (1997) 'The anatomy of stages of change', *American Journal of Health Promotion, 12*: 8–10.

Barraclough, J., Pinder, P., Cruddas, M., Osmond, C., Taylor, I. and Perry, M. (1992) 'Life events and breast cancer prognosis', *British Medical Journal, 304*: 1078–81.

Bates, S. (1997) 'Tobacco sponsorship to end within nine years', *Guardian*: 5 December: 1.

Baum, A. and Spencer, S. (1997) 'Post-traumatic stress disorder', in A. Baum, S. Newman, J. Weinman, R. West and C. McManus (eds), *Cambridge Handbook of Psychology, Health and Medicine.* Cambridge: Cambridge University Press. pp. 550–5.

Bauman, K.E. (1992) 'On the future of applied smoking research: is it up in smoke', *American Journal of Public Health, 82*: 14–16.

Baumeister, R.F. and Newman, L.S. (1994) 'How stories make sense of personal experience: motives that shape autobiographical narratives', *Personality and Social Psychology Bulletin, 20*: 676–90.

Beardsell, S. and Coyle, A. (1996) A review of research on the nature and quality of HIV testing services: a proposal for process-based studies', *Social Science and Medicine, 42*: 733–43.

Beck, N.C., Parker, J.C., Frank, R.A. et al. (1988) 'Patients with rheumatoid arthritis at high risk for non-compliance with salicyclate treatment regimen', *Journal of Rheumatology, 15*: 1981–4.

Becker, M.H. (1992) 'A medical sociologist looks at health promotion', *Journal of Health and Social Behavior, 33*: 1–6.

Becker, M.H. (ed.) (1974) 'The health belief model and personal health behavior', *Health Education Monographs, 2*: 324–508.

Becker, M.H. and Mainman, L.A. (1975) 'Sociobehavioral determinants of compliance with health and medical care recommendations', *Medical Care, 13*: 10–14.

Becker, M.H. and Rosenstock, I.M. (1984) 'Compliance with medical care', in A. Steptoe and A. Matthews (eds), *Health Care and Human Behaviour.* London: Academic Press.

Beisecker, A.E. (1990) 'Patient power in doctor–patient communication: what do we know?', *Health Communication, 2*: 105–27.

Bender, B., Milgrom, H. and Rand, C. (1997) 'Nonadherence in asthmatic patients: is there a solution to the problem?', *Annals of Allergy, Asthma and Immunology, 79*: 177–86.

Bennett, P. and Murphy, S. (1997) *Psychology and Health Promotion.* Buckingham: Open University Press.

Bennett, P., Murphy, S., Carroll, D. and Ground, I. (1995) 'Psychology, health promotion and aesthemiology', *Health Care Analysis, 3*: 15–26.

Benoist, J. and Cathebras, P. (1993) 'The body: from immateriality to another', *Social Science and Medicine, 36*: 857–65.

Bensing, J. (1991) 'Doctor–patient communication and the quality of care, *Social Science and Medicine, 11*: 1301–10.

Bentler, P.M. (1989) *EQS: Structural Equations Program Manual*. Los Angeles: BMDP Statistical Software.

Benzeval, M., Judge, K. and Whitehead, M. (eds) (1995) *Tackling Inequalities in Health: An Agenda for Action*. London: King's Fund. pp. 22–52.

Berger, P. and Luckmann, T. (1966) *The Social Construction of Reality: A Treatise on the Sociology of Knowledge*. New York: Penguin.

Berlin, J.A. and Colditz, G.A. (1990) 'A meta-analysis of physical activity in the prevention of coronary heart disease', *American Journal of Epidemiology, 132*: 612–28.

Bernstein Hyman, R., Baker, S., Ephrain, R., Mondel, A. and Philip, J. (1994) 'Health Belief Model variables as predictors of screening mammography utilization', *Journal of Behavioral Medicine, 17*: 391–406.

Bertakis, K.D. (1991) 'Effect of patient education intervention on appropriate utilization of clinic services', *Journal of American Board of Family Practice, 4*: 411–18.

Bertakis, K.D., Roter, D. and Putnam, S.M. (1991) 'The relationship of physician medical interview style to patient satisfaction', *Journal of Family Practice, 32*: 175–81.

Bibace, R. and Walsh, M.E. (1980) 'Development of children's conceptions of illness', *Pediatrics, 8*: 533–43.

Bird, J.E. and Podmore, V.N. (1990) 'Children's understanding of health and illness', *Psychology and Health, 4*: 175–85.

Bishop, G.D. (1987) 'Lay conceptions of physical symptoms', *Journal of Applied Social Psychology, 17*: 127–46.

Bishop, G.D. (1991a) 'Lay disease representations and responses to victims of disease', *Basic and Applied Social Psychology, 12*: 115–32.

Bishop, G.D. (1991b) 'Understanding the understanding of illness: lay disease representations', in J.A. Skelton and R.T. Croyle (eds), *Mental Representation in Health and Illness*. New York: Springer-Verlag. pp. 32–59.

Bishop, S.D. and Converse, S.A. (1988) 'Illness representations: a prototype approach', *Health Psychology, 5*: 95–114.

Bishop, G.D. and Teng, C.B. (1992) 'Cognitive organization of disease information in young Chinese Singaporeans'. Paper presented at the First Asian Conference in Psychology, Singapore.

Black, D., Morris, J.N., Smith, C., Townsend, P. and Whitehead, M. (1988) *Inequalities in Health: The Black Report: The Health Divide*. London: Penguin.

Black Report, The (1982/1988) in P. Townsend and N. Davidson (eds), *Inequalities in Health*. London: Penguin.

Blackhall, L.J., Murphy, S.T., Frank, G., Michel, V. and Azen, S. (1995) 'Ethnicity and attitudes toward patient autonomy', *Journal of the American Medical Association, 274*: 820–5.

Blair, A. (1993) 'Social class and the contextualization of illness experience', in A. Radley (ed.), *Worlds of Illness: Biographical and Cultural Perspectives on Health and Disease*. London: Routledge. pp. 27–48.

Blair, S.N., Kohl, H.W., Gordon, N.F. and Paffenbarger, R.S. (1992) 'How much physical activity is good for health? *Annual Review of Public Health, 13*: 99–126.

Blane, H.T. and Leonard, K.E. (eds) (1987) *Psychological Theories of Drinking and Alcoholism*. New York: Guilford.

Blane, D., Bartley, M. and Davey Smith, G. (1997) 'Disease aetiology and materialist explanations of socioeconomic mortality differentials', *European Journal of Public Health,* 7: 385–91.

Blane, D., Bartley, M. and Davey Smith, G. (1998) 'Disease aetiology and materialist explanations of socioeconomic mortality differentials: a research note', *European Journal of Public Health,* 8: 259–60.

Blaxter, M. (1983) 'The causes of disease: women talking', *Social Science and Medicine,* 17: 59–69.

Blaxter, M. (1990) *Health and Lifestyles.* London: Routledge.

Blaxter, M. (1993) 'Why do victims blame themselves?', in A. Radley (ed.), *Worlds of Illness: Biographical and Cultural Perspectives on Health and Disease.* London: Sage. pp. 124–42.

Block, G., Patterson, B. and Subar, A. (1992) 'Fruit, vegetables and cancer prevention: a review of the epidemiological evidence', *Nutrition and Cancer,* 18: 1–29.

Blum, K., Noble, E.P., Sheridan, P.J. et al. (1990) 'Allelic association of human dopamine D, receptor gene in alcoholism', *Journal of the American Medical Association,* 263: 2055–60.

Blumhagen, D. (1980) 'Hyper-tension: a folk illness with a medical name', *Culture, Medicine and Psychiatry,* 4: 197–227.

Blumstein, P. and Schwartz, P. (1983) *American Couples.* New York: William Morrow.

Bohman, M., Sigvardsson, S. and Cloninger, C.R. (1981) 'Maternal inheritance of alcohol abuse', *Archives of General Psychiatry,* 38: 965–9.

Bond, C.A. and Monson, R. (1984) 'Sustained improvement in drug documentation, compliance, and disease control: a four-year analysis of an ambulatory care model', *Archives of Internal Medicine,* 144: 1159–62.

Booth, M.L., Macaskill, P., Owen, N., Oldenburg, B., Marcus, B.H. and Bauman, A. (1993) 'Population prevalence and correlates of stages of change in physical activity', *Health Education Quarterly,* 20: 431–40.

Booth-Kewley, S. and Friedman, H.S. (1987) 'Psychological predictors of heart disease: a quantitative review', *Psychological Bulletin,* 101: 343–62.

Boreani, A. and Gangeri, B. (1996) 'Genetic counselling: communication and psychosocial aspects', *Tumori,* 82: 147–50.

Borges, S. and Waitzkin, H. (1995) 'Women's narratives in primary care medical encounters', *Women and Health,* 23: 29–56.

Bostick, R.M., Sprafka, J.M., Virnig, B.A. and Potter, J.D. (1994) 'Predictors of cancer prevention attitudes and participation in cancer screening examinations', *Preventive Medicine,* 23: 816–26.

Bourdieu, P. (1984) *Distinction: A Social Critique of the Judgement of Taste.* London: Routledge & Kegan Paul.

Boureaudhuij, I.D. (1997) 'Family food rules and healthy eating in adolescents', *Journal of Health Psychology,* 2: 45–56.

Bowling, A. (1990) 'Implications of preventive health behaviour for cervical and breast cancer screening programmes: a review', *Family Practice,* 6: 224–31.

Boyle, M.A. and Morris, D.H. (1999) *Community Nutrition in Action. An Entrepreneurial Approach.* Belmont, CA: West/Wadsworth.

Brainard, D., Hyslop, N.E., Mera, R. and Churchill, J. (1997) 'Long-term outcome of inpatients with tuberculosis assigned to outpatient therapy at a local clinic in New Orleans', *Journal of Investigative Medicine,* 45: 381–7.

Breakwell, G.M., Hammond, S. and Fife-Schaw, C. (1995) *Research Methods in Psychology.* London: Sage.

Brehm, J.W. (1966) *A Theory of Psychological Reactance*. New York: Academic Press.

Brehm, S.S. and Brehm, J.W. (1981) *Psychological Reactance: A Theory of Freedom and Control*. New York: Academic Press.

Brenner, C. (1955) *An Elementary Textbook of Psychoanalysis*. New York: International Universities Press.

Breslow, L. (1996) 'Some sequels to the Surgeon General's report on Smoking and Health: thirty years later', *Annals of Epidemiology, 6*: 372–5.

Brewin, C.R., Dalgleish, T. and Joseph, S. (1996) 'A dual representation theory of posttraumatic stress disorder', *Psychological Review, 103*: 670–86.

British Medical Association (1989) *BMA Guide to Alcohol and Accidents*. London: British Medical Association.

Britten, N. (1994) 'Patients' ideas about medicines: a qualitative study in a general practice population', *British Journal of General Practice, 44*: 465–8.

Broman, C.L. (1995) 'Leisure-time physical activity in an African-American population', *Journal of Behavioral Medicine, 18*: 341–52.

Bronfenbrenner, U. (1979) *The Ecology of Human Development*. Cambridge, MA: Harvard University Press.

Broome, A. and Llewellyn, S. (eds) (1995) *Health Psychology: Processes and Applications*, 2nd edn. London: Chapman & Hall.

Brown, G.W. and Harris, T.O. (1978) *Social Origins of Depression: A Study of Psychiatric Disorder in Women*. London: Tavistock.

Brown, G.W. and Harris, T.O. (eds) (1989) *Life Events and Illness*. London: Unwin.

Brown, J.A.C. (1964) *Freud and the Post-Freudians*. London: Penguin.

Brown, M. and Auerback, A. (1981) 'Communication patterns in initiation of marital sex', *Medical Aspects of Human Sexuality, 15*: 105–17.

Brown, M.S. and Goldstein, J.L. (1984) 'How LDL receptors influence cholesterol and atherosclerosis', *Scientific American, 251 (5)*: 52–60.

Brown, S.D. (1996) 'The textuality of stress: drawing between scientific and everyday accounting', *Journal of Health Psychology, 1*: 173–93.

Brownbridge, G., Lilford, R.J. and Tindale-Biscoe, S. (1988) 'Use of a computer to take booking histories in a hospital antenatal clinic', *Medical Care, 26*: 474–87.

Brownell, K. (1991) 'Personal responsibility and control over our bodies: when expectation exceeds reality', *Health Psychology, 10*: 303–10.

Broyard, A. (1992) *Intoxicated by My Illness*. New York: Fawcett Columbine.

Bruun, K., Edwards, G., Lumio, M. et al. (1975) *Alcohol Control Policies in Public Health Perspective*. Helsinki: Finnish Foundation for Alcohol Studies.

Buehler, S.K. and Parsons, W.L. (1997) 'Effectiveness of a call/recall system in improving compliance with cervical cancer screening: a randomized controlled trial', *Canadian Medical Association Journal, 157*: 521–5.

Buller, M.K., and Buller, D.B. (1987) Physicians' communication style and patient satisfaction', *Journal of Health and Social Behavior, 28*: 375–89.

Bunge, M. (1980) *The Mind–Body Problem*. Oxford: Pergamon.

Burbach, D.J. and Peterson, L. (1986) 'Development of children's concepts of illness: a review and critique of the cognitive-developmental literature', *Health Psychology, 5*: 307–25.

Byrne, B.M. (1994) *Structural Equation Modeling with EQS and EQS/Windows*. Thousand Oaks: Sage.

Byrne, P.S. and Long, B.E.L. (1976) *Doctors Talking to Patients*. London: HMSO.

Calnan, M. (1987) *Health and Illness: The Lay Perspective*. London: Tavistock.

Calnan, M. and Williams, S. (1991a) 'Style of life and the salience of health: an exploratory study of health related practices in households from differing socio-economic circumstances', *Sociology of Health and Illness, 7*: 55–75.

Calnan, M. and Williams, S. (1991b) 'Style of life and the salience of health: an exploratory study of health related practices in households from differing socio-economic circumstances', *Sociology of Health and Illness, 13*: 506–29.

Calnan, M. and Williams, S. (1992) 'Images of scientific medicine', *Sociology of Health and Illness, 14*: 233–43.

Camp, D.E., Klesges, R.C. and Relyea, G. (1993) 'The relationship between body weight concerns and adolescent smoking', *Health Psychology, 12*: 24–32.

Campbell, S.M., Peplau, L.A. and DeBro, S.C. (1992) 'Women, men and condoms. Attitudes and experiences of heterosexual college students', *Psychology of Women Quarterly, 16*: 273–88.

Canada Fitness Survey (1984) *Fitness and Aging.* Ottawa: Health Canada.

Cannon, W.B. (1932) *The Wisdom of the Body.* New York: Norton.

Capaldi, E. (1996) 'Conditioned food preferences', in E.D. Capaldi (ed.), *Why We Eat What We Eat: The Psychology of Eating.* Washington, DC: American Psychological Association. pp. 53–80.

Carmelli, D., Swan, G., Robinette, D. and Fabsitz, R. (1992) 'Genetic influence on smoking – a study of male twins', *New England Journal of Medicine, 327*: 829–33.

Carroll, D. and Davey Smith, G, (1997) 'Health and socio-economic position', *Journal of Health Psychology, 2*: 275–82.

Carroll, D., Davey Smith, G. and Bennett, P. (1996) 'Some observations on health and socioeconomic status', *Journal of Health Psychology, 1*: 23–39.

Carton, S., Jouvent, R. and Widlocher, D. (1994) 'Sensation seeking, nicotine dependence, and smoking motivation in female and male smokers', *Addictive Behaviors, 19*: 219–27.

Carver, C.S., Scheier, M.F. and Weintraub, J.K. (1989) 'Assessing coping strategies: a theoretically based approach', *Journal of Personality and Social Psychology, 56*: 267–83.

Caspersen, C.J., Powell, K.E. and Christenson, G.M. (1985) 'Physical activity, exercise, and physical fitness: definitions and distinctions for health-related research', *Public Health Reports, 100*: 126–31.

Catania, J.A., Dolcini, M.M., Coates, T.J., Kegeles, S.M., Greenblatt, R.M. and Puckett, S. (1989) 'Predictors of condom use and multiple partnered sex among sexually-active adolescent women: implications for AIDS-related health interventions', *Journal of Sex Research, 26*: 514–24.

Cattell, R.B. (1950) *Personality: A Systematic Theoretical and Factual Study.* New York: McGraw-Hill.

Cavelaars, A.E.J.M., Kunst, A.E. and Mackenbach, J.P. (1997) 'Socio-economic differences in risk factors for morbidity and mortality in the European Community', *Journal of Health Psychology, 2*: 353–72.

Chalmers, B. (1996) 'Western and African conceptualizations of health', *Psychology and Health, 12*: 1–10.

Chamberlain, K. (1997) 'Socio-economic health differentials: from structure to experience', *Journal of Health Psychology, 2*: 399–411.

Chamberlain, K. and Zika, S. (1990) 'The minor events approach to stress: support for the use of daily hassles', *British Journal of Psychology, 81*: 469–81.

Charlton, A. (1984) 'Smoking and weight control in teenagers', *Public Health, 98*: 277–81.

Charney, D.S., Deutch, A.Y., Krystal, J.H., Southwick, S.M. and Davis, M. (1993)

'Psychobiologic mechanisms of posttraumatic stress disorder', *Archives of General Psychiatry*, 50: 294–305.

Chassin, C., Presson, C.C., Sherman, S.J., Corty, E. and Olshavsky, R.W. (1984) 'Predicting the onset of smoking in adolescence: a longitudinal study', *Journal of Applied Social Psychology*, 14: 224–43.

Chassin, C., Presson, C.C., Rose, J.S. and Sherman, S.J. (1996) 'The natural history of cigarettes from adolescence to adulthood: demographic predictors of continuity and change', *Health Psychology*, 15: 478–84.

Chen, C.C., David, A.S., Nunnerley, H., Michell, M., Dawson, J.L., Berry, H., Dobbs, J. and Fahy, T. (1995) 'Adverse life events and breast cancer: case control study', *British Medical Journal*, 311: 1527–30.

Cheng, Y.H. (1997) 'Explaining disablement in modern times: hand-injured workers' accounts of their injuries in Hong Kong', *Social Science and Medicine*, 45: 739–50.

Cherpitel, C.J. (1993) 'Alcohol and injuries: a review of international emergency room studies', *Addiction*, 88: 923–37.

Chesney, M. (1993) 'Health psychology in the 21st century: acquired immuno-deficiency syndrome as a harbinger of things to come', *Health Psychology*, 12: 259–68.

Christiannse, M.E., Lavigne, J.V. and Lerner, C.V. (1989) 'Psychosocial aspects of compliance in children and adolescents with asthma', *Developmental and Behavioral Pediatrics*, 10: 75–80.

Clark, D.O., Patrick, D.L., Grembowski, D. and Durham, M.L. (1995) 'Socioeconomic status and exercise self-efficacy in late life', *Journal of Behavioral Medicine*, 18: 355–75.

Clark, W.B. and Cahalan, D. (1976) 'Changes in problem drinking over a four year span', *Addictive Behaviours*, 1: 251–60.

Clarke, P. and Eves, F. (1997) 'Applying the transtheoretical model to the study of exercise on prescription', *Journal of Health Psychology*, 2: 195–207.

Cleek, M.G. and Pearson, T.A. (1985) Perceived causes of divorce: an analysis of interrelationships', *Journal of Marriage and the Family*, 47: 179–83.

Cloninger, C.R. (1987) 'Neurogenetic adaptive mechanisms in alcoholism', *Science*, 236: 410–16.

Cloninger, C.R., Bohman, M. and Sigvardsson, S. (1981) 'Inheritance of alcohol abuse', *Archives of General Psychiatry*, 38: 861–8.

Coakley, J. and White, A. (1992) 'Making decisions: gender and sport participation among British adolescents', *Sociology of Sport Journal*, 9: 20–35.

Coan, R.W. (1973) 'Personality variables associated with cigarette smoking', *Journal of Personality and Social Psychology*, 26: 86–104.

Cockburn, J., Gibberd, R.W., Reid, A.L. and Sanson-Fisher, R.W. (1987) 'Determinants of noncompliance with short-term antibiotic regimens', *British Medical Journal*, 295: 814–18.

Cohen, S. and Herbert, T.B. (1996) 'Health psychology: psychological factors and physical disease from the perspective of human psychoneuroimmunology', *Annual Review of Psychology*, 47: 113–42.

Cohen, S. and Williamson, G.M. (1988) 'Perceived stress in a probability sample of the United States', in S. Spacapan and S. Oskamp (eds), *The Social Psychology of Health*. Newbury Park, CA: Sage. pp. 31–67.

Cohen, S. and Williamson, G.M. (1991) 'Stress and infectious disease in humans', *Psychological Bulletin*, 109: 5–24.

Cohen, S. and Wills, T.A. (1985) 'Stress, social support and the buffering hypothesis', *Psychological Bulletin*, 98: 310–57.

Cohen, S., Tyrrell, D.A.J. and Smith, A.P. (1991) 'Psychological stress and susceptibility to the common cold', *New England Journal of Medicine*, 325: 606–12.

Cohen, S., Tyrrell, D.A.J. and Smith, A.P. (1993) 'Negative life events, perceived stress, negative affect, and susceptibility to the common cold', *Journal of Personality and Social Psychology*, 64: 131–40.

Cohen, S., Doyle, W.J., Skoner, D.P., Fireman, P., Gwaltney, J.M. and Newsom, J.T. (1995) 'State and trait negative affect as predictors of objective and subjective symptoms of respiratory viral infections', *Journal of Personality and Social Psychology*, 68: 159–69.

Colby, J.P., Linsky, A.S. and Straus, M.A. (1994) 'Social stress and state-to-state differences in smoking and smoking related mortality in the United States', *Social Science and Medicine*, 38: 373–81.

Coleman, E.M., Hoon, P.W. and Hoon, E.F. (1983) 'Arousability and sexual satisfaction in lesbian and heterosexual women', *Journal of Sex Research*, 19: 58–73.

Colette, M., Godin, G., Bradet, R. and Gionet, N.J. (1994) 'Active living in communities: understanding the intention to take up physical activity as an everyday way of life', *Canadian Journal of Public Health*, 85: 418–21.

COMMIT Research Group (1995) 'Community intervention for smoking cessation (COMMIT) II: changes in adult smoking prevalence', *American Journal of Public Health*, 85: 193–200.

Conner, M. and Norman, P. (eds) (1995) *Predicting Health Behaviour*. Buckingham: Open University Press.

Conner, M. and Sparks, P. (1995) 'The theory of planned behaviour and health behaviours', in M. Conner and P. Norman (eds), *Predicting Health Behaviour*. Buckingham: Open University Press. pp. 121–62.

Conner, M., Holland, C., Wolinsky, A., Thompson, N. and Gilhespy, M. (1994) 'Changing risky driving behaviour in young adults'. Paper presented to the BPS Social Section Annual Conference, University of Cambridge, 20–22 September.

Conner, R. (1994) 'Healthy communities: evaluation research on community-created health promotion projects'. Keynote address at the 23rd International Congress of Applied Psychology, 17–22 July, Madrid, Spain.

Conrad, K.M., Flay, B.R. and Hill, D. (1992) 'Why children start smoking: predictors of onset', *British Journal of Addiction*, 87: 1711–24.

Conrad, P. (1985) 'The meaning of medications: another look at compliance', *Social Science and Medicine*, 20: 29–37.

Corin, E. (1995) 'The cultural frame: context and meaning in the construction of health', in B.C. Amick III, S. Levine, A.R. Tarlov and D. Chapman Walsh (eds), *Society and Health*. New York: Oxford University Press. pp. 272–304.

Cornwell, J. (1984) *Hard-earned Lives*. London: Tavistock.

Costa, P.T., McCrae, R.R. and Bosse, R. (1980) 'Smoking motive factors: a review and replication', *International Journal of the Addictions*, 15: 537–49.

Costanza, M.E. (1992) 'Breast cancer screening in older women: synopsis of a forum', *Cancer Supplement*, 69: 1925–31.

Coulter, A. (1999) 'Paternalism or partnership?', *British Medical Journal*, 319, 719–20.

Coupland, J., Robinson, J.D. and Coupland, N. (1994) 'Frame negotiation in doctor–elderly patient consultations', *Discourse and Society*, 5: 89–124.

Cox, B.D., Blaxter, M., Buckle, A.L.J. et al. (1987) *The Health and Lifestyle Survey*. London: Health Promotion Research Trust.

Cox, C.L. (1982) 'An interaction model of client health behavior: theoretical prescription for nursing', *Advances in Nursing Science*, 5: 519–27.

Cox, T. (1978) *Stress*. London: Macmillan.

Crawford, R. (1980) 'Healthism and the medicalization of everyday life', *International Journal of Health Services*, 10: 365–8.

Crews, F. (1997) *The Memory Wars: Freud's Legacy in Dispute*. London: Granta.

Critchlow, B. (1986) 'The powers of John Barleycorn: beliefs about the effects of alcohol on social behaviour', *American Psychologist*, 41: 751–64.

Cummings, J.H. and Bingham, S.A. (1998) 'Diet and the prevention of cancer', *British Medical Journal*, 317: 1636–40.

Curtis, J.E. and White, P.G. (1992) 'Toward a better understanding of the sport practices of Francophone and Anglophone Canadians', *Sociology of Sport Journal*, 9: 403–22.

Dahl, E., (1993) 'Social inequality in health – the role of the healthy worker effect', *Social Science and Medicine*, 36: 1077–88.

Dahlgren, G. and Whitehead, M. (1991) *Policies and Strategies to Promote Equity in Health*. Stockhom: Institute for Future Studies.

Dasen, P.R., Berry, J.W., Sartorius, N. (eds) (1988) *Health and Cross-cultural Psychology: Towards Applications*. Newbury Park, CA: Sage.

Daughton, J.M., Dughton, D.M. and Patil, K.D. (1997) 'Self-recognition of alcohol and cigarette dependency among high school seniors', *Perceptual and Motor Skills*, 85: 115–20.

Davey Smith, G., Blane, D. and Bartley, M. (1994) 'Explanations for socio-economic differentials in mortality', *European Journal of Public Health*, 4: 131–44.

Davies, D.L. (1962) 'Normal drinking in recovered alcohol addicts', *Quarterly Journal of Studies on Alcohol*, 24: 321–32.

Davies, P. and Project Sigma (1992) 'On relapses: recidivism or rational response?', in P. Aggleton, P. Davies and G. Hart (eds), *AIDS. Rights, Risk and Reason*. London: Falmer Press. pp. 133–41.

Davis, P. (1992) Cited in A. Thomson, 'Let's talk about sex (yes, again)', *The Times*, 3 December.

Davison, C., Macintyre, S. and Davey Smith, G. (1994) 'The potential social impact of predictive genetic testing for susceptibility to common chronic diseases: a review and proposed research agenda', *Sociology of Health and Illness*, 16: 340–71.

Davison, G. and Duffy, M. (1982) 'Smoking habits of long-term survivors of surgery for lung cancer', *Thorax*, 37: 331–3.

De Grasse, C.E., O'Connor, A.M., Perrault, D.J., Aitken, S.E. and Joanisse, S. (1996) 'Changes in women's breast cancer screening, practices, knowledge and attitudes in Ottawa–Carleton since 1991', *Canadian Journal of Public Health*, 37: 338–83.

De La Cancela, V., Chin, J.L. and Jenkins, Y.M. (1998) *Community Health Psychology: Empowerment for Diverse Communities*. London: Routledge.

DelVecchio Good, M.-J., Munakata, T., Kobayashi, Y., Mattingly, C. and Good, B.J. (1994) 'Oncology and narrative time', *Social Science and Medicine*, 38: 855–62.

Department of Health (1998) *Report of the Scientific Committee on Tobacco and Health*. London: Department of Health.

Department of Transport (1992) *The Involvement of Alcohol in Fatal Accidents to Adult Pedestrians*. London: Transport Research Laboratory. Report No. 343.

Department of Transport (1996) *Road Accidents, Great Britain, the Casualty Report*. London: Department of Transport.

Desplanques, G. (1984) *La mortalité des adultes: Résultats de 2 études longitudinales (période 1955–80)*. Paris: INSEE.

Devins, G.M., Styra, R., O'Connor, P., Gray, T., Seland, T.P., Klein, G.M. and Shapiro, C.M. (1996) 'Psychosocial impact of illness intrusiveness moderated by age in multiple sclerosis', *Psychology, Health and Medicine*, 1: 179–92.

D'Houtaud, A. and Field, M.G. (1984) 'The image of health: variations in perception by social class in a French population', *Sociology of Health and Illness*, 6: 30–60.

DiClemente, C.C. (1993) 'Changing addictive behaviors: a process perspective', *Current Directions in Psychological Science*, 2: 101–6.

DiClemente, C.C. and Prochaska, J.O. (1982) 'Self change and therapy change of smoking behavior: a comparison of processes of change in cessation and maintenance', *Addictive Behavior*, 7: 133–42.

DiClemente, C.C. and Velicer, W.F. (1997a) 'The transtheoretical model of health behavior change', *American Journal of Health Promotion*, 12: 38–48.

DiClemente, C.C. and Velicer, W.F. (1997b) 'Misinterpretations and misapplications of the transtheoretical model', *American Journal of Health Promotion*, 12: 11–12.

Dight, S. (1978) *Scottish Drinking Habits*. London: HMSO.

Dijkstra, A., Bakker, M. and De Vries, H. (1997) 'Subtypes within a sample of precontemplating smokers: a preliminary extension of the stages of change', *Addictive Behaviors*, 22: 327–37.

Dijkstra, A., Roijackers, J. and De Vries, H. (1998) 'Smokers in four stages of readiness to change', *Addictive Behaviors*, 23: 339–50.

DiMatteo, M.R. and DiNicola, D.D. (1982) *Achieving Patient Compliance*. New York: Pergamon.

DiMatteo, M.R., Hays, R.D. and Prince, L.M. (1986) 'Relationship of physicians' nonverbal communication skills to patient satisfaction, appointment noncompliance, and physician workload', *Health Psychology*, 5: 581–94.

DiMatteo, M.R., Sherbourne, C.D., Hays, R.D., Ordway, L., Kravitz, R.L., McGlynn, E.A., Kaplan, S. and Rogers, W.H. (1993) 'Physicians' characteristics influence patients' adherence to medical treatment: results from the Medical Outcomes Study', *Health Psychology*, 12: 93–102.

Dishman, R.K. (1986) 'Exercise compliance: a new view for public health', *Physician and Sports Medicine*, 14: 127–45.

Dishman, R.K. and Gettman, L.R. (1980) 'Psychobiologic influences on exercise adherence', *Journal of Sport Psychology*, 2: 295–310.

Doherty, W.J., Schrott, H.C., Metcalf, L. and Iasiello-Vailas, L. (1983) 'Effect of spouse support and health beliefs on medication adherence', *Journal of Family Practice*, 17: 837–41.

Dohrenwend, B.P. and Shrout, P.E. (1985) '"Hassles" in the conceptualization and measurement of life stress variables', *American Psychologist*, 40: 780–5.

Doise, W. (1986) *Levels of Explanation in Social Psychology*. Cambridge: Cambridge University Press.

Dolgin, M.J., Katz, E.R., Doctors, S.R. and Siegel, S.E. (1986) 'Caregivers' perceptions of medical compliance in adolescents with cancer', *Journal of Adolescent Health Care*, 7: 22–7.

Doll, R. and Hill, A.B. (1952) 'A study of the aetiology of carcinoma of the lung', *British Medical Journal*, 2: 1271–86.

Doll, R. and Peto, R. (1981) *The Cause of Human Cancer*. Oxford: Oxford University Press.

Doll, R., Peto, R., Hall, E. and Gray, R. (1994) 'Mortality in relation to consumption of alcohol: 13 years' observation on male British doctors', *British Medical Journal*, 309: 911–18.

Doll, R., Peto, R., Wheatley, K., Gray, R. and Sutherland, I. (1994) 'Mortality in relation to smoking: 40 years' observations on male British doctors', *British Medical Journal*, 309: 901–10.

Donovan, J.L. and Blake, D.R. (1992) 'Patient non-compliance: deviance or reasoned decision-making?', *Social Science and Medicine*, 34: 507–13.

Douglas, M. and Nicod, M. (1974) 'Taking the biscuit: the structure of British meals', *New Society*, 19 December.

Doyal, L. (1979) *The Political Economy of Health*. London: Pluto Press.

Drash, A.L. (1987) *Clinical Care of the Diabetic Child*. Chicago: Yearbook Publishers.

Drummond, D.C., Tiffany, S.T., Glautier, S. and Remington, B. (eds) (1995) *Addictive Behaviour: Cue Exposure Theory and Practice*. London: Wiley.

Dubbert, P.M. (1992) 'Exercise in behavioral medicine', *Journal of Consulting and Clinical Psychology*, 60: 613–18.

Dunbar, J. and Stunkard, A. (1979) 'Adherence to diet and drug regimens', in R. Levy, B. Rifkind, B. Dennis and N. Ernst (eds), *Nutrition, Lipids, and Coronary Heart Disease*. New York: Raven Press. pp. 391–423.

Dzewaltowski, D.A. (1994) 'Physical activity determinants: a social approach, *Medicine and Science in Sports and Exercise*, 26: 1395–9.

Eardley, A. and Elkind, A. (1990) 'A pilot study of attendance for breast cancer screening', *Social Science and Medicine*, 30: 693–9.

Eardley, A., Knopf Elkind, A., Spencer, B., Hobbs, P., Pendleton, L.L. and Haran, D. (1985) 'Attendance for cervical screening – whose problem?', *Social Science and Medicine*, 20: 955–62.

Earker, S.A., Kirscht, J.P. and Becker, M.H. (1984) 'Understanding and improving patient compliance', *Annals of Internal Medicine*, 100: 258–68.

Eckhardt, M.J., Harford, T.C., Kaelber, C.T., Parker, E.S., Rosenthal, L.S., Ryback, R.S., Salmoiraghi, G.C., Vanderveen, E. and Warren, K.R. (1981) 'Health hazards associated with alcohol consumption', *Journal of the American Medical Association*, 246: 648–66.

Edwards, G. (1986) 'The alcohol dependence syndrome: the concept as stimulus to enquiry', *British Journal of Addiction*, 81: 71–84.

Edwards, G. (1998) 'If the drinks industry does not clean up its act, pariah status is inevitable', *British Medical Journal*, 317: 333–9.

Edwards, G. and Gross, M.M. (1976) 'Alcohol dependence: provisional description of a clinical syndrome', *British Medical Journal*, 1: 1058–61.

Edwards, G., Anderson, P., Babor, T.F. et al. (1994) *Alcohol Policy and the Public Good*. Oxford: Oxford University Press.

Egger, G. and Swinburn, B. (1997) 'An ecological approach to the obesity pandemic', *British Medical Journal*, 315: 477–80.

EFPPA (1997) *Meta-Code of Ethics*. Stockholm: European Federation of Professional Psychologists' Associations.

Eisenberg, D., Kessler, R.C. and Foster, C. (1993) 'Unconventional medicine in the United States', *New England Journal of Medicine*, 328: 246–52.

Eiser, C. (1985) *The Psychology of Childhood Illness*. New York: Springer Verlag.

Eiser, C., Patterson, D. and Tripp, J.H. (1984) 'Diabetes and developing knowledge of the body', *Archives of Disease in Childhood*, 59: 167–9.

Eiser, C., Walsh, S. and Eiser, J.R. (1986) 'Young children's understanding of smoking', *Addictive Behaviors, 11*: 119–23.

Elliot, G.R. and Eisdorfer, C. (1982) *Stress and Human Health.* New York: Springer.

Elmore, J.G., Barton, M.B., Moceri, V.M., Polk, S., Arena, P.J. and Fletcher, S.W. (1998) 'Ten year risk of false positive screening mammograms and clinical breast examination', *New England Journal of Medicine, 338*: 1089–96.

Emmons, K.M., Kawachi, I. and Barclay, G. (1997) 'Tobacco control: a brief review of its history and prospects for the future', *Hematology and Oncology Clinics of North America, 11*: 177–95.

Engel, G.L. (1977) 'The need for a new medical model: a challenge for biomedicine', *Science, 196*: 129–36.

Engel, G.L. (1980) 'The clinical application of the biopsychosocial model', *American Journal of Psychiatry, 137*: 535–44.

Environmental Protection Agency (1992) *Respiratory Health Effects of Passive Smoking: Lung Cancer and Other Disorders.* Washington, DC: US Environmental Protection Agency.

Epstein, L.H. (1984) 'The direct effects of compliance on health outcome', *Health Psychology, 3*: 385–93.

Eraker, S.S., Kirscht, J.P. and Becker, M.H. (1984) 'Understanding and improving patient compliance', *Annals of Internal Medicine, 100*: 258–68.

Euripides (1954/414BC) *The Bacchae*, trans. P. Vellacott. London: Penguin.

European Commission (1999) *A Pan-EU Survey of Consumer Attitudes to Physical Activity, Body Weight and Health.* Luxembourg: EC. DGV/F.3.

Eurostat (1992) *Europe in Figures.* Luxembourg: Office for Official Publications of the European Communities.

Evans, P.D. (1990) 'Type A behaviour and coronary heart disease: when will the jury return?', *British Journal of Psychology, 81*: 147–57.

Evans, P., Clow, A. and Hucklebridge, F. (1997) 'Stress and the immune system', *The Psychologist, 10*: 303–7.

Evans, R.I. (1988) 'Health promotion – science or ideology?', *Health Psychology, 7*: 203–19.

Eysenck, H.J. (1947) *Dimensions of Personality.* London: Routledge.

Eysenck, H.J. (1965) *Fact and Fiction in Psychology.* London: Penguin.

Eysenck, H.J. (1988) 'Personality, stress and cancer: prediction and prophylaxis', *British Journal of Medical Psychology, 61*: 57–75.

Eysenck, H.J. and Grossarth-Maticek, R. (1991) 'Creative novation behaviour therapy as a prophylactic treatment for cancer and coronary heart disease: Part II – effects of treatment', *Behaviour Research and Therapy, 29*: 17–31.

Eysenck, H.J., Tarrant, M. and Woolf, M. (1960) 'Smoking and personality', *British Medical Journal, 280*: 1456–60.

Falk, A., Hanson, B.S., Isacsson, S. and Ostergren, P. (1992) 'Job strain and mortality in elderly men: social network, support and influence as buffers', *American Journal of Public Health, 82*: 1136–9.

Farkas, A.J., Pierce, J.P., Zhu, S.-H., Rosbrook, B., Gilpin, E.A., Berry, C. and Kaplan, R.M. (1996) 'Addiction versus stages of change models in predicting smoking cessation', *Addiction, 91*: 1271–80.

Farmer, A. (1994) 'AIDS-talk and the constitution of cultural models', *Social Science and Medicine, 38*: 801–10.

Farmer, P. and Good, B.J. (1991) 'Illness representations in medical anthropology: a critical review and a case study of the representation of AIDS in Haiti', in J.A.

Skelton and R.T. Croyle (eds), *Mental Representation in Health and Illness*. New York: Springer-Verlag. pp. 132–62.

Farr, R.M. (1978) 'Heider, Harré and Herzlich on health and illness: some observations on the structure of "representations collectives"', *European Journal of Social Psychology*, 7: 491–504.

Fava, J.L., Velicer, W.F. and Prochaska, J.O. (1995) 'Applying the transtheoretical model to a representative sample of smokers', *Addictive Behaviors*, 20: 189–203.

Feste, C., and Anderson, R.M. (1995) 'Empowerment: from philosophy to practice', *Patient Education and Counseling*, 26: 139–44.

Fiedler, D.O. (1982) 'Managing medication and compliance: physician–pharmacist–patient interaction', *Journal of the American Geriatrics Society*, 30: S113–S117.

Fieldhouse, P. (1996) *Food and Nutrition: Customs and Culture*, 2nd edn. Cheltenham: Stanley Thornes.

Fillmore, K.M., Golding, J.M., Graves, K.L. and Kniep, S. (1998) 'Alcohol consumption and mortality. II. Studies of male populations', *Addiction*, 93: 205–18.

Fillmore, K.M., Golding, J.M., Graves, K.L., Kniep, S., Leino, E.V., Romelsjo, A., Shoemaker, C., Ager, C.R., Allebeck, P. and Ferrer, H.P. (1998a) 'Alcohol consumption and mortality. I. Characteristics of drinking groups', *Addiction*, 93: 183–203.

Fillmore, K.M., Golding, J.M., Graves, K.L., Kniep, S., Leino, E.V., Romelsjo, A., Shoemaker, C., Ager, C.R., Allebeck, P. and Ferrer, H.P. (1998b) 'Alcohol consumption and mortality. III. Studies of female populations', *Addiction*, 93: 219–29.

Fincham, J.E., and Wertheimer, A.I. (1985) 'Using the Health Belief Model to predict initial drug therapy defaulting', *Social Science and Medicine*, 20: 101–5.

Finney, J.W. and Monahan, S.C. (1996) 'The cost effectiveness of treatment for alcoholism: a second approximation', *Journal of Studies on Alcohol*, 57: 229–43.

Fishbein, M. and Ajzen, I. (1975) *Belief, Attitude, Intention and Behaviour*. New York: Wiley.

Flay, B.R., Hu, F.B., Siddiqui, O., Day, L.E., Hedeker, D., Petratis, J., Richardson, J. and Sussman, S. (1994) 'Differential influence of parental smoking and friends' smoking on adolescent initiation and escalation of smoking', *Journal of Health and Social Behavior*, 35: 248–65.

Flay, B.R., Ockene, J.K. and Tager, I.B. (1992) 'Smoking: epidemiology, cessation, and prevention', *Chest*, 102: 277S–301S.

Fletcher, S. (1997) 'Breast cancer screening in women aged under 50', *British Medical Journal*, 314: 764–5.

Fletcher, S.W., Black, W., Harris, R., Rimer, B.K. and Shapiro, S. (1993) 'Report of the international workshop on screening for breast cancer', *Journal of the National Cancer Institute*, 85: 1644–56.

Fogarty, J.S. (1997) 'Reactance theory and patient non-compliance', *Social Science and Medicine*, 45: 1277–88.

Folsom, A.R., Cook, T.C., Sprafka, J.M., Burke, G.L., Norsted, S.W. and Jacobs, D.R. (1991) 'Differences in leisure-time physical activity levels between blacks and whites in population-based sample: the Minnesota Heart Survey', *Journal of Behavioral Medicine*, 14: 1–9.

Forrest, F., du V Florey, C., McPherson, F. and Young, J.A. (1991) 'Reported alcohol consumption during pregnancy and infants' development at 18 months', *British Medical Journal*, 303: 22–6.

Foucault, M. (1976) *The Birth of the Clinic*. London: Routledge.

Foulds, J. and Ghodse, A. H. (1995) 'The role of nicotine in tobacco smoking: implications for tobacco control policy', *Journal of the Royal Society of Health, 115*: 225–30.

Fox, B.H. (1988) 'Psychogenic factors in cancer, especially its incidence', in S. Maes, D. Spielberger, P.B. Defares and I.G. Sarason (eds), *Topics in Health Psychology*. New York: Wiley. pp. 37–55.

Fox, J. and Benzeval, M. (1995) 'Perspectives on social variations in health', in M. Benzeval, K. Judge and M. Whitehead (eds), *Tackling Inequalities in Health*. London: King's Fund. pp. 10–21.

Francome, C. and Marks, D.F. (1996) *Improving the Health of the Nation*. London: Middlesex University Press.

Frank, A.W. (1993) 'The rhetoric of self-change: illness experience as narrative', *Sociological Quarterly, 34*: 39–52.

Frankenberg, R. (1988) '"Your time or mine?" An anthropological view of the tragic temporal contradictions of biomedical practice', in M. Young and T. Schuller (eds), *The Rhythms of Society*. London: Routledge. pp. 118–52.

Frazier, E.L., Jiles, R.B., and Mayberry, R. (1996) 'Use of screening mammography and clinical breast examination among Black, Hispanic, and White women', *Preventive Medicine, 25*: 118–25.

French, J. and Adams, L. (1986) 'From analysis to synthesis. Theories of health education', *Health Education Journal, 45*: 71–4.

French, S.A., Perry, C.L., Leon, G.R. and Fulkerson, J.A. (1994) 'Weight concerns, dieting behavior, and smoking initiation among adolescents: a prospective study', *American Journal of Public Health, 84*: 1818–20.

Freud, S. (1901) 'The psychopathology of everyday life', in J. Strachey (ed.), *The Standard Edition of the Complete Psychological Works of Sigmund Freud*. London: Hogarth.

Freud, S. (1917) 'Mourning and melancholia', in J. Strachey (ed.), *The Standard Edition of the Complete Psychological Works of Sigmund Freud*. London: Hogarth.

Freud, S. (1930) 'Three contributions to the theory of sex', in J. Strachey (ed.), *The Standard Edition of the Complete Psychological Works of Sigmund Freud*. London: Hogarth.

Freud, S. and Breuer, J. (1895) 'Studies on hysteria', in J. Strachey (ed.), *The Standard Edition of the Complete Psychological Works of Sigmund Freud*. London: Hogarth.

Frey, L.R., Adelman, M.B. and Query, J.L. (1996) 'Communication practices in the social construction of health in an AIDS residence', *Journal of Health Psychology, 1*: 383–97.

Friedman, H.S. and Rosenman, R.H. (1974) *Type A Behaviour and Your Heart*. New York: Knopf.

Friedman, H.S., Tucker, J.S., Tomlinson-Keasey, C., Schwartz, J.E., Wingard, D.L. and Criqui, M.H. (1993) 'Does childhood personality predict longevity?', *Journal of Personality and Social Psychology, 65*: 176–85.

Friedson, E. (1970) *Profession of Medicine*. New York: Harper and Row.

Frye, B.A. (1991) 'Cultural themes in health-care decision making among Cambodian refugee women', *Journal of Community Health Nursing, 8*: 33–44.

Funke, B.L. and Nicholson, M.E. (1993) 'Factors affecting patient compliance among women with abnormal pap smears', *Patient Education and Counseling, 20*: 5–15.

Furnham, A. and Forey, J. (1994) 'The attitudes, behaviours, and beliefs of patients of conventional vs alternative (complementary) medicine', *Journal of Clinical Psychology, 50*: 458–69.

Furnham, A. and Kirkcaldy, B. (1996) 'The health beliefs and behaviours of orthodox and complementary clients', *British Journal of Clinical Psychology, 35*: 49–62.

Gallant, S.J. Keita, G.P. and Royak-Schaler, R. (eds) (1997) *Health Care for Women: Psychological, Social and Behavioral Influences.* Washington, DC: American Psychological Association.

Gallup, G. and Newport, F. (1990) 'Many Americans favor restrictions on smoking in public places', *Gallup Poll Monthly, 298*: 19–27.

Garcia, J., Ervin, R.R. and Koelling, R.A. (1966) 'Learning with prolonged delay of reinforcement', *Psychonomic Science, 5*: 121–2.

Garrity, T.F. (1981) 'Medical compliance and the clinician–patient relationship: a review', *Social Science and Medicine, 15E*: 215–22.

Garro, L.C. (1994) 'Narrative representations of chronic illness experience: cultural models of illness, mind, and body in stories concerning the temporomandibular joint (TMJ)', *Social Science and Medicine, 38*: 775–88.

Gauvin, L. and Spence, J.C. (1996) 'Physical activity and psychological well-being: knowledge base, current issues and caveats', *Nutrition Reviews, 54*: S53–S65.

Gauvin, L., Rejecski, W.J., Norris, J.L. and Lutes, L. (1997) 'The curse of inactivity: failure of acute exercise to enhance feeling states in a community sample of sedentary adults', *Journal of Health Psychology, 2*: 509–23.

Geertz, C. (1973) *The Interpretation of Culture.* New York: Basic Books.

Gergen, K.J. (1985) 'The social constructionist movement in modern psychology', *American Psychologist, 40*: 266–75.

Gergen, K.J. and Gergen, M.M. (1986) 'Narrative form and the construction of psychological science', in T.R. Sarbin (ed.), *Narrative Psychology.* New York: Praeger. pp. 22–44.

Giddens, A. (1992) *The Transformation of Intimacy.* Cambridge: Polity Press.

Gilbert, R.M. (1984) *Caffeine Consumption.* New York: Alan R. Liss.

Gillies, V. and Willig, C. (1997) '"You get the nicotine and that in your blood": constructions of addiction and control in women's accounts of cigarette smoking', *Journal of Community and Applied Social Psychology, 7*: 285–301.

Giovino, G.A., Schooley, M.W., Zhu, B.P., Chrisman, J.H., Tomar, S.L., Peddicord, J.P. et al. (1994) 'Trends and recent patterns in selected tobacco use behaviors – United States 1990–1994', *Morbidity and Mortality Weekly Report, 44 (3)*: 1–42.

Glasgow, R.E., Hampson, S.E., Strycker, L.A. and Ruggiero, L. (1997) 'Personal-model beliefs and social-environmental barriers related to diabetes self-management', *Diabetes Care, 20*: 556–61.

Glendinning, A., Shucksmith, J. and Hendry, L. (1997) 'Family life and smoking in adolescence', *Social Science and Medicine, 44*: 93–101.

Glenister, D. (1996) 'Exercise and mental health: a review', *Journal of the Royal Society of Health, 116*: 7–13.

Gliksman, M., Dwyer, T., Wlodarczyk, T. and Pierce, J. (1989) 'Cigarette smoking in Australian schoolchildren', *Medical Journal of Australia, 150*: 81–4.

Goddard, E. (1990) *Why Children Start Smoking.* London: HMSO.

Godin, G. (1994) 'Theories of reasoned action and planned behavior: usefulness for exercise promotion', *Medicine and Science in Sports and Exercise, 26*: 1391–4.

Goffman, L. (1963) *Stigma: Notes on the Management of Spoiled Identity.* London: Penguin.

Good, B.J. and DelVecchio Good, M. (1994) 'In the subjunctive mode: epilepsy narratives in Turkey', *Social Science and Medicine, 38*: 835–47.

Goodwin, D. (1976) *Is Alcoholism Hereditary?* Oxford: Oxford University Press.

Gordis L., Merkowitz, M. and Lickenfeld, A.M. (1969) 'The inaccuracy in using interviews to estimate patient reliability in taking medication at home', *Medical Care,* 7: 49–54.

Gossop, M. (ed.) (1989) *Relapse and Addictive Behaviour.* London: Tavistock/ Routledge.

Gottlieb, N.H. and Chen, M.S. (1985) 'Socio-cultural correlates of childhood sporting activities: their implications for heart health', *Social Science and Medicine,* 21: 533–9.

Grafstrom, M. (1994) 'The experience of burden in the care of elderly persons with dementia'. Unpublished doctoral dissertation, Karolinska Institute, Stockholm, Sweden.

Graham, H. (1976) 'Smoking in pregnancy: the attitudes of expectant mothers', *Social Science and Medicine,* 10: 399–405.

Graham, H. (1987) 'Women's smoking and family health', *Social Science and Medicine,* 25: 47–56.

Graham, H. (1993) *When Life's a Drag: Women, Smoking and Disadvantage.* London: HMSO.

Graham, H. (1996) 'Smoking prevalence among women in the European community 1950–1980', *Social Science and Medicine,* 43: 243–54.

Gram, I.T., Lund, E. and Slenker, S.E. (1990) 'Quality of life following a false positive mammogram', *British Journal of Cancer,* 62: 1018–22.

Gram, I.T. and Slenker, S.E. (1992) 'Cancer anxiety and attitudes towards mammography among screening attenders, non-attenders, and women never invited', *American Journal of Public Health,* 82: 249–51.

Gray-Sevilla, M.E., Nara, L.E., Malacara, J.M., Huerta, R., Diaz-de-Leon, J., Mena, A. and Fajardo, M.E. (1995) 'Adherence to treatment and social support in patients with non-insulin dependent diabetes mellitus', *Journal of Diabetes Complications,* 9: 81–6.

Greatbatch, D., Heath, C., Campion, P. and Luff, P. (1995) 'How do desk-top computers affect the doctor–patient interaction?', *Family Practice,* 12: 32–6.

Greeley, A.M. (1991) *Faithful Attraction: Discovering Intimacy, Love and Fidelity in American Marriage.* New York: Doherty.

Green, B.L. (1994) 'Psychosocial research in traumatic stress: an update', *Journal of Traumatic Stress,* 7: 341–62.

Greenberg, M.T., Siegel, J.M. and Leitch, C.J. (1983) 'The nature and importance of attachment relationships to parents and peers during adolescence', *Journal of Youth and Adolescence,* 12: 373–86.

Gregg, J. and Curry, R.H. (1994) 'Explanatory models for cancer among African-American women at two Atlanta neighbourhood health centers: the implications for a cancer screening program', *Social Science and Medicine,* 39: 519–26.

Gregory, S. and McKie, L. (1991) 'The smear test: women's views', *Nursing Standards,* 5 (33): 32–6.

Grimm, L.G. and Yarnold, P.R. (eds) (1995) *Reading and Understanding Multivariate Statistics.* Washington, DC: American Psychological Association.

Groddeck, G.W. (1979) *The Book of the It.* London: Vision.

Grossarth-Maticek, R. and Eysenck, H.J. (1991) 'Creative novation behaviour therapy as a prophylactic treatment for cancer and coronary heart disease: Part I – description of treatment', *Behaviour Research and Therapy,* 29: 1–16.

Gryfe, C.I. and Gryfe, B. (1984) Drug therapy of the aged: the problem of compliance and the rules of physicians and pharmacists', *Journal of the American Geriatrics Society, 32*: 301–7.

Haan, M.N. (1988) 'Job strain and ischaemic heart disease: an epidemiologic study of metal workers', *Annals of Clinical Research, 20*: 143–5.

Hajek, P., West, R. and Wilson, J. (1995) 'Regular smokers, lifetime very light smokers, and reduced smokers: comparison of psychosocial and smoking characteristics in women', *Health Psychology, 14*: 195–201.

Hall, J.A., Roter, D.L. and Katz, N.R. (1988) 'Meta-analysis of correlates of provider behavior in medical encounters', *Medical Care, 26*: 1–19.

Hammond, S.L. (1995) Supplementing health campaign messages: recent developments in informing patients about their prescription drugs', in E. Maibach and R.L. Parrott (eds), *Designing Health Messages. Approaches from Communication Theory and Public Health Practice.* Thousand Oaks: Sage. pp. 249–69.

Handmer, J. and Penning-Rowsell, E. (1990) *Hazards and the Communication of Risk.* Aldershot: Gower.

Hans, M.B. and Koeppen, A.H. (1989) 'Huntington's chorea: its impact on the spouse', *Journal of Nervous and Mental Disease, 168*: 209–14.

Harden, A. and Peersman, G. (1997) 'Advancing evidence-based health promotion'. Paper presented at the School of Social Science, Middlesex University, 2 December.

Harlan, L.C., Bernstein, A.M. and Kessler, L.G. (1991) 'Cervical cancer screening: who is not screened and why?', *American Journal of Public Health, 81*: 885–90.

Harper, P. (1992) 'Genetics and public health', *British Medical Journal, 304*: 721.

Harré, R. (1979) *Social Being.* Oxford: Blackwell.

Harris, T.O. (1997) 'Life events and health', in A. Baum, S. Newman, J. Weinman, R. West and C. McManus (eds), *Cambridge Handbook of Psychology, Health and Medicine.* Cambridge: Cambridge University Press. pp. 136–8.

Harris, T.O. and Brown, G.W. (1989) 'The LEDS findings in the context of other research: an overview', in G.W. Brown and T.O. Harris (eds), *Life Events and Illness.* London: Unwin Hyman.

Harrison, J.A., Mullen, P.D. and Green, L.W. (1992) 'A meta-analysis of studies of the health belief model with adults', *Health Education Research, 7*: 107–16.

Hart, C.L., Davey Smith, G., Hole, D.J. and Hawthorne, V.M. (1999) 'Alcohol consumption and mortality from all causes, coronary disease, and stroke: results from a prospective cohort study of Scottish men with 21-years of follow up', *British Medical Journal, 318*: 1725–9.

Hartley, P. (1998) 'Eating disorders and health education', *Psychology, Health and Medicine, 3*: 133–40.

Hartman, F. (1973) *Paracelsus: Life and Prophecies.* New York: Rudolph Steiner.

Hasbrook, C.A. (1986) 'The sport participation–social class relationship: some recent youth sport participation data', *Sociology of Sport Journal, 3*: 154–9.

Hatziandreu, E.J., Pierce, J.P., Lefkopoulou, M. et al. (1990) 'Quitting smoking in the United States in 1986', *Journal of the National Cancer Institute, 82*: 1402–6.

Haug, M. and Lavin, B. (1983) *Consumerism in Medicine: Challenging Physician Authority.* Beverly Hills, CA: Sage.

Hawkes, J. and Holm, K. (1993) 'Gender differences in exercise determinants', *Nursing Research, 42*: 166–72.

Hayes, D. and Ross, C.E. (1987) 'Concern with appearance, health beliefs, and eating habits', *Journal of Health and Social Behavior, 28*: 120–30.

Haynes, R.B (1979a) 'Introduction', in R.B. Haynes, D.W. Taylor and D.L. Sackett (eds), *Compliance in Health Care*. Baltimore, MD: Johns Hopkins University Press. pp. 1–7.

Haynes, R.B. (1979b) 'A critical review of the determinants of patient compliance with therapeutic regimens', in R.B. Haynes, D.W. Taylor and D.L. Sackett (eds), *Compliance in Health Care*. Baltimore, MD: Johns Hopkins University Press. pp. 49–62.

Haynes, S.G., Feinleib, M. and Kannel, W.B. (1980) 'The relationship of psychosocial factors to coronary heart disease in the Framingham study: III. Eight year incidence of coronary heart disease', *American Journal of Epidemiology*, 111: 37–58.

Health Education Authority (1992) *Stopping Smoking Made Easier*. London: HEA.

Heath, A.C. and Madden, P.A.F. (1995) 'Genetic influences on smoking behavior', in J.R. Turner, L.R. Carden and J.K. Hewitt (eds), *Behavior Genetic Approaches in Behavioral Medicine*. New York: Plenum Press. pp. 45–66.

Heath, G.W., Pate, R.R. and Pratt, M. (1993) 'Measuring physical activity among adolescents', *Public Health Reports*, 108 (1): 42–6.

Heather, N. (1995) 'Interpreting the evidence on brief interventions for excessive drinkers: the need for caution', *Alcohol and Alcoholism*, 30: 287–96.

Heather, N. and Robertson, I. (1997) *Problem Drinking*. Oxford: Oxford University Press.

Heckler, M. (1985) *Report of the Secretary's Task Force on Black and Minority Health: Volume 1. Executive Summary*. Washington, DC: US Government Printing Office.

Heelas, P. and Locke, A. (eds) (1981) *Indigenous Psychologies: The Anthropology of the Self*. New York: Academic Press.

Heider, F. (1958) *The Psychology of Interpersonal Relations*. New York: Wiley.

Helakorpi, S., Berg, M.-A., Uutela, A. and Puska, P. (1994) *Health Behavior among Finnish Adult Population*. Helsinki: National Public Health Institute.

Helmert, J. and Shea, S. (1994) 'Social inequalities and health status in Western Germany', *Public Health*, 108: 341–56.

Henningfield, J.E., Gopalan, L. and Shiffman, S. (1998) 'Tobacco dependence: fundamental concepts and recent advances', *Current Opinion in Psychiatry*, 11: 259–63.

Hepburn, S.J. (1988) 'W.H.R. Rivers Prize Essay (1986): western minds, foreign bodies', *Medical Anthropology Quarterly*, 2: 59–74.

Herbert, T.B. and Cohen, S. (1993) 'Stress and immunity in humans: a meta-analytic review', *Psychosomatic Medicine*, 55: 364–79.

Hernes, G. (1998) 'Foreword', in J. Ovretveit, *Evaluating Health Interventions*. Buckingham: Open University Press. p. ix.

Herzlich, C. (1973) *Health and Illness: A Social Psychological Approach*. London: Academic Press.

Herzlich, C. and Pierret, J. (1987) *Illness and Self in Society*. Baltimore, MD: Johns Hopkins University Press.

Hill, L., Casswell, S., Maskill, C., Jones, S. and Wyllie, A.(1998) 'Fruit and vegetables as adolescent food choices in New Zealand', *Health Promotion International*, 13: 55–65.

Hillsdon, M. and Thorogood, M. (1996) 'A systematic review of physical activity promotion strategies', *British Journal of Sports Medicine*, 30: 84–9.

Hillsdon, M., Thorogood, M., Anstiss, T. and Morris, J. (1995) 'Randomised controlled trials of physical activity promotion in free living populations: a review', *Journal of Epidemiology and Community Health*, 49: 448–53.

Hinman, A.R. and Koplan, J.P. (1984) 'Pertussis and pertussis vaccine: further analysis of benefits, risks, and costs', *Journal of the American Medical Association*, 251: 3109–13.

Hite, S. (1976) *The Hite Report: A Nationwide Survey of Female Sexuality*. New York: Dell.

Hjalmarson, A., Franzon, M., Westin, A., Wiklund, A. (1994) 'Effect of nicotine nasal spray on smoking cessation: a randomized placebo-controlled double-blind study', *Archives of Internal Medicine*, 154: 2567–72.

Hobfoll, S.E. (1989) 'Conservation of resources: a new attempt at conceptualising stress', *American Psychologist*, 44: 513–24.

Hofstede, G. (1980) *Culture's Consequences: International Differences in Work-related Values*. Beverly Hills, CA: Sage.

Holbrook, M.L. (1871) *Parturition Without Pain: A Code of Directions for Escaping the Primal Curse*. New York: Wood & Holbrook.

Holder, H.D. and Edwards, G. (1995) *Alcohol and Public Policy: Evidence and Issues*. Oxford: Oxford University Press.

Holland, J.C., Geary, N., Marchini, A. and Tross, S. (1987) 'An international survey of physician attitudes and practice in regard to revealing the diagnosis of cancer', *Cancer Investigation*, 5: 151.

Holland, J., Ramazanoglu, C., Scott, S., Sharpe, S. and Thomson, R. (1991) 'Between embarrassment and trust: young women and the diversity of condom use', in P. Aggleton, G. Hart and P. Davies (eds), *AIDS. Responses, Interventions and Care*. London: Falmer Press. pp. 127–48.

Hollis, J.F., Connett, J.E., Stevens, V.J. and Greenlick, M.R. (1990) 'Stressful life events, Type A behaviour, and the prediction of cardiovascular and total mortality over six years', *Journal of Behavioural Medicine*, 13: 263–81.

Holmes, T.H. and Rahe, R.H. (1967) 'The social readjustment rating scale', *Journal of Psychosomatic Research*, 11: 213–18.

Holroyd, K.A. and Coyne, J. (1987) 'Personality and health in the 1980s: psychosomatic medicine revisited?', *Journal of Personality*, 55: 359–76.

Homans, H. and Aggleton, P. (1988) 'Health education, HIV infection and AIDS', in P. Aggleton and H. Homans (eds), *Social Aspects of AIDS*. London: Falmer Press. pp. 154–76.

Hoon, E.F., Hoon, P.W., Rand, K.H., Johnson, J., Hall, N.R. and Edwards, N.B. (1991) 'A psycho-behavioural model of genital herpes recurrence', *Journal of Psychosomatic Research*, 35: 25–36.

Hooper, J.M. and Veneziano, L. (1995) 'Distinguishing starters from non-starters in an employee physical activity incentive program', *Health Education Quarterly*, 22: 49–60.

Hopkins, N. (1994) 'Peer group processes and adolescent health-related behaviour: more than "peer group pressure"?', *Journal of Community and Applied Social Psychology*, 4: 329–45.

Horton, J.A., Romans, M.C. and Cruess, D.F. (1992) 'Mammography attitudes and usage study', *Women's Health Issues*, 1: 68–73.

House, J.S., Landis, K.R. and Umberson, D. (1988) 'Social relationships and health', *Science*, 241: 540–5.

Hovell, M.F., Sallis, J.F., Hofstetter, C.R., Spry, V.M., Faucher, P. and Casperson, C.J. (1989) 'Identifying correlates of walking for exercise: an epidemiologic prerequisite for physical activity promotion', *Preventive Medicine*, 18: 856–66.

Hudson, W.W., Harrison, D.F. and Crosscup, P.C. (1981) 'A short-form scale to measure sexual discord in dyadic relationships', *Journal of Sex Research, 17*: 157–74.

Huggins, M., Bloch, M., Wigins, S. et al. (1992) 'Predictive testing for Huntington's Disease in Canada: adverse effects and unexpected results in those receiving a decreased result', *American Journal of Human Genetics, 42*: 508–15.

Hughes, J.R. (1991) 'Distinguishing withdrawal relief and direct effects of smoking', *Psychopharmacology, 104*: 409–10.

Hughes. J.R. (1996) 'The future of smoking cessation therapy in the United States', *Addiction, 91*: 1797–1802.

Hulka, B.S. (1979) 'Patient–clinician interactions and compliance', in R.B. Haynes, D.W. Taylor and D.L. Sackett (eds), *Compliance in Health Care*. Baltimore, MD: Johns Hopkins University Press. pp. 63–77.

Hulka, B.S., Cassel, J.C. and Kupper, L.L. (1976a) 'Disparities between medications prescribed and consumed among chronic disease patients', in L. Lasagna (ed.), *Patient Compliance*. Mount Kisco, NY: Futura Publishing. pp. 123–52.

Hulka, B.S., Cassel, J.C., Kupper, L.L. and Burdette, J. (1976b) 'Medication use and misuse: physician–patient discrepancies', *Journal of Chronic Diseases, 28*: 7–14.

Hull, J.G. (1981) 'A self-awareness model of the causes and effects of alcohol consumption', *Journal of Abnormal Psychology, 90*: 586–600.

Hunt, A. and Davis, P. (1991) 'What is a sexual encounter?', in P. Aggleton, G. Hart and P. Davies (eds), *AIDS. Responses, Interventions and Care*. London: Falmer Press. pp. 43–52.

Hunt, L.M., Jordan, B., Irwin, S. and Browner, C. (1989) 'Compliance and the patients' perspective? Controlling symptoms in everyday life', *Culture, Medicine and Psychiatry, 13*: 315–34.

Hunt, S.M. (1993) 'The relationship between research and policy', in J.K. Davies and M.P. Kelly (eds), *Healthy Cities: Research and Practice*. London: Routledge.

Hunter, K.M. (1991) *Doctors' Stories: The Narrative Structure of Medical Knowledge*. Princeton, NJ: Princeton University Press.

Hunter, M.S., O'Dea, I. and Britten, N. (1997) 'Decision-making and hormone replacement therapy: a qualitative analysis', *Social Science and Medicine, 45*: 1541–8.

Hyden, L.-C. (1997) 'Illness and narrative', *Sociology of Health and Illness, 19*: 48–69.

Ikard, F.F., Green, D. and Horn, D. (1969) 'A scale to differentiate between types of smoking as related to management of affect', *International Journal of the Addictions, 4*: 649–59.

Illich, I. (1976a) *Limits to Medicine*. London: Calder and Boyars.

Illich, I. (1976b) *Medical Nemesis: The Expropriation of Health*. New York: Pantheon Books.

Imber, S., Schultz, E., Funderburk, F., Allen, R. and Flanner, R. (1976) 'The fate of the untreated alcoholic: toward a natural history of the disorder', *Journal of Nervous and Mental Disorders, 162*: 238–47.

Ingham, R. and Kirkland, D. (1997) 'Discourses and sexual health: providing for young people', in L. Yardley (ed.), *Material Discourses of Health and Illness*. London: Routledge. pp. 150–75.

Ingham, R., Woodcock, A. and Stenner, K. (1991) 'Getting to know you. Young people's knowledge of their partners at first intercourse', *Journal of Community and Applied Social Psychology, 1*: 117–32.

Ingham, R., Woodcock, A. and Stenner, K. (1992) 'The limitations of rational decision-making models as applied to young people's sexual behaviour', in

P. Aggleton, P. Davies and G. Hart (eds), *AIDS. Rights, Risks and Reason*. London: Falmer Press. pp. 163–73.

International Life Sciences Institute (1998) *Healthy Lifestyles: Nutrition and Physical Activity*. Brussels: ILFI.

Jaber, R., Steinhardt, S. and Trilling, J. (1991) 'Explanatory models of illness: a pilot study', *Family Systems Medicine, 9*: 39–51.

Jackson, R., Scragg, R. and Beaglehole, R. (1991) 'Alcohol consumption and risk of coronary heart disease', *British Medical Journal, 303*: 211–16.

Jain, A. and Ogden, J. (1999) 'General practitioners' experiences of patients' complaints: qualitative study', *British Medical Journal, 318*: 1596–9.

James, J.E. (1997) *Understanding Caffeine. A Biobehavioral Analysis*. Thousand Oaks, CA: Sage.

James, W. (1950/1890) *The Principles of Psychology*. New York: Dover.

Janis, I.L. (1984) 'The patient as decision maker', in W.D. Gentry (ed.), *Handbook of Behavioral Medicine*. New York: Guilford. pp. 326–68.

Janz, N. and Becker, M.H. (1984) 'The health belief model: a decade later', *Health Education Quarterly, 11*: 1–47.

Jarvis, M.J. (1994) 'A profile of tobacco smoking', *Addiction, 89*: 1371–6.

Jarvis, M.J., Raw, M., Russell, M.A.H. and Feyerabend, C. (1982) 'Randomized controlled trial of nicotine chewing gum', *British Medical Journal, 285*: 537–40.

Jarvis, M.J., Goddard, E. and McNeill, A. (1990) 'Do attitudes predict uptake of smoking in teenagers? Case not proven', *Social Science and Medicine, 31*: 997–1001.

Jellinek, E.M. (1960) *The Disease Concept of Alcoholism*. New Haven: Hillhouse Press.

Jerram, K.L. and Coleman, P.G. (1999) 'The big five personality traits and reporting of health problems and health behaviour in old age', *British Journal of Health Psychology, 4*: 181–92.

Joffe, H. (1996) 'AIDS research and prevention: a social representational approach', *British Journal of Medical Psychology, 69*: 169–91.

Johnson, A.M. and Wellings, K. (1994) 'Studying sexual lifestyles', in A.M. Johnson, J. Wadsworth, K. Wellings and J. Field (eds), *Sexual Attitudes and Lifestyles*. Oxford: Blackwell. pp. 1–18.

Johnson, A.M., Wadsworth, J., Wellings, K. and Field, J. (1994) *Sexual Attitudes and Lifestyles*. Oxford: Blackwell.

Johnston, M., Wright, S. and Weinman, J. (1995) *Measures in Health Psychology: A User's Portfolio*. Windsor: NFER-Nelson.

Kabat, G.C., Morabia, A. and Wynder, E.L. (1991) 'Comparison of smoking habits of Blacks and Whites in a case-control study', *American Journal of Public Health, 81*: 1483–6.

Kamin, L.J. (1977) *The Science and Politics of IQ*. London: Penguin.

Kann, L., Warren, W., Collins, J.L., Ross, J., Collins, B. and Kolbe, L.J. (1993) 'Results from the national school-based 1991 Youth Risk Behavior Survey and progress toward achieving health objectives for the nation', *Public Health Reports, 106 (1)*: 47–55.

Kanner, A.D., Coyne, J.C., Schaefer, C. and Lazarus, R.S. (1981) 'Comparison of two modes of stress measurement: daily hassles and uplifts versus major life events', *Journal of Behavioral Medicine, 4*: 1–39.

Kaplan, G.A., Pamuk, E.R., Lynch, J.W., Cohen, R.D. and Balfour, J.L. (1996) 'Inequality in income and mortality in the United States: analysis of mortality and potential pathways', *British Medical Journal, 312*: 999–1003.

Kaplan, S.H., Greenfield, S. and Ware, J.E. (1989) 'Assessing the effects of physician–patient interactions on the outcomes of chronic disease', *Medical Care, 27 (3)*: S110–S127.

Kavanagh, A.M. and Brom, D.H. (1997) 'Women's understanding of abnormal cervical smear test results: a qualitative interview study', *British Medical Journal, 314*: 1388–91.

Keane, T.M. and Wolfe, J. (1990) 'Comorbidity in post-traumatic stress disorder: an analysis of community and clinical studies', *Journal of Applied Social Psychology, 20*: 1776–88.

Keane, V., Stanton, B., Horton, L., Aronson, R., Galbraith, J. and Hughart, N. (1993) 'Perceptions of vaccine efficacy, illness, and health among inner-city parents', *Clinical Pediatrics, 37*: 2–7.

Keefe, R.J., Hauck, E.R., Egert, J., Rimer, B, and Kornguth, P. (1994) 'Mammography pain and discomfort: a cognitive behavioural perspective', *Pain, 56*: 247–60.

Keene, R.J. (1980) 'Follow-up studies of World War II and Korean conflict prisoners', *American Journal of Epidemiology, 111*: 194–200.

Kelder, S.H., Perry, C.L. and Klepp, K.I. (1994) 'Longitudinal tracing of adolescent smoking, physical activity and food choice behaviours', *American Journal of Public Health, 84*: 1121–6.

Kendell, R.E., de Roumanie, M. and Ritson, E.B. (1983a) 'The influence of an increase in excise duty on alcohol consumption and its adverse effects', *British Medical Journal, 287*: 809–11.

Kendell, R.E., de Roumanie, M. and Ritson, E.B. (1983b) 'Effects of economic changes on Scottish drinking habits 1978–1982', *British Journal of Addiction, 78*: 365–79.

Kennedy, B.P, Kawachi, I. and Prothrow-Stith, D. (1996) 'Income distribution and mortality: cross-sectional ecologic study of the Robin Hood index in the United States', *British Medical Journal, 312*: 1004–7.

Kennedy, B.P, Kawachi, I., Glass, R. and Prothrow-Stith, D. (1998) 'Income distribution, socioeconomic status, and self-rated health in the United States: a multilevel analysis', *British Medical Journal, 317*: 917–21.

Kennedy, I. (1981) *The Unmasking of Medicine*. London: George Allen & Unwin.

Kevany, J (1996) 'Extreme poverty: an obligation ignored', *British Medical Journal, 313*: 65–6.

Key, T.J., Fraser, G.E., Thorogood, M., Appleby, P.N., Beral, V., Reeves, G., Burr, M.L., Chang-Claude, J., Frentzel-Beyme, R., Kuzma, J.W., Mann, J. and McPherson, K. (1998) 'Mortality in vegetarians and non-vegetarians: a collaborative analysis of 8,300 deaths among 76,000 men and women in five prospective studies', *Public Health Nutrition, 1*: 33–41.

Keys, A., Anderson, J.T. and Grande, F. (1959) 'Serum cholesterol in man: diet fat and intrinsic responsiveness', *Circulation, 19*: 201–4.

King, A.C. (1994) 'Community and public health approaches to the promotion of physical activity', *Medicine and Science in Sports and Exercise, 26*: 1405–12.

King, A.C., Blair, S.N., Bild, D.E., Dishman, R.K., Dubbert, P.M., Marcus, B.H., Oldridge, N.B., Paffenbarger, R.S., Powell, K.E. and Yeager, K.K. (1992) 'Determinants of physical activity and interventions in adults', *Medicine and Science in Sports and Exercise, 24*: S221–S236.

King, C., Siegel, M., Celebucki, C. and Connolly, G.N. (1998) 'Adolescent exposure to cigarette advertising in magazines: an evaluation of brand-specific advertising in relation to youth readership', *Journal of the American Medical Association, 279*: 516–20.

Kinsey, A.C., Pomeroy, W.B. and Martin, C.E. (1948) *Sexual Behaviour in the Human Male.* Philadelphia: W.B. Saunders.

Kinsey, A.C., Pomeroy, W.B., Martin, C.E. and Gebhard, P.H. (1953) *Sexual Behaviour in the Human Female.* Philadelphia: W.B. Saunders.

Kister, M.C. and Patterson, C.J. (1980) 'Children's conception of the causes of illness: understanding of contagion and use of imminent justice', *Child Development, 51*: 834–46.

Klatsky, A.L., Friedman, G.D. and Siegelaub, A.B. (1981) 'Alcohol and mortality: a ten year Kaiser-Permanente experience', *Annals of Internal Medicine, 95*: 130–45.

Kleinman, A. (1980) *Patients and Healers in the Context of Culture.* Berkeley, CA: University of California Press.

Kleinman, A., Wang, W,-Z., Li, S.-C., Cheng, X.-M., Dai, X.-Y., Li, K.-T. and Kleinman, J. (1995) 'The social course of epilepsy: chronic illness as social experience in interior China', *Social Science and Medicine, 40*: 1319–30.

Klonoff, E.A. and Landrine, H. (1993) 'Cognitive representations of bodily parts and products: implications for health behavior', *Journal of Health Behavior, 16*: 497–508.

Klonoff, E.A. and Landrine, H. (1994) 'Culture and gender diversity in common-sense beliefs about the causes of six illnesses', *Journal of Behavioral Medicine, 17*: 407–18.

Kobasa, S.C. (1979) 'Stressful life events and health: an enquiry into hardiness', *Journal of Personality and Social Psychology, 37*: 1–11.

Krantz, D.S. and Raisen, S.E. (1988) 'Environmental stress, reactivity and ischaemic heart disease', *British Journal of Medical Psychology, 61*: 3–16.

Kreps, G.L. (1988) 'Relational communication in health care', *Southern Speech Communication Journal, 53*: 344–59.

Kreps, G.L. (1996a) 'Promoting a consumer orientation to health care and health promotion', *Journal of Health Psychology, 1*: 41–8.

Kreps, G.L. (1996b) 'Guest editorial. Messages and meanings: health communication and health psychology', *Journal of Health Psychology, 1*: 259–60.

Krieger, (1987) 'Shades of difference: theoretical underpinnings of the medical controversy on black/white differences in the United States, 1830–1870', *International Journal of Health Services, 17*: 259–78.

Kristensson, H., Ohlin, H., Hulten-Nosslin, M.B. et al. (1983) 'Identification and intervention of heavy drinking in middle aged men: results and follow 24, 60 months of long term study with randomised control', *Alcoholism: Clinical and Experimental Research, 7*: 203–9.

Kuhn, T.S. (1970) *The Structure of Scientific Revolutions.* Chicago: University of Chicago Press.

Kunesh, M.A., Hasbrook, C.A. and Lewthwaite, R. (1992) 'Physical activity socialization: peer interactions and affective responses among a sample of sixth grade girls', *Sociology of Sport Journal, 9*: 385–96.

Kunst, A. and Mackenbach, J. (1994) *Measuring Socioeconomic Inequalities in Health.* Copenhagen: World Health Organization Regional Office for Europe.

Kurdek, L.A. (1991a) 'The dissolution of gay and lesbian couples', *Journal of Social and Personal Relationships, 8*: 265–78.

Kurdek, L.A. (1991b) 'Sexuality in homosexual and heterosexual couples', in K.

McKinney and S. Sprecher (eds), *Sexuality in Close Relationships*. Hillsdale, NJ: Lawrence Erlbaum.

Lagasse, R., Humblet, P., Lenaerts, A., Godin, I. and Moens, G. (1990) Health and social inequalities in Belgium', *Social Science and Medicine, 31*: 237–48.

Lalonde, M. (1974) *A New Perspective on the Health of Canadians*. Ottawa: Information Canada.

Lamb, S. and Sington, D. (1998) *Earth Story. The Shaping of our World*. London: BBC Books.

Landrine, H. (1997) 'From the back of the bus', *Journal of Health Psychology, 2*: 428–30.

Landrine, H. and Klonoff, E.A. (1994) 'Cultural diversity in causal attributions for illness: the role of the supernatural', *Journal of Behavioral Medicine, 17*: 181–93.

Larsen, K.M. and Smith, C.K. (1981) Assessment of non-verbal communication in the patient–physician interview', *Journal of Family Practice*: 12, 283–91.

Lau, R.R. and Hartman, K.A. (1983) 'Common sense representations of common illnesses', *Health Psychology, 2*: 167–86.

Laugesen, M. (1992) 'Tobacco advertising bans cut smoking', *British Journal of Addiction, 87*: 965–6.

Law, M. and Tang, J.L. (1995) 'An analysis of the effectiveness of interventions intended to help people stop smoking', *Archives of Internal Medicine, 155*: 1933–41.

Law, M.R., Frost, C.D. and Wald, N.J. (1991) 'By how much does dietary salt lower blood pressure? I – Analysis of observational data among populations', *British Medical Journal, 302*: 811–15.

Lawson, K., Wiggins, S., Green, T., Adam, S., Bloch, M., and Hayden, M.R. (1996) 'Adverse psychological events occurring in the first year after predictive testing for Huntington's disease', *Journal of Medical Genetics, 33*: 856–62.

Lazarus, R.S. (1966) *Psychological Stress and the Coping Process*. New York: McGraw-Hill.

Lazarus, R.S. and Folkman, S. (1984) *Stress, Appraisal and Coping*. New York: Springer.

Lazarus, R.S., Kanner, A.D. and Folkman, S. (1980) 'Emotions: a cognitive-phenomenological analysis', in R. Pluchik and H. Kellerman (eds), *Emotion: Theory, Research and Experience, Vol. 1, Theories of Emotion*. New York: Academic Press. pp. 189–217.

Le Breton, D. (1990) *Anthropologie du corps et modernité*. Paris, Presses Universitaires de France.

Lee, C. (1993) 'Factors related to the adoption of exercise among older women', *Journal of Behavioral Medicine, 16*: 323–34.

Legwold, G. (1995) 'Are we running from the truth about the risks and benefits of exercise?', *Physician and Sports Medicine, 13*: 136–48.

Lehmann, P., Mamboury, C. and Minder, C. (1990) 'Health and social inequalities in Switzerland', *Social Science and Medicine, 31*: 369–86.

Leino, E.V., Romelsjo, A., Shoemaker, C., Ager, C.R., Allebeck, P., Ferrer, H.P. (1998) 'Alcohol consumption and mortality. II. Studies of male populations', *Addiction, 93*: 205–18.

Leitch, A.M. (1995) 'Controversies in breast cancer screening', *Cancer Supplement, 76*: 2064–9.

Lepore, S.J. (1995) 'Cynicism, social support and cardiovascular reactivity', *Health Psychology, 14*: 210–16.

Lerman, C. (1997) 'Psychological aspects of genetic testing: introduction to the special issue', *Health Psychology, 16*: 3–7.

Lerman, C.E. and Rimer, B.K. (1993) 'Psychosocial impact of cancer screening', *Oncology, 7*: 67–72.

Lerman, C., Trock, B., Rimer, B., Boyce, A., Jepson, C. and Engstrom, P.F. (1991) 'Psychological and behavioral implications of abnormal mammograms', *Annals of Internal Medicine, 114*: 657–61.

Lerman, C., Trock, B., Rimer, B.K., Jepson, C., Brody, D. and Boyce, A. (1991) 'Psychological side-effects of breast cancer screening', *Health Psychology, 10*: 259–67.

Lerner, W.D. and Fallon, H.J. (1985) 'The alcohol withdrawal syndrome', *New England Journal of Medicine, 313*: 951–2.

Leshan, L.L. and Worthington, R.E. (1956) 'Personality as a factor in the pathogenesis of cancer: a review of the literature', *British Journal of Medical Psychology, 29*: 49–56.

Lesko, N. (1988) 'The curriculum of the body: lessons from a Catholic high school', in L. Roman, L. Christian-Smith and E. Ellsworth (eds), *Becoming Feminine*. London: Falmer Press. pp. 123–42.

Leslie, C. (1976) *Asian Medical Systems: A Comparative Study*. Los Angeles: University of California Press.

Leslie, C. and Young, A. (eds) (1992) *Paths to Asian Medical Knowledge*. Berkeley, CA: University of California Press.

Levav, I., Friedlander, Y., Kark, J.D. and Peritz, E. (1988) 'An epidemiologic study of mortality among bereaved parents', *New England Journal of Medicine, 319*: 457–61.

Levenson, R.W., Sher, K.J., Grossman, L.M., Newman, J. and Newlin, D.B. (1980) 'Alcohol and stress response dampening: pharmacological effects, expectancy, and tension reduction', *Journal of Abnormal Psychology, 89*: 528–38.

Leventhal, H. (1986) Symptom reporting: a focus on process', in S. McHugh and T.M. Vallis (eds), *Illness Behavior: A Multidisciplinary Model*. New York: Plenum Press. pp. 219–37.

Leventhal, H. (1999) Personal communication.

Leventhal, H. and Cleary, P.D. (1980) 'The smoking problem: a review of the research and theory in behavioral risk modification', *Psychological Bulletin, 88*: 370–405.

Leventhal, H., Meyer, D. and Nerenz, D. (1980) 'The commonsense representation of illness changes', in S. Rachman (ed.), *Contributions to Medical Psychology*, vol. 2. Oxford: Pergamon. pp. 7–30.

Leventhal, H., Leventhal, E.A. and Schaefer, P. (1989) *Vigilant Coping and Health Behaviour: A Lifespan Problem*. New Jersey: State University of New Jersey, Rutgers.

Levine, H.G. (1978) 'The discovery of addiction: changing conceptions of drunkenness in America', *Journal of Studies on Alcohol, 39*: 143–74.

Levine, H.G. (1980) 'Temperance and women in 19th century United States', in O.J. Kalant (ed.), *Alcohol and Drug Problems in Women: Research Advances in Alcohol and Drug Problems*. New York: Plenum Press. pp. 23–51.

Levitt, E.E. (1971) 'Reasons for smoking and not smoking given by school children', *Journal of School Health, 41*: 101–5.

Lewis, T., Osborn, L.M., Lewis, K., Broackert, J., Jacobsen, J. and Cherry, J.D. (1988) 'Influence of parental knowledge and opinions on 12-month diphtheria, tetanus, and pertussis vaccination rates', *American Journal of Diphtheria C, 142*: 283–6.

Ley, P. (1979) 'Memory for medical information', *British Journal of Social and Clinical Psychology, 18*: 245–56.

Ley, P. (1982) 'Satisfaction, compliance and communication', *British Journal of Clinical Psychology, 21*: 241–54.

Ley, P. (1988) *Communicating with Patients. Improving Communication, Satisfaction and Compliance*. London: Chapman & Hall.

Ley, P. and Florio, T. (1996) 'The use of readability formulas in health care', *Psychology, Health and Medicine, 1*: 7–28.

Ley, P. and Morris, L.A. (1985) 'Psychological aspects of written information for patients', in S.J. Rachman (ed.), *Contributions to Medical Psychology*, vol. 3. Oxford: Pergamon.

Li, J. and Taylor, B. (1993) 'Factors affecting uptake of measles, mumps, and rubella immunization', *British Medical Journal, 307*: 168–71.

Lidbrin, E., Elfving, J., Frisell, J. and Jonsson, E. (1996) 'Neglected aspects of false positive findings of mammography in breast cancer screening: analysis of false positive cases from the Stockholm trial', *British Medical Journal, 312*: 273–6.

Lightfoot, N., Steggles, S., Wilkinson, D., Bissett, R., Bakker, D., Darlington, G., Erola, K. and Miller, D. (1994) 'The short-term psychological impact of organized breast cancer screening', *Current Oncology, 1*: 206–11.

Lillard, A. (1998) 'Ethnopsychologies: cultural variations in theories of mind', *Psychological Bulletin, 123*: 3–32.

Lindenthal, J.J., Myers, J.K. and Pepper, J.P. (1972) 'Smoking, psychological status and stress', *Social Science and Medicine, 6*: 583–91.

Lipkus, I.M., Barefoot, J.C., Williams, R.B. and Siegler, I.C. (1994) 'Personality measures as predictors of smoking initiation and cessation in the UNC Alumni Heart Study', *Health Psychology, 13*: 149–55.

Litt, I.F. (1993) 'Health issues for women in the 1990s', in S. Matteo (ed.), *American Women in the Nineties: Today's Critical Issues*. Boston: Northeastern University Press. pp. 139–57.

Livison, N. and Leino, E.V. (1988) 'Cigarette smoking motives: factorial structure and gender differences in a longitudinal study', *International Journal of the Addictions, 23*: 535–44.

Loewenthal, K.M. and Bradley, C. (1996) 'Immunization uptake and doctors' perceptions of uptake in a minority group: implications for intervention', *Psychology, Health and Medicine, 1*: 223–30.

Logie, D.E. and Benatar, S.R. (1997) 'Africa in the 21st century: can despair turn to hope?', *British Medical Journal, 315*: 1444–6.

Low Income Project Team (1996) *Low Income, Food, Nutrition and Health: Strategies for Improvement*. London: Department of Health.

Ludvigsen, C. and Roberts, K. (1996) *Health Care Policies and Europe. The Implications for Practice*. Oxford: Butterworth-Heinemann.

Lugo, N.R. (1996) 'Empowerment education: a case study of the Resources Sisters/ Compañeras Program', *Health Education Quarterly, 23*: 281–9.

Lupton, D. (1995) *The Imperative of Health. Public Health and the Regulated Body*. London: Sage.

Lupton, D. (1997) 'Consumerism, reflexivity and the medical encounter', *Social Science and Medicine, 45*: 373–81.

Lurie, N., Slater, J., McGovern, P., Ekstrum, J., Quam, L. and Margolis, K. (1993) 'Preventive care for women: does the sex of the physician matter?', *New England Journal of Medicine, 329*: 478–82.

Luschen, G., Cockerham, W. and Kunz, G. (1996) 'The socio-cultural context of sport and health: problems of causal relations and structural interdependence', *Sociology of Sport Journal, 13*: 197–213.

Lynch, J.W. and Kaplan, G.A. (1997) 'Understanding how inequality in the distribution of income affects health', *Journal of Health Psychology, 2*: 297–314.

McCaul, K.D., Schroeder, D.M. and Reid, P.A. (1996a) 'Breast cancer worry and screening: some prospective data', *Health Psychology, 15*: 430–3.

McCaul, K.D., Dyche Branstetter, A., Schroeder, D.M. and Glasgow, R.M. (1996b) 'What is the relationship between breast cancer risk and mammography screening? a meta-analytic review', *Health Psychology, 15*: 423–9.

MacAuley, D. (1994) 'A history of physical activity, health and medicine', *Journal of the Royal Society of Medicine, 87*: 32–4.

McCormick, J.S. (1989) 'Cervical smears: a questionable practice? *Lancet, 333*: 207–9.

McCrae, R.R. and Costa, P.T. (1985) 'Updating Norman's "adequate taxonomy": intelligence and personality dimensions in natural language and in questionnaires', *Journal of Personality and Social Psychology, 49*: 710–21.

MacDonald, T.H. (1998) *Rethinking Health Promotion. A Global Approach*: London: Routledge.

McEwan, J., King, E. and Bickler, F. (1989) 'Attendance and non-attendance for breast screening at the South East London breast screening service', *British Medical Journal, 299*: 104–6.

McFadden, E.R. (1995) 'Improper patient techniques with metered dose inhalers: clinical consequences and solutions to misuse', *Journal of Allergy and Clinical Immunology, 96*: 278–83.

McGee, H. and Jenkinson, C. (1997) 'Quality of life: recent advances in theory and methods', *Psychology and Health, 12 (6)*: special issue.

McGinnis, J.M. and Foege, W.H. (1993) 'Actual causes of death in the United States', *Journal of the American Medical Association, 270*: 2207–12.

McGlynn, E. (1988) 'Physician job satisfaction: its measurement and use as an indication of system performance'. Unpublished doctoral dissertation, RAND Graduate School, Santa Monica, CA.

Macintyre, S. and Hunt, K. (1997) 'Socio-economic position, gender and health', *Journal of Health Psychology, 2*: 315–34.

Mackenbach, J. (1993) 'Inequalities in health in the Netherlands according to age, gender, marital status, levels of education, degree of organisation, and region', *European Journal of Public Health, 3*: 112–18.

McKenney, J.W., and Harrison, W.L. (1976) 'Drug-related hospital admissions', *American Journal of Hospital Pharmacy, 33*: 792–5.

McKeown, T. (1979) *The Role of Medicine*. Princeton, NJ: Princeton University Press.

McKie, L. (1993) 'Women's views of the cervical smear test: implications for nursing practice – women who have not had a smear test', *Journal of Advanced Nursing, 18*: 972–9.

McKie, L. (1995) 'The art of surveillance or reasonable prevention? The case of cervical screening', *Sociology of Health and Illness, 17*: 441–57.

McKinlay, J.B. (ed.) (1984) *Issues in the Political Economy of Health Care*. London: Tavistock.

Maclean, U., Sinfield, D., Klein, S., and Harnden, B. (1984) 'Women who decline breast screening', *Journal of Epidemiology and Community Health, 38*: 278–83.

McMurran, M. (1994) *The Psychology of Addiction*. London: Taylor & Francis.

McNeill, A.D. (1991) 'The development of dependence on smoking in children', *British Journal of Addiction, 86*: 589–92.

Maguire, P. (1984) 'Communication skills and patient care', in A. Steptoe and A. Mathews (eds), *Health Care and Human Behaviour*. London: Academic Press. pp. 153–73.

Maguire, P., Fairbairn, S. and Fletcher, C. (1989) 'Consultation skills of young doctors – benefits of undergraduate feedback training', in M Stewart and D. Roter (eds), *Communicating with Medical Patients*. London: Sage. pp. 124–37.

Mah, Z. and Bryant, H. (1992) 'Age as a factor in breast cancer knowledge, attitudes and screening behaviour', *Canadian Medical Association Journal, 146*: 2167–74.

Maheux, B., Dufort, F., Beland, F., Jacques, A. and Levesque, A. (1990) 'Female medical practitioners: more preventive and more patient-oriented?', *Medical Care, 28*: 87–92.

Maier, S.F. and Watkins, L.R. (1998) 'Cytokines for psychologists: implications of bidirectional immune-to-brain communication for understanding behaviour, mood and cognition', *Psychological Review, 105*: 83–107.

Maines, D. (1993) 'Narrative's moment and sociology's phenomena: toward a narrative sociology', *Sociological Quarterly, 34*: 17–38.

Makoul, G., Arntson, P. and Schofield, T. (1995) 'Health promotion in primary care: physician–patient communication and decision-making about prescription medications', *Social Science and Medicine, 41*: 1241–54.

Marcus, B.H. and Simkin, L.R. (1994) 'The transtheoretical model: applications to exercise behavior', *Medicine and Science in Sports and Exercise, 26*: 1400–4.

Marcus, B.H., Selby, V.C., Niaura, R.S. and Rossi, J.S. (1992a) 'Self-efficacy and the stages of exercise behavior change', *Research Quarterly in Exercise and Sport, 63*: 60–6.

Marcus, B.H., Banspach, S.W., Lefebvre, R.L., Rossi, J.S., Carleton, R.A. and Abrams, D.B. (1992b) 'Using the stages of change model to increase the adoption of physical activity among community participants', *American Journal of Health Promotion, 6*: 424–9.

Marcus, B.H., Eaton, C.A., Rossi, J.S. and Harlow, L.L. (1994a) 'Self-efficacy, decision making and stages of change: an integrative model of physical exercise', *Journal of Applied Social Psychology, 24*: 489–508.

Marcus, B.H., Emmons, K.M., Simkin, L.R., Taylor, E.R., Linnan, L., Rossi, J.S. and Abrams, D. (1994b) 'Comparison of stage-matched versus standard care physical activity interventions at the workplace', *Annals of Behavioral Medicine, 16*: S035.

Marcus, B.H., Bock, B.C., Pinto, B.M. and Clark, M.W. (1996) 'Exercise initiation, adoption, and maintenance', in J.L. van Raalte and B.W. Brewer (eds), *Exploring Sport and Exercise Psychology*. Washington, DC: American Psychological Association. pp. 133–58.

Markova, I. and Wilkie, P. (1987) 'Representations, concepts and social change: the phenomenon of AIDS', *Journal for the Theory of Social Behavior, 17*: 389–410.

Marks, D.F. (1992) 'Smoking cessation as a testbed for psychological theory: a group cognitive therapy programme with high long-term abstinence rates', *Journal of Smoking-Related Disorders, 3*: 69–77.

Marks, D.F. (1993) *The QUIT FOR LIFE Programme: An Easier Way to Stop Smoking and not Start Again*. Leicester: British Psychological Society.

Marks, D.F. (1995) 'Mortality and alcohol consumption: the dose-response relation is probably linear', *British Medical Journal, 310*: 325–6.

Marks, D.F. (1996) 'Health psychology in context', *Journal of Health Psychology, 1*: 7–21.

Marks, D.F. (1998) 'Addiction, smoking and health: developing policy-based interventions', *Psychology, Health and Medicine, 3*: 97–111.

Marks, D.F. (1999) 'Health psychology as agent of change. Reconstructing health psychology'. First International Conference on Critical and Qualititative Approaches to Health Psychology. St. John's, Newfoundland, Canada.

Marks, D.F. (2000) 'Settling down: the psychosocial consequences of sedentary living', London: Middlesex University Health Research Centre.

Marks, D.F. and Sykes, C.M. (1999) 'A randomised controlled trial of a psychological therapy for smokers and cost-effectiveness'. Conference of the European Health Psychology Society. Florence, Italy.

Marks, D.F., Brücher-Albers, C., Donker, F.J.S., Jepsen, Z., Rodriguez-Marin, J., Sodit, S. and Wallin Backman, B. (1998) 'Health psychology 2000: the development of professional health psychology', *Journal of Health Psychology, 3*: 149–60.

Marks, J.S., Halpin, T.J., Irvin, J.J. et al. (1979) 'Risk factors associated with failure to receive vaccinations', *Pediatrics, 64*: 304–9.

Marlatt, G.A. and Gordon, J.R. (eds) (1985) *Relapse Prevention.* New York: Guilford.

Marmot, M.G. and Davey Smith, G. (1997) 'Socio-economic differentials in health: the contribution of the Whitehall studies', *Journal of Health Psychology, 2*: 283–96.

Marsh, A. and McKay, S. (1994) *Poor Smokers.* London: Policy Studies Institute.

Marteau, T. (1989) 'Psychological costs of screening', *British Medical Journal, 299*: 527.

Marteau, T. (1990) 'Reducing the psychological costs', *British Medical Journal, 301*: 26–8.

Masek, B.J. (1982) 'Compliance and medicine', in D.M. Doleys, R.L. Meredith and A.R. Ciminero (eds), *Behavioral Medicine: Assessment and Treatment Strategies.* New York: Plenum Press. pp. 208–35.

Mason, J.W. (1971) 'A re-evaluation of the concept of "non-specificity" in stress theory', *Journal of Psychiatric Research, 8*: 323–33.

Mason, J.W. (1975) 'A historical view of the stress field: Parts 1 & 2', *Journal of Human Stress, 1*: 6–12, 22–36.

Masson, J. (1992) *The Assault on Truth: Freud and Sex Abuse.* London: Fontana.

Masters, W.H. and Johnson, V. (1966) *Human Sexual Response.* Boston: Little Brown.

Masunaga, R. (1972) *A Primer of Soto Zen: A Translation of Dogen's Shobogenzo Zuimonki.* London: Routledge.

Matarazzo, J.D. (1980) 'Behavioral health and behavioral medicine: frontiers for a new health psychology', *American Psychologist, 35*: 807–17.

Matarazzo, J.D. (1982) 'Behavioral health's challenge to academic, scientific and professional psychology', *American Psychologist, 37*: 1–14.

Matarazzo, J.D., Weiss, S.H., Herd, J.A., Miller, N.E. and Weiss, S.M. (1984) *Behavioral Health: A Handbook of Health Enhancement and Disease Prevention.* New York: Wiley.

Matsumoto, D., Kudoh, T. and Takeuchi, S. (1996) 'Changing patterns of individualism and collectivism in the United States and Japan', *Culture and Psychology, 2*: 77–107.

Matsumoto, D., Pun, K.K., Nakatani, M., Kadowaki, D., Weissman, M., McCarter, L., Fletcher, D. and Takeuchi, S. (1995) 'Cultural differences in attitudes, values, and beliefs about osteoporosis in first and second generation Japanese-American women', *Women and Health, 23*: 39–56.

Matthews, K.A. (1988) 'Coronary heart disease and Type A behaviours: update on and alternative to the Booth-Kewley and Friedman (1987) quantitative review', *Psychological Bulletin, 104*: 373–80.

May, D.S., Kiete, C.I., Funkhouser, E. and Fouad, M.N. (1999) 'Compliance with mammography guidelines: physician reommendation and patient adherence', *Preventive Medicine, 28*: 386–94.

Mazzulo, J.M. and Lasagna, L. (1972) 'Take thou . . . but is your patient really taking what you prescribed?', *Drug Therapeutics, 2*: 11–15.

Meeuwesen, L., Schaap, C. and van der Staak, C. (1991) 'Verbal analysis of doctor–patient communication', *Social Science and Medicine, 32*: 1143–50.

Meichenbaum, D. (1985) *Stress Innoculation Training*. New York: Pergamon.

Meichenbaum, D. and Turk, D.C. (1987) *Facilitating Treatment Adherence: A Practitioner's Guidebook*. New York: Plenum Press.

Mennella, J.A. and Beauchamp, G.K. (1996) 'The early development of human flavor preferences', in E.D. Capaldi (ed.), *Why We Eat What We Eat: The Psychology of Eating*. Washington, DC: American Psychological Association. pp. 83–112.

Menninger, K. (1938) *Man Against Himself*. New York: Harcourt Brace.

Meszaros, J.R., Asch, D.A., Baron, J., Hershey, J.C., Kunreuther, H. and Schwartz-Buzaglo, J. (1996) 'Cognitive processes and the decisions of some parents to forego pertussis vaccination for their children', *Journal of Clinical Epidemiology, 49*: 697–703.

Meyer, D., Leventhal, H. and Guttmann, M.N. (1985) 'Commonsense models of illness: the example of hypertension', *Health Psychology, 4*: 115–35.

Meyerowitz, B.E., Richardson, J., Hudson, S. and Leedham, B. (1998) 'Ethnicity and cancer outcomes: behavioral and psychosocial considerations', *Psychological Bulletin, 123*: 47–70.

Michell, L. and Amos, A. (1997) 'Girls, pecking order and smoking', *Social Science and Medicine, 44*: 1861–9.

Michie, S. and Marteau, T.M. (1996) 'Predictive genetic testing in children: the need for psychological research', *British Journal of Health Psychology, 1*: 3–14.

Michie, S., McDonald, V. and Marteau, T. (1996a) 'Understanding responses to predictive genetic testing: a grounded theory approach', *Psychology and Health, 11*: 455–70.

Michie, S., Axworthy, D., Weinman, J. and Marteau, T. (1996b) 'Genetic counselling: predicting patient outcomes', *Psychology and Health, 11*: 797–809.

Middleton, D. (1996) 'A discursive analysis of psychosocial issues: talk in a "parent group" for families who have children with chronic renal failure', *Psychology and Health, 11*: 243–60.

Millar, J. (1993) 'The continuing trend in rising poverty', in A. Sinfield (ed.), *Poverty, Inequality, and Justice*. Edinburgh: University of Edinburgh.

Miller, A.B. (1997) 'Canadian National Breast Screening Study: public health implications', *Canadian Journal of Public Health, 84*: 14–16.

Miller, N.H. (1997) 'Compliance with treatment regimens in chronic asymptomatic diseases', *American Journal of Medicine, 102*: 43–9.

Miller, P. McC. and Plant, M. (1996) 'Drinking, smoking, and illicit drug use among 15 and 16 year olds in the United Kingdom', *British Medical Journal, 313*: 394–7.

Miller, T.Q., Smith, T.W., Turner, C.W., Guijarro, M.L. and Hallet, A.J. (1996) 'A meta-analytic review of research on hostility and physical health', *Psychological Bulletin, 119*: 322–48.

Miller, W.R. (1996) 'Motivational interviewing: research, practice and puzzles', *Addictive Behaviours*, 21: 835–42.

Miller, W.R. and Brown, S.A. (1997) 'Why psychologists should treat alcohol and drug problems', *American Psychologist*, 52: 1269–79.

Miller, W.R. and Hester, R.K. (1986) 'The effectiveness of alcoholism treatment: What research reveals', in W.R. Miller and N. Heather (eds), *Treating Addictive Behaviours: Processes of Change*. New York: Plenum Press. pp. 121–74.

Miller, W.R., Brown, J.M., Simpson, T.L., Handmaker, N.S., Bien, T.H., Luckie, L.F., Montgomery, H.A., Hester, R.K. and Tonigan, J.S. (1995) 'What works? A methodological analysis of the alcohol treatment outcome literature', in R.K. Hester and W.R. Miller (eds) *Handbook of Alcoholism Treatment Approaches: Effective Alternatives*. Boston: Allyn and Bacon. pp. 12–44.

Mintz, S. (1997) 'Sugar and morality', in A.M. Brandt and P. Rozin (eds), *Morality and Health*. New York: Routledge. pp. 173–84.

Mirotznik, J., Feldman, L. and Stein, R. (1995) 'The Health Belief Model and adherence with a community center-based supervised coronary heart disease exercise program', *Journal of Community Health*, 20: 233–46.

Mischel, W. (1968) *Personality and Assessment*. New York: Wiley.

Mishler, E. (1984) 'The struggle between the voice of medicine and the voice of the lifeworld', in P. Conrad and R. Kern (eds), *The Sociology of Health and Illness: Critical Perspectives*. New York: St. Martin's Press.

Modood, T., Berthoud, R., Lakey, J., Nazroo, J., Smith, P., Virdee, S. and Beishon, S. (1997) *Ethnic Minorities in Britain: Diversity and Disadvantage*. London: Policy Studies Institute.

Montano, D.E. and Taplin, S.H. (1991) 'A test of an expanded theory of reasoned action to predict mammography participation', *Social Science and Medicine*, 32: 733–41.

Moore, L.L., Lombardi, D.A., White, M.J., Campbell, J.L., Oliveria, S.A. and Ellison, R.C. (1991) 'Influence of parents' activity levels on activity levels of young children', *Journal of Pediatrics*, 118: 215–19.

Morgan, P.P., Sheppard, R.J. and Finucone, R. (1984) 'Health beliefs and exercise habits in an employee fitness programme', *Canadian Journal of Applied Sports Science*, 9: 87–93.

Morgenstern, J., Langenbucher, J., Labouvie, E. and Miller, K.J. (1997) 'The comorbidity of alcoholism and personality disorders in a clinical population: prevalence rates and relation to alcohol typology variables', *Journal of Abnormal Psychology*, 106: 74–84.

Morinis, C.A. and Brilliant, G.E. (1981) 'Smallpox in northern India: diversity and order in a regional medical culture', *Medical Anthropology*, 5: 341–64.

Moscovici, S. (1984) 'The phenomenon of social representations', in R.M. Farr and S. Moscovici (eds), *Social Representations*. Cambridge: Cambridge University Press. pp. 3–70.

Moss-Morris, R., Petrie, K.J. and Weinman, J. (1996) 'Functioning in chronic fatigue syndrome: do illness perceptions play a regulatory role', *British Journal of Health Psychology*, 1: 15–26.

Mulatu, M.S. (1995) 'Lay beliefs about the causes of psychological and physical illnesses in Ethiopia', *Canadian Health Psychologist*, 3: 38–43.

Mulkay, M. (1991) *Sociology of Science: A Sociological Pilgrimage*. Milton Keynes: Open University Press.

Mullen, K. (1992) 'A question of balance: health behaviour and work context among male Glaswegians', *Sociology of Health and Illness, 14*: 73–95.

Murdock, G.P. (1937) 'Comparative data on the division of labour by sex', *Social Forces, 15*: 551–3.

Murdock, G.P. (1980) *Theories of Illness: A World Survey*. Pittsburgh: University of Pittsburgh Press.

Murray, C.J.L. and Lopez, A.D. (1997) 'Alternative projections of mortality and disability by cause 1990–2020: Global Burden of Disease Study', *Lancet, 349*: 1498–504.

Murray, M. (1983) 'The social context of smoking during adolescence', in W.F. Forbes, R.C. Frecker, D. Nostbakken (eds), *Proceedings of the Fifth World Conference on Smoking*. Ottawa: Canadian Council on Smoking and Health.

Murray, M. (1990) 'Lay representations of illness', in P. Bennett, J. Weinman and P. Spurgeon (eds), *Current Developments in Health Psychology*. Chur: Harwood Academic. pp. 63–92.

Murray, M. (1993) 'Social and cognitive representations of health and illness', in H. Schroder, K. Reschke, M. Johnston and S. Maes (eds), *Health Psychology: Potential in Diversity*. Regensburg: S. Roderer Verlag. pp. 124–31.

Murray, M. (1996) 'Autobiography and health psychology', *Canadian Health Psychologist, 4*: 35–7.

Murray, M. (1997a) 'A narrative approach to health psychology: background and potential', *Journal of Health Psychology, 2*: 9–20.

Murray, M. (1997b) *Narrative Health Psychology*. Palmerston North, NZ: Massey University.

Murray, M. and Chamberlain, K. (1998) 'Qualitative research in health psychology: developments and directions', *Journal of Health Psychology, 3*: 291–5.

Murray, M. and Jarrett, L. (1985) 'Young people's perception of health, illness and smoking', *Health Education Journal, 44*: 18–22.

Murray, M. and McMillan, C. (1988) *Working Class Women's Views of Cancer*. Belfast: Ulster Cancer Foundation.

Murray, M. and McMillan, C. (1993a) 'Gender differences in perceptions of cancer', *Journal of Cancer Education, 8*: 53–62.

Murray, M. and McMillan, C. (1993b) 'Health beliefs, locus of control, emotional control and women's cancer screening behaviour', *British Journal of Clinical Psychology, 32*: 87–100.

Murray, M., Kiryluk, S. and Swan, A.V. (1985) 'Relation between parents' and children's smoking behaviour and attitudes', *Journal of Epidemiology and Community Health, 39*: 169–74.

Murray, M., Swan, A.V. and Mattar, N. (1983) 'The task of nursing and risk of smoking', *Journal of Advanced Nursing, 8*: 131–8.

Murray, M., Jarrett, L., Swan, A.V. and Rumun, R. (1988) *Smoking Among Young Adults*. Aldershot: Gower.

Murray, M., Swan, A.V., Johnson, M. and Bewley, B. (1983a) 'Some factors associated with increased risk of smoking by children', *Journal of Child Psychology and Psychiatry, 24*: 223–32.

Murray, M., Swan, A.V., Bewley, B.R. and Johnson, M.R.D. (1983b) 'The development of smoking during adolescence: the MRC/Derbyshire smoking study', *International Journal of Epidemiology, 12*: 185–92.

Najavits, L.M. and Weiss, R.D. (1994) 'Variations in therapist effectiveness in the treatment of patients with substance abuse disorders: an empirical review', *Addiction, 89*: 679–88.

Nakajima, H. (1995) 'Presentation at the House of Commons, 19 June.

National Cancer Institute, Breast Cancer Screening Consortium (1990) 'Screening mammography: a missed clinical opportunity', *JAMA, 264*: 54–8.

National Center for Health Statistics (1994a) *Excess Deaths and other Mortality Measures for the Black Population: 1979–81 and 1991*. Hyattsville, MD: Public Health Service.

National Center for Health Statistics (1994b) *Healthy People 2000 Review, 1993*. Hyattsville, MD: Public Health Service.

National Health Strategy (1992) *Enough to Make You Sick: How Income and Environment Affect Health*. Canberra: Department of Health, Housing and Community Services. (No. 1).

Neimeyer, R.A. (1995) 'Constructivist psychotherapies: features, foundations, and future directions', in R.A. Neimeyer and M.J. Mahoney (eds), *Constructivism in Psychotherapy*. Washington, DC: American Psychological Association. pp. 11–38.

Neisser, U. (1976) *Cognition and Reality*. San Francisco: W.H. Freeman.

Nelson, K.M. and Talbert, R.L. (1996) 'Drug-related hospital admissions', *Pharmacotherapy, 16*: 701–7.

Nesbitt, P.D. (1973) 'Smoking, physiological arousal, and emotional response', *Journal of Personality and Social Psychology, 25*: 137–44.

Ness, A.R. and Powles, J.W. (1997) 'Fruit and vegetables, and cardiovascular disease: a review', *International Journal of Epidemiology, 26*: 1–13.

Neve, M., Nutton, V., Porter, R. and Wear, A. (eds) *The Western Medical Tradition 800 BC to AD 1800*. Cambridge: Cambridge University Press.

New, S.J. and Senior, M. (1991) '"I don't believe in needles": qualitative aspects of study into the uptake of infant immunisation in two English health authorities, *Social Science and Medicine, 33*: 509–18.

Nightingale, D.J. and Cromby, J. (1999) *Social Constructionist Psychology: A Critical Analysis of Theory and Practice*. Milton Keynes: Open University Press.

NIH Consensus Development Panel on Physical Activity and Cardiovascular Health (1996) 'Physical activity and cardiovascular health', *Journal of the American Medical Association, 276*: 241–6.

Nolan, B., (1990) 'Socioeconomic mortality differentials in Ireland', *The Economic and Social Review, 21*: 193–208.

NOP Omnibus Services (1992) *Smoking Habits 1991*. London: NOP.

Nordström, G. and Berglund, M. (1987) 'A prospective study of successful long-term adjustment in alcohol dependence: social drinking versus abstinence', *Journal of Studies on Alcohol, 48*: 95–103.

Norman, P. and Bennett, P. (1996) 'Health locus of control', in M. Conner and P. Norman (eds), *Predicting Health Behaviour*. Buckingham: Open University Press. pp. 62–94.

Norman, P., Bennett, P., Smith, C. and Murphy, S. (1998) 'Health locus of control and health behaviour', *Journal of Health Psychology, 3*: 171–80.

Norton, R.W. (1978) 'Foundation of a communicator style construct', *Human Communication Research, 4*: 99–112.

Nutton, V. (1995) 'Medicine in the Greek world, 800–50BC', in L.I. Conrad, M. Neve, V. Nutton, R. Porter and A. Wear (eds), *The Western Medical Tradition 800 BC–1800 AD*. Cambridge: Cambridge University Press. pp. 11–38.

O'Brien, M. and Petrie, K.J. (1996) 'Examining patient participation in medical consultations: a combined quantitative and qualitative approach', *Psychology and Health*, 11: 871–90.

Odom, S.L., Peck, C.A., Hanson, H., Beckham, P.J., Kaiser, K.P., Lieber, J., Brown, W.H., Horn, E.M. and Schwartz, I.S. (1996) 'Inclusion at the pre-school level: an ecological systems analysis. Social Policy Report', *Society for Research on Child Development*, 10 (2): 18–30.

Office of Inspector General (1990) *Medication Regimens: Causes of Non-compliance.* Washington, DC: Government Printing Office. DHHS Publication no. OEI-04–89–89121.

Office of Population Censuses and Surveys (1985) *General Household Survey 1983.* London: HMSO.

Office of Population Censuses and Surveys (1994) *Mortality Statistics: Cause. Series DH2 No. 19.* London: HMSO.

Ogden, J. (1992) *Fat Chance.* London: Routledge.

Ogden, J. (1997) 'The rhetoric and reality of psychosocial theories: a challenge to biomedicine', *Journal of Health Psychology*, 2: 21–9.

O'Leary, A. (1990) 'Stress, emotion and human immune function', *Psychological Bulletin*, 108: 363–82.

O'Leary, A. and Helgeson, V.S. (1997) 'Psychosocial factors and women's health: integrating mind, heart, and body', in S.J. Gallant, G.P. Keita and R. Royak-Schaler (eds) *Health Care for Women: Psychological, Social, and Behavioral Influences.* Washington, DC: American Psychological Association. pp. 25–40.

Oliver, R.L. and Berger, P.K. (1979) 'A path analysis of preventive care decision models', *Journal of Consumer Research*, 6: 113–22.

Ong, L.M.L., de Haes, J.C.J.M., Hoos, A.M. and Lammes, F.B. (1995) 'Doctor–patient communication: a review of the literature', *Social Science and Medicine*, 40: 903–18.

Orme, C.M. and Binik, Y.M. (1989) 'Consistency of adherence across regimen demands', *Health Psychology*, 8: 27–43.

Otten, J.D.M., van Dijck, J.A., Peer, P.G., Straatman, H., Verbeek, A.L., Mravunac, M., Hendriks, J.H. and Holland, R. (1996) 'Long term breast cancer screening in Nijmegen, The Netherlands: the nine rounds from 1975–92', *Journal of Epidemiology and Community Health*, 50: 353–8.

Ovretveit, J. (1998) *Evaluating Health Interventions.* Buckingham: Open University Press.

Oxfam (1991) *The World: A Third World Guide.* London: Oxfam.

Oygard, L. and Anderssen, N. (1998) 'Social influences and leisure-time physical activity levels in young people: a twelve-year follow-up study', *Journal of Health Psychology*, 3: 59–69.

Pallonen, U.E., Prochaska, J.O., Velicer, W.F., Prokhorov, A.V. and Smith, N.F. (1998) 'Stages of acquisition and cessation for adolescent smoking: an empirical integration', *Addictive Behaviors*, 23: 303–24.

Paludi, M.A. (1992) *The Psychology of Women.* Dubuque, IA: Brown and Benchmark.

Pappas, G., Queen, S., Hadden, W. and Fisher, G. (1993) 'The new increasing disparity in mortality between socioeconomic groups in the United States, 1960 and 1986', *New England Journal of Medicine*, 329: 103–9.

Park, L. (1992) *Cross-cultural Explanations of Illness: Murdock Revisited.* Chicago: Committee on Human Development, University of Chicago.

Park, R.J. (1988) 'How active were early populations?', in R. Malina and H. Eckert (eds), *Physical Activity in Early and Modern Populations*. Champaign: Human Kinetics. pp. 13–21.

Parker, I. (1992) *Discourse Dynamics*. London: Routledge.

Parker, I. (ed.) (1998) *Social Constructionism, Discourse and Realism*. London: Sage.

Parker, S.L., Tong, T., Bolden, S. and Wingo, P.A. (1996) 'Cancer statistics, 1996', *CA Cancer Journal*, 65: 5–27.

Pate, R.R., Pratt, M., Blair, S.N., Haskell, W.L., Macera, C.A., Bouchard, C., Buchner, D., Caspersen, C.J., Ettinger, W., Heath, G.W., King, A.C. et al. (1995) 'Physical activity and public health: a recommendation from the Centers for Disease Control and Prevention and the American College of Sports Medicine', *Journal of the American Medical Association*, 273: 402–7.

Pavlov, I.P. (1927) *Conditioned Reflexes*. Oxford: Oxford University Press.

Peckham, C., Bedford, H., Senturia, Y. and Ades, A. (1989) *National Immunization Study: Factors Influencing Immunization Uptake in Childhood*. Horsham: Action Reserach for the Crippled Child.

Pederson, L.L., Koval, J.J. and O'Connor, K. (1997) 'Are psychosocial factors related to smoking in grade-6 students?', *Addictive Behavior*, 22: 169–81.

Pelosi, A.J. and Appleby, L. (1992) 'Psychological influences on cancer and ischaemic heart disease', *British Medical Journal*, 304: 1295–8.

Pelosi, A.J. and Appleby, L. (1993) 'Personality and fatal diseases', *British Medical Journal*, 306: 1666–7.

Pendleton, D. and Bochner, S. (1980) 'The communication of medical information in general practice consultations as a function of the patients' social class', *Social Science and Medicine*, 14A: 669–73.

Peterson, C., Seligman, M.E.P. and Vaillant, G.E. (1988) 'Pessimistic explanatory style is a risk factor for physical illness: a thirty five year longitudinal study', *Journal of Personality and Social Psychology*, 55: 23–7.

Peto, R., Lopez, A., Borcham, J., Thun, M. and Heath, C. (1992) 'Mortality from tobacco in developed countries: indirect estimates from national vital statistics', *Lancet*, 339: 1268–78.

Petrie, K.J., Weinman, J., Sharpe, N. and Buckley, J. (1996) 'Role of patients' view of their illness in predicting return to work and functioning after myocardial infarction: longitudinal study', *British Medical Journal*, 312: 1191–4.

Petticrew, M., Fraser, J.M. and Regan, M.F. (1999) 'Adverse life events and risk of breast cancer: a meta-analysis', *British Journal of Health Psychology*, 4: 1–17.

Piaget, J. (1930) *The Child's Conception of Physical Causality*. London: Routledge and Kegan Paul.

Pierce, J.P. and Gilpin, E.A. (1995) 'A historical analysis of tobacco marketing and the uptake of smoking by youth in the United States: 1890–1977', *Health Psychology*, 14: 500–8.

Pierce, J.P., Fiore, M.C., Novotny, T.E., Hatziandreu, E.J. and Davis, R.M. (1989) 'Trends in cigarette smoking in the United States: educational differences are increasing', *Journal of the American Medical Association*, 261: 56–60.

Pierce, J.P., Choi, W.S., Gilpin, E.A., Farkas, A.J. and Merritt, R.K. (1996) 'Validation of susceptibility as a predictor of which adolescents take up smoking in the United States', *Health Psychology*, 15: 355–61.

Pierce, J.P., Choi, W.S., Gilpin, E.A., Farkas, A.J. and Berry, C.C. (1998) 'Tobacco industry promotion of cigarettes and adolescent smoking', *Journal of the American Medical Association*, 279: 511–15.

Pill, R. and Stott, N. (1982) 'Concepts of illness causation and responsibility: some preliminary data from a sample of working class mothers', *Social Science and Medicine*, 16: 43–52.

Pinell, P. (1987) 'How do cancer patients express their points of view', *Sociology of Health and Illness*, 9: 25–44.

Pinney, E.M., Gerrard, M. and Denney, N.W. (1987) 'The Pinney Sexual Satisfaction Inventory', *Journal of Sex Research*, 23: 233–51.

Piperno, A. and Di Orio, F. (1990) 'Social differences in health and utilisation of health services in Italy', *Social Science and Medicine*, 31: 305–12.

Pitts, M. (1996) *The Psychology of Preventive Health*. London: Routledge.

Plante, T.G. and Rodin, J. (1990) 'Physical fitness and enhanced psychological health', *Current Psychology: Research and Reviews*, 9: 3–24.

Pleck, J.H., Sonnenstein, F.L. and Ku, L.C. (1990) 'Contraceptive attitudes and intention to use condoms in sexually experienced and inexperienced adolescent males', *Journal of Family Issues*, 11: 294–312.

Plueckhan, V.D. (1982) 'Alcohol consumption and death by drowning in adults: a 24 year epidemiological analysis', *Journal of Studies on Alcohol*, 43: 445–52.

Plummer, K. (1996) *Telling Sexual Stories. Power, Change and Social Worlds*: London: Routledge.

Polich, J.M., Armor, D.J. and Braiker, H.B. (1980) *The Course of Alcoholism: Four Years after Treatment*. Santa Monica, CA: Rand.

Pollock, K. (1988) 'On the nature of social stress: production of a modern mythology', *Social Science and Medicine*, 26: 381–92.

Pomerleau, C.S. (1997) 'Co-factors for smoking and evolutionary psychobiology', *Addiction*, 92: 397–408.

Pomerlau, D.F. (1979) 'Behavioral factors in the establishment, maintenance, and cessation of smoking', in *Smoking and Health: A Report of the Surgeon General*. Washington, DC: US Department of Health, Education and Welfare. pp. 161–2.

Popham, R.E., Schmidt, W. and Israelstam, S. (1984) 'Heavy alcohol consumption and physical health problems: a review of the epidemiological evidence', in R.G. Smart, H.D. Cappell, F.B. Glaser, Y. Israel, H. Kalant, R.E. Popham, W. Schmidt and E.M. Sellers (eds), *Research Advances in Alcohol and Drug Problems, Volume 8*. New York: Plenum Press. pp. 143–59.

Porter, R. (1997) *The Greatest Benefit to Mankind: A Medical History of Humanity*. New York, Norton.

Potter, J. and Wetherell, M. (1987) *Discourse and Social Psychology*. London: Sage.

Potvin, L., Camirand, J. and Beland, F. (1995) 'Patterns of health services utilization and mammography use among women aged 50 to 59 years in the Quebec Medicare system', *Medical Care*, 33: 515–30.

Powell, K.E. and Pratt, M. (1996) 'Physical activity and health', *British Medical Journal*, 313: 126–7.

Powles, J. (1992) 'Changes in disease patterns and related social trends', *Social Science and Medicine*, 35: 377–87.

Pratt, O.E. (1982) 'Alcohol and the developing fetus', *British Medical Bulletin*, 38: 48–52.

Prochaska, J.O. (1984) *Systems of Psychotherapy: A Transtheoretical Analysis*, 2nd edn. Pacific Grove, CA: Brooks-Cole.

Prochaska, J.O. and DiClemente, C.C. (1983) 'Stages and processes of self-change in smoking. Toward an integrative model of change', *Journal of Consulting and Clinical Psychology*, 51: 520–8.

Prochaska, J. and DiClemente, C.C. (1992) *The Transtheoretical Approach: Crossing the Traditional Boundaries of Therapy*. Homewood, IL: Dow Jones/Irwin.

Prochaska, J.O. and Velicer, W.F. (1996) 'On models, methods and premature conclusions', *Addiction, 91*: 1281–3.

Prochaska, J.O. and Velicer, W.F. (1997a) 'Misinterpretations and misapplications of the transtheoretical model', *American Journal of Health Promotion, 12*: 11–12.

Prochaska, J.O. and Velicer, W.F. (1997b) 'The transtheoretical model of health behavior change', *American Journal of Health Promotion, 12*: 38–48.

Prochaska, J.O., Norcross, J.C. and DiClemente, C.C. (1994) *Changing for Good*. New York: William Morrow.

Project MATCH Research Group (1997) 'Matching alcoholism treatments to client heterogeneity: Project MATCH posttreatment drinking outcomes', *Journal of Studies on Alcohol, 58*: 7–29.

Quah, S.-H. and Bishop, G.D. (1996) 'Seeking help for illness: the roles of cultural orientation and illness cognition', *Journal of Health Psychology, 1*: 209–22.

Query, J.L. and Kreps, G.L. (1996) 'Testing a relational model for health communication competence among caregivers for individuals with Alzheimer's disease', *Journal of Health Psychology, 1*: 335–51.

Radley, A. (1993) 'The role of metaphor in adjustment to chronic illness', in A. Radley (ed.), *Worlds of Illness: Biographical and Cultural Perspectives on Health and Disease*. London: Routledge. pp. 27–48.

Radley, A. (1994) *Making Sense of Illness: The Social Psychology of Health and Illness*. London: Sage.

Radley, A. and Billig, M. (1996) 'Accounts of health and illness: dilemmas and representations', *Sociology of Health and Illness, 18*: 220–40.

Raeburn, J. and Rootman, I. (1998) *People-centred Health Promotion*. Chichester: Wiley.

Raffle, D.E. (1997) 'Deaths from cervical cancer began falling before screening programmes were established', *British Medical Journal, 315*: 953–4.

Ragland, D.R. and Brand, R.J. (1988) 'Type A behaviour and mortality from coronary heart disease', *New England Journal of Medicine, 318*: 65–9.

Rakowski, W., Dube, C.E., Marcus, B.H., Prochaska, J.O., Velicer, W.F. and Abrams, D.B. (1992) 'Assessing elements of women's decisions about mammography', *Health Psychology, 11*: 111–18.

Ramirez, A.J., Richards, M.A., Gregory, W. and Craig, T.K.J. (1990) 'Psychological correlates of hormone receptor status in breast cancer', *Lancet, 335*: 1408.

Randhawa, G. (1995) 'Organ donation: social and cultural issues, *Nursing Standard, 9*: 25–7.

Rang, E.H. and Tod, E. (1988) 'Problems of cervical screening programmes', *Journal of the Royal College of General Practitioners, 38*: 267–9.

Rappaport, J. (1987) 'Terms of empowerment/examples of prevention: towards a theory for community psychology', *American Journal of Counseling Psychology, 15*: 121–49.

Ratzan, S.C. (1996) 'Introduction', *Journal of Health Communication. International Perspectives, 1*: v–vii.

Read, D.J., Killoran, A.J., McNeill, A.D. and Chambers, J.S. (1992) 'Choosing the most effective health promotion options for reducing a nation's smoking prevalence', *Tobacco Control, 1*: 185–97.

Reading, R., Calver, A., Openshaw, S. and Jarvis, S. (1994) 'Do interventions that improve immunization uptake also reduce social inequalities in uptake', *British Medical Journal, 308*: 1142–4.

Reddy, C.V. (1989) 'Parents' beliefs about vaccination', *British Medical Journal, 299*: 739.

Reed, D.M., LaCroix, A.Z., Karasek, R.A., Miller, D. and MacLean, C.A. (1989) 'Occupational strain and the incidence of coronary heart disease', *American Journal of Epidemiology, 129*: 495–502.

Reed, G.M., Kemeny, M.E., Taylor, S.E., Wang, H.J. and Visscher, B.R. (1994) 'Realistic acceptance as a predictor of decreased survival time in gay men with AIDS', *Health Psychology, 13*: 299–307.

Reich, W. (1948) *The Cancer Biopathy*. New York: Farrer, Straus & Giroux.

Reich, W. (1949) *Character Analysis*. New York: Farrar, Straus & Giroux.

Reiss, I.L. (1991) 'Sexual pluralism: ending America's sexual crisis', *SIECUS Report*, February–March.

Reynolds, K.D., Killen, J.D., Bryson, S.W., Maron, D.J., Taylor, C.B., Maccoby, N. and Farquhar, J.W. (1990) 'Psycho-social predictors of physical activity in adolescents', *Preventive Medicine, 19*: 541–51.

Rhodes, T. (1994) 'Outreach, community change and community empowerment: contradictions for public health and health promotion', in P. Aggleton, P. Davies and G. Hart (eds), *AIDS. Foundations for the Future*. London: Taylor & Francis. pp. 48–64.

Rhodes, T. and Hartnoll, R. (1991) 'Reaching the hard to reach: models of HIV outreach education', in P. Aggleton, G. Hart and P. Davies (eds), *AIDS. Responses, Interventions and Care*. London: Falmer Press. pp. 233–48.

Richards, T. (1996) 'European health policy: must redefine its raison d'être', *British Medical Journal, 312*: 1622–3.

Richmond, R.L. and Anderson, P. (1994) 'Research in general practice for smokers and excessive drinkers in Australia and the UK. I. Interpretation of results', *Addiction, 89*: 35–40.

Ricoeur, P. (1981) *Hermeneutics and the Human Sciences*. Cambridge: Cambridge University Press.

Rimer, B.K. (1990) 'Perspectives on intrapersonal theories in health education and health behavior', in K. Glanz, F.M. Lewis and B.K. Rimer (eds), *Health Behavior and Health Education*. San Francisco: Jossey-Bass.

Rimer, B.K., Kasper Keintz, M., Kessler, H.B., Engstrom, P.F. and Rosan, J.R. (1989) 'Why women resist screening mammography: patient-related barriers', *Radiology, 172*: 139–51.

Rise, J. (1992) 'An empirical study of the decision to use condoms among Norwegian adolescents using the theory of reasoned action', *Journal of Community and Applied Social Psychology, 2*: 185–97.

Robins, L.N. (1990) 'Steps towards evaluating post-traumatic stress reaction as a psychiatric disorder', *Journal of Applied Social Psychology, 20*: 1674–7.

Robinson, I. (1990) 'Personal narratives, social careers and medical courses: analysing life trajectories in autobiographies of people with multiple sclerosis', *Social Science and Medicine, 30*: 1173–86.

Robinson, J.I. and Rogers, M.A. (1994) 'Adherence to exercise programmes: recommendations', *Sports Medicine, 17*: 39–52.

Robinson, L.A. and Klesges, R.C. (1997) 'Ethnic and gender differences in risk factors for smoking onset', *Health Psychology, 16*: 499–505.

Robinson, T.E. and Berridge, K.C. (1993) 'The neural basis of drug craving: an incentive sensitisation theory of addiction', *Brain Research Reviews, 18*: 247–91.

Rogers, R., (1992) 'Living and dying in the USA: sociodemographic determinants of death among blacks and whites', *Demography, 29*: 287–303.

Room, R. and Day, N. (1974) 'Alcohol and mortality', in M. Keller (ed.), *Second Special Report to the U.S. Congress: Alcohol and Health.* Washington, DC: US Government Printing Office. pp. 123–32.

Rose, G. (1992) *The Strategy of Preventive Medicine.* Oxford: Oxford University Press.

Rose, J.E. (1996) 'Nicotine addiction and treatment', *Annual Review of Medicine, 47*: 493–507.

Rose, S., Kamin, L.J. and Lewontin, R.C. (1984) *Not in our Genes.* London: Penguin.

Rosenberg, H. (1993) 'Prediction of controlled drinking by alcoholics and problem drinkers', *Psychological Bulletin, 113*: 129–39.

Rosengren, A., Tibblin, G. and Wilhelmsen, L. (1991) 'Self-perceived psychological stress and incidence of coronary artery disease in middle-aged men', *American Journal of Cardiology, 68*: 1171–5.

Rosenman, R.H. (1978) 'The interview method of assessment of the coronary-prone behaviour pattern', in T.M. Dembrowski, S.M. Weiss, J.L. Shields, S.G. Haynes and M. Feinleib (eds), *Coronary-prone Behaviour.* New York: Springer-Verlag. pp. 55–70.

Rosenman, R.H., Brand, R.J., Jenkins, C.D., Friedman, M., Straus, R. and Wurm, M. (1975) 'Coronary heart disease in the Western Collaborative Group Study: final follow-up experience of 8.5 years', *Journal of the American Medical Association, 233*: 872–7.

Rosenstock, I.M. (1966) 'Why people use health services', *Millbank Memorial Fund Quarterly, 44*: 94–124.

Ross, L. (1977) 'The intuitive psychologist and his shortcomings: distortion in the attribution process', in L. Berkowitz (ed.), *Advances in Experimental Social Psychology (Vol. 10).* New York: Academic Press. pp. 174–220.

Ross, M.W. and Rosser, B.R.S. (1989) Education and AIDS risks: a review', *Health Education Research. Theory and Practice, 4*: 273–84.

Roter, D.L. (1977) 'Patient-participation in the patient-provider interaction: the effects of patient question-asking on the quality of interaction, satisfaction and compliance', *Health Education Monographs, 5*: 281–330.

Roter, D. (1989) 'Which facets of communication have strong effects on outcome – a meta-analysis', in M. Stewart and D. Roter (eds), *Communicating with Medical Patients.* London: Sage.

Roth, H.P., Caron, H.S. and Hsi, B.P. (1970) 'Measuring intake of a prescribed medication: a bottle count and a tracer technique compared', *Clinical Pharmacology and Therapeutics, 11*: 228–30.

Rotter, J.B. (1954) *Social Learning and Clinical Psychology.* Englewood Cliffs, NJ: Prentice-Hall.

Rounds, J.B. and Zevon, M.A. (1993) 'Cancer stereotypes: a multidimensional scaling analysis', *Journal of Behavioral Medicine, 16*: 485–96.

Royal College of Physicians (1962) *Smoking and Health.* London: RCP.

Royal Colleges of Physicians (1991) *Alcohol and the Heart in Perspective: Sensible Limits Reaffirmed.* London: Royal Colleges of Physicians.

Royal Colleges of Physicians (1995) *Alcohol and the Public Health.* London: Macmillan.

Rozin, E. (1982) 'The structure of cuisine', in L.M. Barker (ed.), *The Psychobiology of Human Food Selection*. Westport, CT: AVI. pp. 192–202.

Rozin, P. (1984) 'The acquisition of food habits and preferences', in J.D. Mattarazzo, S.M. Weiss, J.A. Herd, N.E. Miller and S.M. Weiss (eds), *Behavioral Health: A Handbook of Health Enhancement and Disease Prevention*. New York: Wiley. pp. 590–607.

Rozin, P. (1996) 'Sociocultural influences on human food selection', in E.D. Capaldi (ed.), *Why We Eat What We Eat: The Psychology of Eating*. Washington, DC: American Psychological Association. pp. 233–63.

Ruiz, P. and Ruiz, P.P. (1983) 'Treatment compliance among Hispanics', *Journal of Operational Psychiatry*, 14: 112–14.

Sackett, D.L. and Snow, J.C. (1979) 'The magnitude of compliance and non-compliance', in R.B. Haynes, D.L. Sackett and D.W. Taylor (eds), *Compliance in Health Care*. Baltimore, MD: Johns Hopkins University Press. pp. 11–22.

Saillant, F. (1990) 'Discourse, knowledge and experience of cancer: a life story', *Culture, Medicine and Psychiatry*, 14: 81–104.

St. Clair, L., Watkins, C.J. and Billinghurst, B. (1996) 'Differences in meanings of health: an exploratory study of general practitioners and their patients', *Family Practice*, 13: 511–16.

Salazar, M. (1994) 'A qualitative description of breast self-examination beliefs', *Health Education Quarterly*, 9: 343–54.

Sallis, J.F., Hovell, M.F., Hotstetter, C.R., Fauches, P. et al. (1989) 'A multivariate study of determinants of vigorous exercise in a community sample', *Preventive Medicine*, 18: 20–34.

Sallis, J.F., Hovell, M.F. and Hofstetter, C.R. (1992a) 'Predictors of adoption and maintenance of vigorous physical activity in men and women', *Preventive Medicine*, 21: 237–51.

Sallis, J.F., Simons-Morton, B.G., Stone, E.J., Corbin, C.B., Epstein, L.H., Faucette, N., Iannotti, R.J., Killen, J.D., Klesges, R.C., Petray, C.K., Rowland, T.W. and Taylor, W.C. (1992b) 'Determinants of physical activity and interventions in youth', *Medicine and Science in Sports and Exercise*, 24: Supplement: S248–S257.

Sarason, I.G., Mankowski, E.S., Peterson, A.V. and Dinh, K.T. (1992) 'Adolescents' reasons for smoking', *Journal of School Health*, 62: 185–90.

Sarbin, T.R. (ed.) (1986) *Narrative Psychology: The Storied Nature of Human Conduct*. New York: Praeger.

Saunders, B. (1985) 'The case for controlling alcohol consumption', in N. Heather, I. Robertson and P. Davies (eds), *The Misuse of Alcohol: Crucial Issues in Dependence, Treatment and Prevention*. London: Croom Helm. pp. 214–31.

Sayette, M.A. (1993) 'An appraisal-disruption model of alcohol's effects on stress responses in social drinkers', *Psychological Bulletin*, 114: 459–76.

Sayette, M.A. and Hufford, M.R. (1997) 'Alcohol abuse/alcoholism', in A. Baum, S. Newman, J. Weinman, R. West and C. McManus (eds), *Cambridge Handbook of Psychology, Health and Medicine*. Cambridge: Cambridge University Press. pp. 347–50.

Scaf-Klomp, W., Sanderman, R., van de Wiel, H.B.M., Otter, R. and van den Heuvel, W.J.A. (1997) 'Distressed or relieved? Psychological side effects of breast cancer screening in the Netherlands', *Journal of Epidemiology and Community Health*, 51: 705–10.

Scarpaci, J.L. (1988) Help-seeking behaviour, SSe, and satisfaction among primary care users in Santiago de Chile', *Journal of Health and Social Behaviour*, 29: 199.

Schaal, B. and Orgeur, P. (1992) 'Olfaction in utero: can the rodent model be generalized?', *Quarterly Journal of Experimental Psychology*, *44*: 245–78.

Schachter, S., Silverstein, B. and Perlick, D. (1977) 'Psychological and pharmacological explanations of smoking under stress', *Journal of Experimental Psychology: General*, *106*: 31–40.

Schachter, S., Silverstein, B., Kozlowski, L.T., Herman, C.P. and Liebling, B. (1984) 'Effects of stress on cigarette smoking and urinary pH', *Journal of Experimental Psychology: General*, *106*: 24–30.

Schafe, G.E. and Bernstein, I.L. (1996) 'Taste aversion learning', in E.D. Capaldi (ed.), *Why We Eat What We Eat. The Psychology of Eating*. Washington, DC: American Psychological Association. pp. 31–51.

Schiaffino, K.M. and Cea, C.D. (1995) 'Assessing chronic illness representations: the implicit models of illness questionnaire', *Journal of Behavioral Medicine*, *18*: 531–48.

Schlenker, T.L., Bain, C., Baughman, A.L. and Hadler, S.C. (1992) 'Measles herd immunity: the association of attack rates with immunization rates in preschool children', *Journal of the American Medical Association*, *267*: 823–6.

Schmidt, J.G. (1990) 'The epidemiology of mass breast cancer screening: a plea for a valid measure of benefit', *Journal of Clinical Epidemiology*, *43*: 215–25.

Schmidt, W. (1977) 'Cirrhosis and alcohol consumption: an epidemiological perspective', in G. Edwards and M. Grant (eds), *Alcoholism: New Knowledge and New Responses*. London: Croom Helm. pp. 15–47.

Schober, R. (1997) 'Complementary and conventional medicines working together', *Canadian Health Psychologist*, *5*: 14–18.

Schober, R. and Lacroix, J.M. (1991) 'Lay illness models in the enlightenment and the 20th century: some historical lessons', in J.A. Skelton and R.T. Croyle (eds), *Mental Representation in Health and Illness*. New York: Springer-Verlag. pp. 10–31.

Schönpflug, W. (1986) 'Behaviour economics as an approach to stress theory', in M.H. Appley and R. Trumbull (eds), *Dynamics of Stress: Physiological, Psychological and Social Perspectives*. New York: Plenum Press. pp. 81–100.

Schönpflug, W. and Battmann, W. (1988) 'The costs and benefits of coping', in S. Fisher and J. Reason (eds), *Handbook of Life Stress, Cognition and Health*. London: Wiley. pp. 699–713.

Schroeder, D.H. and Costa, P.T. Jr. (1984) 'Influence of life event stress on physical illness: substantive effects or methodological flaws? *Journal of Personality and Social Psychology*, *46*: 853–63.

Schudson, M. (1993) 'Symbols and smokers: advertising, health messages, and public policy', in R.L. Robin and S.D. Sugarman (eds), *Smoking Policy: Law, Politics, and Culture*. Oxford: Oxford University Press.

Schwartz, G.E. and Weiss, S.M. (1978) 'Behavioral medicine revisited: an amended definition', *Journal of Behavioral Medicine*, *1*: 249–51.

Schwartz, M., Savage, W., George, J. and Emohare, L. (1989) 'Women's knowledge and experience of cervical screening: a failure of health education and medical organization', *Community Medicine*, *11*: 279–89.

Schwarzer, R. (1992) 'Self efficacy in the adaptation and maintenance of health behaviours: theoretical approaches and a new model', in R. Schwarzer (ed.), *Self Efficacy: Thought Control of Action*. Washington, DC: Hemisphere. pp. 217–43.

Schwarzer, R. (1999) 'Self-regulatory processes in the adoption and maintenance of health behaviors', *Journal of Health Psychology*, *4*: 115–27.

Seedhouse, D. (1998) *Ethics: The Heart of Health Care*. Chichester: Wiley.

Segal, L. (1994) *Straight Sex. The Politics of Pleasure*. London: Virago.

Segal, L. (1996) 'Freud and feminism: a century of contradiction', *Feminism and Psychology, 6*: 290–7.

Selye, H. (1956) *The Stress of Life*. New York: McGraw-Hill.

Selye, H. (1976) *Stress in Health and Disease*. Reading, MA: Butterworth.

Semmes, C.E. (1996) *Racism, Health and Post-Industrialism: A Nation of African-American Health*. Westport, CT: Praeger.

Shalev, A.Y. and Rogel-Fuchs, Y. (1993) 'Psychophysiology of the posttraumatic stress disorder: from sulphur fumes to behavioural genetics', *Psychosomatic Medicine, 55*: 413–23.

Shalev, A.Y., Bonne, O. and Eth, S. (1996) 'Treatment of posttraumatic stress disorder: a review', *Psychosomatic Medicine, 58*: 165–82.

Shaper, A.G. (1995) 'Mortality and alcohol consumption: non-drinkers shouldn't be used as baseline', *British Medical Journal, 310*: 325.

Shaper, A.G., Wannamethee, G. and Walker, M. (1988) 'Alcohol and mortality in British men: explaining the U-shaped curve', *Lancet, 3*: 1267–83.

Shapiro, L. (1994) 'A food lover's guide to fat', *Newsweek*, 5 December: 36–43.

Sharp, D.J., Peter, T.J., Bartholomew, J., and Shaw, A. (1996) 'Breast screening: a randomised controlled trial in UK general practice of three generations designed to increase uptake', *Journal of Epidemiology and Community Health, 50*: 72–5.

Shaw, S. (1979) 'A critique of the concept of the alcohol dependence syndrome', *British Journal of Addiction, 74*: 339–48.

Shaw, S. (1985) 'The disease concept of dependence', in N. Heather, I. Robertson and P. Davies (eds), *The Misuse of Alcohol: Crucial Issues in Dependence, Treatment and Prevention*. London: Croom Helm. pp. 35–44.

Sheeran, P. and Abraham, C. (1995) 'The Health Belief Model', in M. Conner and P. Norman (eds), *Predicting Health Behaviour*. Buckingham: Open University Press. pp. 23–61.

Sheeran, P. and Orbell, S. (1996) 'How confidently can we infer health beliefs from questionnaire responses?', *Psychology and Health, 11*: 273–90.

Sheppard, B.H., Hartwick, J. and Warshaw, P.R. (1988) 'The theory of reasoned action: a meta-analysis of past research with recommendations for modifications and future research', *Journal of Consumer Research, 15*: 325–39.

Sheridan, E.P., Matarazzo, J.D., Boll, T.J., Perry, N.W., Weiss, S.M. and Belar, C.D. (1988) 'Postdoctoral education and training for clinical service providers in health psychology', *Health Psychology, 7*: 1–17.

Sher, K.J. (1991) *Children of Alcoholics: A Critical Appraisal of Theory and Research*. Chicago: Chicago University Press.

Sherlock, S. (1995) 'Alcoholic liver disease', *Lancet, 345*: 227–9.

Shorter, E. (1992) *From Paralysis to Fatigue: A History of Psychosomatic Illness in the Modern Era*. New York: Free Press.

Showalter, E. (1997) *Hystories: Hysterical Epidemics and Modern Culture*. London: Picador.

Shweder, R.A., Much, N.C., Mahapatra, M. and Park, L. (1997) 'The "big three" of morality (autonomy, community, divinity) and the "big three" explanations of suffering', in A.M. Brandt and P. Rozin (eds), *Morality and Health*. London: Routledge. pp. 119–72.

Siegal, M., Patty, J. and Eiser, C. (1990) 'A re-examination of children's conceptions of contagion', *Psychology and Health, 4*: 159–65.

Siegel, S. (1975) 'Conditioned insulin effects', *Journal of Comparative Physiology and Psychology*, 89: 189–99.

Siegrist, J., Peter, R., Junge, A., Cremer, P. and Seidel, D. (1990) 'Low status control, high effort at work and ischaemic heart disease: prospective evidence from blue-collar men', *Social Science and Medicine*, 31: 1127–34.

Silverman, D. (1987) *Communication and Medical Practice. Social Relations in the Clinic*: London: Sage.

Silverman, D. (1997) *Discourses of Counselling. HIV Counselling as Social Interaction*. London: Sage.

Silverman, D., Bor, R., Miller, R. and Goldman, E. (1992a) 'Advice-giving and advice-reception in AIDS counselling', in P. Aggleton, P. Davies and G. Hart (eds), *AIDS: Rights, Risks and Reason*. London: Falmer Press. pp. 174–91.

Silverman, D., Perakyla, A. and Bor, R. (1992b) 'Discussing safer sex in HIV coun-selling: assessing three communication formats, *AIDS Care*, 4: 69–82.

Simons-Morton, B.G., McKenzie, T.J., Stone, E., Mitchell, P., Osganian, V., Strikmiller, P.K., Ehlinger, S., Cribb, P. and Nader, P.R. (1997) 'Physical activity in a multiethnic population of third graders in four states', *American Journal of Public Health*, 87: 45–50.

Simpson, N., Lenton, S. and Randall, R. (1995) 'Parental refusal to have children immunised: extent and reasons', *British Medical Journal*, 310: 227.

Skelton, A.M. (1997) 'Patient education for the millennium: beyond control and emancipation?', *Patient Education and Counseling*, 31: 151–8.

Skelton, J.A. and Croyle, R.T. (eds) (1991) *Mental Representation in Health and Illness*. New York: Springer-Verlag.

Skinner, B.F. (1938) *The Behaviour of Organisms*. New York: Appleton Century Crofts.

Skinner, C.S., Champion, V.L., Gonin, R. and Hanna, M. (1997) 'Do perceived barriers and benefits vary by mammography stage?', *Psychology, Health and Medicine*, 2: 65–76.

Skrabanek, P. (1985) 'False premises and false promises of breast cancer screening', *Lancet 2 (8450)*: 316–20.

Slade, J., Bero, L.A., Hanauer, P., Barnes, D.E. and Glantz, S.A. (1995) 'Nicotine and addiction: the Brown and Williamson documents', *Journal of the American Medical Association*, 274: 225–33.

Slenker, S.E. and Grant, M.C. (1989) 'Attitudes, beliefs, and knowledge about mammography among women over forty years of age', *Journal of Cancer Edu-cation*, 4: 61–5.

Slenker, S.E. and Spreitzer, E.A. (1988) 'Public perceptions and behaviors regarding cancer control', *Journal of Cancer Education*, 3: 171–80.

Smart, R.G. (1976) 'Spontaneous recovery in alcoholics: a review and analysis of the available research', *Drug and Alcohol Dependence*, 1: 277–85.

Smith, H.E. and Herbert, C.P. (1993) 'Preventive practice among primary care physicians in British Columbia: relation to recommendations of the Canadian Task Force on the Periodic Health Examination', *Canadian Medical Association Journal*, 149: 1795–800.

Smith, M. (1985) 'The cost of non-compliance and the capacity of improved compliance to reduce health care expenditures', in National Pharmaceutical Council (ed.), *Improving Medication Compliance*. Reston, VA: NPC.

Smith, S., Botha, J.L., Goosey, R. and Dainith, H. (1991) 'Audit of user satisfaction with the Leicestershire Breast Screening Service: women attending for assessment of abnormal mammograms', *Journal of Public Health Medicine, 13*: 166–71.

Smith, T.W. (1992) 'Hostility and health: current status of a psychosomatic hypothesis', *Health Psychology, 11*: 139–50.

Smyth, M. and Browne, F. (1992) *General Household Survey.* London: HMSO.

Snider, J., Beauvais, J., Levy, I., Villeneuve, P. and Pennock, J. (1996) 'Trends in mammography and pap smear utilization in Canada', *Chronic Diseases in Canada, 17*: 108–17.

Somerfield, M.R. (1997) 'The utility of systems models of stress and coping for applied research: the case of cancer adaptation. (with peer criticism and author's response)', *Journal of Health Psychology, 2*: 133–83.

Sontag, S. (1991) *Illness as Metaphor and AIDS and its Metaphors.* London: Penguin.

Spector, R.E. (1991) *Cultural Diversity in Health and Illness,* 4th edn. Stamford, CT: Appleton & Lange.

Spicer, J. and Chamberlain, K. (1996) 'Developing psychosocial theory in health psychology', *Journal of Health Psychology, 1*: 161–71.

Spielberger, C.D. (1966) *Anxiety and Behaviour.* New York: Academic Press.

Spielberger, C.D. (ed.) (1972) *Anxiety: Current Trends in Theory and Research,* vols. 1–2. New York: Academic Press.

Spilker, B. (1991) 'Methods of assessing and improving patient compliance in clinical trials', in J.A. Cramer and B. Spilker (eds), *Patient Compliance in Medical Practice and Clinical Trials.* New York: Raven Press.

Sprecher, S. and McKinney, K. (1993) *Sexuality.* London: Sage.

Stacy, A.W., Bentler, P.M. and Flay, B.R. (1994) 'Attitudes and health behavior in diverse populations: drunk driving, alcohol use, binge eating, marijuana use, and cigarette use', *Health Psychology, 13*: 73–85.

Stainton-Rogers, W. (1991) *Explaining Health and Illness: An Exploration of Diversity.* Hemel Hempstead: Wheatsheaf.

Stainton-Rogers, W. (1996) 'Critical approaches to health psychology', *Journal of Health Psychology, 1*: 65–77.

Standing Conference of Public Health Working Group Report (1994) *Housing, Homelessness and Health.* London: The Nuffield Provincial Hospitals Trust.

Stanley, L. (1995) *Sex Surveyed 1949–1996.* Basingstoke: Taylor & Francis.

Stein, J.A., Fox, S.A., Murata, P.J. and Morisky, D.E. (1992) 'Mammography usage and the health belief model', *Health Education Quarterly, 19*: 447–62.

Steiner, G. (1978) *Heidegger.* London: Faber and Faber.

Steinert, Y. and Rosenberg, E. (1987) 'Psychosocial problems: what do patients want? What do physicians want to provide?', *Family Medicine, 19*: 346–50.

Steinhardt, M.A. and Dishman, R.K. (1989) 'Reliability and validity of expected outcomes and barriers for habitual physical activity', *Journal of Occupational Medicine, 31*: 536–46.

Steptoe, A. and Butler, N. (1996) 'Sports participation and emotional well-being in adolescents', *Lancet, 347*: 1789–92.

Steptoe, A. and Wardle, J. (1996) 'The European Health and Behaviour Survey: the development of an international study in health psychology', *Psychology and Health, 11*: 49–74.

Stewart, J., de Wit, H. and Eikelboom, R. (1984) 'Role of unconditioned and conditioned drug effects in the self-administration of opiates and stimulants', *Psychological Review, 91*: 251–68.

Stewart, M.A. (1984) 'What is a successful doctor–patient interview? A study of interactions and outcomes', *Social Science and Medicine, 19*: 167–75.

Stewart, M.J., Gillis, A., Brosky, G., Johnston, G., Kirkland, S., Leigh, G., Persaud, V., Rootman, I., Jackson, S. and Pawliw-Fry, B.A. (1996) 'Smoking among disadvantaged women: causes and cessation', *Canadian Journal of Nursing Research, 28*: 41–60.

Stiles, W.B. (1996) 'Stability of the verbal exchange structure of medical consultations', *Psychology and Health, 11*: 773–85.

Stiles, W.B., Putnam, S.M. and Jacob, M.C. (1982) 'Verbal exchange structure of initial medical interviews', *Health Psychology, 1*: 315–36.

Stiles, W.B., Putnam, S.M., Wolf, M.H. and James, S.A. (1979) 'Verbal response mode profiles of patients and physicians in medical screening interviews', *Journal of Medical Education, 54*: 81–9.

Stimson, G., Lart, R., Dolan, K. and Donoghoe, M. (1991) 'The future of syringe exchange in the public health prevention of HIV infection', in P. Aggleton, G. Hart and P. Davies (eds), *AIDS. Responses, Interventions and Care*. London: Falmer Press. pp. 225–32.

Stinert, Y.S. and Rosenberg, E. (1987) 'Psychosocial problems: what do patients want? What do physicians want to provide? *Family Medicine, 21*: 103–10.

Stinson, F.S., Dufour, M.C., Steffens, R.A. and DeBakey, S. (1993) 'Alcohol-related mortality in the United States, 1979–1989', *Alcohol Health and Research World, 17*: 251–60.

Stockwell, T. (1996) 'Interventions cannot ignore intentions', *Addiction, 91*: 1283–4.

Stolerman, I.P. and Jarvis, M.J. (1995) 'The scientific case that nicotine is addictive', *Psychopharmacology, 117*: 2–10.

Stone, A.A., Bovbjerg, D.H., Neale, J.M., Napoli, A., Valdimarsdottir, H. et al. (1992) 'Development of common cold symptoms following experimental rhinovirus infection is related to prior stressful life events', *Behavioural Medicine, 8*: 115–20.

Stone, D.H. and Stewart, S. (1996) 'Screening and the new genetics: a public health perspective and the ethical debate', *Journal of Public Health Medicine, 18*: 3–5.

Stone, S.V. and Costa, P.T. (1990) 'Disease-prone personality or distress-prone personality? The role of neuroticism in coronary heart disease', in H.S. Friedman (ed.), *Personality and Disease*. London: Wiley. pp. 178–200.

Street, R.L. (1991) 'Information-giving in medical consultations: the influence of patients' communicative styles and personal characteristics', *Social Science and Medicine, 32 (5)*: 541–8.

Stritzke, W.G., Lang, A.R. and Patrick, C.J. (1996) 'Beyond stress and arousal: a reconceptualisation of alcohol-emotion relations with reference to psychophysiological methods', *Psychological Bulletin, 120*: 376–95.

Stroebe, M.S. and Stroebe, W. (1983) 'Who suffers more? Sex differences in health risks of the widowed', *Psychological Bulletin, 93*: 279–301.

Stroebe, W. and Stroebe, M.S. (1995) *Social Psychology and Health*. Buckingham: Open University Press.

Stucky-Ropp, R.C. and DiLorenzo, T.M. (1993) 'Determinants of exercise in children', *Preventive Medicine, 22*: 880–9.

Sulloway, F.J. (1980) *Freud, Biologist of the Mind*. London: Fontana.

Suls, J. and Mullen, B. (1981) 'Life change and psychological distress: the role of perceived control and desirability', *Journal of Applied Social Psychology, 11*: 379–89.

Suls, J. and Rittenhouse, J.D. (1990) 'Models of linkages between personality and disease', in H.S. Friedman (ed.), *Personality and Disease*. London: Wiley. pp. 38–64.

Sulzberger, P., Marks, D. and Hodgson, I. (1979) *The Isis Smoking Cessation Programme*, 3rd edn. Dunedin, New Zealand: Isis Research Centre.

Suter, E., Marti, B. and Gutzwiller, F. (1994) 'Jogging or walking – comparison of health effects', *AEP, 4*: 375–81.

Sutton, S. (1996) 'Further support for the stages of change model?', *Addiction, 91*: 1287–9.

Sutton, S., Bickler, G., Aldridge, J. and Saidi, G. (1994) 'Prospective study of predictors of attendance for breast screening in inner London', *Journal of Epidemiology and Community Health, 48*: 65–73.

Sutton, S., Saidi, G., Bickler, G. and Hunter, J. (1995) 'Does routine screening for breast cancer raise anxiety? Results from a three wave prospective study in England', *Journal of Epidemiology and Community Health, 49*: 413–18.

Sutton, S.R. (1989) 'Smoking attitudes and behavior: applications of Fishbein and Ajzen's theory of reasoned action in predicting and understanding smoking decisions', in T. Ney and A. Gale (eds), *Smoking and Human Behavior*. Chicester: Wiley. pp. 289–312.

Svarstad, B.L. (1976) 'Physician–patient communication and patient conformity with medical advice', in D. Mechanic (ed.), *Growth of Bureaucratic Medicine*. New York.

Swan, A.V., Cresser, R. and Murray, M. (1990) 'When and why children first start to smoke', *International Journal of Epidemiology, 19*: 323–30.

Swartzman, L.C. and Lees, M.C. (1996) 'Causal dimensions of college students' perceptions of physical symptoms', *Journal of Behavioral Medicine, 19*: 95–110.

Swinburn, B. and Ravusssin, E. (1993) 'Energy balance or fat balance? *American Journal of Clinical Nutrition, 57*: 766–71S.

Swinker, M., Arbogast, J.C. and Murray, S. (1993) 'Why do patients decline screening mammography?', *Family Practice Research Journal, 13*: 165–70.

Taira, D.A., Safran, D.G., Seto, T.B., Rogers, W.H. and Tarlov, A.R. (1997) 'The relationship between patient income and physician discussion of health risk behaviors', *Journal of the American Medical Association, 278*: 1412–17.

Tan, P.E.H. and Bishop, G.D. (1996) 'Disease representations and related behavioural intentions among Chinese Singaporeans', *Psychology and Health, 11*: 671–83.

Tannen, D. (1991) *You Just Don't Understand. Women and Men in Conversation*. London: Virago.

Tatchell, P. (1996) 'It's just a phase: why homosexuality is doomed', in M. Simpson (ed.), *Anti-gay*. London: Freedom Editions.

Tatzer, E., Schubert, M.T., Timischl, W. and Simbruner, G. (1985) 'Discrimination of taste and preference for sweet in premature babies', *Early Human Development, 12*: 23–30.

Taylor, S.E. (1979) 'Hospital patient behavior: reactance, helplessness, or control?', *Journal of Social Issues, 35*: 156–84.

Taylor, S.E. and Brown, J.D. (1988) 'Illusion and well-being: a social psychological perspective on mental health', *Psychological Bulletin, 103*: 193–210.

Taylor, S.E., Lichtman, R.R. and Wood, J.V. (1984) 'Attributions, beliefs about control, and adjustment to breast cancer', *Journal of Personality and Social Psychology, 46*: 499–502.

Taylor, S.E., Repetti, R.L. and Seeman, T. (1997) 'Health psychology: what is an unhealthy environment and how does it get under the skin?, *Annual Review of Psychology, 48*: 411–47.

Terry, D.J., Gallois, C. and McCamish, M. (1993) *The Theory of Reasoned Action: Its Application to AIDS-preventive Behaviour*. Oxford: Pergamon.

Tessaro, I., Eng, E., Smith, J. (1994) 'Breast cancer screening in older African-American women: qualitative research findings', *American Journal of Health Promotion, 8*: 286–93.

Tether, P. and Harrison, L. (1986) 'Alcohol-related fires and drownings', *British Journal of Addiction, 81*: 425–31.

Thomas, L (1979) *The Medusa and the Snail*. New York: Bantam.

Thompson, B. (1997) 'Attitudes and beliefs toward mammography among women using an urban public hospital', *Journal of Health Care for the Poor and Underserved, 8*: 186–201.

Tibben, A., Frets, P.G., van de Kamp, J.J., Niermeijer, M.F., Vegter-van der Vlis, M., Roos, R.A., van Ommen, G.G., Duivenvoorden, H.J., and Verhage, F. (1993) 'Presymptomatic DNA testing for Huntington disease: pre-test attitudes and expectations of applicants and their partners in the Dutch program', *American Journal of Medical Genetics, 48*: 10–16.

Tibben, A., Duinvoorden, M.J., Niermeijer, M.F., Vegter van der Vlis, M., Roos, R.A.C. and Verhage, F. (1994) 'Psychological effects of presymptomatic DNA testing for Huntington's disease in the Dutch program', *Psychosomatic Medicine, 56*: 526–32.

Tibben, A., Timman, R., Banninck, E.C. and Duinvoorden, H.J. (1997) 'Three year follow-up after presymptomatic testing for Huntington's disease in tested individuals and partners', *Health Psychology, 16*: 20–35.

Tiefer, L. (1995) *Sex is not a Natural Act and Other Essays*. Oxford: Westview Press.

Tillotson, L.M. and Smith, M.S. (1996) 'Locus of control, social support, and adherence to the diabetes regimen', *Diabetes Educator, 22*: 133–9.

Tolley, K. (1985) *Health Promotion: How to Measure Cost-effectiveness*. London: Health Education Authority.

Tones, K. (1987) 'Devising strategies for preventing drug misuse: the role of the Health Action Model', *Health Education Research: Theory and Practice, 2*: 305–17.

Townsend, J., Roderick, P. and Cooper, J. (1994) 'Cigarette advertising by socio-economic group, sex, and age: effects of price, income, and health publicity', *British Medical Journal, 309*: 923–7.

Trawick, M. (1992) 'Death and nurturance in Indian systems of healing', in C. Leslie and A. Young (eds), *Paths to Asian Medical Knowledge*. Berkeley, CA: University of California Press. pp. 129–59.

Trostle, J.A. (1998) 'Medical compliance as an ideology', *Social Science and Medicine, 27*: 1299–308.

True, W.R., Heath, A.C., Scherrer, J.F., Waterman, B., Goldberg, J., Lin, N., Eisen, S.A., Lyons, M.J. and Tsuang, M.T. (1997) 'Genetic and environmental contributions to smoking', *Addiction, 92*: 1277–87.

Trumbull, R. and Appley, M.H. (1986) 'A conceptual model for the understanding of stress dynamics', in M.H. Appley and R. Trumbull (eds), *Dynamics of Stress: Physiological, Psychological and Social Perspectives*. New York: Plenum. pp. 21–45.

Tschann, J.M., Adler, N.E., Irwin, C.E., Millstein, S.G., Turner, R.A. and Kegeles, S.M. (1994) 'Initiation of substance use in early adolescence: the roles of pubertal timing and emotional distress', *Health Psychology, 13*: 326–33.

Turk, D.O., Rudy, T.E. and Salovey, P. (1986) 'Implicit models of illness', *Journal of Behavioral Medicine*, 9: 453–74.

Turner, B. (1984) *The Body and Society: Explorations in Social Theory*. Oxford: Blackwell.

Turnquist, D.C., Harvey, J.H. and Anderson, B.L. (1988) 'Attributions and adjustment to life threatening illness', *British Journal of Social Psychology*, 27: 55–6.

US Center for Disease Control and Prevention (1992) 'Retrospective assessment of vaccination coverage among school-aged children: selected US cities, 1991', *Morbidity and Mortality Weekly Report*, 41: 103–7.

US Center for Disease Control and Prevention (1993) 'Prevalence of sedentary lifestyle – behavioral risk factor surveillance system, United States, 1991', *Morbidity and Mortality Weekly Report*, 42: 576–9.

US Center for Disease Control and Prevention (1994) 'Vaccination coverage of 2-year-old children – United States, 1993', *Morbidity and Mortality Weekly Report*, 43: 705–9.

US Center for Disease Control and Prevention (1995) 'Trends in cancer screening – United States, 1987 and 1992', *Morbidity and Mortality Weekly Report*, 45: 57–61.

Uchino, B.N., Cacioppo, J.T. and Kiecolt-Glaser, J.K. (1996) 'The relationship between social support and physiological processes: a review with emphasis on underlying mechanisms and implications for health', *Psychological Bulletin*, 119: 488–531.

United Nations Development Programme (1995) *Human Development Report*. New York: Oxford University Press.

US Department of Health, Education and Welfare (1964) Smoking and health. Report of the Advisory Committee to the Surgeon General of the Public Health Service, Washington, DC. PHS Pub. No. 1103.

US Public Health Service (1990) The health consequences of smoking: a report of the Surgeon General (COL Report No. 90-8416). Rockville, MD: USDHHS.

Vågerö, D. and Lundberg, O. (1989) 'Health inequalities in Britain and Sweden', *The Lancet*, ii: 35–6.

Valach, L., Young, R.A. and Lynam, J. (1996) 'Family health-promotion projects. An action theoretical perspective', *Journal of Health Psychology*, 1: 49–63.

Valkonen, T. (1993) 'Problems in the measurement and international comparisons of socioeconomic differences in mortality', *Social Science and Medicine*, 36, 409–18.

Van der Velde, F.W. and Van der Pligt, J. (1991) 'AIDS-related health behaviour: coping, protection motivation and previous behaviour', *Journal of Behavioural Medicine*, 14: 429–51.

Van Haaften, E.H. and Van de Vijver, F.J.R. (1996) 'Psychological consequences of environmental degradation', *Journal of Health Psychology*, 1: 411–29.

Velicer, W.F., DiClemente, C.C., Rossi, J.S. and Prochaska, J.O. (1990) 'Relapse situations and self-efficacy: an integrative model', *Addictive Behaviors*, 15: 271–83.

Ver Ellen, P. and van Kammen, D.P. (1990) 'The biological findings in post-traumatic stress disorder: a review', *Journal of Applied Social Psychology*, 20: 1789–821.

Vernon, S.W., Laville, E.A. and Jackson, G.L. (1990) 'Participation in breast screening programs: a review', *Social Science and Medicine*, 30: 1107–18.

Vincent, C. and Furnham, A. (1996) 'Why do patients turn to complementary medicine? An empirical study', *British Journal of Clinical Psychology*, 35: 37–48.

Vinck, J., Aricks, M. and Lipkens, D. (1997) 'Health concerns in households', *Journal of Health Psychology*, 2: 435–43.

Waitzkin, H. (1985) 'Information giving in medical care', *Journal of Health and Social Behaviour*, 26: 81–101.

Waitzkin, H. (1989) 'A critical theory of medical discourse: ideology, social control, and the processing of social context in medical encounters', *Journal of Health and Social Behavior*, 30: 220–39.

Wald, N., Kiryluk, S., Darby, S., Doll, R., Pike, M. and Peto, R. (1988) *UK Smoking Statistics*. Oxford: Oxford University Press.

Walker, C.E. and Shelton, T.L. (1985) 'An overview of behavioural medicine', in A.R. Zeiner, D. Bendell and C.E. Walker (eds), *Health Psychology: Treatment and Research Issues*. London: Plenum. pp. 63–81.

Wallace, P., Cutler, S. and Haines, A. (1988) 'Randomised controlled trial of general practitioner intervention in patients with excessive alcohol consumption', *British Medical Journal*, 297: 663–8.

Waller, S., Thom, B., Harris, S. and Kelly, M. (1998) 'Perceptions of alcohol-related attendances in accident and emergency departments in England: a national survey', *Alcohol and Alcoholism* 33: 354–61.

Wallston, K.A., Wallston, B.S. and DeVellis, R. (1978) 'Development of multi-dimensional health locus of control (MHLC) scales', *Health Education Monographs*, 6: 160–70.

Wardle, J. and Pope, R. (1992) 'The psychological costs of screening for cancer', *Journal of Psychosomatic Research*, 36: 609–24.

Warren, R. (1988) 'The debate over mass mammography in Britain: the case for', *British Medical Journal*, 297: 969–72.

Watmough, D.J., Bhargava, S., Memon, A., Syed, F., Roy, S. and Sharma, P. (1997) 'Does breast cancer screening depend on a wobbly hypothesis? *Journal of Public Health Medicine*, 19: 373–9.

Wear, A. (1985) 'Puritan perceptions of illness in seventeenth century England', in R. Porter (ed.), *Patients and Practitioners: Lay Perceptions of Medicine in Pre-industrial Society*. Cambridge: Cambridge University Press. pp. 55–100.

Wearing, B., Wearing, S. and Kelly, K. (1994) 'Adolescent women, identity and smoking: leisure experience as resistance', *Sociology of Health and Illness*, 16: 626–43.

Webb, G.P. (1995) *Nutrition. A Health Promotion Approach*. London: Arnold.

Webster, R. (1995) *Why Freud was Wrong*. London: HarperCollins.

Weeks, J. (1985) *Sexuality and its Discontents. Meanings, Myths and Modern Sexualities*. London: Routledge.

Weiner, B., Frieze, I., Kukla, A., Reed, L., Rest, S. and Rosenbaum, R.M. (1972) 'Perceiving the causes of success and failure', in E.E. Jones, D.E. Kanouse, H.H. Kelley, R.E. Nesbitt, S. Valins and B. Weiner (eds), *Attribution: Perceiving the Causes of Behaviour*. NJ: General Learning Press.

Weinman, J. and Petrie, K.J. (1997) 'Illness perceptions: a new paradigm for psychosomatics? *Journal of Psychosomatic Medicine*, 42: 113–16.

Weinman, J., Petrie, K.J., Moss-Morris, R. and Horne, R. (1996) 'The Illness Perception Questionnaire: a new method for assessing the cognitive representation of illness', *Psychology and Health*, 11: 431–46.

Weinstein, N.D. (1988) 'The precaution adoption process', *Health Psychology*, 7: 355–86.

Weiss, K., Gergen, P. and Hodgson, T. (1992) 'An economic evaluation of asthma in the United States', *New England Journal of Medicine*, 326: 862–8.

Weitkunt, R., Markuzzi, A., Vogel, S., Schlipkoter, U., Koch, H.-J., Meyer, G. and

Ferring, D. (1998) 'Psychological factors associated with the uptake of measles immunization: findings and implications for prevention', *Journal of Health Psychology*, 3: 273–84.

Wellington Women's Health Research Caucus (1997) Cancer screening report. Wellington, New Zealand.

Wennemo, I. (1993) 'Infant mortality, public policy and inequality – a comparison of 18 industralised countries, 1950–85', *Sociology of Health and Illness*, 15: 429–46.

Werner, D. (1992) 'The life and death of primary health care', *Third World Resurgence*, 42: 10–14.

West, C. (1984) *Routine Complications*. Bloomington, IN: Indiana University Press.

West, C. (1990) 'Not just doctors' orders: directive-response sequences in patients' visits to women and men physicians', *Discourse and Society*, 1: 85–113.

White, A., Nicolaas, G., Foster, K., Browne, F. and Carey, S. (1993) *Health Survey for England 1991*. London: HMSO.

Whiteman, M. (1995) 'Tackling inequalities: a review of policy initiatives', in M. Benzeval, K. Judge and M. Whitehead (eds), *Tackling Inequalities in Health: An Agenda for Action*. London: King's Fund. pp. 22–52.

Whitney, H.A.K., Bloss, J.L., Cotting, C.M., Jaworski, P.G., Myers, S.L. and Thorsten, D.J. (eds) (1993) 'Medication compliance: a healthcare problem', *Annals of Pharmacotherapy*, 27: S1–S19.

Wiggins, S., Whyte, P., Huggins, M., Adams, S., Theilmann, J., Bloch, M., Sheps, S.B., Schechter, M.T. and Hayden, M.R. (1992) 'The psychological consequences of predictive testing for Huntington's disease. Canadian Collaborative Study of Predictive Testing', *New England Journal of Medicine*, 327: 1401–5.

Wilhelmsen, L., Sanne, H., Elmfeldt, D., Grimby, G., Tibblin, G. and Wedel, H. (1975) 'A controlled trial of physical training after myocardial infarction: effects of risk factors, nonfatal reinfarction, and death', *Preventive Medicine*, 4: 491–508.

Wilkinson, R. (1992) 'Income distribution and life expectancy', *British Medical Journal*, 304: 165–8.

Wilkinson, R. (1996) *Unhealthy Societies*. London: Routledge.

Wilkinson, S. (1998) 'Focus groups in health research', *Journal of Health Psychology*, 3: 329–48.

Willett, W.C., Stampfer, M.J., Manson, J.E., Colditz, G.A., Speizer, F.E., Rosner, B.A., Sampson, L.A. and Hennekens, C.H. (1993) 'Intake of trans fatty acids and risk of coronary heart disease among women', *Lancet*, 341: 581–5.

Williams, C. and Dowler, E.A. (1994) *Identifying Successful Local Projects and Initiatives on Diet and Low Income: A Review of the Issues. A Working Paper for the Nutrition Task Force Low Income Project Team*. London: Department of Health.

Williams, D.R. and Collins, C. (1995) 'US socioeconomic and racial differences in health: patterns and explanations', *Annual Review of Sociology*, 21: 349–86.

Williams, D.R., Yu, Y., Jackson, J.S. and Anderson, N.B. (1997) 'Racial differences in physical and mental health: socio-economic status, stress and discrimination', *Journal of Health Psychology*, 2: 335–51.

Williams, R.J.L.I., Hittinger, R. and Glouzer, G. (1994) 'Resource implications of head injuries on an acute surgical unit', *Journal of the Royal Society of Medicine*, 87: 83–6.

Williams, S.J. and Calnan, M. (1996) 'The "limits" of medicalization?: modern medicine and the lay populace in "late" modernity', *Social Science and Medicine*, 42: 1609–20.

Willig, C. (1994) Marital discourse and condom use', in P. Aggleton, P. Davies and G. Hart (eds), *AIDS. Foundations for the Future*. London: Taylor & Francis.

Willig, C. (1995) '"I wouldn't have married the guy if I'd have to do that": heterosexual adults' constructions of condom use and their implications for sexual practice', *Journal of Community and Applied Social Psychology*, 5: 75–87.

Willig, C. (1998) 'Constructions of sexual activity and their implications for sexual practice', *Journal of Health Psychology*, 3: 383–92.

Willig, C. (ed.) (1999) *Applied Discourse Analysis. Social and Psychological Interventions*. Buckingham: Open University Press.

Wills, T.A. and Shiffman, S. (1985) 'Coping and substance use: a conceptual framework', in S. Shiffman and T.A. Wills (eds), *Coping and Substance Use*. Orlando, FL: Academic Press. pp. 3–24.

Wills, T.A., McNamara, G. and Vaccaro, D. (1995) 'Parental education related to adolescent stress-coping and substance use: development of a mediational model', *Health Psychology*, 14: 464–78.

Wilson, J. and Jungner, G. (1968) 'Principles and practice of screening for disease'. Geneva, WHO. World Health Organization Public Health Paper 34.

Winefield, H., Murrell, T., Clifford, J and Farmer, E. (1996) 'The search for reliable and valid measures of patient-centredness', *Psychology and Health*, 11: 811–24.

Winett, R.A., King, A.C. and Altman, D.G. (1989) *Health Psychology and Public Health*. New York: Pergamon.

Winkleby, M.A., Schooler, C., Kraemer, H.C., Lin, J. and Fortman, S.P. (1995) 'Hispanic versus white smoking patterns by sex and level of education', *American Journal of Epidemiology*, 142: 410–18.

Winkvist, A. and Akhtar, H.Z. (1997) 'Images of health and health care options among low income women in Punjab, Pakistan', *Social Science and Medicine*, 45: 1483–91.

Winnett, R.A. (1996) 'Activity and exercise guidelines: questions concerning their scientific basis and health outcome efficacy'. Unpublished paper.

Woolf, S.H. (1996) 'Immunizations', in S.H. Woolf, S. Jonas and R.S. Lawrence (eds), *Health Promotion and Disease Prevention in Clinical Practice*. Baltimore: Williams & Wilkins.

World Bank (1993) *World Development Report 1993: Investing in Health*. New York: Oxford University Press.

World Health Organization (1986) Ottawa Charter for Health Promotion. *Health Promotion*, 1, iii–v.

World Health Organization (1989) *World Health Statistics Annual*. Geneva: WHO.

World Health Organization (1995) *World Health Report*. Geneva: WHO.

Wright, E.C. (1993) 'Non-compliance – or how many aunts has Matilda?', *Lancet*, 342: 909–13.

Yardley, L. (ed.) (1997) *Material Discourses of Health and Illness*. London: Routledge.

Young, A. (1980) 'The discourse on stress and the reproduction of conventional knowledge', *Social Science and Medicine*, 14B: 133–46.

Young, A. (1995) *The Harmony of Illusions: Inventing Post-traumatic Stress Disorder*. Princeton, NJ: Princeton University Press.

Zhang, Y., Proenca, R., Maffei, M., Barone, M., Leopold, L. and Friedman, J.M. (1994) 'Positional cloning of the mouse obese gene and its human homologue', *Nature*, 372: 425–32.

Zoller, U. and Maymon, T. (1983) 'Smoking behavior of high school students in Israel', *Journal of School Health*, 53: 613–17.

Zuckerman, M. (1979) *Sensation Seeking: Beyond the Optimal Level of Arousal.* Hillsdale, NJ: Lawrence Erlbaum.

Zuckerman, M. (1984) 'Sensation seeking: a comparative approach to a human trait', *Behavioral and Brain Sciences*, 7: 413–71.

INDEX